MW00848703

EVERYMAN, I will go with thee,

and be thy guide,

In thy most need to go by thy side

JOSEPH ADDISON

Born at Milston in Wiltshire, 1672; educated at Lichfield Grammar School, the Charterhouse and Magdalen College, Oxford, where he was a Demy and Fellow. M.P. for Malmesbury, Under-Secretary of State, Secretary of the Irish Government and Secretary of State in England, he died in 1719 at Holland House, his wife's London residence.

SIR RICHARD STEELE

Born at Dublin in 1672; educated at the Charterhouse and Merton College, Oxford. He was elected M.P. for Stockbridge in 1713, for Boroughbridge in 1715 (in which year he was knighted) and for Wendover in 1722. He died at Llangunnor in 1729.

ADDISON & STEELE
AND OTHERS

The Spectator

IN FOUR VOLUMES · VOLUME ONE

EDITED BY
GREGORY SMITH

INTRODUCTION BY
PETER SMITHERS, D.PHIL.(OXON.)

DENT: LONDON
EVERYMAN'S LIBRARY
DUTTON: NEW YORK

All rights reserved
Made in Great Britain
at the
Aldine Press · Letchworth · Herts
for
J. M. DENT & SONS LTD
Aldine House · Bedford Street · London
First included in Everyman's Library 1907
Reset, with minor revisions, 1945
Last reprinted 1970

NO. *164*

ISBN: 0 460 00164 7

PREFACE

THE purpose of this reprint of the *Spectator* is to preserve the original freshness of the text. Even as early as 1764 'innumerable corruptions' had crept in, to the sorrow of the editor of the *Reliques of Ancient English Poetry*. He was persuaded to undertake a new edition; but his plan was interrupted. It was left to the Bissets and the Chalmerses, and the cheap retailers of their texts, to set a detestable fashion of flamboyant emendation. In this plight the *Spectator* remained till 1868, when the late Mr Henry Morley brought out his one-volume edition, which claimed to reproduce 'the original text, both as first issued, and as corrected by its authors.' An edition in eight volumes appeared in 1897–8, under the care of the present editor, who collated the text and prepared fresh illustrative notes. The edition now offered in four volumes is a reprint of that work. Errors in the first issue have been corrected, and supplementary notes have been included.

The *Spectator* was published daily, in single sheets of foolscap folio, printed, in double columns, on both sides. The first number appeared on 1st March 1711, and the last on 6th December 1712. The sheets were afterwards republished in monthly parts; and in November 1711 a revised edition in octavo volumes was announced. Two volumes, 'well bound and gilt, two guineas,' were issued to the subscribers on 8th January 1712, by 'S. Buckley, at the Dolphin in Little-Britain, and J. Tonson, at Shakespear's-Head, over-against Catherine-street in the Strand.' The third and fourth appeared some time in April of that year; and the fifth, sixth, and seventh early in 1713. These seven volumes constitute the *Second* or *First Collected* edition, and with an eighth, edited by Addison in 1715, from the supplementary papers which he had published from 18th June to 20th December 1714, supply the text of the present edition. The collected edition has the superior interest of showing the final form in which the writers desired to leave their work. In it and its immediate reprints, rather than in the stray sheets of the earlier issue, the contemporaries of Steele and Addison found their amusement and sought their models of style. Had the latter been reprinted, it would have been necessary to incorporate the many errata indicated in the columns of the early issue, with the result that we should have had neither the *Spectator* of the 'tea-equipage' nor the carefully revised edition.

It is hoped that the reproduction of the antique manner of the original in regard to spelling, punctuation, italics, and capital letters will not be condemned as antiquarian pedantry. A slight perusal must convince the reader that these are not to be excused as the caprice of the printer or the lazy fancy of the editors. The punctuation is rhetorical rather than logical, and should not, any more than should the old-fashioned guise of a few words, mar the simple enjoyment of the most modern reader. Printers' errors are, of course, not reproduced: and a few slight alterations (which are duly noted) have been made to avoid misunderstanding. The most serious interference is in the case of such plurals as *Opera's*, and such possessives as *Peoples*, which have been changed to *Operas* and *People's*— forms which are found in the original text. The Latin and Greek mottoes and quotations have been revised. Many of them seem to have been written down, like Steele's story of Mr. Inkle, 'as they dwelt upon the memory,' though not always with the same literary pleasure to the reader. Verbal errors and impossible verses in the quotations in the text have been corrected; but the fashion of contemporary scholarship has been preserved, for it would have been an historical impropriety to supplant the worthy Tonson by the more learned Teubner. The extracts from English writers have been left untouched. The memorial ingenuity shown in these is often too interesting to be lost; and sometimes the passages were intentionally misquoted. The reader will find the chief deviations from the original texts indicated in the Notes. Verses, such as Pope's *Messiah* or Addison's 'Pieces of Divine Poetry,' which were printed for the first time in the *Spectator*, are given in the ordinary type of the Papers; but the quoted passages have been set up in type of a smaller size. The humorous 'Advertisements' which reappeared in the Collected Edition will be found in their places in these volumes. Some of the original advertisements, in small type of the kind which Mr. Bickerstaff commended for 'giving the reader something like the satisfaction of prying into a secret,' are referred to in the Notes, when they illustrate the text of the Papers. The page of this edition is smaller, but it contains a larger portion of the letterpress.

The editor ventures to claim that he has avoided excess in the seductive record of Various Readings, and that he has made the few notes of 'different senses' and 'new elegances' in respectful obedience to Mr Spectator's editorial canon. In the notes proper he has endeavoured, when possible, to explain matters by the aid of contemporary writings. Of these the

Tatler stands first in importance, not merely because it came as a kind of prelude to the *Spectator*, but because it was the direct model for the literary plan and details of the later journal. The older annotated editions of the *Spectator* have been examined with some profit, though not without a fixed suspicion of their authority; and use has been made of Mr Henry Morley's edition, and of Mr Austin Dobson's *Selections from Steele* and other well-known volumes.

The Biographical Index in the fourth volume contains a brief account of all contemporary persons mentioned in the *Spectator*. In the Subject Index only the page references are given, as the addition of a brief description would have seriously increased the bulk of the last volume.

The text is printed from the copy in the Library of the University of Edinburgh; that of the original sixth volume, which is missing, is supplied from the copy in the British Museum. The whole has been collated with the set of original sheets in the Advocates' Library, some of which once graced the tables of Sam's Coffee-house in Ludgate Street.

C. GREGORY SMITH.

Other editions of the *Spectator* appeared in 1729–39; 1744; 1765; 1778; with illustrative notes, and Lives of the Authors, by Bisset, 1793, 1794; with Prefaces, historical and biographical, by A. Chalmers, six volumes, 1864; the original text, with Introduction, Notes, and Index, by H. Morley, 1868, 1887, 1888 (Routledge's Popular Library); the original text, edited and annotated by G. Gregory Smith, and with an introductory essay by Austin Dobson, eight volumes, 1897–8; with introduction and notes by G. A. Aitken, eight volumes, 1898. The *Spectator* has also appeared in several series, among them in the 'British Classics,' and the 'British Essayists.'

INTRODUCTION

THE *Spectator* was the greatest literary triumph of its time. Immediate fame, popularity, admiration, and financial success were the rewards of its authors. During the eighteenth and nineteenth centuries it was a basic text second only to the Bible in its influence upon British manners and morals, and it remained the most popular model for English prose composition. In the twentieth century it is a basic authority for the social historian, unrivalled in its own period for the variety of intimate detail which it reveals either directly or by inference. Its part in the formation of that outlook and character which distinguish the British middle class and which reached their climax, after two centuries of development, in the later Victorian period, would repay a full investigation.

The *Spectator* appeared in an age amply supplied with literature. Writing was a popular part-time occupation of all literate classes, whether as an elegant accomplishment, or in the quest for fame or a living, or for political, social, or scientific purposes. The numerous London presses and some provincial ones poured forth books, pamphlets, broadsheets, and periodicals in astonishing profusion. In this torrent of composition and publication the *Spectator* was easily distinguishable not by reason of any individual novel feature, but because it combined so many points of strength. Based upon Steele's experience in publishing the *Gazette* and the *Tatler*, it was technically efficient as a vehicle for its authors' purpose. The principal authors, Addison and Steele, wrote a direct and elegant prose easily recognized as superior to the main stream of contemporary literature, and perfectly matched with the content of the paper. The purpose of the authors was to amuse and to reform, to extend elegant amusement and rational reform from the circle of wits and divines to that of literate mankind as a whole, and to appeal to women equally with men.

The early *Tatlers* had been composite papers, made up of news, elegant trifles, and more serious items. In the *Spectator* the trumpet of reform was sounded long and clear. Not merely were whole papers devoted to serious subjects, but whole series of papers, such as those upon the 'Pleasures of the Imagination,' dealt with such subjects exhaustively. A complete man or woman was one who had developed the faculties of the mind to the maximum extent of which they were capable.

The *Spectator* explained how that could be done. A virtuous citizen was one who applied those faculties usefully. The reward of virtue would be happiness in this world and the next. But unlike contemporary sermons, whose content and purpose were often similar, the *Spectators* were and remain highly entertaining. Because they sprang from the society of the wits with its connections with the aristocracy alike of birth and intellect, they exhaled the breath of high fashion. The appeal to the reader was thus fourfold: amusement, intellectual and social snobbery, a serious purpose of reform, and the material rewards of virtue.

Addison and Steele were at this time admirably suited to complement and sustain each other. Steele with his knowledge of the gay life, with a ready wit and pen, and with his practical experience of publication, was reinforced by Addison's weighty reputation as a poet, critic, and scholar, now known to be a rising administrator and politician, and by his inimitable gift of humour. Steele's impetuous zeal and initiative were balanced by Addison's cautious yet penetrating wisdom. To the ladies, Steele was the would-be virtuous lover who flattered because his better self fell such an easy victim in the face of female temptation. Addison was the virtuous admirer, who flattered by inviting women to share his world of intellectual distinction upon almost equal terms. Together they combined qualities of creative genius which no single personality could contain, and around them they gathered a circle of occasional contributors who were inspired by their work and wrote in their vein.

It is not difficult to identify the merits of the *Spectator* as literature, as journalism, as morality, or as propaganda. But the external circumstances which enabled its authors to translate merit into immediate success and permanent achievement, are part of the history of Britain. The peculiar conditions which ensured success were two. Firstly, after a century of puritan and cavalier excesses, England was ready for an attitude towards life which would encourage right living without severity and which would equally encourage pleasure without licentiousness. Secondly, John Locke, Isaac Newton, Christopher Wren, and their contemporaries in other arts and sciences had shown how the human mind could expand its faculties by applying the process of reason in every direction. The authors of the *Spectator* took the materials ready to their hands and transformed them into papers which would be understood, enjoyed, and approved by almost all literate men and women.

The permanent achievement of the authors of the *Spectator*

is explained by a single fact. They wrote at the beginning of the rise of a British middle class. They wrote for that class even though it was not particularly numerous by later comparisons. And as the middle class multiplied in strength, wealth, and influence, so did the readers of the *Spectator*. It is probably not a coincidence that when the middle class in the Victorian sense of the word began to decay, the *Spectator* fell abruptly from the first rank of literature prescribed for intensive study by every educated child. Yet there are other reasons for this decline. A temporary one is to be found in the habit, now fortunately dying, of devaluing almost everything which the Victorians admired and respected. As the Victorians and their attitude towards life pass into the perspective of history, the *Spectator* will stand out as a signpost to mankind upon its journey; for it showed Englishmen how to pass beyond the great virtues into that assembly of lesser sound practices which together will always govern the conduct of highly civilized men and women. This task was so completely achieved that much of the teaching of the *Spectator* has been incorporated in the British character and habits of life, and has passed to our generation not through the words of Addison or Steele, but from the teaching of our parents and grandparents who were their pupils.

PETER SMITHERS.

House of Commons,
1956.

CONTENTS

* Volumes of the First Collected edition.

TO THE RIGHT HONOURABLE
JOHN LORD *SOMMERS*,
BARON OF *EVESHAM*.

My LORD,

I SHOULD not act the Part of an impartial Spectator, if I Dedicated the following Papers to one who is not of the most consummate and most acknowledged Merit.

None but a person of a finished Character can be the proper Patron of a Work, which endeavours to Cultivate and Polish Human Life, by promoting Virtue and Knowledge, and by recommending whatsoever may be either Useful or Ornamental to Society.

I know that the Homage I now pay You, is offering a kind of Violence to one who is as solicitous to shun Applause, as he is assiduous to deserve it. But, my Lord, this is perhaps the only Particular in which your Prudence will be always disappointed.

While Justice, Candor, Equanimity, a Zeal for the Good of your Country, and the most persuasive Eloquence in bringing over others to it, are valuable Distinctions, You are not to expect that the Publick will so far comply with your Inclinations, as to forbear celebrating such extraordinary Qualities. It is in vain that You have endeavoured to conceal your Share of Merit, in the many National Services which You have effected. Do what You will, the present Age will be talking of your Virtues, tho' Posterity alone will do them Justice.

Other Men pass through Oppositions and contending Interests in the Ways of Ambition, but Your Great Abilities have been invited to Power, and importuned to accept of Advancement. Nor is it strange that this should happen to your Lordship, who could bring into the Service of Your Sovereign the Arts and Policies of Ancient *Greece* and *Rome*; as well as the most exact Knowledge of our own Constitution in particular, and of the interests of *Europe* in general; to which I must also add, a certain Dignity in Yourself, that (to say the least of it) has been always equal to those great Honours which have been conferred upon You.

It is very well known how much the Church owed to You in the most dangerous Day it ever saw, that of the Arraignment of its Prelates; and how far the Civil Power, in the Late and present Reign, has been indebted to your Counsels and Wisdom.

But to enumerate the great Advantages which the publick has received from your Administration, would be a more proper Work for an History, than for an Address of this Nature.

Your Lordship appears as great in your Private Life, as in the most Important Offices which You have born. I would therefore rather chuse to speak of the Pleasure You afford all who are admitted into your Conversation, of Your Elegant Taste in all the Polite Parts of Learning, of Your great Humanity and Complacency of Manners, and of the surprising Influence which is peculiar to You in making every one who Converses with your Lordship prefer You to himself, without thinking the less meanly of his own Talents. But if I should take notice of all that might be observed in your Lordship, I should have nothing new to say upon any other Character of Distinction.

> I am,
>
> > *My Lord,*
> >
> > > *Your Lordship's*
> > > *most Obedient,*
> > > *most Devoted*
> > > *Humble Servant,*
> > > > THE SPECTATOR.

THE SPECTATOR.

VOL. I.

No. 1.

[ADDISON.]
Thursday, March 1, 17$\frac{10}{11}$

Non fumum ex fulgore, sed ex fumo dare lucem
Cogitat, ut speciosa dehinc miracula promat.—Hor.

I HAVE observed, that a Reader seldom peruses a Book with Pleasure, 'till he knows whether the Writer of it be a black or a fair Man, of a mild or cholerick Disposition, Married or a Batchelor, with other Particulars of the like nature, that conduce very much to the right understanding of an Author. To gratifie this Curiosity, which is so natural to a Reader, I design this Paper, and my next, as Prefatory Discourses to my following Writings, and shall give some Account in them of the several Persons that are engaged in this Work. As the chief Trouble of Compiling, Digesting, and Correcting will fall to my Share, I must do myself the Justice to open the Work with my own History.

I was born to a small Hereditary Estate, which, according to the Tradition of the Village where it lies, was bounded by the same Hedges and Ditches in *William* the Conqueror's Time that it is at present, and has been delivered down from Father to Son whole and entire, without the Loss or Acquisition of a single Field or Meadow, during the Space of six hundred Years. There runs a Story in the Family, that when my Mother was gone with Child of me about three Months, she dreamt that she was brought to Bed of a Judge: Whether this might proceed from a Law-Suit which was then depending in the Family, or my Father's being a Justice of the Peace, I cannot determine; for I am not so vain as to think it presaged any Dignity that I should arrive at in my future Life, though that was the Interpretation which the Neighbourhood put upon it. The Gravity of my Behaviour at my very first Appearance in the World, and all the Time that I sucked, seemed to favour my Mother's Dream: For, as she has often told me, I threw away my Rattle before I was two Months old, and would not make use of my Coral 'till they had taken away the Bells from it.

As for the rest of my Infancy, there being nothing in it

remarkable, I shall pass it over in Silence.   I find, that, during my Nonage, I had the Reputation of a very sullen Youth, but was always a Favourite of my School-master, who used to say, *that my Parts were solid and would wear well.*   I had not been long at the University, before I distinguished my self by a most profound Silence: For during the Space of eight Years, excepting in the publick Exercises of the College, I scarce uttered the Quantity of an hundred Words; and indeed do not remember that I ever spoke three Sentences together in my whole Life. Whilst I was in this Learned Body I applied myself with so much Diligence to my Studies, that there are very few celebrated Books, either in the Learned or the Modern Tongues, which I am not acquainted with.

Upon the Death of my Father I was resolved to travel into Foreign Countries, and therefore left the University, with the Character of an odd unaccountable Fellow, that had a great deal of Learning, if I would but show it.   An insatiable Thirst after Knowledge carried me into all the Countries of *Europe*, in which there was any thing new or strange to be seen; nay, to such a Degree was my Curiosity raised, that having read the Controversies of some great Men concerning the Antiquities of *Egypt*, I made a Voyage to *Grand Cairo*, on purpose to take the Measure of a Pyramid; and as soon as I had set my self right in that Particular, returned to my Native Country with great Satisfaction.

I have passed my latter Years in this City, where I am frequently seen in most Publick Places, tho' there are not above half a dozen of my select Friends that know me; of whom my next Paper shall give a more particular Account.   There is no place of general Resort, wherein I do not often make my appearance; sometimes I am seen thrusting my Head into a Round of Politicians at *Will's*, and listning with great Attention to the Narratives that are made in those little Circular Audiences.   Sometimes I smoak a Pipe at *Child's*; and whilst I seem attentive to nothing but the *Post-Man*, over-hear the Conversation of every Table in the Room.   I appear on *Sunday* nights at St. *James's* Coffee-House, and sometimes join the little Committee of Politicks in the Inner Room, as one who comes there to hear and improve.   My face is likewise very well known at the *Grecian*, the *Cocoa-Tree*, and in the Theatres both of *Drury-Lane* and the *Hay-Market*.   I have been taken for a Merchant upon the *Exchange* for above these ten Years, and sometimes pass for a *Jew* in the Assembly of Stock-Jobbers at *Jonathan's*.   In short, where-ever I see a Cluster of People I always mix with them, though I never open my Lips but in my own Club.

Thus I live in the World, rather as a Spectator of Mankind, than as one of the Species; by which means I have made my self a Speculative Statesman, Soldier, Merchant, and Artizan, without ever medling with any Practical Part in Life. I am very well versed in the Theory of an Husband, or a Father, and can discern the Errors in the Oeconomy, Business and Diversion of others, better than those who are engaged in them; as Standers-by discover Blots, which are apt to escape those who are in the Game. I never espoused any Party with Violence, and am resolved to observe an exact Neutrality between the Whigs and Tories, unless I shall be forced to declare myself by the Hostilities of either Side. In short, I have acted in all the Parts of my Life as a Looker-on, which is the Character I intend to preserve in this Paper.

I have given the Reader just so much of my History and Character, as to let him see I am not altogether unqualified for the Business I have undertaken. As for other Particulars in my Life and Adventures, I shall insert them in following Papers, as I shall see occasion. In the mean time, when I consider how much I have seen, read and heard, I begin to blame my own Taciturnity; and since I have neither Time nor Inclination to communicate the Fulness of my Heart in Speech, I am resolved to do it in Writing; and to Print my self out, if possible, before I Die. I have been often told by my Friends that it is Pity so many useful Discoveries which I have made, should be in the Possession of a Silent Man. For this Reason therefore, I shall publish a Sheet-full of Thoughts every Morning, for the Benefit of my Contemporaries; and if I can any way contribute to the Diversion or Improvement of the Country in which I live, I shall leave it, when I am summoned out of it, with the secret Satisfaction of thinking that I have not Lived in vain.

There are three very material Points which I have not spoken to in this Paper, and which, for several important Reasons, I must keep to my self, at least for some Time: I mean, an Account of my Name, my Age, and my Lodgings. I must confess I would gratifie my Reader in any thing that is reasonable; but as for these three Particulars, though I am sensible they might tend very much to the Embellishment of my Paper, I cannot yet come to a Resolution of communicating them to the Publick. They would indeed draw me out of that Obscurity which I have enjoyed for many Years, and expose me in Publick Places to several Salutes and Civilities, which have been always very disagreeable to me; for the greatest Pain I can suffer, is the being talked to, and being stared at. It is for this Reason likewise, that I keep my

Complexion and Dress, as very great Secrets; tho' it is not impossible, but I may make Discoveries of both, in the Progress of the Work I have undertaken.

After having been thus particular upon my self, I shall in to-Morrow's Paper give an Account of those Gentlemen who are concerned with me in this Work. For, as I have before intimated, a Plan of it is laid and concerted (as all other Matters of Importance are) in a Club. However, as my Friends have engaged me to stand in the Front, those who have a mind to correspond with me, may direct their Letters *To the* SPECTATOR, at Mr. *Buckley's* in *Little Britain*. For I must further acquaint the Reader, that tho' our Club meets only on *Tuesdays* and *Thursdays*, we have appointed a Committee to sit every Night, for the Inspection of all such Papers as may contribute to the Advancement of the Public Weal.   C

No. 2.

[STEELE.]   Friday, March 2.

> . . . *Haec alii sex*
> *Vel plures uno conclamant ore.*—Juv.

THE first of our Society is a Gentleman of *Worcestershire*, of antient Descent, a Baronet, his Name Sir ROGER DE COVERLY. His great Grandfather was Inventor of that famous Country-Dance which is call'd after him. All who know that Shire are very well acquainted with the Parts and Merits of Sir ROGER. He is a Gentleman that is very singular in his Behaviour, but his Singularities proceed from his good Sense, and are Contradictions to the Manners of the World, only as he thinks the World is in the wrong. However, this Humour creates him no Enemies, for he does nothing with Sourness or Obstinacy; and his being unconfined to Modes and Forms, makes him but the readier and more capable to please and oblige all who know him. When he is in town he lives in *Soho-Square*: It is said, he keeps himself a Batchelor by reason he was crossed in Love, by a perverse beautiful Widow of the next County to him. Before this Disappointment, Sir ROGER was what you call a fine Gentleman, had often supped with my Lord *Rochester* and Sir *George Etherege*, fought a Duel upon his first coming to Town, and kick'd Bully *Dawson* in a publick Coffee-house for calling him Youngster. But being ill used by the above-mentioned Widow, he was very serious for a Year and a half; and though, his Temper being naturally jovial, he at last got over it, he grew careless of himself, and never dressed after-

wards; he continues to wear a Coat and Doublet of the same
Cut that were in Fashion at the Time of his Repulse, which,
in his merry Humours, he tells us, has been in and out twelve
Times since he first wore it. 'Tis said Sir ROGER grew humble
in his Desires after he had forgot this cruel Beauty, insomuch
that it is reported he has frequently offended in Point of
Chastity with Beggars and Gypsies: But this is look'd upon by
his Friends rather as Matter of Raillery than Truth. He is
now in his Fifty sixth Year, cheerful, gay, and hearty, keeps a
good House both in Town and Country; a great Lover of Mankind; but there is such a mirthful Cast in his Behaviour, that
he is rather beloved than esteemed: His Tenants grow rich, his
Servants look satisfied, all the young Women profess Love to
him, and the young Men are glad of his Company: When he
comes into a House he calls the Servants by their Names, and
talks all the way up Stairs to a Visit. I must not omit that
Sir ROGER is a Justice of the *Quorum*; that he fills the chair at a
Quarter-Session with great Abilities, and three Months ago
gain'd universal Applause by explaining a Passage in the
Game-Act.

The Gentleman next in Esteem and Authority among us, is
another Batchelor, who is a Member of the *Inner Temple*; a
Man of great Probity, Wit, and Understanding; but he has
chosen his Place of Residence rather to obey the Direction of an
old humoursom Father, than in pursuit of his own Inclinations.
He was placed there to study the Laws of the Land, and is the
most learned of any of the House in those of the Stage. *Aristotle* and *Longinus* are much better understood by him than
Littleton or *Cooke*. The Father sends up every Post Questions
relating to Marriage-Articles, Leases, and Tenures, in the
Neighbourhood; all which Questions he agrees with an Attorney
to answer and take care of in the Lump: He is studying
the Passions themselves, when he should be inquiring into the
Debates among Men which arise from them. He knows the
Argument of each of the Orations of *Demosthenes* and *Tully*,
but not one Case in the Reports of our own Courts. No one
ever took him for a Fool, but none, except his intimate Friends,
know he has a great deal of Wit. This Turn makes him at once
both disinterested and agreeable: As few of his Thoughts are
drawn from Business, they are most of them fit for Conversation. His Taste of Books is a little too just for the Age he
lives in; he has read all, but approves of very few. His
Familiarity with the Customs, Manners, Actions, and Writings
of the Antients, makes him a very delicate Observer of what
occurs to him in the present World. He is an excellent Critick,
and the Time of the Play is his Hour of Business; exactly at

five he passes thro' *New-Inn*, crosses thro' *Russel-Court*, and takes a turn at *Will's* 'till the play begins; he has his Shooes rubbed and his Perriwig powder'd at the Barber's as you go into the *Rose*. It is for the Good of the Audience when he is at a Play, for the Actors have an Ambition to please him.

The Person of next Consideration is Sir ANDREW FREEPORT, a Merchant of great Eminence in the City of *London*. A Person of indefatigable Industry, strong Reason, and great Experience. His Notions of Trade are noble and generous, and (as every rich Man has usually some sly Way of Jesting, which would make no great Figure were he not a rich Man) he calls the Sea the *British Common*. He is acquainted with Commerce in all its Parts, and will tell you that it is a stupid and barbarous Way to extend Dominion by Arms; for true Power is to be got by Arts and Industry. He will often argue, that if this Part of our Trade were well cultivated, we should gain from one Nation; and if another, from another. I have heard him prove, that Diligence makes more lasting Acquisitions than Valour, and that Sloth has ruined more Nations than the Sword. He abounds in several frugal Maxims, among which the greatest Favourite is, 'A Penny saved is a Penny got.' A General Trader of good Sense, is pleasanter company than a general Scholar; and Sir ANDREW having a natural unaffected Eloquence, the Perspicuity of his Discourse gives the same Pleasure that Wit would in another Man. He has made his Fortunes himself; and says that *England* may be richer than other Kingdoms, by as plain Methods as he himself is richer than other Men; tho' at the same Time I can say this of him, that there is not a point in the Compass but blows home a Ship in which he is an Owner.

Next to Sir ANDREW in the Club-room sits Captain SENTRY, a Gentleman of great Courage, good Understanding, but invincible Modesty. He is one of those that deserve very well, but are very awkward at putting their Talents within the Observation of such as should take Notice of them. He was some Years a Captain, and behaved himself with great Gallantry in several Engagements, and at several Sieges; but having a small Estate of his own, and being next Heir to Sir ROGER, he has quitted a Way of Life in which no Man can rise suitably to his Merit, who is not something of a Courtier as well as a Soldier. I have heard him often lament, that in a Profession where Merit is placed in so conspicuous a View, Impudence should get the better of Modesty. When he has talked to this Purpose I never heard him make a sour Expression, but frankly confess that he left the World, because he was not fit for it. A strict Honesty and an even regular Behaviour, are in them-

selves Obstacles to him that must press through Crowds, who
endeavour at the same End with himself, the Favour of a
Commander. He will however in his Way of Talk excuse
Generals, for not disposing according to Men's Desert, or enquiring into it: For, says he, that great Man who has a Mind to help
me, has as many to break through to come at me, as I have to
come at him: Therefore he will conclude, that the Man who
would make a Figure, especially in a military Way, must get
over all false Modesty, and assist his Patron against the Importunity of other Pretenders, by a proper Assurance in his
own Vindication. He says it is a civil Cowardice to be backward in asserting what you ought to expect, as it is a military
Fear to be slow in attacking when it is your Duty. With this
Candour does the Gentleman speak of himself and others.
The same Frankness runs through all his Conversation. The
military Part of his Life has furnish'd him with many Adventures, in the Relation of which he is very agreeable to the Company; for he is never over-bearing, though accustomed to
command Men in the utmost Degree below him; nor ever too
obsequious, from an Habit of obeying Men highly above him.

But that our Society may not appear a Set of Humourists
unacquainted with the Gallantries and Pleasures of the Age,
we have among us the gallant WILL. HONEYCOMB, a Gentleman
who according to his Years should be in the Decline of his Life,
but having ever been very careful of his Person, and always had
a very easie Fortune, Time has made but very little Impression,
either by Wrinkles on his Forehead, or Traces in his Brain.
His Person is well turn'd, of a good Height. He is very ready
at that sort of Discourse with which Men usually entertain
Women. He has all his Life dressed very well, and remembers
Habits as others do Men. He can smile when one speaks to
him, and laughs easily. He knows the History of every Mode,
and can inform you from which of the *French* King's Wenches
our Wives and Daughters had this Manner of curling their
Hair, that Way of placing their Hoods; whose Frailty was
covered by such a Sort of Petticoat, and whose Vanity to shew
her Foot made that Part of the Dress so short in such a Year.
In a Word, all his Conversation and Knowledge has been in
the female World: As other Men of his Age will take Notice to
you what such a Minister said upon such and such an Occasion,
he will tell you when the Duke of *Monmouth* danced at Court
such a Woman was then smitten, another was taken with him
at the Head of his Troop in the *Park*. In all these important
Relations, he has ever about the same Time received a kind
Glance or a Blow of a Fan from some celebrated Beauty,
Mother of the Present Lord such-a-one. If you speak of a

young Commoner that said a lively thing in the House, he starts up, 'He has good Blood in his Veins, *Tom Mirabell* begot him, the Rogue cheated me in that affair; that young Fellow's Mother used me more like a Dog than any Woman I ever made Advances to.' This way of Talking of his very much enlivens the Conversation among us of a more sedate Turn; and I find there is not one of the Company, but my self, who rarely speak at all, but speaks of him as of that Sort of Man, who is usually called a well-bred fine Gentleman. To conclude his Character, where Women are not concern'd, he is an honest worthy Man.

I cannot tell whether I am to account him whom I am next to speak of, as one of our Company; for he visits us but seldom, but when he does it adds to every Man else a new Enjoyment of himself. He is a Clergyman, a very philosophick Man, of general Learning, great Sanctity of Life, and the most exact good Breeding. He has the Misfortune to be of a very weak Constitution, and consequently cannot accept of such Cares and Business as Preferments in his Function would oblige him to: He is therefore among Divines what a Chamber-Counsellor is among Lawyers. The Probity of his Mind, and the Integrity of his Life, create him Followers, as being eloquent or loud advances others. He seldom introduces the Subject he speaks upon; but we are so far gone in Years, that he observes, when he is among us, an Earnestness to have him fall on some divine Topick, which he always treats with much Authority, as one who has no Interests in this World, as one who is hastening to the Object of all his Wishes, and conceives Hope from his Decays and Infirmities. These are my ordinary Companions.

R

No. 3.

[ADDISON.]   Saturday, March 3.

> *Et quo quisque fere studio devinctus adhaeret*
> *Aut quibus in rebus multum sumus ante morati*
> *Atque in ea ratione fuit contenta magis mens,*
> *In somnis eadem plerumque videmur obire.*—Lucr. L. 4.

IN one of my late Rambles, or rather Speculations, I looked into the great Hall where the Bank is kept, and was not a little pleased to see the Directors, Secretaries, and Clerks, with all the other Members of that wealthy Corporation, ranged in their several Stations, according to the Parts they act in that just and regular Oeconomy. This revived in my Memory the many Discourses which I had both read and heard concerning the Decay of Publick Credit, with the Methods of restoring it, and which, in my Opinion, have always been defective, because they have always been made with an Eye to separate Interests, and Party Principles.

The Thoughts of the Day gave my Mind Employment for the whole Night, so that I fell insensibly into a kind of Methodical Dream, which dispos'd all my Contemplations into a Vision or Allegory, or what else the Reader shall please to call it.

Methought I returned to the Great Hall, where I had been the Morning before, but, to my Surprize, instead of the Company that I left there, I saw towards the upper end of the Hall, a beautiful Virgin seated on a Throne of Gold. Her Name (as they told me) was *Publick Credit.* The Walls, instead of being adorn'd with Pictures and Maps, were hung with many Acts of Parliament written in Golden Letters. At the Upper end of the Hall was the *Magna Charta,* with the Act of Uniformity on the right Hand, and the Act of Toleration on the left. At the Lower end of the Hall was the Act of Settlement, which was placed full in the Eye of the Virgin that sat upon the Throne. Both the Sides of the Hall were covered with such Acts of Parliament as had been made for the Establishment of Publick Funds. The Lady seemed to set an unspeakable Value upon these several Pieces of Furniture, insomuch that she often refreshed her Eye with them, and often smiled with a Secret Pleasure, as she looked upon them; but, at the same time, showed a very particular Uneasiness, if she saw any thing approaching that might hurt them. She appeared indeed infinitely timorous in all her Behaviour: And, whether it was from the Delicacy of her Constitution, or that she was troubled with Vapours, as I was afterwards told by one who I found was none of her Well-wishers, she changed Colour, and startled at everything she heard. She was likewise (as I afterwards found) a greater Valetudinarian than any I had ever met with, even in her own Sex, and subject to such Momentary Consumptions, that in the twinkling of an Eye, she would fall away from the most florid Complexion, and the most healthful State of Body, and wither into a Skeleton. Her Recoveries were often as sudden as her Decays, insomuch that she would revive in a Moment out of a wasting Distemper, into a Habit of the highest Health and Vigour.

I had very soon an Opportunity of observing these quick Turns and Changes in her Constitution. There sat at her Feet a Couple of Secretaries, who received every Hour Letters from all Parts of the World, which the one or the other of them was perpetually reading to her; and, according to the News she heard, to which she was exceedingly attentive, she changed Colour, and discovered many Symptoms of Health or Sickness.

Behind the Throne was a prodigious Heap of Bags of Mony, which were piled upon one another so high that they touched the Ceiling. The Floor, on her right Hand and on her left, was covered with vast Sums of Gold that rose up in Pyramids on either side of her: But this I did not so much wonder at, when I heard, upon Enquiry, that she had the same Virtue in her Touch, which the Poets tell us a *Lydian* King was formerly possess'd of; and that she could convert whatever she pleas'd into that precious Metal.

After a little Dizziness, and confused Hurry of Thought, which a Man often meets with in a Dream, methought the Hall was alarm'd, the Doors flew open, and there enter'd half a dozen of the most hideous Phantoms that I had ever seen (even in a Dream) before that Time. They came in two by two, though match'd in the most dissociable Manner, and mingled together in a kind of Dance. It would be tedious to describe their Habits and Persons; for which Reason I shall only inform my Reader that the first Couple were Tyranny and Anarchy, the second were Bigotry and Atheism, the third the Genius of a Common-Wealth, and a young Man of about twenty two Years of Age, whose Name I could not learn. He had a Sword in his right Hand, which in the Dance he often brandished at the Act of Settlement; and a Citizen, who stood by me, whisper'd in my Ear, that he saw a Spunge in his left Hand. The Dance of so many jarring Natures put me in mind of the Sun, Moon, and Earth, in the *Rehearsal*, that danced together for no other end but to eclipse one another.

The Reader will easily suppose, by what has been before said, that the Lady on the Throne would have been almost frighted to Distraction, had she seen but any one of these Spectres; what then must have been her Condition when she saw them all in a body? She fainted and dyed away at the Sight.

> *Et neque jam color est mixto candore rubori;*
> *Nec vigor, & vires, & quae modo visa placebant,*
> *Nec corpus remanet* . . .—Ov. Met. Lib. 3.

There was as great a Change in the Hill of Mony Bags, and the Heaps of Mony, the former shrinking, and falling into so many empty Bags, that I now found not above a tenth part of them had been filled with Mony. The rest that took up the same Space, and made the same Figure as the Bags that were really filled with Mony, had been blown up with Air, and called into my Memory the Bags full of Wind, which *Homer* tells us his Hero receiv'd as a Present from *Aeolus*. The great Heaps of Gold, on either side the Throne, now appeared to be only Heaps of Paper, or little Piles of notched Sticks, bound up together in Bundles, like *Bath*-Faggots.

Whilst I was lamenting this sudden Desolation that had been made before me, the whole Scene vanished: In the Room of the frightful Spectres, there now enter'd a second Dance of Apparitions very agreeably matched together, and made up of very amiable Phantoms. The first Pair was Liberty with Monarchy at her right Hand: The second was Moderation leading in Religion; and the third a Person whom I had never seen, with the genius of *Great Britain*. At their first Entrance the Lady revived, the Bags swell'd to their former Bulk, the Piles of Faggots and Heaps of Paper changed into Pyramids of Guineas: And for my own part I was so transported with Joy, that I awaked, tho', I must confess, I would fain have fallen asleep again to have closed my Vision, if I could have done it.   C

No. 4.
[STEELE.]   Monday, March 5.

>   . . . *Egregii mortalem altique silenti !*—Hor.

An Author, when he first appears in the World, is very apt to believe it has nothing to think of but his Performances. With a good Share of this Vanity in my Heart, I made it my Business these three Days to listen after my own Fame; and, as I have sometimes met with Circumstances which did not displease me, I have been encounter'd by others which gave me as much Mortification. It is incredible to think how empty I have in this Time observed some Part of the Species to be, what mere Blanks they are when they first come abroad in the Morning, how utterly they are at a Stand 'till they are set a going by some Paragraph in a News-Paper: Such Persons are very acceptable to a young Author, for they desire no more in any thing but to be new to be agreeable. If I found Consolation among such, I was as much disquieted by the Incapacity of others. These are Mortals who have a certain Curiosity without Power of Reflection, and perused my Papers like Spectators rather than Readers. But there is so little pleasure in Enquiries that so nearly concern our selves (it being the worst Way in the World to Fame, to be too anxious about it), that upon the whole I resolved for the future to go on in my ordinary Way; and without too much Fear or Hope about the Business of Reputation, to be very careful of the Design of my Actions, but very negligent of the Consequences of them.

It is an endless and frivolous Pursuit to act by any other Rule than the Care of satisfying our own Minds in what we do. One would think a silent Man, who concerned himself with no one breathing, should be very little liable to Misinterpretations; and yet I remember I was once taken up for a Jesuit, for no other reason but my profound Taciturnity. It is from this Misfortune, that to be out of Harm's Way, I have ever since affected Crowds. He who comes into Assemblies only to gratifie his Curiosity, and not to make a Figure, enjoys the Pleasures of Retirement in a more exquisite Degree, than he possibly could in his Closet; the Lover, the Ambitious, and the Miser, are followed thither by a worse Crowd than any they can withdraw from. To be exempt from the Passions with which others are tormented, is the only pleasing Solitude. I can very justly say with the antient Sage, *I am never less alone than when alone.* As I am insignificant to the Company in publick Places, and as it is visible I do not come thither, as most do, to shew my self; I gratify the Vanity of all who pretend to make an Appearance, and have often as kind Looks from well dressed Gentlemen and Ladies, as a Poet would bestow upon one of his Audience. There are so many Gratifications attend this publick sort of Obscurity, that some little Distastes I daily receive have lost their Anguish; and I did the other Day, without the least Displeasure, overhear one say of me, *That strange Fellow*; and another answer, *I have known the Fellow's Face these twelve Years, and so must you; but I believe you are the first ever asked who he was.* There are, I must confess, many to whom my Person is as well known as that of their nearest Relations, who give themselves no further Trouble about calling me by my Name or Quality, but speak of me very currently by Mr. *What-d'ye-call-him.*

To make up for these trivial Disadvantages, I have the high Satisfaction of beholding all Nature with an unprejudic'd Eye; and having nothing to do with Men's Passions or Interests, I can with the greater Sagacity consider their Talents, Manners, Failings, and Merits.

It is remarkable, that those who want any one Sense, possess the others with greater Force and Vivacity. Thus my Want of, or rather Resignation of Speech, gives me all the Advantages of a dumb Man. I have, methinks, a more than ordinary Penetration in Seeing; and flatter my self that I have looked into the Highest and Lowest of Mankind, and make shrewd Guesses, without being admitted to their Conversation, at the inmost Thoughts and Reflections of all whom I behold. It is from hence that good or ill Fortune has no manner of Force towards affecting my Judgment. I see Men flourishing in Courts, and languishing in Jayls, without being prejudiced from their Circumstances to their Favour or Disadvantage; but from their inward Manner of bearing their Condition, often pity the Prosperous and admire the Unhappy.

Those who converse with the Dumb, know from the Turn of their Eyes, and the Changes of their Countenance, their Sentiments of the Objects before them. I have indulged my Silence to such an Extravagance, that the few who are intimate with me, answer my Smiles with concurrent Sentences, and argue to the very Point I shak'd my Head at without my speaking. WILL. HONEYCOMB was very entertaining the other Night at a Play to a Gentleman who sat on his right Hand, while I was at his Left. The Gentleman believed WILL. was talking to himself, when upon my looking with great Approbation at a young thing in a Box before us, he said, 'I am quite of another Opinion: She has, I will allow, a very pleasing Aspect, but methinks that Simplicity in her Countenance is rather childish than innocent.' When I observed her a second time, he said, 'I grant her Dress is very becoming, but perhaps the Merit of that Choice is owing to her Mother; for though,' continued he, 'I allow a Beauty to be as much to be commended for the Elegance of her Dress, as a Wit for that of his Language; yet if she has stolen the Colour of her Ribbands from another, or had Advice about her Trimmings, I shall not allow her the Praise of Dress, any more than I would call a Plagiary an Author.' When I threw my Eye towards the next Woman to her, WILL. spoke what I looked, according to his Romantick Imagination, in the following Manner.

'Behold, you who dare, that charming Virgin. Behold the Beauty of her Person chastised by the Innocence of her Thoughts. Chastity, Good-Nature, and Affability, are the Graces that play in her Countenance; she knows she is handsome, but she knows she is good. Conscious Beauty adorned with conscious Virtue! What a Spirit is there in those Eyes! What a Bloom in that Person! How is the whole Woman expressed in her Appearance! Her Air has the Beauty of Motion, and her Look the Force of Language.'

It was Prudence to turn away my Eyes from this Object, and therefore I turned them to the thoughtless Creatures who make up the Lump of that Sex, and move a knowing Eye no more than the Portraitures of insignificant People by ordinary Painters, which are but Pictures of Pictures.

Thus the working of my own Mind is the general Entertainment of my Life; I never enter into the Commerce of Discourse

with any but my particular Friends, and not in Publick even
with them. Such an Habit has perhaps raised in me uncommon Reflections; but this Effect I cannot communicate
but by my Writings. As my Pleasures are almost wholly
confined to those of the Sight, I take it for a peculiar Happiness
that I have always had an easie and familiar Admittance to the
fair Sex. If I never praised or flatter'd, I never belyed or
contradicted them. As these compose half the World, and are
by the just Complaisance and Gallantry of our Nation the more
powerful Part of our People, I shall dedicate a considerable
Share of these my Speculations to their Service, and shall lead
the Young through all the becoming Duties of Virginity,
Marriage, and Widowhood. When it is a Woman's Day, in
my Works, I shall endeavour at a Stile and Air suitable to their
Understanding. When I say this, I must be understood to
mean, that I shall not lower but exalt the Subjects I treat upon.
Discourse for their Entertainment, is not to be debased but
refined. A Man may appear learned, without talking Sentences; as in his ordinary Gesture he discovers he can Dance,
tho' he does not cut Capers. In a Word, I shall take it for
the greatest Glory of my Work, if among reasonable Women
this Paper may furnish *Tea-Table Talk*. In order to it, I shall
treat on Matters which relate to Females, as they are concern'd
to approach or fly from the other Sex, or as they are tyed to
them by Blood, Interest, or Affection. Upon this Occasion
I think it but reasonable to declare, that whatever Skill I may
have in Speculation, I shall never betray what the Eyes of
Lovers say to each other in my Presence. At the same Time I
shall not think myself obliged, by this Promise, to conceal any
false Protestations which I observe made by Glances in publick
Assemblies; but endeavour to make both Sexes appear in their
Conduct what they are in their Hearts. By this means Love,
during the Time of my Speculations, shall be carried on with
the same Sincerity as any other Affair of less Consideration.
As this is the greatest Concern, Men shall be from henceforth
liable to the greatest Reproach for Misbehaviour in it. Falshood in Love shall hereafter bear a blacker Aspect, than
Infidelity in Friendship, or Villany in Business. For this
great and good End, all Breaches against that noble Passion,
the Cement of Society, shall be severely examined. But this,
and all other Matters loosely hinted at now, and in my
former Papers, shall have their proper Place in my following Discourses: The present Writing is only to admonish the
World, that they shall not find me an idle but a very busie
Spectator.   R

No. 5.

[ADDISON.]   Tuesday, March 6.

Spectatum admissi risum teneatis?—Hor.

An Opera may be allowed to be extravagantly lavish in its
Decorations, as its only Design is to gratifie the Senses, and keep
up an indolent Attention in the Audience. Common Sense
however requires, that there should be nothing in the Scenes
and Machines which may appear Childish and Absurd. How
would the Wits of King *Charles's* Time have laughed, to have
seen *Nicolini* exposed to a Tempest in Robes of Ermin, and
sailing in an open Boat upon a Sea of Paste-Board? What a
Field of Raillery would they have been let into, had they been
entertain'd with painted Dragons spitting Wild-fire, enchanted
Chariots drawn by *Flanders* Mares, and real Cascades in artificial Land-skips? A little Skill in Criticism would inform us,
that Shadows and Realities ought not to be mix'd together in
the same Piece; and that Scenes, which are designed as the
Representations of Nature, should be filled with Resemblances,
and not with the Things themselves. If one would represent a
wide Champian Country filled with Herds and Flocks, it would
be ridiculous to draw the Country only upon the Scenes, and to
crowd several Parts of the Stage with Sheep and Oxen. This
is joining together Inconsistencies, and making the Decoration
partly Real and partly Imaginary. I would recommend what
I have here said, to the Directors, as well as to the Admirers,
of our Modern Opera.

As I was walking in the Streets about a Fortnight ago, I
saw an ordinary Fellow carrying a Cage full of little Birds upon
his Shoulder; and, as I was wondering with my self what Use
he would put them to, he was met very luckily by an Acquaintance, who had the same Curiosity. Upon his asking him
what he had upon his Shoulder, he told him, that he had been
buying Sparrows for the Opera. Sparrows for the Opera, says
his Friend, licking his lips, what, are they to be roasted? No,
no, says the other, they are to enter towards the end of the first
Act, and to fly about the Stage.

This strange Dialogue awakened my Curiosity so far, that I
immediately bought the Opera, by which means I perceived
that the Sparrows were to act the part of Singing Birds in a
delightful Grove: though upon a nearer Enquiry I found the
Sparrows put the same Trick upon the Audience, that Sir
Martin Mar-all practised upon his Mistress; for, though they
flew in Sight, the Musick proceeded from a Consort of Flagel-
lets and Bird-calls which was planted behind the Scenes. At

the same time I made this Discovery, I found by the Discourse of the Actors, that there were great Designs on foot for the Improvement of the Opera; that it had been proposed to break down a part of the Wall, and to surprize the Audience with a Party of an hundred Horse, and that there was actually a Project of bringing the *New-River* into the House, to be employed in Jetteaus and Waterworks. This Project, as I have since heard, is post-poned 'till the Summer-Season; when it is thought the Coolness that proceeds from Fountains and Cascades will be more acceptable and refreshing to People of Quality. In the mean time, to find out a more agreeable Entertainment for the Winter-Season, the Opera of *Rinaldo* is filled with Thunder and Lightning, Illuminations and Fireworks; which the Audience may look upon without catching Cold, and indeed without much Danger of being burnt; for there are several Engines filled with Water, and ready to play at a Minute's warning, in case any such Accident should happen. However, as I have a very great Friendship for the Owner of this Theater, I hope that he has been wise enough to *insure* his House before he would let this Opera be acted in it.

It is no wonder, that those Scenes should be very surprizing, which were contrived by two Poets of different Nations, and raised by two Magicians of different Sexes. *Armida* (as we are told in the Argument) was an *Amazonian* Enchantress, and poor Signior *Cassani* (as we learn from the *Persons represented*) a Christian-Conjuror (*Mago Christiano*). I must confess I am very much puzzled to find how an *Amazon* should be versed in the Black Art, or how a good Christian, for such is the Part of the Magician, should deal with the Devil.

To consider the Poets after the Conjurers, I shall give you a Taste of the *Italian*, from the first Lines of his Preface. *Eccoti, benigno Lettore, un Parto di poche Sere, che se ben nato di Notte, non è però aborto di Tenebre, mà si farà conoscere Figlio d' Apollo con qualche Raggio di Parnasso.* Behold, gentle Reader, *the Birth of a few Evenings, which, tho' it be the Offspring of the Night, is not the Abortive of Darkness, but will make it self known to be the Son of* Apollo, *with a certain Ray of* Parnassus. He afterwards proceeds to call Minheer *Hendel* the *Orpheus* of our Age, and to acquaint us, in the same Sublimity of Stile, that he Composed this Opera in a Fortnight. Such are the Wits, to whose Tastes we so ambitiously conform our selves. The Truth of it is, the finest Writers among the Modern *Italians* express themselves in such a florid Form of Words, and such tedious Circumlocutions, as are used by none but Pedants in our own Country; and at the same time fill their Writings with such poor Imaginations and Conceits, as our Youths are ashamed of before they have been two Years at the University. Some may be apt to think, that it is the difference of Genius which produces this difference in the Works of the two Nations; but to shew there is nothing in this, if we look into the Writings of the old *Italians*, such as *Cicero* and *Virgil*, we shall find that the *English* Writers, in their way of thinking and expressing themselves, resemble those Authors much more than the Modern *Italians* pretend to do.   And as for the Poet himself, from whom the Dreams of this Opera are taken, I must entirely agree with Monsieur *Boileau*, that one verse in *Virgil* is worth all the *Clincant* or Tinsel of *Tasso*.

But to return to the Sparrows; there have been so many Flights of them let loose in this Opera, that it is feared the House will never get rid of them; and that in other Plays they may make their Entrance in very wrong and improper Scenes, so as to be seen flying in a Lady's Bed-Chamber, or pearching upon a King's Throne; besides the Inconveniencies which the Heads of the Audience may sometimes suffer from them.   I am credibly informed, that there was once a Design of casting into an Opera the Story of *Whittington* and his Cat, and that in order to it there had been got together a great Quantity of Mice; but Mr. *Rich*, the Proprietor of the Play-House, very prudently considered that it would be impossible for the Cat to kill them all, and that consequently the Princes of his Stage might be as much infested with Mice, as the Prince of the Island was before the Cat's Arrival upon it; for which Reason he would not permit it to be Acted in his House.   And indeed I cannot blame him; for, as he said very well upon that Occasion, I do not hear that any of the Performers in our Opera pretend to equal the famous Pied Piper, who made all the Mice of a great Town in *Germany* follow his Musick, and by that means cleared the Place of those little Noxious Animals.

Before I dismiss this Paper, I must inform my Reader, that I hear there is a Treaty on foot with *London* and *Wise* (who will be appointed Gardeners of the Play-House) to furnish the Opera of *Rinaldo* and *Armida* with an Orange-Grove; and that the next time it is Acted, the Singing Birds will be Personated by Tom-Tits: The Undertakers being resolved to spare neither Pains nor Mony, for the Gratification of the Audience.   C

No. 6.

[STEELE.]   Wednesday, March 7.

> *Credebant hoc grande nefas & morte piandum,*
> *Si juvenis vetulo non assurrexerat . . .—*Juv.

I KNOW no Evil under the Sun so great as the Abuse of the
Understanding, and yet there is no one Vice more common.
It has diffus'd it self through both Sexes and all Qualities of
Mankind; and there is hardly that Person to be found, who is
not more concern'd for the Reputation of Wit and Sense, than
Honesty and Virtue.   But this unhappy Affectation of being
Wise rather than Honest, Witty than Good-natur'd, is the
Source of most of the ill Habits of Life.   Such false Impres-
sions are owing to the abandon'd Writings of Men of Wit, and
the awkward Imitation of the rest of Mankind.

For this Reason, Sir ROGER was saying last Night, That he
was of Opinion none but Men of fine Parts deserve to be hanged.
The Reflections of such Men are so delicate upon all Occurrences which they are concerned in, that they should be
exposed to more than ordinary Infamy and Punishment, for
offending against such quick Admonitions as their own Souls
give them, and blunting the fine Edge of their Minds in such a
Manner, that they are no more shocked at Vice and Folly,
than Men of slower Capacities.   There is no greater Monster
in Being, than a very ill Man of great Parts: He lives like a
Man in a Palsy, with one Side of him dead.   While perhaps he
enjoys the Satisfaction of Luxury, of Wealth, of Ambition, he
has lost the Taste of Good-will, of Friendship, of Innocence.
Scarecrow, the Beggar in *Lincoln's-Inn-Fields*, who disabled
himself in his Right Leg, and asks Alms all Day to get himself
a warm Supper and a Trull at Night, is not half so despicable
a Wretch as such a Man of Sense.   The Beggar has no Relish
above Sensations; he finds Rest more agreeable than Motion;
and while he has a warm Fire and his Doxy, never reflects that
he deserves to be whipped.   Every Man who terminates his
Satisfactions and Enjoyments within the Supply of his own
Necessities and Passions, is, says Sir ROGER, in my Eye as poor
a Rogue as *Scarecrow*.   But, continued he, for the Loss of
publick and private Virtue we are beholden to your Men of
Parts forsooth; it is with them no matter what is done, so it is
done with an Air.   But to me, who am so whimsical in a corrupt
Age as to act according to Nature and Reason, a selfish Man, in
the most shining Circumstance and Equipage, appears in the
same Condition with the Fellow above-mentioned, but more
contemptible, in Proportion to what more he robs the Publick
of and enjoys above him.   I lay it down therefore for a Rule,

That the whole Man is to move together; that every Action of any Importance is to have a Prospect of publick Good; and that the general Tendency of our indifferent Actions ought to be agreeable to the Dictates of Reason, of Religion, of good Breeding; without this, a Man, as I before have hinted, is hopping instead of walking, he is not in his intire and proper Motion.

While the honest Knight was thus bewildering himself in good Starts, I look'd intentively upon him, which made him, I thought, collect his Mind a little. What I aim at, says he, is to represent, That I am of Opinion, to polish our Understandings and neglect our Manners is of all things the most inexcusable. Reason should govern Passion, but instead of that, you see, it is often subservient to it; and as unaccountable as one would think it, a wise Man is not always a good Man. This Degeneracy is not only the Guilt of particular Persons, but also at some times of a whole People; and perhaps it may appear upon Examination, that the most polite Ages are the least virtuous. This may be attributed to the Folly of admitting Wit and Learning as Merit in themselves, without considering the Application of them. By this Means it becomes a Rule, not so much to regard what we do, as how we do it. But this false Beauty will not pass upon Men of honest Minds and true Taste: Sir *Richard Blackmore* says, with as much good Sense as Virtue, *It is a mighty Dishonour and Shame to employ excellent Faculties and abundance of Wit, to humour and please Men in their Vices and Follies. The great Enemy of Mankind, notwithstanding his Wit and Angelick Faculties, is the most odious Being in the whole Creation.* He goes on soon after to say very generously, That he undertook the writing of his Poem to *rescue the Muses out of the Hands of Ravishers, to restore them to their sweet and chaste Mansions, and to engage them in an Employment suitable to their Dignity.* This certainly ought to be the Purpose of every Man who appears in Publick; and whoever does not proceed upon that Foundation, injures his Country as fast as he succeeds in his Studies. When Modesty ceases to be the chief Ornament of one Sex, and Integrity of the other, Society is upon a wrong Basis, and we shall be ever after without Rules to guide our Judgment in what is really becoming and ornamental. Nature and Reason direct one thing, Passion and Humour another: To follow the Dictates of the two latter, is going into a Road that is both endless and intricate; when we pursue the other, our Passage is delightful, and what we aim at easily attainable.

I do not doubt but *England* is at present as polite a Nation as any in the World; but any Man who thinks can easily see, that the Affectation of being Gay and in Fashion has very near eaten up our good Sense and our Religion. Is there anything so just, as that Mode and Gallantry should be built upon exerting our selves in what is proper and agreeable to the Institutions of Justice and Piety among us? And yet is there any thing more common, than that we run in perfect Contradiction to them? All which is supported by no other Pretension, than that it is done with what we call a good Grace.

Nothing ought to be held laudable or becoming, but what Nature it self should prompt us to think so. Respect to all kind of Superiors is founded, methinks, upon Instinct; and yet what is so ridiculous as Age? I make this abrupt Transition to the Mention of this Vice more than any other, in order to introduce a little Story, which I think a pretty Instance that the most polite Age is in danger of being the most vicious.

'It happen'd at *Athens*, during a publick Representation of some Play exhibited in honour of the Commonwealth, that an old Gentleman came too late for a Place suitable to his Age and Quality. Many of the young Gentlemen who observed the Difficulty and Confusion he was in, made Signs to him that they would accommodate him if he came where they sate: The good Man bustled through the Crowd accordingly; but when he came to the Seats to which he was invited, the Jest was to sit close, and expose him, as he stood out of Countenance, to the whole Audience. The Frolick went round all the *Athenian* Benches. But on those Occasions there were also particular Places assigned for Foreigners: When the good Man skulked towards the Boxes appointed for the *Lacedemonians*, that honest People, more virtuous than polite, rose up all to a Man, and with the greatest Respect received him among them. The *Athenians* being suddenly touch'd with a Sense of the *Spartan* Virtue and their own Degeneracy, gave a Thunder of Applause; and the old Man cried out, *The* Athenians *understand what is good, but the* Lacedemonians *practise it.*' R

No. 7.

[ADDISON.]   Thursday, March 8.

> *Somnia, terrores magicos, miracula, sagas,*
> *Nocturnos lemures, portentaque Thessala rides?*—Hor.

GOING Yesterday to Dine with an old Acquaintance, I had the Misfortune to find his whole Family very much dejected. Upon asking him the Occasion of it, he told me that his Wife had dreamt a very strange Dream the Night before, which they were afraid portended some Misfortune to themselves or to their Children. At her coming into the Room I observed a settled Melancholy in her Countenance, which I should have been troubled for, had I not heard from whence it proceeded. We were no sooner sate down, but, after having looked upon me a little while, *My Dear,* says she, turning to her Husband, *you may now see the Stranger that was in the Candle last Night.* Soon after this, as they began to talk of Family Affairs, a little Boy at the lower end of the Table told her, that he was to go into Join-hand on *Thursday.* Thursday? says she, *No, Child, if it please God, you shall not begin upon* Childermas-day; *tell your Writing-Master that* Friday *will be soon enough.* I was Reflecting with my self on the Oddness of her Fancy, and wondering that any Body would establish it as a Rule to lose a Day in every Week. In the midst of these my Musings she desired me to reach her a little Salt upon the Point of my Knife, which I did in such a Trepidation and Hurry of Obedience, that I let it drop by the Way; at which she immediately startled, and said it fell towards her. Upon this I looked very blank; and, observing the Concern of the whole Table, began to consider my self, with some Confusion, as a Person that had brought a Disaster upon the Family. The Lady however recovering her self after a little space, said to her Husband with a Sigh, *My Dear, Misfortunes never come Single.* My Friend, I found, acted but an under-Part at his Table, and being a Man of more Good-nature than Understanding, thinks himself obliged to fall in with all the Passions and Humours of his Yoke-Fellow: *Do not you remember, Child,* says she, *that the Pidgeon-house fell the very Afternoon that our careless Wench spilt the Salt upon the Table? Yes,* says he, *My Dear, and the next Post brought us an Account of the Battel of* Almanza. The Reader may guess at the figure I made, after having done all this Mischief. I dispatched my Dinner as soon as I could, with my usual Taciturnity; when, to my utter Confusion, the Lady seeing me quitting my Knife and Fork, and laying them across one another upon my Plate, desired me that I would humour her so far as to take them out of that Figure, and place them side by side. What the Absurdity was which I had committed I did not know, but I suppose there was some traditionary Superstition in it; and therefore, in obedience to the Lady of the House, I disposed of my Knife and Fork in two parallel Lines, which is the figure I shall always lay them in for the future, tho' I do not know any Reason for it.

It is not difficult for a Man to see that a Person has conceived an Aversion to him. For my own part, I quickly found, by the Lady's Looks, that she regarded me as a very odd kind of Fellow, with an unfortunate Aspect: For which Reason I took my leave immediately after Dinner, and withdrew to my own Lodgings.   Upon my Return Home, I fell into a profound Contemplation on the Evils that attend these superstitious Follies of Mankind; how they subject us to imaginary Afflictions, and additional Sorrows, that do not properly come within our Lot.   As if the natural Calamities of Life were not sufficient for it, we turn the most indifferent Circumstances into Misfortunes, and suffer as much from trifling Accidents, as from real Evils.   I have known the shooting of a Star spoil a Night's Rest; and have seen a Man in Love grow pale and lose his Appetite, upon the plucking of a Merry-thought.   A Screech-Owl at Midnight has alarm'd a family, more than a Band of Robbers; nay, the Voice of a Cricket hath struck more Terror than the Roaring of a Lion.   There is nothing so inconsiderable, which may not appear dreadful to an Imagination that is filled with Omens and Prognosticks.   A rusty Nail, or a crooked Pin, shoot up into Prodigies.

I remember I was once in a mixt Assembly, that was full of Noise and Mirth, when on a sudden an old Woman unluckily observed there were thirteen of us in Company.   This Remark struck a pannick Terror into several who were present, insomuch that one or two of the Ladies were going to leave the Room; but a Friend of mine taking notice that one of our Female Companions was big with Child, affirm'd there were fourteen in the Room, and that instead of portending one of the Company should die, it plainly foretold one of them should be born.   Had not my Friend found out this Expedient to break the Omen, I question not but half the Women in the Company would have fallen sick that very Night.

An old Maid, that is troubled with the Vapours, produces infinite Disturbances of this kind among her Friends and Neighbours.   I know a Maiden Aunt, of a great Family, who is one of these Antiquated *Sybils*, that forbodes and prophesies from one end of the Year to the other.   She is always seeing Apparitions, and hearing Death-Watches; and was the other Day almost frighted out of her Wits by the great House-Dog, that howled in the Stable at a time when she lay ill of the Tooth-ach.   Such an extravagant Cast of Mind engages Multitudes of People, not only in impertinent Terrors, but in supernumerary Duties of Life; and arises from that Fear and Ignorance which are natural to the Soul of Man.   The Horror with which we entertain the Thoughts of Death (or indeed of any future Evil) and the Uncertainty of its Approach, fill a melancholy Mind with innumerable Apprehensions and Suspicions, and consequently dispose it to the Observation of such groundless Prodigies and Predictions. For as it is the chief Concern of Wise-Men, to retrench the Evils of Life by the Reasonings of Philosophy; it is the Employment of Fools, to multiply them by the Sentiments of Superstition.

For my own part, I should be very much troubled were I endowed with this Divining Quality, though it should inform me truly of every thing that can befal me. I would not anticipate the Relish of any Happiness, nor feel the Weight of any Misery, before it actually arrives.

I know but one way of fortifying my Soul against these gloomy Presages and Terrors of Mind, and that is, by securing to my self the Friendship and Protection of that Being, who disposes of Events, and governs Futurity. He sees, at one View, the whole Thread of my Existence, not only that Part of it which I have already passed through, but that which runs forward into all the Depths of Eternity. When I lay me down to Sleep, I recommend my self to his Care; when I awake, I give my self up to his Direction. Amidst all the Evils that threaten me, I will look up to him for Help, and question not but he will either avert them, or turn them to my Advantage. Though I know neither the Time nor the Manner of the Death I am to die, I am not at all sollicitous about it; because I am sure that he knows them both, and that he will not fail to comfort and support me under them.   C

No. 8.

[ADDISON.]   Friday, March 9.

At Venus obscuro gradientis aere sepsit,
Et multo nebulae circum dea fudit amictu.
Cernere ne quis eos . . .—Virg.

I SHALL here communicate to the World a couple of Letters, which I believe will give the Reader as good an Entertainment as any that I am able to furnish him with, and therefore shall make no Apology for them.

'*To the* SPECTATOR, *&c.*

Sir,

I am one of the Directors of the Society for the Reformation of Manners, and therefore think my self a proper Person for your Correspondence. I have thoroughly examined the present State of Religion in *Great Britain*, and am able to acquaint you with the predominant Vice of every Market-Town in the whole Island. I can tell you the Progress that Virtue has made in all our Cities, Boroughs, and Corporations; and know as well the evil Practices that are committed in *Berwick* or *Exeter*, as what is done in my own Family. In a word, Sir, I have my Correspondents in the remotest Parts of the Nation, who send me up punctual Accounts from time to time of all the little Irregularities that fall under their Notice in their several Districts and Divisions.

I am no less acquainted with the particular Quarters and Regions of this great Town, than with the different Parts and Distributions of the whole Nation. I can describe every Parish by its Impieties, and can tell you in which of our Streets Lewdness prevails, which Gaming has taken the Possession of, and where Drunkenness has got the better of them both. When I am disposed to raise a Fine for the Poor, I know the Lanes and Allies that are inhabited by common Swearers. When I would encourage the Hospital of *Bridewell*, and improve the Hempen Manufacture, I am very well acquainted with all the Haunts and Resorts of Female Night-walkers.

After this short Account of my self, I must let you know, that the Design of this Paper is to give you Information of a certain irregular Assembly which I think falls very properly under your Observation, especially since the Persons it is composed of are Criminals too considerable for the Animadversions of our Society. I mean, Sir, the Midnight Masque, which has of late been very frequently held in one of the most conspicuous Parts of the Town, and which I hear will be continued with Additions and Improvements. As all the Persons who compose this lawless Assembly are masqued, we dare not attack any of them in *our Way*, lest we should send a Woman of Quality to *Bridewell*, or a Peer of *Great-Britain* to the *Counter*: Besides that, their Numbers are so very great, that I am afraid they would be able to rout our whole Fraternity, though we were accompanied with all our Guard of Constables. Both these Reasons, which secure them from our Authority, make them obnoxious to yours; As both their Disguise and their Numbers will give no particular Person Reason to think himself affronted by you.

If we are rightly informed, the Rules that are observed by this new Society are wonderfully contrived for the Advancement of Cuckoldom. The Women either come by themselves or are introduced by Friends, who are obliged to quit them, upon their first Entrance, to the Conversation of any Body that addresses himself to them. There are several Rooms where the Parties may retire, and, if they please, shew their Faces by Consent. Whispers, Squeezes, Nods, and Embraces, are the innocent Freedoms of the Place. In short, the whole Design of this libidinous Assembly seems to terminate in Assignations and Intrigues; and I hope you will take effectual Methods, by your publick Advice and Admonitions, to prevent such a promiscuous Multitude of both Sexes from meeting together in so clandestine a Manner.   I am

> *Your humble Servant,*
>
> *And Fellow-Labourer,*
>
> T. B.'

Not long after the Perusal of this Letter, I receiv'd another upon the same Subject; which by the Date and Stile of it, I take to be written by some young Templer.

'*Sir,*   *Middle-Temple,* 17$\frac{10}{11}$

When a Man has been guilty of any Vice or Folly, I think the best Attonement he can make for it, is to warn others not to fall into the like.   In order to this I must acquaint you, that some time in *February* last I went to the *Tuesday*'s Masquerade. Upon my first going in I was attack'd by half a Dozen female Quakers, who seem'd willing to adopt me for a Brother; but upon a nearer Examination I found they were a Sisterhood of Coquets disguised in that precise Habit.   I was soon after taken out to dance, and, as I fancied, by a Woman of the first Quality, for she was very tall, and moved gracefully.   As soon as the Minuet was over, we ogled one another through our Masques; and as I am very well read in *Waller*, I repeated to her the four following Verses out of his poem to *Vandike*.

> *The heedless Lover does not know*
> *Whose Eyes they are that wound him so;*
> *But, confounded with thy Art,*
> *Enquires her Name that has his Heart.*

I pronounced these Words with such a languishing Air, that I had some Reason to conclude I had made a Conquest.   She told me that she hoped my Face was not akin to my Tongue; and looking upon her Watch, I accidentally discovered the Figure of a Coronet on the back Part of it.   I was so transported with the Thought of such an Amour, that I plied her from one Room to another with all the Gallantries I could invent; and at length brought things to so happy an Issue, that she gave me a private Meeting the next Day, without Page or Footman, Coach or Equipage.   My Heart danced in Raptures; but I had not lived in this golden Dream above three Days, before I found good Reason to wish that I had continued true to my Laundress.   I have since heard, by a very great Accident, that this fine Lady does not live far from

Covent-Garden, and that I am not the first Cully whom she has pass'd her self upon for a Countess.

Thus, Sir, you see how I have mistaken a *Cloud* for a *Juno*; and if you can make any use of this Adventure, for the Benefit of those who may possibly be as vain young Coxcombs as my self, I do most heartily give you Leave. I am, *Sir*,

Your most humble Admirer,

B. L.'

I design to visit the next Masquerade my self, in the same Habit I wore at *Grand Cairo*; and 'till then shall suspend my Judgment of this Midnight Entertainment.   C

No. 9.
[ADDISON.]   Saturday, March 10.

> *. . . Tigris agit rabida cum tigride pacem*
> *Perpetuam; saevis inter se convenit ursis.*—Juv.

MAN is said to be a Sociable Animal, and, as an Instance of it, we may observe, that we take all Occasions and Pretences of forming our selves into those little Nocturnal Assemblies, which are commonly known by the name of *Clubs*. When a Sett of Men find themselves agree in any Particular, tho' never so trivial, they establish themselves into a kind of Fraternity, and meet once or twice a Week, upon the account of such a Fantastick Resemblance. I know a considerable Market-town, in which there was a Club of fat Men, that did not come together (as you may well suppose) to entertain one another with Sprightliness and Wit, but to keep one another in Countenance: The Room where the Club met was something of the largest, and had two Entrances, the one by a Door of a moderate Size, and the other by a Pair of Folding-doors. If a Candidate for this Corpulent Club could make his Entrance through the first, he was looked upon as unqualified; but if he stuck in the Passage, and could not force his Way through it, the Folding-Doors were immediately thrown open for his Reception, and he was saluted as a Brother. I have heard that this Club, though it consisted but of fifteen Persons, weighed above three Tun.

In Opposition to this Society, there sprung up another composed of Scare-crows and Skeletons, who being very meagre and envious, did all they could to thwart the Designs of their Bulky Brethren, whom they represented as Men of Dangerous Principles; till at length they worked them out of the Favour of the People, and consequently out of the Magistracy. These Factions tore the Corporation in Pieces for several Years, till at length they came to this Accommodation; that the two Bailiffs of the Town should be annually chosen out of the two Clubs; by which means the principal Magistrates are at this Day coupled like Rabbets, one fat and one lean.

Every one has heard of the Club, or rather the Confederacy, of the *Kings*. This grand Alliance was formed a little after the Return of King *Charles* the Second, and admitted into it Men of all Qualities and Professions, provided they agreed in this Sirname of *King*, which, as they imagined, sufficiently declared the Owners of it to be altogether untainted with Republican and Anti-Monarchical Principles.

A Christian Name has likewise been often used as a Badge of Distinction, and made the Occasion of a Club. That of the *Georges*, which used to meet at the Sign of the *George*, on St. *George's* Day, and swear *Before George*, is still fresh in every one's Memory.

There are at present in several Parts of this City what they call *Street-Clubs*, in which the chief Inhabitants of the Street converse together every Night. I remember, upon my enquiring after Lodgings in *Ormond-Street*, the Landlord, to recommend that Quarter of the Town, told me, there was at that time a very good Club in it; he also told me, upon further Discourse with him, that two or three noisie Country Squires, who were settled there the Year before, had considerably sunk the Price of House-Rent; and that the Club (to prevent the like Inconveniences for the future) had Thoughts of taking every House that became vacant into their own Hands, till they had found a Tenant for it, of a sociable Nature and good Conversation.

The *Hum-Drum* Club, of which I was formerly an unworthy Member, was made up of very honest Gentlemen, of peaceable Dispositions, that used to sit together, smoak their Pipes, and say nothing till Midnight. The *Mum* Club (as I am informed) is an Institution of the same Nature, and as great an Enemy to Noise.

After these two innocent Societies, I cannot forbear mentioning a very mischievous one, that was erected in the Reign of King *Charles* the Second: I mean *the Club of Duellists*, in which none was to be admitted that had not fought his Man. The President of it was said to have killed half a dozen in single Combat; and as for the other Members, they took their Seats according to the Number of their Slain. There was likewise a Side-Table, for such as had only drawn Blood, and shewn a laudable Ambition of taking the first Opportunity to qualifie themselves for the first Table.   This Club, consisting only of Men of Honour, did not continue long, most of the Members of it being put to the Sword, or hanged, a little after its Institution.

Our Modern celebrated Clubs are founded upon Eating and Drinking, which are Points wherein most Men agree, and in which the Learned and Illiterate, the Dull and the Airy, the Philosopher and the Buffoon, can all of them bear a Part. The *Kit-Cat* it self is said to have taken its Original from a Mutton-Pye.   The *Beef-Steak*, and *October* Clubs, are neither of them averse to Eating and Drinking, if we may form a Judgment of them from their respective Titles.

When Men are thus knit together, by a Love of Society, not a Spirit of Faction, and don't meet to censure or annoy those that are absent, but to enjoy one another;   When they are thus combined for their own Improvement, or for the Good of others, or at least to relax themselves from the Business of the Day, by an innocent and chearful Conversation, there may be something very useful in these little Institutions and Establishments.

I cannot forbear concluding this Paper with a Scheme of Laws that I met with upon a Wall in a little Ale-house: How I came thither I may inform my Reader at a more convenient time.   These Laws were enacted by a Knot of Artizans and Mechanicks, who used to meet every Night; and as there is something in them which gives us a pretty Picture of low Life, I shall transcribe them Word for Word.

Rules *to be observed in the* Two-penny *Club, erected in this Place, for the Preservation of Friendship and good Neighbourhood.*

I. Every Member at his first coming in shall lay down his Two-Pence.

II. Every Member shall fill his Pipe out of his own Box.

III. If any Member absents himself he shall forfeit a Penny for the Use of the Club, unless in case of Sickness or Imprisonment.

IV. If any Member swears or curses, his Neighbour may give him a Kick upon the Shins.

V. If any Member tells Stories in the Club that are not true, he shall forfeit for every third Lie an Halfpenny.

VI. If any Member strikes another wrongfully, he shall pay his Club for him.

VII. If any Member brings his Wife into the Club, he shall pay for whatever she drinks or smoaks.

VIII. If any Member's Wife comes to fetch him home from the Club, she shall speak to him without the Door.

IX. If any Member calls another Cuckold, he shall be turned out of the Club.

X. None shall be admitted into the Club that is of the same Trade with any Member of it.

XI. None of the Club shall have his Cloaths or Shoes made or mended, but by a Brother-Member.

XII. No Non-juror shall be capable of being a Member.

The Morality of this little Club is guarded by such wholesome Laws and Penalties, that I question not but my Reader will be as well pleased with them, as he would have been with the *Leges Convivales* of *Ben. Johnson*, the Regulations of an old *Roman* Club cited by *Lipsius*, or the Rules of a *Symposium* in an ancient *Greek* Author.   C

No. 10.

[ADDISON.]   Monday, March 12.

> *Non aliter quam qui adverso vix flumine lembum*
> *Remigiis subigit, si bracchia forte remisit,*
> *Atque illum praeceps prono rapit alveus amni.*—Virg.

It is with much Satisfaction that I hear this great City inquiring Day by Day after these my Papers, and receiving my Morning Lectures with a becoming Seriousness and Attention. My Publisher tells me, that there are already Three thousand of them distributed every Day: So that if I allow Twenty Readers to every Paper, which I look upon as a modest Computation, I may reckon about Threescore thousand Disciples in *London* and *Westminster*, who I hope will take care to distinguish themselves from the thoughtless Herd of their ignorant and unattentive Brethren.   Since I have raised to myself so great an Audience, I shall spare no Pains to make their Instruction agreeable, and their Diversion useful.   For which Reasons I shall endeavour to enliven Morality with Wit, and to temper Wit with Morality, that my Readers may, if possible, both Ways find their Account in the Speculation of the Day.   And to the End that their Virtue and Discretion may not be short transient intermittent Starts of Thought, I have resolved to refresh their Memories from Day to Day, till I have recovered them out of that desperate State of Vice and Folly into which the Age is fallen.   The Mind that lies fallow but a single Day, sprouts up in Follies that are only to be killed by a constant and assiduous Culture.   It was said of *Socrates*, that he brought Philosophy down from Heaven, to inhabit among Men; and I shall be ambitious to have it said of me, that I have brought Philosophy out of Closets and Libraries, Schools and Colleges, to dwell in Clubs and Assemblies, at Tea-Tables and in Coffee-Houses.

I would therefore in a very particular Manner recommend these my Speculations to all well regulated Families, that set apart an Hour in every Morning for Tea and Bread and Butter; and would earnestly advise them for their Good to order this Paper to be punctually served up, and to be looked upon as a Part of the Tea Equipage.

Sir *Francis Bacon* observes, that a well-written Book, compared with its Rivals and Antagonists, is like *Moses's* Serpent, that immediately swallow'd up and devoured those of the *Aegyptians*. I shall not be so vain as to think, that where the SPECTATOR appears, the other publick Prints will vanish; but shall leave it to my Reader's Consideration, whether, Is it not much better to be let into the Knowledge of one's self, than to hear what passes in *Muscovy* or *Poland*; and to amuse our selves with such Writings as tend to the wearing out of Ignorance, Passion, and Prejudice, than such as naturally conduce to inflame Hatreds, and make Enmities irreconcileable?

In the next Place, I would recommend this Paper to the daily Perusal of those Gentlemen whom I cannot but consider as my good Brothers and Allies, I mean the Fraternity of Spectators who live in the World without having any thing to do in it; and either by the Affluence of their Fortunes, or Laziness of their Dispositions, have no other Business with the rest of Mankind, but to look upon them. Under this Class of Men are comprehended all contemplative Tradesmen, titular Physicians, Fellows of the Royal Society, Templers that are not given to be contentious, and Statesmen that are out of Business; in short, every one that considers the World as a Theatre, and desires to form a right Judgment of those who are the Actors on it.

There is another Set of Men that I must likewise lay a Claim to, whom I have lately called the Blanks of Society, as being altogether unfurnish'd with Ideas, till the Business and Conversation of the Day has supplied them. I have often consider'd these poor Souls with an Eye of great Commiseration, when I have heard them asking the first Man they have met with, whether there was any News stirring? and by that Means gathering together Materials for thinking. These needy Persons do not know what to talk of, 'till about twelve a Clock in the Morning; for by that Time they are pretty good Judges of the Weather, know which Way the Wind sits, and whether the *Dutch* Mail be come in. As they lie at the Mercy of the first Man they meet, and are grave or impertinent all the Day long, according to the Notions which they have imbibed in the Morning, I would earnestly entreat them not to stir out of their Chambers 'till they have read this Paper, and do promise them that I will daily instil into them such sound and wholesom Sentiments, as shall have a good Effect on their Conversation for the ensuing twelve Hours.

But there are none to whom this Paper will be more useful, than to the Female World. I have often thought there has not been sufficient Pains taken in finding out proper Employments and Diversions for the Fair ones. Their Amusements seem contrived for them rather as they are Women, than as they are reasonable Creatures; and are more adapted to the Sex than to the Species. The Toilet is their great Scene of Business, and the right adjusting of their Hair the principal Employment of their Lives. The sorting of a Suit of Ribbons is reckon'd a very good Morning's Work; and if they make an Excursion to a Mercer's or a Toy-shop, so great a Fatigue makes them unfit for any thing else all the Day after. Their more serious Occupations are Sowing and Embroidery, and their greatest Drudgery the Preparation of Jellies and Sweet-meats. This, I say, is the State of ordinary Women; tho' I know there are Multitudes of those of a more elevated Life and Conversation, that move in an exalted Sphere of Knowledge and Virtue, that join all the Beauties of the Mind to the Ornaments of Dress, and inspire a kind of Awe and Respect, as well as Love, into their Male-Beholders. I hope to encrease the Number of these by Publishing this daily Paper, which I shall always endeavour to make an innocent if not an improving Entertainment, and by that Means at least divert the Minds of my Female Readers from greater Trifles. At the same Time, as I would fain give some finishing Touches to those which are already the most beautiful Pieces in human Nature, I shall endeavour to point out all those Imperfections that are the Blemishes, as well as those Virtues which are the Embellishments, of the Sex. In the mean while I hope these my gentle Readers, who have so much Time on their Hands, will not grudge throwing away a Quarter of an Hour in a Day on this Paper, since they may do it without any Hindrance to Business.

I know several of my Friends and Well-wishers are in great Pain for me, lest I should not be able to keep up the Spirit of a Paper which I oblige my self to furnish every Day: But to make them easie in this Particular, I will promise them faithfully to give it over as soon as I grow dull. This I know will be Matter of great Raillery to the small Wits; who will frequently put me in mind of my Promise, desire me to keep my Word, assure me that it is high Time to give over, with many other little

Pleasantries of the like Nature, which Men of a little smart Genius cannot forbear throwing out against their best Friends, when they have such a Handle given them of being witty. But let them remember that I do hereby enter my Caveat against this Piece of Raillery.   C

No. 11.

[STEELE.]   Tuesday, March 13.

Dat veniam corvis, vexat censura columbas.—Juv.

Arietta is visited by all Persons of both Sexes, who have any Pretence to Wit and Gallantry. She is in that time of Life which is neither affected with the Follies of Youth, or Infirmities of Age; and her Conversation is so mixed with Gaiety and Prudence, that she is agreeable both to the Young and the Old. Her Behaviour is very frank, without being in the least blameable; and as she is out of the Tract of any amorous or ambitious Pursuits of her own, her Visitants entertain her with Accounts of themselves very freely, whether they concern their Passions or their Interests. I made her a Visit this Afternoon, having been formerly introduced to the Honour of her Acquaintance, by my Friend WILL. HONEYCOMB, who has prevailed upon her to admit me sometimes into her Assembly, as a civil inoffensive Man. I found her accompanied with one Person only, a Common-Place Talker, who, upon my Entrance, rose, and after a very slight Civility sat down again; then turning to *Arietta*, pursued his Discourse, which I found was upon the old Topick of Constancy in Love. He went on with great Facility in repeating what he talks every Day of his Life; and, with the Ornaments of insignificant Laughs and Gestures, enforced his Arguments by Quotations out of Plays and Songs, which allude to the Perjuries of the Fair, and the general Levity of Women. Methought he strove to shine more than ordinarily in his Talkative Way, that he might insult my Silence, and distinguish himself before a Woman of *Arietta*'s Taste and Understanding. She had often an Inclination to interrupt him, but could find no Opportunity, till the Larum ceased of it self; which it did not 'till he had repeated and murdered the celebrated Story of the *Ephesian* Matron.

Arietta seemed to regard this Piece of Raillery as an Outrage done to her Sex; as indeed I have always observed that Women, whether out of a nicer Regard to their Honour, or what other Reason I cannot tell, are more sensibly touched with those general Aspersions which are cast upon their Sex, than Men are by what is said of theirs.

When she had a little recovered her self from the serious Anger she was in, she replied in the following manner.

Sir, When I consider how perfectly new all you have said on this Subject is, and that the Story you have given us is not quite Two thousand Years old, I cannot but think it a Piece of Presumption to dispute with you: But your Quotations put me in Mind of the Fable of the Lion and the Man. The Man walking with that noble Animal, shewed him, in the Ostentation of Human Superiority, a Sign of a Man killing a Lion. Upon which the Lion said very justly, *We Lions are none of us Painters, else we could shew a hundred Men killed by Lions, for one Lion killed by a Man.* You Men are Writers, and can represent us Women as Unbecoming as you please in your Works, while we are unable to return the Injury. You have twice or thrice observed in your Discourse, that Hypocrisie is the very Foundation of our Education; and that an Ability to dissemble our Affections, is a professed Part of our Breeding. These, and such other Reflections, are sprinkled up and down the Writings of all Ages, by Authors, who leave behind them Memorials of their Resentment against the Scorn of particular Women, in Invectives against the whole Sex. Such a Writer, I doubt not, was the celebrated *Petronius*, who invented the pleasant Aggravations of the Frailty of the *Ephesian* Lady; but when we consider this Question between the Sexes, which has been either a Point of Dispute or Raillery ever since there were Men and Women, let us take Facts from plain People, and from such as have not either Ambition or Capacity to embellish their Narrations with any Beauties of Imagination. I was the other Day amusing my self with *Ligon*'s Account of *Barbadoes*; and, in Answer to your well-wrought Tale, I will give you (as it dwells upon my Memory) out of that honest Traveller, in his fifty fifth Page, the History of *Inkle* and *Yarico*.

Mr. *Thomas Inkle*, of *London*, aged twenty Years, embarked in the *Downs* on the good Ship called the *Achilles*, bound for the *West-Indies*, on the 16th of *June*, 1647, in order to improve his Fortune by Trade and Merchandize. Our Adventurer was the third Son of an eminent Citizen, who had taken particular Care to instill into his Mind an early Love of Gain, by making him a perfect Master of Numbers, and consequently giving him a quick View of Loss and Advantage, and preventing the natural Impulses of his Passions, by Prepossession towards his Interests. With a Mind thus turned, young *Inkle* had a Person every way agreeable, a ruddy Vigour in his Countenance, Strength in his Limbs, with Ringlets of fair Hair loosely flowing on his Shoulders. It happened, in the Course of the Voyage,

that the *Achilles*, in some Distress, put into a Creek on the Main
of *America*, in Search of Provisions: The Youth, who is the
Hero of my Story, among others, went ashore on this Occasion.
From their first Landing they were observed by a Party of
Indians, who hid themselves in the Woods for that Purpose.
The *English* unadvisedly marched a great distance from the
Shore into the Country, and were intercepted by the Natives,
who slew the greatest Number of them. Our Adventurer
escaped among others, by flying into a Forest. Upon his
coming into a remote and pathless Part of the Wood, he threw
himself, tired and breathless, on a little Hillock, when an
Indian Maid rushed from a Thicket behind him: After the
first Surprize, they appeared mutually agreeable to each other.
If the *European* was highly Charmed with the Limbs, Features,
and wild Graces of the Naked *American*; the *American* was no
less taken with the Dress, Complexion, and Shape of an
European, covered from Head to Foot. The *Indian* grew immediately enamoured of him, and consequently sollicitous for
his Preservation: She therefore conveyed him to a Cave, where
she gave him a delicious Repast of Fruits, and led him to a
Stream to slake his Thirst. In the midst of these good Offices,
she would sometimes play with his Hair, and delight in the
Opposition of its Colour to that of her Fingers: Then open his
Bosom, then laugh at him for covering it. She was, it seems,
a Person of Distinction, for she every Day came to him in a
different Dress, of the most beautiful Shells, Bugles, and Bredes.
She likewise brought him a great many Spoils, which her other
Lovers had presented to her; so that his Cave was richly
adorned with all the spotted Skins of Beasts, and most Party-
coloured Feathers of Fowls, which that World afforded. To
make his Confinement more tolerable, she would carry him in
the dusk of the Evening, or by the favour of Moonlight, to unfrequented Groves and Solitudes, and shew him where to lye
down in Safety, and sleep amidst the Falls of Waters, and
Melody of Nightingales. Her Part was to watch and hold him
awake in her Arms, for fear of her Countrymen, and awake him
on Occasions to consult his Safety. In this manner did the
Lovers pass away their Time, till they had learn'd a Language
of their own, in which the Voyager communicated to his Mistress, how happy he should be to have her in his Country,
where she should be Cloathed in such Silks as his Wastecoat
was made of, and be carried in Houses drawn by Horses, without being exposed to Wind or Weather. All this he promised
her the Enjoyment of, without such Fears and Alarms as they
were there tormented with. In this tender Correspondence
these Lovers lived for several Months, when *Yarico*, instructed

by her Lover, discovered a Vessel on the Coast, to which she
made Signals; and in the Night, with the utmost Joy and
Satisfaction, accompanied him to a Ship's-Crew of his Countrymen, bound for *Barbadoes*. When a Vessel from the Main
arrives in that Island, it seems the Planters come down to the
Shoar, where there is an immediate Market of the *Indians* and
other Slaves, as with us of Horses and Oxen.

To be short, Mr. *Thomas Inkle*, now coming into *English*
Territories, began seriously to reflect upon his loss of Time, and
to weigh with himself how many Days Interest of his Money
he had lost during his Stay with *Yarico*. This Thought made
the young Man very pensive, and careful what Account he
should be able to give his Friends of his Voyage. Upon which
Considerations, the prudent and frugal young Man sold *Yarico*
to a *Barbadian* Merchant; notwithstanding that the poor Girl,
to incline him to commiserate her Condition, told him that she
was with Child by him: But he only made use of that Information, to rise in his Demands upon the Purchaser.

I was so touch'd with this Story, (which I think should be
always a Counterpart to the *Ephesian* Matron) that I left the
Room with Tears in my Eyes; which a Woman of *Arietta*'s
good Sense, did, I am sure, take for greater Applause, than any
Compliments I could make her.   R

No. 12.
ADDISON.]   Wednesday, March 14.

> . . . *Veteres avias tibi de pulmone revello.*—Pers.

At my coming to *London*, it was some time before I could
settle my self in a House to my liking. I was forced to quit
my first Lodgings, by reason of an officious Landlady, that
would be asking me every Morning how I had slept. I then
fell into an honest Family, and lived very happily for above a
Week; when my Landlord, who was a jolly good-natured Man,
took it into his Head that I wanted Company, and therefore
would frequently come into my Chamber to keep me from
being alone. This I bore for two or three Days; but telling
me one Day that he was afraid I was melancholy, I thought
it was high time for me to be gone, and accordingly took new
Lodgings that very Night. About a Week after, I found my
jolly Landlord, who, as I said before, was an honest hearty
Man, had put me into an Advertisement of the *Daily Courant*,
in the following Words. *Whereas a melancholy Man left his
Lodgings on* Thursday *last in the Afternoon, and was afterwards*

seen going towards Islington; *If any one can give Notice of him
to R. B. Fishmonger in the* Strand, *he shall be very well rewarded
for his pains.* As I am the best Man in the World to keep
my own Counsel, and my Landlord the Fishmonger not knowing my Name, this Accident of my Life was never discovered
to this very Day.

I am now settled with a Widow-woman, who has a great
many Children, and complies with my Humour in every thing.
I do not remember that we have exchanged a Word together
these Five Years; my Coffee comes into my Chamber every
Morning without asking for it; if I want Fire I point to my
Chimney, if Water to my Bason: Upon which my Landlady
nodds, as much as to say she takes my Meaning, and immediately obeys my Signals. She has likewise model'd her Family
so well, that when her little Boy offers to pull me by the Coat,
or prattle in my Face, his eldest Sister immediately calls him
off, and bids him not disturb the Gentleman. At my first
entring into the Family, I was troubled with the Civility of
their rising up to me every time I came into the Room; but my
Landlady observing that upon these Occasions I always cried
Pish, and went out again, has forbidden any such Ceremony to
be used in the House; so that at present I walk into the
Kitchen or Parlour without being taken notice of, or giving
any Interruption to the Business or Discourse of the Family.
The Maid will ask her Mistress (tho' I am by) whether the
Gentleman is ready to go to Dinner, as the Mistress (who is
indeed an excellent Housewife) scolds at the Servants as
heartily before my Face as behind my Back. In short, I move
up and down the House and enter into all Companies, with the
same Liberty as a Cat or any other Domestick Animal, and am
as little suspected of telling any thing that I hear or see.

I remember last Winter there were several young Girls of
the Neighbourhood sitting about the Fire with my Landlady's
Daughters, and telling Stories of Spirits and Apparitions.
Upon my opening the Door the young Women broke off their
Discourse, but my Landlady's Daughters telling them that it
was no Body but the Gentleman (for that is the Name which I
go by in the Neighbourhood as well as in the Family) they went
on without minding me. I seated my self by the Candle that
stood on a Table at one end of the Room; and pretending to
read a Book that I took out of my Pocket, heard several
dreadful Stories of Ghosts as pale as Ashes that had stood at
the Feet of a Bed, or walked over a Church-yard by Moonlight: And of others that had been conjured into the *Red-
Sea*, for disturbing People's Rest, and drawing their Curtains
at Midnight; with many other old Women's Fables of the like

nature. As one Spirit raised another, I observed that at the
End of every Story the whole Company closed their Ranks, and
crouded about the Fire: I took Notice in particular of a little
Boy, who was so attentive to every Story, that I am mistaken
if he ventures to go to Bed by himself this Twelve-month.
Indeed they talked so long, that the Imaginations of tho whole
Assembly were manifestly crazed, and I am sure will be the
worse for it as long as they live. I heard one of the Girls,
that had looked upon me over her Shoulder, asking the Company how long I had been in the Room, and whether I did
not look paler than I used to do. This put me under some
Apprehensions that I should be forced to explain my self if I
did not retire; for which Reason I took the Candle in my Hand,
and went up into my Chamber, not without wondering at this
unaccountable Weakness in reasonable Creatures, that they
should love to astonish and terrifie one another. Were I a
Father, I should take a particular Care to preserve my Children
from these little Horrors of Imagination, which they are apt to
contract when they are young, and are not able to shake off
when they are in Years. I have known a Soldier that has
entered a Breach, affrighted at his own Shadow; and look pale
upon a little scratching at his Door, who the Day before had
marched up against a Battery of Cannon. There are Instances
of Persons, who have been terrified, even to Distraction, at the
Figure of a Tree, or the shaking of a Bull-rush. The Truth of
it is, I look upon a sound Imagination as the greatest Blessing
of Life, next to a clear Judgment and a good Conscience. In
the mean time, since there are very few whose Minds are not
more or less subject to these dreadful Thoughts and Apprehensions, we ought to arm our selves against them by the
Dictates of Reason and Religion, *to pull the old Woman out of
our Hearts* (as *Persius* expresses it in the Motto of my Paper)
and extinguish those impertinent Notions which we imbibed
at a Time that we were not able to judge of their Absurdity.
Or if we believe, as many wise and good Men have done, that
there are such Phantoms and Apparitions as those I have been
speaking of, let us endeavour to establish to our selves an Interest in him who holds the Reins of the whole Creation in
his Hand, and moderates them after such a Manner, that it is
impossible for one Being to break loose upon another without
his Knowledge and Permission.

For my own Part, I am apt to join in Opinion with those
who believe that all the Regions of Nature swarm with Spirits;
and that we have Multitudes of Spectators on all our Actions,
when we think our selves most alone: But instead of terrifying
myself with such a Notion, I am wonderfully pleased to think

that I am always engaged with such an innumerable Society, in searching out the Wonders of the Creation, and joining in the same Consort of Praise and Adoration.

Milton has finely described this mixed Communion of Men and Spirits in Paradise; and had doubtless his Eye upon a Verse in old *Hesiod*, which is almost Word for Word the same with his third Line in the following Passage.

> . . . *Nor think, though Men were none,*
> *That Heav'n would want Spectators, God want Praise;*
> *Millions of spiritual Creatures walk the Earth*
> *Unseen, both when we wake and when we sleep;*
> *All these with ceaseless Praise his Works behold*
> *Both Day and Night. How often from the Steep*
> *Of echoing Hill or Thicket have we heard*
> *Celestial Voices to the midnight Air,*
> *Sole, or responsive each to other's Note,*
> *Singing their great Creator? Oft in Bands*
> *While they keep Watch, or nightly rounding walk*
> *With heav'nly Touch of instrumental Sounds,*
> *In full harmonick Number join'd their Songs*
> *Divide the Night, and lift our Thoughts to Heav'n.*

C

No. 13.

[ADDISON.]   Thursday, March 15.

Dic mihi, si fias tu leo, qualis eris?—Mart.

THERE is nothing that of late Years has afforded Matter of greater Amusement to the Town than Signior *Nicolini*'s Combat with a Lion in the *Hay-Market*, which has been very often exhibited to the general Satisfaction of most of the Nobility and Gentry in the Kingdom of *Great Britain*. Upon the first Rumour of this intended Combat, it was confidently affirmed, and is still believed by many in both Galleries, that there would be a tame Lion sent from the *Tower* every Opera Night, in order to be killed by *Hydaspes*; this Report, though altogether groundless, so universally prevailed in the upper Regions of the Play-house, that some of the most refined Politicians in those Parts of the Audience gave it out in Whisper, that the Lion was a Cousin-German of the Tyger who made his Appearance in King *William*'s Days, and that the Stage would be supplied with Lions at the publick Expence, during the whole Session. Many likewise were the Conjectures of the Treatment which this Lion was to meet with from the Hands of Signior *Nicolini*; some supposed that he was to subdue him in *Recitativo*, as *Orpheus* used to serve the wild Beasts in his time, and afterwards to knock him on

the Head; some fancied that the Lion would not pretend to
lay his Paws upon the Hero, by reason of the received Opinion,
that a Lion will not hurt a Virgin: Several, who pretended to
have seen the Opera in *Italy*, had informed their Friends, that
the Lion was to act a Part in *High-Dutch*, and roar twice or
thrice to a *Thorough Base*, before he fell at the Feet of *Hydaspes*.
To clear up a Matter that was so variously reported, I have
made it my Business to examine whether this pretended Lion
is really the Savage he appears to be, or only a Counterfeit.

But before I communicate my Discoveries, I must acquaint
the Reader, that upon my walking behind the Scenes last
Winter, as I was thinking on something else, I accidentally
justled against a monstrous Animal that extreamly startled
me, and upon my nearer Survey of it, appeared to be a Lion
Rampant. The Lion, seeing me very much surprized, told me,
in a gentle Voice, that I might come by him if I pleased: *For*
(says he) *I do not intend to hurt any body*. I thanked him very
kindly, and passed by him. And in a little time after saw him
leap upon the Stage, and act his Part with very great Applause.
It has been observed by several, that the Lion has changed his
manner of Acting twice or thrice since his first Appearance;
which will not seem strange, when I acquaint my Reader that
the Lion has been changed upon the Audience three several
times. The first Lion was a Candle-snuffer, who being a Fellow
of a testy cholerick Temper over-did his Part, and would not
suffer himself to be killed so easily as he ought to have done;
besides, it was observed of him, that he grew more surly every
time he came out of the Lion; and having dropt some Words in
ordinary Conversation, as if he had not fought his best, and
that he suffered himself to be thrown upon his Back in the
Scuffle, and that he would wrestle with Mr. *Nicolini* for what he
pleased, out of his Lion's Skin, it was thought proper to discard
him: And it is verily believed to this Day, that had he been
brought upon the Stage another time, he would certainly have
done Mischief. Besides, it was objected against the first Lion,
that he reared himself so high upon his hinder Paws, and walked
in so erect a Posture, that he looked more like an old Man
than a Lion.

The second Lion was a Taylor by Trade, who belonged to
the Play-house, and had the Character of a mild and peaceable
Man in his Profession. If the former was too furious, this was
too sheepish, for his Part; insomuch that after a short modest
Walk upon the Stage, he would fall at the first Touch of
Hydaspes, without grapling with him, and giving him an
Opportunity of showing his Variety of *Italian* Tripps: It is
said indeed, that he once gave him a Ripp in his flesh-colour

Doublet, but this was only to make Work for himself, in his
private Character of a Taylor.   I must not omit that it was
this second Lion who treated me with so much Humanity
behind the Scenes.

The Acting Lion at present is, as I am informed, a Country
Gentleman, who does it for his Diversion, but desires his Name
may be concealed.   He says very handsomely in his own Excuse
that he does not Act for Gain, that he indulges an innocent
Pleasure in it, and that it is better to pass away an Evening
in this manner, than in Gaming and Drinking: But at the
same time says, with a very agreeable Raillery upon himself,
that if his Name should be known, the ill-natured World might
call him, *The Ass in the Lion's Skin.*   This Gentleman's
Temper is made out of such a happy Mixture of the Mild and
the Cholerick, that he out-does both his Predecessors, and has
drawn together greater Audiences than have been known in
the Memory of Man.

I must not conclude my Narrative, without taking Notice of
a groundless Report that has been raised, to a Gentleman's
Disadvantage, of whom I must declare my self an Admirer;
namely, that Signior *Nicolini* and the Lion have been seen
sitting peaceably by one another, and smoaking a Pipe together,
behind the Scenes; by which their common Enemies would
insinuate, that it is but a sham Combat which they represent
upon the Stage: But upon Enquiry I find, that if any such
Correspondence has passed between them, it was not till the
Combat was over, when the Lion was to be looked upon as
dead, according to the received Rules of the *Drama.*   Besides,
this is what is practised every Day in *Westminster-Hall,* where
nothing is more usual than to see a Couple of Lawyers, who have
been tearing each other to pieces in the Court, embracing one
another as soon as they are out of it.

I would not be thought, in any part of this Relation, to
reflect upon Signior *Nicolini,* who in Acting this Part only
complies with the wretched Taste of his Audience; he knows
very well, that the Lion has many more Admirers than himself; as they say of the famous *Equestrian* Statue on the *Pont-
Neuf* at *Paris,* that more People go to see the Horse, than the
King who sits upon it.   On the contrary, it gives me a just
Indignation, to see a Person whose Action gives new Majesty
to Kings, Resolution to Heroes, and Softness to Lovers, thus
sinking from the Greatness of his Behaviour, and degraded
into the Character of *the* London *Prentice.*   I have often
wished, that our Tragoedians would copy after this great
Master in Action.   Could they make the same use of their
Arms and Legs, and inform their Faces with as significant

Looks and Passions, how glorious would an *English* Tragedy appear with that Action, which is capable of giving a Dignity to the forced Thoughts, cold Conceits, and unnatural Expressions of an *Italian* Opera. In the mean time, I have related this Combat of the Lion, to shew what are at present the reigning Entertainments of the Politer Part of *Great Britain.*

Audiences have often been reproached by Writers for the Coarseness of their Taste, but our present Grievance does not seem to be the Want of a good Taste, but of Common Sense.

C

No. 14.

[STEELE.] Friday, March 16.

. . . *Teque his infelix exue monstris.*—Ovid.

I was reflecting this Morning upon the Spirit and Humour of the publick Diversions Five and twenty Years ago, and those of the present Time; and lamented to my self, that though in those Days they neglected their Morality, they kept up their Good Sense; but that the *beau Monde* at present is only grown more childish, not more innocent, than the former. While I was in this Train of Thought, an odd Fellow, whose Face I have often seen at the Play-house, gave me the following Letter with these Words, *Sir, The Lion presents his humble Service to you, and desired me to give this into your own Hands.*

'*From my Den in the* Hay-Market, March 15.

Sir,

I have read all your Papers, and have stifled my Resentment against your Reflections upon Operas, 'till that of this Day, wherein you plainly insinuate that Signior *Grimaldi* and my self have a Correspondence more friendly than is consistent with the Valour of his Character, or the Fierceness of mine. I desire you would for your own Sake forbear such Intimations for the future; and must say it is a great Piece of Ill-nature in you, to shew so great an Esteem for a Foreigner, and to discourage a *Lion* that is your own Country-man.

I take notice of your Fable of the Lion and Man, but am so equally concerned in that Matter, that I shall not be offended to which soever of the Animals the Superiority is given. You have misrepresented me, in saying that I am a Country Gentleman who act only for my Diversion; whereas, had I still the same Woods to range in which I once had when I was a Foxhunter, I should not resign my Manhood for a Maintenance;

and assure you, as low as my Circumstances are at present, I
am so much a Man of Honour, that I would scorn to be any
Beast for Bread but a Lion.

Yours, &c.'

I had no sooner ended this, than one of my Landlady's
Children brought me in several others, with some of which I
shall make up my present Paper, they all having a Tendency
to the same Subject, *viz.* the Elegance of our present Diversions.

'Sir, *Covent-Garden, March* 13.

I have been for twenty Years Under-Sexton of this Parish of
St. *Paul's, Covent-Garden,* and have not missed tolling in to
Prayers six times in all those Years; which Office I have performed to my great Satisfaction, till this Fortnight last past,
during which Time I find my Congregation take the Warning
of my Bell, Morning and Evening, to go to a Puppet-Show set
forth by one *Powell* under the *Piazzas.* By this Means I have
not only lost my two Customers, whom I used to place for
Six-pence a-piece over-against Mrs. *Rachel Eye-bright,* but Mrs.
Rachel her self is gone thither also. There now appear among
us none but a few ordinary People, who come to Church only
to say their Prayers, so that I have no Work worth speaking
of but on *Sundays.* I have placed my Son at the *Piazzas,* to
acquaint the Ladies that the Bell rings for Church, and that it
stands on the other Side of the *Garden;* but they only laugh
at the Child.

I desire you would lay this before all the World, that I may
not be made such a Tool for the future, and that Punchinello
may chuse Hours less canonical. As things are now, Mr.
Powell has a full Congregation, while we have a very thin
House; which if you can remedy, you will very much oblige,

Sir,

Your, &c.'

The following Epistle I find is from the Undertaker of the
Masquerade.

'Sir,

I have observed the Rules of my Masque so carefully (in not
enquiring into Persons) that I cannot tell whether you were one
of the Company or not last *Tuesday;* but if you were not, and
still design to come, I desire you would, for your own Entertainment, please to admonish the Town, that all Persons
indifferently are not fit for this sort of Diversion. I could
wish, Sir, you could make them understand, that it is a kind of
acting to go in Masquerade, and a Man should be able to say or
do things proper for the Dress in which he appears. We have

now and then Rakes in the Habit of *Roman* Senators, and grave
Politicians in the Dress of Rakes. The Misfortune of the thing
is, that People dress themselves in what they have a Mind to
be, and not what they are fit for. There is not a Girl in the
Town, but let her have her Will in going to a Masque, and she
shall dress as a Shepherdess. But let me beg of them to read
the *Arcadia*, or some other good Romance, before they appear
in any such Character at my House. The last Day we presented, every Body was so rashly habited, that when they came
to speak to each other, a Nymph with a Crook had not a Word
to say but in the pert Stile of the Pit Bawdry; and a Man in
the Habit of a Philosopher was speechless, till an Occasion
offered of expressing himself in the Refuse of the Tyring-Rooms.
We had a Judge that danced a Minuet, with a Quaker for his
Partner, while half a dozen Harlequins stood by as Spectators:
A *Turk* drank me off two Bottles of Wine, and a *Jew* eat me up
half a Ham of Bacon. If I can bring my Design to bear, and
make the Masquers preserve their Characters in my Assemblies,
I hope you will allow there is a Foundation laid for more elegant
and improving Gallantries than any the Town at present
affords; and consequently, that you will give your Approbation to the Endeavours of,

Sir,

Your most obedient humble Servant.'

I am very glad the following Epistle obliges me to mention
Mr. *Powell* a second Time in the same Paper; for indeed there
cannot be too great Encouragement given to his Skill in Motions,
provided he is under proper Restrictions.

' *Sir,*

The Opera at the *Hay-Market,* and that under the little
Piazza in *Covent-Garden,* being at present the two leading
Diversions of the Town, and Mr. *Powell* professing in his
Advertisements to set up *Whittington and his Cat* against
Rinaldo and *Armida,* my Curiosity led me the Beginning of last
Week to view both these Performances, and make my Observa-
tions upon them.

First therefore, I cannot but observe that Mr. *Powell* wisely
forbearing to give his Company a Bill of Fare before-hand,
every Scene is new and unexpected; whereas it is certain, that
the Undertakers of the *Hay-Market,* having raised too great an
Expectation in their printed Opera, very much disappoint their
Audience on the Stage.

The King of *Jerusalem* is obliged to come from the City on
foot, instead of being drawn in a triumphant Chariot by white

Horses, as my Opera-Book had promised me; and thus while
I expected *Armida's* Dragons should rush forward towards
Argantes, I found the Hero was obliged to go to *Armida*, and
hand her out of her Coach. We had also but a very short
Allowance of Thunder and Lightning; tho' I cannot in this
Place omit doing Justice to the Boy who had the Direction of
the Two painted Dragons, and made them spit Fire and Smoke:
He flash'd out his Rosin in such just Proportions and in such
due Time, that I could not forbear conceiving Hopes of his
being one Day a most excellent Player. I saw indeed but Two
things wanting to render his whole Action compleat, I mean the
keeping his Head a little lower, and hiding his Candle.

I observe that Mr. *Powell* and the Undertakers had both the
same Thought, and I think much about the same time, of
introducing Animals on their several Stages, tho' indeed with
very different Success. The Sparrows and Chaffinches at the
Hay-Market fly as yet very irregularly over the Stage; and
instead of perching on the Trees and performing their Parts,
these young Actors either get into the Galleries or put out the
Candles; whereas Mr. *Powell* has so well disciplin'd his Pig,
that in the first Scene he and Punch dance a Minuet together.
I am informed however, that Mr. *Powell* resolves to excell
his Adversaries in their own Way; and introduce Larks in his
next Opera of *Susanna*, or *Innocence betrayed*, which will be
exhibited next Week with a Pair of new Elders.

The Moral of Mr. *Powell's* Drama is violated, I confess, by
Punch's national Reflections on the *French*, and King *Harry's*
laying his Leg upon the Queen's Lap in too ludicrous a manner
before so great an Assembly.

As to the Mechanism and Scenary, every thing indeed was
uniform and of a Piece, and the Scenes were managed very
dexterously; which calls on me to take notice, that at the
Hay-Market the Undertakers forgetting to change their Side-
Scenes, we were presented with a Prospect of the Ocean in the
midst of a delightful Grove; and tho' the Gentlemen on the
Stage had very much contributed to the Beauty of the Grove
by walking up and down between the Trees, I must own I was
not a little astonished to see a well-dressed young Fellow, in
a full-bottom'd Wigg, appear in the midst of the Sea, and without any visible Concern taking Snuff.

I shall only observe one thing further, in which both Dramas
agree; which is, that by the Squeak of their Voices the Heroes
of each are Eunuchs; and as the Wit in both Pieces is equal,
I must prefer the Performance of Mr. *Powell*, because it is in
our own Language.

R   *I am, &c.'*

No. 15.

[ADDISON.]   Saturday, March 17.

Parva leves capiunt animos.—Ovid.

WHEN I was in *France*, I used to gaze with great Astonishment at the Splendid Equipages, and Party-coloured Habits, of that Fantastick Nation.   I was one Day in particular contemplating a Lady, that sate in a Coach adorned with gilded *Cupids*, and finely painted with the Loves of *Venus* and *Adonis*.   The Coach was drawn by six milk-white Horses, and loaden behind with the same Number of powder'd Footmen.   Just before the Lady were a Couple of beautiful Pages, that were stuck among the Harness, and, by their gay Dresses and smiling Features, looked like the elder Brothers of the little Boys that were carved and painted in every corner of the Coach.

The Lady was the unfortunate *Cleanthe*, who afterwards gave an Occasion to a pretty melancholy Novel.   She had, for several Years, received the Addresses of a Gentleman, whom, after a long and intimate Acquaintance she forsook, upon the Account of this shining Equipage, which had been offered to her by one of Great Riches, but a Crazy Constitution.   The Circumstances in which I saw her, were, it seems, the Disguises only of a broken Heart, and a kind of Pageantry to cover Distress; for in two Months after she was carried to her Grave with the same Pomp and Magnificence; being sent thither partly by the Loss of one Lover, and partly by the Possession of another.

I have often reflected with my self on this unaccountable Humour in Woman-kind, of being smitten with every thing that is showy and superficial; and on the numberless Evils that befal the Sex, from this light fantastical Disposition.   I my self remember a young Lady, that was very warmly sollicited by a Couple of importunate Rivals, who for several Months together did all they could to recommend themselves, by Complacency of Behaviour, and Agreeableness of Conversation.   At length, when the Competition was doubtful, and the Lady undetermined in her Choice, one of the young Lovers very luckily bethought himself of adding a supernumerary Lace to his Liveries, which had so good an Effect that he Married her the very Week after.

The usual Conversation of ordinary Women very much cherishes this natural Weakness of being taken with Outside and Appearance.   Talk of a new-married Couple, and you immediately hear whether they keep their Coach and six, or eat in Plate: Mention the Name of an absent Lady, and it is ten to one but you learn something of her Gown and Petticoat.

A Ball is a great Help to Discourse, and a Birth-Day furnishes Conversation for a Twelve-month after. A Furbelow of precious Stones, an Hat buttoned with a Diamond, a Brocade Waistcoat or Petticoat, are standing Topicks. In short, they consider only the Drapery of the Species, and never cast away a Thought on those Ornaments of the Mind, that make Persons Illustrious in themselves, and Useful to others. When Women are thus perpetually dazling one another's Imaginations, and filling their Heads with nothing but Colours, it is no Wonder that they are more attentive to the superficial Parts of Life, than the solid and substantial Blessings of it. A Girl, who has been trained up in this kind of Conversation, is in danger of every Embroidered Coat that comes in her Way. A Pair of fringed Gloves may be her Ruin. In a word, Lace and Ribbons, Silver and Gold Galloons, with the like glittering Gew-gaws, are so many Lures to Women of weak Minds or low Educations, and, when artificially displayed, are able to fetch down the most airy Coquet from the wildest of her Flights and Rambles.

True Happiness is of a retired Nature, and an Enemy to Pomp and Noise; it arises, in the first place, from the Enjoyment of one's self; and, in the next, from the Friendship and Conversation of a few select Companions. It loves Shade and Solitude, and naturally haunts Groves and Fountains, Fields and Meadows: In short, it feels every thing it wants within it self, and receives no Addition from Multitudes of Witnesses and Spectators. On the contrary, false Happiness loves to be in a Crowd, and to draw the Eyes of the World upon her. She does not receive any Satisfaction from the Applauses which she gives her self, but from the Admiration which she raises in others. She flourishes in Courts and Palaces, Theatres and Assemblies, and has no Existence but when she is looked upon.

Aurelia, though a Woman of great Quality, delights in the Privacy of a Country Life, and passes away a great part of her Time in her own Walks and Gardens. Her husband, who is her Bosom Friend, and Companion in her Solitudes, has been in Love with her ever since he knew her. They both abound with good Sense, consummate Virtue, and a mutual Esteem; and are a perpetual Entertainment to one another. Their Family is under so regular an Oeconomy, in its Hours of Devotion and Repast, Employment and Diversion, that it looks like a little Common-wealth within it self. They often go into Company, that they may return with the greater Delight to one another; and sometimes live in Town, not to enjoy it so properly as to grow weary of it, that they may renew in themselves the Relish of a Country Life. By this means they are

happy in each other, beloved by their Children, adored by their
Servants, and are become the Envy, or rather the Delight, of
all that know them.

How different to this is the Life of *Fulvia!* she considers her
Husband as her Steward, and looks upon Discretion and good
Housewifery as little domestick Virtues, unbecoming a Woman
of Quality.   She thinks Life lost in her own Family, and fancies
her self out of the World when she is not in the Ring, the Play-
house, or the Drawing-Room: She lives in a perpetual Motion
of Body, and Restlessness of Thought, and is never easie in
any one Place when she thinks there is more Company in
another.   The missing of an Opera the first Night, would be
more afflicting to her than the Death of a Child.   She pities
all the valuable Part of her own Sex, and calls every Woman
of a prudent modest retired Life, a poor-spirited unpolished
Creature.   What a Mortification would it be to *Fulvia*, if she
knew that her setting her self to View is but exposing her self,
and that she grows Contemptible by being Conspicuous.

I cannot conclude my Paper, without observing that *Virgil*
has very finely touched upon this Female Passion for Dress
and Show, in the Character of *Camilla*; who, though she seems
to have shaken off all the other Weaknesses of her Sex, is still
described as a Woman in this Particular.   The Poet tells us,
that after having made a great Slaughter of the Enemy, she
unfortunately cast her Eye on a *Trojan* who wore an embroidered Tunick, a beautiful Coat of Mail, with a Mantle of
the finest Purple.   *A Golden Bow,* says he, *hung upon his
Shoulder; his Garment was buckled with a Golden Clasp, and his
Head was covered with an Helmet of the same shining Metal.*
The *Amazon* immediately singled out this well-dressed Warrior,
being seized with a Woman's Longing for the pretty Trappings
that he was adorned with:

> . . . *totumque incauta per agmen*
> *Femineo praedae & spoliorum ardebat amore.*

This heedless Pursuit after these glittering Trifles, the Poet (by
a nice concealed Moral) represents to have been the Destruc-
tion of his Female Hero.   C

No. 16.

[ADDISON.]   Monday, March 19.

Quid verum atque decens curo & rogo & omnis in hoc sum.—Hor

I HAVE received a Letter, desiring me to be very satyrical upon
the little Muff that is now in Fashion; another informs me of a

Pair of silver Garters buckled below the Knee, that have been lately seen at the *Rainbow* Coffee-house in *Fleetstreet*; a third sends me an heavy Complaint against fringed Gloves. To be brief, there is scarce an Ornament of either Sex which one or other of my Correspondents has not inveighed against with some Bitterness, and recommended to my Observation. I must therefore, once for all, inform my Readers, that it is not my Intention to sink the Dignity of this my Paper with Reflections upon Red-heels or Top-knots, but rather to enter into the Passions of Mankind, and to correct those depraved Sentiments that give Birth to all those little Extravagances which appear in their outward Dress and Behaviour. Foppish and fantastick Ornaments are only Indications of Vice, not criminal in themselves. Extinguish Vanity in the Mind, and you naturally retrench the little Superfluities of Garniture and Equipage. The Blossoms will fall of themselves, when the Root that nourishes them is destroyed.

I shall therefore, as I have said, apply my Remedies to the first Seeds and Principles of an affected Dress, without descending to the Dress it self; though at the same time I must own, that I have thoughts of creating an Officer under me, to be entituled, *The Censor of small Wares*, and of allotting him one Day in a Week for the Execution of such his Office. An Operator of this Nature might act under me, with the same Regard as a Surgeon to a Physician; the one might be employed in healing those Blotches and Tumours which break out in the Body, while the other is sweetning the Blood and rectifying the Constitution. To speak truly, the young People of both Sexes are so wonderfully apt to shoot out into long Swords or sweeping Trains, bushy Head-dresses or full-bottom'd Perriwigs, with several other Incumbrances of Dress, that they stand in need of being pruned very frequently, lest they should be oppressed with Ornaments, and over-run with the Luxuriency of their Habits. I am much in doubt, whether I should give the Preference to a Quaker, that is trimmed close and almost cut to the Quick, or to a Beau that is loaden with such a Redundance of Excrescences. I must therefore desire my Correspondents to let me know how they approve my Project, and whether they think the erecting of such a petty Censorship may not turn to the Emolument of the Publick; for I would not do any thing of this Nature rashly and without Advice.

There is another Set of Correspondents to whom I must address my self in the second Place; I mean, such as fill their Letters with private Scandal, and black Accounts of particular Persons and Families. The World is so full of Ill-nature, that I have Lampoons sent me by People who cannot spell, and

Satyrs compos'd by those who scarce know how to write. By the last Post in particular I received a Packet of Scandal which is not legible; and have a whole Bundle of Letters in Women's Hands that are full of Blots and Calumnies, insomuch that when I see the Name *Caelia, Phillis, Pastora,* or the like, at the Bottom of a Scrawl, I conclude on course that it brings me some Account of a fallen Virgin, a faithless Wife, or an amorous Widow. I must therefore inform these my Correspondents, that it is not my Design to be a Publisher of Intreagues and Cuckoldoms, or to bring little infamous Stories out of their present lurking Holes into broad Day-light. If I attack the Vicious, I shall only set upon them in a Body; and will not be provoked by the worst Usage I can receive from others, to make an Example of any particular Criminal. In short, I have so much of a *Drawcansir* in me, that I shall pass over a single Foe to charge whole Armies. It is not *Lais* or *Silenus,* but the Harlot and the Drunkard, whom I shall endeavour to expose; and shall consider the Crime as it appears in a Species, not as it is circumstanced in an Individual. I think it was *Caligula* who wished the whole City of *Rome* had but one Neck, that he might behead them at a Blow. I shall do out of Humanity, what that Emperor would have done in the Cruelty of his Temper, and aim every Stroke at a collective Body of Offenders. At the same time I am very sensible, that nothing spreads a Paper like private Calumny and Defamation; but as my Speculations are not under this Necessity, they are not exposed to this Temptation.

In the next Place I must apply my self to my Party-Correspondents, who are continually teazing me to take Notice of one another's Proceedings. How often am I asked by both Sides, if it is possible for me to be an unconcerned Spectator of the Rogueries that are committed by the Party which is opposite to him that writes the Letter. About two Days since I was reproached with an old *Grecian* Law, that forbids any Man to stand as a Neuter or a Looker-on in the Divisions of his Country. However, as I am very sensible my Paper would lose its whole Effect, should it run into the Outrages of a Party, I shall take care to keep clear of every thing which looks that Way. If I can any way asswage private Inflamations, or allay publick Ferments, I shall apply my self to it with my utmost Endeavours; but will never let my Heart reproach me, with having done any thing towards encreasing those Feuds and Animosities that extinguish Religion, deface Government, and make a Nation miserable.

What I have said under the three foregoing Heads, will, I am afraid, very much retrench the Number of my Correspondents:

I shall therefore acquaint my Reader, that if he has started any Hint which he is not able to pursue, if he has met with any surprizing Story which he does not know how to tell, if he has discovered any Epidemical Vice which has escaped my Observation, or has heard of any uncommon Virtue which he would desire to publish; in short, if he has any Materials that can furnish out an innocent Diversion, I shall promise him my best Assistance in the working of them up for a publick Entertainment.

This Paper my Reader will find was intended for an Answer to a Multitude of Correspondents; but I hope he will pardon me if I single out one of them in particular, who has made me so very humble a Request, that I cannot forbear complying with it.

'To the SPECTATOR.

Sir,   March 15, $17\frac{10}{11}$

I am at present so unfortunate, as to have nothing to do but to mind my own Business; and therefore beg of you that you will be pleased to put me into some small Post under you. I observe that you have appointed your Printer and Publisher to receive Letters and Advertisements for the City of *London*; and shall think my self very much honoured by you, if you will appoint me to take in Letters and Advertisements for the City of *Westminster* and the Dutchy of *Lancaster*. Though I cannot promise to fill such an Employment with sufficient Abilities, I will endeavour to make up with Industry and Fidelity what I want in Parts and Genius.   I am,

Sir,

Your most obedient Servant,

C   Charles Lillie.'

No. 17.
[STEELE.]   Tuesday, March 20.

. . . *Tetrum ante omnia vultum.*—Juv.

SINCE our Persons are not of our own Making, when they are such as appear Defective or Uncomely, it is, methinks, an honest and laudable Fortitude to dare to be Ugly; at least to keep our selves from being abashed with a Consciousness of Imperfections which we cannot help, and in which there is no Guilt. I would not defend an haggard Beau, for passing away much time at a Glass, and giving Softnesses and Languishing Graces to Deformity: All I intend is, that we ought to be contented with our Countenance and Shape, so far, as never to give our selves an uneasie Reflection on that Subject.   It is to the ordinary People who are not accustomed to make very proper Remarks on any Occasion, matter of great Jest, if a Man enters with a prominent Pair of Shoulders into an Assembly, or is distinguished by an Expansion of Mouth, or Obliquity of Aspect.   It is happy for a Man, that has any of these Oddnesses about him, if he can be as merry upon himself, as others are apt to be upon that Occasion: When he can possess himself with such a Chearfulness, Women and Children, who were at first frighted at him, will afterwards be as much pleased with him.   As it is barbarous in others to railly him for natural Defects, it is extreamly agreeable when he can Jest upon himself for them.

Madam *Maintenon's* first Husband was an Hero in this Kind, and has drawn many Pleasantries from the Irregularity of his Shape, which he describes as very much resembling the Letter Z.   He diverts himself likewise by representing to his Reader the Make of an Engine and Pully, with which he used to take off his Hat.   When there happens to be anything ridiculous in a Visage, and the Owner of it thinks it an Aspect of Dignity, he must be of very great Quality to be exempt from Raillery: The best Expedient therefore is to be pleasant upon himself. Prince *Harry* and *Falstaffe*, in *Shakespear*, have carried the Ridicule upon Fat and Lean as far as it will go.   *Falstaffe* is humourously called *Woolsack, Bed-presser*, and *Hill of Flesh*; *Harry*, a *Starveling*, an *Elves-Skin*, a *Sheath*, a *Bow-case*, and a *Tuck*.   There is, in several Incidents of the Conversation between them, the Jest still kept up upon the Person.   Great Tenderness and Sensibility in this Point is one of the greatest Weaknesses of Self-love.   For my own part, I am a little unhappy in the Mold of my Face, which is not quite so long as it is broad: Whether this might not partly arise from my opening my Mouth much seldomer than other People, and by Consequence not so much lengthning the Fibres of my Visage, I am not at leisure to determine.   However it be, I have been often out of Countenance by the Shortness of my Face, and was formerly at great Pains in concealing it by wearing a Periwig with an high Foretop, and letting my Beard grow.   But now I have thoroughly got over this Delicacy, and could be contented it were much shorter, provided it might qualifie me for a Member of the Merry Club, which the following Letter gives me an Account of.   I have received it from *Oxford*, and as it abounds with the Spirit of Mirth and good Humour which is natural to that Place, I shall set it down Word for Word as it came to me.

'*Most Profound Sir,*

Having been very well entertained, in the last of your Speculations that I have yet seen, by your Specimen upon Clubs, which I therefore hope you will continue, I shall take the Liberty to furnish you with a brief Account of such a one as perhaps you have not seen in all your Travels, unless it was your Fortune to touch upon some of the woody Parts of the *African* Continent, in your Voyage to or from *Grand Cairo*. There have arose in this University (long since you left us without saying any thing) several of these inferior Hebdomadal Societies, as *the Punning Club, the Witty Club,* and amongst the rest *the Handsome Club*; as a Burlesque upon which, a certain merry Species, that seem to have come into the World in Masquerade, for some Years last past have associated themselves together, and assumed the Name of *the Ugly Club*: This ill-favoured Fraternity consists of a President and twelve Fellows; the Choice of which is not confined by Patent to any particular Foundation (as St. *John's* Men would have the World believe, and have therefore erected a separate Society within themselves) but Liberty is left to elect from any School in *Great Britain*, provided the Candidates be within the Rules of the Club, as set forth in a Table, entituled, *The Act of Deformity*. A Clause or two of which I shall transmit to you.

I. That no Person whatsoever shall be admitted without a visible Quearity in his Aspect, or peculiar Cast of Countenance; of which the President and Officers for the time being are to determine, and the President to have the casting Voice.

II. That a singular Regard be had, upon Examination, to the Gibbosity of the Gentlemen that offer themselves, as Founder's Kinsmen; or to the Obliquity of their Figure, in what sort soever.

III. That if the Quantity of any Man's Nose be eminently miscalculated, whether as to Length or Breadth, he shall have a just Pretence to be elected.

Lastly, That if there shall be two or more Competitors for the same Vacancy, *caeteris paribus,* he that has the thickest Skin to have the Preference.

Every fresh Member, upon his first night, is to entertain the Company with a Dish of Cod-fish, and a Speech in Praise of *Aesop*; whose Portraiture they have in full Proportion, or rather Disproportion, over the Chimney; and their Design is, as soon as their Funds are sufficient, to purchase the Heads of *Thersites, Duns Scotus, Scarron, Hudibras,* and the old Gentleman in *Oldham*, with all the celebrated ill Faces of Antiquity, as Furniture for the Club Room.

As they have always been professed Admirers of the other

Sex, so they unanimously declare that they will give all possible Encouragement to such as will take the Benefit of the Statute, though none yet have appeared to do it.

The worthy President, who is their most devoted Champion, has lately shewn me two Copies of Verses composed by a Gentlemen of this Society; the first, a Congratulatory Ode inscribed to Mrs. *Touchwood*, upon the loss of her two Foreteeth; the other, a Panegyrick upon Mrs. *Andiron*'s left Shoulder. Mrs. *Vizard* (he says) since the Small Pox, is grown tolerably ugly, and a top Toast in the Club; but I never heard him so lavish of his fine things, as upon old *Nell Trot*, who constantly officiates at their Table; her he even adores, and extols as the very counterpart of Mother *Shipton*; in short, *Nell* (says he) is one of the Extraordinary Works of Nature; but as for Complexion, Shape, and Features, so valued by others, they are all meer Outside and Symmetry, which is his Aversion. Give me leave to add, that the President is a facetious pleasant Gentleman, and never more so, than when he has got (as he calls 'em) his dear Mummers about him; and he often protests it does him good to meet a Fellow with a right genuine Grimace in his Air (which is so agreeable in the generality of the *French* Nation); and, as an Instance of his Sincerity in this particular, he gave me a sight of a List in his Pocket-book of all of this Class, who for these five Years have fallen under his Observation, with himself at the Head of 'em, and in the Rear (as one of a promising and improving Aspect)

Sir,

Oxford,
March 12, 1710.

Your Obliged and

Humble Servant,

Alexander Carbuncle.

R

No. 18.
[ADDISON.]   Wednesday, March 21.

> . . . *Equitis quoque jam migravit ab aure voluptas*
> *Omnis ad incertos oculos & gaudia vana.*—Hor.

It is my Design in this Paper to deliver down to Posterity a faithful Account of the *Italian* Opera, and of the gradual Progress which it has made upon the *English* Stage: for there is no question but our great Grand-children will be very curious to know the Reason why their Forefathers used to sit together like an Audience of Foreigners in their own Country, and to hear whole Plays acted before them in a Tongue which they did not understand.

Arsinoe was the first Opera that gave us a Taste of *Italian* Musick. The great Success this Opera met with, produced some Attempts of forming Pieces upon *Italian* Plans, which should give a more natural and reasonable Entertainment than what can be met with in the elaborate Trifles of that Nation. This alarmed the Poetasters and Fidlers of the Town, who were used to deal in a more ordinary kind of Ware; and therefore laid down an established Rule, which is received as such to this Day, *That nothing is capable of being well set to Musick, that is not Nonsense.*

This Maxim was no sooner received, but we immediately fell to translating the *Italian* Operas; and as there was no great Danger of hurting the Sense of those extraordinary Pieces, our Authors would often make Words of their own which were entirely foreign to the Meaning of the Passages they pretended to translate; their chief Care being to make the Numbers of the *English* Verse answer to those of the *Italian*, that both of them might go to the same Tune. Thus the famous Song in *Camilla*,

> *Barbara si t'intendo* &c.
>
> *Barbarous Woman, yes, I know your Meaning,*

which expresses the Resentments of an angry Lover, was translated into that *English* Lamentation,

> *Frail are a Lover's Hopes* &c.

And it was pleasant enough to see the most refined Persons of the *British* Nation dying away and languishing to Notes that were filled with a Spirit of Rage and Indignation. It happened also very frequently, where the Sense was rightly translated, the necessary Transposition of Words, which were drawn out of the Phrase of one Tongue into that of another, made the Musick appear very absurd in one Tongue that was very natural in the other. I remember an *Italian* Verse that ran thus Word for Word,

> *And turn'd my Rage into Pity;*

which the *English* for Rhime sake translated,

> *And into Pity turn'd my Rage.*

By this means the soft Notes that were adapted to *Pity* in the *Italian*, fell upon the Word *Rage* in the *English*; and the angry Sounds that were tuned to *Rage* in the Original, were made to express *Pity* in the Translation. It oftentimes happened likewise, that the finest Notes in the Air fell upon the most insignificant Words in the Sentence. I have known the Word *And* pursued through the whole Gamut, have been entertained with many a melodious *The*, and have heard the most beautiful Graces, Quavers, and Divisions bestowed upon *Then, For*, and *From*; to the eternal Honour of our *English* Particles.

The next Step to our Refinement was the introducing of *Italian* Actors into our Opera; who sung their Parts in their own Language, at the same time that our Countrymen performed theirs in our native Tongue. The King or Hero of the Play generally spoke in *Italian*, and his Slaves answered him in *English*: The Lover frequently made his Court, and gained the Heart of his Princess, in a Language which she did not understand.   One would have thought it very difficult to have carried on Dialogues after this manner, without an Interpreter between the Persons that convers'd together; but this was the State of the *English* Stage for about three Years.

At length the Audience grew tired of understanding Half the Opera, and therefore to ease themselves intirely of the Fatigue of Thinking, have so ordered it at present, that the whole Opera is performed in an unknown Tongue.   We no longer understand the Language of our own Stage; insomuch that I have often been afraid, when I have seen our *Italian* Performers chattering in the Vehemence of Action, that they have been calling us Names, and abusing us among themselves; but I hope, since we do put such an entire Confidence in them, they will not talk against us before our Faces, though they may do it with the same Safety as if it were behind our Backs.   In the mean time, I cannot forbear thinking how naturally an Historian who writes two or three hundred Years hence, and does not know the Taste of his wise Forefathers, will make the following Reflection, *In the Beginning of the Eighteenth Century the* Italian *Tongue was so well understood in* England, *that Operas were acted on the publick Stage in that Language.*

One scarce knows how to be serious in the Confutation of an Absurdity that shews it self at the first Sight.   It does not want any great measure of Sense to see the Ridicule of this monstrous Practice; but what makes it the more astonishing, it is not the Taste of the Rabble, but of Persons of the greatest Politeness, which has established it.

If the *Italians* have a Genius for Musick above the *English*, the *English* have a Genius for other Performances of a much higher Nature, and capable of giving the Mind a much nobler Entertainment.   Would one think it was possible (at a Time when an Author lived that was able to write the *Phaedra and Hippolitus*) for a People to be so stupidly fond of the *Italian* Opera, as scarce to give a third Day's Hearing to that admirable Tragedy?   Musick is certainly a very agreeable Entertainment, but if it would take the entire Possession of our

Ears, if it would make us incapable of hearing Sense, if it would exclude Arts that have a much greater Tendency to the Refinement of Human Nature; I must confess I would allow it no better Quarter than *Plato* has done, who banishes it out of his Common-wealth.

At present, our Notions of Musick are so very uncertain, that we do not know what it is we like; only, in general, we are transported with any thing that is not *English*: So it be of foreign Growth, let it be *Italian, French,* or *High-Dutch,* it is the same thing. In short, our *English* Musick is quite rooted out, and nothing yet planted in its stead.

When a Royal Palace is burnt to the Ground, every Man is at liberty to present his Plan for a new one; and though it be but indifferently put together, it may furnish several Hints that may be of Use to a good Architect. I shall take the same Liberty in a following Paper, of giving my Opinion upon the Subject of Musick; which I shall lay down only in a problematical Manner, to be considered by those who are Masters in the Art.   C

No. 19.

[STEELE.]   Thursday, March 22.

Di bene fecerunt, inopis me quodque pusilli
Finxerunt animi, raro & perpauca loquentis.—Hor.

OBSERVING one Person behold another, who was an utter Stranger to him, with a Cast of his Eye, which, methought, expressed an Emotion of Heart very different from what could be raised by an Object so agreeable as the Gentleman he looked at, I began to consider, not without some secret Sorrow, the Condition of an Envious Man. Some have fancied that Envy has a certain Magical Force in it, and that the Eyes of the Envious have by their Fascination blasted the Enjoyments of the Happy. Sir *Francis Bacon* says, Some have been so curious as to remark the Times and Seasons when the Stroke of an envious Eye is most effectually pernicious, and have observed that it has been when the Person envied has been in any Circumstance of Glory and Triumph. At such a time the Mind of the prosperous Man goes, as it were, abroad, among things without him, and is more exposed to the Malignity. But I shall not dwell upon Speculations so abstracted as this, or repeat the many excellent Things which one might collect out of Authors upon this miserable Affection; but keeping in the Road of common Life, consider the Envious Man with relation to these three Heads, His Pains, His Reliefs, and His Happiness.

The Envious Man is in Pain upon all Occasions which ought to give him Pleasure. The Relish of his Life is inverted; and the Objects which administer the highest Satisfaction to those who are exempt from this Passion, give the quickest Pangs to Persons who are subject to it. All the Perfections of their Fellow-Creatures are odious: Youth, Beauty, Valour and Wisdom are Provocations of their Displeasure. What a Wretched and Apostate State is this! To be offended with Excellence, and to hate a Man because we approve him! The Condition of the Envious Man is the most emphatically miserable; he is not only incapable of rejoicing in another's Merit or Success, but lives in a World wherein all Mankind are in a Plot against his Quiet, by studying their own Happiness and Advantage. *Will. Prosper* is an honest Tale-bearer, he makes it his Business to join in Conversation with Envious Men. He points to such an handsom young Fellow, and whispers that he is secretly married to a great Fortune: When they doubt, he adds Circumstances to prove it; and never fails to aggravate their Distress, by assuring 'em, that to his Knowledge he has an Uncle will leave him some Thousands. *Will.* has many Arts of this kind to torture this sort of Temper, and delights in it. When he finds them change Colour, and say faintly they wish such a Piece of News is true, he has the Malice to speak some good or other of every Man of their Acquaintance.

The Reliefs of the Envious Man are those little Blemishes and Imperfections that discover themselves in an Illustrious Character. It is a matter of great Consolation to an Envious Person, when a Man of known Honour does a thing unworthy himself: Or when any Action which was well executed, upon better Information appears so altered in its Circumstances, that the Fame of it is divided among many, instead of being attributed to One. This is a secret Satisfaction to these Malignants; for the Person whom they before could not but admire, they fancy is nearer their own Condition as soon as his Merit is shared among others. I remember some Years ago there came out an excellent Poem without the Name of the Author. The little Wits, who were incapable of Writing it, began to pull in Pieces the supposed Writer. When that would not do, they took great Pains to suppress the Opinion that it was his. That again failed. The next Refuge was to say it was overlooked by one Man, and many Pages wholly written by another. An honest Fellow, who sate among a Cluster of them in debate on this Subject, cryed out, *Gentlemen, if you are sure none of you your selves had an hand in it, you are but where you were, whoever writ it.* But the most usual Succour to the Envious, in cases of nameless Merit in this kind, is to keep the Property, if possible, unfixed, and by that means to hinder the Reputation of it from falling upon any particular Person. You see an Envious Man clear up his Countenance, if in the Relation of any Man's Great Happiness in one Point, you mention his Uneasiness in another. When he hears such a one is very rich he turns Pale, but recovers when you add that he has many Children. In a word, the only sure Way to an Envious Man's Favour, is not to deserve it.

But if we consider the Envious Man in Delight, it is like reading the Seat of a Giant in a Romance; the Magnificence of his House consists in the many Limbs of Men whom he has slain. If any who promised themselves Success in any Uncommon Undertaking miscarry in the Attempt, or he that aimed at what would have been Useful and Laudable, meets with Contempt and Derision, the Envious Man, under the Colour of hating Vain-glory, can smile with an inward Wantonness of Heart at the ill Effect it may have upon an honest Ambition for the future.

Having thoroughly considered the Nature of this Passion, I have made it my Study how to avoid the Envy that may accrue to me from these my Speculations; and if I am not mistaken in my self, I think I have a Genius to escape it. Upon hearing in a Coffee-house one of my Papers commended, I immediately apprehended the Envy that would spring from that Applause; and therefore gave a Description of my Face the next Day; being resolved, as I grow in Reputation for Wit, to resign my Pretensions to Beauty. This, I hope, may give some Ease to those unhappy Gentlemen, who do me the Honour to torment themselves upon the Account of this my Paper. As their Case is very deplorable, and deserves Compassion, I shall sometimes be dull, in Pity to them, and will from time to time administer Consolations to them by further Discoveries of my Person. In the mean while, if any one says the SPECTATOR has Wit, it may be some Relief to them, to think that he does not shew it in Company. And if any one praises his Morality, they may comfort themselves by considering that his Face is none of the longest.   R

No. 20.

[STEELE.]   *Friday, March* 23.

. . . Κυνὸς ὄμματ' ἔχων . . .—Hom.

AMONG the other hardy Undertakings which I have proposed to myself, that of the Correction of Impudence is what I have very much at Heart. This in a particular Manner is my Province as SPECTATOR; for it is generally an Offence committed by the Eyes, and that against such as the Offenders would perhaps never have an Opportunity of injuring any other Way. The following Letter is a Complaint of a young Lady, who sets forth a Trespass of this kind, with that Command of herself as befits Beauty and Innocence, and yet with so much Spirit as sufficiently expresses her Indignation. The whole Transaction is performed with the Eyes; and the Crime is no less than employing them in such a Manner, as to divert the Eyes of others from the best Use they can make of them, even looking up to Heaven.

' *Sir,*

There never was (I believe) an acceptable Man, but had some awkard Imitators. Ever since the SPECTATOR appeared, have I remarked a kind of Men, whom I chuse to call *Starers*; that without any regard to Time, Place, or Modesty, disturb large Company with their impertinent Eyes. Spectators make up a proper Assembly for a Puppet-Show or a Bear-Garden; but devout Supplicants and attentive Hearers are the Audience one ought to expect in Churches. I am, Sir, Member of a small pious Congregation near one of the North Gates of this City; much the greater Part of us indeed are females, and used to behave ourselves in a regular attentive Manner, till very lately one whole Isle has been disturbed with one of these monstrous Starers; He 's the Head taller than any one in the Church; but for the greater Advantage of exposing himself, stands upon a Hassock, and commands the whole Congregation, to the great Annoyance of the devoutest Part of the Auditory; for what with Blushing, Confusion, and Vexation, we can neither mind the Prayers nor Sermon. Your Animadversion upon this Insolence would be a great Favour to,

Sir,

Your most humble Servant,

S. C.'

I have frequently seen of this sort of Fellows; and do not think there can be a greater Aggravation of an Offence, than that it is committed where the Criminal is protected by the Sacredness of the Place which he violates. Many Reflections of this sort might be very justly made upon this kind of Behaviour, but a *Starer* is not usually a Person to be convinced by the Reason of the thing; and a Fellow that is capable of shewing an impudent Front before a whole Congregation, and can bear being a publick Spectacle, is not so easily rebuked as to amend by Admonitions. If therefore my Correspondent does not inform me, that within seven Days after this Date the Barbarian does not at least stand upon his own Legs only, without an Eminence, my friend *Will. Prosper* has promised to take an Hassock opposite to him, and stare against him in Defence of the Ladies.   I have given him Directions, according to the most exact Rules of Opticks, to place himself in such a manner that he shall meet his Eyes where-ever he throws them: I have Hopes that when *Will.* confronts him, and all the Ladies, in whose Behalf he engages him, cast kind Looks and Wishes of Success at their Champion, he will have some Shame, and feel a little of the Pain he has so often put others to, of being out of Countenance.

It has indeed been Time out of Mind generally remarked, and as often lamented, that this Family of Starers have infested Publick Assemblies: And I know no other Way to obviate so great an Evil, except, in the Case of fixing their Eyes upon Women, some Male Friend will take the Part of such as are under the Oppression of Impudence, and encounter the Eyes of the Starers where-ever they meet them.   While we suffer our Women to be thus impudently attacked, they have no Defence, but in the End to cast yielding Glances at the Starers: And in this Case, a Man who has no Sense of Shame has the same Advantage over his Mistress, as he who has no regard for his own Life has over his Adversary.   While the Generality of the World are fettered by Rules, and move by proper and just Methods; he who has no Respect to any of them, carries away the Reward due to that Propriety of Behaviour, with no other Merit, but that of having neglected it.

I take an impudent Fellow to be a sort of Outlaw in Goodbreeding, and therefore what is said of him no Nation or Person can be concerned for.   For this Reason, one may be free upon him.   I have put myself to great Pains in considering this prevailing Quality which we call Impudence, and have taken notice that it exerts it self in a different Manner, according to the different Soils wherein such Subjects of these Dominions, as are Masters of it, were born.   Impudence in an *English-man* is sullen and insolent; in a *Scotch-man* it is untractable and rapacious; in an *Irish-man* absurd and fawning: As the Course of the World now runs, the impudent *English-man* behaves like a surly Landlord, the *Scot* like an ill-received Guest, and the *Irish-man* like a Stranger who knows he is not welcome.   There is seldom any thing entertaining either in the Impudence of a *South* or *North Briton*; but that of an *Irish-man* is always Comick: A true and genuine Impudence is ever the Effect of Ignorance, without the least Sense of it: The best and most successful Starers now in this Town, are of that

Nation; they have usually the Advantage of the Stature mentioned in the above Letter of my Correspondent, and generally take their Stands in the Eye of Women of Fortune: Insomuch that I have known one of them, three Months after he came from Plough, with a tolerable good Air lead out a Woman from a Play, which one of our own Breed, after four Years at *Oxford*, and two at the *Temple*, would have been afraid to look at.

I cannot tell how to account for it, but these People have usually the Preference to our own Fools, in the Opinion of the sillier Part of Womankind. Perhaps it is that an *English* Coxcomb is seldom so obsequious as an *Irish* one; and when the Design of pleasing is visible, an Absurdity in the Way toward it is easily forgiven.

But those who are downright impudent, and go on without Reflection that they are such, are more to be tolerated, than a Set of Fellows among us who profess Impudence with an Air of Humour, and think to carry off the most inexcusable of all Faults in the World, with no other Apology than saying in a gay Tone, *I put an impudent Face upon the Matter.* No; no Man shall be allowed the Advantages of Impudence, who is conscious that he is such: If he knows he is impudent, he may as well be otherwise; and it shall be expected that he blush, when he sees he makes another do it. For nothing can attone for the Want of Modesty; without which Beauty is ungraceful, and Wit detestable.

No. 21.

[ADDISON.]   Saturday, March 24.

. . . *Locus est & pluribus umbris.*—Hor.

I AM sometimes very much troubled, when I reflect upon the three great Professions of Divinity, Law, and Physick; how they are each of them over-burdened with Practitioners, and filled with multitudes of Ingenious Gentlemen that starve one another.

We may divide the Clergy into Generals, Field-Officers, and Subalterns. Among the first we may reckon Bishops, Deans and Arch-Deacons. Among the second are Doctors of Divinity, Prebendaries, and all that wear Scarfs. The rest are comprehended under the Subalterns. As for the first Class, our Constitution preserves it from any redundancy of Incumbents, notwithstanding Competitors are numberless. Upon a strict Calculation, it is found that there has been a great Exceeding of late Years in the second Division, several Brevets having been granted for the converting of Subalterns into Scarf-

Officers; insomuch that within my Memory the Price of Lutestring is raised above two Pence in a Yard. As for the Subalterns they are not to be numbred. Should our Clergy once enter into the corrupt Practice of the Laity, by the splitting of their Freeholds, they would be able to carry most of the Elections in *England*.

The Body of the Law is no less incumbered with superfluous Members, that are like *Virgil's* Army, which he tells us was so crouded, many of them had not Room to use their Weapons. This prodigious Society of Men may be divided into the Litigious and Peaceable. Under the first are comprehended all those who are carried down in Coach-fulls to *Westminster-Hall*, every Morning in Term-time. *Martial's* Description of this Species of Lawyers is full of Humour:

Iras & verba locant.

Men that hire out their Words and Anger; that are more or less passionate according as they are paid for it, and allow their Client a quantity of Wrath proportionable to the Fee which they receive from him. I must however observe to the Reader, that above three Parts of those whom I reckon among the Litigious, are such as are only quarrelsome in their Hearts, and have no Opportunity of shewing their Passion at the Bar. Nevertheless, as they do not know what Strifes may arise, they appear at the Hall every Day, that they may show themselves in a Readiness to enter the Lists, whenever there shall be Occasion for them.

The Peaceable Lawyers are, in the first place, many of the Benchers of the several Inns of Court, who seem to be the Dignitaries of the Law, and are endowed with those Qualifications of Mind that accomplish a Man rather for a Ruler, than a Pleader. These Men live peaceably in their Habitations, Eating once a Day, and Dancing once a Year, for the Honour of their respective Societies.

Another numberless Branch of Peaceable Lawyers, are those young Men who being placed at the Inns of Court in order to study the Laws of their Country, frequent the Play-house more than *Westminster-Hall*, and are seen in all publick Assemblies, except in a Court of Justice. I shall say nothing of those Silent and Busie Multitudes that are employed within Doors in the drawing up of Writings and Conveyances; nor of those greater Numbers that palliate their want of Business with a Pretence to such Chamber-practice.

If, in the third place, we look into the Profession of Physick, we shall find a most formidable Body of Men: The Sight of them is enough to make a Man serious, for we may lay it down as a

Maxim, that when a Nation abounds in Physicians it grows thin of People.   Sir *William Temple* is very much puzzled to find out a Reason why the Northern Hive, as he calls it, does not send out such prodigious Swarms, and over-run the World with *Goths* and *Vandals*, as it did formerly; but had that excellent Author observed that there were no Students in Physick among the Subjects of *Thor* and *Woden*, and that this Science very much flourishes in the North at present, he might have found a better Solution for this Difficulty, than any of those he has made use of.   This Body of Men, in our own Country, may be described like the *British* Army in *Caesar's* time: Some of them slay in Chariots, and some on Foot.   If the Infantry do less Execution than the Charioteers, it is because they cannot be carried so soon into all Quarters of the Town, and dispatch so much Business in so short a Time.   Besides this Body of Regular Troops, there are Stragglers, who without being duly listed and enrolled, do infinite Mischief to those who are so unlucky as to fall into their Hands.

There are, besides the above-mentioned, innumerable Retainers to Physick, who, for want of other Patients, amuse themselves with the stifling of Cats in an Air Pump, cutting up Dogs alive, or impaling of Insects upon the Point of a Needle for Microscopical Observations; besides those that are employed in the gathering of Weeds, and the Chace of Butterflies: Not to mention the Cockleshell-Merchants and Spidercatchers.

When I consider how each of these Professions are crouded with Multitudes that seek their Livelihood in them, and how many Men of Merit there are in each of them, who may be rather said to be of the Science, than the Profession; I very much wonder at the humour of Parents, who will not rather chuse to place their Sons in a way of Life where an honest Industry cannot but thrive, than in Stations where the greatest Probity, Learning, and Good Sense may miscarry.   How many Men are Country-Curates, that might have made themselves Aldermen of *London*, by a right Improvement of a smaller Sum of Mony than what is usually laid out upon a learned Education?   A sober, frugal Person, of slender Parts and a slow Apprehension, might have thrived in Trade, though he starves upon Physick; as a Man would be well enough pleased to buy Silks of one, whom he would not venture to feel his Pulse.   *Vagellius* is careful, studious and obliging, but withal a little thickskull'd; he has not a single Client, but might have had abundance of Customers.   The Misfortune is, that Parents take a liking to a particular Profession, and therefore desire their Sons may be of it.   Whereas, in so great an Affair of Life, they should consider the Genius and Abilities of their Children, more than their own Inclinations.

It is the great Advantage of a trading Nation, that there are very few in it so dull and heavy, who may not be placed in Stations of Life which may give them an Opportunity of making their Fortunes. A well-regulated Commerce is not, like Law, Physick, or Divinity, to be over-stocked with Hands; but, on the contrary, flourishes by Multitudes, and gives Employment to all its Professors. Fleets of Merchantmen are so many Squadrons of floating Shops, that vend our Wares and Manufactures in all the Markets of the World, and find out Chapmen under both the Tropicks.　　　　　　　　　　C

No. 22.

[STEELE.]　　　　　　　　　　　　　　　Monday, March 26.

　. . . *Quodcunque ostendis mihi sic, incredulus odi.*—Hor.

The Word Spectator being most usually understood as one of the Audience at publick Representations in our Theatres, I seldom fail of many Letters relating to Plays and Operas. But indeed there are such monstrous things done in both, that if one had not been an Eye-witness of them, one could not believe that such Matters had really been exhibited. There is very little which concerns Human Life, or is a Picture of Nature that is regarded by the greater Part of the Company. The Understanding is dismissed from our Entertainments. Our Mirth is the Laughter of Fools, and our Admiration the Wonder of Idiots; else such improbable, monstrous, and incoherent Dreams could not go off as they do, not only without the utmost Scorn and Contempt, but even with the loudest Applause and Approbation. But the Letters of my Correspondents will represent this Affair in a more lively manner than any Discourse of my own; I shall therefore give them to my Reader with only this Preparation, that they all come from Players, and that the Business of Playing is now so managed, that you are not to be surprised when I say one or two of them are rational, others sensitive and vegetative Actors, and others wholly inanimate. I shall not place these as I have named them, but as they have Precedence in the Opinion of their Audiences.

　' *Mr.* Spectator,

Your having been so humble as to take notice of the Epistles of other Animals, emboldens me, who am the wild Boar that was killed by Mrs. *Tofts*, to represent to you, That I think I was hardly used in not having the Part of the Lion in *Hydaspes* given to me. It would have been but a natural Step for me to have personated that noble Creature, after having behaved my self to Satisfaction in the Part above-mentioned: But that of a Lion is too great a Character for one that never trod the Stage before but upon two Legs. As for the little Resistance which I made, I hope it may be excused, when it is considered that the Dart was thrown at me by so fair an Hand. I must confess I had but just put on my Brutality; and *Camilla*'s Charms were such, that beholding her erect Mien, hearing her charming Voice, and astonished with her graceful Motion, I could not keep up to my assumed Fierceness, but died like a Man.

> *I am, Sir,*
>> *Your most humble Servant,*
>>> Thomas Prone.'

'*Mr.* SPECTATOR,

This is to let you understand, that the Play-house is a Representation of the World in nothing so much as in this Particular, that no one rises in it according to his Merit. I have acted several Parts of Houshold-stuff with great Applause for many Years: I am one of the Men in the Hangings in the *Emperor of the Moon*; I have twice performed the third Chair in an *English* Opera; and have rehearsed the Pump in the *Fortune Hunters*. I am now grown old, and hope you will recommend me so effectually, as that I may say something before I go off the Stage: In which you will do a great Act of Charity to

> *Your most humble Servant,*
>> William Screne.'

'*Mr.* SPECTATOR,

Understanding that Mr. *Screne* has writ to you, and desired to be raised from dumb and still Parts; I desire, if you give him Motion or Speech, that you would advance me in my Way, and let me keep on in what I humbly presume I am a Master, to wit, in representing human and still Life together. I have several times acted one of the finest Flower-pots in the same Opera wherein Mr. *Screne* is a Chair; therefore upon his Promotion, request that I may succeed him in the Hangings, with my Hand in the Orange-Trees.

> *Your humble Servant,*
>> Ralph Simple.'

'*Sir,*   *Drury-Lane, March* 24, 17$\frac{10}{11}$

I saw your Friend the Templer this Evening in the Pit, and thought he looked very little pleased with the Representation of the mad Scene of the *Pilgrim*. I wish, Sir, you would do us the Favour to animadvert frequently upon the false Taste the Town is in, with Relation to Plays as well as Operas. It certainly requires a Degree of Understanding to play justly; but such is our Condition, that we are to suspend our Reason to perform our Parts. As to Scenes of Madness, you know, Sir, there are noble Instances of this Kind in *Shakespear*; but then it is the Disturbance of a noble Mind, from generous and human Resentments: It is like that Grief which we have for the Decease of our Friends: It is no Diminution, but a Recommendation of human Nature, that in such Incidents Passion gets the better of Reason; and all we can think to comfort our selves, is impotent against half what we feel. I will not mention that we had an Idiot in the Scene, and all the Sense it is represented to have, is that of Lust. As for my self, who have long taken Pains in personating the Passions, I have to Night acted only an Appetite: The Part I play is Thirst, but it is represented as written rather by a Dray-man than a Poet. I come in with a Tub about me, that Tub hung with Quart-pots, with a full Gallon at my Mouth. I am ashamed to tell you that I pleased very much, and this was introduced as a Madness; but sure it was not human Madness, for a Mule or an Ass may have been as dry as ever I was in my Life.

> *I am, Sir,*
> *Your most obedient*
> *and humble Servant.'*

From the Savoy *in the* Strand.

'Mr. SPECTATOR,

If you can read it with dry Eyes, I give you this Trouble to acquaint you, that I am the unfortunate King *Latinus*, and believe I am the first Prince that dated from this Palace since *John* of *Gaunt*. Such is the Uncertainty of all human Greatness, that I who lately never moved without a Guard, am now pressed as a common Soldier, and am to sail with the first fair Wind against my Brother *Lewis* of *France*. It is a very hard thing to put off a Character which one has appeared in with Applause: This I experienced since the loss of my Diadem; for upon quarrelling with another Recruit, I spoke my Indignation out of my Part in *recitativo*;

> *. . . Most audacious Slave,*
> *Dar'st thou an angry Monarch's Fury brave?*

The Words were no sooner out of my Mouth, when a Serjeant knock'd me down, and asked me if I had a Mind to mutiny, in talking things no body understood. You see, Sir, my unhappy

Circumstances; and if by your Mediation you can procure a Subsidy for a Prince (who never failed to make all that beheld him merry at his Appearance) you will merit the Thanks of

Your Friend,

The King of *Latium.'*

ADVERTISEMENT.

For the Good of the Publick.

Within two Doors of the Masquerade, lives an eminent Italian *Chirurgeon, arrived from the Carnaval at* Venice, *of great Experience in private Cures. Accommodations are provided, and Persons admitted in their Masquing Habits.*

He has cured since his coming thither, in less than a Fortnight, Four Scaramouches, a Mountebank Doctor, Two Turkish *Bassas, three Nuns, and a Morris Dancer.*

Venienti occurrite Morbo.

N.B. *Any Person may agree by the Great, and be kept in Repair by the Year. The Doctor draws Teeth without pulling off your Mask.* R

No. 23.

[ADDISON.] Tuesday, March 27

*Saevit atrox Volscens, nec teli conspicit usquam
Auctorem, nec quo se ardens immittere possit.*—Virg.

THERE is nothing that more betrays a base ungenerous Spirit than the giving of secret Stabs to a Man's Reputation. Lampoons and Satyrs, that are written with Wit and Spirit, are like poisoned Darts, which not only inflict a Wound, but make it incurable. For this Reason I am very much troubled when I see the Talents of Humour and Ridicule in the Possession of an ill-natured Man. There cannot be a greater Gratification to a barbarous and inhuman Wit, than to stir up Sorrow in the Heart of a private Person, to raise Uneasiness among near Relations, and to expose whole Families to Derision, at the same time that he remains unseen and undiscovered. If, besides the Accomplishments of being witty and ill-natured, a Man is vicious into the bargain, he is one of the most mischievous Creatures that can enter into a Civil Society. His Satyr will then chiefly fall upon those who ought to be the most exempt from it. Virtue, Merit, and every thing that is Praiseworthy, will be made the Subject of Ridicule and Buffoonry.

It is impossible to enumerate the Evils which arise from these Arrows that fly in the dark, and I know no other Excuse that is or can be made for them, than that the Wounds they give are only imaginary, and produce nothing more tnan a secret Shame or Sorrow in the Mind of the suffering Person.   It must indeed be confess'd, that a Lampoon or Satyr do not carry in them Robbery or Murder; but at the same time, how many are there that would not rather lose a considerable Sum of Mony, or even Life it self, than be set up as a Mark of Infamy and Derision?   And in this Case a Man should consider, that an Injury is not to be measured by the Notions of him that gives, but of him that receives it.

Those who can put the best Countenance upon the Outrages of this nature which are offered them, are not without their secret Anguish.   I have often observed a Passage in *Socrates*'s Behaviour at his Death, in a Light wherein none of the Criticks have considered it.   That excellent Man, entertaining his Friends, a little before he drank the Bowl of Poison, with a Discourse on the Immortality of the Soul, at his entering upon it says, that he does not believe any the most Comick Genius can censure him for talking upon such a Subject at such a time. This Passage, I think, evidently glances upon *Aristophanes*, who writ a Comedy on purpose to ridicule the Discourses of that Divine Philosopher.   It has been observed by many Writers, that *Socrates* was so little moved at this piece of Buffoonry, that he was several times present at its being acted upon the Stage, and never expressed the least Resentment of it. But with Submission, I think the Remark I have here made shews us that this unworthy Treatment made an Impression upon his Mind, though he had been too wise to discover it.

When *Julius Caesar* was lampooned by *Catullus*, he invited him to a Supper, and treated him with such a generous Civility, that he made the Poet his Friend ever after.   Cardinal *Mazarine* gave the same kind of Treatment to the Learned *Quillet*, who had reflected upon his Eminence in a famous *Latin* Poem.   The Cardinal sent for him, and after some kind Expostulations upon what he had written, assured him of his Esteem, and dismissed him with a Promise of the next good Abby that should fall, which he accordingly conferred upon him in a few Months after.   This had so good an Effect upon the Author, that he dedicated the second Edition of his Book to the Cardinal, after having expunged the Passages which had given him offence.

Sextus Quintus was not of so generous and forgiving a Temper. Upon his being made Pope, the Statue of *Pasquin* was one Night dressed in a very dirty Shirt, with an Excuse written under it, that he was forced to wear foul Linnen because his Laundress was made a Princess.   This was a Reflection upon the Pope's Sister, who, before the Promotion of her Brother, was in those mean Circumstances that *Pasquin* represented her. As this Pasquinade made a great Noise in *Rome*, the Pope offered a considerable Sum of Mony to any Person that should discover the Author of it.   The Author relying upon his Holiness's Generosity, as also on some private Overtures which he had received from him, made the Discovery himself; upon which the Pope gave him the Reward he had promised, but at the same time, to disable the Satyrist for the future, ordered his Tongue to be cut out, and both his Hands to be chopped off.   *Aretine* is too trite an Instance.   Every one knows that all the Kings in *Europe* were his Tributaries.   Nay, there is a Letter of his extant, in which he makes his Boasts that he had laid the Sophy of *Persia* under Contribution.

Though in the various Examples which I have here drawn together, these several great Men behaved themselves very differently towards the Wits of the Age who had reproached them; they all of them plainly shewed that they were very sensible of their Reproaches, and consequently that they received them as very great Injuries.   For my own part, I would never trust a Man that I thought was capable of giving these secret Wounds; and cannot but think that he would hurt the Person, whose Reputation he thus assaults, in his Body or in his Fortune, could he do it with the same Security.   There is indeed something very barbarous and inhuman in the ordinary Scriblers of Lampoons.   An innocent young Lady shall be exposed, for an unhappy Feature.   A Father of a Family turned to Ridicule, for some domestick Calamity. A Wife be made uneasie all her Life, for a misinterpreted Word or Action.   Nay, a good, a temperate, and a just Man, shall be put out of Countenance, by the Representation of those Qualities that should do him Honour.   So pernicious a thing is Wit, when it is not tempered with Virtue and Humanity.

I have indeed heard of heedless inconsiderate Writers, that without any Malice have sacrificed the Reputation of their Friends and Acquaintance, to a certain Levity of Temper, and a silly Ambition of distinguishing themselves by a Spirit of Raillery and Satyr: As if it were not infinitely more honourable to be a good-natured Man, than a Wit.   Where there is this little petulant Humour in an Author, he is often very mischievous without designing to be so.   For which Reason I always lay it down as a Rule, that an indiscreet Man is more hurtful than an ill-natured one; for as the latter will only attack his Enemies, and those he wishes ill to, the other injures indifferently both Friends and Foes.   I cannot forbear, on this Occasion, transcribing a Fable out of Sir *Roger l'Estrange,* which accidentally lyes before me.   'A Company of waggish Boys were watching of Frogs at the side of a Pond, and still as any of 'em put up their Heads, they 'd be pelting them down again with Stones.   *Children* (says one of the Frogs) *you never consider that tho' this may be Play to you, 'tis Death to us.'*

As this Week is in a manner set apart and dedicated to Serious Thoughts, I shall indulge my self in such Speculations as may not be altogether unsuitable to the Season: and in the mean time, as the settling in our selves a Charitable Frame of Mind is a Work very proper for the Time, I have in this Paper endeavoured to expose that particular Breach of Charity which has been generally overlooked by Divines, because they are but few who can be guilty of it.   C

No. 24.
[STEELE.]   Wednesday, March 28.

Accurrit quidam, notus mihi nomine tantum,
Arreptaque manu, Quid agis, dulcissime rerum?—Hor.

THERE are in this Town a great Number of insignificant People who are by no Means fit for the better sort of Conversation, and yet have an impertinent Ambition of appearing with those to whom they are not welcome.   If you walk in the *Park,* one of them will certainly join with you, tho' you are in Company with Ladies; if you drink a Bottle, they will find your Haunts. What makes such Fellows the more burdensome, is, that they neither offend nor please so far as to be taken Notice of for either.   It is, I presume, for this Reason that my Correspondents are willing by my Means to be rid of them.   The two following Letters are writ by Persons who suffer by such Impertinence.   A worthy old Batchelor, who sets in for his Dose of Claret every Night at such an Hour, is teized by a Swarm of them; who, because they are sure of Room and good Fire, have taken it in their Heads to keep a sort of Club in his Company; tho' the sober Gentleman himself is an utter Enemy to such Meetings.

' *Mr.* SPECTATOR,

The Aversion I for some Years have had to Clubs in general gave me a perfect Relish for your Speculation on that Subject but I have since been extreamly mortified, by the malicious World's ranking me amongst the Supporters of such impertinent Assemblies.   I beg leave to state my Case fairly; and that done, I shall expect Redress from your judicious Pen.

I am, Sir, a Batchelor of some standing, and a Traveller; my Business, to consult my own Humour, which I gratifie without controlling other People's; I have a Room and a whole Bed to my self; and I have a Dog, a Fiddle, and a Gun; they please me, and injure no Creature alive.   My chief Meal is a Supper, which I always make at a Tavern.   I am constant to an Hour, and not ill-humour'd; for which Reasons, tho' I invite no Body, I have no sooner supp'd, than I have a Crowd about me of that sort of good Company that know not whither else to go.   It is true every Man pays his Share; yet as they are Intruders, I have an undoubted Right to be the only Speaker, or at least the loudest; which I maintain, and that to the great Emolument of my Audience.   I sometimes tell them their own in pretty free Language; and sometimes divert them with merry Tales, according as I am in Humour.   I am one of those who live in Taverns to a great Age, by a sort of regular Intemperance; I never go to Bed drunk, but always fluster'd; I wear away very gently; am apt to be peevish, but never angry.   *Mr.* SPECTA-TOR, If you have kept various Company, you know there is in every Tavern in Town some old Humourist or other, who is Master of the House as much as he that keeps it.   The Drawers are all in Awe of him; and all the Customers who frequent his Company, yield him a sort of comical obedience.   I do not know but I may be such a Fellow as this my self.   But I appeal to you, whether this is to be called a Club, because so many Impertinents will break in upon me, and come without Appointment?   *Clinch* of *Barnet* has a nightly Meeting, and shows to every one that will come in and pay; but then he is the only Actor.   Why should People miscall things?   If his is allow'd to be a Consort, why mayn't mine be a Lecture? However, Sir, I submit to you, and am,

Sir,

Your most obedient, &c.

Tho. Kimbow.'

'*Good Sir,*

You and I were press'd against each other last Winter in a Crowd, in which uneasie Posture we suffered together for almost half an Hour.   I thank you for all your Civilities ever since, in being of my Acquaintance wherever you meet me.   But the other Day you pull'd off your Hat to me in the *Park,* when I was walking with my Mistress: She did not like your Air, and said she wondered what strange Fellows I was acquainted with. Dear Sir, consider it as much as my Life is worth, if she should think we were intimate; therefore I earnestly intreat you for the future to take no manner of Notice of,

Sir,

Your obliged humble Servant,

Will. Fashion.'

A like Impertinence is also very troublesom to the superior and more intelligent Part of the fair Sex. It is, it seems, a great Inconvenience, that those of the meanest Capacities will pretend to make Visits, tho' indeed they are qualified rather to add to the Furniture of the House (by filling an empty Chair) than to the Conversation they come into when they visit. A Friend of mine hopes for Redress in this Case, by the Publication of her Letter in my Paper; which she thinks those she would be rid of will take to themselves. It seems to be written with an Eye to one of those pert giddy unthinking Girls, who upon the Recommendation only of an agreeable Person, and a fashionable Air, take themselves to be upon a Level with Women of the greatest Merit.

'*Madam,*

I take this Way to acquaint you with what common Rules and Forms would never permit me to tell you otherwise; to wit, that you and I, tho' Equals in Quality and Fortune, are by no Means suitable Companions. You are, 'tis true, very pretty, can dance, and make a very good Figure in a publick Assembly; but alas, Madam, you must go no further; Distance and Silence are your best Recommendations; therefore let me beg of you never to make me any more Visits. You come in a literal Sense to see one, for you have nothing to say. I do not say this, that I would by any Means lose your Acquaintance; but I would keep it up with the strictest Forms of good Breeding. Let us pay Visits, but never see one another: If you will be so good as to deny your self always to me, I shall return the Obligation by giving the same Orders to my Servants. When Accident makes us meet at a third Place, we may mutually lament the Misfortune of never finding one another at home, go in the same Party to a Benefit-Play, and smile at each other, and put down Glasses as we pass in our Coaches. Thus we may enjoy as much of each other's Friendship as we are capable: For there are some People who are to be known only by Sight, with which sort of Friendship I hope you will always honour,

Madam,

Your most obedient humble Servant,

Mary Tuesday,

P. S. I subscribe my self by the Name of the Day I keep, that my supernumerary Friends may know who I am.'

ADVERTISEMENT.

To prevent all Mistakes that may happen among Gentlemen of the other End of the Town, who come but once a Week to St. James's *Coffee-house, either by miscalling the Servants, or requiring such things from them as are not properly within their respective Provinces; this is to give Notice, that* Kidney, *Keeper of the Book-Debts of the outlying Customers, and Observer of those who go off without paying, having resign'd that Employment, is succeeded by* John Sowton; *to whose Place of Enterer of Messages and first Coffee-Grinder* William Bird *is promoted; and* Samuel Burdock *comes as Shoe-Cleaner in the Room of the said* Bird. R

No. 25.
[ADDISON.]   Thursday, March 29.

. . . *Aegrescitque medendo.*—Virg.

THE following Letter will explain it self, and needs no Apology.

'*Sir,*

I am one of that sickly Tribe who are commonly known by the name of *Valetudinarians*; and do confess to you, that I first contracted this ill Habit of Body, or rather of Mind, by the Study of Physick. I no sooner began to peruse Books of this Nature, but I found my Pulse was irregular, and scarce ever read the Account of any Disease that I did not fancy my self afflicted with. Doctor *Sydenham's* learned Treatise of Fevers threw me into a lingring Hectick, which hung upon me all the while I was reading that excellent Piece. I then applied my self to the Study of several Authors, who have written upon Phthisical Distempers, and by that means fell into a Consumption; till at length, growing very fat, I was in a manner shamed out of that Imagination. Not long after this I found in my self all the Symptoms of the Gout, except Pain; but was cured of it by a Treatise upon the Gravel, written by a very Ingenious Author, who (as it is usual for Physicians to convert one Distemper into another) eased me of the Gout by giving me the Stone. I at length studied my self into a Complication of Distempers; but, accidentally taking into my Hand that Ingenious Discourse written by *Sanctorius*, I was resolved to direct my self by a Scheme of Rules, which I had collected from his Observations. The Learned World are very well acquainted with that Gentleman's Invention; who, for the better carrying on of his Experiments, contrived a certain Mathematical Chair, which was so Artificially hung upon Springs, that it would weigh any thing as well as a Pair of Scales. By this means he discovered how many Ounces of his Food pass'd by Perspiration, what quantity of it was turned into Nourishment, and how much went away by the other Channels and Distributions of Nature.

Having provided my self with this Chair, I used to Study, Eat, Drink, and Sleep in it; insomuch that I may be said, for these three last Years, to have lived in a Pair of Scales. I compute my self, when I am in full Health, to be precisely Two hundred Weight, falling short of it about a Pound after a Day's Fast, and exceeding it as much after a very full Meal; so that it is my continual Employment to trim the Ballance between these two Volatile Pounds in my Constitution. In my ordinary Meals I fetch my self up to Two hundred Weight and a half Pound; and if after having dined I find my self fall short of it, I drink just so much Small Beer, or eat such a quantity of Bread, as is sufficient to make me weight. In my greatest Excesses I do not trangress more than the other half Pound; which, for my Health's sake, I do the first *Monday* in every Month. As soon as I find my self duly poised after Dinner, I walk till I have perspired five Ounces and four Scruples; and when I discover, by my Chair, that I am so far reduced, I fall to my Books, and study away three Ounces more. As for the remaining Parts of the Pound, I keep no accompt of them. I do not dine and sup by the Clock, but by my Chair; for when that informs me my Pound of Food is exhausted I conclude my self to be hungry, and lay in another with all Diligence. In my Days of Abstinence I lose a Pound and an half, and on solemn Fasts am two Pound lighter than on other Days in the Year.

I allow my self, one Night with another, a Quarter of a Pound of Sleep within a few Grains more or less; and if upon my rising I find that I have not consumed my whole quantity, I take out the rest in my Chair. Upon an exact Calculation of what I expended and received the last Year, which I always register in a Book, I find the Medium to be Two hundred Weight, so that I cannot discover that I am impaired one Ounce in my Health during a whole Twelve-month. And yet, Sir, notwithstanding this my great Care to ballast my self equally every Day, and to keep my Body in its proper Poise, so it is that I find my self in a sick and languishing Condition. My Complexion is grown very sallow, my Pulse low, and my Body Hydropical. Let me therefore beg you, Sir, to consider me as your Patient, and to give me more certain Rules to walk by than those I have already observed, and you will very much oblige

Your Humble Servant.'

This Letter puts me in mind of an *Italian* Epitaph written on the Monument of a *Valetudinarian*; *Stavo ben, ma per star meglio, sto qui*: Which it is impossible to translate. The Fear of Death often proves Mortal, and sets People on Methods to save their Lives, which infallibly destroy them. This is a Reflection made by some Historians, upon observing that there are many more thousands killed in a Flight than in a Battel; and may be applied to those Multitudes of Imaginary Sick Persons that break their Constitutions by Physick, and throw themselves into the Arms of Death, by endeavouring to escape it. This Method is not only dangerous, but below the practice of a Reasonable Creature. To consult the Preservation of Life, as the only End of it, To make our Health our Business, To engage in no Action that is not part of a Regimen, or course of Physick; are Purposes so abject, so mean, so unworthy human Nature, that a generous Soul would rather die than submit to them. Besides, that a continual Anxiety for Life vitiates all the Relishes of it, and casts a Gloom over the whole Face of Nature; as it is impossible we should take Delight in any thing that we are every Moment afraid of losing.

I do not mean, by what I have here said, that I think any one to blame for taking due Care of their Health. On the contrary, as Cheerfulness of Mind, and Capacity for Business, are in a great measure the Effects of a well-tempered Constitution, a Man cannot be at too much Pains to cultivate and preserve it. But this Care, which we are prompted to, not only by common Sense, but by Duty and Instinct, should never engage us in groundless Fears, melancholy Apprehensions, and imaginary Distempers, which are natural to every Man who is more anxious to live than how to live. In short, the Preservation of Life should be only a secondary Concern, and the Direction of it our Principal. If we have this Frame of Mind, we shall take the best Means to preserve Life, without being over-sollicitous about the Event; and shall arrive at that Point of Felicity which *Martial* has mentioned as the Perfection of Happiness, of neither fearing nor wishing for Death.

In answer to the Gentleman, who tempers his Health by
Ounces and by Scruples, and instead of complying with those
natural Sollicitations of Hunger and Thirst, Drowsiness or Love
of Exercise, governs himself by the Prescriptions of his Chair,
I shall tell him a short Fable.   *Jupiter*, says the Mythologist,
to reward the Piety of a certain Countryman, promised to give
him whatever he would ask.   The Countryman desired that he
might have the Management of the Weather in his own Estate:
He obtained his Request, and immediately distributed Rain,
Snow, and Sunshine among his several Fields, as he thought
the nature of the Soil required.   At the end of the Year, when
he expected to see a more than ordinary Crop, his Harvest fell
infinitely short of that of his Neighbours: Upon which (says
the Fable) he desired *Jupiter* to take the Weather again
into his own Hands, or that otherwise he should utterly ruin
himself.   C

No. 26.
[ADDISON.]   Friday, March 30.

> *Pallida mors aequo pulsat pede pauperum tabernas*
>   *Regumque turres.   O beate Sesti,*
> *Vitae summa brevis spem nos vetat incohare longam.*
>   *Jam te premet nox, fabulaeque manes,*
> *Et domus exilis Plutonia . . .*—Hor.

WHEN I am in a serious Humour, I very often walk by my self
in *Westminster* Abby; where the Gloominess of the Place, and
the Use to which it is applied, with the Solemnity of the Building, and the Condition of the People who lye in it, are apt to
fill the Mind with a kind of Melancholy, or rather Thoughtful-
ness, that is not disagreeable.   I Yesterday pass'd a whole
Afternoon in the Church-yard, the Cloysters, and the Church,
amusing my self with the Tomb-stones and Inscriptions that
I met with in those several Regions of the Dead.   Most of them
recorded nothing else of the buried Person, but that he was
born upon one Day and died upon another: The whole History
of his Life being comprehended in those two Circumstances,
that are common to all Mankind.   I could not but look upon
these Registers of Existence, whether of Brass or Marble, as a
kind of Satyr upon the departed Persons; who had left no other
Memorial of them, but that they were born and that they died.
They put me in mind of several Persons mentioned in the
Battels of Heroic Poems, who have sounding Names given
them, for no other Reason but that they may be killed,

and are celebrated for nothing but being knocked on the Head.

Γλαῦκόν τε Μέδοντά τε Θερσίλοχόν τε.—Hom.
Glaucumque, Medontaque, Thersilochumque.—Virg.

The Life of these Men is finely described in Holy Writ by *the Path of an Arrow*, which is immediately closed up and lost.

Upon going into the Church, I entertained my self with the digging of a Grave; and saw in every Shovel-full of it that was thrown up, the Fragment of a Bone or Skull intermixt with a kind of fresh mouldering Earth that some time or other had a place in the Composition of an human Body. Upon this, I began to consider with my self what innumerable Multitudes of People lay confused together under the Pavement of that ancient Cathedral; how Men and Women, Friends and Enemies, Priests and Soldiers, Monks and Prebendaries, were crumbled amongst one another, and blended together in the same common Mass; how Beauty, Strength, and Youth, with Old-age, Weakness, and Deformity, lay undistinguished in the same promiscuous Heap of Matter.

After having thus surveyed this great Magazine of Mortality, as it were, in the Lump, I examined it more particularly by the Accounts which I found on several of the Monuments which are raised in every Quarter of that ancient Fabrick. Some of them were covered with such extravagant Epitaphs, that, if it were possible for the dead Person to be acquainted with them, he would blush at the Praises which his Friends have bestowed upon him.   There are others so excessively modest, that they deliver the Character of the Person departed in *Greek* or *Hebrew*, and by that means are not understood once in a Twelve-month. In the Poetical Quarter, I found there were Poets who had no Monuments, and Monuments which had no Poets.   I observed indeed that the present War had filled the Church with many of these uninhabited Monuments, which had been erected to the Memory of Persons whose Bodies were perhaps buried in the Plains of *Blenheim*, or in the Bosom of the Ocean.

I could not but be very much delighted with several modern Epitaphs, which are written with great Elegance of Expression and Justness of Thought, and therefore do Honour to the Living as well as to the Dead.   As a Foreigner is very apt to conceive an Idea of the Ignorance or Politeness of a Nation from the Turn of their publick Monuments and Inscriptions, they should be submitted to the Perusal of Men of Learning and Genius before they are put in Execution.   Sir *Cloudesley Shovel*'s Monument has very often given me great Offence: Instead of the brave rough *English* Admiral, which was the distinguishing Character of that plain gallant Man, he is represented on his Tomb by the Figure of a Beau, dress'd in a long Perriwig, and reposing himself upon Velvet Cushions under a Canopy of State. The Inscription is answerable to the Monument; for instead of celebrating the many remarkable Actions he had performed in the Service of his Country, it acquaints us only with the Manner of his Death, in which it was impossible for him to reap any Honour. The *Dutch*, whom we are apt to despise for want of Genius, shew an infinitely greater Taste of Antiquity and Politeness in their Buildings and Works of this Nature, than what we meet with in those of our own Country. The Monuments of their Admirals, which have been erected at the publick Expence, represent them like themselves; and are adorned with rostral Crowns and naval Ornaments, with beautiful Festoons of Seaweed, Shells, and Coral.

But to return to our Subject. I have left the Repository of our *English* Kings for the Contemplation of another Day, when I shall find my Mind disposed for so serious an Amusement. I know that Entertainments of this nature are apt to raise dark and dismal Thoughts in timorous Minds, and gloomy Imaginations; but for my own part, though I am always serious, I do not know what it is to be melancholy; and can therefore take a View of Nature in her deep and solemn Scenes, with the same Pleasure as in her most gay and delightful ones. By this means I can improve my self with those Objects, which others consider with Terror. When I look upon the Tombs of the Great, every Emotion of Envy dies in me; when I read the Epitaphs of the Beautiful, every inordinate Desire goes out; when I meet with the Grief of Parents upon a Tomb-stone, my Heart melts with Compassion; when I see the Tomb of the Parents themselves, I consider the Vanity of grieving for those whom we must quickly follow: When I see Kings lying by those who deposed them, when I consider rival Wits placed Side by Side, or the holy Men that divided the World with their Contests and Disputes, I reflect with Sorrow and Astonishment on the little Competitions, Factions, and Debates of Mankind. When I read the several Dates of the Tombs, of some that died Yesterday, and some six hundred Years ago, I consider that great Day when we shall all of us be Contemporaries, and make our Appearance together.   C

No. 27.

[STEELE.] Saturday, March 31.

> *Ut nox longa quibus mentitur amica, diesque*
> *Longa videtur opus debentibus, ut piger annus*
> *Pupillis quos dura premit custodia matrum;*
> *Sic mihi tarda fluunt ingrataque tempora, quae spem*
> *Consiliumque morantur agendi naviter, id quod*
> *Aeque pauperibus prodest, locupletibus aeque,*
> *Aeque neglectum pueris senibusque nocebit.*—Hor.

THERE is scarce a thinking Man in the World, who is involved in the Business of it, but lives under a secret Impatience of the Hurry and Fatigue he suffers, and has formed a Resolution to fix himself, one time or other, in such a State as is suitable to the End of his Being. You hear Men every Day in Conversation profess, that all the Honour, Power and Riches which they propose to themselves, cannot give Satisfaction enough to reward them for half the Anxiety they undergo in the Pursuit, or Possession of them. While Men are in this Temper (which happens very frequently) how inconsistent are they with themselves? They are wearied with the Toil they bear, but cannot find in their Hearts to relinquish it; Retirement is what they want, but they cannot betake themselves to it: While they pant after Shade and Covert, they will affect to appear in the most glittering Scenes of Life: But sure this is but just as reasonable as if a Man should call for more Lights, when he has a mind to go to Sleep.

Since then it is certain that our own Hearts deceive us in the Love of the World, and that we cannot command our selves enough to resign it, though we every Day wish our selves disengaged from its Allurements; let us not stand upon a Formal taking of Leave, but wean our selves from them, while we are in the midst of them.

It is certainly the general Intention of the greater Part of Mankind to accomplish this Work, and live according to their own Approbation, as soon as they possibly can: But since the Duration of Life is so uncertain, and that has been a common Topick of Discourse ever since there was such a thing as Life it self, how is it possible that we should defer a Moment the beginning to Live according to the Rules of Reason?

The Man of Business has ever some one Point to carry, and then he tells himself he 'll bid adieu to all the Vanity of Ambition: The Man of Pleasure resolves to take his Leave at least, and part civilly with his Mistress: But the Ambitious Man is entangled every Moment in a fresh Pursuit, and the Lover sees new Charms in the Object he fancy'd he could abandon. It is therefore a fantastical way of thinking, when we promise our selves an Alteration in our Conduct from change of Place, and difference of Circumstances; the same Passions will attend us where-ever we are, 'till they are Conquer'd; and we can never live to our Satisfaction in the deepest Retirement, unless we are capable of living so in some measure amidst the Noise and Business of the World.

I have ever thought Men were better known, by what could be observed of them from a Perusal of their private Letters, than any other way. My Friend, the Clergyman, the other Day, upon serious Discourse with him concerning the Danger of Procrastination, gave me the following Letters from Persons with whom he lives in great Friendship and Intimacy, according to the good Breeding and good Sense of his Character.   The first is from a Man of Business, who is his Convert: The second from one of whom he conceives good Hopes: The third from one who is in no State at all, but carried one way and another by starts.

'*Sir*,
I know not with what Words to express to you the Sense I have of the high Obligation you have laid upon me, in the Penance you enjoined me of doing some Good or other, to a Person of Worth, every Day I live.   The Station I am in, furnishes me with daily Opportunities of this kind: And the Noble Principle with which you have inspired me, of Benevolence to all I have to deal with, quickens my Application in every thing I undertake.   When I relieve Merit from Discountenance, when I assist a friendless Person, when I produce concealed Worth, I am displeased with my self, for having designed to leave the World in order to be Virtuous.   I am sorry you decline the Occasions which the Condition I am in might afford me of enlarging your Fortunes; but know I contribute more to your Satisfaction, when I acknowledge I am the better Man, from the Influence and Authority you have over,
                    Sir,
                         Your most Obliged and
                              Most Humble Servant,
                                        R. O.'

'*Sir*,
I am intirely convinced of the Truth of what you were pleased to say to me, when I was last with you alone.   You told me then of the silly way I was in; but you told me so, as I saw you loved me, otherwise I could not obey your Commands in letting you know my Thoughts so sincerely as I do at present.

I know *the Creature for whom I resign so much of my Character,* is all that you said of her; but then the Trifler has something in her so undesigning and harmless, that her Guilt in one kind disappears by the Comparison of her Innocence in another. Will you, Virtuous Men, allow no alteration of Offences? Must Dear *Chloe* be called by the hard Name you pious People give to common Women? I keep the solemn Promise I made you, in writing to you the State of my Mind, after your kind Admonition; and will endeavour to get the better of this Fondness, which makes me so much her humble Servant, that I am almost asham'd to Subscribe my self yours,

T. D.'

'*Sir,*

There is no State of Life so Anxious as that of a Man who does not live according to the Dictates of his own Reason. It will seem odd to you, when I assure you that my Love of Retirement first of all brought me to Court; but this will be no Riddle, when I acquaint you that I placed my self here with a Design of getting so much Mony as might enable me to Purchase a handsome Retreat in the Country. At present my Circumstances enable me, and my Duty prompts me, to pass away the remaining Part of my Life in such a Retirement as I at first proposed to my self; but to my great Misfortune I have intirely lost the Relish of it, and should now return to the Country with greater Reluctance than I at first came to Court. I am so unhappy, as to know that what I am fond of are Trifles, and that what I neglect is of the greatest Importance: In short, I find a Contest in my own Mind between Reason and Fashion. I remember you once told me, that I might live in the World and out of it, at the same time. Let me beg of you to explain this Paradox more at large to me, that I may conform my Life, if possible, both to my Duty and my Inclination. I am

Your most humble Servant,

R   *R. B.'*

No. 28.
[ADDISON.]   Monday, April 2.

> . . . *Neque semper arcum*
> *Tendit Apollo.*—Hor.

I SHALL here present my Reader with a Letter from a Projector, concerning a new Office which he thinks may very much contribute to the Embellishment of the City, and to the driving

Barbarity out of our Streets. I consider it as a Satyr upon Projectors in general, and a lively Picture of the whole Art of Modern Criticism.

'*Sir*,

Observing that you have Thoughts of creating certain Officers under you, for the Inspection of several petty Enormities which you your self cannot attend to; and finding daily Absurdities hung out upon the Sign-Posts of this City, to the great Scandal of Foreigners, as well as those of our own Country, who are curious Spectators of the same: I do humbly propose, that you would be pleased to make me your Superintendant of all such Figures and Devices as are or shall be made use of on this Occasion; with full Powers to rectifie or expunge whatever I shall find irregular or defective. For want of such an Officer, there is nothing like sound Literature and good Sense to be met with in those Objects, that are every where thrusting themselves out to the Eye, and endeavouring to become visible. Our Streets are filled with blue Boars, black Swans, and red Lions; not to mention flying Pigs, and Hogs in Armour, with many other Creatures more extraordinary than any in the Desarts of *Africk*. Strange! that one who has all the Birds and Beasts in Nature to chuse out of, should live at the Sign of an *Ens Rationis!*

My first Task therefore should be, like that of *Hercules*, to clear the City from Monsters. In the second Place I would forbid, that Creatures of jarring and incongruous Natures should be joined together in the same Sign; such as the Bell and the Neats-Tongue, the Dog and Gridiron. The Fox and Goose may be supposed to have met; but what has the Fox and the Seven Stars to do together? And when did the Lamb and Dolphin ever meet, except upon a Sign-Post? As for the Cat and Fiddle, there is a Conceit in it; and therefore I do not intend that any thing I have here said should affect it. I must however observe to you upon this Subject, that it is usual for a young Tradesman, at his first setting up, to add to his own Sign that of the Master whom he serv'd; as the Husband after Marriage, gives a Place to his Mistress's Arms in his own Coat. This I take to have given Rise to many of those Absurdities which are committed over our Heads; and, as I am informed, first occasioned the three Nuns and a Hare, which we see so frequently joined together. I would therefore establish certain Rules, for the determining how far one Tradesman may *give* the Sign of another, and in what Cases he may be allowed to quarter it with his own.

In the third Place, I would enjoin every Shop to make use

of a Sign which bears some Affinity to the Wares in which it deals. What can be more inconsistent, than to see a Bawd at the Sign of the Angel, or a Taylor at the Lion? A Cook should not live at the Boot, nor a Shoemaker at the roasted Pig; and yet, for want of this Regulation, I have seen a Goat set up before the Door of a Perfumer, and the *French* King's Head at a Sword-Cutler's.

An Ingenious Foreigner observes, that several of those Gentlemen who value themselves upon their Families, and overlook such as are bred to Trade, bear the Tools of their Forefathers in their Coats of Arms. I will not examine how true this is in Fact: But though it may not be necessary for Posterity thus to set up the Sign of their Forefathers; I think it highly proper for those who actually profess the Trade, to show some such Marks of it before their Doors.

When the Name gives an Occasion for an ingenious Sign-Post, I would likewise advise the Owner to take that Opportunity of letting the World know who he is. It would have been ridiculous for the Ingenious Mrs. *Salmon* to have lived at the Sign of the Trout; for which Reason she has erected before her House the Figure of the Fish that is her Name-sake. Mr. *Bell* has likewise distinguish'd himself by a Device of the same Nature: And here, Sir, I must beg Leave to observe to you, that this particular Figure of a Bell has given Occasion to several Pieces of Wit in this kind. A Man of your Reading must know that *Abel Drugger* gained great Applause by it in the Time of *Ben. Johnson*. Our Apocryphal Heathen God is also represented by this Figure; which, in Conjunction with the Dragon, makes a very handsome Picture in several of our Streets. As for the Bell-Savage, which is the Sign of a Savage Man standing by a Bell, I was formerly very much puzzled upon the Conceit of it, till I accidentally fell into the reading of an old Romance translated out of the *French*; which gives an Account of a very beautiful Woman who was found in a Wilderness, and is called in the *French la belle Sauvage*; and is every where translated by our Country-men the Bell-Savage. This Piece of Philology will, I hope, convince you that I have made Sign-Posts my Study, and consequently qualified my self for the Employment which I sollicit at your Hands. But before I conclude my Letter, I must communicate to you another Remark which I have made upon the Subject with which I am now entertaining you, namely, that I can give a shrewd Guess at the Humour of the Inhabitant by the Sign that hangs before his Door. A surly cholerick Fellow generally makes Choice of a Bear; as Men of milder Dispositions frequently live at the Lamb. Seeing a Punch-Bowl painted upon a Sign near

Charing-Cross, and very curiously garnished, with a Couple of Angels hovering over it and squeezing a Lemmon into it, I had the Curiosity to ask after the Master of the House, and found upon Enquiry, as I had guessed by the little *Agréemens* upon his Sign, that he was a *Frenchman*. I know, Sir, it is not requisite for me to enlarge upon these Hints to a Gentleman of your great Abilities; so humbly recommending my self to your Favour and Patronage,

I remain, &c.'

I shall add to the foregoing Letter, another which came to me by the same Penny-Post.

'From my own Apartment near Charing-Cross.

Honoured Sir,

Having heard that this Nation is a great Encourager of Ingenuity, I have brought with me a Rope-Dancer that was caught in one of the Woods belonging to the Great *Mogul*. He is by Birth a Monkey; but swings upon a Rope, takes a Pipe of Tobacco, and drinks a Glass of Ale, like any reasonable Creature. He gives great Satisfaction to the Quality; and if they will make a Subscription for him, I will send for a Brother of his out of *Holland* that is a very good Tumbler; and also for another of the same Family whom I design for my *Merry-Andrew*, as being an excellent Mimick, and the greatest Drole in the Country where he now is. I hope to have this Entertainment in a Readiness for the next Winter; and doubt not but it will please more than the Opera or Puppet-Show. I will not say that a Monkey is a better Man than some of the Opera Heroes; but certainly he is a better Representative of a Man, than the most artificial Composition of Wood and Wire. If you will be pleased to give me a good Word in your Paper, you shall be every Night a Spectator at my Show for nothing.

C   *I am*, &c.'

No. 29.
[ADDISON.]   Tuesday, April 3.

. . . Sermo lingua concinnus utraque
Suavior, ut Chio nota si commixta Falerni est.—Hor.

THERE is nothing that has more startled our *English* Audience, than the *Italian Recitativo* at its first Entrance upon the Stage. People were wonderfully surprized to hear Generals singing the Word of Command, and Ladies delivering Messages in Musick. Our Countrymen could not forbear laughing when they heard a Lover chanting out a Billet-doux, and even the

Superscription of a Letter set to a Tune.   The Famous Blunder in an old Play of *Enter a King and two Fidlers solus*, was now no longer an Absurdity; when it was impossible for a Hero in a Desart, or a Princess in her Closet, to speak any thing unaccompanied with Musical Instruments.

But however this *Italian* Method of acting in *Recitativo* might appear at first hearing, I cannot but think it much more just than that which prevailed in our *English* Opera before this Innovation: The Transition from an Air to Recitative Musick being more natural, than the passing from a Song to plain and ordinary Speaking, which was the common Method in *Purcell's* Operas.

The only Fault I find in our present Practice, is the making use of the *Italian Recitativo* with *English* Words.

To go to the Bottom of this Matter, I must observe, that the Tone, or (as the *French* call it) the Accent of every Nation in their ordinary Speech, is altogether different from that of every other People; as we may see even in the *Welsh* and *Scotch*, who border so near upon us.   By the Tone or Accent, I do not mean the Pronunciation of each particular Word, but the Sound of the whole Sentence.   Thus it is very common for an *English* Gentleman, when he hears a *French* Tragedy, to complain that the Actors all of them speak in a Tone; and therefore he very wisely prefers his own Country-men, not considering that a Foreigner complains of the same Tone in an *English* Actor.

For this Reason, the Recitative Musick, in every Language, should be as different as the Tone or Accent of each Language; for otherwise, what may properly express a Passion in one Language, will not do it in another.   Every one who has been long in *Italy* knows very well, that the Cadences in the *Recitativo* bear a remote Affinity to the Tone of their Voices in ordinary Conversation; or, to speak more properly, are only the Accents of their Language made more Musical and Tuneful.

Thus the Notes of Interrogation, or Admiration, in the *Italian* Musick (if one may so call them) which resemble their Accents in Discourse on such Occasions, are not unlike the ordinary Tones of an *English* Voice when we are angry; insomuch that I have often seen our Audiences extreamly mistaken as to what has been doing upon the Stage, and expecting to see the Hero knock down his Messenger, when he has been asking him a Question; or fancying that he quarrels with his Friend, when he only bids him Good-morrow.

For this Reason the *Italian* Artists cannot agree with our *English* Musicians, in admiring *Purcell's* Compositions, and thinking his Tunes so wonderfully adapted to his Words;

because both Nations do not always express the same Passions by the same Sounds.

I am therefore humbly of Opinion, that an *English* Composer should not follow the *Italian* Recitative too servilely, but make use of many gentle Deviations from it, in Compliance with his own Native Language. He may Copy out of it all the lulling Softness and *Dying Falls* (as *Shakespear* calls them), but should still remember that he ought to accommodate himself to an *English* Audience; and by humouring the Tone of our Voices in ordinary Conversation, have the same Regard to the Accent of his own Language, as those Persons had to theirs whom he professes to imitate. It is observed, that several of the singing Birds of our own Country learn to sweeten their Voices, and mellow the Harshness of their natural Notes, by practising under those that come from warmer Climates. In the same manner I would allow the *Italian* Opera to lend our *English* Musick as much as may grace and soften it, but never entirely to annihilate and destroy it. Let the Infusion be as strong as you please, but still let the Subject Matter of it be *English*.

A Composer should fit his Musick to the Genius of the People, and consider that the Delicacy of Hearing, and Taste of Harmony, has been formed upon those Sounds which every Country abounds with: In short, that Musick is of a Relative Nature, and what is Harmony to one Ear, may be Dissonance to another.

The same Observations which I have made upon the Recitative Part of Musick, may be applied to all our Songs and Airs in general.

Signior *Baptist Lully* acted like a Man of Sense in this Particular. He found the *French* Musick extreamly defective and very often barbarous: However, knowing the Genius of the People, the Humour of their Language, and the prejudiced Ears he had to deal with, he did not pretend to extirpate the *French* Musick and plant the *Italian* in its stead; but only to Cultivate and Civilize it with innumerable Graces and Modulations which he borrowed from the *Italian*. By this means the *French* Musick is now perfect in its kind; and when you say it is not so good as the *Italian*, you only mean that it does not please you so well, for there is scarce a *Frenchman* who would not wonder to hear you give the *Italian* such a Preference. The Musick of the *French* is indeed very properly adapted to their Pronunciation and Accent, as their whole Opera wonderfully favours the Genius of such a gay airy People. The Chorus in which that Opera abounds, gives the Parterre frequent Opportunities of joining in Concert with the Stage. This Inclination of the Audience to sing along with the Actors, so

prevails with them, that I have sometimes known the Performer on the Stage do no more in a Celebrated Song, than the
Clerk of a Parish Church, who serves only to raise the Psalm,
and is afterwards drowned in the Musick of the Congregation.
Every Actor that comes on the Stage is a Beau.   The Queens
and Heroines are so Painted, that they appear as Ruddy and
Cherry-cheek'd as Milk-maids.   The Shepherds are all Embroidered, and acquit themselves in a Ball better than our
English Dancing-Masters.   I have seen a Couple of Rivers
appear in red Stockings; and *Alpheus*, instead of having his
Head covered with Sedge and Bull-Rushes, making Love in a
fair full-bottomed Perriwig, and a Plume of Feathers, but with
a Voice so full of Shakes and Quavers that I should have
thought the Murmurs of a Country Brook the much more
agreeable Musick.

I remember the last Opera I saw in that merry Nation, was
the Rape of *Proserpine*, where *Pluto*, to make the more tempting Figure, puts himself in a *French* Equipage, and brings
Ascalaphus along with him as his *Valet de Chambre*.   This is
what we call Folly and Impertinence; but what the *French*
look upon as Gay and Polite.

I shall add no more to what I have here offered, than that
Musick, Architecture and Painting, as well as Poetry and
Oratory, are to deduce their Laws and Rules from the general
Sense and Taste of Mankind, and not from the Principles of
those Arts themselves; or in other Words, the Taste is not to
conform to the Art, but the Art to the Taste.   Musick is not
designed to please only Chromatick Ears, but all that are
capable of distinguishing harsh from disagreeable Notes.   A
Man of an ordinary Ear is a Judge whether a Passion is expressed in proper Sounds, and whether the Melody of those
Sounds be more or less pleasing.   C

No. 30.

[STEELE.]   Wednesday, April 4.

Si, Mimnermus uti censet, sine amore jocisque
Nil est jucundum, vivas in amore jocisque.—Hor.

ONE common Calamity makes Men extreamly affect each other,
though they differ in every other Particular.   The Passion of
Love is the most general Concern among Men; and I am glad
to hear by my last Advices from *Oxford*, that there are a Set
of Sighers in that University, who have erected themselves into
a Society in Honour of that tender Passion.   These Gentlemen
are of that Sort of Inamoratos, who are not so very much lost

to common Sense, but that they understand the Folly they are
guilty of; and for that Reason separate themselves from all
other Company, because they will enjoy the Pleasure of talking
incoherently, without being ridiculous to any but each other.
When a Man comes into the Club, he is not obliged to make any
Introduction to his Discourse, but at once, as he is seating
himself in his Chair, speaks in the Thread of his own Thoughts,
'She gave me a very obliging Glance, She never looked so well
in her Life as this Evening,' or the like Reflection, without
Regard to any other Member of the Society; for in this Assembly they do not meet to talk to each other, but every Man
claims the full Liberty of talking to himself. Instead of Snuff-
boxes and Canes, which are usual Helps to Discourse with other
young Fellows, these have each some Piece of Ribbon, a broken
Fan, or an old Girdle, which they play with while they talk
of the fair Person remembered by each respective Token.
According to the Representation of the Matter from my
Letters, the Company appear like so many Players rehearsing
behind the Scenes; one is sighing and lamenting his Destiny
in beseeching Terms, another declaring he will break his Chain,
and another in dumb-Show striving to express his Passion by
his Gesture. It is very ordinary in the Assembly for one of a
sudden to rise, and make a Discourse concerning his Passion in
general, and describe the Temper of his Mind in such a manner,
as that the whole Company shall join in the Description, and
feel the Force of it. In this Case, if any Man has declared the
Violence of his Flame in more pathetick Terms, he is made
President for that Night, out of respect to his superior Passion.

We had some Years ago in this Town a Set of People who
met and dressed like Lovers, and were distinguished by the
Name of the *Fringe-Glove Club*; but they were Persons of such
moderate Intellects, even before they were impaired by their
Passion, that their Irregularities could not furnish sufficient
Variety of Folly to afford daily new Impertinences; by which
Means that Institution dropped. These Fellows could express
their Passion in nothing but their Dress; but the *Oxonians*
are phantastical now they are Lovers, in proportion to their
Learning and Understanding before they become such. The
Thoughts of the ancient Poets on this agreeable Phrenzy, are
translated in honour of some modern Beauty; and *Chloris*
is won to Day, by the same Compliment that was made to
Lesbia a thousand Years ago. But as far as I can learn, the
Patron of the Club is the renowned Don *Quixote*. The Adventures of that gentle Knight are frequently mentioned in the
Society, under the Colour of laughing at the Passion and
themselves: But at the same time, though they are sensible

of the Extravagancies of that unhappy Warrior, they do not observe, that to turn all the Reading of the best and wisest Writings into Rhapsodies of Love, is a Phrenzy no less diverting than that of the aforesaid accomplished *Spaniard*. A Gentleman who, I hope, will continue his Correspondence, is lately admitted into the Fraternity, and sent me the following Letter.

'*Sir*,

Since I find you take Notice of Clubs, I beg leave to give you an Account of one in *Oxford*, which you have no where mentioned, and perhaps never heard of. We distinguish our selves by the Title of the *Amorous Club*, are all Votaries of *Cupid*, and Admirers of the Fair Sex. The Reason that we are so little known in the World, is the Secresie which we are obliged to live under in the University. Our Constitution runs counter to that of the Place wherein we live: For in Love there are no Doctors, and we all possess so high Passion, that we admit of no Graduates in it. Our Presidentship is bestowed according to the Dignity of Passion; our Number is unlimited; and our Statutes are like those of the *Druids*, recorded in our own Breasts only, and explained by the Majority of the Company. A Mistress, and a Poem in her Praise, will introduce any Candidate: Without the latter no one can be admitted; for he that is not in Love enough to rhime, is unqualified for our Society. To speak disrespectfully of any Woman is Expulsion from our gentle Society. As we are at present all of us Gown-men, instead of duelling when we are Rivals, we drink together the Health of our Mistress. The Manner of doing this sometimes indeed creates Debates; on such Occasions we have Recourse to the Rules of Love among the Antients.

Naevia sex cyathis, septem Justina bibatur.

This Method of a Glass to every Letter of her Name, occasioned the other Night a Dispute of some Warmth. A young Student, who is in Love with Mrs. *Elizabeth Dimple*, was so unreasonable as to begin her Health under the Name of *Elizabetha*; which so exasperated the Club, that by common Consent we retrenched it to *Betty*. We look upon a Man as no Company, that does not sigh five times in a Quarter of an Hour; and look upon a Member as very absurd, that is so much himself as to make a direct Answer to a Question. In fine, the whole Assembly is made up of absent Men, that is, of such Persons as have lost their Locality, and whose Minds and Bodies never keep Company with one another. As I am an unfortunate Member

of this distracted Society, you cannot expect a very regular
Account of it; for which Reason, I hope you will pardon me
that I so abruptly subscribe my self,

Sir,

Your most obedient,

humble Servant,

T. B.

I forgot to tell you, that *Albina*, who has six Votaries in this
Club, is one of your Readers.'   R

No. 31.
[ADDISON.]   Thursday, April 5.

Sit mihi fas audita loqui.—Virg.

LAST Night, upon my going into a Coffee-house not far from
the *Hay-Market* Theatre, I diverted my self for above half an
Hour by overhearing the Discourse of one, who, by the
Shabbiness of his Dress, the Extravagance of his Conceptions,
and the Hurry of his Speech, I discovered to be of that Species
who are generally distinguished by the Title of Projectors.
This Gentleman, for I found he was treated as such by his
Audience, was entertaining a whole Table of Listners with the
Project of an Opera, which he told us had not cost him above
two or three Mornings in the Contrivance, and which he was
ready to put in Execution, provided he might find his Account
in it. He said, that he had observed the great Trouble and
Inconvenience which Ladies were at, in travelling up and down
to the several Shows that are exhibited in different Quarters
of the Town. The dancing Monkies are in one Place; the
Puppet Show in another; the Opera in a third; not to mention
the Lions, that are almost a whole Day's Journey from the
politer Part of the Town. By this means People of Figure
are forced to lose half the Winter after their coming to Town,
before they have seen all the strange Sights about it. In order
to remedy this great Inconvenience, our Projector drew out of
his Pocket the Scheme of an Opera, Entitled, *The Expedition of*
Alexander *the Great*; in which he had disposed all the remarkable Shows about Town, among the Scenes and Decorations
of his Piece. The Thought, he confest, was not originally his
own, but that he had taken the Hint of it from several Performances which he had seen upon our Stage: In one of which
there was a Rary-Show; in another, a Ladder-dance; and in
others a Posture-Man, a moving Picture, with many Curiosities
of the like Nature.

This *Expedition of Alexander* opens with his consulting the

Oracle at *Delphos*, in which the dumb Conjurer, who has been visited by so many Persons of Quality of late Years, is to be introduced as telling him his Fortune: At the same time *Clench* of *Barnet* is represented in another Corner of the Temple, as ringing the Bells of *Delphos*, for joy of his Arrival.   The Tent of *Darius* is to be Peopled by the Ingenious Mrs. *Salmon*, where *Alexander* is to fall in Love with a Piece of Wax-work, that represents the beautiful *Statira*.   When *Alexander* comes into that Country, in which *Quintus Curtius* tells us the Dogs were so exceeding fierce that they would not loose their Hold, though they were cut to pieces Limb by Limb, and that they would hang upon their Prey by their Teeth when they had nothing but a Mouth left, there is to be a Scene of *Hockley in the Hole*, in which is to be represented all the Diversions of that Place, the Bull-baiting only excepted, which cannot possibly be exhibited in the Theatre, by reason of the Lowness of the Roof.   The several Woods in *Asia*, which *Alexander* must be supposed to pass through, will give the Audience a Sight of Monkies dancing upon Ropes, with the many other Pleasantries of that ludicrous Species.   At the same time, if there chance to be any Strange Animals in Town, whether Birds or Beasts, they may be either let loose among the Woods, or driven across the Stage by some of the Country People of *Asia*.   In the last great Battel, *Pinkethman* is to personate King *Porus* upon an Elephant, and is to be encountered by *Powell*, representing *Alexander* the Great, upon a Dromedary, which nevertheless Mr. *Powell* is desired to call by the Name of *Bucephalus*.   Upon the Close of this great decisive Battel, when the two Kings are thoroughly reconciled, to shew the mutual Friendship and good Correspondence that reigns between them, they both of them go together to a Puppet Show, in which the ingenious Mr. *Powell, Junior*, may have an Opportunity of displaying his whole Art of Machinery, for the Diversion of the two Monarchs. Some at the Table urged, that a Puppet Show was not a suitable Entertainment for *Alexander* the Great; and that it might be introduced more properly, if we suppose the Conqueror touched upon that Part of *India* which is said to be inhabited by the Pigmies.   But this Objection was looked upon as frivolous, and the Proposal immediately overruled.   Our Projector further added, that after the Reconciliation of these two Kings they might invite one another to Dinner, and either of them entertain his Guest with the *German* Artist, Mr. *Pinkethman*'s Heathen Gods, or any of the like Diversions, which shall then chance to be in vogue.

This Project was received with very great Applause by the whole Table.   Upon which the Undertaker told us, that he

had not yet communicated to us above half his Design; for
that *Alexander* being a *Greek*, it was his Intention that the
whole Opera should be acted in that Language, which was a
Tongue he was sure would wonderfully please the Ladies,
especially when it was a little raised and rounded by the
Ionick Dialect; and could not but be acceptable to the whole
Audience, because there are fewer of them who understand
Greek than *Italian*. The only Difficulty that remained, was,
how to get Performers, unless we could persuade some Gentlemen of the Universities to learn to Sing, in order to qualifie
themselves for the Stage; but this Objection soon vanished,
when the Projector informed us that the *Greeks* were at present
the only Musicians in the *Turkish* Empire, and that it would
be very easie for our Factory at *Smyrna* to furnish us every
Year with a Colony of Musicians, by the Opportunity of the
Turkey Fleet; besides, says he, if we want any single Voice for
any lower Part in the Opera, *Lawrence* can learn to speak
Greek, as well as he does *Italian*, in a Fortnight's time.

The Projector having thus settled Matters, to the good
liking of all that heard him, he left his Seat at the Table, and
planted himself before the Fire, where I had unluckily taken
my Stand for the Convenience of overhearing what he said.
Whether he had observed me to be more attentive than
ordinary, I cannot tell, but he had not stood by me above a
quarter of a Minute, but he turned short upon me on a sudden,
and catching me by a Button of my Coat, attacked me very
abruptly after the following manner: Besides, Sir, I have heard
of a very extraordinary Genius for Musick that lives in *Switzerland*, who has so strong a Spring in his Fingers, that he can
make the Board of an Organ sound like a Drum, and if I could
but procure a Subscription of about Ten thousand Pound
every Winter, I would undertake to fetch him over, and oblige
him by Articles to set everything that should be sung upon the
English Stage. After this he looked full in my Face, expecting
I would make an Answer; when by good Luck, a Gentleman
that had entered the Coffee-house since the Projector applied
himself to me, hearing him talk of his *Swiss* Compositions,
cry'd out with a kind of Laugh, Is our Musick then to receive
farther Improvements from *Switzerland*? This alarmed the
Projector, who immediately let go my Button, and turned about
to answer him. I took the Opportunity of the Diversion, which
seemed to be made in favour of me, and laying down my Penny
upon the Bar, retired with some Precipitation.   C

No. 32.

[STEELE.]   Friday, April 6.

Nil illi larva aut tragicis opus esse cothurnis.—Hor.

THE late Discourse concerning the Statutes of the *Ugly Club*
having been so well received at *Oxford,* that, contrary to the
strict Rules of the Society, they have been so partial as to take
my own Testimonial, and admit me into that select Body; I
could not restrain the Vanity of publishing to the World the
Honour which is done me. It is no small Satisfaction, that I
have given Occasion for the President's shewing both his
Invention and Reading to such Advantage as my Correspondent reports he did: But it is not to be doubted there were
many very proper Hums and Pauses in his Harangue, which
lose their Ugliness in the Narration, and which my correspondent (begging his Pardon) has no very good Talent at representing. I very much approve of the Contempt the Society
has of Beauty: Nothing ought to be laudable in a Man, in which
his Will is not concerned; therefore our Society can follow
Nature, and where she has thought fit, as it were, to mock her
self, we can do so too, and be merry upon the Occasion.

'*Mr.* SPECTATOR,

Your making publick the late Trouble I gave you, you will
find to have been the Occasion of this: Who should I meet at
the Coffee-house Door t'other Night, but my old Friend Mr.
President? I saw somewhat had pleased him; and as soon as
he had cast his Eye upon me, "Oho, Doctor, rare News from
London, (says he); the SPECTATOR has made honourable Mention
of the Club (Man) and published to the World his sincere
Desire to be a Member, with a recommendatory Description
of his Phiz: And though our Constitution has made no particular Provision for short Faces, yet, his being an extraordinary
Case, I believe we shall find an Hole for him to creep in at;
for I assure you he is not against the Canon; and if his Sides are
as compact as his Joles, he need not disguise himself to make one
of us." I presently called for the Paper to see how you looked
in Print; and after we had regaled our selves awhile upon the
pleasant Image of our Proselite, Mr. President told me I should
be his Stranger at the next Night's Club: Where we were no
sooner come, and Pipes brought, but Mr. President began an
Harangue upon your Introduction to my Epistle, setting forth
with no less Volubility of Speech than Strength of Reason,
"That a Speculation of this Nature was what had been long
and much wanted; and that he doubted not but it would be of
inestimable Value to the Publick, in reconciling even of Bodies

I—*D ¹⁶⁴

and Souls; in composing and quieting the Minds of Men under all corporal Redundancies, Deficiencies, and Irregularities whatsoever; and making every one sit down content in his own Carcass, though it were not perhaps so mathematically put together as he could wish." And again, "How that for want of a due Consideration of what you first advance, *viz.* that our Faces are not of our own chusing, People had been transported beyond all good Breeding, and hurried themselves into un-accountable and fatal Extravagances: As, how many impartial Looking-glasses had been censured and calumniated, nay, and sometimes shivered into ten thousand Splinters, only for a fair Representation of the Truth? how many Headstrings and Garters had been made accessary, and actually forfeited, only because Folks must needs quarrel with their own Shadows? And who (continues he) but is deeply sensible, that one great Source of the Uneasiness and Misery of human Life, especially amongst those of Distinction, arises from nothing in the world else, but too severe a Contemplation of an indefeasible Con-texture of our external Parts, or certain natural and invincible Dispositions to be fat or lean? When a little more of Mr. Spectator's Philosophy would take off all this; and in the mean time let them observe, that there's not one of their Grievances of this Sort, but perhaps, in some Ages of the World has been highly in vogue: and may be so again, nay, in some Country or other ten to one is so at this Day.   My Lady *Ample* is the most miserable Woman in the World, purely of her own making: She even grudges her self Meat and Drink, for fear she should thrive by them; and is constantly crying out, In a Quarter of a Year more I shall be quite out of all manner of Shape!   Now the Lady's Misfortune seems to be only this, that she is planted in a wrong Soil; for, go but t'other Side of the Water, it's a Jest at *Harlem* to talk of a Shape under eighteen Stone.   These wise Traders regulate their Beauties as they do their Butter, by the Pound; and Miss *Cross*, when she first arrived in the *Low-Countries*, was not computed to be so handsom as Madam *Van Brisket* by near half a Tun.   On the other hand, there's 'Squire *Lath*, a proper Gentleman, of Fifteen hundred Pound *per Annum*, as well as of an unblameable Life and Conversation; yet would not I be the Esquire for half his Estate; for if it was as much more, he'd freely part with it all for a Pair of Legs to his Mind: Whereas in the Reign of our first King *Edward* of glorious Memory, nothing more modish than a Brace of your fine taper Supporters; and his Majesty, without an Inch of Calf, managed Affairs in Peace and War as laudably as the bravest and most politick of his Ancestors; and was as terrible to his Neighbours under the Royal Name of *Long-*

shanks, as *Cœur de Lion* to the *Saracens* before him. If we look farther back into History we shall find, that *Alexander* the Great wore his Head a little over the left Shoulder; and then not a Soul stirred out till he had adjusted his Neck Bone; the whole Nobility addressed the Prince and each other obliquely, and all Matters of Importance were concerted and carried on in the *Macedonian* Court with their Polls on one Side. For about the first Century nothing made more Noise in the World than *Roman* Noses, and then not a Word of them till they revived again in Eighty eight. Nor is it so very long since *Richard* the Third set up half the Backs of the Nation; and high Shoulders, as well as high Noses, were the Top of the Fashion. But to come to our selves, Gentlemen, tho' I find by my quinquennial Observations, that we shall never get Ladies enough to make a Party in our own Country, yet might we meet with better Success among some of our Allies. And what think you if our Board sate for a *Dutch* Piece? Truly I am of Opinion, that as odd as we appear in Flesh and Blood, we should be no such strange things in Metzo-Tinto. But this Project may rest till our Number is compleat; and this being our Election Night, give me leave to propose Mr. SPECTATOR: You see his Inclinations, and perhaps we may not have his Fellow."

I found most of them (as is usual in all such Cases) were prepared; but one of the Seniors (whom by the by Mr. President had taken all this Pains to bring over) sate still, and cocking his Chin, which seemed only to be levelled at his Nose, very gravely declared, "That in case he had had sufficient Knowledge of you, no Man should have been more willing to have served you; but that he, for his Part, had always had regard to his own Conscience, as well as other People's Merit; and he did not know that but you might be a handsome Fellow; for as for your own Certificate, it was every Body's Business to speak for themselves." Mr. President immediately retorted, "A handsome Fellow! why he is a Wit (Sir) and you know the Proverb:" and to ease the old Gentleman of his Scruples, cried, "That for Matter of Merit it was all one, you might wear a Mask." This threw him into a Pause, and he looked desirous of three Days to consider on it; but Mr. President improved the Thought, and followed him up with an old Story, "That Wits were privileged to wear what Masks they pleased in all Ages; and that a Vizard had been the constant Crown of their Labours, which was generally presented them by the Hand of some Satyr, and sometimes of *Apollo* himself:" For the Truth of which he appealed to the Frontispiece of several Books, and particularly to the *English Juvenal*, to which he referred him;

and only added; "That such Authors were the *Larvati*, or *Larva donati* of the Antients." This cleared up all, and in the Conclusion you were chose Probationer; and Mr. President put round your Health as such, protesting, "That though indeed he talked of a Vizard, he did not believe all the while you had any more Occasion for it than the Cat-a-mountain;" so that all you have to do now is to pay your Fees, which here are very reasonable if you are not imposed upon; and you may stile your self *Informis Societatis Socius:* Which I am desired to acquaint you with; and upon the same I beg you to accept of the Congratulation of,

Sir,

Oxford,   *Your obliged humble Servant,*
March 21.   A. C.'
R

No. 33.
[STEELE.]   Saturday, April 7.

> *Fervidus tecum puer & solutis*
> *Gratiae zonis properentque Nymphae*
> *Et parum comis sine te Juventas*
>   *Mercuriusque.*—Hor. ad Venerem.

A FRIEND of mine has two Daughters, whom I will call *Laetitia* and *Daphne*; The Former is one of the Greatest Beauties of the Age in which she lives, the Latter no way remarkable for any Charms in her Person. Upon this one Circumstance of their Outward Form, the Good and Ill of their Life seems to turn. *Laetitia*, has not from her very Childhood, heard any thing else but Commendations of her Features and Complexion; by which means she is no other than Nature made her, a very beautiful Outside. The Consciousness of her Charms has rendered her insupportably Vain and Insolent towards all who have to do with her. *Daphne*, who was almost Twenty before one civil thing had ever been said to her, found her self obliged to acquire some Accomplishments, to make up for the want of those Attractions which she saw in her Sister. Poor *Daphne* was seldom submitted to in a Debate wherein she was concerned; her Discourse had nothing to recommend it but the good Sense of it, and she was always under a necessity to have very well considered what she was to say before she uttered it; while *Laetitia* was listened to with Partiality, and Approbation sat in the Countenances of those she conversed with, before she communicated what she had to say. These Causes have produced suitable Effects, and *Laetitia* is as insipid a Companion, as *Daphne* is an agreeable one. *Laetitia*, confident of Favour,

has studied no Arts to please; *Daphne*, despairing of any In
clination towards her Person, has depended only on her Merit.
Laetitia has always something in her Air that is sullen, grave,
and disconsolate.   *Daphne* has a Countenance that appears
cheaiful, open, and unconcerned.   A Young Gentleman saw
Laetitia this Winter at a Play, and became her Captive.   His
Fortune was such, that he wanted very little Introduction to
speak his Sentiments to her Father.   The Lover was admitted
with the utmost Freedom into the Family, where a constrained
Behaviour, severe Looks, and distant Civilities, were the
highest Favours he could obtain of *Laetitia*; while *Daphne*
used him with the good Humour, Familiarity, and Innocence
of a Sister: Insomuch, that he would often say to her, *Dear*
Daphne, *wert thou but as Handsome as* Laetitia!——She received
such Language with that ingenuous and pleasing Mirth, which
is natural to a Woman without Design.   He still sighed in vain
for *Laetitia*, but found certain Relief in the agreeable Conversation of *Daphne*.   At length, heartily tired with the haughty
Impertinence of *Laetitia*, and charmed with repeated Instances
of good Humour he had observed in *Daphne*, he one Day told
the latter, that he had something to say to her he hoped she
would be pleased with——   *Faith* Daphne, continued he, *I am
in Love with thee, and despise thy Sister sincerely*.   The manner
of his declaring himself gave his Mistress occasion for a very
hearty Laughter.——*Nay*, says he, *I knew you would Laugh
at me, but I'll ask your Father*.   He did so; the Father received
his Intelligence with no less Joy than Surprize, and was very
glad he had now no Care left but for his *Beauty*, which he
thought he could carry to Market at his Leisure.   I do not
know any thing that has pleased me so much a great while,
as this Conquest of my Friend *Daphne*'s.   All her Acquaintance
congratulate her upon her Chance-Medley, and laugh at that
premeditating Murderer her Sister.   As it is an Argument of a
light Mind, to think the worse of our selves for the Imperfections of our Persons, it is equally below us to value our selves
upon the Advantages of them.   The Female World seem to be
almost incorrigibly gone astray in this Particular; for which
Reason, I shall recommend the following Extract out of a
Friend's Letter to the Profess'd Beauties, who are a People
almost as unsufferable as the Profess'd Wits.

'Monsieur *St. Evremont* has concluded one of his Essays,
with affirming, that the last Sighs of a handsom Woman are
not so much for the Loss of her Life, as of her Beauty.   Perhaps this Raillery is pursued too far, yet it is turned upon a
very obvious Remark, that Woman's strongest Passion is for
her own Beauty, and that she values it as her Favourite

Distinction. From hence it is that all Arts, which pretend to improve or preserve it, meet with so general a Reception among the Sex. To say nothing of many false Helps, and Contraband Wares of Beauty, which are daily vended in this great Mart, there is not a Maiden-Gentlewoman, of a good Family in any Country of *South-Britain*, who has not heard of the Virtues of *May*-Dew, or is unfurnished with some Receipt or other in Favour of her Complexion; and I have known a Physician of Learning and Sense, after Eight Years Study in the University, and a Course of Travels into most Countries of *Europe*, owe the first raising of his Fortunes to a Cosmetick Wash.

This has given me Occasion to consider how so Universal a Disposition in Womankind, which springs from a laudable Motive, the Desire of Pleasing, and proceeds upon an Opinion, not altogether groundless, that Nature may be helped by Art, may be turned to their Advantage. And, methinks, it would be an acceptable Service to take them out of the Hands of Quacks and Pretenders, and to prevent their imposing upon themselves, by discovering to them the true Secret and Art of improving Beauty.

In order to this, before I touch upon it directly, it will be necessary to lay down a few Preliminary Maxims, *viz.*

That no Woman can be Handsome by the Force of Features alone, any more than she can be Witty only by the Help of Speech.

That Pride destroys all Symmetry and Grace, and Affectation is a more terrible Enemy to fine faces than the Small-Pox.

That no Woman is capable of being Beautiful, who is not incapable of being False.

And, That what would be Odious in a Friend, is Deformity in a Mistress.

From these few Principles, thus laid down, it will be easie to prove, that the true Art of assisting Beauty consists in Embellishing the whole Person by the proper Ornaments of virtuous and commendable Qualities. By this Help alone it is, that those who are the Favourite Work of Nature, or, as Mr. *Dryden* expresses it, the Porcelain Clay of human Kind, become animated, and are in a Capacity of exerting their Charms: And those who seem to have been neglected by her, like Models wrought in haste, are capable, in a great measure, of finishing what She has left imperfect.

It is, methinks, a low and degrading Idea of that Sex, which was created to refine the Joys, and soften the Cares of Humanity, by the most agreeable Participation, to consider them meerly as Objects of Sight. This is abridging them of their natural Extent of Power, to put them upon a Level with their Pictures at *Kneller's*.   How much nobler is the Contemplation of Beauty heightened by Virtue, and commanding our Esteem and Love, while it draws our Observation?   How faint and spiritless are the Charms of a Coquet, when compared with the real Loveliness of *Sophronia's* Innocence, Piety, good Humour and Truth; Virtues which add a new Softness to her Sex, and even beautifie her Beauty!   That Agreeableness, which must otherwise have appeared no longer in the modest Virgin, is now preserved in the tender Mother, the prudent Friend, and the faithful Wife.   Colours artfully spread upon Canvas may entertain the Eye, but not affect the Heart; and she, who takes no Care to add to the natural Graces of her Person any excelling Qualities, may be allowed still to amuse, as a Picture, but not to triumph as a Beauty.

When *Adam* is introduced by *Milton* describing *Eve* in Paradise, and relating to the Angel the Impressions he felt upon seeing her at her first Creation, he does not represent her like a *Grecian Venus*, by her Shape or Features, but by the Lustre of her Mind which shone in them, and gave them their Power of charming.

> *Grace was in all her Steps, Heaven in her Eye,*
> *In all her Gestures Dignity and Love.*

Without this irradiating Power the proudest Fair One ought to know, whatever her Glass may tell her to the contrary, that her most perfect Features are Uninform'd and Dead.

I cannot better close this Moral, than by a short Epitaph written by *Ben. Johnson*, with a Spirit which nothing could inspire but such an Object as I have been describing;

> *Underneath this Stone doth lye*
> *As much Virtue as cou'd die:*
> *Which when alive did Vigour give*
> *To as much Beauty as cou'd live.*

> *I am, Sir,*
>
> > *Your most humble Servant,*

R   R. B.'

No. 34.
[ADDISON.]   Monday, April 9.

Parcit
Cognatis maculis similis fera . . .—Juv.

THE Club of which I am a Member, is very luckily composed of such Persons as are engaged in different Ways of Life, and deputed as it were out of the most conspicuous Classes of

Mankind: By this Means I am furnished with the greatest Variety of Hints and Materials, and know every thing that passes in the different Quarters and Divisions, not only of this great City, but of the whole Kingdom. My Readers too have the Satisfaction to find, that there is no Rank or Degree among them who have not their Representative in this Club, and that there is always some Body present who will take Care of their respective Interests, that nothing may be written or published to the Prejudice or Infringement of their just Rights and Privileges.

I last Night sat very late in Company with this select Body of Friends, who entertained me with several Remarks which they and others had made upon these my Speculations, as also with the various Success which they had met with among their several Ranks and Degrees of Readers. WILL. HONEYCOMB told me, in the softest manner he could, that there were some Ladies (but for your Comfort, says WILL. they are not those of the most Wit) that were offended at the Liberties I had taken with the Opera and the Puppet-Show: That some of them were likewise very much surprised, that I should think such serious Points as the Dress and Equipage of Persons of Quality, proper Subjects for Raillery.

He was going on, when Sir ANDREW FREEPORT took him up short, and told him, that the Papers he hinted at had done great Good in the City, and that all their Wives and Daughters were the better for them: And further added, that the whole City thought themselves very much obliged to me for declaring my generous Intentions to scourge Vice and Folly as they appear in a Multitude, without condescending to be a Publisher of particular Intreagues and Cuckoldoms. In short, says Sir ANDREW, if you avoid that foolish beaten Road of falling upon Aldermen and Citizens, and employ your Pen upon the Vanity and Luxury of Courts, your Paper must needs be of general Use.

Upon this my Friend the TEMPLER told Sir ANDREW, That he wondered to hear a Man of his Sense talk after that manner; that the City had always been the Province for Satyr; and that the Wits of King *Charles*'s Time jested upon nothing else during his whole Reign. He then shewed, by the Examples of *Horace*, *Juvenal*, *Boileau*, and the best Writers of every Age, that the Follies of the Stage and Court had never been accounted too sacred for Ridicule, how great soever the Persons might be that patroniz'd them. But after all, says he, I think your Raillery has made too great an Excursion, in attacking several Persons of the Inns of Court; and I do not believe you can shew me any Precedent for your Behaviour in that Particular.

My good Friend Sir ROGER DE COVERLEY, who had said nothing all this while, began his Speech with a Pish! and told us, That he wondered to see so many Men of Sense so very serious upon Fooleries. Let our good Friend, says he, attack every one that deserves it: I would only advise you, Mr. SPECTATOR, applying himself to me, to take care how you meddle with Country Squires: They are the Ornaments of the *English* Nation; Men of Good Heads and sound Bodies! and let me tell you, some of them take it ill of you, that you mention Fox-hunters with so little Respect.

Captain SENTRY spoke very sparingly on this Occasion. What he said was only to commend my Prudence in not touching upon the Army, and advised me to continue to act discreetly in that Point.

By this time I found every Subject of my Speculations was taken away from me, by one or other of the Club; and began to think my self in the Condition of the good Man that had one Wife who took a Dislike to his grey Hairs, and another to his black, till by their picking out what each of them had an Aversion to, they left his Head altogether bald and naked.

While I was thus musing with my self, my worthy Friend the Clergyman, who, very luckily for me, was at the Club that Night, undertook my Cause. He told us, that he wondered any Order of Persons should think themselves too considerable to be advis'd: That it was not Quality, but Innocence, which exempted Men from Reproof: That Vice and Folly ought to be attacked where-ever they could be met with, and especially when they were placed in high and conspicuous Stations of Life. He further added, That my Paper would only serve to aggravate the Pains of Poverty, if it chiefly exposed those who are already depress'd, and in some measure turned into Ridicule, by the Meanness of their Conditions and Circumstances. He afterwards proceeded to take Notice of the great Use this Paper might be of to the Publick, by reprehending those Vices which are too trivial for the Chastisement of the Law, and too fantastical for the Cognizance of the Pulpit. He then advised me to prosecute my Undertaking with Chearfulness; and assured me, that whoever might be displeased with me, I should be approved by all those whose Praises do Honour to the Persons on whom they are bestowed.

The whole Club pays a particular Deference to the Discourse of this Gentleman, and are drawn into what he says, as much by the candid ingenuous Manner with which he delivers himself, as by the Strength of Argument and Force of Reason which he makes use of. WILL. HONEYCOMB immediately agreed, that what he had said was right; and that for his Part, he would not insist upon the Quarter which he had demanded for the Ladies. Sir ANDREW gave up the City with the same Frankness. The TEMPLER would not stand out; and was followed by Sir ROGER and the CAPTAIN: Who all agreed that I should be at Liberty to carry the War into what Quarter I pleased; provided I continued to combat with Criminals in a Body, and to assault the Vice without hurting the Person.

This Debate, which was held for the Good of Mankind, put me in mind of that which the *Roman* Triumvirate were formerly engaged in, for their Destruction. Every Man at first stood hard for his Friend, till they found that by this Means they should spoil their Proscription: And at length, making a Sacrifice of all their Acquaintance and Relations, furnished out a very decent Execution.

Having thus taken my Resolutions to march on boldly in the Cause of Virtue and good Sense, and to annoy their Adversaries in whatever Degree or Rank of Men they may be found: I shall be deaf for the future to all the Remonstrances that shall be made to me on this Account. If *Punch* grows extravagant, I shall reprimand him very freely: If the Stage becomes a Nursery of Folly and Impertinence, I shall not be afraid to animadvert upon it. In short, If I meet with any thing in City, Court, or Country, that shocks Modesty or good Manners, I shall use my utmost Endeavours to make an Example of it. I must however intreat every particular Person, who does me the Honour to be a Reader of this Paper, never to think himself, or any one of his Friends or Enemies, aimed at in what is said: For I promise him, never to draw a faulty Character which does not fit at least a Thousand People; or to publish a single Paper, that is not written in the Spirit of Benevolence, and with a love to Mankind.   C

No. 35.
[ADDISON.]   Tuesday, April 10.
Risu inepto res ineptior nulla est.—Catull.

AMONG all kinds of Writing, there is none in which Authors are more apt to miscarry than in Works of Humour, as there is none in which they are more ambitious to excel. It is not an Imagination that teems with Monsters, an Head that is filled with extravagant Conceptions, which is capable of furnishing the World with Diversions of this nature; and yet if we look into the Productions of several Writers, who set up for Men of Humour, what wild irregular Fancies, what unnatural Distortions of Thoughts, do we meet with? If they speak

Nonsense, they believe they are talking Humour; and when they have drawn together a Scheme of absurd inconsistent Ideas, they are not able to read it over to themselves without laughing. These poor Gentlemen endeavour to gain themselves the Reputation of Wits and Humourists, by such monstrous Conceits as almost qualifie them for *Bedlam*; not considering that Humour should always lye under the Check of Reason, and that it requires the Direction of the nicest Judgment, by so much the more as it indulges it self in the most boundless Freedoms. There is a kind of Nature that is to be observed in this sort of Compositions, as well as in all other; and a certain Regularity of Thought which must discover the Writer to be a Man of Sense, at the same time that he appears altogether given up to Caprice: For my part, when I read the delirious Mirth of an unskilful Author, I cannot be so barbarous as to divert my self with it, but am rather apt to pity the Man, than to laugh at any thing he writes.

The Deceased Mr. *Shadwell*, who had himself a great deal of the Talent which I am treating of, represents an empty Rake, in one of his Plays, as very much surprized to hear one say that breaking of Windows was not Humour; and I question not but several *English* Readers will be as much startled to hear me affirm, that many of those raving incoherent Pieces, which are often spread among us, under odd Chymerical Titles, are rather the Offsprings of a distempered Brain, than Works of Humour.

It is indeed much easier to describe what is not Humour, than what is; and very difficult to define it otherwise than as *Cowley* has done Wit, by Negatives. Were I to give my own Notions of it, I would deliver them after *Plato*'s manner, in a kind of Allegory, and by supposing Humour to be a Person, deduce to him all his Qualifications, according to the following Genealogy. TRUTH was the Founder of the Family, and the Father of GOOD SENSE. GOOD SENSE was the Father of WIT who married a Lady of a Collateral Line called MIRTH, by whom he had issue HUMOUR. HUMOUR therefore being the youngest of the Illustrious Family, and descended from Parents of such different Dispositions, is very various and unequal in his Temper; sometimes you see him putting on grave Looks and a solemn Habit, sometimes airy in his Behaviour and fantastick in his Dress: Insomuch that at different times he appears as serious as a Judge, and as jocular as a *Merry-Andrew*. But as he has a great deal of the Mother in his Constitution, whatever Mood he is in, he never fails to make his Company laugh.

But since there is an Impostor abroad, who takes upon him

the Name of this young Gentleman, and would willingly pass for him in the World; to the end that well-meaning Persons may not be imposed upon by Cheats, I would desire my Readers, when they meet with this Pretender, to look into his Parentage, and to examine him strictly, whether or no he be remotely allied to Truth, and lineally descended from Good Sense; if not, they may conclude him a Counterfeit. They may likewise distinguish him by a loud and excessive Laughter, in which he seldom gets his Company to join with him. For as True Humour generally looks serious, while every Body laughs about him; False Humour is always laughing, whilst every Body about him looks serious. I shall only add, if he has not in him a Mixture of both Parents, that is, if he would pass for the Offspring of Wit without Mirth, or Mirth without Wit, you may conclude him to be altogether Spurious, and a Cheat.

The Impostor of whom I am speaking, descends Originally from Falsehood, who was the Mother of Nonsense, who was brought to Bed of a Son called Frenzy, who Married one of the Daughters of Folly, commonly known by the Name of Laughter, on whom he begot that Monstrous Infant of which I have been here speaking. I shall set down at length the Genealogical Table of False Humour, and, at the same time, place under it the Genealogy of True Humour, that the Reader may at one View behold their different Pedigrees and Relations.

Falsehood.
Nonsense.
Frenzy.————Laughter.
False Humour.

Truth.
Good Sense.
Wit.————Mirth.
Humour.

I might extend the Allegory, by mentioning several of the Children of False Humour, who are more in Number than the Sands of the Sea, and might in particular enumerate the many Sons and Daughters which he has begot in this Island. But as this would be a very invidious Task, I shall only observe in general, that False Humour differs from the True, as a Monkey does from a Man.

First of all, He is exceedingly given to little Apish Tricks and Buffooneries.

Secondly, He so much delights in Mimickry, that it is all one to him whether he exposes by it Vice and Folly, Luxury, and

Avarice; or, on the contrary, Virtue and Wisdom, Pain and Poverty.

Thirdly, He is wonderfully unlucky, insomuch that he will bite the Hand that feeds him, and endeavour to ridicule both Friends and Foes indifferently. For having but small Talents, he must be merry where he *can,* not where he *should.*

Fourthly, Being entirely void of Reason, he pursues no Point either of Morality or Instruction, but is Ludicrous only for the sake of being so.

Fifthly, Being incapable of having any thing but Mock-Representations, his Ridicule is always Personal, and aimed at the Vicious Man, or the Writer; not at the Vice, or at the Writing.

I have here only pointed at the whole Species of False Humourists, but as one of my principal Designs in this Paper is to beat down that malignant Spirit, which discovers it self in the Writings of the present Age, I shall not scruple, for the future, to single out any of the small Wits, that infest the World with such Compositions as are ill-natured, immoral, and absurd. This is the only Exception which I shall make to the General Rule I have prescribed my self, of *attacking Multitudes*: Since every honest Man ought to look upon himself as in a Natural State of War with the Libeller and Lampooner, and to annoy them where-ever they fall in his way. This is but retaliating upon them, and treating them as they treat others.   C

No. 36.

[STEELE.]   Wednesday, April 11.

. . *Immania monstra*
Perferimus . . .—Virg.

I SHALL not put my self to any further Pains for this Day's Entertainment, than barely to publish the Letters and Titles of Petitions from the Play-house, with the Minutes I have made upon the Latter for my Conduct in Relation to them.

'*Drury-Lane, March the 9th.*

Upon reading the Project which is set forth in one of your late Papers, of making an Alliance between all the Bulls, Bears, Elephants, and Lions, which are separately exposed to publick View in the Cities of *London* and *Westminster*; together with the other Wonders, Shows, and Monsters, whereof you made respective Mention in the said Speculation; We, the chief Actors of this Play-house, met and sate upon the said Design. It is with great Delight that we expect the Execution of this

Work; and in order to contribute to it, we have given Warning to all our Ghosts to get their Livelihoods where they can, and not to appear among us after Daybreak of the 16th Instant. We are resolved to take this Opportunity to part with every thing which does not contribute to the Representation of human Life; and shall make a free Gift of all animated Utensils to your Projector. The Hangings you formerly mentioned are run away; as are likewise a Sett of Chairs, each of which was met upon two Legs going through the *Rose* Tavern at two this Morning. We hope, Sir, you will give proper Notice to the Town that we are endeavouring at these Regulations; and that we intend for the future to shew no Monsters, but Men who are converted into such by their own Industry and Affectation. If you please to be at the House to Night, you will see me do my Endeavour to shew some unnatural Appearances which are in vogue among the Polite and Well-bred. I am to represent, in the Character of a fine Lady dancing, all the Distortions which are frequently taken for Graces in Mien and Gesture. This, Sir, is a Specimen of the Method we shall take to expose the Monsters which come within the Notice of a regular Theatre; and we desire nothing more gross may be admitted by you Spectators for the future. We have cashier'd three Companies of Theatrical Guards, and design our Kings shall for the future make Love, and sit in Council, without an Army; and wait only your Direction, whether you will have them reinforce King *Porus*, or join the Troops of *Macedon*. Mr. *Pinkethman* resolves to consult his *Pantheon* of Heathen Gods in Opposition to the Oracle of *Delphos*, and doubts not but he shall turn the Fortunes of *Porus*, when he personates him. I am desired by the Company to inform you, that they submit to your Censures; and shall have you in greater Veneration than *Hercules* was in of old, if you can drive Monsters from the Theatre; and think your Merit will be as much greater than his, as to convince is more than to conquer.

> *I am, Sir,*
>
> *Your most obedient Servant,*
>
> T. D.

'Sir,

When I acquaint you with the great and unexpected Vicissitudes of my Fortune, I doubt not but I shall obtain your Pity and Favour. I have for many Years last past been Thunderer to the Play-house; and have not only made as much Noise out of the Clouds as any Predecessor of mine in the Theatre that ever bore that Character, but also have descended and spoke on the Stage, as the bold Thunder in the *Rehearsal*. When they got me down thus low, they thought fit to degrade me further, and make me a Ghost. I was contented with this for these two last Winters; but they carry their Tyranny still further, and not satisfied that I am banished from above Ground, they have given me to understand that I am wholly to depart their Dominions, and taken from me even my subterraneous Employment. Now, Sir, what I desire of you is, that if your Undertaker thinks fit to use Fire-Arms (as other Authors have done) in the Time of *Alexander*, I may be a Cannon against *Porus*, or else provide for me in the Burning of *Persepolis*, or what other Method you shall think fit.

Salmoneus of *Covent-Garden*.'

The Petition of all the Devils of the Play-house in behalf of themselves and Families, setting forth their Expulsion from thence, with Certificates of their good Life and Conversation, and praying Relief.

The Merit of this Petition referred to Mr. Chr. Rich, *who made them Devils.*

The Petition of the Grave-digger in *Hamlet*, to command the Pioneers in the Expedition of *Alexander*.

Granted.

The Petition of *William Bullock*, to be *Hephestion* to *Pinkethman the Great.*

Granted.

ADVERTISEMENT.

A Widow Gentlewoman, well born both by Father and Mother's Side, being the Daughter of Thomas Prater, *once an eminent Practitioner in the Law, and of* Letitia Tattle, *a Family well known in all Parts of this Kingdom, having been reduced by Misfortunes to wait on several great Persons, and for some time to be Teacher at a Boarding-School of young Ladies, giveth Notice to the Publick, That she hath lately taken a House near* Bloomsbury-Square, *commodiously situated next the Fields in a good Air; where she teaches all Sorts of Birds of the loquacious Kind, as Parrots, Starlings, Magpies, and others, to imitate human Voices in greater Perfection than ever yet was practised. They are not only instructed to pronounce Words distinctly, and in a proper Tone and Accent, but to speak the Language with great Purity and Volubility of Tongue, together with all the fashionable Phrases and Compliments now in use either at Tea-Tables or visiting Days. Those that have good Voices may be taught to sing the newest Opera-Airs, and, if required, to speak either* Italian *or* French, *paying something extraordinary above the common Rates. They whose Friends are not able to pay the full Prices may be taken as*

Half-Boarders. She teaches such as are designed for the Diversion of the Publick, and to act in enchanted Woods on the Theatres, by the Great. As she has often observed with much Concern how indecent an Education is usually given these innocent Creatures, which in some Measure is owing to their being placed in Rooms next the Street, where, to the great Offence of chaste and tender Ears, they learn Ribaldry, obscene Songs, and immodest Expressions from Passengers and idle People, as also to cry Fish and Card-matches, with other useless Parts of Learning to Birds who have rich Friends, she has fitted up proper and neat Apartments for them in the back Part of her said House; where she suffers none to approach them but her self, and a Servant Maid who is deaf and dumb, and whom she provided on purpose to prepare their Food and cleanse their Cages; having found by long Experience how hard a thing it is for those to keep Silence who have the Use of Speech, and the Dangers her Scholars are exposed to by the strong Impressions that are made by harsh Sounds and vulgar Dialects. In short, if they are Birds of any Parts or Capacity, she will undertake to render them so accomplished in the Compass of a Twelvemonth, that they shall be fit Conversation for such Ladies as love to chuse their Friends and Companions out of this Species.

No. 37.

[ADDISON.]   Thursday, April 12.

> . . . *Non illa colo calathisve Minervae*
> *Femineas assueta manus . . .*—Virg.

SOME Months ago, my Friend Sir ROGER, being in the Country, enclosed a Letter to me, directed to a certain Lady whom I shall here call by the Name of *Leonora*, and as it contained Matters of Consequence, desired me to deliver it to her with my own Hand. Accordingly I waited upon her Ladyship pretty early in the Morning, and was desired by her Woman to walk into her Lady's Library, till such time as she was in a Readiness to receive me. The very sound of a *Lady's Library* gave me a great Curiosity to see it; and, as it was some time before the Lady came to me, I had an Opportunity of turning over a great many of her Books, which were ranged together in a very beautiful Order. At the End of the *Folios* (which were finely bound and gilt) were great Jars of *China* placed one above another in a very noble piece of Architecture. The *Quartos* were separated from the *Octavos* by a pile of smaller Vessels, which rose in a delightful Pyramid. The *Octavos* were bounded by Tea Dishes of all Shapes Colours and Sizes, which were so disposed on a wooden Frame, that they looked like one con-

tinued Pillar indented with the finest Strokes of Sculpture, and
stained with the greatest Variety of Dyes. That Part of the
Library which was designed for the Reception of Plays and
Pamphlets, and other loose Papers, was inclosed in a kind of
Square, consisting of one of the prettiest Grotesque Works
that ever I saw, and made up of Scaramouches, Lions, Monkies,
Mandarines, Trees, Shells, and a thousand other odd Figures
in *China* Ware. In the midst of the Room was a little Japan
Table, with a Quire of gilt Paper upon it, and on the Paper a
Silver Snuff-box made in the Shape of a little Book. I found
there were several other Counterfeit Books upon the upper
Shelves, which were carved in Wood, and served only to fill up
the Number, like Faggots in the Muster of a Regiment. I was
wonderfully pleased with such a mixt kind of Furniture, as
seemed very suitable both to the Lady and the Scholar, and
did not know at first whether I should fancy my self in a Grotto,
or in a Library.

Upon my looking into the Books, I found there were some
few which the Lady had bought for her own use, but that most
of them had been got together, either because she had heard
them praised, or because she had seen the Authors of them.
Among several that I examined, I very well remember these
that follow.

Ogleby's *Virgil*.

Dryden's *Juvenal*.

Cassandra.

Cleopatra.

Astraea.

Sir *Isaac Newton*'s Works.

The *Grand Cyrus*: with a Pin stuck in one of the middle
Leaves.

Pembroke's *Arcadia*.

Lock of Human Understanding: with a Paper of Patches in it.

A Spelling Book.

A Dictionary for the Explanation of hard Words.

Sherlock upon Death.

The fifteen Comforts of Matrimony.

Sir *William Temple*'s Essays.

Father *Malbranche*'s Search after Truth, translated into
English.

A Book of Novels.

The Academy of Compliments.

Culpepper's Midwifery.

The Ladies' Calling.

Tales in Verse by Mr. *Durfey*: Bound in Red Leather, gilt
on the Back, and doubled down in several Places

All the Classick Authors in Wood.

A Set of *Elzivers* by the same Hand.

Clelia: Which opened of it self in the Place that describes two Lovers in a Bower.

Baker's Chronicle.

Advice to a Daughter.

The New *Atalantis*, with a Key to it.

Mr. *Steele*'s Christian Heroe.

A Prayer Book: With a Bottle of *Hungary* Water by the side of it.

Dr. *Sacheverell*'s Speech.

Fielding's Tryal.

Seneca's Morals.

Taylor's Holy Living and Dying.

La Ferte's Instructions for Country Dances.

I was taking a Catalogue in my Pocket-Book of these, and several other Authors, when *Leonora* entred, and upon my presenting her with the Letter from the Knight, told me, with an unspeakable Grace, that she hoped Sir ROGER was in good Health: I answered *Yes*, for I hate long Speeches, and after a Bow or two retired.

Leonora was formerly a celebrated Beauty, and is still a very lovely Woman. She has been a Widow for two or three Years, and being unfortunate in her first Marriage, has taken a Resolution never to venture upon a second. She has no Children to take care of, and leaves the Management of her Estate to my good Friend Sir ROGER. But as the Mind naturally sinks into a kind of Lethargy, and falls asleep, that is not agitated by some Favourite Pleasures and Pursuits, *Leonora* has turned all the Passions of her Sex into a love of Books and Retirement. She converses chiefly with Men (as she has often said herself) but it is only in their Writings; and admits of very few Male-Visitants, except my Friend Sir ROGER, whom she hears with great Pleasure, and without Scandal. As her Reading has lain very much among Romances, it has given her a very particular Turn of Thinking, and discovers it self even in her House, her Gardens, and her Furniture. Sir ROGER has entertained me an Hour together with a Description of her Country-Seat, which is situated in a kind of Wilderness, about an hundred Miles distant from *London*, and looks like a little enchanted Palace. The Rocks about her are shaped into Artificial Grottoes, covered with Woodbines and Jessamines. The woods are cut into shady Walks, twisted into Bowers, and filled with Cages of Turtles. The Springs are made to run among Pebbles, and by that means taught to murmur very agreeably. They are likewise collected into a beautiful Lake, that is inhabited by a Couple of Swans, and empties it self by a little Rivulet which runs through a green Meadow, and is known in the Family by the Name of *The Purling Stream.* The Knight likewise tells me, that this Lady preserves her Game better than any of the Gentlemen in the Country; not (says Sir ROGER) that she sets so great a Value upon her Partridges and Pheasants, as upon her Larks and Nightingales. For she says that every Bird which is killed in her Ground, will spoil a Consort, and that she shall certainly miss him the next Year.

When I think how odly this Lady is improved by Learning, I look upon her with a mixture of Admiration and Pity. Amidst these innocent Entertainments which she has formed to her self, how much more Valuable does she appear than those of her Sex, who employ themselves in Diversions that are less Reasonable, though more in Fashion? What improvements would a Woman have made, who is so susceptible of Impressions from what she reads, had she been guided to such Books as have a tendency to enlighten the Understanding and rectifie the Passions, as well as to those which are of little more use than to divert the Imagination?

But the manner of a Lady's employing her self usefully in Reading shall be the Subject of another Paper, in which I design to recommend such particular Books as may be proper for the Improvement of the Sex. And as this is a Subject of a very nice Nature, I shall desire my Correspondents to give me their Thoughts upon it.

No. 38.
[STEELE.]   Friday, April 13.

. . . *Cupias non placuisse nimis.*—Mart.

A LATE Conversation which I fell into, gave me an Opportunity of observing a great deal of Beauty in a very handsome Woman, and as much Wit in an ingenious Man, turned into Deformity in the one, and Absurdity in the other, by the meer Force of Affectation. The Fair One had something in her Person upon which her Thoughts were fixed, that she attempted to shew to Advantage in every Look, Word, and Gesture. The Gentleman was as diligent to do Justice to his fine Parts, as the Lady to her beauteous Form: You might see his Imagination on the Stretch to find out something uncommon, and what they call bright, to entertain her; while she writhed her self into as many different Postures to engage him. When she laughed, her Lips were to sever at a greater Distance than ordinary to shew her Teeth: Her Fan was to point to somewhat at a Distance, that in the Reach she may discover the Roundness of her Arm; then she is utterly mistaken in what she saw, falls back, smiles at her own Folly, and is so wholly discomposed, that her Tucker is to be adjusted, her Bosom exposed, and the whole Woman put into new Airs and Graces. While she was doing all this, the Gallant had time to think of something very pleasant to say next to her, or make some unkind Observation on some other Lady to feed her Vanity. These unhappy Effects of Affectation naturally led me to look into that strange State of Mind which so generally discolours the Behaviour of most People we meet with.

The learned Dr. *Burnet*, in his Theory of the Earth, takes occasion to observe, That every Thought is attended with Consciousness and Representativeness; the Mind has nothing presented to it but what is immediately followed by a Reflection or Conscience, which tells you whether that which was so presented is graceful or unbecoming. This Act of the Mind discovers it self in the Gesture, by a proper Behaviour in those whose Consciousness goes no further than to direct them in the just Progress of their present Thought or Action; but betrays an Interruption in every second Thought, when the Consciousness is employ'd in too fondly approving a Man's own Conceptions; which sort of Consciousness is what we call Affectation.

As the Love of Praise is implanted in our Bosoms as a strong Incentive to worthy Actions, it is a very difficult Task to get above a Desire of it for things that should be wholly indifferent. Women, whose Hearts are fixed upon the Pleasure they have in the Consciousness that they are the Objects of Love and Admiration, are ever changing the Air of their Countenances, and altering the Attitude of their Bodies, to strike the Hearts of their Beholders with new Sense of their Beauty. The dressing Part of our Sex, whose Minds are the same with the sillier Part of the other, are exactly in the like uneasie Condition to be regarded for a well-tied Cravat, an Hat cocked with an unusual Briskness, a very well-chosen Coat, or other Instances of Merit, which they are impatient to see unobserved.

But this apparent Affectation, arising from an ill-governed Consciousness, is not so much to be wondered at in such loose and trivial Minds as these: But when you see it reign in Characters of Worth and Distinction, it is what you cannot but lament, not without some Indignation. It creeps into the Heart of the wise Man as well as that of the Coxcomb. When you see a Man of Sense look about for Applause, and discover an itching Inclination to be commended; lay Traps for a little

Incense, even from those whose Opinion he values in nothing but his own Favour; Who is safe against this Weakness? or who knows whether he is guilty of it or not? The best way to get clear of such a light Fondness for Applause, is, to take all possible Care to throw off the Love of it upon Occasions that are not in themselves laudable; but, as it appears, we hope for no Praise from them. Of this Nature are all Graces in Men's Persons, Dress, and bodily Deportment; which will naturally be winning and attractive if we think not of them, but lose their Force in proportion to our Endeavour to make them such.

When our Consciousness turns upon the main Design of Life, and our Thoughts are employed upon the chief Purpose either in Business or Pleasure, we shall never betray an Affectation, for we cannot be guilty of it: But when we give the Passion for Praise an unbridled Liberty, our Pleasure in little Perfections robs us of what is due to us for great Virtues, and worthy Qualities. How many excellent Speeches and honest Actions are lost, for want of being indifferent where we ought? Men are oppressed with regard to their Way of speaking and acting, instead of having their Thought bent upon what they should do or say; and by that means bury a Capacity for great things, by their fear of failing in indifferent things. This, perhaps, cannot be called Affectation; but it has some Tincture of it, at least so far, as that their fear of erring in a thing of no Consequence, argues they would be too much pleased in performing it.

It is only from a thorough Disregard to himself in such Particulars, that a Man can act with a laudable Sufficiency: His Heart is fixed upon one Point in view; and he commits no Errors, because he thinks nothing an Error but what deviates from that Intention.

The wild Havock Affectation makes in that Part of the World which should be most polite, is visible where-ever we turn our Eyes: It pushes Men not only into Impertinences in Conversation, but also in their premeditated Speeches. At the Bar it torments the Bench, whose Business it is to cut off all Superfluities in what is spoken before it by the Practitioner; as well as several little Pieces of Injustice which arise from the Law it self. I have seen it make a Man run from the Purpose before a Judge, who was, when at the Bar himself, so close and logical a Pleader, that with all the Pomp of Eloquence in his Power, he never spoke a Word too much.

It might be born even here, but it often ascends the Pulpit it self; and the Declaimer, in that sacred Place, is frequently so impertinently witty, speaks of the last Day it self with so many quaint Phrases, that there is no Man who understands

Raillery, but must resolve to sin no more: Nay, you may behold him sometimes in Prayer, for a proper Delivery of the great Truths he is to utter, humble himself with so very well turned Phrase, and mention his own Unworthiness in a Way so very becoming, that the Air of the pretty Gentleman is preserved, under the Lowliness of the Preacher.

I shall end this with a short Letter I writ the other Day to a very witty Man, over-run with the Fault I am speaking of.

'*Dear Sir*,

I spent some Time with you the other Day, and must take the Liberty of a Friend to tell you of the unsufferable Affectation you are guilty of in all you say and do. When I gave you an Hint of it, you asked me whether a Man is to be cold to what his Friends think of him? No; but Praise is not to be the Entertainment of every Moment: He that hopes for it must be able to suspend the Possession of it till proper Periods of Life, or Death it self. If you would not rather be commended than be Praise-worthy, contemn little Merits; and allow no Man to be so free with you, as to praise you to your Face. Your Vanity by this Means will want its Food. At the same time your Passion for Esteem will be more fully gratified; Men will praise you in their Actions: Where you now receive one Compliment, you will then receive twenty Civilities. Till then you will never have of either further than,

Sir,

R *Your humble Servant.*'

No. 39.
[ADDISON.] Saturday, April 14.

Multa fero, ut placeam genus irritabile vatum.
Cum scribo . . .—Hor.

As a perfect Tragedy is the noblest Production of human Nature, so it is capable of giving the Mind one of the most delightful and most improving Entertainments. A virtuous Man (says *Seneca*) strugling with Misfortunes, is such a Spectacle as Gods might look upon with Pleasure: And such a Pleasure it is which one meets with in the Representation of a well-written Tragedy. Diversions of this kind wear out of our Thoughts every thing that is mean and little. They cherish and cultivate that Humanity which is the Ornament of our Nature. They soften Insolence, sooth Affliction, and subdue the Mind to the Dispensations of Providence.

It is no Wonder therefore that in all the Polite Nations of the World, this Part of the *Drama* has met with Publick Encouragement.

The Modern Tragedy excels that of *Greece* and *Rome,* in the Intricacy and Disposition of the Fable: but, what a Christian Writer would be ashamed to own, falls infinitely short of it in the Moral Part of the Performance.

This I may shew more at large hereafter; and in the mean time, that I may contribute something towards the Improvement of the *English* Tragedy, I shall take notice, in this and in other following Papers, of some particular Parts in it that seem liable to Exception.

Aristotle observes, that the *Iambick* Verse in the *Greek* Tongue was the most proper for Tragedy: Because at the same time that it lifted up the Discourse from Prose, it was that which approached nearer to it than any other kind of Verse. For, says he, we may observe that Men in ordinary Discourse very often speak *Iambicks,* without taking Notice of it. We may make the same Observation of our *English* Blank Verse, which often enters into our common Discourse, though we do not attend to it, and is such a due Medium between Rhyme and Prose, that it seems wonderfully adapted to Tragedy. I am therefore very much offended when I see a Play in Rhyme; which is as absurd in *English* as a Tragedy of *Hexameters* would have been in *Greek* or *Latin.* The Soloecism is, I think, still greater, in those Plays that have some Scenes in Rhyme and some in Blank Verse, which are to be looked upon as two several Languages; or where we see some particular Similies dignified with Rhyme, at the same time that every thing about them lyes in Blank Verse. I would not however debar the Poet from concluding his Tragedy, or, if he pleases, every Act of it, with two or three Couplets, which may have the same Effect as an Air in the *Italian* Opera after a long *Recitativo,* and give the Actor a graceful *Exit.* Besides, that we see a Diversity of Numbers in some Parts of the Old Tragedy, in order to hinder the Ear from being tired with the same continued Modulation of Voice. For the same Reason I do not dislike the Speeches in our *English* Tragedy that close with an *Hemistick,* or half Verse, notwithstanding the Person who speaks after it begins a new Verse, without filling up the preceding one; nor with abrupt Pauses and Breakings-off in the middle of a Verse, when they humour any Passion that is expressed by it.

Since I am upon this Subject, I must observe that our *English* Poets have succeeded much better in the Stile, than in the Sentiments of their Tragedies. Their Language is very often noble and sonorous, but the Sense either very trifling or very common. On the contrary, in the ancient Tragedies, and indeed in those of *Corneille* and *Racine*, tho' the Expressions are very great, it is the Thought that bears them up and swells them. For my own part, I prefer a noble Sentiment that is depressed with homely Language, infinitely before a vulgar one that is blown up with all the Sound and Energy of Expression. Whether this Defect in our Tragedies may arise from Want of Genius, Knowledge, or Experience in the Writers, or from their Compliance with the vicious Taste of their Readers, who are better Judges of the Language than of the Sentiments, and consequently relish the one more than the other, I cannot determine. But I believe it might rectifie the Conduct both of the one and of the other, if the Writer laid down the whole Contexture of his Dialogue in plain *English*, before he turned it into Blank Verse; and if the Reader, after the Perusal of a Scene, would consider the naked Thought of every Speech in it, when divested of all its Tragick Ornaments: By this means, without being imposed upon by Words, we may judge impartially of the Thought, and consider whether it be natural or great enough for the Person that utters it, whether it deserves to shine in such a Blaze of Eloquence, or shew it self in such a variety of Lights as are generally made use of by the Writers of our *English* Tragedy.

I must in the next place observe, that when our Thoughts are great and just, they are often obscured by the sounding Phrases, hard Metaphors, and forced Expressions in which they are cloathed. *Shakespear* is often very faulty in this Particular. There is a fine Observation in *Aristotle* to this purpose, which I have never seen quoted. The Expression, says he, ought to be very much laboured in the unactive Parts of the Fable, as in Descriptions, Similitudes, Narrations, and the like; in which the Opinions, Manners, and Passions of Men are not represented; for these (namely the Opinions, Manners, and Passions) are apt to be obscured by pompous Phrases and elaborate Expressions. *Horace*, who copy'd most of his Criticisms after *Aristotle*, seems to have had his Eye on the foregoing Rule, in the following Verses:

> *Et tragicus plerumque dolet sermone pedestri*
> *Telephus & Peleus, cum pauper & exsul uterque*
> *Projicit ampullas & sesquipedalia verba,*
> *Si curat cor spectantis tetigisse querela.*

> *Tragoedians too lay by their State, to grieve.*
> Peleus *and* Telephus, *exil'd and poor,*
> *Forget their swelling and gigantick Words.*

Ld. Roscommon.

Among our Modern *English* Poets, there is none who was better turned for Tragedy than *Lee;* if instead of favouring the Impetuosity of his Genius, he had restrained it, and kept it within its proper Bounds. His Thoughts are wonderfully suited to Tragedy, but frequently lost in such a Cloud of Words, that it is hard to see the Beauty of them: There is an infinite Fire in his Works, but so involved in Smoak, that it does not appear in half its Lustre. He frequently succeeds in the passionate Parts of the Tragedy, but more particularly where he slackens his Efforts, and eases the Stile of those Epithets and Metaphors, in which he so much abounds. What can be more natural, more soft, or more passionate, than that Line in *Statira*'s Speech, where she describes the Charms of *Alexander*'s Conversation?

> *Then he would talk: Good Gods! how he would talk!*

That unexpected Break in the Line, and turning the Description of his manner of Talking into an Admiration of it, is inexpressibly beautiful, and wonderfully suited to the fond Character of the Person that speaks it. There is a Simplicity in the Words, that outshines the utmost Pride of Expression.

Otway has followed Nature in the Language of his Tragedy, and therefore shines in the Passionate Parts, more than any of our *English* Poets. As there is something Familiar and Domestick in the Fable of his Tragedy, more than in those of any other Poet, he has little Pomp, but great Force in his Expressions. For which Reason, tho' he has admirably succeeded in the tender and melting Part of his Tragedies, he sometimes falls into too great a Familiarity of Phrase in those Parts, which, by *Aristotle*'s Rule, ought to have been raised and supported by the Dignity of Expression.

It has been observed by others, that this Poet has founded his Tragedy of *Venice Preserved* on so wrong a Plot, that the greatest Characters in it are those of Rebels and Traitors. Had the Hero of his Play discovered the same good Qualities in the Defence of his Country, that he shewed for its Ruin and Subversion, the Audience could not enough pity and admire him: But as he is now represented, we can only say of him what the *Roman* Historian says of *Catiline*, that his Fall would have been glorious (*si pro Patria sic concidisset*) had he so fallen in the Service of his Country.   C

No. 40.

[ADDISON.]   Monday, April 16.

> *Ac ne forte putes me, quae facere ipse recusem,*
> *Cum recte tractent alii, laudare maligne;*
> *Ille per extentum funem mihi posse videtur*
> *Ire poeta, meum qui pectus inaniter angit,*
> *Irritat, mulcet, falsis terroribus implet,*
> *Ut magus, & modo me Thebis, modo ponit Athenis.*—Hor.

THE *English* Writers of Tragedy are possessed with a Notion, that when they represent a virtuous or innocent Person in Distress, they ought not to leave him till they have delivered him out of his Troubles, or made him triumph over his Enemies. This Error they have been led into by a ridiculous Doctrine in Modern Criticism, that they are obliged to an equal Distribution of Rewards and Punishments, and an impartial Execution of Poetical Justice. Who were the first that established this Rule I know not; but I am sure it has no Foundation in Nature, in Reason, or in the Practice of the Ancients. We find that Good and Evil happen alike to all Men on this Side the Grave; and as the principal Design of Tragedy is to raise Commiseration and Terror in the Minds of the Audience, we shall defeat this great End, if we always make Virtue and Innocence happy and successful. Whatever Crosses and Disappointments a good Man suffers in the Body of the Tragedy, they will make but small Impression on our Minds, when we know that in the last Act he is to arrive at the End of his Wishes and Desires. When we see him engaged in the Depth of his Afflictions, we are apt to comfort our selves, because we are sure he will find his Way out of them; and that his Grief, how great soever it may be at present, will soon terminate in Gladness. For this Reason, the ancient Writers of Tragedy treated Men in their Plays, as they are dealt with in the World, by making Virtue sometimes happy and sometimes miserable, as they found it in the Fable which they made choice of, or as it might affect their Audience in the most agreeable Manner. *Aristotle* considers the Tragedies that were written in either of these Kinds, and observes, that those which ended unhappily, had always pleased the People, and carried away the Prize in the publick Disputes of the Stage, from those that ended happily. Terror and Commiseration leave a pleasing Anguish in the Mind; and fix the Audience in such a serious Composure of Thought, as is much more lasting and delightful than any little transient Starts of Joy and Satisfaction. Accordingly we find, that more of our *English* Tragedies have succeeded, in which the Favourites of the Audience sink under their Calamities, than those in which they recover themselves out of them. The best Plays of this Kind are the *Orphan, Venice Preserved, Alexander the Great, Theodosius, All for Love, Oedipus, Oroonoko, Othello*, etc. *King Lear* is an admirable Tragedy of the same Kind, as *Shakespear* wrote it; but as it is reformed according to the chymerical Notion of Poetical Justice, in my humble Opinion it has lost half its Beauty. At the same time I must allow, that there are very noble Tragedies, which have been framed upon the other Plan, and have ended happily; as indeed most of the good Tragedies, which have been written since the starting of the above-mentioned Criticism, have taken this Turn: As the *Mourning Bride, Tamerlane, Ulysses, Phaedra and Hyppolitus*, with most of Mr. *Dryden*'s. I must also allow, that many of *Shakespear*'s, and several of the celebrated Tragedies of Antiquity, are cast in the same Form. I do not therefore dispute against this way of writing Tragedies, but against the criticism that would establish this as the only Method; and by that Means would very much cramp the *English* Tragedy, and perhaps give a wrong Bent to the Genius of our Writers.

The Tragi-Comedy, which is the Product of the *English* Theatre, is one of the most monstrous Inventions that ever entered into a Poet's Thoughts. An Author might as well think of weaving the Adventures of *Aeneas* and *Hudibras* into one Poem, as of writing such a motly Piece of Mirth and Sorrow. But the Absurdity of these Performances is so very visible, that I shall not insist upon it.

The same Objections which are made to Tragi-Comedy, may in some Measure be applied to all Tragedies that have a double Plot in them; which are likewise more frequent upon the *English* Stage, than upon any other: For though the Grief of the Audience, in such Performances, be not changed into another Passion, as in Tragi-Comedies; it is diverted upon another Object, which weakens their Concern for the principal Action, and breaks the Tide of Sorrow, by throwing it into different Channels. This Inconvenience, however, may in a great Measure be cured, if not wholly removed, by the skilful Choice of an Under-Plot, which may bear such a near Relation to the principal Design, as to contribute towards the Completion of it, and be concluded by the same Catastrophe.

There is also another Particular, which may be reckoned among the Blemishes, or rather the false Beauties, of our *English* Tragedy: I mean those particular Speeches which are commonly known by the Name of *Rants*. The warm and passionate Parts of a Tragedy, are always the most taking with the Audience; for which Reason we often see the Players pronouncing, in all the Violence of Action, several Parts of the Tragedy which the Author writ with great Temper, and designed that they should have been so acted. I have seen *Powell* very often raise himself a loud Clap by this Artifice. The Poets that were acquainted with this Secret, have given frequent Occasion for such Emotions in the Actor, by adding Vehemence to Words where there was no Passion, or inflaming a real Passion into Fustian. This hath filled the Mouths of our Heroes with Bombast; and given them such Sentiments, as proceed rather from a Swelling than a Greatness of Mind. Unnatural Exclamations, Curses, Vows, Blasphemies, a Defiance of Mankind, and an Outraging of the Gods, frequently pass upon the Audience for tow'ring Thoughts, and have accordingly met with infinite Applause.

I shall here add a Remark, which I am afraid our Tragick Writers may make an ill use of. As our Heroes are generally Lovers, their Swelling and Blustring upon the Stage very much recommends them to the fair Part of their Audience. The Ladies are wonderfully pleased to see a Man insulting Kings, or affronting the Gods, in one Scene, and throwing himself at the Feet of his Mistress in another. Let him behave himself insolently towards the Men, and abjectly towards the Fair One, and it is ten to one but he proves a Favourite of the Boxes. *Dryden* and *Lee*, in several of their Tragedies, have practised this Secret with good Success.

But to shew how a *Rant* pleases beyond the most just and natural Thought that is not pronounced with Vehemence, I would desire the Reader, when he sees the Tragedy of *Oedipus,* to observe how quietly the Hero is dismissed at the End of the third Act, after having pronounced the following Lines, in which the Thought is very natural, and apt to move Compassion:

> *To you, good Gods, I make my last Appeal,*
> *Or clear my Virtues, or my Crimes reveal.*
> *If in the Maze of Fate I blindly run,*
> *And backward trod those Paths I sought to shun;*
> *Impute my Errors to your own Decree:*
> *My Hands are guilty, but my Heart is free.*

Let us then observe with what Thunder-claps of Applause he leaves the Stage, after the Impieties and Execrations at the End of the fourth Act; and you will wonder to see an Audience so cursed and so pleased at the same time.

> *O that as oft I have at* Athens *seen,*
> [Where, by the way, there was no Stage till many
>   Years after *Oedipus.*]

The Stage arise, and the big Clouds descend;
So now, in very deed, I might behold
This pond'rous Globe, and all yon marble Roof,
Meet, like the Hands of Jove, and crush Mankind.
For all the Elements, &c.

ADVERTISEMENT.

Having spoken of Mr. Powell, *as sometimes raising himself Applause from the ill Taste of an Audience; I must do him the Justice to own, that he is excellently formed for a Tragoedian, and, when he pleases, deserves the Admiration of the best Judges; as I doubt not but he will in the* Conquest of Mexico, *which is acted for his own Benefit To-morrow Night.*   C

No. 41.
[STEELE.]   Tuesday, April 17.

. . . *Tu non inventa reperta es.*—Ovid.

COMPASSION for the Gentleman who writes the following Letter, should not prevail upon me to fall upon the Fair Sex, if it were not that I find they are frequently Fairer than they ought to be. Such Impostures are not to be tolerated in Civil Society; and I think his Misfortune ought to be made publick, as a Warning for other Men always to Examine into what they Admire.

'Sir,

Supposing you to be a Person of general Knowledge, I make my Application to you on a very particular Occasion. I have a great mind to be rid of my Wife, and hope, when you consider my Case, you will be of Opinion I have very just Pretensions to a Divorce. I am a mere Man of the Town, and have very little Improvement, but what I have got from Plays. I remember in *The Silent Woman*, the Learned Dr. *Cutberd*, or Dr. *Otter* (I forget which) makes one of the Causes of Separation to be *Error Personae*, when a Man marries a Woman, and finds her not to be the same Woman whom he intended to marry, but another. If that be Law, it is, I presume, exactly my Case. For you are to know, Mr. SPECTATOR, that there are Women who do not let their Husbands see their Faces till they are married.

Not to keep you in Suspense, I mean plainly, that Part of the Sex who paint. They are some of them so exquisitely skilful this Way, that give them but a tolerable Pair of Eyes

to set up with, and they will make Bosom, Lips, Cheeks, and
Eyebrows, by their own Industry. As for my Dear, never
Man was so inamour'd as I was of her fair Forehead, Neck and
Arms, as well as the bright Jett of her Hair; but to my great
Astonishment, I find they were all the Effect of Art: Her Skin
is so tarnished with this Practice, that when she first wakes in
a Morning, she scarce seems young enough to be the Mother
of her whom I carried to Bed the Night before. I shall take
the Liberty to part with her by the first Opportunity, unless her
Father will make her Portion suitable to her real, not her assumed, Countenance. This I thought fit to let him and her
know by your Means. I am,

> Sir,
>
> *Your most Obedient Humble Servant.'*

I cannot tell what the Law, or the Parents of the Lady will
do for this Injured Gentleman, but must allow he has very
much Justice on his side. I have indeed very long observed
this Evil, and distinguished those of our Women who wear
their own, from those in borrowed Complexions, by the *Picts*
and the *British*. There does not need any great Discernment
to judge which are which. The *British* have a lively animated
Aspect; The *Picts*, though never so Beautiful, have dead uninformed Countenances. The Muscles of a real Face sometimes swell with soft Passion, sudden Surprize, and are flushed
with agreeable Confusions, according as the Objects before
them, or the Ideas presented to them, affect their Imagination.
But the *Picts* behold all things with the same Air, whether they
are Joyful or Sad; the same fixed Insensibility appears upon
all Occasions. A *Pict*, though she takes all that Pains to
invite the Approach of Lovers, is obliged to keep them at a
certain Distance; a Sigh in a Languishing Lover, if fetched too
near her, would dissolve a Feature; and a Kiss snatched by a
Forward one, might transfer the Complexion of the Mistress
to the Admirer. It is hard to speak of these false Fair Ones,
without saying something uncomplaisant, but I would only
recommend to them to consider how they like coming into a
Room new Painted; they may assure themselves, the near
Approach of a Lady who uses this Practice is much more
offensive.

WILL. HONEYCOMB told us, one Day, an Adventure he once
had with a *Pict*. This Lady had Wit, as well as Beauty, at
Will; and made it her Business to gain Hearts, for no other
Reason, but to railly the Torments of her Lovers. She would
make great Advances to insnare Men, but without any manner
of Scruple break off when there was no Provocation. Her Ill-

Nature and Vanity made my Friend very easily Proof against the Charms of her Wit and Conversation; but her beauteous Form, instead of being blemished by her Falshood and Inconstancy, every Day increased upon him, and she had new Attractions every time he saw her. When she observed WILL. irrevocably her Slave, she began to use him as such, and after many Steps toward such a Cruelty, she at last utterly banished him. The unhappy Lover strove in vain, by servile Epistles, to revoke his Doom; till at length he was forced to the last Refuge, a round Sum of Mony to her Maid. This corrupt Attendant placed him early in the Morning behind the Hangings in her Mistress's Dressing-Room. He stood very conveniently to observe, without being seen. The *Pict* begins the Face she designed to wear that Day, and I have heard him protest she had worked a full half Hour before he knew her to be the same Woman. As soon as he saw the Dawn of that Complexion, for which he had so long languished, he thought fit to break from his Concealment, repeating that of *Cowley*:

> *Th' adorning Thee with so much Art,*
> *Is but a barb'rous Skill;*
> *'Tis like the Pois'ning of a Dart,*
> *Too apt before to kill.*

The *Pict* stood before him in the utmost Confusion, with the prettiest Smirk imaginable on the finish'd side of her Face, pale as Ashes on the other. HONEYCOMB seized all her Gally-pots and Washes, and carried off his Handkerchief full of Brushes, Scraps of *Spanish* Wooll, and Phials of Unguents. The Lady went into the Country; the Lover was cured.

It is certain no Faith ought to be kept with Cheats, and an Oath made to a *Pict* is of it self void. I would therefore exhort all the *British* Ladies to single them out, nor do I know any but *Lindamira* who should be exempt from Discovery; for her own Complexion is so delicate, that she ought to be allowed the Covering it with Paint, as a Punishment for chusing to be the worst Piece of Art extant, instead of the Masterpiece of Nature. As for my Part, who have no Expectations from Women, and consider them only as they are Part of the Species, I do not half so much fear offending a Beauty as a Woman of Sense; I shall therefore produce several Faces which have been in Publick this many Years, and never appeared; it will be a very pretty Entertainment in the Play-house (when I have abolished this Custom) to see so many Ladies, when they first lay it down, *incog.* in their own Faces.

In the mean time, as a Pattern for improving their Charms, let the Sex study the agreeable *Statira*. Her Features are enlivened with the Chearfulness of her Mind, and good Humour gives an Alacrity to her Eyes. She is Graceful without affecting an Air, and Unconcerned without appearing Careless. Her having no manner of Art in her Mind, makes her want none in her Person.

How like is this Lady, and how unlike is a *Pict*, to that Description Dr. *Donne* gives of his Mistress?

> . . . *Her pure and eloquent Blood*
> *Spoke in her Cheeks, and so distinctly wrought,*
> *That one would almost say her Body thought.*

ADVERTISEMENT.

A young Gentlewoman of about Nineteen Years of Age (bred in the Family of a Person of Quality lately deceased) who Paints the Finest Flesh-colour, wants a Place, and is to be heard of at the House of Minheer Grotesque, *a* Dutch *Painter in* Barbican.

N.B. *She is also well skilled in the Drapery-part, and puts on Hoods, and mixes Ribbons so as to suit the Colours of the Face with Great Art and Success.* R

No. 42.
[ADDISON.] Wednesday, April 18.

> *Garganum mugire putes nemus aut mare Tuscum.*
> *Tanto cum strepitu ludi spectantur, & artes,*
> *Divitiaeque peregrinae: quibus oblitus actor*
> *Cum stetit in scena, concurrit dextera laevae.*
> *Dixit adhuc aliquid? Nil sane. Quid placet ergo?*
> *Lana Tarentino violas imitata veneno.*—Hor.

Aristotle has observed, that ordinary Writers in Tragedy endeavour to raise Terror and Pity in their Audience, not by proper Sentiments and Expressions, but by the Dresses and Decorations of the Stage. There is something of this kind very ridiculous in the *English* Theatre. When the Author has a mind to terrifie us, it thunders; when he would make us melancholy, the Stage is darkened. But among all our Tragick Artifices, I am the most offended at those which are made use of to inspire us with magnificent Ideas of the Persons that speak. The ordinary Method of making an Hero, is to clap a huge Plume of Feathers upon his Head, which rises so very high, that there is often a greater Length from his Chin to the Top of his Head, than to the Sole of his Foot. One would believe, that we thought a great Man and a tall Man the same thing. This very much embarrasses the Actor, who is forced to hold his Neck extremaly stiff and steady all the while he

speaks; and notwithstanding any Anxieties which he pretends
for his Mistress, his Country, or his Friends, one may see by his
Action, that his greatest Care and Concern is to keep the Plume
of Feathers from falling off his Head.   For my own part, when
I see a Man uttering his Complaints under such a Mountain
of Feathers, I am apt to look upon him rather as an unfortunate Lunatick, than a Distressed Hero.   As these superfluous Ornaments upon the Head make a great Man, a Princess
generally receives her Grandeur from those additional incumbrances that fall into her Tail: I mean the broad sweeping
Train that follows her in all her Motions, and finds constant
Employment for a Boy who stands behind her to open and
spread it to Advantage.   I do not know how others are affected
at this Sight, but I must confess, my Eyes are wholly taken
up with the Page's Part; and as for the Queen, I am not so
attentive to any thing she speaks, as to the right adjusting of
her Train, lest it should chance to trip up her Heels, or incom-
mode her, as she walks to and fro upon the Stage.   It is, in
my Opinion, a very odd Spectacle, to see a Queen venting her
Passion in a disordered Motion, and a little Boy taking Care
all the while that they do not ruffle the Tail of her Gown.
The Parts that the two Persons act on the Stage at the same
Time, are very different: The Princess is afraid lest she should
incur the Displeasure of the King her Father, or lose the Hero
her Lover, whilst her Attendant is only concerned lest she
should entangle her Feet in her Petticoat.

   We are told, that an ancient Tragick Poet, to move the Pity
of his Audience for his exiled Kings and distressed Heroes, used
to make the Actors represent them in Dresses and Cloaths
that were thread-bare and decayed.   This Artifice for moving
Pity seems as ill contrived, as that we have been speaking of
to inspire us with a great Idea of the Persons introduced upon
the Stage.   In short, I would have our Conceptions raised by
the Dignity of Thought and Sublimity of Expression, rather
than by a Train of Robes or a Plume of Feathers.

   Another Mechanical Method of making great Men, and adding
Dignity to Kings and Queens, is to accompany them with
Halberts and Battel-axes.   Two or three Shifters of Scenes,
with the two Candle-Snuffers, make up a compleat Body of
Guards upon the *English* Stage; and by the Addition of a few
Porters dressed in Red Coats, can represent above a dozen
Legions.   I have sometimes seen a couple of Armies drawn up
together upon the Stage, when the Poet has been disposed to do
Honour to his Generals.   It is impossible for the Reader's
Imagination to multiply twenty Men into such prodigious
Multitudes, or to fancy that two or three hundred thousand

Soldiers are fighting in a Room of forty or fifty Yards in Compass. Incidents of such a nature should be told, not represented.

> . . . *Non tamen intus*
> *Digna geri promes in scenam: multaque tolles*
> *Ex oculis, quae mox narret facundia praesens.*—Hor.

> *Yet there are things improper for a Scene,*
> *Which Men of Judgment only will relate.*—Ld. Roscommon.

I should therefore, in this Particular, recommend to my Countrymen the Example of the *French* Stage, where the Kings and Queens always appear unattended, and leave their Guards behind the Scenes. I should likewise be glad if we imitated the *French* in banishing from our Stage the Noise of Drums, Trumpets, and Huzzas; which is sometimes so very great, that when there is a Battel in the *Hay-Market* Theatre, one may hear it as far as *Charing-Cross*.

I have here only touched upon those Particulars which are made use of to raise and aggrandize the Persons of a Tragedy; and shall shew in another Paper the several Expedients which are practised by Authors of a vulgar Genius to move Terror, Pity, or Admiration, in their Hearers.

The Taylor and the Painter often contribute to the Success of a Tragedy more than the Poet. Scenes affect ordinary Minds as much as Speeches; and our Actors are very sensible, that a well-dressed Play has sometimes brought them as full Audiences, as a well-written one. The *Italians* have a very good Phrase to express this Art of imposing upon the Spectators by Appearances: They call it the *Fourberia della Scena, The Knavery or trickish Part of the Drama.* But however the Show and Outside of the Tragedy may work upon the Vulgar, the more understanding Part of the Audience immediately see through it, and despise it.

A good Poet will give the Reader a more lively Idea of an Army or a Battel in a Description, than if he actually saw them drawn up in Squadrons and Battalions, or engaged in the Confusion of a Fight. Our Minds should be opened to great Conceptions, and inflamed with glorious Sentiments, by what the Actor speaks, more than by what he appears. Can all the Trappings or Equipage of a King or Hero, give *Brutus* half that Pomp and Majesty which he receives from a few Lines in *Shakespear?*   C

No. 43.

[STEELE.] Thursday, April 19.

Hae tibi erunt artes; pacisque imponere morem,
Parcere subjectis, & debellare superbos.—Virg.

THERE are Crowds of Men, whose great Misfortune it is that they were not bound to Mechanick Arts or Trades; it being absolutely necessary for them to be led by some continual Task or Employment. These are such as we commonly call Dull Fellows; Persons, who for want of something to do, out of a certain Vacancy of thought, rather than Curiosity, are ever meddling with things for which they are unfit. I cannot give you a Notion of them better than by presenting you with a Letter from a Gentleman, who belongs to a Society of this Order of Men, residing at *Oxford*.

'Oxford, April 13, 1711.

Sir, *Four a clock in the Morning.*

In some of your late Speculations, I find some Sketches towards an History of Clubs: But you seem to me to shew them in somewhat too ludicrous a Light. I have well weighed that Matter, and think that the most important Negotiations may best be carried on in such Assemblies. I shall, therefore, for the Good of Mankind (which, I trust, you and I are equally concerned for) propose an Institution of that Nature for Example sake.

I must confess, the Design and Transactions of too many Clubs are trifling, and manifestly of no Consequence to the Nation or publick Weal: Those I 'll give you up. But you must do me then the Justice to own, that nothing can be more useful or laudable, than the Scheme we go upon. To avoid Nicknames and Witticisms, we call our selves *The Hebdomadal Meeting*: Our President continues for a Year at least, and sometimes four or five: We are all Grave, Serious, Designing Men, in our Way: We think it our Duty, as far as in us lies, to take care the Constitution receives no Harm—*Ne quid detrimenti Res capiat publica*—. To censure Doctrines or Facts, Persons or Things, which we don't like; to settle the Nation at home, and to carry on the War abroad, where and in what manner we see fit: If other People are not of our Opinion, we can't help that. 'Twere better they were. Moreover, we now and then condescend to direct, in some measure, the little Affairs of our own University.

Verily, Mr. SPECTATOR, we are much offended at the Act for importing *French* Wines: A Bottle or two of good solid Edifying Port at honest *George*'s, made a night cheerful, and threw off Reserve. But this plaguy *French* Claret will not only cost us more Mony, but do us less Good: Had we been aware of it, before it had gone too far, I must tell you we would have petitioned to be heard upon that Subject. But let that pass.

I must let you know likewise, good Sir, that we look upon a certain Northern Prince's March, in Conjunction with Infidels, to be palpably against our good Will and Liking; and for all Monsieur *Palmquist*, a most dangerous Innovation; and we are by no means yet sure, that some People are not at the Bottom on 't. At least, my own private Letters leave Room for a Politician, well vers'd in matters of this nature, to suspect as much, as a penetrating Friend of mine tells me.

We think we have at last done the Business with the Male-contents in *Hungary*, and shall clap up a Peace there.

What the Neutrality Army is to do, or what the Army in *Flanders*, and what two or three other Princes, is not yet fully determined among us; and we wait impatiently for the coming in of the next *Dyer*'s, who, you must know, is our Authentick Intelligence, our *Aristotle* in Politicks. And 'tis indeed but fit there should be some dernier Resort, the absolute Decider of all Controversies.

We were lately informed, that the Gallant Train'd-Bands had patroll'd all Night long about the Streets of *London*: We indeed could not imagine any Occasion for it, we guess'd not a Tittle on 't aforehand, we were in nothing of the Secret; and that City Tradesmen, or their Apprentices should do Duty, or work, during the Holidays, we thought absolutely impossible: But *Dyer* being positive in it, and some Letters from other People, who had talked with some who had it from those who should know, giving some Countenance to it, the Chairman reported from the Committee, appointed to examine into that Affair, That 'twas Possible there might be something in 't. I have much more to say to you, but my two good Friends and Neighbours, *Dominic* and *Slyboots*, are just come in, and the Coffee 's ready.

I am, in the mean time,

Mr. Spectator,

Your Admirer, and

Humble Servant,

Abraham Froth.'

You may observe the Turn of their Minds tends only to Novelty, and not Satisfaction in any thing. It would be Disappointment to them, to come to Certainty in any thing, for that would gravel them, and put an end to their Enquiries, which dull Fellows do not make for Information, but for Exercise. I do not know but this may be a very good way of accounting for what we frequently see, to wit, that dull Fellows prove very good Men of Business.   Business relieves them from their own natural Heaviness, by furnishing them with what to do; whereas Business to Mercurial Men, is an Interruption from their real Existence and Happiness.   Tho' the dull Part of Mankind are harmless in their Amusements, it were to be wished they had no vacant Time, because they usually undertake something that makes their Wants conspicuous, by their manner of supplying them.   You shall seldom find a dull Fellow of good Education, but (if he happens to have any Leisure upon his Hands) will turn his Head to one of those two Amusements, for all Fools of Eminence, Politicks or Poetry. The former of these Arts, is the Study of all dull People in general; but when Dulness is lodged in a Person of a quick Animal Life, it generally exerts it self in Poetry.   One might here mention a few Military Writers, who give great Entertainment to the Age, by reason that the Stupidity of their Heads is quickened by the Alacrity of their Hearts. This Constitution in a dull Fellow, gives Vigour to Nonsense, and makes the Puddle boil, which would otherwise Stagnate.   The *British Prince*, that Celebrated Poem, which was written in the Reign of King *Charles* the Second, and deservedly called by the Wits of that Age *Incomparable*, was the Effect of such an happy Genius as we are speaking of.   From among many other Disticks no less to be quoted on this Account, I cannot but recite the two following Lines.

> *A painted Vest Prince* Voltager *had on,*
> *Which from a Naked* Pict *his Grandsire won.*

Here if the Poet had not been Vivacious, as well as Stupid, he could not, in the Warmth and Hurry of Nonsense, have been capable of forgetting that neither Prince *Voltager*, nor his Grandfather, could strip a Naked Man of his Doublet; but a Fool of a colder Constitution would have staied to have Fleaed the *Pict*, and made Buff of his Skin, for the Wearing of the Conqueror.

To bring these Observations to some useful Purpose of Life, what I would propose should be, that we imitated those wise Nations, wherein every Man learns some Handicraft Work. Would it not employ a Beau prettily enough, if instead of eternally playing with a Snuff-Box, he spent some part of his Time in making one?   Such a Method as this would very much conduce to the publick Emolument, by making every Man Living good for something; for there would then be no one Member of human Society, but would have some little Pretension for some Degree in it; like him who came to *Will's* Coffee-house, upon the Merit of having writ a Posie of a Ring.

R

No. 44.

[ADDISON.]   Friday, April 20.

Tu quid ego & populus mecum desideret audi.—Hor.

AMONG the several Artifices which are put in Practice by the
Poets to fill the Minds of an Audience with Terror, the first
Place is due to Thunder and Lightning, which are often made
use of at the Descending of a God, or the Rising of a Ghost, at
the Vanishing of a Devil, or at the Death of a Tyrant.   I have
known a Bell introduced into several Tragedies with good
Effect; and have seen the whole Assembly in a very great
Alarm all the while it has been ringing.   But there is nothing
which delights and terrifies our *English* Theatre so much as a
Ghost, especially when he appears in a bloody Shirt.   A
Spectre has very often saved a Play, though he has done
nothing but stalked across the Stage, or rose through a Cleft of
it, and sunk again without speaking one Word.   There may be
a proper Season for these several Terrors; and when they only
come in as Aids and Assistances to the Poet, they are not only
to be excused, but to be applauded.   Thus the sounding of
the Clock in *Venice Preserved*, makes the Hearts of the whole
Audience quake; and conveys a stronger Terror to the Mind,
than it is possible for Words to do.   The Appearance of the
Ghost in *Hamlet* is a Master-piece in its kind, and wrought up
with all the Circumstances that can create either Attention or
Horror.   The Mind of the Reader is wonderfully prepared for
his Reception, by the Discourses that precede it: His dumb
Behaviour at his first Entrance, strikes the Imagination very
strongly; but every time he enters, he is still more terrifying.
Who can read the Speech with which young *Hamlet* accosts
him, without trembling?

> Hor. *Look, my Lord, it comes!*
> Ham. *Angels and Ministers of Grace defend us!*
> *Be thou a Spirit of Health, or Goblin damn'd;*
> *Bring with thee Airs from Heav'n, or Blasts from Hell;*
> *Be thy Events wicked or charitable;*
> *Thou com'st in such a questionable Shape*
> *That I will speak to thee.   I'll call thee* Hamlet.
> *King, Father, Royal* Dane: *Oh! Oh! Answer me,*
> *Let me not burst in Ignorance; but tell*
> *Why thy canoniz'd Bones, hearsed in Death,*
> *Have burst their Cearments?   Why the Sepulchre,*
> *Wherein we saw thee quietly inurn'd,*
> *Hath op'd his ponderous and marble Jaws*
> *To cast thee up again!   What may this mean?*
> *That thou dead Coarse again in complete Steel*
> *Revisit'st thus the Glimpses of the Moon,*
> *Making Night hideous?*

I do not therefore find Fault with the Artifices above-mentioned when they are introduced with Skill, and accompanied by proportionable Sentiments and Expressions in the Writing.

For the moving of Pity, our principal Machine is the Handkerchief; and indeed in our common Tragedies, we should not know very often that the Persons are in Distress by any thing they say, if they did not from time to time apply their Handkerchiefs to their Eyes. Far be it from me to think of banishing this Instrument of Sorrow from the Stage; I know a Tragedy could not subsist without it: All that I would contend for, is to keep it from being misapplied. In a Word, I would have the Actor's Tongue sympathize with his Eyes.

A disconsolate Mother, with a Child in her Hand, has frequently drawn Compassion from the Audience, and has therefore gained a Place in several Tragedies. A Modern Writer, that observed how this had took in other Plays, being resolved to double the Distress, and melt his Audience twice as much as those before him had done, brought a Princess upon the Stage with a little Boy in one Hand and a Girl in the other. This too had a very good Effect. A third Poet, being resolved to outwrite all his Predecessors, a few Years ago introduced three Children with great Success: And, as I am informed, a young Gentleman, who is fully determined to break the most obdurate Hearts, has a Tragedy by him, where the first Person that appears upon the Stage is an afflicted Widow in her Mourning-Weeds, with half a Dozen fatherless Children attending her, like those that usually hang about the Figure of Charity. Thus several Incidents that are beautiful in a good Writer, become ridiculous by falling into the Hands of a bad one.

But among all our Methods of moving Pity or Terror, there is none so absurd and barbarous, and what more exposes us to the Contempt and Ridicule of our Neighbours, than that dreadful butchering of one another, which is so very frequent upon the *English* Stage. To delight in seeing Men stabbed, poisoned, racked, or impaled, is certainly the Sign of a cruel Temper: And as this is often practised before the *British* Audience, several *French* Criticks, who think these are grateful Spectacles to us, take Occasion from them to represent us as a People that delight in Blood. It is indeed very odd, to see our Stage strowed with Carcasses in the last Scene of a Tragedy; and to observe in the Ward-robe of the Play-house several Daggers, Poniards, Wheels, Bowls for Poison, and many other Instruments of Death. Murders and Executions are always transacted behind the Scenes in the *French* Theatre; which in general is very agreeable to the Manners of a polite and civilised People: But as there are no Exceptions to this Rule on the

French Stage, it leads them into Absurdities almost as ridiculous as that which falls under our present Censure. I remember in the famous Play of *Corneille*, written upon the Subject of the *Horatii* and *Curiatii*; the fierce young Hero who had overcome the *Curiatii* one after another, (instead of being congratulated by his Sister for his Victory, being upbraided by her for having slain her Lover) in the height of his Passion and Resentment kills her. If any thing could extenuate so brutal an Action, it would be the doing of it on a sudden, before the Sentiments of Nature, Reason, or Manhood could take Place in him. However, to avoid *publick Bloodshed*, as soon as his Passion is wrought to its Height, he follows his Sister the whole length of the Stage, and forbears killing her till they are both withdrawn behind the Scenes. I must confess, had he murder'd her before the Audience, the Indecency might have been greater; but as it is, it appears very unnatural, and looks like killing in cold Blood. To give my Opinion upon this Case; the Fact ought not to have been represented, but to have been told, if there was any Occasion for it.

It may not be unacceptable to the Reader, to see how *Sophocles* has conducted a Tragedy under the like delicate Circumstances. *Orestes* was in the same Condition with *Hamlet* in *Shakespear*, his Mother having murdered his Father, and taken Possession of his Kingdom in Conspiracy with her Adulterer. That young Prince therefore, being determined to revenge his Father's Death upon those who filled his Throne, conveys himself by a beautiful Stratagem into his Mother's Apartment, with a Resolution to kill her. But because such a Spectacle would have been too shocking for the Audience, this dreadful Resolution is executed behind the Scenes: The Mother is heard calling out to her Son for Mercy; and the Son answering her, that she shewed no Mercy to his Father. After which she shrieks out that she is wounded, and by what follows we find that she is slain. I do not remember that in any of our Plays there are Speeches made behind the Scenes, though there are other Instances of this Nature to be met with in those of the Ancients: And I believe my Reader will agree with me, that there is something infinitely more affecting in this dreadful Dialogue between the Mother and her Son behind the Scenes, than could have been in any thing transacted before the Audience. *Orestes* immediately after meets the Usurper at the Entrance of his Palace; and by a very happy Thought of the Poet avoids killing him before the Audience, by telling him that he should live some Time in his present Bitterness of Soul before he would dispatch him, and by ordering him to retire into that Part of the Palace where he had slain his Father, whose Murther he would revenge in the very same Place where it was committed. By this Means the Poet observes that Decency, which *Horace* afterwards established by a Rule, of forbearing to commit Parricides or unnatural Murthers before the Audience.

> *Nec coram populo natos Medea trucidet.*
>
> *Let not* Medea *draw her murth'ring Knife,*
> *And spill her Children's Blood upon the Stage.*

The *French* have therefore refined too much upon *Horace's* Rule, who never designed to banish all Kinds of Death from the Stage; but only such as had too much Horror in them, and which would have a better Effect upon the Audience when transacted behind the Scenes. I would therefore recommend to my Countrymen the Practice of the ancient Poets, who were very sparing of their publick Executions, and rather chose to perform them behind the Scenes, if it could be done with as great an Effect upon the Audience. At the same Time I must observe, that though the devoted Persons of the Tragedy were seldom slain before the Audience, which has generally something ridiculous in it, their Bodies were often produced after their Death, which has always in it something melancholy or terrifying; so that the killing on the Stage does not seem to have been avoided only as an Indecency, but also as an Improbability.

> *Nec pueros coram populo Medea trucidet,*
> *Aut humana palam coquat exta nefarius Atreus,*
> *Aut in avem Progne vertatur, Cadmus in anguem.*
> *Quodcunque ostendis mihi sic, incredulus odi.*—Hor.
>
> Medea *must not draw her murth'ring Knife,*
> *Nor* Atreus *there his horrid Feast prepare.*
> Cadmus *and* Progne's *Metamorphosis,*
> *(She to a Swallow turn'd, he to a Snake)*
> *And whatsoever contradicts my Sense,*
> *I hate to see, and never can believe.*—Ld. Roscommon.

I have now gone through the several dramatick Inventions which are made use of by the ignorant Poets to supply the place of Tragedy, and by the skilful to improve it; some of which I could wish entirely rejected, and the rest to be used with Caution. It would be an endless Task to consider Comedy in the same Light, and to mention the innumerable Shifts that small Wits put in practice to raise a Laugh. *Bullock* in a short Coat, and *Norris* in a long one, seldom fail of this Effect. In ordinary Comedies, a broad and a narrow brim'd Hat are different Characters. Sometimes the Wit of the Scene lies in a Shoulder-Belt, and sometimes in a Pair of Whiskers. A

Lover running about the Stage, with his Head peeping out of a Barrel, was thought a very good jest in King *Charles* the Second's Time; and invented by one of the first Wits of that Age. But because Ridicule is not so delicate as Compassion, and because the Objects that make us laugh are infinitely more numerous than those that make us weep, there is a much greater Latitude for comick than tragick Artifices, and by Consequence a much greater Indulgence to be allowed them.

C

No. 45.
[ADDISON.]

Saturday, April 21.

Natio comoeda est . . .—Juv.

THERE is nothing which I more desire than a safe and honourable Peace, tho' at the same time I am very apprehensive of many ill Consequences that may attend it. I do not mean in regard to our Politicks, but to our Manners. What an Inundation of Ribbons and Brocades will break in upon us? What Peals of Laughter and Impertinence shall we be exposed to? For the Prevention of these great Evils, I could heartily wish that there was an Act of Parliament for Prohibiting the Importation of *French* Fopperies.

The Female Inhabitants of our Island have already received very strong Impressions from this ludicrous Nation, though by the Length of the War (as there is no Evil which has not some Good attending it) they are pretty well worn out and forgotten. I remember the time when some of our well-bred Country Women kept their *Valet de Chambre*, because, forsooth, a Man was much more handy about them than one of their own Sex. I my self have seen one of these Male *Abigails* tripping about the Room with a Looking-Glass in his Hand, and combing his Lady's Hair a whole Morning together. Whether or no there was any Truth in the Story of a Lady's being got with Child by one of these her Hand-maids, I cannot tell, but I think at present the whole Race of them is extinct in our own Country.

About the time that several of our Sex were taken into this kind of Service, the Ladies likewise brought up the Fashion of receiving Visits in their Beds. It was then looked upon as a piece of Ill Breeding, for a Woman to refuse to see a Man, because she was not stirring; and a Porter would have been thought unfit for his Place, that could have made so awkard an Excuse. As I love to see every thing that is new, I once prevailed upon my Friend WILL. HONEYCOMB to carry me along with him to one of these Travelled Ladies, desiring him, at the same time, to present me as a Foreigner who could not speak *English*, that so I might not be obliged to bear a Part in the Discourse. The Lady, tho' willing to appear undrest, had put on her best Looks, and painted her self for our Reception. Her Hair appeared in a very nice Disorder, as the Night-Gown which was thrown upon her Shoulders, was ruffled with great Care. For my part, I am so shocked with every thing that looks immodest in the Fair Sex, that I could not forbear taking off my Eye from her when she moved in her Bed, and was in the greatest Confusion imaginable every time she stirred a Leg or an Arm. As the Coquets who introduced this Custom, grew old, they left it off by Degrees; well knowing that a Woman of Threescore may kick and tumble her Heart out, without making any Impressions.

Sempronia is at present the most profest Admirer of the *French* Nation, but is so modest as to admit her Visitants no farther than her Toilet. It is a very odd Sight that beautiful Creature makes, when she is talking Politicks with her Tresses flowing about her Shoulders, and examining that Face in the Glass, which does such Execution upon all the Male Standers-by. How prettily does she divide her Discourse between her Woman and her Visitants? What sprightly Transitions does she make from an Opera or a Sermon, to an Ivory Comb or a Pin Cushion? How have I been pleased to see her interrupted in an Account of her Travels, by a Message to her Footman; and holding her Tongue in the midst of a Moral Reflexion, by applying the tip of it to a Patch?

There is nothing which exposes a Woman to greater Dangers, than that Gaiety and Airiness of Temper, which are natural to most of the Sex. It should be therefore the Concern of every wise and virtuous Woman, to keep this Sprightliness from degenerating into Levity. On the contrary, the whole Discourse and Behaviour of the *French* is to make the Sex more Fantastical, or (as they are pleased to term it) *more awaken'd*, than is consistent either with Virtue or Discretion. To speak Loud in Publick Assemblies, to let every one hear you Talk of Things that should only be mentioned in Private, or in Whisper, are looked upon as Parts of a refined Education. At the same time, a Blush is unfashionable, and Silence more ill-bred than any thing that can be spoken. In short, Discretion and Modesty, which in all other Ages and Countries have been regarded as the greatest Ornaments of the Fair Sex, are considered as the Ingredients of narrow Conversation, and Family Behaviour.

Some Years ago, I was at the Tragedy of *Mackbeth*, and unfortunately placed my self under a Woman of Quality that is since Dead; who, as I found by the Noise she made, was newly returned from *France*.   A little before the rising of the Curtain, she broke out into a loud Soliloquy, *When will the dear Witches enter?* and immediately upon their first Appearance, asked a Lady that sate three Boxes from her, on her Right Hand, if those Witches were not charming Creatures.   A little after, as *Betterton* was in one of the finest Speeches of the Play, she shook her Fan at another Lady, who sate as far on her Left Hand, and told her with a Whisper, that might be heard all over the Pit, We must not expect to see *Balloon* to Night.   Not long after, calling out to a young Baronet by his Name, who sate three Seats before me, she asked him whether *Mackbeth*'s Wife was still alive; and before he could give an Answer, fell a talking of the Ghost of *Banquo*.   She had by this time formed a little Audience to her self, and fixed the Attention of all about her. But as I had a mind to hear the Play, I got out of the Sphere of her Impertinence, and planted my self in one of the remotest Corners of the Pit.

This pretty Childishness of Behaviour is one of the most refined Parts of Coquetry, and is not to be attained in Perfection by Ladies that do not Travel for their Improvement. A natural and unconstrained Behaviour has something in it so agreeable, that it is no wonder to see People endeavouring after it.   But at the same time, it is so very hard to hit, when it is not Born with us, that People often make themselves Ridiculous in attempting it.

A very Ingenious *French* Author tells us, that the Ladies of the Court of *France*, in his Time, thought it ill Breeding, and a kind of Female Pedantry, to pronounce an hard Word right; for which Reason they took frequent occasion to use hard Words, that they might show a Politeness in murdering them. He further adds, that a Lady of some Quality at Court, having accidentally made use of an hard Word in a proper Place, and Pronounced it right, the whole Assembly was out of Countenance for her.

I must however be so just as to own, that there are many Ladies who have Travelled several thousands of Miles without being the worse for it, and have brought Home with them all the Modesty, Discretion, and good Sense, that they went abroad with.   As on the contrary, there are great Numbers of *Travelled* Ladies, who have lived all their Days within the Smoak of *London*.   I have known a Woman that never was out of the Parish of *St. James*'s betray as many Foreign Fopperies in her Carriage, as she could have Gleaned up in half the Countries of *Europe*.   C

No. 46.

[ADDISON.]   Monday, April 23.

Non bene junctarum discordia semina rerum.—Ovid.

WHEN I want Materials for this Paper, it is my Custom to go Abroad in quest of Game; and when I meet any proper Subject, I take the first Opportunity of setting down an Hint of it upon Paper. At the same Time I look into the Letters of my Correspondents, and if I find any thing suggested in them that may afford Matter of Speculation, I likewise enter a Minute of it in my Collection of Materials. By this Means I frequently carry about me a whole Sheet-full of Hints, that would look like a Rhapsody of Nonsense to any Body but my self: There is nothing in them but Obscurity and Confusion, Raving and Inconsistency. In short, they are my Speculations in the first Principles, that (like the World in its Chaos) are void of all Light, Distinction and Order.

About a Week since there happened to me a very odd Accident, by Reason of one of these my Papers of Minutes which I had accidentally dropped at *Lloyd*'s Coffee-house, where the Auctions are usually kept. Before I missed it, there was a Cluster of People who had found it, and were diverting themselves with it at one End of the Coffee-house: It had raised so much Laughter among them, before I had observed what they were about, that I had not the Courage to own it. The Boy of the Coffee-house, when they had done with it, carried it about in his Hand, asking every Body if they had dropped a written Paper; but no Body challenging it, he was ordered by those merry Gentlemen who had before perused it, to get up into the Auction-Pulpit, and read it to the whole Room, that if any one would own it, they might. The Boy accordingly mounted the Pulpit, and with a very audible Voice read as follows.

MINUTES.

Sir ROGER DE COVERLY's Country-Seat—Yes, for I hate long Speeches—Query, if a good Christian may be a Conjurer—*Childermas-day*, Saltseller, House-Dog, Screech-Owl, Cricket,—Mr. *Thomas Inkle* of *London*, in the good Ship called the *Achilles*. *Yarico*—*Aegrescitque medendo*—Ghosts—The Lady's Library—Lion by Trade a Taylor—Dromedary called *Bucephalus*—Equipage the Lady's *summum bonum*—*Charles Lillie* to be taken Notice of—Short Face a Relief to Envy—Redundancies in the three Professions—King *Latinus* a Recruit—Jew devouring an Ham of Bacon—*Westminster-Abby*—*Grand*

Cairo—Procrastination—*April* Fools—Blue Boars, Red Lyons.
Hogs in Armour—Enter a King and two Fidlers *solus*—Admission into the Ugly Club—Beauty, how improveable—Families
of true and false Humour—The Parrot's School-Mistress—
Face half *Pict* half *British*—No Man to be an Hero of a Tragedy
under six Foot—Club of Sighers—Letters from Flower-Pots,
Elbow-Chairs, Tapestry-Figures, Lion, Thunder—The Bell
rings to the Puppet-Show—Old Woman with a Beard Married
to a Smock-faced Boy—My next Coat to be turn'd up with
Blue — Fable of Tongs and Gridiron — Flower Dyers — the
Soldier's Prayer—Thank ye for nothing, says the Gally-Pot—
Pactolus in Stockings, with golden Clocks to them—Bamboos,
Cudgels, Drum-sticks—Slip of my Land-lady's eldest Daughter
—The black Mare with a Star in her Forehead—The Barber's
Pole—WILL. HONEYCOMB's Coat-Pocket—*Caesar's* Behaviour
and my own in Parallel Circumstances—Poem in Patch-work
—*Nulli gravis est percussus Achilles*—The Female Conventicler
—The Ogle-Master.

The reading of this Paper made the whole Coffee-house very
merry; some of them concluded it was written by a Madman,
and others by some Body that had been taking Notes out of
the Spectator. One who had the Appearance of a very substantial Citizen, told us, with several politick Winks and Nods,
that he wished there was no more in the Paper than what was
expressed in it: That for his Part, he looked upon the Dromedary, the Gridiron, and the Barber's Pole, to signifie something
more than what was usually meant by those Words; and that
he thought the Coffee-man could not do better, than to carry
the Paper to one of the Secretaries of State. He further added,
that he did not like the name of the outlandish Man with the
Golden Clock in his Stockings. A young *Oxford* Scholar, who
chanced to be with his Uncle at the Coffee-house, discovered
to us who this *Pactolus* was; and by that Means turned the
whole Scheme of this worthy Citizen into Ridicule. While
they were making their several Conjectures upon this innocent
Paper, I reached out my Arm to the Boy, as he was coming
out of the Pulpit, to give it me; which he did accordingly.
This drew the eyes of the whole Company upon me; but after
having cast a cursory Glance over it, and shook my Head twice
or thrice at the reading of it, I twisted it into a kind of Match,
and litt my Pipe with it. My profound Silence, together with
the Steadiness of my Countenance, and the Gravity of my
Behaviour during this whole Transaction, raised a very loud
Laugh on all Sides of me; but as I had escaped all Suspicion of
being the Author, I was very well satisfied, and applying my

self to my Pipe and the *Post-Man*, took no further Notice of anything that passed about me.

My Reader will find, that I have already made use of above half the Contents of the foregoing Paper; and will easily suppose, that those Subjects which are yet untouched, were such Provisions as I had made for his future Entertainment. But as I have been unluckily prevented by this Accident, I shall only give him the Letters which relate to the two last Hints. The first of them I should not have published, were I not informed that there is many an Husband who suffers very much in his private Affairs by the indiscreet Zeal of such a Partner as is hereafter mentioned; to whom I may apply the barbarous inscription quoted by the Bishop of *Salisbury* in his Travels; *Dum nimia pia est, facta est impia.*

'*Sir*,

I am one of those unhappy Men that are plagued with a Gospel-Gossip, so common among Dissenters (especially Friends). Lectures in the Morning, Church-Meetings at Noon, and Preparation-Sermons at Night, take up so much of her Time, 'tis very rare she knows what we have for Dinner, unless when the Preacher is to be at it. With him come a Tribe, all Brothers and Sisters it seems; while others, really such, are deemed no Relations. If at any time I have her Company alone, she is a meer Sermon Popgun, repeating and discharging Texts, Proofs, and Applications so perpetually, that however weary I may go to Bed, the Noise in my Head will not let me sleep till towards Morning. The Misery of my Case, and great Numbers of such Sufferers, plead your Pity and speedy Relief; otherwise must expect, in a little Time, to be lectured, preached and prayed into Want, unless the Happiness of being sooner talked to Death prevent it.

I am, &c.

R. G.'

The second Letter, relating to the Ogling Master, runs thus.

'*Mr.* Spectator,

I am an *Irish* Gentleman, that have travelled many Years for my Improvement; during which Time I have accomplished my self in the whole Art of Ogling, as it is at present practised in all the polite Nations of *Europe*. Being thus qualified, I intend, by the Advice of my Friends, to set up for an Ogling-Master. I teach the Church Ogle in the Morning, and the Play-house Ogle by Candle-light. I have also brought over with me a new flying Ogle fit for the Ring; which I teach in the

Dusk of the Evening, or in any Hour of the Day by darkning one of my Windows. I have a Manuscript by me called *The compleat Ogler*, which I shall be ready to shew you upon any Occasion: In the mean time, I beg you will publish the Substance of this Letter in an Advertisement, and you will very much oblige,

C   *Yours,* &c.'

No. 47.

[ADDISON.]   Tuesday, April 24.

Ride si sapis . . .—Mart.

Mr. *Hobbs*, in his Discourse of Human Nature, which, in my humble Opinion, is much the best of all his Works, after some very curious Observations upon Laughter, concludes thus: 'The Passion of Laughter is nothing else but sudden Glory arising from some sudden Conception of some Eminency in our selves, by Comparison with the Infirmity of others, or with our own formerly: For Men laugh at the Follies of themselves past, when they come suddenly to Remembrance, except they bring with them any present Dishonour.'

According to this Author therefore, when we hear a Man laugh excessively, instead of saying he is very Merry, we ought to tell him he is very Proud. And indeed, if we look into the bottom of this Matter, we shall meet with many Observations to confirm us in his Opinion. Every one laughs at some-body that is in an inferior State of Folly to himself. It was formerly the Custom for every great House in *England* to keep a tame Fool dressed in Petticoats, that the Heir of the Family might have an Opportunity of joking upon him, and diverting himself with his Absurdities. For the same Reason Ideots are still in request in most of the Courts of *Germany*, where there is not a Prince of any great Magnificence who has not two or three dressed, distinguished, undisputed Fools in his Retinue, whom the rest of the Courtiers are always breaking their Jests upon.

The *Dutch*, who are more famous for their Industry and Application, than for Wit and Humour, hang up in several of their Streets what they call the Sign of the *Gaper*, that is, the head of an Ideot dressed in a Cap and Bells, and gaping in a most immoderate manner: This is a standing Jest at *Amsterdam*.

Thus every one diverts himself with some Person or other that is below him in Point of Understanding, and triumphs in the Superiority of his Genius, whilst he has such Objects o:

Derision before his Eyes. Mr. *Dennis* has very well expressed this in a Couple of humorous Lines, which are part of a Translation of a Satyr in Monsieur *Boileau*.

> *Thus one Fool lolls his Tongue out at another,*
> *And shakes his empty Noddle at his Brother.*

Mr. *Hobbs*'s Reflection gives us the Reason why the insignificant People above-mentioned are Stirrers up of Laughter among Men of a gross Taste: But as the more understanding Part of Mankind do not find their Risibility affected by such ordinary Objects, it may be worth the while to examine into the several Provocatives of Laughter in Men of superior Sense and Knowledge.

In the first Place I must observe, that there is a Sett of merry Drolls, whom the common People of all Countries admire, and seem to love so well, *that they could eat them,* according to the old Proverb; I mean those circumforaneous Wits whom every Nation calls by the Name of that Dish of Meat which it loves best. In *Holland* they are termed *Pickled Herrings*; in *France, Jean Pottages*; in *Italy, Maccaronies*; and in *Great Britain, Jack Puddings*. These merry Wags, from whatsoever Food they receive their Titles, that they may make their Audiences laugh, always appear in a Fool's Coat, and commit such Blunders and Mistakes in every step they take, and every Word they utter, as those who listen to them would be ashamed of.

But this little Triumph of the Understanding, under the Disguise of Laughter, is no where more visible than in that Custom which prevails every where among us on the first Day of the present Month, when every Body takes it in his Head to make as many Fools as he can. In proportion as there are more Follies discovered, so there is more Laughter raised on this Day than on any other in the whole Year. A Neighbour of mine, who is a Haberdasher by Trade, and a very shallow conceited Fellow, makes his Boasts that for these ten Years successively he has not made less than an hundred *April* Fools. My Landlady had a falling out with him about a Fortnight ago, for sending every one of her Children upon some *Sleeveless Errand*, as she terms it. Her eldest Son went to buy an Half-penny worth of Inkle at a Shoe-maker's; the eldest Daughter was dispatched half a Mile to see a Monster; and in short, the whole Family of innocent Children made *April* Fools. Nay, my landlady her self did not escape him. This empty Fellow has laughed upon these Conceits ever since.

This Art of Wit is well enough, when confined to one Day in Twelve-month; but there is an ingenious Tribe of Men sprung up of late Years, who are for making *April* Fools every Day in the Year. These Gentlemen are commonly distinguished by the Name of *Biters*; a Race of Men that are perpetually employed in laughing at those Mistakes which are of their own Production.

Thus we see, in proportion as one Man is more refined than another, he chuses his Fool out of a lower or higher Class of Mankind; or, to speak in a more Philosophical Language, That secret Elation and Pride of Heart which is generally called Laughter, arises in him from his comparing himself with an Object below him, whether it so happens that it be a Natural or an Artificial Fool. It is indeed very possible, that the Persons we laugh at may in the main of their Characters be much wiser Men than our selves; but if they would have us laugh at them, they must fall short of us in those Respects which stir up this Passion.

I am afraid I shall appear too Abstracted in my Speculations, if I shew that when a Man of Wit makes us laugh, it is by betraying some Oddness or Infirmity in his own Character, or in the Representation which he makes of others; and that when we laugh at a Brute or even at an inanimate thing, it is at some Action or Incident that bears a remote Analogy to any Blunder or Absurdity in reasonable Creatures.

But to come into common Life: I shall pass by the Consideration of those Stage Coxcombs that are able to shake a whole Audience, and take notice of a particular sort of Men who are such Provokers of Mirth in Conversation, that it is impossible for a Club or Merry-meeting to subsist without them; I mean, those honest Gentlemen that are always exposed to the Wit and Raillery of their Well-wishers and Companions; that are pelted by Men, Women, and Children, Friends, and Foes, and, in a word, stand as *Butts* in Conversation, for every one to shoot at that pleases. I know several of these *Butts* who are Men of Wit and Sense, though by some odd Turn of Humour, some unlucky Cast in their Person or Behaviour, they have always the Misfortune to make the Company merry. The Truth of it is, a Man is not qualified for a *Butt*, who has not a good deal of Wit and Vivacity, even in the ridiculous Side of his Character. A stupid *Butt* is only fit for the Conversation of ordinary People: Men of Wit require one that will give them Play, and bestir himself in the absurd Part of his Behaviour. A *Butt* with these Accomplishments frequently gets the Laugh of his Side, and turns the Ridicule upon him that attacks him. Sir *John Falstaff* was an Hero of this Species, and gives a good Description of himself in his Capacity of a *Butt*, after the following manner; *Men of all sorts* (says that merry Knight) *take a Pride to gird at me. The Brain of Man is not able to invent any thing that tends to Laughter more than I invent, or is invented on me. I am not only Witty in my self, but the Cause that Wit is in other Men.* C

No. 48.
[STEELE.] Wednesday, April 25.

> . . . *Per multas aditum sibi saepe figuras*
> *Repperit . . .*—Ovid.

My Correspondents take it ill if I do not, from time to time, let them know I have received their Letters. The most effectual way will be to publish some of them that are upon important Subjects; which I shall introduce with a Letter of my own, that I writ a Fortnight ago to a Fraternity who thought fit to make me an honorary Member.

'To the President and Fellows of the *UGLY CLUB.*

> *May it please your Deformities,*

I have received the Notification of the Honour you have done me, in admitting me into your Society. I acknowledge my Want of Merit, and for that Reason shall endeavour at all times to make up my own Failures, by introducing and recommending to the Club Persons of more undoubted Qualifications than I can pretend to. I shall next Week come down in the Stage Coach, in order to take my Seat at the Board; and shall bring with me a Candidate of each Sex. The Persons I shall present to you, are an old Beau and a modern *Pict.* If they are not so eminently gifted by Nature as our Assembly expects, give me Leave to say, their acquired Ugliness is greater than any that has ever appeared before you. The Beau has varied his Dress every Day of his Life for these thirty Years last past, and still added to the Deformity he was born with. The *Pict* has still greater Merit towards us; and has, ever since she came to Years of Discretion, deserted the handsome Party, and taken all possible Pains to acquire the Face in which I shall present her to your Consideration and Favour. I am, Gentlemen,

> *Your most Obliged Humble Servant,*

> *The* Spectator.

P. S. I desire to know whether you admit People of Quality.'

'*Mr.* Spectator, *April* 17.

To shew you there are among us of the vain weak Sex, some that have Honesty and Fortitude enough to dare to be ugly, and willing to be thought so; I apply my self to you, to beg your Interest and Recommendation to the *Ugly Club*. If my own Word will not be taken, (tho' in this Case a Woman's may) I can bring credible Witness of my Qualifications for their Company, whether they insist upon Hair, Forehead, Eyes, Cheeks, or Chin; to which I must add, that I find it easier to lean to my left Side, than my Right. I hope I am in all Respects agreeable: And for Humour and Mirth, I 'll keep up to the President himself. All the Favour I 'll pretend to is, that as I am the first Woman has appeared desirous of good Company and agreeable Conversation, I may take and keep the upper End of the Table. And indeed I think they want a Carver, which I can be after as ugly a Manner as they can wish. I desire your Thoughts of my Claim as soon as you can. Add to my Features the Length of my Face, which is full half Yard; tho' I never knew the Reason of it till you gave one for the Shortness of yours. If I knew a Name ugly enough to belong to the above described Face, I would feign one; but, to my unspeakable Misfortune, my Name is the only disagreeable Prettiness about me; so prithee make one for me, that signifies all the Deformity in the World: You understand *Latin*, but be sure bring it in with my being, in the Sincerity of my Heart,

> *Your most frightful Admirer,*
> *and Servant,*
>
> Hecatissa.'

'*Mr.* SPECTATOR,

I read your Discourse upon Affectation, and from the Remarks made in it examined my own Heart so strictly, that I thought I had found out its most secret Avenues, with a Resolution to be aware of you for the future. But alas! to my Sorrow I now understand, that I have several Follies which I do not know the Root of. I am an old Fellow, and extreamly troubled with the Gout; but having always a strong Vanity towards being pleasing in the Eyes of Women, I never have a Moment's Ease, but I am mounted in high-heel'd Shoes with a glased Wax-leather Instep. Two Days after a severe Fit I was invited to a Friend's House in the City, where I believed I should see Ladies; and with my usual Complaisance crippled my self to wait upon them: A very sumptuous Table, agreeable Company, and kind Reception, were but so many importunate Additions to the Torment I was in. A Gentleman of the Family observed my Condition; and soon after the Queen's Health, he, in the Presence of the whole Company, with his own Hands degraded me into an old Pair of his own Shoes. This Operation, before fine Ladies, to me (who am by Nature a Coxcomb) was suffered with the same Reluctance as they admit the Help of Men in their greatest Extremity. The Return of Ease made me forgive the rough Obligation laid upon me, which at that time relieved my Body from a Distemper, and will my mind for ever from a Folly. For the Charity received I return my Thanks this way.

Your most humble Servant.'

  'Sir,   *Epping, April 18.*

We have your Papers here the Morning they come out, and we have been very well entertained with your last, upon the false Ornaments of Persons who represent Heroes in a Tragedy. What made your Speculation come very seasonably among us is, that we have now at this Place a Company of Strolers, who are very far from offending in the impertinent Splendor of the Drama. They are so far from falling into these false Gallantries, that the Stage is here in its Original Situation of a Cart. *Alexander* the Great was acted by a Fellow in a Paper Cravat. The next Day, the Earl of *Essex* seemed to have no Distress but his Poverty: And my Lord *Foppington* the same Morning wanted any better Means to shew himself a Fop, than by wearing Stockings of different Colours. In a Word, tho' they have had a full Barn for many Days together, our Itinerants are still so wretchedly poor, that without you can prevail to send us the Furniture you forbid at the Playhouse, the Heroes appear only like sturdy Beggars, and the Heroins Gipsies. We have had but one Part which was performed and dressed with Propriety, and that was Justice *Clodpate*: This was so well done that it offended Mr. Justice *Overdo*, who, in the midst of our whole Audience, was (like *Quixote* in the Puppet Show) so highly provoked, that he told them, If they would move Compassion, it should be in their own Persons, and not in the Characters of distressed Princes and Potentates: He told them, If they were so good at finding the way to People's Hearts, they should do it at the End of Bridges or Church-Porches, in their proper Vocation of Beggars. This, the Justice says, they must expect, since they could not be contented to act Heathen Warriors, and such Fellows as *Alexander*, but must presume to make a Mockery of one of the *Quorum.*

R   *Your Servant.'*

No. 49.

[STEELE.]   Thursday, April 26.

> . . . *Hominem pagina nostra sapit.*—Mart.

IT is very natural for a Man, who is not turned for Mirthful
Meetings of Men, or Assemblies of the fair Sex, to delight in
that sort of Conversation which we find in Coffee-houses.
Here a Man, of my Temper, is in his Element; for, if he cannot
talk, he can still be more agreeable to his Company, as well as
pleased in himself, in being only an Hearer.   It is a Secret
known but to few, yet of no small use in the Conduct of Life,
that when you fall into a Man's Conversation, the first thing
you should consider is, whether he has a greater Inclination
to hear you, or that you should hear him.   The latter is the
more general Desire, and I know very able Flatterers that never
speak a Word in Praise of the Persons from whom they obtain
daily Favours, but still practise a skilful Attention to whatever
is uttered by those with whom they converse.   We are very
Curious to observe the Behaviour of Great Men and their
Clients; but the same Passions and Interests move Men in
lower Spheres; and I (that have nothing else to do, but make
Observations) see in every Parish, Street, Lane, and Alley of
this Populous City, a little Potentate that has his Court, and
his Flatterers who lay Snares for his Affection and Favour,
by the same Arts that are practised upon Men in higher
Stations.

In the Place I most usually frequent, Men differ rather in
the Time of Day in which they make a Figure, than in any
real Greatness above one another.   I, who am at the Coffee-
house at Six in a Morning, know that my Friend *Beaver* the
Haberdasher has a Levy of more undissembled Friends and
Admirers, than most of the Courtiers or Generals of *Great
Britain*.   Every Man about him has, perhaps, a News-Paper
in his Hand; but none can pretend to guess what Step will be
taken in any one Court of *Europe*, 'till Mr. *Beaver* has thrown
down his Pipe, and declares what Measures the Allies must
enter into upon this new Posture of Affairs.   Our Coffee-house
is near one of the Inns of Court, and *Beaver* has the Audience
and Admiration of his Neighbours from Six 'till within a
Quarter of Eight, at which time he is interrupted by the
Students of the House; some of whom are ready dress'd for
Westminster, at eight in a Morning, with Faces as busie as if
they were retained in every Cause there; and others come in
their Night-Gowns to saunter away their Time, as if they
never designed to go thither.   I do not know that I meet, in
any of my Walks, Objects which move both my Spleen and

Laughter so effectually, as those Young Fellows at the *Grecian,
Squire's, Searle's*, and all other Coffee-houses adjacent to the
Law, who rise early for no other Purpose but to publish their
Laziness. One would think these young *Virtuosos* take a
gay Cap and Slippers, with a Scarf and Party-coloured Gown,
to be Ensigns of Dignity; for the vain Things approach each
other with an Air, which shews they regard one another for
their Vestments. I have observed, that the Superiority among
these proceeds from an Opinion of Gallantry and Fashion:
The Gentleman in the Strawberry Sash, who presides so much
over the rest, has, it seems, subscribed to every Opera this last
Winter, and is supposed to receive Favours from one of the
Actresses.

When the Day grows too busie for these Gentlemen to enjoy
any longer the Pleasures of their *Deshabilé*, with any manner of
Confidence, they give place to Men who have Business or good
Sense in their Faces, and come to the Coffee-house either to
transact Affairs, or enjoy Conversation. The Persons to whose
Behaviour and Discourse I have most regard, are such as are
between these two sorts of Men: Such as have not Spirits too
Active to be happy and well pleased in a private Condition,
nor Complexions too warm to make them neglect the Duties
and Relations of Life. Of these sort of Men consist the
worthier Part of Mankind; of these are all good Fathers,
generous Brothers, sincere Friends, and faithful Subjects.
Their Entertainments are derived rather from Reason than
Imagination: Which is the Cause that there is no Impatience or
Instability in their Speech or Action. You see in their Countenances they are at home, and in quiet Possession of the
present Instant, as it passes, without desiring to quicken it by
gratifying any Passion, or prosecuting any new Design. These
are the Men formed for Society, and those little Communities
which we express by the Word *Neighbourhoods*.

The Coffee-house is the Place of Rendezvous to all that live
near it, who are thus turned to relish calm and ordinary Life.
Eubulus presides over the middle Hours of the Day, when this
Assembly of Men meet together. He enjoys a great Fortune
handsomely, without launching into Expence; and exerts many
noble and useful Qualities, without appearing in any publick
Employment. His Wisdom and Knowledge are serviceable to
all that think fit to make use of them; and he does the Office
of a Council, a Judge, an Executor, and a Friend to all his
Acquaintance, not only without the Profits which attend such
Offices, but also without the Deference and Homage which are
usually paid to them. The giving of Thanks is displeasing to
him. The greatest Gratitude you can shew him, is to let him

see you are the better Man for his Services; and that you are
as ready to oblige others, as he is to oblige you.

In the private Exigencies of his Friends he lends, at legal
Value, considerable Sums, which he might highly increase by
rolling in the Publick Stocks. He does not consider in whose
Hands his Mony will improve most, but where it will do
most Good.

Eubulus has so great an Authority in his little Diurnal
Audience, that when he shakes his Head at any Piece of
Publick News, they all of them appear dejected; and on the
contrary, go home to their Dinners with a good Stomach and
chearful Aspect, when *Eubulus* seems to intimate that Things
go well. Nay, their Veneration towards him is so great, that
when they are in other Company they speak and act after him;
are Wise in his Sentences, and are no sooner sate down at their
own Tables, but they hope or fear, rejoice or despond as they
saw him do at the Coffee-house. In a word, every Man is
Eubulus as soon as his Back is turned.

Having here given an Account of the several Reigns that
succeed each other from Day-break 'till Dinner-time, I shall
mention the Monarchs of the Afternoon on another occasion,
and shut up the whole Series of them with the History of *Tom*
the Tyrant; who, as first Minister of the Coffee-house, takes
the Government upon him between the Hours of Eleven and
Twelve at Night, and gives his Orders in the most Arbitrary
manner to the Servants below him, as to the Disposition of
Liquors, Coal and Cinders.   R

No. 50.
[ADDISON.]   Friday, April 27.

Nunquam aliud natura, aliud sapientia dicit.—Juv.

WHEN the four *Indian* Kings were in this Country about a
Twelvemonth ago, I often mixed with the Rabble, and followed
them a whole Day together, being wonderfully struck with the
Sight of every thing that is new or uncommon. I have, since
their Departure, employed a Friend to make many Enquiries of
their Landlord the Upholsterer, relating to their Manners and
Conversation, as also concerning the Remarks which they made
in this Country: For, next to the forming a right Notion of
such Strangers, I should be desirous of learning what Ideas
they have conceived of us.

The Upholsterer finding my Friend very inquisitive about
these his Lodgers, brought him some time since a little Bundle
of Papers, which he assured him were written by King *Sa Ga*

Yean Qua Rash Tow, and, as he supposes, left behind by some Mistake. These Papers are now translated, and contain abundance of very odd Observations, which I find this little Fraternity of Kings made during their Stay in the Isle of *Great Britain*. I shall present my Reader with a short Specimen of them in this Paper, and may, perhaps, communicate more to him hereafter. In the Article of *London* are the following Words, which without doubt are meant of the Church of St. *Paul*.

'On the most rising Part of the Town there stands a huge House, big enough to contain the whole Nation of which I am King. Our good Brother *E Tow O Koam*, King of the *Rivers*, is of Opinion it was made by the Hands of that great God to whom it is consecrated. The Kings of *Granajah* and of the *Six Nations* believe that it was created with the Earth, and produced on the same Day with the Sun and Moon. But for my own Part, by the best Information that I could get of this Matter, I am apt to think that this prodigious Pile was fashioned into the Shape it now bears by several Tools and Instruments of which they have a wonderful Variety in this Country. It was probably at first an huge mis-shapen Rock that grew upon the Top of the Hill, which the Natives of the Country (after having cut it into a kind of regular Figure) bored and hollowed with incredible Pains and Industry, till they had wrought in it all those beautiful Vaults and Caverns into which it is divided at this Day. As soon as this Rock was thus curiously scooped to their Liking, a prodigious Number of Hands must have been employed in chipping the Outside of it, which is now as smooth as the Surface of a Pebble; and is in several Places hewn out into Pillars that stand like the Trunks of so many Trees bound about the Top with Garlands of Leaves. It is probable that when this great Work was begun, which must have been many Hundred Years ago, there was some Religion among this People; for they give it the Name of a Temple, and have a Tradition that it was designed for Men to pay their Devotions in. And indeed, there are several Reasons which make us think, that the Natives of this Country had formerly among them some sort of Worship; for they set apart every seventh Day as sacred: But upon my going into one of these holy Houses on that Day, I could not observe any Circumstance of Devotion in their Behaviour; There was indeed a Man in Black who was mounted above the rest, and seemed to utter something with a great deal of Vehemence; but as for those underneath him, instead of paying their Worship to the Deity of the Place, they were most of them bowing and curtsying to one another, and a considerable Number of them fast asleep.

The Queen of the Country appointed two Men to attend us, that had enough of our Language to make themselves understood in some few Particulars. But we soon perceived these two were great Enemies to one another, and did not always agree in the same Story. We could make a Shift to gather out of one of them, that this Island was very much infested with a monstrous Kind of Animals, in the Shape of Men, called *Whigs*; and he often told us, that he hoped we should meet with none of them in our Way, for that if we did, they would be apt to knock us down for being Kings.

Our other Interpreter used to talk very much of a kind of Animal called a *Tory*, that was as great a Monster as the *Whig*, and would treat us as ill for being Foreigners. These two Creatures, it seems, are born with a secret Antipathy to one another, and engage when they meet as naturally as the Elephant and the Rhinoceros. But as we saw none of either of these Species, we are apt to think that our Guides deceived us with Misrepresentations and Fictions, and amused us with an Account of such Monsters as are not really in their Country.

These Particulars we made a Shift to pick out from the Discourse of our Interpreters; which we put together as well as we could, being able to understand but here and there a Word of what they said, and afterwards making up the meaning of it among ourselves. The Men of the Country are very cunning and ingenious in handicraft Works, but withal so very idle, that we often saw young lusty raw-boned Fellows carried up and down the Streets in little covered Rooms by a Couple of Porters, who are hired for that Service. Their Dress is likewise very barbarous, for they almost strangle themselves about the Neck, and bind their Bodies with many Ligatures, that we are apt to think are the Occasion of several Distempers among them which our Country is entirely free from. Instead of those beautiful Feathers with which we adorn our Heads, they often buy up a monstrous Bush of Hair, which covers their Heads, and falls down in a large Fleece below the Middle of their Backs; with which they walk up and down the Streets, and are as proud of it as if it was of their own Growth.

We were invited to one of their publick Diversions, where we hoped to have seen the great Men of their Country running down a Stag or pitching a Bar, that we might have discovered who were the Persons of the greatest Abilities among them; but instead of that they conveyed us into a huge Room lighted up with abundance of Candles, where this lazy People sate still above three Hours to see several Feats of Ingenuity performed by others, who it seems were paid for it.

As for the Women of the Country, not being able to talk with them, we could only make our Remarks upon them at a Distance. They let the Hair of their Heads grow to a great Length; but as the Men make a great Show with Heads of Hair that are none of their own, the Women, who they say have very fine Heads of Hair, tie it up in a Knot, and cover it from being seen. The Women look like Angels, and would be more beautiful than the Sun, were it not for little black Spots that are apt to break out in their Faces, and sometimes rise in very odd Figures. I have observed that those little Blemishes wear off very soon; but when they disappear in one Part of the Face, they are very apt to break out in another, insomuch that I have seen a Spot upon the Forehead in the Afternoon, which was upon the Chin in the Morning.'

The Author then proceeds to shew the Absurdity of Breeches and Petticoats, with many other curious Observations, which I shall reserve for another Occasion. I cannot however conclude this Paper without taking notice, That amidst these wild Remarks there now and then appears something very reasonable. I cannot likewise forbear observing, That we are all guilty in some measure of the same narrow way of Thinking, which we meet with in this Abstract of the *Indian* Journal when we fancy the Customs, Dresses, and Manners of other Countries are ridiculous and extravagant, if they do not resemble those of our own.   C

No. 51.

[STEELE.]   Saturday, April 28.

Torquet ab obscenis jam nunc sermonibus aurem.—Hor.

'Mr. SPECTATOR,

My Fortune, Quality, and Person are such, as render me as conspicuous as any young Woman in Town. It is in my Power to enjoy it in all its Vanities; but I have, from a very careful Education, contracted a great Aversion to the forward Air and Fashion which is practised in all Publick Places and Assemblies. I attribute this very much to the Stile and Manners of our Plays: I was last Night at the *Funeral*, where a Confident Lover in the Play, speaking of his Mistress, Cries out——*Oh that* Harriot! *To fold these Arms about the Waste of that beauteous, strugling, and at last yielding Fair!* Such an Image as this ought, by no means, to be presented to a Chaste and Regular Audience. I expect your Opinion of this Sentence, and recommend to your

Consideration, as a SPECTATOR, the Conduct of the Stage at present, with Relation to Chastity and Modesty.

I am, Sir,

Your Constant Reader,

and Well-wisher.'

The Complaint of this Young Lady is so just, that the Offence is gross enough to have displeased Persons who cannot pretend to that Delicacy and Modesty, of which she is Mistress. But there is a great deal to be said in Behalf of an Author: If the Audience would but consider the Difficulty of keeping up a sprightly Dialogue for five Acts together, they would allow a Writer, when he wants Wit, and can't please any otherwise, to help it out with a little Smuttiness. I will answer for the Poets, that no one ever writ Bawdry for any other Reason but Dearth of Invention. When the Author cannot strike out of himself any more of that which he has superior to those who make up the Bulk of his Audience, his natural Recourse is to that which he has in common with them; and a Description which gratifies a sensual Appetite will please, when the Author has nothing about him to delight a refined Imagination. It is to such a Poverty we must impute this and all other Sentences in Plays, which are of this Kind, and which are commonly termed Luscious Expressions.

This Expedient, to supply the Deficiencies of Wit, has been used, more or less, by most of the Authors who have succeeded on the Stage; tho' I know but one who has professedly writ a Play upon the Basis of the Desire of Multiplying our Species, and that is the Polite Sir *George Etherege*; if I understand what the Lady would be at, in the Play called *She would if she could.* Other Poets have, here and there, given an Intimation that there is this Design, under all the Disguises and Affectations which a Lady may put on; but no Author, except this, has made sure Work of it, and put the Imaginations of the Audience upon this one Purpose, from the Beginning to the End of the Comedy. It has always fared accordingly; for whether it be, that all who go to this Piece would if they could, or that the Innocents go to it, to guess only what *She would if she could*, the Play has always been well received.

It lifts an heavy, empty Sentence, when there is added to it a lascivious Gesture of Body; and when it is too low to be raised even by that, a flat Meaning is enlivened by making it a double one. Writers, who want *Genius*, never fail of keeping this Secret in reserve, to create a Laugh, or raise a Clap. I, who know nothing of Women but from seeing Plays, can give great guesses at the whole Structure of the fair Sex, by being innocently placed in the Pit, and insulted by the Petticoats of their Dancers; the Advantages of whose pretty Persons are a great help to a dull Play. When a Poet flags in writing Lusciously, a pretty Girl can move Lasciviously, and have the same good Consequence for the Author. Dull Poets in this Case use their Audiences, as dull Parasites do their Patrons; when they cannot longer divert them with their Wit or Humour, they bait their Ears with something which is agreeable to their Temper, though below their Understanding. *Apicius* cannot resist being pleased, if you give him an Account of a delicious Meal: or *Clodius*, if you describe a wanton Beauty: Tho' at the same time, if you do not awake those Inclinations in them, no Men are better Judges of what is just and delicate in Conversation. But, as I have before observed, it is easier to talk to the Man, than to the Man of Sense.

It is remarkable, that the writers of least Learning are best skill'd in the luscious Way. The Poetesses of the Age have done Wonders in this kind; and we are obliged to the Lady who writ *Ibrahim*, for introducing a preparatory Scene to the very Action, when the Emperor throws his Handkerchief as a Signal for his Mistress to follow him into the most retired Part of the Seraglio. It must be confessed his *Turkish* Majesty went off with a good Air, but, methought, we made but a sad Figure who waited without. This Ingenious Gentlewoman, in this piece of Bawdry, refined upon an Author of the same Sex, who, in the *Rover*, makes a Country Squire strip to his Holland Drawers. For *Blunt* is disappointed, and the Emperor is understood to go on to the utmost. The Pleasantry of Stripping almost Naked has been since practised (where indeed it should have begun) very successfully at *Bartholomew Fair*.

It is not here to be omitted, that in one of the abovementioned Female Compositions, the *Rover* is very frequently sent on the same Errand; as I take it, above once every Act. This is not wholly unnatural; for, they say, the Men-Authors draw themselves in their chief Characters, and the Women-Writers may be allowed the same Liberty. Thus, as the Male Wit gives his Hero a good Fortune, the Female gives her Heroin a good Gallant, at the End of the Play. But, indeed, there is hardly a Play one can go to, but the Hero or fine Gentleman of it struts off upon the same account, and leaves us to consider what good Office he has put us to, or to employ our selves as we please. To be plain, a Man who frequents Plays, would have a very respectful Notion of himself, were he to recollect how often he has been used as a Pimp to ravishing Tyrants, or successful Rakes. When the Actors make their

Exit on this good Occasion, the Ladies are sure to have an examining Glance from the Pit, to see how they relish what passes; and a few lewd Fools are very ready to employ their Talents upon the Composure or Freedom of their Looks. Such Incidents as these make some Ladies wholly absent themselves from the Play-house; and others never miss the first Day of a Play, lest it should prove too luscious to admit their going with any Countenance to it on the Second.

If Men of Wit, who think fit to write for the Stage, instead of this pitiful way of giving Delight, would turn their Thoughts upon raising it from good natural Impulses as are in the Audience, but are choaked up by Vice and Luxury, they would not only please, but befriend us at the same time. If a Man had a mind to be new in his way of Writing, might not he who is now represented as a fine Gentleman, tho' he betrays the Honour and Bed of his Neighbour and Friend, and lies with half the Women in the Play, and is at last rewarded with her of the best Character in it; I say, upon giving the Comedy another Cast, might not such a one divert the Audience quite as well, if at the Catastrophe he were found out for a Traytor, and met with Contempt accordingly? There is seldom a Person devoted to above one Darling Vice at a time, so that there is room enough to catch at Men's Hearts to their Good and Advantage, if the Poets will attempt it with the Honesty which becomes their Characters.

There is no Man who loves his Bottle or his Mistress, in a manner so very abandoned as not to be capable of relishing an agreeable Character, that is no way a Slave to either of those Pursuits. A Man that is Temperate, Generous, Valiant, Chaste, Faithful and Honest, may, at the same time, have Wit, Humour, Mirth, good Breeding, and Gallantry. While he exerts these latter Qualities, twenty Occasions might be invented to shew he is Master of the other noble Virtues. Such Characters would smite and reprove the Heart of a Man of Sense, when he is given up to his Pleasures. He would see he has been mistaken all this while, and be convinced that a sound Constitution and an innocent Mind are the true Ingredients for becoming and enjoying Life. All Men of true Taste would call a Man of Wit, who should turn his Ambition this way, a Friend and Benefactor to his Country; but I am at a loss what Name they would give him, who makes use of his Capacity for contrary Purposes. R

No. 52.

[STEELE.] Monday, April 30.

> *Omnes ut tecum meritis pro talibus annos*
> *Exigat, & pulchra faciat te prole parentem.*—Virg.

AN ingenious Correspondent, like a sprightly Wife, will always
have the last Word. I did not think my last Letter to the
deformed Fraternity would have occasioned any Answer,
especially since I had promised them so sudden a Visit: But
as they think they cannot shew too great a Veneration for my
Person, they have already sent me up an Answer. As to the
Proposal of a Marriage between my self and the matchless
Hecatissa, I have but one Objection to it; which is, That all the
Society will expect to be acquainted with her; and who can
be sure of keeping a Woman's Heart long, where she may have
so much Choice? I am the more alarmed at this, because the
Lady seems particularly smitten with Men of their Make.

I believe I shall set my Heart upon her; and think never the
worse of my Mistress for an Epigram a smart Fellow writ, as
he thought, against her; it does but the more recommend her
to me. At the same time I cannot but discover that his
Malice is stolen from *Martial*.

> *Tacta places, audita places, si non videare,*
> *Tota places: neutro, si videare, places.*

> *Whilst in the Dark on thy soft Hand I hung,*
> *And heard the tempting Syren in thy Tongue,*
> *What Flames, what Darts, what Anguish I endur'd?*
> *But when the Candle enter'd I was cur'd.*

'Your Letter to us we have received, as a signal Mark of
your Favour and brotherly Affection. We shall be heartily
glad to see your short Face in *Oxford*: And since the Wisdom
of our Legislature has been immortalized in your Speculations,
and our personal Deformities in some sort by you recorded to
all Posterity; we hold our selves in Gratitude bound to receive,
with the highest Respect, all such Persons as for their extraordinary Merit you shall think fit, from Time to Time, to
recommend unto the Board. As for the Pictish Damsel, we
have an easie Chair prepared at the upper End of the Table;
which we doubt not but she will grace with a very hideous
Aspect, and much better become the Seat in the native and
unaffected Uncomeliness of her Person, than with all the
superficial Airs of the Pencil, which (as you have very ingeniously observed) vanish with a Breath; and the most
innocent Adorer may deface the Shrine with a Salutation, and,

in the literal Sense of our Poets, snatch and imprint his balmy Kisses, and devour her melting Lips: In short, the only Faces of the Pictish Kind that will endure the Weather, must be of Dr. *Carbuncle's* Die; though his, in truth, has cost him a World the Painting; but then he boasts with *Zeuxis, In eternitatem pingo*; and oft jocosely tells the Fair Ones, Would they acquire Colours that would stand kissing, they must no longer Paint but Drink for a Complexion: A Maxim that in this our Age has been pursued with no ill Success; and has been as admirable in its Effects, as the famous Cosmetick mentioned in the *Post-Man*, and invented by the renowned *British Hippocrates* of the Pestle and Mortar; making the Party, after a due Course, rosie, hale, and airy; and the best and most approved Receipt now extant for the Fever of the Spirits. But to return to our female Candidate, who, I understand, is returned to her self, and will no longer hang out false Colours; as she is the first of her Sex that has done us so great an Honour, she will certainly, in a very short time, both in Prose and Verse, be a Lady of the most celebrated Deformity now living; and meet with Admirers here as frightful as her self. But being a long-headed Gentlewoman, I am apt to imagine she has some further Design than you have yet penetrated; and perhaps has more Mind to the SPECTATOR than any of his Fraternity, as the Person of all the World she could like for a Paramour: And if so, really I cannot but applaud her Choice; and should be glad, if it might lie in my Power, to effect an amicable Accommodation betwixt two Faces of such different Extremes, as the only possible Expedient, to mend the Breed, and rectifie the Physiognomy of the Family on both Sides. And again, as she is a Lady of a very fluent Elocution, you need not fear that your first Child will be born dumb, which otherwise you might have some Reason to be apprehensive of. To be plain with you, I can see nothing shocking in it; for though she has not a Face like a *John-Apple*, yet as a late Friend of mine, who at Sixty five ventured on a Lass of Fifteen, very frequently, in the remaining Five Years of his Life, gave me to understand, That, as old as he then seemed, when they were first married he and his Spouse could make but Fourscore; so may Madam *Hecatissa* very justly alledge hereafter, That, as long visaged as she may then be thought, upon their Wedding-day Mr. SPECTATOR and she had but Half an Ell of Face betwixt them: And this my very worthy Predecessor, Mr. Sergeant *Chin*, always maintained to be no more than the true oval Proportion between Man and Wife. But as this may be a new thing to you, who have hitherto had no Expectations from Women, I shall allow you what Time you think fit to consider on it; not without some Hope of seeing at last your Thoughts hereupon subjoined to mine, and which is an Honour much desired by,

Sir,

Your assured Friend,

and most humble Servant,

Hugh Goblin, Praeses.'

The following Letter has not much in it, but as it is written in my own Praise I cannot from my Heart suppress it.

'*Sir,*

You proposed in your SPECTATOR of last *Tuesday* Mr. *Hobbs*'s Hypothesis, for solving that very odd Phaenomenon of Laughter. You have made the Hypothesis valuable by espousing it your self; for had it continued Mr. *Hobbs*'s, no Body would have minded it. Now here this perplexed Case arises. A certain Company laughed very heartily upon the Reading of that very Paper of yours: And the Truth on it is, he must be a Man of more than ordinary Constancy that could stand it out against so much Comedy, and not do as we did. Now there are few Men in the World so far lost to all good Sense, as to look upon you to be a Man in a State of Folly *inferior to himself*. Pray then, how do you justify your Hypothesis of Laughter?

Thursday, *the 26th of*   *Your most humble,*

    the Month of Fools.   Q. R.'

'*Sir,*

In answer to your Letter, I must desire you to recollect your self; and you will find, that when you did me the Honour to be so merry over my Paper, you laughed at the Idiot, the *German* Courtier, the Gaper, the Merry-Andrew, the Haberdasher, the Biter, the Butt, and not at

Your humble Servant,

The SPECTATOR.'

No. 53.

[STEELE.]   Tuesday, May 1.

. . . *Quandoque bonus dormitat Homerus.*—Hor.

MY Correspondents grow so numerous, that I cannot avoid frequently inserting their Applications to me.

'*Mr.* SPECTATOR,

I am glad I can inform you, that your Endeavours to adorn that Sex, which is the fairest Part of the visible Creation, are well received, and like to prove not unsuccessful. The Triumph of *Daphne* over her Sister *Letitia* has been the Subject

I—*F   164

of Conversation at several Tea-Tables where I have been present; and I have observed the fair Circle not a little pleased to find you considering them as reasonable Creatures, and endeavouring to banish that *Mahometan* Custom, which had too much prevailed even in this Island, of treating Women as if they had no Souls. I must do them the Justice to say, that there seems to be nothing wanting to the finishing of these lovely Pieces of human Nature, besides the turning and applying their Ambition properly, and the keeping them up to a Sense of what is their true Merit. *Epictetus*, that plain honest Philosopher, as little as he had of Gallantry, appears to have understood them, as well as the polite *St. Evremont*, and has hit this Point very luckily. *When Young Women*, says he, *arrive at a certain Age, they hear themselves called* Mistresses, *and are made to believe that their only Business is to please the Men; they immediately begin to Dress, and place all their Hopes in the adorning of their Persons; it is therefore,* continues he, *worth the while to endeavour by all Means to make them sensible, that the Honour paid to them is only upon Account of their conducting themselves with Virtue, Modesty, and Discretion.*

Now to pursue the Matter yet further, and to render your Cares for the Improvement of the Fair Ones more effectual, I would propose a new Method, like those Applications which are said to convey their Virtue by Sympathy; and that is, that in order to embellish the Mistress, you should give a new Education to the Lover, and teach the Men not to be any longer dazled by false Charms and unreal Beauty. I cannot but think that if our Sex knew always how to place their Esteem justly, the other would not be so often wanting to themselves in deserving it. For as the being enamoured with a Woman of Sense and Virtue is an Improvement to a Man's Understanding and Morals, and the Passion is ennobled by the Object which inspires it; so on the other side, the appearing amiable to a Man of a wise and elegant Mind, carries in it self no small Degree of Merit and Accomplishment. I conclude therefore, that one way to make the Women yet more agreeable is, to make the Men more virtuous.

I am, Sir,

Your most Humble Servant,

R. B.'

'*Sir,* *April* 26.

Yours of *Saturday* last I read, not without some Resentment; but I will suppose when you say you expect an Inundation of Ribbons and Brocades, and to see many new Vanities which the Women will fall into upon a Peace with *France*, that you intend only the unthinking Part of our Sex; And what Methods can reduce them to Reason is hard to imagine.

But, Sir, there are others yet that your Instructions might be of great Use to, who, after their best Endeavours, are sometimes at a Loss to acquit themselves to a Censorious World: I am far from thinking you can altogether disapprove of Conversation between Ladies and Gentlemen, regulated by the Rules of Honour and Prudence; and have thought it an Observation not ill made, that where that was wholly denied, the Women lost their Wit, and the Men their good Manners. 'Tis sure, from those improper Liberties you mentioned, that a sort of undistinguishing People shall banish from their Drawing-Rooms the best bred Men in the World, and condemn those that do not. Your stating this Point might, I think, be of good use, as well as much oblige,

Sir,

Your Admirer, and

Most Humble Servant,

ANNA BELLA.'

No Answer to this, 'till Anna Bella *sends a Description of those she calls the Best bred Men in the World.*

'*Mr.* SPECTATOR,

I am a Gentleman who for many Years last past have been well known to be truly Splenatick, and that my Spleen arises from having contracted so great a Delicacy, by reading the best Authors, and keeping the most refined Company, that I cannot bear the least Impropriety of Language, or Rusticity of Behaviour. Now, Sir, I have ever looked upon this as a wise Distemper; but by late Observations find that every heavy Wretch, who has nothing to say, excuses his Dulness by complaining of the Spleen. Nay, I saw, the other Day, two Fellows in a Tavern Kitchen set up for it, call for a Pint and Pipes, and only by Guzling Liquor to each other's Health, and wasting Smoak in each other's Face, pretend to throw off the Spleen. I appeal to you, whether these Dishonours are to be done to the Distemper of the Great and the Polite. I beseech you, Sir, to inform these Fellows that they have not the Spleen, because they cannot talk without the help of a Glass at their Mouths, or convey their Meaning to each other without the Interposition of Clouds. If you will not do this with all speed, I assure you, for my part, I will wholly quit the Disease, and for the future be merry with the Vulgar.

Sir,

Your Humble Servant.'

'*Sir,*

This is to let you understand, that I am a reformed Starer, and conceived a Detestation for that Practice from what you have writ upon the Subject.   But as you have been very severe upon the Behaviour of us Men at Divine Service, I hope you will not be so apparently partial to the Women, as to let them go wholly unobserved.   If they do every thing that is possible to attract our Eyes, are we more culpable than they, for looking at them?   I happened last *Sunday* to be shut into a Pew, which was full of young Ladies in the Bloom of Youth and Beauty.   When the Service began, I had not Room to kneel at the Confession, but as I stood kept my Eyes from wandring as well as I was able, till one of the young Ladies, who is a Peeper, resolved to bring down my Looks, and fix my Devotion on her self.   You are to know, Sir, that a Peeper works with her Hands, Eyes, and Fan; one of which is continually in motion, while she thinks she is not actually the Admiration of some Ogler or Starer in the Congregation.   As I stood utterly at a loss how to behave my self, surrounded as I was, this Peeper so placed herself as to be kneeling just before me.   She displayed the most beautiful Bosom imaginable, which heaved and fell with some Fervour, while a delicate well-shaped Arm held a Fan over her Face.   It was not in Nature to command one's Eyes from this Object.   I could not avoid taking notice also of her Fan, which had on it various Figures, very improper to behold on that occasion.   There lay in the Body of the Piece a *Venus,* under a Purple Canopy furled with curious Wreaths of Drapery, half naked, attended with a Train of *Cupids,* who were busied in Fanning her as she slept.   Behind her was drawn a Satyr peeping over the silken Fence, and threatening to break through it.   I frequently offered to turn my Sight another way, but was still detained by the Fascination of the Peeper's Eyes, who had long practised a Skill in them, to recal the parting Glances of her Beholders. You see my Complaint, and hope you will take these mischievous People, the Peepers, into your Consideration: I doubt not but you will think a Peeper as much more pernicious than a Starer, as an Ambuscade is more to be feared than an open Assault.

I am, Sir,

Your most Obedient Servant.'

This Peeper using both Fan and Eyes to be considered as a Pict, *and proceed accordingly.*

'*King* Latinus *to the* Spectator, *Greeting.*

Though some may think we descend from our Imperial

Dignity, in holding Correspondence with a private *Litterato*; yet as we have great Respect to all good Intentions for our Service, we do not esteem it beneath us to return you our Royal Thanks for what you published in our Behalf, while under Confinement in the inchanted Castle of the *Savoy*, and for your Mention of a Subsidy for a Prince in Misfortune. This your timely Zeal has inclined the Hearts of divers to be aiding unto us, if we could propose the Means. We have taken their Good-will into Consideration, and have contrived a Method which will be easie to those who shall give the Aid, and not unacceptable to us who receive it. A Consort of Musick shall be prepared at *Haberdashers-Hall* for *Wednesday* the Second of *May*, and we will honour the said Entertainment with our own Presence, where each Person shall be assessed but at two Shillings and six Pence. What we expect from you is, that you publish these our Royal Intentions, with Injunction that they be read at all Tea-Tables within the Cities of *London* and *Westminster*; and so we bid you heartily Farewel.

Latinus, *King of the* Volscians.

Given at our Court in Vinegar-Yard, *Story the Third from the Earth.* April 28, 1711.' R

No. 54.
[STEELE.] Wednesday, May 2.

Strenua nos exercet inertia.—Hor.

THE following Letter being the first that I have received from the learned University of *Cambridge*, I could not but do my self the Honour of publishing it. It gives an Account of a new Sect of Philosophers which has arose in that famous Residence of Learning; and is, perhaps, the only Sect this Age is likely to produce.

'*Mr.* SPECTATOR, *Cambridge, April* 26.
Believing you to be an universal Encourager of liberal Arts and Sciences, and glad of any Information from the learned World, I thought an Account of a Sect of Philosophers very frequent among us, but not taken notice of, as far as I can remember, by any Writers either ancient or modern, would not be unacceptable to you. The Philosophers of this Sect are, in the Language of our University called *Lowngers*. I am of Opinion, that, as in many other things, so likewise in this, the Ancients have been defective; *viz.* in mentioning no Philosophers of this sort. Some indeed will affirm that they are a kind

of Peripateticks, because we see them continually walking about. But I would have these Gentlemen consider, that tho' the ancient Peripateticks walked much, yet they wrote much also; (witness, to the Sorrow of this Sect, *Aristotle* and others): Whereas it is notorious that most of our Professors never lay out a Farthing either in Pen, Ink, or Paper. Others are for deriving them from *Diogenes*, because several of the leading Men of the Sect have a great deal of the Cynical Humour in them, and delight much in Sun-shine. But then again, *Diogenes* was content to have his constant Habitation in a narrow Tub, whilst our Philosophers are so far from being of his Opinion, that it 's Death to them to be confined within the Limits of a good handsome convenient Chamber but for half an Hour. Others there are, who from the Clearness of their Heads deduce the Pedigree of *Lowngers* from that great Man (I think it was either *Plato* or *Socrates*) who after all his Study and Learning professed, That all he then knew was, that he knew nothing. You easily see this is but a shallow Argument, and may be soon confuted.

I have with great Pains and Industry made my Observations, from time to time, upon these Sages; and having now all Materials ready, am compiling a Treatise, wherein I shall set forth the Rise and Progress of this famous Sect, together with their Maxims, Austerities, Manner of living, &c. Having prevailed with a Friend who designs shortly to publish a new Edition of *Diogenes Laertius*, to add this Treatise of mine by way of Supplement; I shall now, to let the World see what may be expected from me (first begging Mr. SPECTATOR'S Leave that the World may see it) briefly touch upon some of my chief Observations, and then subscribe my self your humble Servant. In the first Place I shall give you two or three of their Maxims: The fundamental one, upon which their whole System is built, is this, *viz.* That Time being an implacable Enemy to and Destroyer of all things, ought to be paid in his own Coin, and be destroyed and murdered without Mercy, by all the Ways that can be invented. Another favourite Saying of theirs is, That Business was designed only for Knaves, and Study for Blockheads. A Third seems to be a ludicrous one, but has a great Effect upon their Lives; and is this, That the Devil is at home. Now for their Manner of Living: And here I have a large Field to expatiate in; but I shall reserve Particulars for my intended Discourse, and now only mention one or two of their principal Exercises. The elder Proficients employ themselves in inspecting *mores hominum multorum*, in getting acquainted with all the Signs and Windows in the Town. Some are arrived to so great

Knowledge, that they can tell every time any Butcher kills a Calf, every time an old Woman's Cat is in the Straw; and a thousand other Matters as important. One ancient Philosopher contemplates two or three Hours every Day over a Sun-Dial; and is true to the Dial,

> *. . . As the Dial to the Sun,*
> *Although it be not shone upon.*

Our younger Students are content to carry their Speculations as yet no farther than Bowling-Greens, Billiard-Tables, and such like Places. This may serve for a Sketch of my Design; in which I hope I shall have your Encouragement.

> *I am, Sir,*
> *Yours.'*

I must be so just as to observe I have formerly seen of this Sect at our other University; tho' not distinguished by the Appellation which the learned Historian, my Correspondent, reports they bear at *Cambridge.* They were ever looked upon as a People that impaired themselves more by their strict Application to the Rules of their Order, than any other Students whatever. Others seldom hurt themselves any further than to gain weak Eyes and sometimes Head-aches; but these Philosophers are seized all over with a general Inability, Indolence, and Weariness, and a certain Impatience of the Place they are in, with an Heaviness in removing to another.

The *Lowngers* are satisfied with being merely Part of the Number of Mankind, without distinguishing themselves from amongst them. They may be said rather to suffer their Time to pass, than to spend it, without Regard to the past, or Prospect of the future. All they know of Life is only the present Instant, and do not taste even that. When one of this Order happens to be a Man of Fortune, the Expence of his Time is transferred to his Coach and Horses, and his Life is to be measured by their Motion, not his own Enjoyments or Sufferings. The chief Entertainment one of these Philosophers can possibly propose to himself, is to get a Relish of Dress: This, methinks, might diversifie the Person he is weary of (his own dear self) to himself. I have known these two Amusements make one of these Philosophers make a tolerable Figure in the World; with Variety of Dresses in publick Assemblies in Town, and quick Motion of his Horses out of it, now to *Bath,* now to *Tunbridge,* then to *New-Market,* and then to *London,* he has in Process of time brought it to pass, that his Coach and his Horses have been mentioned in all those Places. When the

Lowngers leave an Academick Life, and instead of this more elegant way of appearing in the polite World, retire to the Seats of their Ancestors, they usually join a Pack of Dogs, and employ their Days in defending their Poultry from Foxes: I do not know any other Method that any of this Order has ever taken to make a Noise in the World; but I shall enquire into such about this Town as have arrived at the Dignity of being *Lowngers* by the Force of natural Parts, without having ever seen an University; and send my Correspondent, for the Embellishment of his Book, the Names and History of those who pass their Lives without any Incidents at all; and how they shift Coffee-houses and Chocolate-houses from Hour to Hour, to get over the insupportable Labour of doing nothing.

R

No. 55.
[ADDISON.]   Thursday, May 3.

> . . . *Intus & in jecore aegro*
> *Nascuntur domini* . . .—Pers.

Most of the Trades, Professions, and Ways of Living among Mankind, take their Original either from the Love of Pleasure, or the Fear of Want.   The former, when it becomes too violent, degenerates into *Luxury*, and the latter into *Avarice*.   As these two Principles of Action draw different Ways, *Persius* has given us a very humorous Account of a young Fellow who was rouzed out of his Bed, in order to be sent upon a long Voyage by *Avarice*, and afterwards over-persuaded and kept at Home by *Luxury*.   I shall set down at length the Pleadings of these two imaginary Persons, as they are in the Original, with Mr. Dryden's Translation of them.

> *Mane, piger, stertis.   Surge, inquit Avaritia; eja*
> *Surge.   Negas.   Instat; surge inquit.   Non queo.   Surge*
> *Et quid agam?   Rogitas?   Saperdas advehe Ponto,*
> *Castoreum, stuppas, hebenum, thus, lubrica Coa.*
> *Tolle recens primus piper e sitiente camelo.*
> *Verte aliquid; jura.   Sed Jupiter audiet.   Eheu!*
> *Baro, regustatum digito terebrare salinum*
> *Contentus perages, si vivere cum Jove tendis.*
> *Jam pueris pellem succinctus & oenophorum aptas;*
> *Ocyus ad navem.   Nil obstat, quin trabe vasta*
> *Aegaeum rapias, nisi solers Luxuria ante*
> *Seductum moneat; Quo deinde, insane, ruis?   Quo?*
> *Quid tibi vis?   Calido sub pectore mascula bilis*
> *Intumuit, quam non extinxerit urna cicutae.*

Tun' mare transilias?   Tibi torta cannabe fulto
Coena sit in transtro?   Veientanumque rubellum
Exhalet vapida laesum pice sessilis obba?
Quid petis?   Ut nummi, quos hic quincunce modesto
Nutrieras, pergant avidos sudare deunces?
Indulge genio; carpamus dulcia; nostrum est
Quod vivis; cinis, & manes, & fabula fles.
Vine memor lethi: fugit hora.   Hoc quod loquor, inde est
En quid agis?   Duplici in diversum scinderis hamo.
Huncine, an hunc sequeris? . . .

  Whether alone, or in thy Harlot's Lap,
When thou would'st take a lazy Morning's Nap,
Up, Up, says *AVARICE*; thou snor'st again,
Stretchest thy Limbs, and yawn'st, but all in vain.
The rugged Tyrant no Denial takes;
At his Command th' unwilling Sluggard wakes.
What must I do? he cries; What? says his Lord:
Why rise, make ready, and go straight Aboard:
With Fish, from *Euxine* Seas, thy Vessel freight;
Flax, Castor, *Coan* Wines, the precious Weight
Of Pepper, and *Sabean* Incense, take
With thy own Hands, from the tir'd Camel's Back,   }
And with Poste-haste thy running Markets make.   }
Be sure to turn the Penny; Lye and Swear,
'Tis wholsom Sin: But *Jove*, thou say'st, will hear.
Swear, Fool, or Starve; for the *Dilemma*'s even:
A Tradesman thou! and hope to go to Heav'n?

  Resolv'd for Sea, the Slaves thy Baggage pack,
Each saddled with his Burden on his Back:
Nothing retards thy Voyage, now; but He,
That soft voluptuous Prince, call'd *LUXURY*;
And he may ask this civil Question; Friend,
What dost thou make a Shipboard? To what end?
Art thou of *Bethlem*'s noble College free?
Stark, staring mad, that thou would'st tempt the Sea?
Cubb'd in a Cabbin, on a Mattress laid,
On a brown *George*, with lowsie Swobbers fed,
Dead Wine that stinks of the *Borachio*, sup
From a foul Jack, or greasie Maple Cup?
Say, would'st thou bear all this, to raise thy Store,
From Six i' th' Hundred, to Six Hundred more?
Indulge, and to thy Genius freely give:
For, not to live at Ease, is not to live:
Death stalks behind thee, and each flying Hour
Does some loose Remnant of thy Life devour.
Live, while thou liv'st; for Death will make us all
A Name, a Nothing but an Old Wife's Tale.
  Speak; wilt thou *Avarice* or *Pleasure* chuse
To be thy Lord?   Take one, and one refuse.

When a Government flourishes in Conquests, and is secure from Foreign Attacks, it naturally falls into all the Pleasures of Luxury; and as these Pleasures are very expensive, they put those who are addicted to them upon raising fresh Supplies of Mony, by all the Methods of Rapaciousness and Corruption; so that Avarice and Luxury very often become one complicated Principle of Action, in those whose Hearts are wholly set upon Ease, Magnificence, and Pleasure. The most Elegant and Correct of all the *Latin* Historians observes, that in his time, when the most formidable States of the World were subdued by the *Romans*, the Republick sunk into those two Vices of a quite different Nature, Luxury and Avarice: And accordingly describes *Catiline* as one who coveted the Wealth of other Men, at the same time that he squandred away his own. This Observation on the Commonwealth, when it was in its height of Power and Riches, holds good of all Governments that are settled in a State of Ease and Prosperity. At such times Men naturally endeavour to outshine one another in Pomp and Splendor, and having no Fears to alarm them from Abroad, indulge themselves in the Enjoyment of all the Pleasures they can get into their Possession; which naturally produces Avarice, and an immoderate Pursuit after Wealth and Riches.

As I was humouring my self in the Speculation of these two great Principles of Action, I could not forbear throwing my Thoughts into a little kind of Allegory or Fable, with which I shall here present my Reader.

There were two very powerful Tyrants engaged in a perpetual War against each other: The Name of the first was *Luxury*, and of the second *Avarice*. The Aim of each of them was no less than Universal Monarchy over the Hearts of Mankind. *Luxury* had many Generals under him, who did him great Service, as *Pleasure, Mirth, Pomp*, and *Fashion*. *Avarice* was likewise very strong in his Officers, being faithfully served by *Hunger, Industry, Care* and *Watchfulness*: He had likewise a Privy-Counsellor who was always at his Elbow, and whispering something or other in his Ear: the Name of this Privy-Counsellor was *Poverty*. As *Avarice* conducted himself by the Counsels of *Poverty*, his Antagonist was entirely guided by the Dictates and Advice of *Plenty*, who was his first Counsellor and Minister of State, that concerted all his Measures for him, and never departed out of his Sight. While these two great Rivals were thus contending for Empire, their Conquests were very various. *Luxury* got Possession of one Heart, and *Avarice* of another. The Father of a Family would often range himself under the Banners of *Avarice*, and the Son under those of *Luxury*. The Wife and Husband would often declare themselves on the two different Parties; nay, the same Person would very often side with one in his Youth, and revolt to the other in his old Age.   Indeed the wise Men of the World stood *Neuter*; but alas! their Numbers were not considerable.   At length, when these two Potentates had wearied themselves with waging War upon one another, they agreed upon an Interview, at which neither of their Counsellors were to be present.   It is said that *Luxury* began the Parly, and after having represented the endless State of War in which they were engaged, told his Enemy, with a Frankness of Heart which is natural to him, that he believed these two should be very good Friends, were it not for the Instigations of *Poverty*, that pernicious Counsellor, who made an ill use of his Ear, and filled him with ground-less Apprehensions and Prejudices.   To this *Avarice* replied, that he looked upon *Plenty* (the first Minister of his Antagonist) to be a much more destructive Counsellor than *Poverty*, for that he was perpetually suggesting Pleasures, banishing all the necessary Cautions against Want, and consequently under-mining those Principles on which the Government of *Avarice* was founded.   At last, in order to an Accommodation, they agreed upon this Preliminary; That each of them should immediately dismiss his Privy-Counsellor.   When things were thus far adjusted towards a Peace, all other Differences were soon accommodated, insomuch that for the future they resolved to live as good Friends and Confederates, and to share between them whatever Conquests were made on either side.   For this Reason, we now find *Luxury* and *Avarice* taking Possession of the same Heart, and dividing the same Person between them. To which I shall only add, that since the discarding of the Counsellors above-mentioned, *Avarice* supplies *Luxury* in the room of *Plenty*, as *Luxury* prompts *Avarice* in the place of *Poverty*.   C

No. 56.
[ADDISON.]   Friday, May 4.

*Felices errore suo . . .—*Lucan.

THE *Americans* believe that all Creatures have Souls, not only Men and Women, but Brutes, Vegetables, nay even the most inanimate things, as Stocks and Stones.   They believe the same of all the Works of Art, as of Knives, Boats, Looking-glasses: And that as any of these Things perish, their Souls go into another World, which is inhabited by the Ghosts of Men and Women.   For this Reason they always place by the Corpse of their dead Friend a Bow and Arrows, that he may make use of the Souls of them in the other World, as he did of their wooden Bodies in this. How absurd soever such an Opinion as this may appear, our *European* Philosophers have maintained several Notions altogether as improbable. Some of *Plato's* Followers in particular, when they talk of the World of Ideas, entertain us with Substances and Beings no less extravagant and chymerical. Many *Aristotelians* have likewise spoken as unintelligibly of their substantial Forms. I shall only instance *Albertus Magnus*, who in his Dissertation upon the Load-stone observing that Fire will destroy its Magnetick Virtues, tells us that he took particular Notice of one as it lay glowing amidst an Heap of burning Coals, and that he perceived a certain blue Vapour to arise from it, which he believed might be the *substantial Form*, that is, in our *West-Indian* Phrase, the *Soul* of the Load-stone.

There is a Tradition among the *Americans*, that one of their Countrymen descended in a Vision to the great Repository of Souls, or, as we call it here, to the other World; and that upon his Return he gave his Friends a distinct Account of every thing he saw among those Regions of the Dead. A Friend of mine, whom I have formerly mentioned, prevailed upon one of the Interpreters of the *Indian* Kings to enquire of them, if possible, what Tradition they have among them of this Matter: Which, as well as he could learn by those many Questions which he asked them at several Times, was in Substance as follows.

The Visionary, whose Name was *Marraton*, after having travelled for a long Space under an hollow Mountain, arrived at length on the Confines of this World of Spirits, but could not enter it by reason of a thick Forest made up of Bushes, Brambles, and pointed Thorns, so perplexed and interwoven with one another that it was impossible to find a Passage through it. Whilst he was looking about for some Track or Pathway that might be worn in any Part of it, he saw an huge Lion crouched under the Side of it, who kept his Eye upon him in the same Posture as when he watches for his Prey. The *Indian* started back, whilst the Lion rose with a Spring, and leaped towards him. Being wholly destitute of all other Weapons, he stooped down to take up an huge Stone in his Hand; but to his infinite Surprize grasped nothing, and found the supposed Stone to be only the Apparition of one. If he was disappointed on this Side, he was as much pleased on the other, when he found the Lion, which had seized on his left Shoulder, had no Power to hurt him, and was only the Ghost of that ravenous Creature which it appeared to be. He no sooner got rid of his impotent Enemy, but he marched up to the

Wood, and after having surveyed it for some time, endeavoured to press into one Part of it that was a little thinner than the rest; when again, to his great Surprize, he found the Bushes made no Resistance, but that he walked through Briars and Brambles with the same Ease as through the open Air; and, in short, that the whole Wood was nothing else but a Wood of Shades. He immediately concluded, that this huge Thicket of Thorns and Brakes was designed as a kind of Fence or quick-set Hedge to the Ghosts it inclosed; and that probably their soft Substances might be torn by these subtle Points and Prickles, which were too weak to make any Impressions in Flesh and Blood. With this Thought he resolved to travel through this intricate Wood; when by degrees he felt a Gale of Perfumes breathing upon him, that grew stronger and sweeter in proportion as he advanced. He had not proceeded much further when he observed the Thorns and Briars to end, and give Place to a thousand beautiful green Trees covered with Blossoms of the finest Scents and Colours, that formed a Wilderness of Sweets, and were a kind of Lining to those ragged Scenes which he had before passed through. As he was coming out of this delightful Part of the Wood, and entering upon the Plains it inclosed, he saw several Horsemen rushing by him, and a little while after heard the Cry of a Pack of Dogs. He had not listened long before he saw the Apparition of a milk-white Steed, with a young Man on the Back of it, advancing upon full Stretch after the Souls of about an hundred Beagles that were hunting down the Ghost of an Hare, which ran away before them with an unspeakable Swiftness. As the Man on the milk-white Steed came by him, he looked upon him very attentively, and found him to be the young Prince *Nicharagua*, who died about half a Year before, and by reason of his great Virtues, was at that time lamented over all the Western Parts of *America*.

He had no sooner got out of the Wood, but he was entertained with such a Landskip of flowry Plains, green Meadows, running Streams, sunny Hills, and shady Vales, as were not to be represented by his own Expressions, nor, as he said, by the Conceptions of others. This happy Region was peopled with innumerable Swarms of Spirits, who applied themselves to Exercises and Diversions according as their Fancies led them. Some of them were tossing the Figure of a Coit; others were pitching the Shadow of a Bar; others were breaking the Apparition of a Horse; and Multitudes employing themselves upon ingenious Handicrafts with the Souls of *departed Utensils*; for that is the Name which in the *Indian* Language they give their Tools when they are burnt or broken. As he travelled thro' this delightful Scene, he was very often tempted to pluck the Flowers that rose every where about him in the greatest Variety and Profusion, having never seen several of them in his own Country. But he quickly found that though they were Objects of his Sight, they were not liable to his Touch. He at length came to the Side of a great River, and being a good Fisherman himself, stood upon the Banks of it some time to look upon an Angler that had taken a great many Shapes of Fishes, which lay flouncing up and down by him.

I should have told my Reader, that this *Indian* had been formerly married to one of the greatest Beauties of his Country, by whom he had several Children. This Couple were so famous for their Love and Constancy to one another, that the *Indians* to this Day, when they give a married Man Joy of his Wife, wish that they may live together like *Marraton* and *Yaratilda*. *Marraton* had not stood long by the Fisherman when he saw the Shadow of his beloved *Yaratilda*, who had for some time fixed her Eye upon him, before he discovered her. Her Arms were stretched out towards him, Floods of Tears ran down her Eyes; her Looks, her Hands, her Voice called him over to her; and at the same time seemed to tell him that the River was unpassable. Who can describe the Passion made up of Joy, Sorrow, Love, Desire, Astonishment, that rose in the *Indian* upon the Sight of his dear *Yaratilda*? He could express it by nothing but his Tears, which ran like a River down his Cheeks as he looked upon her. He had not stood in this Posture long, before he plunged into the Stream that lay before him; and finding it to be nothing but the Phantom of a River, walked on the Bottom of it till he arose on the other Side. At his Approach *Yaratilda* flew into his Arms, whilst *Marraton* wished himself disencumbered of that Body which kept her from his Embraces. After many Questions and Endearments on both Sides, she conducted him to a Bower which she had dressed with her own Hands, with all the Ornaments that could be met with in those blooming Regions. She had made it gay beyond Imagination, and was every Day adding something new to it. As *Marraton* stood astonished at the unspeakable Beauty of her Habitation, and ravished with the Fragrancy that came from every Part of it, *Yaratilda* told him that she was preparing this Bower for his Reception, as well knowing that his Piety to his God, and his faithful Dealing towards Men, would certainly bring him to that happy Place, whenever his Life should be at an End. She then brought two of her Children to him, who died some Years before, and resided with her in the same delightful Bower; advising him to breed up those others which were still with him in such a manner, that they might hereafter all of them meet together in this happy Place.

The Tradition tells us further, that he had afterwards a Sight of those dismal Habitations which are the Portion of ill Men after Death; and mentions several Molten Seas of Gold, in which were plunged the Souls of barbarous *Europeans*, who put to the Sword so many Thousands of poor *Indians* for the sake of that precious Metal: But having already touched upon the chief Points of this Tradition, and exceeded the Measure of my Paper, I shall not give any further Account of it.   C

No. 57.
[ADDISON.]   Saturday, May 5.

> *Quem praestare potest mulier galeata pudorem,*
> *Quae fugit a sexu? . . .* —Juv.

WHEN the Wife of *Hector*, in *Homer's Iliads*, discourses with her Husband about the Battel in which he was going to engage, the Hero, desiring her to leave that Matter to his Care, bids her go to her Maids and mind her Spinning: By which the Poet intimates, that Men and Women ought to busie themselves in their proper Spheres, and on such Matters only as are suitable to their respective Sex.

I am at this time acquainted with a young Gentleman, who has passed a great Part of his Life in the Nursery, and, upon Occasion, can make a Caudle or a Sack Posset better than any Man in *England*. He is likewise a wonderful Critick in Cambrick and Muslins, and will talk an Hour together upon a Sweet-meat. He entertains his Mother every Night with Observations that he makes both in Town and Court: As what Lady shows the nicest Fancy in her Dress; what Man of Quality wears the fairest Wig; who has the finest Linnen, who the prettiest Snuff-box, with many other the like curious Remarks that may be made in good Company.

On the other hand I have very frequently the Opportunity of seeing a Rural *Andromache*, who came up to Town last Winter, and is one of the greatest Fox Hunters in the Country. She talks of Hounds and Horses, and makes nothing of leaping over a Six-bar Gate. If a Man tells her a waggish Story, she gives him a Push with her Hand in jest, and calls him an impudent Dog; and if her Servant neglects his Business, threatens to kick him out of the House. I have heard her, in her Wrath, call a Substantial Trades-man a Lousie Cur; and remember one Day, when she could not think of the Name of a

Person, she described him, in a large Company of Men and Ladies, by the Fellow with the Broad Shoulders.

If those Speeches and Actions, which in their own Nature are indifferent, appear ridiculous when they proceed from a wrong Sex, the Faults and Imperfections of one Sex transplanted into another, appear black and monstrous. As for the Men, I shall not in this Paper any further concern my self about them; but as I would fain contribute to make Woman-kind, which is the most beautiful Part of the Creation, entirely amiable, and wear out all those little Spots and Blemishes that are apt to rise among the Charms which Nature has poured out upon them, I shall dedicate this Paper to their Service. The Spot which I would here endeavour to clear them of, is that Party-Rage which of late Years is very much crept into their Conversation. This is, in its Nature, a Male Vice, and made up of many angry and cruel Passions that are altogether repugnant to the Softness, the Modesty, and those other endearing Qualities which are natural to the Fair Sex. Women were formed to temper Mankind, and sooth them into Tenderness and Compassion; not to set an Edge upon their Minds, and blow up in them those Passions which are too apt to rise of their own Accord. When I have seen a pretty Mouth uttering Calumnies and Invectives, what would I not have given to have stopt it? How have I been troubled to see some of the finest Features in the World grow pale, and tremble with Party-Rage? *Camilla* is one of the greatest Beauties in the *British* Nation, and yet values her self more upon being the *Virago* of one Party, than upon being the Toast of both. The Dear Creature, about a Week ago, encountred the fierce and beautiful *Penthesilea* across a Tea-Table; but in the height of her Anger, as her Hand chanced to shake with the Earnestness of the Dispute, she scalded her Fingers, and spilt a Dish of Tea upon her Petticoat. Had not this Accident broke off the Debate, no Body knows where it would have ended.

There is one Consideration which I would earnestly recommend to all my Female Readers, and which, I hope, will have some weight with them. In short, it is this, that there is nothing so bad for the Face as Party-Zeal. It gives an ill-natured Cast to the Eye, and a disagreeable Sourness to the Look; besides, that it makes the Lines too strong, and flushes them worse than Brandy. I have seen a Woman's Face break out in Heats, as she has been talking against a great Lord, whom she had never seen in her Life; and indeed never knew a Party-Woman that kept her Beauty for a Twelve-month. I would therefore advise all my Female Readers, as they value their Complexions, to let alone all Disputes of this Nature;

though, at the same time, I would give free Liberty to all superannuated motherly Partizans to be as violent as they please, since there will be no danger either of their spoiling their Faces, or of their gaining Converts.

For my own part, I think a Man makes an odious and despicable Figure, that is violent in a Party; but a Woman is too sincere to mitigate the Fury of her Principles with Temper and Discretion, and to act with that Caution and Reservedness which are requisite in our Sex. When this unnatural Zeal gets into them, it throws them into ten thousand Heats and Extravagances; their generous Souls set no Bounds to their Love, or to their Hatred; and whether a Whig or Tory, a Lap-Dog or a Gallant, an Opera or a Puppet-Show, be the Object of it, the Passion, while it reigns, engrosses the whole Woman.

I remember when Dr. *Titus Oates* was in all his Glory, I accompanied my Friend WILL. HONEYCOMB in a Visit to a Lady of his Acquaintance: We were no sooner sate down, but upon casting my Eyes about the Room, I found in almost every Corner of it a Print that represented the Doctor in all Magnitudes and Dimensions. A little after, as the Lady was discoursing my Friend, and held her Snuff-Box in her Hand, who should I see in the Lid of it but the Doctor. It was not long after this, when she had occasion for her Handkerchief, which upon the first opening discovered among the Plaites of it the Figure of the Doctor. Upon this my Friend WILL. who loves Raillery, told her, That if he was in Mr. *Truelove's* Place (for that was the Name of her Husband) he should be made as uneasie by a Handkerchief as ever *Othello* was. *I am afraid,* said she, *Mr.* HONEYCOMB, *you are a Tory; tell me truly, are you a Friend to the Doctor or not?* WILL. instead of making her a Reply, smiled in her Face (for indeed she was very pretty) and told her that one of her Patches was dropping off. She immediately adjusted it, and looking a little seriously, *Well,* says she, *I 'll be hanged if you and your silent Friend there are not against the Doctor in your Hearts, I suspected as much by his saying nothing.* Upon this she took her Fan into her Hand, and upon the opening of it again displayed to us the Figure of the Doctor, who was placed with great Gravity among the Sticks of it. In a word, I found that the Doctor had taken Possession of her Thoughts, her Discourse, and most of her Furniture; but finding my self pressed too close by her Question, I winked upon my Friend to take his Leave, which he did accordingly. C

No. 58.

[ADDISON.]   Monday, May 7.

Ut pictura poesis erit . . .—Hor.

NOTHING is so much admired, and so little understood, as Wit.
No Author that I know of has written professedly upon it;
and as for those who make any Mention of it, they only treat
on the Subject as it has accidentally fallen in their Way, and
that too in little short Reflections, or in general declamatory
Flourishes, without entring into the Bottom of the Matter.
I hope therefore I shall perform an acceptable Work to my
Countrymen, if I treat at large upon this Subject; which I shall
endeavour to do in a Manner suitable to it, that I may not
incur the Censure which a famous Critick bestows upon one
who had written a Treatise upon *the Sublime* in a low groveling
Stile.   I intend to lay aside a whole Week for this Undertaking, that the Scheme of my Thoughts may not be broken
and interrupted; and I dare promise my self, if my Readers
will give me a Week's Attention, that this great City will be
very much changed for the better by next *Saturday* Night.
I shall endeavour to make what I say intelligible to ordinary
Capacities; but if my Readers meet with any Paper that in
some Parts of it may be a little out of their Reach, I would not
have them discouraged, for they may assure themselves the
next shall be much clearer.

As the great and only End of these my Speculations is to
banish Vice and Ignorance out of the Territories of *Great
Britain*, I shall endeavour as much as possible to establish
among us a Taste of polite Writing.   It is with this View that
I have endeavoured to set my Readers right in several Points
relating to Operas and Tragedies; and shall from Time to Time
impart my Notions of Comedy, as I think they may tend to its
Refinement and Perfection.   I find by my Bookseller that these
Papers of Criticism, with that upon Humour, have met with a
more kind Reception than indeed I could have hoped for from
such Subjects; for which Reason I shall enter upon my present
Undertaking with greater Chearfulness.

In this, and one or two following Papers, I shall trace out
the History of false Wit, and distinguish the several Kinds of
it as they have prevailed in different Ages of the World.   This
I think the more necessary at present, because I observed
there were Attempts on foot last Winter to revive some of
those antiquated Modes of Wit that have been long exploded
out of the Commonwealth of Letters.   There were several
Satyrs and Panegyricks handed about in Acrostick, by which

Means some of the most arrant undisputed Blockheads about the Town began to entertain ambitious Thoughts, and to set up for polite Authors. I shall therefore describe at length those many Arts of false Wit, in which a Writer does not shew himself a Man of a beautiful Genius, but of great Industry.

The first Species of false Wit which I have met with is very venerable for its Antiquity, and has produced several Pieces which have lived very near as long as the *Iliad* it self: I mean those short Poems printed among the minor *Greek* Poets, which resemble the Figure of an Egg, a Pair of Wings, an Ax, a Shepherd's Pipe, and an Altar.

As for the first, it is a little oval Poem, and may not improperly be called a Scholar's Egg. I would endeavour to hatch it, or, in more intelligible Language, to translate it into *English*, did not I find the Interpretation of it very difficult; for the Author seems to have been more intent upon the Figure of his Poem, than upon the Sense of it.

The Pair of Wings consist of twelve Verses, or rather Feathers, every Verse decreasing gradually in its Measure according to its Situation in the Wing. The Subject of it (as in the rest of the Poems which follow) bears some remote Affinity with the Figure, for it describes a God of Love, who is always painted with Wings.

The Ax methinks would have been a good Figure for a Lampoon, had the Edge of it consisted of the most satyrical Parts of the Work; but as it is in the Original, I take it to have been nothing else but the Posie of an Ax which was consecrated to *Minerva*, and was thought to have been the same that *Epeus* made use of in the building of the *Trojan* Horse; which is a Hint I shall leave to the Consideration of the Criticks. I am apt to think that the Posie was written originally upon the Ax, like those which our modern Cutlers inscribe upon their Knives; and that therefore the Posie still remains in its ancient Shape, though the Ax it self is lost.

The Shepherd's Pipe may be said to be full of Musick, for it is composed of nine different Kinds of Verses, which by their several Lengths resemble the nine Stops of the old musical Instrument, that is likewise the Subject of the Poem.

The Altar is inscribed with the Epitaph of *Troilus* the son of *Hecuba*; which, by the way, makes me believe, that these false Pieces of Wit are much more ancient than the Authors to whom they are generally ascribed; at least I will never be perswaded, that so fine a Writer as *Theocritus* could have been the Author of any such simple Works.

It was impossible for a Man to succeed in these Performances who was not a kind of Painter, or at least a Designer: He was

first of all to draw the Outline of the Subject which he intended
to write upon, and afterwards conform the Description to the
Figure of his Subject. The Poetry was to contract or dilate
it self according to the Mould in which it was cast. In a Word,
the Verses were to be cramped or extended to the Dimensions
of the Frame that was prepared for them; and to undergo the
Fate of those Persons whom the Tyrant *Procrustes* used to
lodge in his Iron Bed; if they were too short he stretched them
on a Rack, and if they were too long chopped off a Part of their
Legs, till they fitted the Couch which he had prepared for them.

Mr. *Dryden* hints at this obsolete kind of Wit in one of the
following Verses in his *Mac Fleckno*; which an *English* Reader
cannot understand, who does not know that there are those
little Poems abovementioned in the Shape of Wings and Altars.

> . . . *Chuse for thy Command*
> *Some peaceful Province in Acrostick Land;*
> *There may'st thou* Wings *display, and* Altars *raise,*
> *And torture one poor Word a thousand Ways.*

This Fashion of false Wit was revived by several Poets of the
last Age, and in particular may be met with among Mr. *Herbert*'s Poems; and, if I am not mistaken, in the Translation of
Du Bartas. I do not remember any other Kind of Work
among the Moderns which more resembles the Performances
I have mentioned, than that famous Picture of King *Charles* I.
which has the whole Book of *Psalms* written in the Lines of
the Face and the Hair of the Head. When I was last at
Oxford I perused one of the Whiskers; and was reading the
other, but could not go so far in it as I would have done, by
reason of the Impatience of my Friends and Fellow-Travellers,
who all of them pressed to see such a Piece of Curiosity. I
have since heard, that there is now an eminent Writing-Master
in Town, who has transcribed all the *Old Testament* in a full-
bottomed Perriwig; and if the Fashion should introduce the
thick Kind of Wigs which were in Vogue some few Years ago,
he promises to add two or three supernumerary Locks that shall
contain all the *Apocrypha*. He designed this Wig originally
for King *William*, having disposed of the two Books of *Kings*
in the two Forks of the Foretop; but that glorious Monarch
dying before the Wig was finished, there is a Space left in
it for the Face of any one that has a mind to purchase it.

But to return to our ancient Poems in Picture, I would
humbly propose, for the Benefit of our modern Smatterers
in Poetry, that they would imitate their Brethren among the
Ancients in those ingenious Devices. I have communicated
this Thought to a young Poetical Lover of my Acquaintance

who intends to present his Mistress with a Copy of Verses made in the shape of her Fan; and, if he tells me true, has already finished the three first Sticks of it.   He has likewise promised me to get the Measure of his Mistress's Marriage-Finger, with a Design to make a Posie in the Fashion of a Ring which shall exactly fit it.   It is so very easie to enlarge upon a good Hint, that I do not question but my ingenious Readers will apply what I have said to many other Particulars; and that we shall see the Town filled in a very little time with Poetical Tippets, Handkerchiefs, Snuff-Boxes, and the like Female-Ornaments.   I shall therefore conclude with a Word of Advice to those admirable *English* Authors who call themselves Pindarick Writers, that they would apply themselves to this Kind of Wit without Loss of Time, as being provided better than any other Poets with Verses of all Sizes and Dimensions.   C

No. 59.
[ADDISON.]   Tuesday, May 8.

Operose nihil agunt.—Sen.

THERE is nothing more certain than that every Man would be a Wit if he could, and notwithstanding Pedants of a pretended Depth and Solidity are apt to decry the Writings of a polite Author, as *Flash* and *Froth,* they all of them shew upon Occasion that they would spare no Pains to arrive at the Character of those whom they seem to despise.   For this Reason we often find them endeavouring at Works of Fancy, which cost them infinite Pangs in the Production.   The Truth of it is, a Man had better be a Gally-Slave than a Wit, were one to gain that Title by those Elaborate Trifles which have been the Inventions of such Authors as were often Masters of Great Learning but no Genius.

In my last Paper I mentioned some of those false Wits among the Ancients, and in this shall give the Reader two or three other Species of them, that flourished in the same early Ages of the World.   The first I shall produce are the *Lipogrammatists* or *Letter-droppers* of Antiquity, that would take an exception, without any Reason, against some particular Letter in the Alphabet, so as not to admit it once into a whole Poem.   One *Tryphiodorus* was a great Master in this kind of Writing.   He composed an *Odissey* or Epick Poem on the Adventures of *Ulysses,* consisting of four and twenty Books, having entirely banished the letter *A* from his first Book, which was called *Alpha* (as *Lucus a non lucendo*) because there was not an *Alpha* in it. His second Book was inscribed *Beta*, for the same Reason. In short, the Poet excluded the whole four and twenty Letters in their turns, and shewed them, one after another, that he could do his Business without them.

It must have been very pleasant to have seen this Poet avoiding the reprobate Letter, as much as another would a false Quantity, and making his Escape from it through the several *Greek* Dialects, when he was pressed with it in any particular Syllable. For the most apt and elegant Word in the whole Language was rejected, like a Diamond with a Flaw in it, if it appeared blemished with a wrong Letter. I shall only observe upon this Head, that if the Work I have here mentioned had been now extant, the *Odissey* of *Tryphiodorus*, in all probability, would have been oftner quoted by our learned Pedants, than the *Odissey* of *Homer*. What a perpetual Fund would it have been of obsolete Words and Phrases, unusual Barbarisms and Rusticities, absurd Spellings and complicated Dialects? I make no Question but it would have been looked upon as one of the most valuable Treasuries of the *Greek* Tongue.

I find likewise among the Ancients that ingenious kind of Conceit, which the Moderns distinguish by the Name of a *Rebus*, that does not sink a Letter but a whole Word, by substituting a Picture in its place. When *Caesar* was one of the Masters of the *Roman* Mint, he placed the Figure of an Elephant upon the Reverse of the Publick Mony; the Word *Caesar* signifying an Elephant in the *Punick* Language. This was artificially contrived by *Caesar*, because it was not lawful for a private Man to stamp his own Figure upon the Coin of the Commonwealth. *Cicero*, who was so called from the Founder of his Family, that was marked on the Nose with a little Wenn like a Vetch (which is *Cicer* in *Latin*) instead of *Marcus Tullius Cicero*, ordered the Words *Marcus Tullius* with the Figure of a Vetch at the end of 'em to be inscribed on a Publick Monument. This was done probably to shew that he was neither ashamed of his Name or Family, notwithstanding the Envy of his Competitors had often reproached him with both. In the same manner we read of a famous Building that was marked in several Parts of it with the Figures of a Frog and a Lizard: Those Words in *Greek* having been the Names of the Architects, who by the Laws of their Country were never permitted to inscribe their own Names upon their Works. For the same Reason it is thought, that the Forelock of the Horse in the Antique-Equestrian Statue of *Marcus Aurelius*, represents at a distance the Shape of an Owl, to intimate the Country of the Statuary, who, in all probability, was an *Athenian*. This kind of Wit was very much in Vogue among our own Country-men

about an Age or two ago, who did not practise it for any oblique
Reason, as the Ancients above-mentioned, but purely for the
sake of being Witty.   Among innumerable Instances that may
be given of this Nature, I shall produce the Device of one Mr.
Newberry, as I find it mentioned by our learned *Camden* in his
Remains   Mr *Newberry*, to represent his Name by a Picture,
hung up at his Door the Sign of a Yew-tree, that had several
Berries upon it, and in the midst of them a great golden *N* hung
upon a Bough of the Tree, which by the help of a little false
Spelling made up the Word *N-ew-berry*.

I shall conclude this Topick with a *Rebus*, which has been
lately hewn out in Free-stone, and erected over two of the
Portals of *Blenheim* House, being the Figure of a monstrous
Lion tearing to Pieces a little Cock.   For the better understanding of which Device, I must acquaint my *English* Reader
that a Cock has the Misfortune to be called in *Latin* by the same
Word that signifies a *French*-Man, as a Lion is the Emblem of
the *English* Nation.   Such a Device in so noble a Pile of Building looks like a Punn in an Heroick Poem; and I am very sorry
the truly ingenious Architect would suffer the Statuary to
blemish his excellent Plan with so poor a Conceit: But I hope
what I have said will gain Quarter for the Cock, and deliver
him out of the Lion's Paw.

I find likewise in ancient Times the Conceit of making an
Eccho talk sensibly, and give rational Answers.   If this could
be excusable in any Writer, it would be in *Ovid*, where he introduces the Eccho as a Nymph, before she was worn away
into nothing but a Voice.   The learned *Erasmus*, tho' a Man of
Wit and Genius, has composed a Dialogue upon this silly kind
of Device, and made use of an Eccho who seems to have been
a very extraordinary Linguist, for she answers the Person she
talks with in *Latin*, *Greek*, and *Hebrew*, according as she found
the Syllables which she was to repeat in any of those learned
Languages.   *Hudibras*, in Ridicule of this false kind of Wit,
has described *Bruin* bewailing the Loss of his Bear to a solitary
Eccho, who is of great use to the Poet in several Disticks, as
she does not only repeat after him, but helps out his Verse,
and furnishes him with *Rhymes*.

> *He rag'd, and kept as heavy a Coil as*
> *Stout* Hercules *for loss of* Hylas *;*
> *Forcing the Vallies to repeat*
> *The Accents of his sad Regret:*
> *He beat his Breast, and tore his Hair,*
> *For loss of his dear Crony Bear,*
> *That Eccho from the hollow Ground*
> *His doleful Wailings did resound*

> *More wistfully, by many times,*
> *Than in small Poets Splay-foot Rhymes,*
> *That make her, in their rueful Stories,*
> *To answer to Int'rogatories,*
> *And most unconscionably depose*
> *Things of which she nothing knows:*
> *And when she has said all she can say,*
> *'Tis wrested to the Lover's Fancy.*
> *Quoth he, O whither, wicked* Bruin,
> *Art thou fled to my —— Eccho,* Ruin?
> *I thought th' hadst scorn'd to budge a Step*
> *For Fear.   (Quoth Eccho)* Marry guep.
> *Am I not here to take thy Part!*
> *Then what has quell'd thy stubborn Heart?*
> *Have these Bones rattled, and this Head*
> *So often in thy Quarrel bled?*
> *Nor did I ever winch or grudge it,*
> *For thy dear Sake?   (Quoth she)* Mum budget.
> *Think'st thou 'twill not be laid i' th' Dish*
> *Thou turn'dst thy Back?   Quoth Eccho,* Pish.
> *To run from those th' hadst overcome*
> *Thus cowardly?   Quoth Eccho,* Mum.
> *But what a-vengeance makes thee fly*
> *From me too, as thine Enemy?*
> *Or if thou hadst no Thought of me,*
> *Nor what I have endur'd for Thee,*
> *Yet Shame and Honour might prevail*
> *To keep thee thus from turning Tail:*
> *For who wou'd grudge to spend his Blood in*
> *His Honour's Cause?   Quoth she, A* Pudding.

C.

No. 60.

[ADDISON.]   Wednesday, May 9.

Hoc est quod palles?   Cur quis non prandeat, hoc est?—Per. Sat. 3.

SEVERAL kinds of false Wit that vanished in the refined Ages
of the World, discovered themselves again in the Times of
Monkish Ignorance.

As the Monks were the Masters of all that little Learning
which was then extant, and had their whole Lives entirely
disengaged from Business, it is no Wonder that several of
them, who wanted Genius for higher Performances, employed
many Hours in the Composition of such Tricks in Writing as
required much Time and little Capacity.   I have seen half the
Aeneid turned into *Latin* Rhymes by one of the *Beaux Esprits*
of that dark Age; who says in his Preface to it, that the *Aeneid*
wanted nothing but the Sweets of Rhyme to make it the most

perfect Work in its kind.   I have likewise seen an Hymn in Hexameters to the Virgin *Mary*, which filled a whole Book, tho' it consisted but of the eight following Words;

> *Tot, tibi, sunt, Virgo, dotes, quot, sidera, Coelo.*
> *Thou hast as many Virtues, O Virgin, as there are Stars in Heaven.*

The Poet rung the Changes upon these eight several Words and by that Means made his Verses almost as numerous as the Virtues and the Stars which they celebrated.   It is no Wonder that Men who had so much Time upon their Hands, did not only restore all the antiquated Pieces of false Wit, but enriched the World with Inventions of their own.   It was to this Age that we owe the Production of Anagrams, which is nothing else but a Transmutation of one Word into another, or the turning of the same Set of Letters into different Words; which may change Night into Day, or Black into White, if Chance, who is the Goddess that presides over these Sorts of Composition, shall so direct.   I remember a witty Author, in Allusion to this kind of Writing, calls his Rival, who (it seems) was distorted, and had his Limbs set in Places that did not properly belong to them, *The Anagram of a Man.*

When the Anagrammatist takes a Name to work upon, he considers it at first as a Mine not broken up, which will not shew the Treasure it contains till he shall have spent many Hours in the Search of it: For it is his Business to find out one Word that conceals it self in another, and to examine the Letters in all the Variety of Stations in which they can possibly be ranged.   I have heard of a Gentleman who, when this Kind of Wit was in fashion, endeavoured to gain his Mistress's Heart by it.   She was one of the finest Women of her Age, and known by the Name of the Lady *Mary Boon.*   The Lover not being able to make any thing of *Mary*, by certain Liberties indulged to this kind of Writing converted it into *Moll*; and after having shut him self up for half a Year, with indefatigable Industry produced an Anagram.   Upon the presenting it to his Mistress, who was a little vexed in her Heart to see her self degraded into *Moll Boon*, she told him, to his infinite Surprize, that he had mistaken her Sirname, for that it was not *Boon* but *Bohun*

> *. . . Ibi omnis*
> *Effusus labor . . .*

The Lover was thunder-struck with his Misfortune, insomuch that in a little Time after he lost his Senses, which indeed had been very much impaired by that continual Application he had given to his Anagram.

The Acrostick was probably invented about the same time with the Anagram, though it is impossible to decide whether the Inventor of the one or the other were the greater Block-head. The *Simple* Acrostick is nothing but the Name or Title of a Person or Thing made out of the initial Letters of several Verses, and by that Means written, after the Manner of the *Chinese*, in a perpendicular Line. But besides these there are *Compound* Acrosticks, where the principal Letters stand two or three deep. I have seen some of them where the Verses have not only been edged by a Name at each Extremity, but have had the same Name running down like a Seam through the Middle of the Poem.

There is another near Relation of the Anagrams and Acros-ticks, which is commonly called a Chronogram. This kind of Wit appears very often on many modern Medals, especially those of *Germany*, when they represent in the Inscription the Year in which they were coined. Thus we see on a Medal of *Gustaphus Adolphus* the following Words, CHRISTVS DVX ERGO TRIVMPHVS. If you take the pains to pick the Figures out of the several Words, and range them in their proper Order, you will find they amount to MDCXVVVII, or 1627, the Year in which the Medal was stamped: For as some of the Letters distinguish themselves from the rest, and overtop their Fellows, they are to be considered in a double Capacity, both as Letters and as Figures. Your laborious *German* Wits will turn over a whole Dictionary for one of these ingenious Devices. A Man would think they were searching after an apt classical Term, but instead of that they are looking out a Word that has an L, an M, or a D in it. When therefore we meet with any of these Inscriptions, we are not so much to look in 'em for the Thought, as for the Year of the Lord.

The *Bouts Rimez* were the Favourites of the *French* Nation for a whole Age together, and that at a Time when it abounded in Wit and Learning. They were a List of Words that rhyme to one another, drawn up by another Hand, and given to a Poet, who was to make a Poem to the Rhymes in the same Order that they were placed upon the List: The more uncom-mon the Rhymes were, the more extraordinary was the Genius of the Poet that could accommodate his Verses to them. I do not know any greater Instance of the Decay of Wit and Learning among the *French* (which generally follows the Declension of Empire) than the endeavouring to restore this foolish Kind of Wit. If the Reader will be at the Trouble to see Examples of it, let him look into the new *Mercure Galant*; where the Author every Month gives a List of Rhymes to be filled up by the Ingenious, in order to be communicated to the

Publick in the *Mercure* for the succeeding Month. That for the Month of *November* last, which now lies before me, is as follows.

.	.	.	.	.	.	.	.	.	.	.	.	.	.	.	*Lauriers*
.	.	.	.	.	.	.	.	.	.	.	.	.	.	.	*Guerriers*
.	.	.	.	.	.	.	.	.	.	.	.	.	.	.	*Musette*
.	.	.	.	.	.	.	.	.	.	.	.	.	.	.	*Lisette*
.	.	.	.	.	.	.	.	.	.	.	.	.	.	.	*Cesars*
.	.	.	.	.	.	.	.	.	.	.	.	.	.	.	*Etendars*
.	.	.	.	.	.	.	.	.	.	.	.	.	.	.	*Houlette*
.	.	.	.	.	.	.	.	.	.	.	.	.	.	.	*Folette*

One would be amazed to see so learned a Man as *Menage* talking seriously on this Kind of Trifle in the following Passage.

Monsieur de la Chambre has told me, that he never knew what he was going to write when he took his Pen into his Hand; but that one Sentence always produced another. For my own Part, I never knew what I should write next when I was making Verses. In the first Place I got all my Rhymes together, and was afterwards perhaps three or four Months in filling them up. I one Day shewed Monsieur Gombaud a Composition of this Nature, in which among others I had made use of the four following Rhymes, Amaryllis, Phillis, Marne, Arne, *desiring him to give me his Opinion of it. He told me immediately, That my Verses were good for nothing. And upon my asking his Reason, he said, Because the Rhymes are too common; and for that Reason easie to be put into Verse. Marry, says I, if it be so, I am very well rewarded for all the Pains I have been at. But by Monsieur Gombaud's Leave, notwithstanding the Severity of the Criticism, the Verses were good.* Vid. MENAGIANA. Thus far the learned *Menage*, whom I have translated Word for Word.

The first Occasion of these *Bouts Rimez* made them in some Manner excusable, as they were Tasks which the *French* Ladies used to impose on their Lovers. But when a grave Author, like him above-mentioned, tasked himself, could there be any thing more ridiculous? Or would not one be apt to believe that the Author played booty, and did not make his List of Rhymes till he had finished his Poem?

I shall only add, that this Piece of false Wit has been finely ridiculed by Monsieur *Sarasin*, in a Poem entituled, *La Defaite des Bouts-Rimez, The Rout of the Bouts-Rimez.*

I must subjoin to this last Kind of Wit the double Rhymes, which are used in Doggerel Poetry, and generally applauded by ignorant Readers. If the Thought of the Couplet in such Compositions is good, the Rhyme adds little to it; and if bad it will not be in the Power of the Rhyme to recommend it. I am afraid that great Numbers of those who admire the incomparable *Hudibras,* do it more on account of these Doggerel Rhymes than of the Parts that really deserve Admiration. I am sure I have heard the

> *Pulpit, Drum Ecclesiastick,*
> *Was beat with Fist instead of a Stick.*

and

> *There was an antient sage Philosopher*
> *Who had read* Alexander Ross *over,*

more frequently quoted, than the finest Pieces of Wit in the whole Poem. C

No. 61.

[ADDISON.]   Thursday, May 10.

> *Non equidem hoc studeo, pullatis ut mihi nugis*
> *Pagina turgescat, dare pondus idonea fumo.*—Pers.

THERE is no kind of false Wit which has been so recommended by the Practice of all Ages, as that which consists in a Jingle of Words, and is comprehended under the general Name of *Punning.* It is indeed impossible to kill a Weed, which the Soil has a natural Disposition to produce. The Seeds of Punning are in the Minds of all Men, and tho' they may be subdued by Reason, Reflection, and good Sense, they will be very apt to shoot up in the greatest Genius, that is not broken and cultivated by the Rules of Art. Imitation is natural to us, and when it does not raise the Mind to Poetry, Painting, Musick, or other more noble Arts, it often breaks out in Punns and Quibbles.

Aristotle, in the Eleventh Chapter of his Book of Rhetorick, describes two or three kinds of Punns, which he calls Paragrams, among the Beauties of good Writing, and produces Instances of them out of some of the greatest Authors in the *Greek* Tongue. *Cicero* has sprinkled several of his Works with Punns, and in his Book where he lays down the Rules of Oratory, quotes abundance of Sayings as Pieces of Wit, which also upon Examination prove arrant Punns. But the Age in which *the Punn* chiefly flourished, was the Reign of King *James* the First. That learned Monarch was himself a tolerable Punnster, and made very few Bishops or Privy-Counsellors that had not some time or other signalized themselves by a

Clinch, or a *Conundrum*. It was therefore in this Age that the
Punn appeared with Pomp and Dignity. It had before been
admitted into merry Speeches and ludicrous Compositions,
but was now delivered with great Gravity from the Pulpit, or
pronounced in the most solemn manner at the Council-Table.
The greatest Authors, in their most serious Works, made
frequent use of Punns. The Sermons of Bishop *Andrews*, and
the Tragedies of *Shakespear*, are full of them. The Sinner was
punned into Repentance by the former, as in the latter nothing
is more usual than to see a Hero weeping and quibbling for a
dozen Lines together.

I must add to these great Authorities, which seem to have
given a kind of Sanction to this Piece of false Wit, that all the
Writers of Rhetorick have treated of Punning with very great
Respect, and divided the several kinds of it into hard Names,
that are reckoned among the Figures of Speech, and recommended as Ornaments in Discourse. I remember a Country
School-master of my Acquaintance told me once, that he had
been in Company with a Gentleman whom he looked upon to
be the greatest *Paragrammatist* among the Moderns. Upon
Enquiry, I found my learned Friend had dined that day with
Mr. *Swan*, the famous Punnster; and desiring him to give me
some Account of Mr. *Swan's* Conversation, he told me that he
generally talked in the *Paronomasia*, that he sometimes gave
into the *Plocè*, but that in his humble Opinion he shined most
in the *Antanaclasis*.

I must not here omit, that a famous University of this Land
was formerly very much infested with Punns; but whether or
no this might not arise from the Fens and Marshes in which it
was situated, and which are now drained, I must leave to the
Determination of more skilful Naturalists.

After this short History of Punning, one would wonder how
it should be so entirely banished out of the Learned World,
as it is at present, especially since it had found a Place in the
Writings of the most ancient Polite Authors. To account
for this, we must consider, that the first Race of Authors,
who were the great Heroes in Writing, were destitute of all
Rules and Arts of Criticism; and for that Reason, though they
excel later Writers in Greatness of Genius, they fall short of
them in Accuracy and Correctness. The Moderns cannot
reach their Beauties, but can avoid their Imperfections. When
the World was furnished with these Authors of the first Eminence, there grew up another Set of Writers, who gained themselves a Reputation by the Remarks which they made on the
Works of those who preceded them. It was one of the Employments of these Secondary Authors, to distinguish the

several kinds of Wit by Terms of Art, and to consider them as more or less perfect, according as they were founded in Truth. It is no wonder therefore, that even such Authors as *Isocrates, Plato,* and *Cicero,* should have such little Blemishes as are not to be met with in Authors of a much inferior Character, who have written since those several Blemishes were discovered. I do not find that there was a proper Separation made between Punns and true Wit by any of the ancient Authors, except *Quintilian* and *Longinus.* But when this Distinction was once settled, it was very natural for all Men of Sense to agree in it. As for the Revival of this false Wit, it happened about the time of the Revival of Letters; but as soon as it was once detected, it immediately vanished and disappeared. At the same time there is no question, but as it has sunk in one Age and rose in another, it will again recover it self in some distant Period of Time, as Pedantry and Ignorance shall prevail upon Wit and Sense. And, to speak the Truth, I do very much apprehend, by some of the last Winter's Productions, which had their Sets of Admirers, that our Posterity will in a few Years degenerate into a Race of Punnsters: At least, a Man may be very excusable for any Apprehensions of this kind, that has seen *Acrosticks* handed about the Town with great Secrecie and Applause; to which I must also add a little *Epigram* called the *Witches Prayer,* that fell into Verse when it was read either backward or forward, excepting only that it Cursed one way and Blessed the other. When one sees there are actually such Pains-takers among our *British* Wits, who can tell what it may end in? If we must Lash one another, let it be with the manly Strokes of Wit and Satyr; for I am of the old Philosopher's Opinion, That if I must suffer from one or the other, I would rather it should be from the Paw of a Lion, than the Hoof of an Ass. I do not speak this out of any Spirit of Party. There is a most crying Dulness on both Sides. I have seen Tory *Acrosticks* and Whig *Anagrams,* and do not quarrel with either of them, because they are *Whigs* or *Tories,* but because they are *Anagrams* and *Acrosticks.*

But to return to Punning. Having pursued the History of a Punn, from its Original to its Downfal, I shall here define it to be a Conceit arising from the use of two Words that agree in the Sound, but differ in the Sense. The only way therefore to try a Piece of Wit, is to translate it into a different Language: If it bears the Test you may pronounce it true; but if it vanishes in the Experiment you may conclude it to have been a Punn. In short, one may say of a Punn as the Country-man described his Nightingale, that it is *vox & praeterea nihil,* a Sound, and nothing but a Sound. On the contrary, one may represent true

Wit by the Description which *Aristinetus* makes of a fine Woman, When she is *dressed* she is Beautiful, when she is *undressed* she is Beautiful: Or, as *Mercerus* has translated it more Emphatically, *Induitur, formosa est: Exuitur, ipsa forma est.*   C

No. 62.
[ADDISON.]   Friday, May 11.

Scribendi recte sapere est & principium & fons.—Hor.

MR. *Lock* has an admirable Reflection upon the Difference of Wit and Judgment, whereby he endeavours to shew the Reason why they are not always the Talents of the same Person. His Words are as follow: *And hence, perhaps, may be given some Reason of that common Observation, That Men who have a great deal of Wit and prompt Memories, have not always the clearest Judgment, or deepest Reason. For Wit lying most in the Assemblage of Ideas, and putting those together with Quickness and Variety, wherein can be found any Resemblance or Congruity, thereby to make up pleasant Pictures and agreeable Visions in the Fancy; Judgment, on the contrary, lies quite on the other Side, In separating carefully one from another, Ideas, wherein can be found the least Difference, thereby to avoid being mis-led by Similitude, and by Affinity to take one thing for another. This is a Way of proceeding quite contrary to Metaphor and Allusion; wherein, for the most Part, lies that Entertainment and Pleasantry of Wit which strikes so lively on the Fancy, and is therefore so acceptable to all People.*

This is, I think, the best and most philosophical Account that I have ever met with of Wit, which generally, though not always, consists in such a Resemblance and Congruity of Ideas as this Author mentions. I shall only add to it, by way of Explanation; That every Resemblance of Ideas is not that which we call Wit, unless it be such an one that gives *Delight* and *Surprize* to the Reader: These two Properties seem essential to Wit, more particularly the last of them. In order therefore that the Resemblance in the Ideas be Wit, it is necessary that the Ideas should not lie too near one another in the Nature of things; for where the Likeness is obvious, it gives no Surprize. To compare one Man's Singing to that of another, or to represent the Whiteness of any Object by that of Milk and Snow, or the Variety of its Colours by those of the Rainbow, cannot be called Wit, unless, besides this obvious Resemblance, there be some further Congruity discovered in the two Ideas that is capable of giving the Reader some Surprize. Thus when a Poet tells us, the Bosom of his Mistress is as white as Snow, there is no Wit in the Comparison; but when he adds, with a Sigh, that it is as cold too, it then grows into Wit. Every Reader's Memory may supply him with innumerable Instances of the same Nature. For this Reason, the Similitudes in Heroick Poets, who endeavour rather to fill the Mind with great Conceptions, than to divert it with such as are new and surprizing, have seldom any thing in them that can be called Wit. Mr. *Lock*'s Account of Wit, with this short Explanation, comprehends most of the Species of Wit, as Metaphors, Similitudes, Allegories, Aenigmas, Mottos, Parables, Fables, Dreams, Visions, dramatick Writings, Burlesque, and all the Methods of Allusion: As there are many other Pieces of Wit (how remote soever they may appear at first Sight from the foregoing Description) which upon Examination will be found to agree with it.

As *true Wit* generally consists in this Resemblance and Congruity of Ideas, *false Wit* chiefly consists in the Resemblance and Congruity sometimes of single Letters, as in Anagrams, Chronograms, Lipograms, and Acrosticks: Sometimes of Syllables, as in Ecchos and Doggerel Rhymes: Sometimes of Words, as in Punns and Quibbles; and sometimes of whole Sentences or Poems, cast into the Figures of *Eggs*, *Axes* or *Altars*: Nay, some carry the Notion of Wit so far, as to ascribe it even to external Mimickry; and to look upon a Man as an ingenious Person, that can resemble the Tone, Posture, or Face of another.

As *true Wit* consists in the Resemblance of Ideas, and *false Wit* in the Resemblance of Words, according to the foregoing Instances; there is another kind of Wit which consists partly in the Resemblance of Ideas, and partly in the Resemblance of Words; which for Distinction Sake I shall call *mixt Wit*. This Kind of Wit is that which abounds in *Cowley*, more than in any Author that ever wrote. Mr. *Waller* has likewise a great deal of it. Mr. *Dryden* is very sparing in it. *Milton* had a Genius much above it. *Spencer* is in the same class with *Milton*. The *Italians*, even in their Epic Poetry, are full of it. Monsieur *Boileau*, who formed himself upon the Ancient Poets, has every where rejected it with Scorn. If we look after mixt Wit among the *Greek* Writers, we shall find it no where but in the Epigrammatists. There are indeed some Strokes of it in the little Poem ascribed to *Musaeus*, which by that, as well as many other Marks, betrays it self to be a modern Composition. If we look into the *Latin* Writers, we find none of this mixt Wit in *Virgil*,

Lucretius, or *Catullus;* very little in Horace, but a great deal of it in *Ovid,* and scarce any thing else in *Martial.*

Out of the innumerable Branches of *mixt Wit,* I shall chuse one Instance which may be met with in all the Writers of this Class. The Passion of Love in its Nature has been thought to resemble Fire; for which Reason the Words Fire and Flame are made use of to signifie Love. The witty Poets therefore have taken an Advantage from the doubtful Meaning of the Word Fire, to make an infinite Number of Witticisms. *Cowley* observing the cold Regard of his Mistress's Eyes, and at the same Time their Power of producing Love in him, considers them as Burning-Glasses made of Ice; and finding himself able to live in the greatest Extremities of Love, concludes the Torrid Zone to be habitable. When his Mistress has read his Letter written in Juice of Lemmon by holding it to the Fire, he desires her to read it over a second time by Love's Flames. When she weeps, he wishes it were inward Heat that distilled those Drops from the Limbeck. When she is absent he is beyond eighty, that is, thirty Degrees nearer the Pole than when she is with him. His ambitious Love is a Fire that naturally mounts upwards; his happy Love is the Beams of Heaven, and his unhappy Love Flames of Hell. When it does not let him sleep, it is a Flame that sends up no Smoak; when it is opposed by Counsel and Advice, it is a Fire that rages the more by the Wind's blowing upon it. Upon the dying of a Tree in which he had cut his Loves, he observes that his written Flames had burnt up and withered the Tree. When he re-solves to give over his Passion, he tells us that one burnt like him for ever dreads the Fire. His Heart is an *Aetna,* that instead of *Vulcan's* Shop encloses *Cupid's* Forge in it. His endeavouring to drown his Love in Wine, is throwing Oil upon the Fire. He would insinuate to his Mistress, that the Fire of Love, like that of the Sun (which produces so many living Creatures) should not only warm but beget. Love in another Place cooks Pleasure at his Fire. Sometimes the Poet's Heart is frozen in every Breast, and sometimes scorched in every Eye. Sometimes he is drowned in Tears, and burnt in Love, like a Ship set on Fire in the Middle of the Sea.

The Reader may observe in every one of these Instances, that the Poet mixes the Qualities of Fire with those of Love; and in the same Sentence speaking of it both as a Passion, and as real Fire, surprizes the Reader with those seeming Re-semblances or Contradictions that make up all the Wit in this kind of Writing. Mixt Wit therefore is a Composition of Punn and true Wit, and is more or less perfect as the Resemblance lies in the Ideas or in the Words: Its Foundations are laid partly in Falsehood and partly in Truth: Reason puts in her Claim for one Half of it, and Extravagance for the other. The only Province therefore for this kind of Wit, is Epigram, or those little occasional Poems that in their own Nature are nothing else but a Tissue of Epigrams. I cannot conclude this Head of *mixt Wit*, without owning that the admirable Poet out of whom I have taken the Examples of it, had as much true Wit as any Author that ever writ; and indeed all other Talents of an extraordinary Genius.

It may be expected, since I am upon this Subject, that I should take Notice of Mr. *Dryden*'s Definition of Wit; which, with all the Deference that is due to the Judgment of so great a Man, is not so properly a Definition of Wit, as of good Writing in general. Wit, as he defines it, is ' a Propriety of Words and Thoughts adapted to the Subject.' If this be a true Definition of Wit, I am apt to think that *Euclid* was the greatest Wit that ever set Pen to Paper: It is certain that never was a greater Propriety of Words and Thoughts adapted to the Subject, than what that Author has made use of in his Elements. I shall only appeal to my Reader, if this Definition agrees with any Notion he has of Wit: If it be a true one, I am sure Mr. *Dryden* was not only a better Poet, but a greater Wit than Mr. *Cowley*; and *Virgil* a much more facetious Man than either *Ovid* or *Martial*.

Bouhours, whom I look upon to be the most penetrating of all the *French* Criticks, has taken Pains to shew, That it is impossible for any Thought to be beautiful which is not just, and has not its Foundation in the Nature of Things: That the Basis of all Wit is Truth; and that no Thought can be valuable, of which good Sense is not the Ground-work. *Boileau* has endeavoured to inculcate the same Notion in several Parts of his Writings, both in Prose and Verse. This is that natural Way of Writing, that beautiful Simplicity, which we so much admire in the Compositions of the Ancients; and which no Body deviates from, but those who want Strength of Genius to make a Thought shine in its own natural Beauties. Poets who want this Strength of Genius to give that Majestick Simplicity to Nature, which we so much admire in the Works of the Ancients, are forced to hunt after foreign Ornaments, and not to let any Piece of Wit of what Kind soever escape them. I look upon these Writers as *Goths* in Poetry, who, like those in Architecture, not being able to come up to the beautiful Simplicity of the old *Greeks* and *Romans*, have endeavoured to supply its Place with all the Extravagances of an irregular Fancy. Mr. *Dryden* makes a very handsom Observation on *Ovid*'s Writing a Letter from *Dido* to *Aeneas*, in the following

Words: '*Ovid* (says he, speaking of *Virgil*'s Fiction of *Dido* and *Aeneas*) takes it up after him, even in the same Age, and makes an Ancient Heroine of *Virgil*'s new-created *Dido*; dictates a Letter for her just before her Death to the ungrateful Fugitive; and, very unluckily for himself, is for measuring a Sword with a Man so much superior in Force to him, on the same Subject. I think I may be Judge of this, because I have translated both. The famous Author of the Art of Love has nothing of his own; he borrows all from a greater Master in his own Profession, and, which is worse, improves nothing which he finds: Nature fails him, and being forced to his old Shift, he has Recourse to Witticism. This passes indeed with his soft Admirers, and gives him the Preference to *Virgil* in their Esteem.'

Were not I supported by so great an Authority as that of Mr. *Dryden*, I should not venture to observe, That the Taste of most of our *English* Poets, as well as Readers, is extremely *Gothick*. He quotes Monsieur *Segrais* for a threefold Distinction of the Readers of Poetry: In the first of which he comprehends the Rabble of Readers, whom he does not treat as such with regard to their Quality, but to their Numbers and the Coarseness of their Taste. His Words are as follow: '*Segrais* has distinguished the Readers of Poetry, according to their Capacity of judging, into three Classes. [He might have said the same of Writers too, if he had pleased.] In the lowest Form he places those whom he calls *Les Petits Esprits*, such things as are our Upper-Gallery Audience in a Play-house; who like nothing but the Husk and Rind of Wit, prefer a Quibble, a Conceit, an Epigram, before solid Sense and elegant Expression: These are Mob-Readers. If *Virgil* and *Martial* stood for Parliament-Men, we know already who would carry it. But though they make the greatest Appearance in the Field, and cry the loudest, the best on 't is they are but a sort of *French* Huguenots, or *Dutch* Boors, brought over in Herds, but not Naturalized; who have not Lands of two Pounds *per Annum* in *Parnassus*, and therefore are not privileged to Poll. Their Authors are of the same Level, fit to represent them on a Mountebank's Stage, or to be Masters of the Ceremonies in a Bear-Garden: Yet these are they who have the most Admirers. But it often happens, to their Mortification, that as their Readers improve their Stock of Sense (as they may by reading better Books, and by Conversation with Men of Judgment) they soon forsake them.'

I must not dismiss this Subject without observing, that as Mr. *Lock* in the Passage above-mentioned has discovered the most fruitful Source of Wit, so there is another of a quite contrary Nature to it, which does likewise branch it self out into several Kinds. For not only the *Resemblance*, but the *Opposition* of Ideas does very often produce Wit; as I could shew in several little Points, Turns, and Antitheses, that I may possibly enlarge upon in some future Speculation. C

No. 63.
[ADDISON.] Saturday, May 12.

> *Humano capiti cervicem pictor equinam*
> *Jungere si velit, & varias inducere plumas*
> *Undique collatis membris, ut turpiter atrum*
> *Desinat in piscem mulier formosa superne:*
> *Spectatum admissi risum teneatis, amici?*
> *Credite, Pisones, isti tabulae fore librum*
> *Persimilem, cujus, velut aegri somnia, vanae*
> *Fingentur species . . .*—Hor.

It is very hard for the Mind to disengage itself from a Subject in which it has been long employed. The Thoughts will be rising of themselves from time to time, tho' we give them no Encouragement; as the Tossings and Fluctuations of the Sea continue several Hours after the Winds are laid.

It is to this that I impute my last Night's Dream or Vision, which formed into one continued Allegory the several Schemes of Wit, whether False, Mixed, or True, that have been the Subject of my late Papers.

Methought I was transported into a Country that was filled with Prodigies and Enchantments, governed by the Goddess of FALSEHOOD, and entitled *The Region of False Wit*. There was nothing in the Fields, the Woods, and the Rivers, that appeared natural. Several of the Trees blossomed in Leaf-Gold, some of them produced Bone-Lace, and some of them precious Stones. The Fountains bubbled in an Opera Tune, and were filled with Stags, Wild-Boars, and Mermaids, that lived among the Waters; at the same time that Dolphins and several kinds of Fish played upon the Banks, or took their Pastime in the Meadows. The Birds had many of them golden Beaks, and human Voices. The Flowers perfumed the Air with Smells of Incense, Amber-greese, and Pulvillios; and were so interwoven with one another, that they grew up in Pieces of Embroidery. The Winds were filled with Sighs and Messages of distant Lovers. As I was walking to and fro in this enchanted Wilderness, I could not forbear breaking out into Soliloquies upon the several Wonders which lay before me, when to my great Surprise, I found there were artificial Ecchoes in every Walk, that by Repetitions of certain Words which I spoke, agreed with me, or contradicted me, in every thing I said. In the midst of my Conversation with these invisible Companions, I discovered in the Centre of a very dark Grove a monstrous Fabrick built after the *Gothick* manner, and covered with innumerable Devices in that barbarous kind of Sculpture. I immediately went up to it, and found it to be a kind of Heathen Temple consecrated to the God of *Dullness*. Upon my Entrance I saw the Deity of the Place dressed in the Habit of a Monk, with a Book in one Hand and a Rattle in the other. Upon his right Hand was *Industry*, with a Lamp burning before her; and on his left *Caprice*, with a Monky sitting on her Shoulder. Before his Feet there stood an *Altar* of a very odd Make, which, as I afterwards found, was shaped in that manner, to comply with the Inscription that surrounded it. Upon the Altar there lay several Offerings of *Axes*, *Wings*, and *Eggs*, cut in Paper, and inscribed with Verses. The Temple was filled with Votaries, who applied themselves to different Diversions, as their Fancies directed them. In one Part of it I saw a Regiment of *Anagrams*, who were continually in motion, turning to the Right or to the Left, facing about, doubling their Ranks, shifting their Stations, and throwing themselves into all the Figures, and Counter-marches of the most changeable and perplexed Exercise.

Not far from these was a Body of *Acrosticks*, made up of very disproportioned Persons. It was disposed into three Columns, the Officers planting themselves in a Line on the left Hand of each Column. The Officers were all of them at least Six Foot high, and made three Rows of very proper Men; but the Common Soldiers, who filled up the Spaces between the Officers, were such Dwarfs, Cripples, and Scarecrows, that one could hardly look upon them without laughing. There were behind the *Acrosticks* two or three Files of *Chronograms*, which differed only from the former, as their Officers were equipped (like the Figure of Time) with an Hour-glass in one Hand, and a Scythe in the other, and took their Posts promiscuously among the private Men whom they commanded.

In the Body of the Temple, and before the very Face of the Deity, methought I saw the Phantom of *Tryphiodorus* the *Lipogrammatist*, engaged in a Ball with four and twenty Persons, who pursued him by turns thro' all the Intricacies and Labyrinths of a Country Dance, without being able to overtake him.

Observing several to be very busie at the Western End of the *Temple*, I enquired into what they were doing, and found there was in that Quarter the great Magazine of *Rebus*'s. These were several things of the most different Natures tied up in Bundles, and thrown upon one another in heaps like Faggots. You might behold an Anchor, a Night-rail, and an Hobby-horse bound up together. One of the Workmen seeing me very much surprised, told me, there was an infinite deal of Wit in several of those Bundles, and that he would explain them to me if I pleased: I thanked him for his Civility, but told him I was in very great haste at that time. As I was going out of the Temple, I observed in one Corner of it a Cluster of Men and Women laughing very heartily, and diverting themselves at a game of *Crambo*. I heard several *Double Rhymes* as I passed by them, which raised a great deal of Mirth.

Not far from these was another Set of merry People engaged at a Diversion, in which the whole Jest was to mistake one Person for another. To give Occasion for these ludicrous Mistakes, they were divided into Pairs, every Pair being covered from Head to Foot with the same kind of Dress, though perhaps there was not the least Resemblance in their Faces. By this means an old Man was sometimes mistaken for a Boy, a Woman for a Man, and a Black-a-moor for an *European*, which very often produced great Peals of Laughter. These I guessed to be a Party of *Punns*. But being very desirous to get out of this World of Magick, which had almost turned my Brain, I left the Temple, and crossed over the Fields that lay about it with all the Speed I could make. I was not gone far before I heard the Sound of Trumpets and Alarms, which seemed to proclaim the March of an Enemy; and, as I afterwards found, was in reality what I apprehended it. There appeared at a great Distance a very shining Light, and in the midst of it a Person of a most beautiful Aspect; her Name was TRUTH. On her Right Hand there marched a Male Deity, who bore several Quivers on his Shoulders, and grasped several Arrows in his Hand. His Name was *Wit*. The Approach of these two Enemies filled all the Territories of *False Wit* with an unspeakable Consternation, insomuch that the Goddess of those Regions appeared in Person upon her Frontiers, with the several inferior Deities, and the different Bodies of Forces which I had before seen in the Temple, who were now drawn up in Array, and prepared to give their Foes a warm Reception. As the March of the Enemy was very slow, it gave time to the several Inhabitants who bordered upon the *Regions* of FALSEHOOD to draw their Forces into a Body, with a Design to stand upon their Guard as Neuters, and attend the issue of the Combat.

I must here inform my Reader, that the Frontiers of the Enchanted Region, which I have before described, were inhabited by the Species of MIXED WIT, who made a very odd

Appearance when they were mustered together in an Army. There were Men whose Bodies were stuck full of Darts, and Women whose Eyes were Burning-glasses: Men that had Hearts of Fire, and Women that had Breasts of Snow. It would be endless to describe several Monsters of the like Nature, that composed this great Army; which immediately fell asunder and divided itself into two Parts; the one half throwing themselves behind the Banners of TRUTH, and the others behind those of FALSEHOOD.

The Goddess of FALSEHOOD was of a Gigantick Stature, and advanced some Paces before the Front of her Army; but as the dazling Light, which flowed from TRUTH, began to shine upon her, she faded insensibly; insomuch that in a little Space she looked rather like an huge Phantom, than a real Substance. At length, as the Goddess of TRUTH approached still nearer to her, she fell away entirely, and vanished amidst the Brightness of her Presence; so that there did not remain the least Trace or Impression of her Figure in the Place where she had been seen.

As at the rising of the Sun the Constellations grow thin, and the Stars go out one after another, till the whole Hemisphere is extinguished; such was the vanishing of the Goddess: and not only of the Goddess herself, but of the whole Army that attended her, which sympathized with their Leader, and shrunk into Nothing, in proportion as the Goddess disappeared. At the same time the whole Temple sunk, the Fish betook themselves to the Streams, and the wild Beasts to the Woods; the Fountains recovered their Murmurs, the Birds their Voices, the Trees their Leaves, the Flowers their Scents, and the whole Face of Nature its true and genuine Appearance. Tho' I still continued asleep, I fancied my self as it were awakened out of a Dream, when I saw this Region of Prodigies restored to Woods and Rivers, Fields and Meadows.

Upon the Removal of that wild Scene of Wonders, which had very much disturbed my Imagination, I took a full Survey of the Persons of WIT and TRUTH; for indeed it was impossible to look upon the first, without seeing the other at the same time. There was behind them a strong and compact Body of Figures. The Genius of *Heroic Poetry* appeared with a Sword in her Hand, and a Lawrel on her Head. *Tragedy* was crowned with a Cypress, and covered with Robes dipped in Blood. *Satyr* had Smiles in her Look, and a Dagger under her Garment. *Rhetorick* was known by her Thunderbolt; and *Comedy* by her Mask. After several other Figures, *Epigram* marched up in the Rear, who had been posted there at the Beginning of the Expedition, that he might not revolt to the Enemy, whom he was suspected to favour in his Heart. I was very much awed

and delighted with the Appearance of the God of *Wit*; there
was something so amiable and yet so piercing in his Looks, as
inspired me at once with Love and Terror.   As I was gazing
on him to my unspeakable Joy, he took a Quiver of Arrows
from his Shoulder, in order to make me a Present of it; but as
I was reaching out my Hand to receive it of him, I knocked it
against a Chair, and by that means awaked.   C

No. 64.

[STEELE.]   Monday, May 14

> . . . *Hic vivimus ambitiosa*
> *Paupertate omnes* . . .—Juv.

THE most improper things we commit in the Conduct of our
Lives, we are led into by the Force of Fashion.   Instances
might be given, in which a prevailing Custom makes us act
against the Rules of Nature, Law, and common Sense: But at
present I shall confine my Consideration of the Effect it has
upon Men's Minds, by looking into our Behaviour when it is the
Fashion to go into Mourning.   The Custom of representing the
Grief we have for the Loss of the Dead by our Habits, certainly
had its Rise from the real Sorrow of such as were too much
distressed to take the proper Care they ought of their Dress.
By Degrees it prevailed, that such as had this inward Oppression upon their Minds, made an Apology for not joining with the
rest of the World in their ordinary Diversions, by a Dress
suited to their Condition.   This therefore was at first assumed
by such only as were under real Distress, to whom it was a
Relief that they had nothing about them so light and gay as to
be irksome to the Gloom and Melancholy of their inward Reflections, or that might misrepresent them to others.   In
Process of Time this laudable Distinction of the Sorrowful
was lost, and Mourning is now worn by Heirs and Widows.
You see nothing but Magnificence and Solemnity in the
Equipage of the Relict, and an Air of Release from Servitude
in the Pomp of a Son who has lost a wealthy Father.   This
Fashion of Sorrow is now become a generous Part of the
Ceremonial between Princes and Sovereigns, who in the
Language of all Nations are stiled Brothers to each other, and
put on the Purple upon the Death of any Potentate with whom
they live in Amity.   Courtiers, and all who wish themselves
such, are immediately seized with Grief from Head to Foot
upon this Disaster to their Prince; so that one may know by
the very Buckles of a Gentleman-Usher, what Degree of Friend-

ship any deceased Monarch maintained with the Court to which
he belongs. A good Courtier's Habit and Behaviour is hiero-
glyphical on these Occasions: He deals much in Whispers, and
you may see he dresses according to the best Intelligence.

The general Affectation among Men, of appearing greater
than they are, makes the whole World run into the Habit of
the Court. You see the Lady, who the Day before was as
various as a Rainbow, upon the Time appointed for beginning
to mourn, as dark as a Cloud. This Humour does not prevail
only on those whose Fortunes can support any Change in their
Equipage, not on those only whose Incomes demand the
Wantonness of new Appearances; but on such also who have
just enough to cloath them. An old Acquaintance of mine, of
Ninety Pounds a Year, who has naturally the Vanity of being
a Man of Fashion deep at his Heart, is very much put to it to
bear the Mortality of Princes. He made a new black Suit
upon the Death of the King of *Spain*, he turned it for the
King of *Portugal*, and he now keeps his Chamber while it is
scowring for the Emperor. He is a good Oeconomist in his
Extravagance, and makes only a fresh black Button upon his
iron-grey Suit for any Potentate of small Territories; he indeed
adds his Crape Hatband for a Prince whose Exploits he has
admired in the *Gazette*. But whatever Compliments may be
made on these Occasions, the true Mourners are the Mercers,
Silkmen, Lacemen and Milliners. A Prince of a merciful and
royal Disposition would reflect with great Anxiety upon the
Prospect of his Death, if he considered what Numbers would
be reduced to Misery by that Accident only: He would think
it of Moment enough to direct, that in the Notification of his
Departure, the Honour done to him might be restrained to
those of the Houshold of the Prince to whom it should be
signified. He would think a general Mourning to be in a less
Degree the same Ceremony which is practised in barbarous
Nations, of killing their Slaves to attend the Obsequies of
their Kings.

I had been wonderfully at a Loss for many Months together,
to guess at the Character of a Man who came now and then to
our Coffee-house: He ever ended a News-paper with this Reflexion, *Well, I see all the Foreign Princes are in good Health.*
If you asked, Pray, Sir, What says the *Postman* from *Vienna?*
he answered, *Make us thankful, the* German *Princes are all well:*
What does he say from *Barcelona? He does not speak but that
the Country agrees very well with the new Queen.* After very
much Enquiry, I found this Man of universal Loyalty was a
wholesale Dealer in Silks and Ribbons: His Way is, it seems,
if he hires a Weaver or Workman, to have it inserted in his

Articles, 'That all this shall be well and truly performed, provided no foreign Potentate shall depart this Life within the Time above-mentioned.' It happens in all publick Mournings, that the many Trades which depend upon our Habits, are during that Folly either pinched with present Want, or terrified with the apparent Approach of it. All the Atonement which Men can make for wanton Expences (which is a Sort of insulting the Scarcity under which others labour) is, that the Superfluities of the Wealthy give Supplies to the Necessities of the Poor; but instead of any other Good arising from the Affectation of being in courtly Habits of Mourning, all Order seems to be destroyed by it; and the true Honour, which one Court does to another on that Occasion, loses its Force and Efficacy. When a foreign Minister beholds the Court of a Nation (which flourishes in Riches and Plenty) lay aside, upon the Loss of his Master, all Marks of Splendor, and Magnificence, though the head of such a joyful People, he will conceive a greater Idea of the Honour done his Master, than when he sees the Generality of the People in the same Habit. When one is afraid to ask the Wife of a Tradesman whom she has lost of her Family; and after some Preparation endeavours to know whom she mourns for; how ridiculous is it to hear her explain her self, That we have lost one of the House of *Austria*? Princes are elevated so highly above the rest of Mankind, that it is a presumptuous Distinction to take a Part in Honours done to their Memories, except we have authority for it, by being related in a particular Manner to the Court which pays that Veneration to their Friendship; and seems to express on such an Occasion the Sense of the Uncertainty of human Life in general, by assuming the Habit of Sorrow though in the full Possession of Triumph and Royalty. R

No. 65.

[STEELE.]   Tuesday, May 15.

> . . . *Demetri, teque, Tigelli,*
> *Discipularum inter jubeo plorare cathedras.*—Hor.

AFTER having at large explained what Wit is, and described the false Appearances of it, all that Labour seems but an useless Enquiry, without some Time be spent in considering the Application of it. The Seat of Wit, when one speaks as a Man of the Town and the World, is the Play-house; I shall therefore fill this Paper with Reflections upon the Use of it in that Place. The Application of Wit in the Theatre has as strong an Effect upon the Manners of our Gentlemen, as the Taste of it has upon the Writings of our Authors. It may, perhaps, look like a very presumptuous Work, though not Foreign from the Duty of a SPECTATOR, to tax the Writings of such as have long had the general Applause of a Nation: But I shall always make Reason, Truth, and Nature the Measures of Praise and Dispraise; if those are for me, the Generality of Opinion is of no Consequence against me; if they are against me, the general Opinion cannot long support me.

Without further Preface, I am going to look into some of our most applauded Plays, and see whether they deserve the Figure they at present bear in the Imaginations of Men, or not.

In reflecting upon these Works, I shall chiefly dwell upon that for which each respective Play is most celebrated. The present Paper shall be employed upon Sir *Foplin Flutter*. The received Character of this Play is, That it is the Pattern of Gentile Comedy. *Dorimant* and *Harriot* are the Characters of greatest Consequence, and if these are Low and Mean, the Reputation of the Play is very Unjust.

I will take for granted, that a fine Gentleman should be honest in his Actions, and refined in his Language. Instead of this, our Hero, in this Piece, is a direct Knave in his Designs, and a Clown in his Language. *Bellair* is his Admirer and Friend; in return for which, because he is forsooth a greater Wit than his said Friend, he thinks it reasonable to perswade him to Marry a young Lady, whose Virtue, he thinks, will last no longer than till she is a Wife, and then she cannot but fall to his Share, as he is an irresistible fine Gentleman. The Falshood to Mrs. *Loveit*, and the Barbarity of Triumphing over her Anguish for losing him, is another Instance of his Honesty, as well as his good Nature. As to his fine Language; he calls the Orange Woman, who, it seems, is inclined to grow Fat, *An Over-grown Jade, with a Flasket of Guts before her*; and salutes her with a pretty Phrase of, *How now, Double Tripe?* Upon the Mention of a Country Gentlewoman, whom he knows nothing of, (no one can imagine why) he *will lay his Life she is some awkward, ill-fashioned Country Toad, who not having above four dozen of Hairs on her Head, has adorned her baldness with a large white Fruz, that she may look Sparkishly in the Fore-front of the King's Box at an old Play*. Unnatural Mixture of senseless Common Place!

As to the Generosity of his Temper, he tells his poor Footman, *If he did not wait better*——he would turn him away, in the insolent Phrase of, *I'll Uncase you.*

Now for Mrs. *Harriot*: She laughs at Obedience to an absent Mother, whose Tenderness *Busie* describes to be very exquisite, for *that she is so pleased with finding* Harriot *again, that she cannot chide her for being out of the Way.*   This Witty Daughter, and Fine Lady, has so little Respect for this good Woman, that she Ridicules her Air in taking Leave, and cries, *In what Struggle is my poor Mother yonder?   See, see, her Head tottering, her Eyes staring, and her under Lip trembling.*   But all this is atoned for, because *she has more Wit than is usual in her Sex, and as much Malice, though she is as wild as you would wish her, and has a Demureness in her Looks that makes it so surprising!*   Then to recommend her as a fit Spouse for his Hero, the Poet makes her speak her Sense of Marriage very ingeniously: *I think*, says she, *I might be brought to endure him, and that is all a reasonable Woman should expect in an Husband.*   It is, methinks, unnatural that we are not made to understand how she that was bred under a silly pious old Mother, that would never trust her out of her sight, came to be so Polite.

It cannot be denied, but that the Negligence of every thing, which engages the Attention of the sober and valuable Part of Mankind, appears very well drawn in this Piece: But it is denied, that it is necessary to the Character of a Fine Gentleman, that he should in that manner Trample upon all Order and Decency.   As for the Character of *Dorimant*, it is more of a Coxcomb than that of *Foplin*.   He says of one of his Companions, that a good Correspondence between them is their mutual Interest.   Speaking of that Friend, he declares, their being much together *makes the Women think the better of his Understanding, and judge more favourably of my Reputation. It makes him pass upon some for a Man of very good Sense, and me upon others for a very civil Person.*

This whole celebrated Piece is a perfect Contradiction to good Manners, good Sense, and common Honesty; and as there is nothing in it but what is built upon the Ruin of Virtue and Innocence, according to the Notion of Merit in this Comedy, I take the Shooe-maker to be, in reality, the Fine Gentleman of the Play: For it seems he is an Atheist, if we may depend upon his Character as given by the Orange-Woman, who is her self far from being the lowest in the Play.   She says of a Fine Man who is *Dorimant's* Companion, There *is not such another Heathen in the Town, except the Shooe-maker.*   His Pretention to be the Hero of the *Drama* appears still more in his own Description of his way of Living with his Lady. *There is*, says he, *never a Man in Town lives more like a Gentleman with his Wife than I do; I never mind her Motions; she never enquires into mine.   We speak to one another civilly, hate one another heartily; and because it is Vulgar to Lye and Soak together, we have each of us our several Settle-Bed.*   That of

Soaking together is as good as if *Dorimant* had spoken it himself; and, I think, since he puts human Nature in as ugly a Form as the Circumstance will bear, and is a stanch Unbeliever, he is very much Wronged in having no part of the good Fortune bestowed in the last Act.

To speak plainly of this whole Work, I think nothing but being lost to a Sense of Innocence and Virtue can make any one see this Comedy, without observing more frequent Occasion to move Sorrow and Indignation, than Mirth and Laughter. At the same time I allow it to be Nature, but it is Nature in its utmost Corruption and Degeneracy.   R

No. 66.
[STEELE.]   Wednesday, May 16.

> *Motus doceri gaudet Ionicos*
> *Matura virgo, & fingitur artibus*
> *Jam nunc & incestos amores*
> *De tenero meditatur ungui.*—Hor.

THE two following Letters are upon a Subject of very great Importance, tho' expressed without any Air of Gravity.

'*To the* SPECTATOR.

Sir,

I take the Freedom of asking your Advice in Behalf of a Young Country Kinswoman of mine who is lately come to Town, and under my Care for her Education. She is very pretty, but you can't imagine how unformed a Creature it is. She comes to my Hands just as Nature left her, half finished, and without any acquired Improvements. When I look on her I often think of the *Belle Sauvage* mentioned in one of your Papers. Dear *Mr.* SPECTATOR, help me to make her comprehend the visible Graces of Speech, and the dumb Eloquence of Motion; for she is at present a perfect Stranger to both. She knows no Way to express her self but by her Tongue, and that always to signifie her Meaning. Her Eyes serve her yet only to see with, and she is utterly a Foreigner to the Language of Looks and Glances. In this I fancy you could help her better than any Body. I have bestowed two Months in teaching her to Sigh when she is not concerned, and to Smile when she is not pleased; and am ashamed to own she makes little or no Improvement. Then she is no more able now to walk, than she was to go at a Year old. By Walking you will easily know I mean that regular but easie Motion, which gives our Persons so irresistible a Grace as if we moved to Musick, and is a kind of disengaged Figure, or, if I may so speak, recitative Dancing. But the want of this I cannot blame in her, for I find she has no Ear, and means nothing by Walking but to change her Place. I could pardon too her Blushing, if she knew how to carry her self in it, and if it did not manifestly injure her Complexion.

They tell me you are a Person who have seen the World, and you are a Judge of fine Breeding; which makes me ambitious of some Instructions from you for her Improvement: Which when you have favoured me with, I shall further advise with you about the Disposal of this fair Forrester in Marriage; for I will make it no Secret to you, that her Person and Education are to be her Fortune.

> I am, Sir,
>> *Your very Humble Servant,*
>>> CELIMENE.'

'*Sir,*

Being employed by *Celimene* to make up and send to you her Letter, I make bold to recommend the Case therein mentioned to your Consideration, because she and I happen to differ a little in our Notions. I, who am a rough Man, am afraid the young Girl is in a fair Way to be spoiled: Therefore pray, Mr. Spectator, let us have your Opinion of this fine thing called *Fine Breeding*; for I am afraid it differs too much from that plain thing called *Good Breeding*.

> *Your most humble Servant.*'

The general Mistake among us in the Educating our Children, is, That in our Daughters we take Care of their Persons and neglect their Minds; in our Sons, we are so intent upon adorning their Minds, that we wholly neglect their Bodies. It is from this that you shall see a young Lady Celebrated and admired in all the Assemblies about Town; when her elder Brother is afraid to come into a Room. From this ill Management it arises, That we frequently observe a Man's Life is half spent before he is taken Notice of; and a Woman in the Prime of her Years is out of Fashion and neglected. The Boy I shall consider upon some other Occasion, and at present stick to the Girl: And I am the more inclined to this, because I have several Letters which complain to me that my Female Readers have not understood me for some Days last past, and take themselves to be unconcerned in the present Turn of my Writings. When a Girl is safely brought from her Nurse, before she is capable of forming one simple Notion of any thing in Life, she is delivered to the Hands of her Dancing-Master; and with a Collar round her Neck, the pretty wild Thing is taught a fantastical Gravity of Behaviour, and forced to a particular Way of holding her Head, heaving her Breast, and moving with her whole Body; and all this under Pain of never having an Husband, if she steps, looks or moves awry. This gives the young Lady wonderful Workings of Imagination, what is to pass between her and this Husband, that she is every Moment told of, and for whom she seems to be educated. Thus her Fancy is engaged to turn all her Endeavours to the Ornament of her Person, as what must determine her Good and Ill in this Life; and she naturally thinks, if she is tall enough, she is wise enough for any thing for which her Education makes her think she is designed. To make her an agreeable Person is the main Purpose of her Parents; to that is all their Cost, to that all their Care directed; and from this general Folly of Parents we owe our present numerous Race of Coquets. These Reflections puzzle me, when I think of giving my Advice on the Subject of managing the wild Thing mentioned in the Letter of my Correspondent. But sure there is a middle Way to be followed; the Management of a young Lady's Person is not to be overlooked, but the Erudition of her Mind is much more to be regarded. According as this is managed, you will see the Mind follow the Appetites of the Body, or the Body express the Virtues of the Mind.

Cleomira dances with all the Elegance of Motion imaginable; but her Eyes are so chastised with the Simplicity and Innocence of her Thoughts, that she raises in her Beholders Admiration and good Will, but no loose Hope or wild Imagination. The true Art in this Case is, To make the Mind and Body improve together; and if possible, to make Gesture follow Thought, and not let Thought be employed upon Gesture.   R

No. 67.

[BUDGELL.]   Thursday, May 17.

Saltare elegantius quam necesse est probae.—Sal.

Lucian, in one of his Dialogues, introduces a Philosopher chiding his Friend for his being a Lover of Dancing, and a Frequenter of Balls. The other undertakes the Defence of his Favourite Diversion, which, he says, was at first invented by the Goddess *Rhea*, and preserved the Life of *Jupiter* himself, from the Cruelty of his Father *Saturn*. He proceeds to shew, that it had been approved by the greatest Men in all ages; that *Homer* calls *Merion* a *Fine Dancer*; and says, That the graceful Mein and great Agility which he had acquired by that Exercise, distinguished him above the rest in the Armies, both of *Greeks* and *Trojans.*

He adds, that *Pyrrhus* gained more Reputation by Inventing the Dance which is called after his Name, than by all his other Actions: That the *Lacedemonians,* who were the bravest People in *Greece,* gave great Encouragement to this Diversion, and made their *Hormus* (a Dance much resembling the *French Brawl*) famous over all *Asia:* That there were still extant some *Thessalian* Statues erected to the Honour of their best Dancers: And that he wondred how his Brother Philosopher could declare himself against the Opinions of those two Persons, whom he professed so much to Admire, *Homer* and *Hesiod;* the latter of which compares Valour and Dancing together; and says, That *the Gods have bestowed Fortitude on some Men, and on others a Disposition for Dancing.*

Lastly, He puts him in mind that *Socrates* (who, in the Judgment of *Apollo,* was the Wisest of Men) was not only a professed Admirer of this Exercise in others, but learned it himself when he was an old Man.

The Morose Philosopher is so much affected by these, and some other Authorities, that he becomes a Convert to his Friend, and desires he would take him with him when he went to his next Ball.

I love to shelter my self under the Examples of great Men; and, I think, I have sufficiently shewed that it is not below the Dignity of these my Speculations, to take Notice of the following Letter, which, I suppose, is sent me by some substantial Tradesman about *Change.*

'*Sir,*

I am a Man in Years, and by an honest Industry in the World have acquired enough to give my Children a liberal Education, though I was an utter Stranger to it my self. My eldest Daughter, a Girl of Sixteen, has for some time been under the Tuition of Monsieur *Rigadoon,* a Dancing-Master in the City; and I was prevailed upon by her and her Mother to go last Night to one of his Balls. I must own to you, Sir, that having never been at any such Place before, I was very much pleased and surprized with that part of his Entertainment which he called *French Dancing.* There were several young Men and Women, whose Limbs seemed to have no other Motion, but purely what the Musick gave them. After this Part was over, they began a Diversion which they call *Country Dancing,* and wherein there were also some things not disagreeable, and divers *Emblematical Figures,* Composed, as I guess, by Wise Men, for the Instruction of Youth.

Among the rest I observed one, which, I think, they call *Hunt the Squirrel*, in which while the Woman flies the Man pursues her, but as soon as she turns, he runs away, and she is obliged to follow.

The Moral of this Dance does, I think, very aptly recommend Modesty and Discretion to the Female Sex.

But as the best Institutions are liable to Corruptions, so, Sir, I must acquaint you, that very great Abuses are crept into this Entertainment. I was amazed to see my Girl handed by, and handing young Fellows with so much Familiarity; and I could not have thought it had been in the Child. They have often made use of a most impudent and lascivious Step called *Setting*, which I know not how to describe to you, but by telling you that it is the very reverse of *Back to Back*. At last an impudent young Dog bid the Fidlers play a Dance called *Mol. Pately*, and after having made two or three Capers, ran to his Partner, locked his Arms in hers, and whisked her round cleverly above Ground in such manner, that I, who sate upon one of the lowest Benches, saw further above her Shooe than I can think fit to acquaint you with. I could no longer endure these Enormities, wherefore just as my Girl was going to be made a Whirligig, I ran in, seized on the Child, and carried her home.

Sir, I am not yet old enough to be a Fool. I suppose this Diversion might be at first invented to keep up a good Understanding between young Men and Women, and so far I am not against it; but I shall never allow of these things. I know not what you will say to this Case at present, but am sure that had you been with me you would have seen matter of great Speculation. I am,

Yours, &c.'

I must confess I am afraid that my Correspondent had too much Reason to be a little out of Humour at the Treatment of his Daughter, but I conclude that he would have been much more so, had he seen one of those *kissing Dances* in which WILL HONEYCOMB assures me they are obliged to dwell almost a Minute on the Fair One's Lips, or they will be too quick for the Musick, and dance quite out of Time.

I am not able however to give my final Sentence against this Diversion; and am of Mr. *Cowley*'s Opinion, that so much of Dancing, at least, as belongs to the Behaviour and an handsome Carriage of the Body, is extreamly useful, if not absolutely necessary.

We generally form such Ideas of People at first Sight, as we are hardly ever perswaded to lay aside afterwards: For this Reason, a Man would wish to have nothing disagreeable or uncomely in his Approaches, and to be able to enter a Room with a good Grace.

I might add, that a moderate Knowledge in the little Rules of Good-breeding gives a Man some Assurance, and makes him easy in all Companies. For Want of this, I have seen a Professor of a Liberal Science at a Loss to salute a Lady; and a most excellent Mathematician not able to determine whether he should stand or sit while my Lord drank to him.

It is the proper Business of a Dancing Master to regulate these Matters; tho' I take it to be a just Observation, that unless you add something of your own to what these fine Gentlemen teach you, and which they are wholly ignorant of themselves, you will much sooner get the Character of an Affected Fop, than of a Well-bred Man.

As for *Country Dancing*, it must indeed be confessed, that the great Familiarities between the two Sexes on this Occasion may sometimes produce very dangerous Consequences; and I have often thought that few Ladies' Hearts are so obdurate as not to be melted by the Charms of Musick, the Force of Motion, and an handsome young Fellow who is continually playing before their Eyes, and convincing them that he has the perfect Use of all his Limbs.

But as this kind of Dance is the particular Invention of our own Country, and as every one is more or less a Proficient in it, I would not Discountenance it; but rather suppose it may be practised innocently by others, as well as my self, who am often Partner to my Landlady's Eldest Daughter.

POSTSCRIPT.

Having heard a good Character of the Collection of Pictures which is to be exposed to Sale on *Friday* next; and concluding from the following Letter, that the Person who Collected them is a Man of no unelegant Taste, I will be so much his Friend as to Publish it, provided the Reader will only look upon it as filling up the Place of an Advertisement.

' *From the Three Chairs in the Piazza* Covent-Garden.

Sir,   May 16, 1711.

As you are a SPECTATOR, I think we, who make it our Business to exhibit any thing to publick View, ought to apply our selves to you for your Approbation. I have travelled *Europe* to furnish out a Show for you, and have brought with me what has been admired in every Country thro' which I passed. You have declared in many Papers, that your greatest

Delights are those of the Eye, which I do not doubt but I shall gratifie with as Beautiful Objects as yours ever beheld.   If Castles, Forests, Ruins, Fine Women, and Graceful Men, can please you, I dare promise you much Satisfaction, if you will appear at my Auction on *Friday* next.   A Sight is, I suppose, as grateful to a SPECTATOR, as a Treat to another Person, and therefore I hope you will pardon this Invitation from,

> Sir,
>
> > *Your most Obedient*
> >
> > *Humble Servant,*
> >
> > > J. GRAHAM.'

No. 68.

[ADDISON.]   Friday, May 18.

Nos duo turba sumus . . .—Ovid.

ONE would think that the larger the Company is in which we are engaged, the greater Variety of Thoughts and Subjects would be started in Discourse; but instead of this, we find that Conversation is never so much streightned and confined as in numerous Assemblies.   When a Multitude meet together upon any Subject of Discourse, their Debates are taken up chiefly with Forms and general Positions; nay, if we come into a more contracted Assembly of Men and Women, the Talk generally runs upon the Weather, Fashions, News, and the like publick Topicks.   In proportion, as Conversation gets into Clubs and Knots of Friends, it descends into Particulars, and grows more free and communicative: But the most open, instructive, and unreserved Discourse, is that which passes between two Persons who are familiar and intimate Friends.   On these Occasions, a Man gives a Loose to every Passion and every Thought that is uppermost, discovers his most retired Opinions of Persons and Things, tries the Beauty and Strength of his Sentiments, and exposes his whole Soul to the Examination of his Friend.

Tully was the first who observed, that Friendship improves Happiness and abates Misery, by the doubling of our Joy and dividing of our Grief; a Thought in which he hath been followed by all the Essayers upon Friendship, that have written since his Time.   Sir *Francis Bacon* has finely described other Advantages, or, as he calls them, Fruits of Friendship; and indeed there is no Subject of Morality which has been better handled and more exhausted than this.   Among the several fine things which have been spoken of it, I shall beg Leave to quote some out of a very ancient Author, whose Book would be

regarded by our Modern Wits as one of the most shining Tracts
of Morality that is extant, if it appeared under the Name of a
Confucius, or of any celebrated *Grecian* Philosopher: I mean
the little Apocryphal Treatise entitled, *The Wisdom of the Son
of Sirach*. How finely has he described the Art of making
Friends, by an obliging and affable Behaviour? And laid down
that Precept which a late excellent Author has delivered as his
own,' That we should have many Well-wishers, but few Friends.'
*Sweet Language will multiply Friends; and a fair-speaking
Tongue will encrease kind Greetings. Be in Peace with many,
nevertheless have but one Counsellor of a thousand.* With what
Prudence does he caution us in the Choice of our Friends?
And with what Strokes of Nature (I could almost say of
Humour) has he described the Behaviour of a treacherous and
self-interested Friend? *If thou would'st get a Friend, prove him
first, and be not hasty to credit him: For some Man is a Friend
for his own Occasion, and will not abide in the Day of thy Trouble.
And there is a Friend who being turned to Enmity and Strife will
discover thy reproach.* Again, *Some Friend is a Companion at
the Table, and will not continue in the Day of thy Affliction;
But in thy Prosperity he will be as thy self, and will be bold over
thy Servants. If thou be brought low he will be against thee, and
hide himself from thy Face.* What can be more strong and
pointed than the following Verse? *Separate thy self from thine
Enemies, and take heed of thy Friends.* In the next Words he
particularizes one of those Fruits of Friendship which is described at length by the two famous Authors above-mentioned,
and falls into a general Elogium of Friendship, which is very
just as well as very sublime. *A faithful Friend is a strong
Defence; and he that hath found such an one, hath found a
Treasure. Nothing doth countervail a faithful Friend, and his
Excellency is unvaluable. A faithful Friend is the Medicine of
Life; and they that fear the Lord shall find him. Whoso feareth
the Lord shall direct his Friendship aright; for as he is, so shall his
Neighbour* (that is his Friend) *be also.* I do not remember to
have met with any Saying that has pleased me more than that
of a Friend's being the Medicine of Life, to express the Efficacy
of Friendship in healing the Pains and Anguish which naturally
cleave to our Existence in this World; and am wonderfully
pleased with the Turn in the last Sentence, That a virtuous
Man shall as a Blessing meet with a Friend who is as virtuous
as himself. There is another Saying in the same Author
which would have been very much admired in an Heathen
Writer; *Forsake not an old Friend, for the new is not comparable
to him: A new Friend is as new Wine; when it is old thou shalt
drink it with Pleasure.* With what Strength of Allusion, and

Force of Thought, has he described the Breaches and Viola-
tions of Friendship? *Whoso casteth a Stone at the Birds frayeth
them away; and he that upbraideth his Friend, breaketh Friendship. Tho' thou drawest a Sword at a Friend yet despair not,
for there may be a returning to Favour: If thou hast opened thy
Mouth against thy Friend fear not, for there may be a Reconcilia
tion; except for upbraiding, or Pride, or disclosing of Secrets, or a
treacherous Wound; for, for these things every Friend will depart.*
We may observe in this and several other Precepts in this
Author, those little familiar Instances and Illustrations which
are so much admired in the moral Writings of *Horace* and
Epictetus. There are very beautiful Instances of this Nature
in the following Passages, which are likewise written upon the
same Subject: *Whoso discovereth Secrets loseth his Credit, and
shall never find a Friend to his Mind. Love thy Friend, and be
faithful unto him; but if thou bewrayest his Secrets, follow no
more after him: For as a Man hath destroyed his Enemy, so
hast thou lost the Love of thy Friend: as one that letteth a Bird go
out of his Hand, so hast thou let thy Friend go, and shall not get
him again: Follow after him no more, for he is too far off; he is
as a Roe escaped out of the Snare. As for a Wound, it may be
bound up, and after reviling there may be Reconciliation; but he
that bewrayeth Secrets, is without Hope.*

Among the several Qualifications of a good Friend, this wise
Man has very justly singled out Constancy and Faithfulness
as the principal: To these, others have added Virtue, Knowledge, Discretion, Equality in Age and Fortune, and as *Cicero*
calls it, *Morum Comitas*, a Pleasantness of Temper. If I were
to give my Opinion upon such an exhausted Subject, I should
join to these other Qualifications a certain Aequability or
Evenness of Behaviour. A Man often contracts a Friendship
with one whom perhaps he does not find out till after a
Year's Conversation; when on a sudden some latent ill Humour
breaks out upon him, which he never discovered or suspected
at his first entering into an Intimacy with him. There are
several Persons who in some certain Periods of their Lives are
inexpressibly agreeable, and in others as odious and detestable.
Martial has given us a very pretty Picture of one of this Species
in the following Epigram:

> *Difficilis, facilis, jucundus, acerbus es idem,
> Nec tecum possum vivere, nec sine te.*

> *In all thy Humours, whether grave or mellow,
> Thou 'rt such a touchy, testy, pleasant Fellow;
> Hast so much Wit, and Mirth, and Spleen about thee,
> There is no living with thee, nor without thee.*

It is very unlucky for a Man to be entangled in a Friendship with one, who by these Changes and Vicissitudes of Humour is sometimes amiable and sometimes odious: And as most Men are at some Times in an admirable Frame and Disposition of Mind, it should be one of the greatest Tasks of Wisdom to keep our selves well when we are so, and never to go out of that which is the agreeable Part of our Character.   C

No. 69.

[ADDISON.]   Saturday, May 19.

> *Hic segetes, illic veniunt felicius uvae;*
> *Arborei foetus alibi atque injussa virescunt*
> *Gramina.   Nonne vides, croceos ut Tmolus odores,*
> *India mittit ebur, molles sua thura Sabaei?*
> *At Chalybes nudi ferrum, virosaque Pontus*
> *Castorea, Eliadum palmas Epirus equarum?*
> *Continuo has leges aeternaque foedera certis*
> *Imposuit Natura locis . . .*—Virg.

THERE is no Place in the Town which I so much love to frequent as the *Royal Exchange.* It gives me a secret Satisfaction, and, in some measure, gratifies my Vanity, as I am an *Englishman,* to see so rich an Assembly of Country-men and Foreigners consulting together upon the private Business of Mankind, and making this Metropolis a kind of *Emporium* for the whole Earth.   I must confess I look upon High-Change to be a great Council, in which all considerable Nations have their Representatives.   Factors in the Trading World are what Ambassadors are in the Politick World; they negotiate Affairs, conclude Treaties, and maintain a good Correspondence between those wealthy Societies of Men that are divided from one another by Seas and Oceans, or live on the different Extremities of a Continent.   I have often been pleased to hear Disputes adjusted between an Inhabitant of *Japan* and an Alderman of *London,* or to see a Subject of the *Great Mogul* entering into a League with one of the *Czar* of *Muscovy.*   I am infinitely delighted in mixing with these several Ministers of Commerce, as they are distinguished by their different Walks and different Languages: Sometimes I am justled among a Body of *Armenians*: Sometimes I am lost in a Crowd of *Jews*; and sometime make one in a Groupe of *Dutch-men.*   I am a *Dane, Swede,* or *Frenchman* at different times, or rather fancy my self like the old Philosopher, who upon being asked what Country-man he was, replied, That he was a Citizen of the World.

Though I very frequently visit this busie Multitude of People, I am known to no Body there but my Friend Sir ANDREW, who often smiles upon me as he sees me bustling in the Croud, but at the same time connives at my Presence without taking any further Notice of me. There is indeed a Merchant of *Egypt*, who just knows me by sight, having formerly remitted me some Mony to *Grand Cairo*; but as I am not versed in the Modern *Coptick*, our Conferences go no further than a Bow and a Grimace.

This grand Scene of Business gives me an infinite Variety of solid and substantial Entertainments. As I am a great Lover of Mankind, my Heart naturally overflows with Pleasure at the sight of a prosperous and happy Multitude, insomuch that at many publick Solemnities I cannot forbear expressing my Joy with Tears that have stoln down my Cheeks. For this Reason I am wonderfully delighted to see such a Body of Men thriving in their own private Fortunes, and at the same time promoting the Publick Stock; or in other Words, raising Estates for their own Families, by bringing into their Country whatever is wanting, and carrying out of it whatever is superfluous.

Nature seems to have taken a particular Care to disseminate her Blessings among the different Regions of the World, with an Eye to this mutual Intercourse and Traffick among Mankind, that the Natives of the several Parts of the Globe might have a kind of Dependance upon one another, and be united together by their common Interest. Almost every *Degree* produces something peculiar to it. The Food often grows in one Country, and the Sauce in another. The Fruits of *Portugal* are corrected by the Products of *Barbadoes*: The Infusion of a *China* Plant sweetned with the Pith of an *Indian* Cane. The *Philippick* Islands give a Flavour to our *European* Bowls. The single Dress of a Woman of Quality is often the Product of an Hundred Climates. The Muff and the Fan come together from the different Ends of the Earth. The Scarf is sent from the Torrid Zone, and the Tippet from beneath the Pole. The Brocade Petticoat rises out of the Mines of *Peru*, and the Diamond Necklace out of the Bowels of *Indostan*.

If we consider our own Country in its natural Prospect, without any of the Benefits and Advantages of Commerce, what a barren uncomfortable Spot of Earth falls to our Share! Natural Historians tell us, that no Fruit grows originally among us, besides Hips and Haws, Acorns and Pig-nutts, with other Delicacies of the like Nature; That our climate of it self, and without the Assistances of Art, can make no further Advances towards a Plumb than to a Sloe, and carries an Apple to no greater a Perfection than a Crab: That our Melons, our Peaches, our Figs, our Apricots, and Cherries, are Strangers among us, imported in different Ages, and naturalized in our *English* Gardens: and that they would all degenerate and fall away into the Trash of our own Country, if they were wholly neglected by the Planter, and left to the Mercy of our Sun and Soil. Nor has Traffick more enriched our Vegetable World, than it has improved the whole Face of Nature among us. Our Ships are laden with the Harvest of every Climate: Our Tables are stored with Spices, and Oils, and Wines: Our Rooms are filled with Pyramids of *China*, and adorned with the Workmanship of *Japan*: Our Morning's-Draught comes to us from the remotest Corners of the Earth: We repair our Bodies by the Drugs of *America*, and repose our selves under *Indian* Canopies. My Friend Sir ANDREW calls the Vineyards of *France* our Gardens: the Spice-Islands our Hot-beds; the *Persians* our Silk-Weavers, and the *Chinese* our Potters. Nature indeed furnishes us with the bare Necessaries of Life, but Traffick gives us a great Variety of what is Useful, and at the same time supplies us with every thing that is Convenient and Ornamental. Nor is it the least Part of this our Happiness that whilst we enjoy the remotest Products of the North and South, we are free from those Extremities of Weather which give them Birth: That our Eyes are refreshed with the green Fields of *Britain*, at the same time that our Palates are feasted with Fruits that rise between the Tropicks.

For these Reasons there are not more useful Members in a Commonwealth than Merchants. They knit Mankind together in a mutual Intercourse of good Offices, distribute the Gifts of Nature, find Work for the Poor, add Wealth to the Rich, and Magnificence to the Great. Our *English* Merchant converts the Tin of his own Country into Gold, and exchanges his Wool for Rubies. The *Mahometans* are cloathed in our *British* Manufacture, and the Inhabitants of the Frozen Zone warmed with the Fleeces of our Sheep.

When I have been upon the *'Change*, I have often fancied one of our old Kings standing in Person, where he is represented in Effigy, and looking down upon the wealthy Concourse of People with which that Place is every Day filled. In this Case, how would he be surprized to hear all the Languages of *Europe* spoken in this little Spot of his former Dominions, and to see so many private Men, who in his Time would have been the Vassals of some powerful Baron, Negotiating like Princes for greater Sums of Mony than were formerly to be met with in the Royal Treasury! Trade, without enlarging the *British* Territories, has given us a kind of additional Empire: It has multiplied the Number of the Rich, made our Landed Estates

infinitely more Valuable than they were formerly, and added
to them an Accession of other Estates as valuable as the Lands
themselves.   C

No. 70.
[ADDISON.]   Monday, May 21.
Interdum vulgus rectum videt.—Hor.

WHEN I travelled, I took a particular Delight in hearing the
Songs and Fables that are come from Father to Son, and are
most in vogue among the common People of the Countries
through which I passed; for it is impossible that any thing
should be universally tasted and approved by a Multitude,
tho' they are only the Rabble of a Nation, which hath not in it
some peculiar Aptness to please and gratifie the Mind of Man.
Human Nature is the same in all reasonable Creatures; and
whatever falls in with it, will meet with Admirers amongst
Readers of all Qualities and Conditions. *Moliere*, as we are
told by Monsieur *Boileau*, used to read all his Comedies to an
old Woman who was his House-keeper, as she sat with him
at her Work by the Chimney-Corner; and could foretel the
Success of his Play in the Theatre, from the Reception it met
at his Fire-Side: For he tells us the Audience always followed
the old Woman, and never failed to laugh in the same Place.

I know nothing which more shews the essential and inherent
Perfection of Simplicity of Thought, above that which I call
the Gothick Manner in Writing, than this, that the first pleases
all Kinds of Palates, and the latter only such as have formed to
themselves a wrong artificial Taste upon little fanciful Authors
and Writers of Epigram. *Homer*, *Virgil*, or *Milton*, so far as
the Language of their Poems is understood, will please a
Reader of plain common Sense, who would neither relish nor
comprehend an Epigram of *Martial* or a Poem of *Cowley*:
So, on the contrary, an ordinary Song or Ballad that is the
Delight of the common People, cannot fail to please all such
Readers as are not unqualified for the Entertainment by their
Affectation or Ignorance; and the Reason is plain. because the
same Paintings of Nature which recommend it to the most
ordinary Reader, will appear Beautiful to the most refined.

The old Song of *Chevy-Chase* is the favourite Ballad of the
common People of *England*; and *Ben Johnson* used to say he
had rather have been the Author of it than of all his Works.
Sir *Philip Sidney* in his Discourse of Poetry speaks of it in the
following Words: *I never heard the old Song of* Piercy *and*
Douglas, *that I found not my Heart more moved than with a*

Trumpet; and yet it is sung by some blind Crowder with no rougher Voice than rude Stile; which being so evil apparelled in the Dust and Cobweb of that uncivil Age, what would it work trimmed in the gorgeous Eloquence of Pindar? For my own Part, I am so professed an Admirer of this antiquated Song, that I shall give my Reader a Critick upon it, without any further Apology for so doing.

The greatest Modern Criticks have laid it down as a Rule, That an Heroick Poem should be founded upon some important Precept of Morality, adapted to the Constitution of the Country in which the Poet writes. *Homer* and *Virgil* have formed their Plans in this View. As *Greece* was a Collection of many Governments, who suffered very much among themselves, and gave the *Persian* Emperor, who was their common Enemy, many Advantages over them by their mutual Jealousies and Animosities, *Homer*, in order to establish among them an Union, which was so necessary for their Safety, grounds his Poem upon the Discords of the several *Grecian* Princes who were engaged in a Confederacy against an *Asiatick* Prince, and the several Advantages which the Enemy gained by such their Discords. At the Time the Poem we are now treating of was written, the Dissentions of the Barons, who were then so many petty Princes, ran very high, whether they quarrelled among themselves, or with their Neighbours, and produced unspeakable Calamities to the Country: The Poet, to deter Men from such unnatural Contentions, describes a bloody Battel and dreadful Scene of Death, occasioned by the mutual Feuds which reigned in the Families of an *English* and *Scotch* Nobleman. That he designed this for the Instruction of his Poem, we may learn from his four last Lines, in which, after the Example of the modern Tragedians, he draws from it a Precept for the Benefit of his Readers.

> *God save the King, and bless the Land*
> *In Plenty, Joy, and Peace;*
> *And grant henceforth that foul Debate*
> *'Twixt Noblemen may cease.*

The next Point observed by the greatest Heroic Poets, hath been to celebrate Persons and Actions which do Honour to their Country: Thus *Virgil*'s Hero was the Founder of *Rome*, *Homer*'s a Prince of *Greece*; and for this Reason *Valerius Flaccus* and *Statius*, who were both *Romans*, might be justly derided for having chosen the Expedition of the *Golden Fleece* and the *Wars of Thebes*, for the Subjects of their Epic Writing.

The Poet before us has not only found out an Hero in his own Country, but raises the Reputation of it by several

beautiful Incidents.   The *English* are the first who take the
Field, and the last who quit it.   The *English* bring only
Fifteen hundred to the Battel, the *Scotch* Two thousand.   The
English keep the Field with Fifty three: The *Scotch* retire with
Fifty five: All the rest on each side being slain in Battel.   But
the most remarkable Circumstance of this Kind is the different
Manner in which the *Scotch* and *English* Kings receive the News
of this Fight, and of the great Men's Deaths who commanded
in it.

> *This News was brought to* Edinburgh,
> *Where* Scotland's *King did reign,*
> *That brave Earl* Douglas *suddenly*
> *Was with an Arrow slain.*
>
> *O heavy News, King* James *did say,*
> Scotland *can Witness be,*
> *I have not any Captain more*
> *Of such Account as he.*
>
> *Like Tydings to King* Henry *came*
> *Within as short a Space,*
> *That* Piercy *of* Northumberland
> *Was slain in* Chevy-Chace.
>
> *Now God be with him, said our King,*
> *Sith 'twill no better be,*
> *I trust I have within my Realm*
> *Five hundred as good as he.*
>
> *Yet shall not* Scot *nor* Scotland *say*
> *But I will Vengeance take,*
> *And be revenged on them all*
> *For brave Lord* Piercy's *sake.*
>
> *This Vow full well the King perform'd*
> *After on* Humble-down,
> *In one Day fifty Knights were slain*
> *With Lords of great Renown.*
>
> *And of the rest of small Account*
> *Did many Thousands dye,* &c.

At the same time that our Poet shews a laudable Partiality to
his Country-men, he represents the *Scots* after a Manner not
unbecoming so bold and brave a People.

> *Earl* Douglas *on a milk-white Steed,*
> *Most like a Baron bold,*
> *Rode foremost of the Company*
> *Whose Armour shone like Gold.*

His Sentiments and Actions are every Way suitable to an
Hero. One of us two, says he, must dye: I am an Earl as
well as your self, so that you can have no Pretence for refusing
the Combat: However, says he, 'tis Pity, and indeed would be
a Sin, that so many innocent Men should perish for our Sakes,
rather let you and I end our Quarrel in single Fight.

> *E'er thus I will out-braved be,*
> *One of us two shall dye:*
> *I know thee well, an Earl thou art,*
> *Lord* Piercy, *so am I.*

> *But trust me,* Piercy, *Pity it were,*
> *And great Offence, to kill*
> *Any of these our harmless Men,*
> *For they have done no Ill.*

> *Let thou and I the Battel try,*
> *And set our Men aside;*
> *Accurst be he, Lord* Piercy *said,*
> *By whom this is deny'd.*

When these brave Men had distinguished themselves in the
Battel and in single Combat with each other, in the Midst of a
generous Parly, full of heroic Sentiments, the *Scotch* Earl
falls; and with his Dying Words encourages his Men to revenge
his Death, representing to them, as the most bitter Circumstance of it, that his Rival saw him fall.

> *With that there came an Arrow keen*
> *Out of an* English *bow,*
> *Which struck Earl* Douglas *to the Heart*
> *A deep and deadly Blow.*

> *Who never spoke more Words than these,*
> *Fight on my merry Men all,*
> *For why, my Life is at an End,*
> *Lord* Piercy *sees my fall.*

Merry Men, in the Language of those Times, is no more than
a chearful Word for Companions and Fellow-Soldiers. A
Passage in the Eleventh Book of *Virgil*'s *Aeneid* is very much
to be admired, where *Camilla* in her last Agonies, instead of
weeping over the Wound she had received, as one might have
expected from a Warrior of her Sex, considers only (like the
Hero of whom we are now speaking) how the Battel should be
continued after her Death.

Tum sic expirans, &c.

A gathering Mist o'erclouds her chearful Eyes;
And from her Cheeks the rosy colour flies.
Then, turns to her, whom, of her Female Train,
She trusted most, and thus she speaks with Pain.
Acca, 'tis past! He swims before my Sight,
Inexorable Death; and claims his Right.
Bear my last Words to Turnus, *fly with speed,*
And bid him timely to my Charge succeed:
Repel the Trojans, *and the Town relieve:*
Farewell. . . .

Turnus did not die in so heroic a Manner; tho' our Poet seems to have had his eye upon *Turnus's* Speech in the last Verse.

Lord Piercy *sees my Fall.*

. . . *Vicisti, & victum tendere palmas*
    Ausonii videre . . .

Earl *Piercy's* Lamentation over his Enemy is generous, beautiful, and passionate; I must only caution the Reader not to let the Simplicity of the Stile, which one may well pardon in so old a Poet, prejudice him against the Greatness of the Thought.

Then leaving Life Earl Piercy *took*
    The dead Man by the Hand,
And said, Earl Douglas *for thy Life*
    Would I had lost my Land.

O Christ! My very Heart doth bleed
    With Sorrow for thy Sake;
For sure a more renowned Knight
    Mischance did never take.

That beautiful Line *Taking the dead Man by the Hand,* will put the Reader in Mind of *Aeneas's* Behaviour towards *Lausus,* whom he himself had Slain as he came to the Rescue of his aged Father.

At vero ut vultum vidit morientis, & ora,
Ora modis Anchisiades pallentia miris,
Ingemuit, miserans graviter, dextramque tetendit, &c.

The pious Prince beheld young Lausus *dead;*
He griev'd, he wept; then grasp'd his Hand, and said,
Poor hapless Youth! What Praises can be paid
To Worth so great! . . .

I shall take another Opportunity to consider the other Parts of this old Song.

C

No. 71.

. . . Scribere jussit amor.—Ovid.

THE entire Conquest of our Passions is so difficult a Work, that they who despair of it should think of a less difficult Task, and only attempt to Regulate them.   But there is a third thing which may contribute not only to the Ease, but also to the Pleasure of our Life; and that is, refining our Passions to a greater Elegance, than we receive them from Nature.   When the Passion is Love, this Work is performed in innocent, tho' rude and uncultivated Minds, by the mere Force and Dignity of the Object.   There are Forms which naturally create Respect in the Beholders, and at once inflame and chastise the Imagination.   Such an Impression as this gives an immediate Ambition to deserve, in order to please.   This Cause and Effect are beautifully described by Mr. *Dryden* in the Fable of *Cymon* and *Iphigenia*.   After he has represented *Cymon* so stupid, that

> *He whistled as he went, for want of Thought,*

he makes him fall into the following Scene, and shews its Influence upon him so excellently, that it appears as Natural as Wonderful.

> *It happen'd on a Summer's Holiday,*
> *That to the Greenwood-shade he took his way;*
> *His Quarter-staff, which he cou'd ne'er forsake,*
> *Hung half before, and half behind his Back.*
> *He trudg'd along unknowing what he sought,*
> *And whistled as he went, for want of Thought,*
> *   By Chance conducted, or by Thirst constrain'd,*
> *The deep Recesses of the Grove he gain'd:*
> *Where in a Plain, defended by the Wood*
> *Crept thro' the matted Grass a Crystal Flood,* }
> *By which an Alablaster Fountain stood:*
> *And on the Margin of the Fount was laid*
> *(Attended by her Slaves) a sleeping Maid,*
> *Like* Dian, *and her Nymphs, when tir'd with Sport.*
> *To rest by cool* Eurotas *they resort;*
> *The Dame her self the Goddess well express'd,*
> *Not more distinguish'd by her Purple Vest,*
> *Than by the charming Features of her Face,*
> *And ev'n in Slumber a superior Grace:*
> *Her comely Limbs compos'd with decent Care,* }
> *Her Body shaded with a slight Cymarr;*
> *Her Bosom to the View was only bare;*
> *The Fanning Wind upon her Bosom blows,*
> *To meet the Fanning Wind the Bosom rose;*
> *The Fanning Wind and purling Streams continue her*
> *   Repose.*

The Fool of Nature stood with stupid Eyes
And gaping Mouth, that testify'd Surprize,
Fix'd on her Face, nor could remove his Sight,
New as he was to Love, and Novice in Delight;
Long mute he stood, and, leaning on his Staff,
His Wonder witness'd with an Idoot Laugh;
Then would have spoke, but by his glimm'ring Sense
First found his want of Words, and fear'd Offence:
Doubted for what he was he should be known,
By his Clown-Accent, and his Country-Tone.

But lest this fine Description should be excepted against, as the Creation of that great Master Mr. *Dryden*, and not an Account of what has really ever happened in the World; I shall give you, *verbatim*, the Epistle of an enamoured Footman in the Country, to his Mistress. Their Sirnames shall not be incerted, because their Passion demands a greater Respect than is due to their Quality. *James* is Servant in a great Family, and *Elizabeth* waits upon the Daughter of one as numerous, some Miles off of her Lover. *James*, before he beheld *Betty*, was vain of his Strength, a rough Wrestler, and quarrelsome Cudgel-Player; *Betty* a publick Dancer at Maypoles, a Romp at Stool Ball: He always following idle Women, she playing among the Peasants: He a Country Bully, she a Country Coquette. But Love has made her constantly in her Mistress's Chamber, where the young Lady gratified a secret Passion of her own by making *Betty* talk of *James*; and *James* is become a constant Waiter near his Master's Apartment, in reading, as well as he can, Romances. I cannot learn who *Molly* is, who it seems walked Ten Mile to carry the angry Message, which gave Occasion to what follows.

'To *ELIZABETH* ——

My Dear Betty,   *May* 14, 1711.

Remember your bleeding Lover, who lyes bleeding at the Wounds *Cupid* made with the Arrows he borrowed at the Eyes of *Venus*, which is your sweet Person.

Nay more, with the Token you sent me for my Love and Service offered to your sweet Person, which was your base Respects to my ill Conditions, when alas! there is no ill Conditions in me, but quite contrary; all Love and Purity, especially to your sweet Person; but all this I take as a Jest.

But the sad and dismal News which *Molly* brought me, struck me to the Heart, which was, it seems, and is your ill Conditions for my Love and Respects to you.

For she told me, if I came Forty times to you, you would not peak with me, which Words I am sure is a great Grief to me.

222 THE SPECTATOR No. 71. *Tuesday, May 22,* 1711

Now, my Dear, if I may not be permitted to your sweet Company, and to have the Happiness of speaking with your sweet Person, I beg the Favour of you to accept of this my secret Mind and Thoughts, which hath so long lodged in my Breast; the which if you do not accept, I believe will go nigh to break my Heart.

For indeed, my Dear, I love you above all the Beauties I ever saw in all my Life.

The young Gentleman, and my Master's Daughter, the *Londoner* that is come down to marry her, sate in the Arbour most part of last Night. Oh! dear *Betty,* must the Nightingales sing to those who marry for Mony, and not to us true Lovers! Oh my dear *Betty,* that we could meet this Night where we used to do in the Wood!

Now, my Dear, if I may not have the Blessing of kissing your sweet Lips, I beg I may have the Happiness of kissing your fair Hand, with a few Lines from your dear self, presented by whom you please or think fit. I believe, if Time would permit me, I could write all Day; but the Time being short, and Paper little, no more from your never-failing Lover till Death,

James ——'

Poor *James!* Since his Time and Paper were so short; I, that have more than I can use well of both, will put the Sentiments of his kind Letter (the Stile of which seems to be confused with Scraps he had got in hearing and reading what he did not understand) into what he meant to express.

'*Dear Creature,*

Can you then neglect him who has forgot all his Recreations and Enjoyments, to pine away his Life in thinking of you? When I do so, you appear more amiable to me than Venus does in the most beautiful Description that ever was made of her. All this Kindness you return with an Accusation, that I do not love you: But the contrary is so manifest, that I cannot think you in earnest. But the Certainty given me in your Message by *Molly,* that you do not love me, is what robs me of all Comfort. She says you will not see me: If you can have so much Cruelty, at least write to me, that I may kiss the Impression made by your fair Hand. I love you above all things, and, in my Condition, what you look upon with Indifference is to me the most exquisite Pleasure or Pain. Our young Lady, and a fine Gentleman from *London,* who are to marry for mercenary Ends, walk about our Gardens, and hear the Voice of Evening Nightingales, as if for Fashion-sake they

courted those Solitudes, because they have heard Lovers do so.
Oh *Betty*! could I hear these Rivulets murmur, and Birds sing
while you stood near me, how little sensible should I be that
we are both Servants, that there is any thing on Earth above us.
Oh! I could write to you as long as I love you, till Death it self.

JAMES'

  N.B. By the Words *Ill Conditions*, James means in a Woman
Coquetry, in a Man *Inconstancy*. R

No. 72.

[ADDISON.] Wednesday, May 23.

> . . . *Genus immortale manet, multosque per annos*
> *Stat fortuna domus, & avi numerantur avorum.*—Virg.

HAVING already given my Reader an Account of several
extraordinary Clubs both ancient and modern, I did not design
to have troubled him with any more Narratives of this Nature;
but I have lately received Information of a Club which I can
call neither ancient nor modern, that I dare say will be no less
surprising to my Reader than it was to my self; for which
Reason I shall communicate it to the Publick as one of the
greatest Curiosities in its kind.

A Friend of mine complaining of a Tradesman who is related
to him, after having represented him as a very idle worthless
Fellow, who neglected his Family, and spent most of his Time
over a Bottle, told me, to conclude his Character, that he was a
Member of the *Everlasting Club*. So very odd a Title raised
my Curiosity to enquire into the Nature of a Club that had
such a sounding Name; upon which my Friend gave me the
following Account.

The *Everlasting Club* consists of an hundred Members, who
divide the whole twenty four Hours among them in such a
manner, that the Club sits Day and Night from one end of the
Year to another; no Party presuming to rise till they are relieved by those who are in course to succeed them. By this
means a Member of the *Everlasting Club* never wants Company;
for tho' he is not upon Duty himself, he is sure to find some who
are; so that if he be disposed to take a Whet, a Nooning, an
Evening's Draught, or a Bottle after Midnight, he goes to the
Club, and finds a Knot of Friends to his Mind.

It is a Maxim in this Club That the Steward never dies; for
as they succeed one another by way of Rotation, no Man is
to quit the great Elbow-chair which stands at the upper End

of the Table, till his Successor is in a Readiness to fill it; insomuch that there has not been a *Sede vacante* in the Memory of Man.

This Club was instituted towards the End (or, as some of them say, about the Middle) of the Civil Wars, and continued without Interruption till the Time of the *Great Fire*, which burnt them out, and dispersed them for several Weeks. The Steward at that time maintained his Post till he had like to have been blown up with a neighbouring House (which was demolished in order to stop the Fire); and would not leave the Chair at last, till he had emptied all the Bottles upon the Table, and received repeated Directions from the Club, to withdraw himself. This Steward is frequently talked of in the Club, and looked upon by every Member of it as a greater Man, than the famous Captain mentioned in my Lord *Clarendon*, who was burnt in his Ship because he would not quit it without orders. It is said that towards the Close of 1700, being the great Year of Jubilee, the Club had it under Consideration whether they should break up or continue their Session; but after many Speeches and Debates, it was at length agreed to sit out the other Century. This Resolution passed in a general Club *Nemine Contradicente*.

Having given this short Account of the Institution and Continuation of the *Everlasting Club*, I should here endeavour to say something of the Manners and Characters of its several Members, which I shall do according to the best Lights I have received in this Matter.

It appears by their Books in general, that since their first Institution they have smoaked Fifty Tun of Tobacco, drank Thirty Thousand Butts of Ale, One Thousand Hogsheads of Red Port, Two hundred Barrels of Brandy, and a Kilderkin of small Beer: There has been likewise a great Consumption of Cards. It is also said, that they observe the Law in *Ben. Johnson*'s Club, which orders the Fire to be always kept in (*focus perennis esto*) as well for the Convenience of lighting their Pipes, as to cure the Dampness of the Club-Room. They have an old Woman in the nature of a Vestal, whose Business it is to cherish and perpetuate the Fire, which burns from Generation to Generation, and has seen the Glass-house Fires in and out above an Hundred times.

The *Everlasting Club* treats all other Clubs with an Eye of Contempt, and talks even of the *Kit-Cat* and *October* as of a couple of Upstarts. Their ordinary Discourse (as much as I have been able to learn of it) turns altogether upon such Adventures as have passed in their own Assembly: of Members who have taken the Glass in their Turns for a Week together without stirring out of the Club; of others who have smoaked an hundred Pipes at a Sitting; of others who have not missed their Morning's Draught for Twenty Years together: Sometimes they speak in Raptures of a Run of Ale in King *Charles*'s Reign; and sometimes reflect with Astonishment upon Games at Whisk, which have been miraculously recovered by Members of the Society, when in all human Probability the Case was desperate.

They delight in several old Catches, which they sing at all Hours to encourage one another to moisten their Clay, and grow immortal by drinking; with many other edifying Exhortations of the like nature.

There are four general Clubs held in a Year, at which Times they fill up Vacancies, appoint Waiters, confirm the old Fire-Maker, or elect a new one, settle Contributions for Coals, Pipes, Tobacco, and other Necessaries.

The Senior Member has out-lived the whole Club twice over, and has been drunk with the Grandfathers of some of the present sitting Members.   C

No. 73.
[ADDISON.]   Thursday, May 24.

. . . O Dea certe!—Virg.

It is very strange to consider, that a Creature like Man, who is sensible of so many Weaknesses and Imperfections, should be actuated by a Love of Fame: That Vice and Ignorance, Imperfection and Misery should contend for Praise, and endeavour as much as possible to make themselves Objects of Admiration.

But notwithstanding Man's Essential Perfection is but very little, his Comparative Perfection may be very considerable. If he looks upon himself in an abstracted Light, he has not much to boast of; but if he considers himself with regard to others, he may find Occasion of glorying, if not in his own Virtues, at least in the Absence of another's Imperfections. This gives a different Turn to the Reflections of the Wise Man and the Fool. The first endeavours to shine in himself, and the last to out-shine others. The first is humbled by the Sense of his own Infirmities, the last is lifted up by the Discovery of those which he observes in other Men. The Wise Man considers what he wants, and the Fool what he abounds in. The Wise Man is happy when he gains his own Approbation, and the Fool when he Recommends himself to the Applause of those about him.

But however unreasonable and absurd this Passion for Admiration may appear in such a Creature as Man, it is not wholly to be discouraged; since it often produces very good Effects, not only as it restrains him from doing any thing which is mean and contemptible, but as it pushes him to Actions which are great and glorious. The Principle may be defective or faulty, but the Consequences it produces are so good, that, for the Benefit of Mankind, it ought not to be extinguished.

It is observed by *Cicero*, that Men of the greatest and the most shining Parts are the most actuated by Ambition; and if we look into the two Sexes, I believe we shall find this Principle of Action stronger in Women than in Men.

The Passion for Praise, which is so very vehement in the fair Sex, produces excellent Effects in Women of Sense, who desire to be admired for that only which deserves Admiration: and I think we may observe, without a Compliment to them, that many of them do not only live in a more uniform Course of Virtue, but with an infinitely greater Regard to their Honour, than what we find in the Generality of our own Sex. How many Instances have we of Chastity, Fidelity, Devotion? How many Ladies distinguish themselves by the Education of their Children, Care of their Families, and Love of their Husbands, which are the great Qualities and Atchievements of Womankind: As the making of War, the carrying on of Traffick, the Administration of Justice, are those by which Men grow famous, and get themselves a Name.

But as this Passion for Admiration, when it works according to Reason, improves the beautiful Part of our Species in every thing that is Laudable; so nothing is more Destructive to them when it is governed by Vanity and Folly. What I have therefore here to say, only regards the vain Part of the Sex, whom for certain Reasons, which the Reader will hereafter see at large, I shall distinguish by the name of *Idols*. An *Idol* is wholly taken up in the Adorning of her Person. You see in every Posture of her Body, Air of her Face, and Motion of her Head, that it is her Business and Employment to gain Adorers. For this Reason your *Idols* sppear in all publick Places and Assemblies, in order to seduce Men to their Worship. The Playhouse is very frequently filled with *Idols*; several of them are carried in Procession every Evening about the Ring, and several of them set up their Worship even in Churches. They are to be accosted in the Language proper to the Deity. Life and Death are in their Power: Joys of Heaven and Pains of Hell are at their disposal: Paradise is in their Arms, and Eternity in every Moment that you are present with them. Raptures Transports, and Extasies are the Rewards which they confer

Sighs and Tears, Prayers and broken Hearts are the Offerings which are paid to them. Their Smiles make Men happy; their Frowns drive them to despair. I shall only add under this Head, that *Ovid*'s Book of the Art of Love is a kind of Heathen Ritual, which contains all the Forms of Worship which are made use of to an *Idol*.

It would be as difficult a Task to reckon up these different kinds of *Idols*, as *Milton*'s was to number those that were known in *Canaan*, and the Lands adjoining. Most of them are Worshipped, like *Moloch*, in Fires and Flames. Some of them, like *Baal*, love to see their Votaries cut and slashed, and shedding their Blood for them. Some of them, like the *Idol* in the *Apocrypha*, must have Treats and Collations prepared for them every Night. It has indeed been known, that some of them have been used by their incensed Worshippers like the *Chinese Idols*, who are Whipped and Scourged when they refuse to comply with the Prayers that are offered to them.

I must observe, that those Idolaters who devote themselves to the *Idols* I am here speaking of, differ very much from all other kinds of Idolaters. For as others fall out because they Worship different *Idols*, these Idolaters quarrel because they Worship the same.

The Intention therefore of the *Idol* is quite contrary to the wishes of the Idolater; as the one desires to confine the *Idol* to himself, the whole Business and Ambition of the other is to multiply Adorers. This Humour of an *Idol* is prettily described in a Tale of *Chaucer*: He represents one of them sitting at a Table with three of her Votaries about her, who are all of them courting her Favour, and paying their Adorations: She smiled upon one, drank to another, and trod upon the other's Foot which was under the Table. Now which of these three, says the old Bard, do you think was the Favourite? In troth, says he, not one of all the three.

The Behaviour of this old *Idol* in *Chaucer*, puts me in mind of the Beautiful *Clarinda*, one of the greatest *Idols* among the Moderns. She is Worshipped once a Week by Candle-light in the midst of a large Congregation generally called an Assembly. Some of the gayest Youths in the Nation endeavour to plant themselves in her Eye, while she sits in form with multitudes of Tapers burning about her. To encourage the Zeal of her Idolaters, she bestows a Mark of her Favour upon every one of them, before they go out of her Presence. She asks a Question of one, tells a Story to another, glances an Ogle upon a third, takes a Pinch of Snuff from the fourth, lets her Fan drop by accident to give the fifth an occasion of taking it up. In short, every one goes away satisfied with his Success, and encouraged to renew his Devotions on the same Canonical Hour that Day Sevennight.

An *Idol* may be Undeified by many accidental Causes. Marriage in particular is a kind of Counter-*Apotheosis*, or a Deification inverted.   When a Man becomes familiar with his Goddess, she quickly sinks into a Woman.

Old Age is likewise a great Decayer of your *Idol:* The truth of it is, there is not a more unhappy Being than a super-annuated *Idol*, especially when she has contracted such Airs and Behaviour as are only Graceful when her Worshippers are about her.

Considering therefore that in these and many other Cases the *Woman* generally out-lives the *Idol*, I must return to the Moral of this Paper, and desire my fair Readers to give a proper Direction to their Passion for being admired: In order to which, they must endeavour to make themselves the Objects of a reasonable and lasting Admiration.   This is not to be hoped for from Beauty, or Dress, or Fashion, but from those inward Ornaments which are not to be defaced by Time or Sickness, and which appear most amiable to those who are most acquainted with them.   C

No. 74.
[ADDISON.]   Friday, May 25.

. . . *Pendent opera interrupta* . . .—Virg.

In my last *Monday*'s Paper I gave some general Instances of those beautiful Strokes which please the Reader in the old Song of *Chevy-Chase*; I shall here, according to my Promise, be more particular, and shew that the Sentiments in that Ballad are extreamly Natural and Poetical, and full of the majestick Simplicity which we admire in the greatest of the ancient Poets; For which Reason I shall quote several Passages of it, in which the Thought is altogether the same with what we meet in several Passages of the *Aeneid*; not that I would infer from thence, that the Poet (whoever he was) proposed to himself any Imitation of those Passages, but that he was directed to them in general, by the same kind of Poetical Genius, and by the same Copyings after Nature.

Had this old Song been filled with Epigrammatical Turns and Points of Wit, it might perhaps have pleased the wrong Taste of some Readers; but it would never have become the Delight of the common People, nor have warmed the Heart of Sir *Philip Sidney* like the Sound of a Trumpet; it is only Natur

that can have this Effect, and please those Tastes which are
the most unprejudiced or the most refined.   I must however
beg leave to dissent from so great an Authority as that of Sir
Philip Sidney, in the Judgment which he has passed as to the
rude Stile and evil Apparel of this Antiquated Song; for there
are several Parts in it where not only the Thought but the
Language is majestick, and the Numbers sonorous; at least,
the *Apparel* is much more *gorgeous* than many of the Poets made
use of in Queen *Elizabeth*'s Time, as the Reader will see in
several of the following Quotations.

What can be greater than either the Thought or the Expression in that Stanza,

> *To drive the Deer with Hound and Horn*
> *Earl* Piercy *took his Way;*
> *The Child may rue that was unborn*
> *The Hunting of that Day!*

This Way of considering the Misfortunes which this Battel
would bring upon Posterity, not only on those who were born
immediately after the Battel and lost their Fathers in it, but
on those also who perished in future Battels which took their
rise from this Quarrel of the two Earls, is wonderfully beautiful,
and conformable to the Way of Thinking among the ancient
Poets.

> *Audiet pugnas vitio parentum*
> *Rara juventus.*—Hor.

What can be more sounding and poetical, or resemble more
the majestick Simplicity of the Ancients, than the following
Stanzas?

> *The stout Earl of* Northumberland,
> *A Vow to God did make,*
> *His Pleasure in the* Scottish *Woods*
> *Three Summer's Days to take.*

> *With fifteen hundred Bowmen bold,*
> *All chosen Men of Might,*
> *Who knew full well, in Time of Need,*
> *To aim their Shaftes aright.*

> *The Hounds ran swiftly thro' the Woods*
> *The nimble Deer to take,*
> *And with their Cries the Hills and Dales*
> *An Eccho shrill did make.*

> . . Vocat ingenti clamore Cithaeron,
> Taygetique canes, domitrixque Epidaurus equorum:
> Et vox assensu nemorum ingeminata remugit.

> *Lo, yonder doth Earl* Dowglas *come,*
> *His Men in Armour bright:*
> *Full twenty hundred* Scottish *Spears,*
> *All marching in our Sight.*
>
> *All Men of pleasant* Tividale,
> *Fast by the River* Tweed, &c.

The Country of the *Scotch* Warriors, described in these two last Verses, has a fine romantick Situation, and affords a Couple of smooth Words for Verse. If the Reader compares the foregoing six Lines of the Song with the following *Latin* Verses, he will see how much they are written in the Spirit of *Virgil.*

> *Adversi campo apparent, hastasque reductis*
> *Protendunt longe dextris, & spicula vibrant:*
>
> *Quique altum Preneste viri, quique arva Gabinae*
> *Junonis, gelidumque Anienem, & roscida rivis*
> *Hernica saxa olunt:*
>   . . . *qui rosea rura Velini,*
> *Qui Tetricæ horrentes rupes, montemque Severum,*
> *Casperiamque colunt, Forulosque & flumen Himellæ:*
> *Qui Tiberim Fabarimque bibunt.* . . .

But to proceed.

> *Earl* Dowglas *on a milk-white Steed,*
> *Most like a Baron bold,*
> *Rode foremost of the Company*
> *Whose Armour shone like Gold.*

Turnus ut antevolans tardum praecesserat agmen, &c.

Vidisti, quo Turnus equo, quibus ibat in armis
Aureus . . .

> *Our* English *Archers bent their Bows,*
> *Their Hearts were good and true;*
> *At the first Flight of Arrows sent,*
> *Full threescore* Scots *they slew.*
>
> *They clos'd full fast on ev'ry Side,*
> *No Slackness there was found;*
> *And many a gallant Gentleman*
> *Lay gasping on the Ground.*
>
> *With that there came an Arrow keen*
> *Out of an* English *Bow,*
> *Which struck Earl* Dowglas *to the Heart*
> *A deep and deadly Blow.*

Aeneas was wounded after the same Manner by an unknown Hand in the midst of a Parly.

> *Has inter voces, media inter talia verba,*
> *Ecce viro stridens alis allapsa sagitta est,*
> *Incertum qua pulsa manu . . .*

But of all the descriptive Parts of this Song, there are none more beautiful than the four following Stanzas, which have a great Force and Spirit in them, and are filled with very natural Circumstances. The Thought in the third Stanza was never touched by any other Poet, and is such an one as would have shined in *Homer* or in *Virgil*.

> *So thus did both those Nobles die,*
> *Whose Courage none could stain;*
> *An* English *Archer then perceiv'd*
> *The noble Earl was slain.*

> *He had a Bow bent in his Hand,*
> *Made of a trusty Tree,*
> *An Arrow of a Cloth-yard long*
> *Unto the Head drew he.*

> *Against Sir* Hugh Montgomery
> *So right his Shaft he set,*
> *The grey-goose Wing that was thereon*
> *In his Heart-blood was wet.*

> *This Fight did last from Break of Day*
> *Till setting of the Sun;*
> *For when they rung the Evening Bell*
> *The Battel scarce was done.*

One may observe likewise, that in the Catalogue of the Slain the Author has followed the Example of the greatest ancient Poets, not only in giving a long List of the Dead, but by diversifying it with little Characters of particular Persons.

> *And with Earl* Douglas *there was slain*
> *Sir* Hugh Montgomery,
> *Sir* Charles Carrel, *that from the Field*
> *One foot would never fly:*

> *Sir* Charles Murrel *of* Ratcliff *too,*
> *His Sister's Son was he,*
> *Sir* David Lamb, *so well esteem'd,*
> *Yet saved could not be.*

The familiar Sound in these Names destroys the Majesty of the Description; for this Reason I do not mention this Part of the Poem but to shew the natural Cast of Thought which appears in it, as the two last Verses look almost like a Translation of *Virgil*.

> *. . . Cadit & Ripheus justissimus unus*
> *Qui fuit in Teucris & servantissimus aequi,*
> *Diis aliter visum . . .*

In the Catalogue of the *English* who fell, *Witherington's* Behaviour is in the same Manner particularized very artfully, as the Reader is prepared for it by that Account which is given of him in the Beginning of the Battel; though I am satisfied your little Buffoon Readers (who have seen that Passage ridiculed in *Hudibras*) will not be able to take the Beauty of it: For which Reason I dare not so much as quote it.

> *Then stept a gallant Squire forth,*
>   Witherington *was his Name,*
> *Who said, I would not have it told*
>   To Henry *our King for Shame,*
>
> *That e'er my Captain fought on Foot,*
>   *And I stood looking on.*

We meet with the same Heroick Sentiments in *Virgil.*

> *Non pudet, O Rutuli, pro cunctis talibus unam*
> *Objectare animam? numerone an viribus æqui*
> *Non sumus?*

What can be more natural or more moving, than the Circumstances in which he describes the Behaviour of those Women who had lost their Husbands on this fatal Day?

> *Next Day did many Widows come*
>   *Their Husbands to bewail,*
> *They wash'd their Wounds in brinish Tears,*
>   *But all would not prevail.*
>
> *Their Bodies bath'd in purple Blood*
>   *They bore with them away:*
> *They kiss'd them dead a thousand times,*
>   *When they were clad in Clay.*

Thus we see how the Thoughts of this Poem, which naturally arise from the Subject, are always simple, and sometimes exquisitely noble; that the Language is often very sounding, and that the whole is written with a true Poetical Spirit.

If this Song had been written in the *Gothic* Manner, which is the Delight of all our little Wits, whether Writers or Readers, it would not have hit the Taste of so many Ages, and have pleased the Readers of all Ranks and Conditions.   I shall only beg Pardon for such a Profusion of *Latin* Quotations; which I should not have made use of, but that I feared my own Judgment would have looked too singular on such a Subject, had not I supported it by the Practice and Authority of *Virgil.* C

No. 75.

[STEELE.]   Saturday, May 26.

Omnis Aristippum decuit color & status & res.—Hor.

It was with some Mortification that I suffered the Raillery of a
Fine Lady of my Acquaintance, for Calling, in one of my Papers,
Dorimant a Clown. She was so unmerciful as to take Advan-
tage of my invincible Taciturnity, and on that occasion, with
great Freedom to consider the Air, the Height, the Face, the
Gesture of him who could pretend to judge so arrogantly of
Gallantry. She is full of Motion, Janty and lively in her Im-
pertinence, and one of those that commonly pass, among the
Ignorant, for Persons who have a great deal of Humour. She
had the Play of Sir *Fopling* in her Hand, and after she had said
it was happy for her there was not so charming a Creature as
Dorimant now living, she began with a Theatrical Tone of
Voice to read, by way of Triumph over me, some of his
Speeches. *'Tis she, that lovely Hair, that easie Shape, those
wanton Eyes, and all those melting Charms about her Mouth,
which* Medley *spoke of; I'll follow the Lottery, and put in for a
Prize with my Friend* Bell-air.

> *In Love the Victors from the Vanquish'd fly;*
> *They fly that wound, and they pursue that dye.*

Then turning over the Leaves, she reads alternately, and speaks,

> *And you and* Loveit *to her Cost shall find,*
> *I fathom all the Depths of Womankind.*

Oh the Fine Gentleman! But here, continues she, is the
Passage I admire most, where he begins to Teize *Loveit*, and
Mimick Sir *Fopling*. Oh the pretty Satyr, in his resolving to
be a Coxcomb to please, since Noise and Nonsense have such
powerful charms!

> *I, that I may Successful prove,*
> *Transform my self to what you love.*

Then how like a Man of the Town, so Wild and Gay is that!

> *The Wife will find a Difference in our Fate,*
> *You Wed a Woman, I a good Estate.*

It would have been a very wild Endeavour for a Man of my
Temper to offer any Opposition to so nimble a Speaker as my
Fair Enemy is, but her Discourse gave me very many Reflections, when I had left her Company. Among others, I could
not but consider, with some Attention, the false Impressions

the generality (the Fair Sex more especially) have of what should be intended, when they say a *Fine Gentleman*; and could not help revolving that Subject in my Thoughts, and settling, as it were, an Idea of that Character in my own Imagination.

No Man ought to have the Esteem of the rest of the World, for any Actions which are disagreeable to those Maxims which prevail, as the Standards of Behaviour, in the Country wherein he lives. What is opposite to the eternal Rules of Reason and good Sense, must be excluded from any Place in the Carriage of a Well-bred Man. I did not, I confess, explain my self enough on this Subject, when I called *Dorimant* a Clown, and made it an Instance of it, that he called the *Orange Wench, Double-Tripe*: I should have shewed, that Humanity obliges a Gentleman to give no Part of Humankind Reproach, for what they, whom they Reproach, may possibly have in common with the most Virtuous and Worthy amongst us. When a Gentleman speaks Coarsly, he has dressed himself Clean to no purpose: The Cloathing of our Minds certainly ought to be regarded before that of our Bodies. To betray in a Man's Talk a corrupted Imagination, is a much greater Offence against the Conversation of Gentlemen, than any Negligence of Dress imaginable. But this Sense of the Matter is so far from being received among People even of Condition, that *Vocifer* passes for a Fine Gentleman. He is Loud, Haughty, Gentle, Soft, Lewd, and Obsequious by turns, just as a little Understanding and great Impudence prompt him at the present Moment. He passes among the Silly Part of our Women for a Man of Wit, because he is generally in Doubt. He Contradicts with a Shrug, and confutes with a certain Sufficiency, in professing such or such a Thing is above his Capacity. What makes his Character the pleasanter is, that he is a professed Deluder of Women; and because the empty Coxcomb has no Regard to any thing that is of it self Sacred and Inviolable. I have heard an unmarried Lady of Fortune say, it is Pity so fine a Gentleman as *Vocifer* is so great an Atheist. The Crowds of such inconsiderable Creatures that infest all Places of Assembling, every Reader will have in his Eye from his own Observation; but would it not be worth considering what Sort of Figure a Man who formed himself upon those Principles among us, which are agreeable to the Dictates of Honour and Religion, would make in the familiar and ordinary Occurrences of Life?

I hardly have observed any one fill his several Duties of Life better than *Ignotus*. All the Under parts of his Behaviour, and such as are exposed to common Observation, have their rise in him from great and noble Motives. A firm and unshaken Expectation of another Life, makes him become this; Humanity and good Nature, fortified by the Sense of Virtue, has the same Effect upon him, as the Neglect of all Goodness has upon many others. Being firmly Established in all Matters of Importance, that certain Inattention which makes Men's Actions look easie appears in him with greater Beauty: By a thorough Contempt of little Excellencies, he is perfectly Master of them. This Temper of Mind leaves him under no necessity of Studying his Air, and he has this peculiar Distinction, that his Negligence is unaffected.

He that can work himself into a Pleasure in considering this Being as an uncertain one, and think to reap an Advantage by its Discontinuance, is in a fair way of doing all Things with a graceful Unconcern, and Gentleman-like Ease. Such a one does not behold his Life as a short, transient, perplexing State, made up of trifling Pleasures, and great Anxieties: but sees it in quite another Light; his Griefs are Momentary and his Joys Immortal. Reflection upon Death is not a gloomy and sad thought of Resigning every Thing that he Delights in, but it is a short Night followed by an endless Day. What I would here contend for is, that the more Virtuous the Man is, the nearer he will naturally be to the Character of Genteel and Agreeable. A Man whose Fortune is Plentiful, shews an Ease in his Countenance, and Confidence in his Behaviour, which he that is under Wants and Difficulties cannot assume. It is thus with the State of the Mind; he that governs his Thoughts with the everlasting Rules of Reason and Sense, must have something so inexpressibly Graceful in his Words and Actions, that every Circumstance must become him. The Change of Persons or Things around him do not at all alter his Situation, but he looks disinterested in the Occurrences with which others are distracted, because the greatest purpose of his Life is to maintain an Indifference both to it and all its Enjoyments. In a word, to be a Fine Gentleman, is to be a Generous and a Brave Man. What can make a Man so much in constant Humour and Shine, as we call it, than to be supported by what can never fail him, and to believe that whatever happens to him was the best thing that could possibly befal him, or else he on whom it depends would not have permitted it to have befallen him at all?

R

No. 76.
[STEELE.]   Monday, May 28.

Ut tu fortunam, sic nos te, Celse, feremus.—Hor.

THERE is nothing so common as to find a Man whom in the
general Observation of his Carriage you take to be of an uniform Temper, subject to such unaccountable Starts cf Humour
and Passion, that he is as much unlike himself, and differs as
much from the Man you at first thought him, as any two
distinct Persons can differ from each other. This proceeds
from the Want of forming some Law of Life to our selves, or
fixing some Notion of things in general, which may affect us in
such manner, as to create proper Habits both in our Minds and
Bodies. The Negligence of this, leaves us exposed not only to
an unbecoming Levity in our usual Conversation, but also to
the same Instability in our Friendships, Interests, and Alliances.
A Man who is but a meer Spectator of what passes around him,
and not engaged in Commerces of any Consideration, is but an
ill Judge of the secret Motions of the Heart of Man, and by what
Degrees it is actuated to make such visible Alterations in the
same Person: But at the same time, when a Man is no way
concerned in the Effect of such Inconsistences in the Behaviour
of Men of the World, the Speculation must be in the utmost
Degree both diverting and instructive; yet to enjoy such
Observations in the highest Relish, he ought to be placed in a
Post of Direction, and have the dealing of their Fortunes to
them. I have therefore been wonderfully diverted with some
Pieces of secret History, which an Antiquary, my very good
Friend, lent me as a Curiosity. They are Memoirs of the
private Life of *Pharamond of France*. '*Pharamond*,' says my
Author, 'was a Prince of infinite Humanity and Generosity,
and at the same time the most pleasant and facetious Companion of his Time. He had a peculiar Taste in him (which
would have been unlucky in any Prince but himself), he thought
there could be no exquisite Pleasure in Conversation but among
Equals; and would pleasantly bewail himself that he always
lived in a Crowd, but was the only Man in *France* that never
could get into Company. This Turn of Mind made him delight
in Midnight Rambles, attended only with one Person of his
Bed-chamber: He would in these Excursions get acquainted
with Men (whose Temper he had a Mind to try) and recommend them privately to the particular Observation of his
first Minister. He generally found himself neglected by his
new Acquaintance, as soon as they had hopes of growing
great; and used on such Occasions to remark, That it was a

great Injustice to tax Princes of forgetting themselves in their
high Fortunes, when there were so few that could with Constancy bear the Favour of their very Creatures.' My Author
in these loose Hints has one Passage that gives us a very lively
Idea of the uncommon Genius of *Pharamond*. He met with
one Man whom he had put to all the usual Proofs he made of
those he had a Mind to know throughly, and found him for
his Purpose: In Discourse with him one Day, he gave him
Opportunity of saying how much would satisfie all his Wishes.
The Prince immediately revealed himself, doubled the Sum,
and spoke to him in this manner. '*Sir, You have twice what
you desired, by the Favour of* Pharamond *; but look to it that you
are satisfied with it, for 'tis the last you shall ever receive. I from
this Moment consider you as mine; and to make you truly so, I
give you my Royal Word you shall never be greater or less than you
are at present. Answer me not* (concluded the Prince smiling)
*but enjoy the Fortune I have put you in, which is above my own
Condition; for you have hereafter nothing to hope or to fear.*'

His Majesty having thus well chosen and bought a Friend
and Companion, he enjoyed alternately all the Pleasures of an
agreeable private Man and a great and powerful Monarch:
He gave himself, with his Companion, the Name of the merry
Tyrant; for he punished his Courtiers for their Insolence and
Folly, not by any Act of publick Disfavour, but by humorously
practising upon their Imaginations. If he observed a Man
untractable to his Inferiors, he would find an Opportunity to
take some favourable Notice of him, and render him insupportable. He knew all his own Looks, Words and Actions
had their Interpretations; and his Friend Monsieur *Eucrate*
(for so he was called) having a great Soul without Ambition, he
could communicate all his Thoughts to him, and fear no artful
Use would be made of that Freedom. It was no small Delight,
when they were in private, to reflect upon all which had passed
in publick.

Pharamond would often, to satisfie a vain Fool of Power in
his Country, talk to him in a full Court, and with one Whisper
make him despise all his old Friends and Acquaintance. He was
come to that Knowledge of Men by long Observation, that he
would profess altering the whole Mass of Blood in some Tempers
by thrice speaking to them. As Fortune was in his Power, he
gave himself constant Entertainment in managing the mere
Followers of it with the Treatment they deserved. He would,
by a skilful Cast of his Eye and half a Smile, make two Fellows
who hated, embrace and fall upon each other's Neck with as
much Eagerness, as if they followed their real Inclinations, and
intended to stifle one another. When he was in high good

Humour, he would lay the Scene with *Eucrate*, and on a publick Night exercise the Passions of his whole Court. He was pleased to see an haughty Beauty watch the Looks of the Man she had long despised, from Observation of his being taken notice of by *Pharamond*; and the Lover conceive higher Hopes, than to follow the Woman he was dying for the Day before. In a Court, where Men speak Affection in the strongest Terms, and Dislike in the faintest, it was a comical Mixture of Incidents, to see Disguises thrown aside in one Case and encreased on the other, according as Favour or Disgrace attended the respective Objects of Men's Approbation or Disesteem. *Pharamond*, in his Mirth, upon the Meanness of Mankind, used to say, 'As he could take away a Man's Five Senses, he could give him an Hundred. The Man in Disgrace shall immediately lose all his Natural Endowments, and he that finds Favour have the Attributes of an Angel.' He would carry it so far as to say, 'It should not be only so in the Opinion of the lower Part of his Court, but the Men themselves shall think thus meanly or greatly of themselves, as they are out or in the good Graces of a Court.'

A Monarch who had Wit and Humour like *Pharamond*, must have Pleasures which no Man else can ever have Opportunity of enjoying. He gave Fortune to none but those whom he knew could receive it without Transport; he made a noble and generous Use of his Observations; and did not regard his Ministers as they were agreeable to himself, but as they were useful to his Kingdom: By this Means the King appeared in every Officer of State; and no Man had a Participation of the Power, who had not a Similitude of the Virtue of *Pharamond*.

R

No. 77.
[BUDGELL.]   Tuesday, May 29.

> *Non convivere . . .*
> *. . . licet, nec urbe tota*
> *Quisquam est tam prope tam proculque nobis.*—Mart.

MY Friend WILL. HONEYCOMB is one of those Sort of Men who are very often absent in Conversation, and what the *French* call *a reveur* and *a distrait*. A little before our Club-time last Night we were walking together in *Somerset* Garden, where WILL. had picked up a small Pebble of so odd a Make, that he said he would present it to a Friend of his, an eminent *Virtuoso*. After we had walked some time, I made a full stop with my Face towards the West, which WILL. knowing to be my usual

Method of asking what's a Clock, in an Afternoon, immediately pulled out his Watch, and told me we had seven Minutes good. We took a turn or two more, when, to my great Surprize, I saw him squir away his Watch a considerable way into the Thames, and with great Sedateness in his Looks put up the Pebble, he had before found, in his Fob. As I have naturally an Aversion to much Speaking, and do not love to be the Messenger of ill News, especially when it comes too late to be useful, I left him to be convinced of his Mistake in due time, and continued my Walk, reflecting on these little Absences and Distractions in Mankind, and resolving to make them the Subject of a future Speculation.

I was the more confirmed in my Design, when I considered that they were very often Blemishes in the Characters of Men of excellent Sense; and helped to keep up the Reputation of that *Latin* Proverb, which Mr. *Dryden* has Translated in the following Lines:

> *Great Wit to Madness sure is near ally'd,*
> *And thin Partitions do their Bounds divide.*

My Reader does, I hope, perceive, that I distinguish a Man who is *Absent*, because he thinks of something else, from one who is *Absent*, because he thinks of nothing at all: The latter is too Innocent a Creature to be taken notice of; but the Distractions of the former may, I believe, be generally accounted for from one of these Reasons.

Either their Minds are wholly fixed on some particular Science, which is often the Case of Mathematicians and other Learned Men; or are wholly taken up with some Violent Passion, such as Anger, Fear, or Love, which ties the Mind to some distant Object; or, lastly, these Distractions proceed from a certain Vivacity and Fickleness in a Man's Temper, which while it raises up infinite Numbers of *Ideas* in the Mind, is continually pushing it on, without allowing it to rest on any particular Image. Nothing therefore is more unnatural than the Thoughts and Conceptions of such a Man, which are seldom occasioned either by the Company he is in, or any of those Objects which are placed before him. While you fancy he is Admiring a Beautiful Woman, 'tis an even Wager that he is solving a Proposition in *Euclid*; and while you may imagine he is reading the *Paris Gazette*, 'tis far from being impossible, that he is pulling down and rebuilding the Front of his Country-House.

At the same time that I am endeavouring to expose this Weakness in others, I shall readily confess that I once laboured under the same Infirmity my self. The Method I took to

Conquer it was a firm Resolution to learn something from whatever I was obliged to see or hear. There is a way of Thinking, if a Man can attain to it, by which he may strike somewhat out of any thing. I can at present observe those Starts of good Sense and Struggles of unimproved Reason in the Conversation of a Clown, with as much Satisfaction as the most shining Periods of the most finished Orator; and can make a shift to command my Attention at a *Puppet-Show* or an *Opera*, as well as at *Hamlet* or *Othello*. I always make one of the Company I am in; for though I say little my self, my Attention to others, and those Nods of Approbation which I never bestow unmerited, sufficiently shew that I am among them. Whereas WILL. HONEYCOMB, tho' a Fellow of good Sense, is every Day doing and saying an hundred Things, which he afterwards confesses, with a well-bred Frankness, were somewhat *mal a propos*, and undesigned.

I chanced the other Day to go into a Coffee-house, where WILL. was standing in the midst of several Auditors whom he had gathered round him, and was giving them an Account of the Person and Character of *Moll Hinton*. My Appearance before him just put him in Mind of me, without making him reflect that I was actually present. So that keeping his Eyes full upon me, to the great Surprize of his Audience, he broke off his first Harangue, and proceeded thus,—'Why now there's my Friend (mentioning me by Name) he is a Fellow that thinks a great deal, but never opens his Mouth; I warrant you he is now thrusting his short Face into some Coffee-house about '*Change*. I was his Bail in the time of the *Popish-Plot*, when he was taken up for a Jesuit.' If he had looked on me a little longer, he had certainly described me so particularly, without ever considering what led him into it, that the whole Company must necessarily have found me out; for which reason remembring the old Proverb, *Out of Sight out of Mind*, I left the Room; and upon meeting him an Hour afterwards, was asked by him, with a great deal of good Humour, in what Part of the World I had lived, that he had not seen me these three Days.

Monsieur *Bruyere* has given us the Character of *an absent Man*, with a great deal of Humour, which he has pushed to an agreeable Extravagance; with the Heads of it I shall conclude my present Paper.

'*Menalcas* (says that excellent Author) comes down in a Morning, opens his Door to go out, but shuts it again, because he perceives that he has his Night-cap on; and examining himself further, finds that he is but half shaved, that he has stuck his Sword on his Right Side, that his Stockings are about his heels, and that his Shirt is over his Breeches. When he is dressed he goes to Court, comes into the Drawing-room, and walking bolt upright under a branch of Candlesticks, his Wig is caught up by one of them, and hangs dangling in the Air. All the Courtiers fall a laughing, but *Menalcas* laughs louder than any of them, and looks about for the Person that is the Jest of the Company. Coming down to the Court-gate he finds a Coach, which taking for his own he whips into it; and the Coachman drives off, not doubting but he carries his Master. As soon as he stops, *Menalcas* throws himself out of the Coach, crosses the Court, ascends the Stair-case, and runs thro' all the Chambers with the greatest Familiarity, reposes himself on a Couch, and fancies himself at Home. The Master of the House at last comes in, *Menalcas* rises to receive him, desires him to sit down; he talks, muses, and then talks again. The Gentleman of the House is tired and amazed; *Menalcas* is no less so, but is every Moment in hopes that his impertinent Guest will at last end his tedious Visit. Night comes on, when *Menalcas* is hardly undeceived.

When he is playing at Backgammon, he calls for a full Glass of Wine and Water; 'tis his turn to throw, he has the Box in one Hand, and his Glass in the other, and being extremely dry, and unwilling to lose Time, he swallows down both the Dice, and at the same Time throws his Wine into the Tables. He writes a Letter, and flings the Sand into the Inkbottle; he writes a second, and mistakes the Superscription. A Noble-man receives one of them, and upon opening it reads as follows. *I would have you, honest* Jack, *immediately upon the Receipt of this, take in Hay enough to serve me the Winter.* His Farmer receives the other, and is amazed to see in it, *My Lord, I received your Grace's Commands with an intire Submission to* . . . If he is at an Entertainment, you may see the Pieces of Bread continually multiplying round his Plate: 'Tis true, the rest of the Company want it, as well as their Knives and Forks, which *Menalcas* does not let them keep long. Sometimes in a Morning he puts his whole Family in an hurry, and at last goes out without being able to stay for his Coach or Dinner; and for that Day you may see him in every part of the Town, except the very Place where he had appointed to be upon a Business of Importance. You would often take him for everything that he is not; for a Fellow quite Stupid, for he hears nothing; for a Fool, for he talks to himself, and has an hundred Grimaces and Motions with his Head, which are altogether involuntary; for a proud Man, for he looks full upon you, and takes no Notice of your saluting him: The Truth on 't is, his Eyes are open, but he makes no use of them, and

neither sees you, nor any Man, nor any thing else.   He came
once from his Country-house, and his own Footmen undertook
to rob him, and succeeded: They held a Flambeau to his Throat,
and bid him deliver his Purse: he did so, and coming home told
his Friends he had been robbed; they desire to know the
Particulars, *Ask my Servants*, says *Menalcas, for they were
with me.'*   X

No. 78.

[STEELE.]   Wednesday, May 30.

Cum talis sis, utinam noster esses!

THE following Letters are so pleasant, that I doubt not but
the Reader will be as much diverted with them as I was.   I
have nothing to do in this Day's Entertainment, but taking the
Sentence from the End of the *Cambridge* Letter, and placing it
at the Front of my Paper; to shew the Author I wish him my
Companion with as much Earnestness as he invites me to be his.

  'Sir,

I send you the inclosed, to be inserted (if you think them
worthy of it) in your SPECTATORS; in which so surprising a
Genius appears, that it is no wonder if all Mankind endeavours
to get somewhat into a Paper which will always live.

As to the *Cambridge* Affair, the Humour was really carried
on in the Way I describe it.   However, you have a full Commission to put out or in, and to do whatever you think fit with
it.   I have already had the Satisfaction of seeing you take
that Liberty with some things I have before sent you.

  Go on, Sir, and prosper.   You have the best Wishes of,
                    Sir,
                         Your very Affectionate and
                                     Obliged Humble Servant.'

  '*Mr.* SPECTATOR,   *Cambridge.*

You well know it is of great Consequence to clear Titles, and
it is of Importance that it be done in the proper Season; On
which Account this is to assure you, that the CLUB OF UGLY
FACES was instituted originally at *CAMBRIDGE* in the merry
Reign of K—g *Ch—les* II.   As in great Bodies of Men it is not
difficult to find Members enow for such a Club, so (I remember)
it was then feared, upon their intention of dining together,
that the Hall belonging to *CLARE HALL*, (the ugliest *then* in
the Town, tho' *now* the neatest) would not be large enough

HANDSOMELY to hold the Company. Invitations were made to great Numbers, but very few accepted them without much Difficulty. ONE pleaded, that being at *London* in a Bookseller's Shop, a Lady going by with a great Belly longed to kiss him, HE had certainly been excused, but that Evidence appeared, That indeed one in *London* did pretend she longed to kiss him, but that it was only a *Pickpocket*, who during his kissing her stole away all his Money. ANOTHER would have got off by a Dimple in his Chin; but it was proved upon *him*, that he had by coming into a Room made a Woman miscarry, and frighted two Children into Fits. A THIRD alledged, That he was taken by a Lady for another Gentleman, who was one of the handsomest in the University: But upon Enquiry it was found, That the Lady had actually lost one Eye, and the other was very much upon the Decline. A FOURTH produced Letters out of the Country in his Vindication, in which a Gentleman offered him his Daughter, who had lately fallen in Love with him, with a good Fortune: But it was made appear that the young Lady was amorous, and had like to have run away with her Father's Coachman; so that 'twas supposed, that her Pretence of falling in Love with him was only in order to be well married. It was pleasant to hear the several Excuses which were made, insomuch that some made as much Interest to be excused, as they would from serving Sheriff; however, at last the Society was formed, and proper Officers were appointed; and the Day was fixed for the Entertainment, which was in *Venison Season*. A pleasant *Fellow* of *King's College* (commonly called CRAB from his sour Look, and the only Man who did not pretend to get off) was nominated for Chaplain; and nothing was wanting but some one to sit in the Elbow-Chair, by way of PRESIDENT, at the upper end of the Table; and there the Business stuck, for there was no Contention for Superiority *there*. This affair made so great a Noise, that the K—g, who was then at *New-Market*, heard of it, and was pleased merrily and graciously to say, HE COULD NOT BE THERE HIMSELF, BUT HE WOULD SEND THEM A BRACE OF BUCKS.

I would desire you, Sir, to set this Affair in a true Light, that Posterity may not be mis-led in so important a Point: For when *the Wise Man who shall write your true History* shall acquaint the World, That you had a DIPLOMA sent from the *Ugly Club at Oxford*, and That by Vertue of it you were admitted into it; what a learned War will there be among *future Criticks* about the Original of that Club, which both Universities will contend so warmly for? And perhaps some hardy *Cantabrigian* Author may then boldly affirm, That the Word *OXFORD* was an Interpolation of some *Oxonian* instead of

CAMBRIDGE. This Affair will be best adjusted in your Lifetime; but I hope your Affection to your MOTHER will not make you partial to your AUNT.

To tell you, Sir, my own Opinion: Tho' I cannot find any ancient Records of any Acts of the SOCIETY OF THE UGLY FACES, considered in a *publick* Capacity; yet in a *private* one they have certainly Antiquity on their Side. I am perswaded they will hardly give Place to the LOWNGERS, and the LOWNGERS are of the same Standing with the University it self.

Though we well know, Sir, you want no Motives to do Justice, yet I am commissioned to tell you, that you are invited to be admitted *ad eundem* at *CAMBRIDGE*; and I believe I may venture safely to deliver this as the Wish of our whole University.'

'*To Mr.* SPECTATOR.

The humble Petition of WHO and WHICH.

Sheweth,

That your Petitioners being in a forlorn and destitute Condition, know not to whom we should apply our selves for Relief, because there is hardly any Man alive who has not injured us. Nay, we speak it with Sorrow, even YOU your self, whom we should suspect of such a Practice the last of all Mankind, can hardly acquit your self of having given us some Cause of Complaint. We are descended of ancient Families, and kept up our Dignity and Honour many Years, till the Jacksprat THAT supplanted us. How often have we found our selves slighted by the Clergy in their Pulpits, and the Lawyers at the Bar? Nay, how often have we heard in one of the most polite and august Assemblies in the Universe, to our great Mortification, these Words, *That THAT that noble L—d urged?* which if one of us had had Justice done, would have sounded nobler thus, *That WHICH that noble L—d urged.* Senates themselves, the Guardians of *British* Liberty, have degraded us, and preferred THAT to us; and yet no Decree was ever given against us. In the very Acts of Parliament, in which the utmost Right should be done to every *Body, WORD,* and *Thing,* we find ourselves often either not used, or used one instead of another. In the first and best Prayer Children are taught, they learn to misuse us: *Our Father WHICH art in Heaven,* should be, *Our Father WHO art in Heaven*; and even a CONVOCATION, after long Debates, refused to consent to an Alteration of it. In our *general Confession* we say,—*Spare Thou them, O God, WHICH confess their Faults*; which ought to be, *WHO confess their Faults.* What Hopes then have we of having Justice done us, when the Makers of our very Prayers and Laws, and the most learned in all Faculties, seem to be in a Confederacy against us, and our Enemies themselves must be our Judges?

The *Spanish* Proverb says *Il sabio muda conscio, il necio no:* i.e. *A wise Man changes his Mind, a Fool never will.* So that we think You, Sir, a very proper Person to address to, since we know you to be capable of being convinced, and changing your Judgment. You are well able to settle this Affair, and to you we submit our Cause. We desire you to assign the Butts and Bounds of each of us; and that for the future we may both enjoy our own. We would desire to be heard by our Council, but that we fear in their very Pleadings they would betray our Cause: Besides, we have been oppressed so many Years, that we can appear no other Way, but *in forma pauperis.* All which considered, we hope you will be pleased to do that which to Right and Justice shall appertain.

R   *And Your Petitioners,* &c.'

No. 79.
[STEELE.]   Thursday, May 31.

Oderunt peccare boni virtutis amore.—Hor.

I HAVE received very many Letters of late from my Female Correspondents, most of whom are very angry with me for Abridging their Pleasures, and looking severely upon things, in themselves indifferent. But I think they are extreamly Unjust to me in this Imputation: All that I contend for is, that those Excellencies, which are to be regarded but in the second Place, should not precede more weighty Considerations. The Heart of Man deceives him in spite of the Lectures of half a Life spent in Discourses on the Subjection of Passion; and I do not know why one may not think the Heart of Woman as unfaithful to it self. If we grant an Equality in the Faculties of both Sexes, the Minds of Women are less Cultivated with Precepts, and consequently may, without Disrespect to them, be accounted more liable to Illusion in Cases wherein natural Inclination is out of the Interest of Virtue. I shall take up my present Time in commenting upon a Billet or two which came from Ladies, and from thence leave the Reader to judge whether I am in the right or not, in thinking it is possible Fine Women may be mistaken.

The following Address seems to have no other Design in it, but to tell me the Writer will do what she pleases for all me.

'Mr. SPECTATOR,

I am Young, and very much inclined to follow the Paths of Innocence; but at the same time, as I have a plentiful Fortune, and am of Quality, I am unwilling to resign the Pleasures of Distinction, some little Satisfaction in being Admired in general, and much greater in being beloved by a Gentleman, whom I design to make my Husband. But I have a mind to put off entring into Matrimony 'till another Winter is over my Head, which (whatever, musty Sir, you may think of the Matter) I design to pass away in hearing Musick, going to Plays, Visiting, and all other Satisfactions which Fortune and Youth, protected by Innocence and Virtue, can procure for,

Sir,

Your most Humble Servant,

M. T.

My Lover does not know I like him, therefore having no Engagements upon me, I think to stay, and know whether I may not like any one else better.'

I have heard WILL. HONEYCOMB say, *A Woman seldom writes her Mind but in her Postscript.* I think this Gentlewoman has sufficiently discovered hers in this. I 'll lay what Wager she pleases against her present Favourite, and can tell her that she will Like Ten more before she is fixed, and then will take the worst Man she ever liked in her Life. There is no end of Affection taken in at the Eyes only; and you may as well satisfie those Eyes with seeing, as control any Passion received by them only. It is from Loving by Sight that Coxcombs so frequently succeed with Women, and very often a Young Lady is bestowed by her Parents to a Man who weds her (as Innocence it self) tho' she has, in her own Heart, given her Approbation of a different Man in every Assembly she was in the whole Year before. What is wanting among Women, as well as among Men, is the Love of laudable Things, and not to rest only in the Forbearance of such as are Reproachful.

How far removed from a Woman of this light Imagination is *Eudosia*! *Eudosia* has all the Arts of Life and good Breeding with so much ease, that the Virtue of her Conduct looks more like an Instinct than Choice. It is as little difficult to her to think justly of Persons and Things, as it is to a Woman of different Accomplishments to move ill or look awkard. That which was, at first, the effect of Instruction is grown into an Habit; and it would be as hard for *Eudosia* to indulge a wrong Suggestion of Thought, as it would be for *Flavia* the Fine Dancer, to come into a Room with an unbecoming Air.

But the Misapprehensions People themselves have of their own State of Mind, is laid down with much discerning in the following Letter, which is but an Extract of a kind Epistle from my charming Mistress *Hecatissa*, who is above the Vanity of external Beauty, and is the better Judge of the Perfections of the Mind.

'*Mr.* SPECTATOR,

I write this to acquaint you, that very many Ladies, as well as my self, spend many Hours more than we used at the Glass, for want of the Female Library of which you promised us a Catalogue. I hope, Sir, in the Choice of Authors for us, you will have a particular Regard to Books of Devotion. What they are, and how many, must be your chief Care; for upon the Propriety of such Writings depends a great deal. I have known those among us who think, if they every Morning and Evening spend an Hour in their Closet, and read over so many Prayers in Six or Seven Books of Devotion, all equally non-sensical, with a sort of Warmth (that might as well be raised by a Glass of Wine, or a Drachm of Citron) they may all the rest of their time go on in whatever their particular Passion leads them to. The Beauteous *Philauthia*, who is (in your Language) an *Idol*, is one of these Votaries; she has a very pretty furnished Closet, to which she retires at her appointed Hours; This is her Dressing-room, as well as Chappel; she has constantly before her a large Looking-glass, and upon the Table, according to a very witty Author,

> *Together lye her Prayer-Book and Paint*
> *At once t' improve the Sinner and the Saint.*

It must be a good Scene, if one could be present at it, to see this *Idol* by turns lift up her Eyes to Heav'n, and steal Glances at her own dear Person. It cannot but be a pleasing Conflict between Vanity and Humiliation. When you are upon this Subject, chuse Books which elevate the Mind above the World, and give a pleasing Indifference to little things in it. For want of such Institutions, I am apt to believe so many People take it in their Heads to be sullen, cross and angry, under Pretence of being abstracted from the Affairs of this Life; when at the same time they betray their Fondness for them by doing their Duty as a Task, and Pouting and reading good Books for a Week together. Much of this I take to pro-ceed from the Indiscretion of the Books themselves, whose very Titles of Weekly Preparations, and such limited Godliness, lead People of ordinary Capacities into great Errors, and raise in them a Mechanical Religion, intirely distinct from Morality. I know a Lady so given up to this sort of Devotion, that tho' she employs six or eight Hours of the twenty four at Cards, she never misses one constant Hour of Prayer, for which time another holds her Cards, to which she returns with no little Anxiousness 'till two or three in the Morning. All these Acts are but empty Shows, and, as it were, Compliments made to Virtue; the Mind is all the while untouched with any true Pleasure in the Pursuit of it. From hence I presume it arises that so many People call themselves Virtuous, from no other Pretence to it but an Absence of Ill. There is *Dulcianara* is the most insolent of all Creatures to her Friends and Domesticks, upon no other Pretence in Nature, but that (as her silly Phrase is) no one can say Black is her Eye. She has no Secrets, forsooth, which should make her afraid to speak her Mind, and therefore she is impertinently Blunt to all her Acquaintance, and unseasonably Imperious to all her Family. Dear Sir, be pleased to put such Books in our Hands, as may make our Virtue more inward, and convince some of us that in a Mind truly Virtuous the Scorn of Vice is always accompanied with the Pity of it. This, and other things, are impatiently expected from you by our whole Sex, among the rest by, Sir,

Your most humble Servant,

B. D.'

No. 80.

[STEELE.]   Friday, June 1.

Coelum, non animum mutant, qui trans mare currunt.—Hor.

In the Year 1688, and on the same Day of that Year, were born in *Cheapside, London,* two Females of exquisite Feature and Shape; the one we shall call *Brunetta*; the other *Phillis.* A close Intimacy between their Parents made each of them the first Acquaintance the other knew in the World: They Played, dressed Babies, acted Visitings, learned to Dance and make Curtsies, together. They were inseparable Companions in all the little Entertainments their tender Years were capable of: Which innocent Happiness continued till the Beginning of their fifteenth Year, when it happened that Mrs. *Phillis* had an Head-dress on which became her so very well, that instead of being beheld any more with Pleasure for their Amity to each other, the Eyes of the Neighbourhood were turned to remark them with Comparison of their Beauty. They now no longer

enjoyed the Ease of Mind and pleasing Indolence in which they
were formerly happy, but all their Words and Actions were
misinterpreted by each other, and every Excellence in their
Speech and Behaviour was looked upon as an Act of Emulation to surpass the other. These Beginnings of Dis-inclination
soon improved into a Formality of Behaviour, a general Coldness, and by natural Steps into an irreconcileable Hatred.

These two Rivals for the Reputation of Beauty, were in their
Stature, Countenance and Mein so very much alike, that if
you were speaking of them in their Absence, the Words in
which you described the one must give you an Idea of the other.
They were hardly distinguishable, you would think, when they
were apart, tho' extreamly different when together. What
made their Enmity the more entertaining to all the rest of
their Sex was, that in Detraction from each other neither could
fall upon Terms which did not hit her self as much as her
Adversary. Their Nights grew restless with Meditation of new
Dresses to out-vie each other, and inventing new Devices to
recall Admirers, who observed the Charms of the one rather
than those of the other on the last Meeting. Their Colours
failed at each other's Appearance, flushed with Pleasure at the
Report of a Disadvantage, and their Countenances withered
upon Instances of Applause. The Decencies to which Women
are obliged, made these Virgins stifle their Resentment so far
as not to break into open Violences, while they equally suffered
the Torments of a regulated Anger. Their Mothers, as it is
usual, engaged in the Quarrel, and supported the several Pretensions of the Daughters with all that ill-chosen sort of
Expence which is common with People of plentiful Fortunes
and mean taste. The Girls preceded their Parents like Queens
of *May*, in all the gaudy Colours imaginable, on every *Sunday*
to Church, and were exposed to the Examination of the
Audience for Superiority of Beauty.

During this constant Struggle it happened, that *Phillis* one
Day at publick Prayers smote the Heart of a gay *West-Indian*,
who appeared in all the Colours which can affect an Eye that
could not distinguish between being fine and tawdry. This
American in a Summer-Island Suit was too shining and too
gay to be resisted by *Phillis*, and too intent upon her Charms
to be diverted by any of the laboured Attractions of *Brunetta*.
Soon after, *Brunetta* had the Mortification to see her Rival
disposed of in a Wealthy Marriage, while she was only addressed to in a Manner that shewed she was the Admiration of
all Men, but the Choice of none. *Phillis* was carried to the
Habitation of her Spouse in *Barbadoes*: *Brunetta* had the ill
Nature to enquire for her by every Opportunity, and had the

Misfortune to hear of her being attended by numerous Slaves, fanned into Slumbers by successive Hands of them, and carried from Place to Place in all the Pomp of barbarous Magnificence. *Brunetta* could not endure these repeated Advices, but employed all her Arts and Charms in laying Baits for any of Condition of the same Island, out of a meer Ambition to confront her once more before she died. She at last succeeded in her Design, and was taken to Wife by a Gentleman whose Estate was continuous to that of her Enemy's Husband. It would be endless to ennumerate the many Occasions on which these irreconcileable Beauties laboured to excel each other; but in Process of Time it happened, that a Ship put into the Island consigned to a Friend of *Phillis*, who had Directions to give her the Refusal of all Goods for Apparel, before *Brunetta* could be alarmed of their Arrival. He did so, and *Phillis* was dressed in a few Days in a Brocade more gorgeous and costly than had ever before appeared in that Latitude. *Brunetta* languished at the Sight, and could by no Means come up to the Bravery of her Antagonist. She communicated her Anguish of Mind to a faithful Friend, who by an Interest in the Wife of *Phillis*'s Merchant, procured a Remnant of the same Silk for *Brunetta*. *Phillis* took Pains to appear in all publick Places where she was sure to meet *Brunetta*; *Brunetta* was now prepared for the Insult, and came to a publick Ball in a plain black Silk Mantua, attended by a beautiful Negro Girl in a Petticoat of the same Brocade with which *Phillis* was attired. This drew the Attention of the whole Company; upon which the unhappy *Phillis* swooned away, and was immediately conveyed to her House. As soon as she came to herself she fled from her Husband's House, went on board a Ship in the Road, and is now landed in inconsolable Despair at *Plymouth*.

POSTSCRIPT.

After the above melancholy Narration, it may perhaps be a Relief to the Reader to peruse the following Expostulation.

'To Mr. SPECTATOR.

The just Remonstrance of affronted That.

Tho' I deny not the Petition of Mr. *Who* and *Which*, yet You should not suffer them to be rude, and to call honest People Names; For that bears very hard on some of those Rules of Decency, which You are justly famous for establishing. They may find Fault, and correct Speeches in the Senate and at the Bar: But let them try to get *themselves* so *often* and with s much *Eloquence* repeated in a Sentence, as a great Orator doth frequently introduce me.

My Lords! (says he) with humble Submission, *That* that I say is this: that, *That* that, that Gentleman has advanced, is not *That*, that he should have proved to your Lordships. Let those two questionary Petitioners try to do thus with their *Whos* and their *Whiches*.

What great Advantage was I of to Mr. *Dryden* in his *Indian Emperor*,

> *You force me still to answer You in* That,

to furnish out a Rhime to *Morat*? And what a poor Figure would Mr. *Bayes* have made without his *Egad and all That*? How can a judicious Man distinguish one thing from another, without saying *This here*, or *That there*? And how can a sober Man, without using the *Expletives* of Oaths (in which indeed the Rakes and Bullies have a great Advantage over others) made a Discourse of any tolerable Length, without *That is*; and if he be a very grave Man indeed, without *That is to say*? And how instructive as well as entertaining are those usual Expressions, in the Mouths of great Men, *Such things as That* and *The like of That*.

I am not against reforming the Corruptions of Speech You mention, and own there are proper Seasons for the Introduction of other Words besides *That*; but I scorn as much to supply the place of a *Who* or a *Which* at every Turn, as they are *unequal* always to fill mine; and I expect good Language and civil Treatment, and hope to receive it for the future: *That*, that I shall only add is, that I am,

> *Yours,*

R   THAT.'

The End of the First Volume.

TO THE RIGHT HONOURABLE

CHARLES LORD *HALLIFAX.*

My LORD,

SIMILITUDE of Manners and Studies is usually mentioned as one of the strongest Motives to Affection and Esteem; but the passionate Veneration I have for Your Lordship, I think, flows from an Admiration of Qualities in You, of which in the whole Course of these Papers I have acknowledged my self incapable. While I busie my self as a Stranger upon Earth, and can pretend to no other than being a Looker on, You are conspicuous in the Busy and Polite World, both in the World of Men and that of Letters: While I am silent and unobserved in publick Meetings, You are admired by all that approach You as the Life and Genius of the Conversation. What an happy Conjunction of different Talents meets in him whose whole Discourse is at once animated by the Strength and Force of Reason, and adorned with all the Graces and Embellishments of Wit? When Learning irradiates common Life, it is then in its highest Use and Perfection; and it is to such as Your Lordship that the Sciences owe the Esteem which they have with the active Part of Mankind. Knowledge of Books in recluse Men, is like that sort of Lanthorn which hides him who carries it, and serves only to pass through secret and gloomy Paths of his own; but in the Possession of a Man of Business, it is as a Torch in the Hand of one who is willing and able to shew those, who are bewildered, the Way which leads to their Prosperity and Welfare. A generous Concern for Your Country, and a Passion for every thing which is truly Great and Noble, are what actuate all Your Life and Actions; and I hope You will forgive me that I have an Ambition this Book may be placed in the Library of so good a Judge of what is valuable, in that Library where the Choice is such that it will not be a Disparagement to be the meanest Author in it. Forgive me, my Lord, for taking this Occasion of telling all the World how ardently I Love and Honour You; and that I am with the utmost Gratitude for all Your Favours,

> *My Lord,*
> > *Your Lordship's*
> > > *most Obliged,*
> > > > *most Obedient,*
> > > > > *and most Humble Servant,*

> > > > > > *THE SPECTATOR.*

THE SPECTATOR.

VOL. II.

No. 81.

[ADDISON.]   Saturday, June 2, 1711.

Qualis ubi audito venantum murmure tigris
Horruit in maculas . . .—Statius.

ABOUT the middle of last Winter I went to see an *Opera* at
the Theatre in the *Hay-Market*, where I could not but take
notice of two Parties of very Fine Women, that had placed
themselves in the opposite Side-Boxes, and seemed drawn up
in a kind of Battle-Array one against another. After a short
Survey of them, I found they were *Patched* differently; the
Faces, on one Hand, being Spotted on the Right Side of the
Forehead, and those upon the other on the Left. I quickly
perceived that they cast Hostile Glances upon one another;
and that their Patches were placed in those different Situations,
as Party-Signals to distinguish Friends from Foes. In the
Middle-Boxes, between these two opposite Bodies, were several
Ladies who Patched indifferently on both sides of their Faces,
and seemed to sit there with no other Intention but to see
the *Opera*. Upon Enquiry I found, that the Body of *Amazons*
on my Right Hand, were Whigs; and those on my Left,
Tories; and that those who had placed themselves in the
Middle-Boxes were a Neutral Party, whose Faces had not yet
declared themselves. These last, however, as I afterwards
found, diminished daily, and took their Party with one Side
or the other; insomuch that I observed in several of them, the
Patches which were before dispersed equally, are now all gone
over to the Whig, or Tory Side of the Face. The Censorious
say, That the Men whose Hearts are aimed at are very often
the Occasions that one part of the Face is thus Dishonoured,
and lyes under a kind of Disgrace, while the other is so much
Set off and Adorned by the Owner; and that the Patches turn to
the Right or to the Left, according to the Principles of the Man
who is most in Favour. But whatever may be the Motives of
a few Fantastical Coquets, who do not Patch for the Publick
Good, so much as for their own Private Advantage; it is certain,
that there are several Women of Honour who Patch out of

Principle, and with an Eye to the Interest of their Country. Nay, I am informed, that some of them adhere so steadfastly to their Party, and are so far from Sacrificing their Zeal for the Publick to their Passion for any particular Person, that in a late Draught of Marriage-Articles a Lady has stipulated with her Husband, That, whatever his Opinions are, she shall be at Liberty to Patch on which side she pleases.

I must here take notice, that *Rosalinda*, a Famous Whig Partizan, has most unfortunately a very beautiful Mole on the Tory part of her Forehead; which, being very conspicuous, has occasioned many Mistakes, and given an Handle to her Enemies to misrepresent her Face, as tho' it had Revolted from the Whig Interest. But whatever this natural Patch may seem to intimate, it is well known that her Notions of Government are still the same. This unlucky Mole however has mis-led several Coxcombs; and, like the hanging out of false Colours, made some of them converse with *Rosalinda* in what they thought the Spirit of her Party, when on a sudden she has given them an unexpected Fire, that has sunk them all at once. If *Rosalinda* is unfortunate in her Mole, *Nigranilla* is as unhappy in a Pimple, which forces her, against her Inclinations, to Patch on the Whig side.

I am told that many Virtuous Matrons, who formerly have been taught to believe that this Artificial Spotting of the Face was unlawful, are now reconciled by a Zeal for their Cause, to what they could not be prompted by a Concern for their Beauty. This way of declaring War upon one another, puts me in mind of what is reported of the Tigress, that several Spots rise in her Skin when she is angry; or as Mr. *Cowley* has imitated the Verses that stand as the Motto of this Paper,

> . . . *She Swells with angry Pride,*
> *And calls forth all her Spots on ev'ry side.*

When I was in the Theatre the time above-mentioned, I had the Curiosity to count the Patches on both Sides, and found the Tory patches to be about twenty Stronger than the Whig; but to make amends for this small Inequality, I the next Morning found the whole Puppet-show filled with the Faces spotted after the Whiggish manner. Whether or no the Ladies had retreated hither in order to rally their Forces I cannot tell: but the next Night they came in so great a Body to the Opera, that they outnumbered the Enemy.

This Account of Party-Patches will, I am afraid, appear improbable to those who live at a distance from the fashionable World; but as it is a Distinction of a very singular Nature, and what perhaps may never meet with a Parallel, I think I should not have discharged the Office of a faithful Spectator had I not recorded it.

I have, in former Papers, endeavoured to expose this Party-Rage in Women, as it only serves to aggravate the Hatreds and Animosities that reign among Men, and in a great measure deprives the Fair Sex of those peculiar Charms with which Nature has endowed them.

When the *Romans* and *Sabines* were at War, and just upon the point of giving Battle, the Women, who were allied to both of them, interposed with so many Tears and Intreaties, that they prevented the mutual Slaughter which threatned both Parties, and united them together in a firm and lasting Peace.

I would recommend this noble Example to our *British* Ladies, at a time when their Country is torn with so many unnatural Divisions, that if they contiue, it will be a Misfortune to be born in it. The *Greeks* thought it so improper for Women to interest themselves in Competitions and Contentions, that for this Reason, among others, they forbad them, under Pain of Death, to be present at the *Olympick* Games, notwithstanding these were the publick Diversions of all *Greece*.

As our *English* Women excel those of all Nations in Beauty, they should endeavour to outshine them in all other Accomplishments proper to the Sex, and to distinguish themselves as tender Mothers and faithful Wives, rather than as furious Partizans. Female Virtues are of a Domestick turn. The Family is the proper Province for Private Women to Shine in. If they must be showing their Zeal for the Publick, let it not be against those who are perhaps of the same Family, or at least of the same Religion or Nation, but against those who are the open, professed, undoubted Enemies of their Faith, Liberty, and Country. When the *Romans* were pressed with a Foreign Enemy, the Ladies voluntarily contributed all their Rings and Jewels to assist the Government under a publick Exigence; which appeared so laudable an Action in the Eyes of their Countrymen, that from thenceforth it was permitted by a Law to pronounce publick Orations at the Funeral of a Woman in Praise of the deceased Person, which till that time was peculiar to Men. Would our *English* Ladies, instead of sticking on a Patch against those of their own Country, shew themselves so truly Publick-spirited as to Sacrifice every one her Necklace against the Common Enemy, what Decrees ought not to be made in favour of them?

Since I am recollecting upon this Subject such Passages as occur to my Memory out of ancient Authors, I cannot omit a Sentence in the Celebrated Funeral Oration of *Pericles*, which he made in Honour of those Brave *Athenians* that were Slain

in a Fight with the *Lacedemonians*.   After having addressed
himself to the several Ranks and Orders of his Countrymen,
and shewn them how they should behave themselves in the
Publick Cause, he turns to the Female part of his Audience;
'And as for you (says he) I shall advise you in very few Words:
Aspire only to those Virtues that are peculiar to your Sex:
follow your natural Modesty, and think it your greatest
Commendation not to be talked of one way or other.'   C

No. 82.
[STEELE.]   Monday, June 4.
      . . . Caput domina venale sub hasta.—Juv.

PASSING under *Ludgate* the other Day I heard a Voice bawling
for Charity, which I thought I had somewhere heard before.
Coming near to the Grate, the Prisoner called me by my Name,
and desired I would throw something into the Box: I was out of
Countenance for him, and did as he bid me, by putting in half
a Crown.   I went away reflecting upon the strange Constitution of some Men, and how meanly they behave themselves in
all Sorts of Conditions.   The Person who begged of me is
now, as I take it, Fifty: I was well acquainted with him till
about the Age of Twenty five; at which Time a good Estate
fell to him, by the Death of a Relation.   Upon coming to this
unexpected good Fortune, he ran into all the Extravagancies imaginable; was frequently in drunken Disputes, broke
Drawers' Heads, talked and swore loud; was unmannerly to
those above him, and insolent to those below him.   I could
not but remark, that it was the same Baseness of Spirit which
worked in his Behaviour in both Fortunes: The same little
Mind was insolent in Riches, and shameless in Poverty.   This
Accident made me muse upon the Circumstance of being in
Debt in general, and solve in my Mind what Tempers were most
apt to fall into this Errour of Life, as well as the Misfortune it
must needs be to languish under such Pressures.   As for my
self, my natural Aversion to that Sort of Conversation which
makes a Figure with the Generality of Mankind, exempts me
from any Temptations to Expence; and all my Business lies
within a very narrow Compass, which is, only to give an honest
Man who takes care of my Estate proper Vouchers for his
quarterly Payments to me, and observe what Linnen my
Laundress brings and takes away with her once a Week: My
Steward brings his Receipt ready for my signing, and I have a
pretty Implement with the respective Names of Shirts, Cravats,
Handkerchiefs and Stockings, with proper Numbers to know

how to reckon with my Laundress. This being almost all the Business I have in the World for the Care of my own Affairs, I am at full Leisure to observe upon what others do, with Relation to their Equipage and Oeconomy.

When I walk the Street, and observe the Hurry about me in this Town,

> *Where with like Haste, tho' different Ways, they run;*
> *Some to undo, and some to be undone,*

I say, when I behold this vast Variety of Persons and Humours, with the Pains they both take for the Accomplishment of the Ends mentioned in the above Verses of *Denham*, I cannot much wonder at the Endeavour after Gain; but am extreamly astonished that Men can be so insensible of the Danger of running into Debt. One would think it impossible a Man who is given to contract Debts should know, that his Creditor has from that Moment in which he transgresses Payment, so much as that Demand comes to in his Debtor's Honour, Liberty and Fortune. One would think he did not know, that his Creditor can say the worst thing imaginable of him, to wit, *That he is unjust*, without Defamation; and can sieze his Person, without being guilty of an Assault. Yet such is the loose and abandoned Turn of some Men's Minds, that they can live under these constant Apprehensions, and still go on to encrease the Cause of them. Can there be a more low and servile Condition, than to be ashamed, or afraid, to see any one Man breathing? Yet he that is much in debt, is in that Condition with relation to twenty different People. There are indeed Circumstances wherein Men of honest Natures may become liable to Debts, by some unadvised Behaviour in any great Point of their Life, or mortgaging a Man's Honesty as a Security for that of another, and the like; but these Instances are so particular and circumstantiated, that they cannot come within general Considerations: For one such Case as one of these, there are ten, where a Man, to keep up a Farce of Retinue and Grandeur within his own House, shall shrink at the Expectation of surly Demands at his Doors. The Debtor is the Creditor's Criminal, and all the Officers of Power and State whom we behold make so great a Figure, are no other than so many Persons in Authority to make good his Charge against him. Humane Society depends upon his having the Vengeance Law allots him; and the Debtor owes his Liberty to his Neighbour, as much as the Murdrer does his Life to his Prince.

Our Gentry are, generally speaking, in debt; and many Families have put it into a kind of Method of being so from Generation to Generation. The Father mortgages when his

Son is very young; and the Boy is to marry as soon as he is at Age, to redeem it, and find Portions for his Sisters. This, forsooth, is no great Inconvenience to him; for he may wench, keep a publick Table, or feed Dogs, like a worthy *English* Gentleman, till he has outrun half his Estate, and leave the same Incumbrance upon his First-born; and so on, till one Man of more Vigour than ordinary goes quite through the Estate, or some Man of Sense comes into it, and scorns to have an Estate in Partnership, that is to say, liable to the Demand or Insult of any Man living. There is my friend Sir ANDREW, tho' for many Years a great and general Trader, was never the Defendant in a Law Suit, in all the Perplexity of Business, and the Iniquity of Mankind at present: No one had any Colour for the least Complaint against his Dealings with him. This is certainly as uncommon, and in its Proportion as laudable in a Citizen, as it is in a General never to have suffered a Disadvantage in Fight. How different from this Gentleman is *Jack Truepenny*, who has been an old Acquaintance of Sir ANDREW and my self from Boys, but could never learn our Caution. *Jack* has a whorish unresisting good Nature, which makes him incapable of having a Property in any thing. His Fortune, his Reputation, his Time and his Capacity, are at any Man's Service that comes first. When he was at School, he was whipp'd thrice a Week for Faults he took upon him to excuse others; since he came into the Business of the World, he has been arrested twice or thrice a Year for Debts he had nothing to do with but as Surety for others; and I remember when a Friend of his had suffered in the Vice of the Town, all the Physick his Friend took was conveyed to him by *Jack*, and inscribed, 'A Bolus or an Electuary for Mr. *Truepenny*.' *Jack* had a good Estate left him, which came to nothing; because he believed all who pretended to Demands upon it. This Easiness and Credulity destroy all the other Merit he has: and he has all his Life been a Sacrifice to others, without ever receiving Thanks or doing one good Action.

I will end this Discourse with a Speech which I heard *Jack* make to one of his Creditors (of whom he deserved gentler Usage) after lying a whole Night in Custody at his Suit.

'Sir,

Your Ingratitude for the many Kindnesses I have done you, shall not make me unthankful for the Good you have done me, in letting me see there is such a Man as you in the World I am obliged to you for the Diffidence I shall have all the rest of my Life: *I shall hereafter trust no Man so far as to be in his Debt.*'

No. 83.

[ADDISON.]   Tuesday, June 5.

> . . . *Animum* pictura *pascit* inani.—Virg.

WHEN the Weather hinders me from taking my Diversions
without Doors, I frequently make a little Party with two or
three select Friends, to visit any thing curious that may be
seen under Covert.   My principal Entertainments of this
Nature are Pictures, insomuch that when I have found the
Weather set in to be very bad, I have taken a whole Day's
Journey to see a Galley that is furnished by the Hands of great
Masters.   By this Means, when the Heavens are filled with
Clouds, when the Earth swims in Rain, and all Nature wears a
lowring Countenance, I withdraw my self from these uncomfortable Scenes into the visionary Worlds of Art; where I meet
with shining Landskips, gilded Triumphs, beautiful Faces, and
all those other Objects that fill the Mind with gay Ideas, and
disperse that Gloominess which is apt to hang upon it in those
dark disconsolate Seasons.

I was some Weeks ago in a Course of these Diversions; which
had taken such an entire Possession of my Imagination, that
they formed in it a short Morning's Dream, which I shall communicate to my Reader, rather as the first Sketch and Outlines
of a Vision than as a finished Piece.

I dreamt that I was admitted into a long spacious Gallery,
which had one Side covered with Pieces of all the famous
Painters who are now living, and the other with the Works
of the greatest Masters that are dead.

On the side of the *Living* I saw several Persons busy in
Drawing, Colouring, and Designing; on the Side of the *Dead*
Painters I could not discover more than one Person at work,
who was exceeding slow in his Motions, and wonderfully nice
in his Touches.

I was resolved to examine the several Artists that stood
before me, and accordingly applied my self to the Side of the
Living.   The first I observed at work in this Part of the
Gallery was VANITY, with his Hair tied behind him in a
Ribbon, and dressed like a *Frenchman*.   All the Faces he
drew, were very remarkable for their Smiles, and a certain
smirking Air which he bestowed indifferently on every Age
and Degree of either Sex.   The *Toujours Gai* appeared even
in his Judges, Bishops, and Privy-Counsellors: In a Word, all
his Men were *Petits Maitres*, and all his Women *Coquets*.
The Drapery of his Figures was extreamly well suited to his
Faces, and was made up of all the glaring Colours that could be

mixt together; every Part of the Dress was in a Flutter, and endeavoured to distinguish it self above the rest.

On the Left-hand of VANITY stood a laborious Workman, who I found was his humble Admirer, and copied after him. He was dressed like a *German*, and had a very hard Name that sounded something like STUPIDITY.

The third Artist that I looked over was FANTASQUE, dressed like a *Venetian* Scaramouch. He had an excellent Hand at a *Chimera*, and dealt very much in Distortions and Grimaces. He would sometimes affright himself with the Phantoms that flowed from his Pencil. In short, the most elaborate of his Pieces was at best but a terrifying Dream; and one could say nothing more of his finest Figures, than that they were agreeable Monsters.

The fourth Person I examined was very remarkable for his hasty Hand, which left his Pictures so unfinished, that the Beauty in the Picture (which was designed to continue as a Monument of it to Posterity) faded sooner than in the Person after whom it was drawn. He made so much Haste to dispatch his Business, that he neither gave himself Time to clean his Pencils nor mix his Colours. The Name of this expeditious Workman was AVARICE.

Not far from this Artist I saw another of a quite different Nature, who was dressed in the Habit of a *Dutchman*, and known by the Name of INDUSTRY. His Figures were wonderfully laboured: If he drew the Portraiture of a Man, he did not omit a single Hair in his Face; if the Figure of a Ship, there was not a Rope among the Tackle that escaped him. He had likewise hung a great Part of the Wall with Night-Pieces, that seemed to show themselves by the Candles which were lighted up in several Parts of them; and were so inflamed by the Sun-shine which accidentally fell upon them, that at first Sight I could scarce forbear crying out *Fire*.

The five foregoing Artists were the most considerable on this Side the Gallery; there were indeed several others whom I had not Time to look into. One of them however I could not forbear observing, who was very busy in retouching the finest Pieces, though he produced no Originals of his own. His Pencil aggravated every Feature that was before over-charged, loaded every Defect, and poisoned every Colour it touched. Though this Workman did so much Mischief on the Side of the Living, he never turned his Eye towards that of the Dead. His Name was ENVY.

Having taken a cursory View of one Side of the Gallery, I turned my self to that which was filled by the Works of those great Masters that were dead; when immediately I fancied my self standing before a Multitude of Spectators, and thousands of Eyes looking upon me at once; for all before me appeared so like Men and Women, that I almost forgot they were Pictures. *Raphael*'s Figures stood in one Row, *Titian*'s in another, *Guido Rheni*'s in a third. One part of the Wall was peopled by *Hanibal Carrache*, another by *Correggio*, and another by *Rubens*. To be short, there was not a great Master among the Dead who had not contributed to the Embellishment of this Side of the Gallery. The Persons that owed their Being to these several Masters, appeared all of them to be real and alive, and differed among one another only in the Variety of their Shapes, Complexions, and Cloaths; so that they looked like different Nations of the same Species.

Observing an old Man (who was the same Person I before mentioned, as the only Artist that was at work on this Side of the Gallery) creeping up and down from one Picture to another, and re-touching all the fine Pieces that stood before me, I could not but be very attentive to all his Motions. I found his Pencil was so very light that it worked imperceptibly, and after a thousand Touches scarce produced any visible Effect in the Picture on which he was employ'd. However, as he busied himself incessantly, and repeated Touch after Touch without Rest or Intermission, he wore off insensibly every little disagreeable Gloss that hung upon a Figure: He also added such a beautiful Brown to the Shades, and Mellowness to the Colours, that he made every Picture appear more perfect than when it came fresh from the Master's Pencil. I could not forbear looking upon the Face of this ancient Workman, and immediately by the long Lock of Hair upon his Forehead discovered him to be TIME.

Whether it were because the Thread of my Dream was at an end I cannot tell, but upon my taking a Survey of this imaginary old Man my Sleep left me. C

No. 84.

[STEELE.]

Wednesday, June 6.

> . . . *Quis talia fando*
> *Myrmidonum Dolopumve aut duri miles Ulyssei*
> *Temperet a lachrymis.*—Virg.

LOOKING over the old Manuscript wherein the private Actions of *Pharamond* are set down by way of Table-book, I found many things which gave me great Delight; and as human

Life turns upon the same Principles and Passions in all Ages, I thought it very proper to take Minutes of what passed in that Age, for the Instruction of this. The Antiquary who lent me these Papers gave me a Character of *Eucrate*, the Favourite of *Pharamond*, extracted from an Author who lived in that Court. The Account he gives both of the Prince and this his faithful Friend, will not be improper to insert here, because I may have Occasion to mention many of their Conversations, into which these Memorials of them may give Light.

'*Pharamond*, when he had a Mind to retire for an Hour or two from the Hurry of Business and Fatigue of Ceremony, made a Signal to *Eucrate*, by putting his Hand to his Face, placing his Arm negligently on a Window, or some such Action as appeared indifferent to all the rest of the Company. Upon such Notice, unobserved by others (for their entire Intimacy was always a Secret), *Eucrate* repaired to his own Apartment to receive the King. There was a secret Access to this Part of the Court, at which *Eucrate* used to admit many whose mean Appearance in the Eyes of the ordinary Waiters and Door-keepers made them be repulsed from other Parts of the Palace. Such as these were let in here by Order of *Eucrate*, and had Audiences of *Pharamond*. This Entrance *Pharamond* called the Gate of the Unhappy, and the Tears of the Afflicted who came before him, he would say were Bribes received by *Eucrate*; for *Eucrate* had the most compassionate Spirit of all Men living, except his generous Master, who was always kindled at the least Affliction which was communicated to him. In the Regard for the Miserable, *Eucrate* took particular Care, that the common Forms of Distress, and the idle Pretenders to Sorrow, about Courts, who wanted only Supplies to Luxury, should never obtain Favour by his Means: But the Distresses which arise from the many inexplicable Occurrences that happen among Men, the unaccountable Alienation of Parents from their Children, Cruelty of Husbands to Wives, Poverty occasioned from Shipwreck or Fire, the falling out of Friends, or such other terrible Disasters to which the Life of Man is exposed; In Cases of this Nature, *Eucrate* was the Patron; and enjoyed this Part of the royal Favour so much without being envied, that it was never enquired into by whose Means, what no one else cared for doing, was brought about.

One Evening when *Pharamond* came into the Apartment of *Eucrate*, he found him extremely dejected; upon which he asked (with a Smile which was natural to him) "What, is there any one too miserable to be relieved by *Pharamond*, that *Eucrate* is melancholy?" "I fear there is," answered the

Favourite; "a Person without, of a good Air, well dressed, and tho' a Man in the Strength of his Life, seems to faint under some inconsolable Calamity: All his Features seem suffused with Agony of Mind; but I can observe in him, that it is more inclined to break away in Tears than Rage. I asked him what he would have; he said he would speak to *Pharamond*. I desired his Business; he could hardly say to me, *Eucrate*, carry me to the King, my Story is not to be told twice, I fear I shall not be able to speak it at all." *Pharamond* commanded *Eucrate* to let him enter; he did so, and the Gentleman approached the King with an Air which spoke him under the greatest concern in what manner to demean himself. The King, who had a quick Discerning, relieved him from the Oppression he was under; and with the most beautiful Complacency said to him, "Sir, do not add to that Load of Sorrow I see in your Countenance, the Awe of my Presence: Think you are speaking to your Friend; if the Circumstances of your Distress will admit of it, you shall find me so." To whom the Stranger: "Oh excellent *Pharamond*, name not a Friend to the unfortunate *Spinamont*: I had one but he is dead by my own Hand; but, oh *Pharamond*, tho' it was by the Hand of *Spinamont*, it was by the Guilt of *Pharamond*. I come not, oh excellent Prince, to implore your Pardon; I come to relate my Sorrow, a Sorrow too great for humane Life to support: From henceforth shall all Occurrences appear Dreams or short Intervals of Amusement, from this one Affliction which has siez'd my very Being. Pardon me, oh *Pharamond*, if my Griefs give me Leave, that I lay before you, in the Anguish of a wounded Mind, that you, Good as you are, are guilty of the generous Blood spilt this Day by this unhappy Hand: Oh that it had perished before that Instant!" Here the Stranger paused, and recollecting his Mind after some little Meditation, he went on in a calmer Tone and Gesture as follows.

"There is an Authority due to Distress; and as none of humane Race is above the Reach of Sorrow, none should be above the hearing the Voice of it: I am sure *Pharamond* is not. Know then, that I have this Morning unfortunately killed in a Duel the Man whom of all Men living I most loved. I command my self too much in your Royal Presence, to say *Pharamond* give me my Friend! *Pharamond* has taken him from me! I will not say, shall the merciful *Pharamond* destroy his own Subjects? Will the Father of his Country murder his People? But, the merciful *Pharamond* does destroy his Subjects, the Father of his Country does murder his People. Fortune is so much the Pursuit of Mankind, that all Glory and Honour is in the Power of a Prince, because he has the Distribution of their Fortunes. It is therefore the Inadvertency, Negligence or Guilt of Princes, to let any thing grow into Custom which is against their Laws. A Court can make Fashion and Duty walk together; it can never, without the Guilt of a Court, happen, that it shall not be unfashionable to do what is unlawful. But alas! in the Dominions of *Pharamond*, by the Force of a Tyrant Custom, which is misnamed a Point of Honour, the Duellist kills his Friend whom he loves; and the Judge condemns the Duellist, while he approves his Behaviour. Shame is the greatest of all Evils; what avail Laws, when Death only attends the Breach of them, and Shame Obedience to them? As for me, oh *Pharamond*, were it possible to describe the nameless Kinds of Compunctions and Tendernesses I feel, when I reflect upon the little Accidents in our former Familiarity, my Mind swells into Sorrow which cannot be resisted enough to be silent in the Presence of *Pharamond*.' With that he fell into a Flood of Tears, and wept aloud. 'Why should not *Pharamond* hear the Anguish he only can relieve others from in time to come? Let him hear from me, what they feel who have given Death by the false Mercy of his Administration, and form to himself the Vengeance called for by those who have perished by his Negligence.''   P

No. 85.

[ADDISON.]   Thursday, June, 7.

> *Interdum speciosa locis morataque recte*
> *Fabula nullius Veneris, sine pondere & arte,*
> *Valdius oblectat populum meliusque moratur,*
> *Quam versus inopes rerum nugaeque canorae.*—Hor.

It is the Custom of the *Mahometans*, if they see any printed or written Paper upon the Ground, to take it up and lay it aside carefully, as not knowing but it may contain some Piece of their *Alcoran*. I must confess I have so much of the *Mussulman* in me, that I cannot forbear looking into every Printed Paper which comes in my way, under whatsoever despicable Circumstances it may appear: For as no Mortal Author, in the ordinary Fate and Vicissitude of Things, knows to what use his Works may, some time or other, be applied, a Man may often meet with very celebrated Names in a Paper of Tobacco. I have lighted my Pipe more than once with the Writings of a Prelate; and know a Friend of mine who, for these several Years, has converted the Essays of a Man of Quality into a kind of Fringe for his Candlesticks. I remember, in particular, after having read over a Poem of an Eminent Author on a Victory, I met with several Fragments of it upon the next Rejoycing-day, which had been employed in Squibs and Crackers, and by that means celebrated its Subject in a double Capacity. I once met with a Page of Mr. *Baxter* under a *Christmas* Pye. Whether or no the Pastry-Cook had made use of it through Chance, or Waggery, for the defence of that superstitious *Viande*, I know not; but, upon the Perusal of it, I conceived so good an Idea of the Author's Piety, that I bought the whole Book. I have often profited by these accidental Readings, and have sometimes found very Curious Pieces, that are either out of Print, or not to be met with in the Shops of our *London* Booksellers. For this Reason, when my Friends take a Survey of my Library, they are very much surprised to find, upon the Shelf of Folios, two long Band-boxes standing upright among my Books; till I let them see that they are both of them lined with deep Erudition and abstruse Literature. I might likewise mention a Paper Kite, from which I have received great Improvement; and a Hat-case, which I would not exchange for all the Beavers in *Great Britain*. This my inquisitive Temper, or rather impertinent Humour of prying into all sorts of Writing, with my natural Aversion to Loquacity, give me a good deal of Employment when I enter any House in the Country; for I can't, for my Heart, leave a Room before I have thoroughly studied the Walls of it, and examined the several printed Papers which are usually pasted upon them. The last Piece that I met with upon this Occasion, gave me a most exquisite Pleasure. My Reader will think I am not serious, when I acquaint him that the Piece I am going to speak of was the old Ballad of the *Two Children in the Wood*, which is one of the Darling Songs of the Common People, and has been the Delight of most *Englishmen* in some Part of their Age.

This Song is a plain simple Copy of Nature, destitute of all the Helps and Ornaments of Art. The Tale of it is a pretty Tragical Story; and pleases for no other Reason, but because it is a Copy of Nature. There is even a despicable Simplicity in the Verse; and yet, because the Sentiments appear genuine and unaffected, they are able to move the Mind of the most polite Reader with inward Meltings of Humanity and Compassion. The Incidents grow out of the Subject, and are such as are the most proper to excite Pity. For which Reason the whole Narration has something in it very moving; notwithstanding the Author of it (whoever he was) has delivered it in such an abject Phrase, and poorness of Expression, that the quoting any part of it would look like a Design of turning it into Ridicule. But though the Language is mean, the Thoughts, as I have said, from one end to the other are natural: and therefore cannot fail to please those who are not Judges of Language, or those who notwithstanding they are Judges of Language, have a true and unprejudiced Taste of Nature. The Condition, Speech, and Behaviour of the dying Parents, with the Age, Innocence, and Distress of the Children, are set forth in such tender Circumstances, that it is impossible for a Reader of common Humanity not to be affected with them. As for the Circumstance of the *Robin-red-breast*, it is indeed a little Poetical Ornament; and to shew the Genius of the Author amidst all his Simplicity, it is just the same kind of Fiction which one of the greatest of the *Latin* Poets has made use of upon a Parallel Occasion; I mean that Passage in *Horace*, where he describes himself when he was a Child, fallen asleep in a Desart Wood, and covered with Leaves by the Turtles that took pity on him.

> *Me fabulosae Vulture in Apulo*
> *Altricis extra limen Apuliae*
> *Ludo fatigatumque somno*
> *Fronde nova puerum palumbes*
>
> *Texere . . .*

I have heard that the late Lord DORSET, who had the greatest Wit tempered with the greatest Candour, and was one of the finest Criticks as well as the best Poets of his Age, had a numerous Collection of old *English* Ballads, and took a particular Pleasure in the Reading of them. I can affirm the same of Mr. DRYDEN; and know several of the most refined Writers of our present Age, who are of the same Humour.

I might likewise refer my Reader to MOLIERE's Thoughts on this Subject, as he has expressed them in the Character of the *Misanthrope*; but those only who are endowed with a true Greatness of Soul and Genius, can divest themselves of the little Images of Ridicule, and admire Nature in her Simplicity and Nakedness. As for the little conceited Wits of the Age, who can only shew their Judgment by finding Fault; they cannot be supposed to admire these Productions which have nothing to recommend them, but the Beauties of Nature, when they do not know how to relish even those Compositions that, with all the Beauties of Nature, have also the additional Advantages of Art.   L

No. 86.

[ADDISON.]   Friday, June 8.

Heu quam difficile est crimen non prodere vultu!—Ovid.

THERE are several Arts which all Men are in some Measure
Masters of, without having been at the Pains of learning them.
Every one that speaks or reasons is a Grammarian and a
Logician, though he may be wholly unacquainted with the
Rules of Grammar or Logick, as they are delivered in Books
and Systems.   In the same Manner, every one is in some Degree a Master of that Art, which is generally distinguished by
the Name of Physiognomy; and naturally forms to himself the
Character or Fortune of a Stranger, from the Features and
Lineaments of his Face.   We are no sooner presented to any
one we never saw before, but we are immediately struck
with the Idea of a proud, a reserved, an affable, or a good-
natured Man; and upon our first going into a Company of
Strangers, our Benevolence or Aversion, Awe or Contempt,
rises naturally towards several particular Persons, before we
have heard them speak a single Word, or so much as know
who they are.

Every Passion gives a particular Cast to the Countenance,
and is apt to discover itself in some Feature or other.   I have
seen an Eye curse for half an Hour together, and an Eye-brow
call a Man Scoundrel.   Nothing is more common than for
Lovers to complain, resent, languish, despair, and dye, in
dumb Show.   For my own Part, I am so apt to frame a Notion
of every Man's Humour or Circumstances by his Looks, that I
have sometimes employed my self from *Charing-Cross* to the
Royal-Exchange in drawing the Characters of those who have
passed by me.   When I see a Man with a sour rivell'd Face,
I cannot forbear pitying his Wife; and when I meet with an
open ingenuous Countenance, think on the Happiness of his
Friends, his Family, and Relations.

I cannot recollect the Author of a famous Saying to a
Stranger who stood silent in his Company, *Speak that I may see
thee*: But with Submission, I think we may be better known by
our Looks than by our Words; and that a Man's Speech is much
more easily disguised than his Countenance.   In this Case however, I think the Air of the whole Face is much more expressive
than the Lines of it: The Truth of it is, the Air is generally
nothing else but the inward Disposition of the Mind made
visible.

Those who have established Physiognomy into an Art, and
laid down Rules of judging Men's Tempers by their Faces,

have regarded the Features much more than the Air.   *Martial* has a pretty Epigram on this Subject.

> *Crine ruber, niger ore, brevis pede, lumine laesus,*
>   *Rem magnam praestas, Zoile, si bonus es.*
>
> *Thy Beard and Head are of a different Die;*
>   *Short of one Foot, distorted in an Eye:*
> *With all these Tokens of a Knave compleat,*
>   *Should'st thou be honest, thou'rt a dev'lish Cheat.*

I have seen a very ingenious Author on this Subject, who founds his Speculations on the Supposition, That as a Man hath in the Mould of his Face a remote Likeness to that of an Ox, a Sheep, a Lyon, an Hog, or any other Creature; he hath the same Resemblance in the Frame of his Mind, and is subject to those Passions which are predominant in the Creature that appears in his Countenance.   Accordingly he gives the Prints of several Faces that are of a different Mould; and by a little overcharging the Likeness, discovers the Figures of these several Kinds of brutal Faces in human Features.   I remember in the Life of the famous Prince of *Conde* the Writer observes, the Face of that Prince was like the Face of an Eagle, and that the Prince was very well pleased to be told so.   In this Case therefore we may be sure, that he had in his Mind some general implicit Notion of this Art of Physiognomy which I have just now mentioned; and that when his Courtiers told him his Face was made like an Eagle's, he understood them in the same Manner as if they had told him, there was something in his Looks which shewed him to be strong, active, piercing, and of a royal Descent.   Whether or no the different Motions of the Animal Spirits in different Passions, may have any Effect on the Mould of the Face when the Lineaments are pliable and tender, or whether the same Kind of Souls require the same Kind of Habitations, I shall leave to the Consideration of the Curious.   In the mean Time I think nothing can be more glorious than for a Man to give the Lie to his Face, and to be an honest, just, good-natured Man, in spite of all those Marks and Signatures which Nature seems to have set upon him for the Contrary.   This very often happens among those, who instead of being exasperated by their own Looks, or envying the Looks of others, apply themselves entirely to the cultivating of their Minds, and getting those Beauties which are more lasting and more ornamental.   I have seen many an amiable Piece of Deformity; and have observed a certain Chearfulness in as bad a System of Features as ever was clap'd together, which hath appeared more lovely than all the

blooming Charms of an insolent Beauty. There is a double
Praise due to Virtue, when it is lodged in a Body that seems
to have been prepared for the Reception of Vice; in many such
Cases the Soul and the Body do not seem to be Fellows.

Socrates was an extraordinary Instance of this Nature.
There chanced to be a great Physiognomist in his Time at
Athens, who had made strange Discoveries of Men's Tempers
and Inclinations by their outward Appearances. *Socrates's*
Disciples, that they might put this Artist to the Trial, carried
him to their Master, whom he had never seen before, and did
not know he was then in Company with him. After a short
Examination of his Face, the Physiognomist pronounced him
the most lewd, libidinous, drunken old Fellow that he had ever
met with in his whole Life. Upon which the Disciples all
burst out a laughing, as thinking they had detected the
Falshood and Vanity of his Art: But *Socrates* told them, That
the Principles of his Art might be very true, notwithstanding
his present Mistake; for that he himself was naturally inclined
to those particular Vices which the Physiognomist had discovered in his Countenance, but that he had conquered the
strong Dispositions he was born with, by the Dictates of
Philosophy.

We are indeed told by an ancient Author, that *Socrates*
very much resembled *Silenus* in his Face; which we find to
have been very rightly observed from the Statues and Busts
of both, that are still extant; as well as on several antique
Seals and precious Stones, which are frequently enough to be
met with in the Cabinets of the Curious. But however Observations of this Nature may sometimes hold, a wise Man
should be particularly cautious how he gives Credit to a Man's
outward Appearance. It is an irreparable Injustice we are
guilty of towards one another, when we are prejudiced by the
Looks and Features of those whom we do not know. How
often do we conceive Hatred against a Person of Worth, or
fancy a Man to be proud and ill-natured by his Aspect, whom
we think we cannot esteem too much when we are acquainted
with his real Character? Dr. *Moore,* in his admirable System
of Ethicks, reckons this particular Inclination to take a
Prejudice against a Man for his Looks, among the smaller
Vices in Morality; and, if I remember, gives it the Name of a
Prosopolepsia.   L

No. 87.

[STEELE.]   Saturday, June 9.

. . . *Nimium ne crede colori.*—Virg.

IT has been the Purpose of several of my Speculations to bring
People to an unconcerned Behaviour, with relation to their
Persons, whether Beautiful or Defective. As the Secrets of
the Ugly Club were exposed to the Publick, that Men might
see there were some Noble Spirits in the Age, who were not at
all displeased with themselves upon Considerations which they
had no Choice in; So the Discourse concerning *Idols*, tended to
lessen the Value People put upon themselves from personal
Advantages, and Gifts of Nature. As to the latter Species of
Mankind, the Beauties, whether Male or Female; they are
generally the most untractable People of all others. You
are so excessively perplexed with the Particularities in their
Behaviour, that, to be at Ease, one would be apt to wish
there were no such Creatures. They expect so great Allowances, and give so little to others, that they who have to do
with them find in the main, a Man with a better Person than
ordinary, and a Beautiful Woman, might be very happily
changed for such to whom Nature has been less Liberal. The
Handsome Fellow is usually so much a Gentleman, and the
fine Woman has something so becoming, that there is no
enduring either of them. It has therefore been generally
my Choice to mix with chearful Ugly Creatures, rather than
Gentlemen who are Graceful enough to omit or do what they
please; or Beauties who have Charms enough to do and say
what would be disobliging in any but themselves.

Diffidence and Presumption, upon account of our Persons,
are equally Faults; and both arise from the want of knowing,
or rather endeavouring to know, our selves, and for what we
ought to be valued or neglected. But indeed, I did not
imagine these little Considerations and Coqueteries could have
the ill Consequence as I find they have by the following Letters
of my Correspondents, where it seems Beauty is thrown into
the Accompt, in Matters of Sale, to those who receive no
Favour from the Charmers.

'*Mr.* SPECTATOR,   *June* 4.

After I have assured you I am in every respect one of the
Handsomest young Girls about Town—, I need be particular
in nothing but the Make of my Face, which has the Misfortune
to be exactly Oval. This I take to proceed from a Temper
that naturally inclines me both to speak and to hear.

With this Account you may wonder how I can have the Vanity to offer my self as a Candidate, which I now do, to a Society, where the *Spectator* and *Hecatissa* have been admitted with so much Applause. I don't want to be put in mind how very Defective I am in every thing that is Ugly; I am too sensible of my own Unworthiness in this Particular, and therefore I only propose my self as a Foil to the Club.

You see how honest I have been to confess all my Imperfections, which is a great deal to come from a Woman, and what, I hope, you will encourage with the Favour of your Interest.

There can be no Objection made on the side of the Matchless *Hecatissa*, since it is certain I shall be in no danger of giving her the least occasion of Jealousie: And then, a Joint-Stool in the very lowest Place at the Table, is all the Honour that is coveted by

> *Your most Humble*
> *and Obedient Servant,*
>
> Rosalinda.

P.S. I have sacrificed my Necklace to put into the Publick Lottery against the Common Enemy. And last *Saturday*, about Three a Clock in the Afternoon, I began to Patch indifferently on both sides of my Face.'

'*Mr.* SPECTATOR, *London, June* 7, 1711.

Upon reading your late Dissertation concerning *Idols*, I cannot but complain to you that there are, in six or seven Places of this City, Coffee-houses kept by Persons of that Sisterhood. These Idols sit and receive all day long the Adoration of the Youth within such and such Districts: I know, in particular, Goods are not entered as they ought to be at the Custom-house, nor Law-Reports perused at the Temple; by reason of one Beauty who detains the young Merchants too long near Change, and another Fair one, who keeps the Students at her House when they should be at Study. It would be worth your while to see how the Idolaters alternately offer Incense to their *Idols*, and what Heart-burnings arise in those who wait for their Turn to receive kind Aspects from those little Thrones, which all the Company, but these Lovers, call the Bars. I saw a Gentleman turn as pale as Ashes, because an *Idol* turned the Sugar in a Tea-Dish for his Rival, and carelessly called the Boy to serve him, with a *Sirrah! Why don't you give the Gentleman the Box to please himself?* Certain it is, that a very hopeful young Man was taken with Leads in his Pockets below Bridge, where he intended to drown himself, because his *Idol* would wash the Dish in which she had just before drank Tea, before she would let him use it.

I am, Sir, a Person past being Amorous, and do not give this Information out of Envy or Jealousy, but I am a real Sufferer by it. These Lovers take any thing for Tea and Coffee; I saw one Yesterday surfeit to make his Court; and all his Rivals, at the same time, loud in the Commendation of Liquors that went against every body in the Room that was not in Love. While these young Fellows resign their Stomachs with their Hearts, and drink at the *Idol* in this manner, we who come to do Business, or talk Politicks, are utterly Poisoned: They have also Drams for those who are more enamoured than ordinary; and it is very common for such as are too low in Constitution to Ogle the *Idol* upon the strength of Tea, to fluster themselves with warmer Liquors: Thus all Pretenders advance, as fast as they can, to a Feaver or a Diabetes. I must repeat to you, that I do not look with an Evil Eye upon the Profit of the *Idols*, or the Diversions of the Lovers; what I hope from this Remonstrance, is only that we plain People may not be served as if we were Idolaters; but that from the time of Publishing this in your Paper, the *Idols* would mix Ratsbane only for their Admirers, and take more care of us who don't Love them. *I am,*

Sir,

Yours,

R   T. T.'

No. 88.

[STEELE.]   Monday, June 11.

Quid domini facient, audent cum talia fures?—Virg.

'*Mr.* Spectator,   *May* 30, 1711.

I have no small Value for your Endeavours to lay before the World what may escape their Observation, and yet highly conduces to their Service. You have, I think, succeeded very well on many Subjects; and seem to have been conversant in very different Scenes of Life. But in the Considerations of Mankind, as a Spectator, you should not omit Circumstances which relate to the inferiour Part of the World, any more than those which concern the greater. There is one thing in particular which I wonder you have not touched upon, and that is, the general Corruption of Manners in the Servants of *Great Britain.* I am a Man that have travelled and seen many Nations, but have for seven Years last past resided constantly

in *London* or within twenty Miles of it: In this Time I have contracted a numerous Acquaintance among the best Sort of
People, and have hardly found one of them happy in their
Servants. This is Matter of great Astonishment to Foreigners,
and all such as have visited foreign Countries; especially since
we cannot but observe, That there is no Part of the World
where Servants have those Privileges and Advantages as in
England: They have no where else such plentiful Diet, large
Wages, or indulgent Liberty: There is no Place wherein they
labour less, and yet where they are so little respectful, more
wasteful, more negligent, or where they so frequently change
their Masters. To this I attribute, in a great Measure, the
frequent Robberies and Losses which we suffer on the high
Road and in our own Houses. That indeed which gives me
the present Thought of this Kind, is, that a careless Groom of
mine has spoiled me the prettiest Pad in the World, with only
riding him ten Miles; and I assure you, if I were to make a
Register of all the Horses I have known thus abused by Negligence of Servants, the Number would mount a Regiment. I
wish you would give us your Observations, that we may know
how to treat these Rogues, or that we Masters may enter into
Measures to reform them. Pray give us a Speculation in
general about Servants, and you make me

Yours,

Pray do not omit the
Mention of Grooms in   Philo-Britannicus.
particular.'

This honest Gentleman, who is so desirous that I should
write a Satyr upon Grooms, has a great deal of Reason for his
Resentment; and I know no Evil which touches all Mankind
so much, as this of the Misbehaviour of Servants.

The Complaint of this Letter runs wholly upon Men-
Servants; and I can attribute the Licentiousness which has
at present prevailed among them, to nothing but what an
hundred before me have ascribed it to, The Custom of giving
Board-Wages: This one Instance of false Oeconomy, is sufficient to debauch the whole Nation of Servants, and makes
them as it were but for some Part of their Time in that Quality.
They are either attending in Places where they meet and run
into Clubs, or else, if they wait at Taverns, they eat after their
Masters, and reserve their Wages for other Occasions. From
hence it arises, That they are but in a lower Degree what their
Masters themselves are; and usually affect an Imitation of their
Manners: And you have in Liveries Beaux, Fops, and Coxcombs, in as high Perfection, as among People that keep

Equipages. It is a common Humour among the Retinue of People of Quality, when they are in their Revels, that is when they are out of their Masters' Sight, to assume in an humourous Way the Names and Titles of those whose Liveries they wear. By which Means Characters and Distinctions become so familiar to them, that it is to this, among other Causes, one may impute a certain Insolence among our Servants, that they take no Notice of any Gentlemen though they know him ever so well, except he is an Acquaintance of their Masters.

My Obscurity and Taciturnity leave me at Liberty, without Scandal, to dine, if I think fit, at a common Ordinary, in the meanest as well as the most sumptuous House of Entertainment. Falling in the other Day at a Victualling-house near the House of Peers, I heard the Maid come down and tell the Landlady at the Bar, That my Lord Bishop swore he would throw her out at Window if she did not bring up more Mild-beer, and that my Lord Duke would have a double Mug of Purle. My Surprise was encreased, in hearing loud and rustick Voices speak and answer to each other upon the publick Affairs, by the Names of the most Illustrious of our Nobility; till of a sudden one came running in, and cryed the House was rising. Down came all the Company together, and away: The Alehouse was immediately filled with Clamour, and scoring one Mug to the Marquis of such a Place, Oyl and Vinegar to such an Earl, three Quarts to my new Lord for wetting his Title, and so forth. It is a thing too notorious to mention the Crowds of Servants, and their Insolence, near the Courts of Justice, and the Stairs towards the supreme Assembly; where there is an universal Mockery of all Order, such riotous Clamour and licentious Confusion, that one would think the whole Nation lived in Jest, and there were no such thing as Rule and Distinction among us.

The next Place of Resort, wherein the servile World are let loose, is at the Entrance of *Hide-Park*, while the Gentry are at the Ring. Hither People bring their Lacqueys out of State, and here it is that all they say at their Tables and act in their Houses is communicated to the whole Town. There are Men of Wit in all Conditions of Life; and mixing with these People at their Diversions, I have heard Coquets and Prudes as well rallied, and Insolence and Pride exposed, (allowing for their want of Education) with as much Humour and good Sense, as in the politest Companies. It is a general Observation, That all Dependants run in some Measure into the Manners and Behaviour of those whom they serve: You shall frequently meet with Lovers and Men of Intrigue among the Lacqueys, as well as at *White*'s or in the Side-Boxes. I remember some Years ago an Instance of this Kind. A Footman to a Captain of the Guard used frequently, when his Master was out of the Way, to carry on Amours and make Assignations in his Master's Cloaths. The Fellow had a very good Person, and there are very many Women that think no further than the Outside of a Gentleman; besides which, he was almost as learned a Man as the Collonel himself. I say, thus qualified, the Fellow could scrawl *Billets doux* so well, and furnish a Conversation on the common Topicks, that he had, as they call it, a great deal of good Business on his Hands. It happened one Day, that coming down a Tavern-stairs in his Master's fine Guard-Coat, with a well-dressed Woman masked, he met the Collonel coming up with other Company; but with a ready Assurance he quitted his Lady, came up to him, and said, *Sir, I know you have too much Respect for your self to cane me in this honourable Habit: But you see there is a Lady in the Case, and I hope on that Score also you will put off your Anger till I have told you all another Time.* After a little Pause the Collonel cleared up his Countenance, and with an Air of Familiarity whispered his Man apart, *Sirrah, bring the Lady with you to ask Pardon for you;* then aloud, *Look to it* Will. *I'll never forgive you else.* The Fellow went back to his Mistress, and telling her with a loud Voice and an Oath, That was the honestest Fellow in the World, conveyed her to an Hackney-Coach.

But the many Irregularities committed by Servants in the Places above-mentioned, as well as in the Theatres, of which Masters are generally the Occasions, are too various not to need being resumed on another Occasion. R

No. 89.
[ADDISON.] Tuesday, June 12.

> *. . . Petite hinc puerique senesque*
> *Finem animo certum, miserisque viatica canis.*
> *Cras hoc fiet. Idem cras fiet. Quid? quasi magnum*
> *Nempe diem donas. Sed cum lux altera venit,*
> *Jam cras hesternum consumpsimus ; ecce aliud cras*
> *Egerit hos annos, & semper paulum erit ultra.*
> *Nam quamvis prope te, quamvis temone sub uno*
> *Vertentem sese frustra sectabere canthum.*—Per.

As my Correspondents upon the Subject of Love are very numerous, it is my Design, if possible, to range them under several Heads, and address my self to them at different Times. The first Branch of them, to whose Service I shall dedicate this Paper, are those that have to do with Women of dilatory Tempers, who are for spinning out the Time of Courtship to an

immoderate Length, without being able either to close with
their Lovers, or to dismiss them. I have many Letters by me
filled with Complaints against this sort of Women. In one
of them no less a Man than a Brother of the Coiff tells me, that
he began his Suit *Vicessimo nono Caroli secundi*, before he had
been a Twelve-month at the *Temple*; that he prosecuted it for
many Years after he was called to the Bar; that at present he
is a Serjeant at Law; and notwithstanding he hoped that
Matters would have been long since brought to an Issue, the
Fair one still *demurrs*. I am so well pleased with this Gentleman's Phrase, that I shall distinguish this Sect of Women by
the Title of *Demurrers*. I find by another Letter from one who
calls himself *Thirsis*, that his Mistress has been demurring
above these seven Years. But among all my Plaintiffs of this
Nature, I most pity the unfortunate *Philander*, a Man of constant Passion and plentiful Fortune, who sets forth that the
timorous and irresolute *Sylvia* has demurred till she is past
Child-bearing. *Strephon* appears by his Letter to be a very
cholerick Lover, and irrevocably smitten with one that demurrs
out of Self-interest. He tells me with great Passion that she
has bubbled him out of his Youth; that she drilled him on to
five and fifty, and that he verily believes she will drop him in
his old Age if she can find her Account in another. I shall
conclude this Narrative with a Letter from honest SAM. HOPE-
WELL, a very pleasant Fellow, who it seems has at last married
a *Demurrer*: I must only premise, that SAM. who is a very
good Bottle-Companion, has been the Diversion of his Friends,
upon account of his Passion, ever since the Year One thousand
Six hundred and Eighty one.

'*Dear Sir,*

You know very well my Passion for Mrs. *Martha*, and what
a Dance she has led me: She took me out at the Age of Two
and Twenty, and dodged with me above Thirty Years. I have
loved her till she is grown as grey as a Cat, and am with much
ado become the Master of her Person, such as it is at present.
She is however in my Eye a very charming old Woman. We
often lament that we did not marry sooner, but she has no
Body to blame for it but her self: You know very well that she
would never think of me whilst she had a Tooth in her Head.
I have put the Date of my Passion (*Anno Amoris Trigesimo
primo*) instead of a Posy, on my Wedding-Ring. I expect
you should send me a congratulatory Letter, or, if you please,
an *Epithalamium* upon this Occasion.

Mrs. Martha's *and Yours eternally,*

Sam. Hopewell.'

In order to banish an Evil out of the World, that does not only produce great Uneasiness to private Persons, but has also a very bad Influence on the Publick, I shall endeavour to shew the Folly of *Demurrage* from two or three Reflections, which I earnestly recommend to the Thoughts of my fair Readers.

First of all I would have them seriously think on the Shortness of their Time. Life is not long enough for a Coquet to play all her Tricks in. A timorous Woman drops into her Grave before she has done deliberating. Were the Age of Man the same that it was before the Flood, a Lady might sacrifice half a Century to a Scruple, and be two or three Ages in demurring. Had she Nine Hundred Years good, she might hold out to the Conversion of the *Jews* before she thought fit to be prevailed upon. But alas! she ought to play her Part in haste, when she considers that she is suddenly to quit the Stage, and make Room for others.

In the second Place, I would desire my female Readers to consider, that as the Term of Life is short, that of Beauty is much shorter. The finest Skin wrinkles in a few Years, and loses the Strength of its Colouring so soon, that we have scarce Time to admire it. I might embellish this Subject with Roses and Rain-bows, and several other ingenious Conceits, which I may possibly reserve for another Opportunity.

There is a third Consideration which I would likewise recommend to a Demurrer, and that is the great Danger of her falling in Love when she is about Three-score, if she cannot satisfy her Doubts and Scruples before that Time. There is a kind of *latter Spring*, that sometimes gets into the Blood of an old Woman, and turns her into a very odd sort of an Animal. I would therefore have the Demurrer consider what a strange Figure she will make, if she chances to get over all Difficulties, and comes to a final Resolution in that unseasonable Part of her Life.

I would not however be understood, by any thing I have here said, to discourage that natural Modesty in the Sex, which renders a Retreat from the first Approaches of a Lover both fashionable and graceful: All that I intend, is, to advise them, when they are prompted by Reason and Inclination, to demurr only out of Form, and so far as Decency requires. A virtuous Woman should reject the first Offer of Marriage, as a good Man does that of a Bishoprick; but I would advise neither the one nor the other to persist in refusing what they secretly approve. I would in this Particular propose the Example of *Eve* to all her Daughters, as *Milton* has represented her in the following Passage, which I cannot forbear transcribing entire, tho' only the twelve last Lines are to my present Purpose.

> *The Rib he form'd and fashion'd with his Hands:*
> *Under his forming Hands a Creature grew,*
> *Manlike, but diff'rent Sex, so lovely fair,*
> *That what seem'd fair in all the World, seem'd now*
> *Mean, or in her summ'd up, in her contain'd*
> *And in her Looks, which from that Time infus'd*
> *Sweetness into my Heart unfelt before.*
> *And into all things from her Aire inspir'd*
> *The Spirit of Love and amorous Delight.*
> *   She disappear'd, and left me dark; I wak'd*
> *To find her, or for ever to deplore*
> *Her Loss, and other Pleasures all abjure:*
> *When out of Hope, behold her, not far off,*
> *Such as I saw her in my Dream, adorn'd*
> *With what all Earth or Heaven could bestow*
> *To make her amiable.   On she came,*
> *Led by her heav'nly Maker, though unseen,*
> *And guided by his Voice, nor uninform'd*
> *Of nuptial Sanctity and marriage Rites:*
> *Grace was in all her Steps, Heav'n in her Eye.*
> *In every Gesture Dignity and Love.*
> *I overjoy'd could not forbear aloud.*
> *   This Turn hath made Amends; thou hast fulfill'd*
> *Thy Words, Creator bounteous and benign,*
> *Giver of all things fair, but fairest this*
> *Of all thy Gifts, nor enviest.   I now see*
> *Bone of my Bone, Flesh of my Flesh, my Self . . .*
> *   She heard me thus, and tho' divinely brought,*
> *Yet Innocence and Virgin Modesty,*
> *Her Virtue and the Conscience of her Worth,*
> *That would be woo'd, and not unsought be won,*
> *Not obvious, not obtrusive, but retir'd,*
> *The more desirable, or to say all,*
> *Nature her self, though pure of sinful Thought,*
> *Wrought in her so, that seeing me she turn'd;*
> *I follow'd her: She what was Honour knew,*
> *And with obsequious Majesty approv'd*
> *My pleaded Reason.   To the nuptial Bow'r*
> *I led her blushing like the Morn. . . .*

L

No. 90.

[ADDISON.]   Wednesday, June 13.

> *. . . Magnus sine viribus ignis*
> *Incassum furit. . . .*—Virg.

THERE is not, in my Opinion, a Consideration more effectua
to extinguish inordinate Desires in the Soul of Man, than the
Notions of *Plato* and his Followers upon that Subject.   They

tell us, that every Passion which has been contracted by the Soul during her Residence in the Body, remains with her in her separate State; and that the Soul, in the Body or out of the Body, differs no more than the Man does from himself when he is in his House or in open Air. When therefore the obscene Passions in particular have once taken Root and spread themselves in the Soul, they cleave to her inseparably, and remain in her for ever after the Body is cast off and thrown aside. As an Argument to confirm this their Doctrine they observe, that a lewd Youth who goes on in a continued Course of Voluptuousness, advances by Degrees into a libidinous old Man; and that the Passion survives in the Mind when it is altogether dead in the Body; nay, that the Desire grows more violent, and (like all other Habits) gathers Strength by Age, at the same Time that it has no Power of executing its own Purposes. If, they say, the Soul is the most subject to these Passions at a Time when it has the least Instigations from the Body, we may well suppose she will still retain them when she is entirely divested of it. The very Substance of the Soul is festered with them; the Gangrene is gone too far to be ever cured: the Inflammation will rage to all Eternity.

In this therefore (say the *Platonists*) consists the Punishment of a voluptuous Man after Death: He is tormented with Desires which it is impossible for him to gratify, sollicited by a Passion that has neither Objects nor Organs adapted to it: He lives in a State of invincible Desire and Impotence, and always burns in the Pursuit of what he always despairs to possess. It is for this Reason (says *Plato*) that the Souls of the Dead appear frequently in Coemiteries, and hover about the Places where their Bodies are buried, as still hankering after their old brutal Pleasures, and desiring again to enter the Body that gave them an Opportunity of fulfilling them.

Some of our most eminent Divines have made use of this *Platonick* Notion, so far as it regards the Subsistence of our Passions after Death, with great Beauty and Strength of Reason. *Plato* indeed carries the Thought very far, when he grafts upon it his Opinion of Ghosts appearing in Places of Burial; though, I must confess, if one did believe that the departed Souls of Men and Women wandered up and down these lower Regions, and entertained themselves with the Sight of their Species, one could not devise a more proper Hell for an impure Spirit, than that which *Plato* has touched upon.

The Ancients seem to have drawn such a State of Torments in the Description of *Tantalus*, who was punished with the Rage of an eternal Thirst, and set up to the Chin in Water that fled from his Lips whenever he attempted to drink it.

Virgil, who has cast the whole System of *Platonick* Philosophy, so far as it relates to the Soul of Man, into beautiful Allegories; in the sixth Book of his *Aeneid* gives us the Punishment of a Voluptuary after Death, not unlike that which we are here speaking of.

> . . . *Lucent genialibus altis*
> *Aurea fulcra toris, epulaeque ante ora paratae*
> *Regifico luxu.   Furiarum maxima juxta*
> *Accubat, & manibus prohibet contingere mensas;*
> *Exurgitque facem attollens, atque intonat ore.*

> *They lie below on Golden Beds display'd,*
> *And genial Feasts with regal Pomp are made,*
> *The Queen of Furies by their Side is set,*
> *And snatches from their Mouths th' untasted Meat;*
> *Which if they touch, her hissing Snakes she rears,*
> *Tossing her Torch, and Thund'ring in their Ears.*—Dryd.

That I may a little alleviate the Severity of this my Speculation (which otherwise may lose me several of my polite Readers) I shall translate a Story that has been quoted upon another Occasion by one of the most learned Men of the present Age, as I find it in the Original.   The Reader will see it is not foreign to my present Subject, and I dare say will think it a lively Representation of a Person lying under the Torments of such a Kind of Tantalism, or *Platonick* Hell, as that which we have now under Consideration.   Monsieur *Pontignan* speaking of a Love-Adventure that happened to him in the Country, gives the following account of it.

'When I was in the Country last Summer, I was often in Company with a couple of charming Women who had all the Wit and Beauty one could desire in Female Companions, with a Dash of Coquetry, that from time to time gave me a great many agreeable Torments.   I was, after my Way, in love with both of them, and had such frequent Opportunities of pleading my Passion to them when they were asunder, that I had reason to hope for particular Favours from each of them.   As I was walking one Evening in my Chamber with nothing about me but my Night-Gown, they both came into my Room and told me, they had a very pleasant Trick to put upon a Gentleman that was in the same House, provided I would bear a Part in it.   Upon this they told me such a plausible Story, that I laughed at their Contrivance, and agreed to do whatever they should require of me: They immediately began to swaddle me up in my Night-Gown with long Pieces of Linnen, which they folded about me till they had wrapt me in above an hundred Yards of Swathe: My Arms were pressed to my Sides, and my

Legs closed together by so many Wrappers one over another, that I looked like an *Aegyptian* Mummy. As I stood bolt upright upon one End in this antique Figure, one of the Ladies burst out a Laughing, "And now, *Pontignan,*" says she, "we intend to perform the Promise that we find you have extorted from each of us. You have often asked the Favour of us, and I dare say you are a better bred Cavalier than to refuse to go to Bed to Ladies that desire it of you." After having stood a Fit of Laughter, I begg'd them to uncase me, and do with me what they pleased. "No, no," say they, "we like you very well as you are"; and upon that ordered me to be carried to one of their Houses, and put to Bed in all my Swaddles. The Room was lighted up on all Sides; and I was laid very decently between a Pair of Sheets, with my Head (which was indeed the only Part I could move) upon a very high Pillow: This was no sooner done, but my two Female Friends came into Bed to me in their finest Night-Clothes. You may easily guess at the Condition of a Man, that saw a couple of the most beautiful Women in the World undrest and abed with him, without being able to stir Hand or Foot. I begged them to release me, and struggled all I could to get loose; which I did with so much Violence, that about Midnight they both leaped out of the Bed crying out they were undone: But seeing me safe they took their Posts again, and renewed their Raillery. Finding all my Prayers and Endeavours were lost, I compos'd my self as well as I could; and told them, that if they would not unbind me, I would fall asleep between them, and by that means disgrace them for ever: But alas! this was impossible; could I have been disposed to it, they would have prevented me by several little ill-natured Caresses and Endearments which they bestow'd upon me. As much devoted as I am to Womankind, I would not pass such another Night to be Master of the whole Sex. My Reader will doubtless be curious to know what became of me the next Morning: Why truly my Bed-fellows left me about an Hour before Day, and told me if I would be good and lie still, they would send somebody to take me up as soon as it was Time for me to rise: Accordingly about Nine a Clock in the Morning an old Woman came to unswathe me. I bore all this very patiently, being resolved to take my Revenge of my Tormentors, and to keep no Measures with them as soon as I was at Liberty; but upon asking my old Woman what was become of the two Ladies, she told me she believ'd they were by that Time within Sight of *Paris,* for that they went away in a Coach and six, before five a Clock in the morning.'   L

No. 91.

[STEELE.] Thursday, June 14.

In furias ignemque ruunt. Amor on.nibus idem.—Virg.

THO' the Subject I am now going upon would be much more
properly the Foundation of a Comedy, I cannot forbear inserting the Circumstances which pleased me in the Account a
young Lady gave me of the Loves of a Family in Town, which
shall be nameless; or rather for the better Sound, and Elevation
of the History, instead of Mr. and Mrs. such a one, I shall call
them by feigned Names. Without further Preface, you are to
know that within the Liberties of the City of *Westminster* lives
the Lady *Honoria*, a Widow about the Age of Forty, of a
healthy Constitution, gay Temper, and elegant Person. She
dresses a little too much like a Girl, affects a Childish Fondness
in the Tone of her Voice, sometimes a pretty Sullenness in the
leaning of her Head, and now and then a Down-cast of her Eyes
on her Fan: Neither her Imagination nor her Health would ever
give her to know that she is turned of Twenty; but that in the
midst of these pretty Softnesses, and Airs of Delicacy and
Attraction, she has a tall Daughter within a Fortnight of
Fifteen, who impertinently comes into the Room, and towers
so much towards Woman, that her Mother is always checked
by her Presence, and every Charm of *Honoria* droops at the
Entrance of *Flavia*. The agreeable *Flavia* would be what she
is not, as well as her Mother *Honoria*; but all their Beholders
are more partial to an Affectation of what a Person is growing
up to, than of what has been already enjoyed, and is gone for
ever. It is therefore allowed to *Flavia* to look forward, but not
to *Honoria* to look back. *Flavia* is no way dependant on her
Mother, with Relation to her Fortune, for which Reason they
live almost upon an Equality in Conversation; and as *Honoria*
has given *Flavia* to understand, that it is ill-bred to be always
calling Mother, *Flavia* is as well pleased never to be called
Child. It happens, by this means, that these Ladies are generally Rivals in all Places where they appear; and the Words
Mother and Daughter never pass between them, but out of
Spite. *Flavia* one Night at a Play observing *Honoria* draw the
Eyes of several in the Pit, called to a Lady who sat by her, and
bid her ask her Mother to lend her her Snuff-Box for one
Moment. Another time, when a Lover of *Honoria* was on his
Knees beseeching the Favour to Kiss her Hand, *Flavia* rush-
ing into the Room kneeled down by him and asked Blessing.
Several of these Contradictory Acts of Duty have raised be-
tween them such a Coldness, that they generally converse

when they are in mixed Company, by way of Talking at one another, and not to one another.   *Honoria* is ever complaining of a certain Sufficiency in the young women of this Age, who assume to themselves an Authority of carrying all things before them, as if they were Possessors of the Esteem of Mankind; and all, who were but a Year before them in the World, were neglected or deceased.   *Flavia*, upon such a Provocation, is sure to observe that there are People who can resign nothing, and know not how to give up what they know they cannot hold; that there are those who will not allow Youth their Follies, not because they are themselves past them, but because they love to continue in them.   These Beauties rival each other on all Occasions, not that they have always had the same Lovers, but each has kept up a Vanity to shew the other the Charms of her Lover.   *Dick Crastin* and *Tom Tulip*, among many others, have of late been Pretenders in this Family: *Dick* to *Honoria*, *Tom* to *Flavia*.   *Dick* is the only surviving Beau of the last Age, and *Tom* almost the only one that keeps up that Order of Men in this.

I wish I could repeat the little Circumstances of a Conversation of the four Lovers with the Spirit in which the young Lady, I had my Account from, represented it at a Visit where I had the Honour to be present; but it seems *Dick Crastin* the Admirer of *Honoria*, and *Tom Tulip* the Pretender to *Flavia*, were purposely admitted together by the Ladies; that each might shew the other that her Lover had the Superiority in the Accomplishments of that sort of Creature, whom the sillier part of Women call a Fine Gentleman.   As this Age has a much more gross Taste in Courtship, as well as in everything else, than the last had, these Gentlemen are Instances of it in their different manner of Application.   *Tulip* is ever making Allusions to the Vigour of his Person, the sinewy Force of his Make, while *Crastin* professes a wary Observation of the Turns of his Mistress's Mind.   *Tulip* gives himself the Air of a resistless Ravisher, *Crastin* practises that of a skilful Lover.   Poetry is the inseparable Property of every Man in Love; and as Men of Wit write Verses on those Occasions, the rest of the World repeat the Verses of others.   These Servants of the Ladies were used to imitate their Manner of Conversation; and allude to one another, rather than interchange discourse in what they said when they met.   *Tulip*, the other day, seized his Mistress's Hand, and repeated out of *Ovid's Art of Love*,

> *'Tis I can in soft Battels pass the Night,*
> *Yet rise next Morning Vigorous for the Fight,*
> *Fresh as the Day, and active as the Light.*

Upon hearing this, *Crastin*, with an Air of Deference, played *Honoria's* Fan, and repeated,

> *Sidley has that prevailing gentle Art,*
> *That can, with a resistless Charm, impart*   }
> *The loosest Wishes to the chastest Heart:*   }
> *Raise such a Conflict, kindle such a Fire,*
> *Between declining Virtue and Desire,*
> *'Till the poor vanquish'd Maid dissolves away*
> *In Dreams all Night, in Sighs and Tears all Day.*

When *Crastin* had uttered these Verses, with a Tenderness which at once spoke Passion and Respect, *Honoria* cast a Triumphant Glance at *Flavia*, as exulting in the Elegance of *Crastin's* Courtship, and upbraiding her with the Homeliness of *Tulip's. Tulip* understood the Reproach, and in return began to applaud the Wisdom of old amorous Gentlemen, who turned their Mistress's Imagination, as far as possible, from what they had long themselves forgot, and ended his Discourse with a sly Commendation of the Doctrine of *Platonick Love*; at the same time he ran over, with a laughing Eye, *Crastin's* thin Legs, meagre Looks and spare Body. The old Gentleman immediately left the Room with some Disorder, and the Conversation fell upon untimely Passion, after Love, and unseasonable Youth. *Tulip* sung, danced, moved before the Glass, led his Mistress half a Minuet, humm'd

> *Celia the Fair, in the Bloom of fifteen;*

when there came a Servant with a Letter to him, which was as follows.

'*Sir*,

I Understand very well what you meant by your Mention of *Platonick* Love. I shall be glad to meet you immediately in *Hide-Park*, or behind *Montague-House*, or attend you to *Barn Elmes*, or any other fashionable Place that 's fit for a Gentleman to dye in, that you shall appoint for,

Sir,
Your most Humble Servant,
Richard Crastin.'

Tulip's Colour changed at the reading of this Epistle; for which Reason his Mistress snatched it to read the Contents. While she was doing so *Tulip* went away, and the Ladies now agreeing in a Common Calamity, bewailed together the Danger of their Lovers. They immediately undressed to go out, and took Hackneys to prevent Mischief; but, after alarming all Parts of the Town, *Crastin* was found by his Widow in his

Pumps at *Hide-Park*, which Appointment *Tulip* never kept,
but made his Escape into the Country. *Flavia* tears her
Hair for his Inglorious Safety, curses and despises her Charmer,
is fallen in Love with *Crastin*: Which is the first Part of the
History of the *Rival Mother*.   R

No. 92.
[ADDISON.]   Friday, June 15.

> . . . *Convivae prope dissentire videntur,*
> *Poscentes vario multum diversa palato.*
> *Quid dem?   Quid non dem?* . . .—Hor.

'*Mr.* SPECTATOR,

Your Paper is a Part of my Tea-Equipage; and my Servant
knows my Humour so well, that calling for my Breakfast this
Morning (it being past my usual Hour) she answered, the
SPECTATOR was not yet come in; but that the Tea-Kettle
boiled, and she expected it every Moment.   Having thus in
Part signified to you the Esteem and Veneration which I have
for you, I must put you in Mind of the Catalogue of Books
which you have promised to recommend to our Sex: For I have
deferred furnishing my Closet with Authors, till I receive your
Advice in this Particular; being your daily Disciple and humble
Servant,

                                    LEONORA.'

In answer to my fair Disciple, whom I am very proud of, I
must acquaint her and the rest of my Readers, that since I
have called out for Help in my Catalogue of a Lady's Library,
I have received many Letters upon that Head; some of which
I shall give an Account of.

In the first Class I shall take Notice of those which come to
me from eminent Booksellers, who every one of them mention
with Respect the Authors they have printed; and consequently
have an Eye to their own Advantage more than to that of the
Ladies.   One tells me, that he thinks it absolutely necessary
for Women to have true Notions of Right and Equity, and
that therefore they cannot peruse a better Book than *Dalton's
Country Justice*.   Another thinks they cannot be without *The
Compleat Jockey*.   A third observing the Curiosity and Desire
of prying into Secrets, which he tells me is natural to the fair
Sex, is of Opinion this Female Inclination, if well directed,
might turn very much to their Advantage, and therefore
recommends to me *Mr. Mede upon the Revelations*.   A fourth

lays it down as an unquestioned Truth, that a Lady cannot be thoroughly accomplished who has not read *The Secret Treaties and Negotiations of the Marshal D'Estrades.* Mr. *Jacob Tonson,* Junr. is of Opinion, that *Bayle's Dictionary* might be of very great Use to the Ladies, in order to make them general Scholars. Another, whose Name I have forgotten, thinks it highly proper that every Woman with Child should read *Mr. Wall's History of Infant Baptism*: As another is very importunate with me, to recommend to all my Female Readers, *The finishing Stroke: Being a Vindication of the Patriarchal Scheme,* &c.

In the second Class I shall mention Books which are recommended by Husbands, if I may believe the Writers of them. Whether or no they are real Husbands or personated ones I cannot tell, but the Books they recommend are as follow. *A Paraphrase on the History of Susanna. Rules to keep Lent. The Christian's Overthrow prevented. A Dissuasive from the Play-House. The Virtues of Camphire, with Directions to make Camphire Tea. The Pleasures of a Country Life. The Government of the Tongue.* A Letter dated from *Cheapside* desires me that I would advise all young Wives to make themselves Mistresses of *Wingate's Arithmetick,* and concludes with a Postscript, that he hopes I will not forget *The Countess of Kent's Receipts.*

I may reckon the Ladies themselves as a third Class among these my Correspondents and Privy-Counsellors. In a Letter from one of them, I am advised to place *Pharamond* at the Head of my Catalogue, and, if I think proper, to give the second place to *Cassandra. Coquetilla* begs me not to think of nailing Women upon their Knees with Manuals of Devotion, nor of scorching their Faces with Books of Housewifery. *Florella* desires to know if there are any Books written against Prudes, and intreates me, if there are, to give them a Place in my Library. Plays of all Sorts have their several Advocates: *All for Love* is mentioned in above fifteen Letters; *Sophonisba,* or *Hannibal's Overthrow,* in a Dozen; the *Innocent Adultery* is likewise highly approved of: *Mithridates King of Pontus* has many Friends; *Alexander the Great* and *Aurenzebe* have the same Number of Voices; but *Theodosius,* or *the Force of Love,* carries it from all the rest.

I should, in the last Place, mention such Books as have been proposed by Men of Learning, and those who appear competent Judges of this Matter; and must here take Occasion to thank *A. B.,* whoever it is that conceals himself under those two Letters, for his Advice upon this Subject; But as I find the Work I have undertaken to be very difficult, I shall defer the executing of it till I am further acquainted with the Thoughts of my judicious Contemporaries, and have Time to examine the several Books they offer to me; being resolved, in an Affair of this Moment, to proceed with the greatest Caution.

In the mean while, as I have taken the Ladies under my particular Care, I shall make it my Business to find out in the best Authors ancient and modern such Passages as may be for their use, and endeavour to accommodate them as well as I can to their Taste; not questioning but the valuable Part of the Sex will easily pardon me, if from Time to Time I laugh at those little Vanities and Follies which appear in the Behaviour of some of them, and which are more proper for Ridicule than a serious Censure. Most Books being calculated for Male Readers, and generally written with an Eye to Men of Learning, makes a Work of this Nature the more necessary; besides, I am the more encouraged, because I flatter my self that I see the Sex daily improving by these my Speculations. My fair Readers are already deeper Scholars than the Beaus: I could name some of them who talk much better than several Gentlemen that make a Figure at *Will*'s; and as I frequently receive Letters from the *fine Ladies*, and *pretty Fellows*, I cannot but observe that the former are superior to the others not only in the Sense but in the Spelling. This cannot but have a good Effect upon the female World, and keep them from being charmed by those empty Coxcombs that have hitherto been admired among the Women, tho' laugh'd at among the Men.

I am credibly informed that *Tom Tattle* passes for an impertinent Fellow, that *Will Trippit* begins to be smoaked, and that *Frank Smoothly* himself is within a Month of a Coxcomb, in case I think fit to continue this Paper. For my Part, as it is my Business in some Measure to detect such as would lead astray weak Minds by their false Pretences to Wit and Judgment, Humour and Gallantry, I shall not fail to lend the best Lights I am able to the fair Sex for the Continuation of these their Discoveries.   L

No. 93.
[ADDISON.]
                                                    Saturday, June 16.

         . . . *Spatio brevi*
Spem longam reseces; dum loquimur, fugerit invida
Aetas: carpe diem, quam minimum credula postero.—Hor.

WE all of us complain of the Shortness of Time, saith *Seneca*, and yet have much more than we know what to do with. Our Lives, says he, are spent either in doing nothing at all, or in doing nothing to the purpose, or in doing nothing that we ought to do; We are always Complaining our Days are few, and Acting as though there would be no End of them. That noble Philosopher has described our Inconsistency with our selves in this Particular, by all those various turns of Expression and Thought which are peculiar to his Writings.

I often consider Mankind as wholly inconsistent with it self in a Point that bears some Affinity to the former. Though we seem grieved at the Shortness of Life in general, we are wishing every Period of it at an end. The Minor longs to be at Age, then to be a Man of Business, then to make up an Estate, then to arrive at Honours, then to retire. Thus although the whole of Life is allowed by every one to be short, the several Divisions of it appear long and tedious. We are for lengthening our Span in general, but would fain contract the Parts of which it is composed. The Usurer would be very well satisfyed to have all the Time annihilated that lies between the present Moment and next Quarter-day. The Politician would be contented to lose three Years in his Life, could he place things in the Posture which he fancies they will stand in after such a Revolution of Time. The Lover would be glad to strike out of his Existence all the Moments that are to pass away before the happy Meeting. Thus, as fast as our Time runs, we should be very glad in most parts of our Lives that it ran much faster than it does. Several Hours of the Day hang upon our Hands, nay we wish away whole Years; and travel through Time as through a Country filled with many wild and empty Wastes, which we would fain hurry over, that we may arrive at those several little Settlements or imaginary Points of Rest which are dispersed up and down in it.

If we divide the Life of most Men into twenty Parts, we shall find that at least nineteen of them are meer Gaps and Chasms, which are neither filled with Pleasure nor Business. I do not however include in this Calculation the Life of those Men who are in a perpetual Hurry of Affairs, but of those who only are not always engaged in Scenes of Action; and I hope I shall not do an unacceptable Piece of Service to these Persons, if I point out to them certain Methods for the filling up their empty Spaces of Life. The Methods I shall propose to them, are as follow.

The first is the Exercise of Virtue, in the most general Acceptation of the Word. That Particular Scheme which comprehends the Social Virtues may give Employment to the most industrious Temper, and find a Man in Business more than the most active Station of Life. To advise the Ignorant, relieve the Needy, comfort the Afflicted, are Duties that fall in

our way almost every Day of our Lives. A Man has frequent
Opportunities of mitigating the Fierceness of a Party; of doing
Justice to the Character of a deserving Man; of softning the
Envious, quieting the Angry, and rectifying the Prejudiced;
which are all of them Employments suited to a reasonable
Nature, and bring great Satisfaction to the Person who can
busy himself in them with Discretion.

There is another kind of Virtue that may find Employment
for those Retired Hours in which we are altogether left to our
selves, and destitute of Company and Conversation; I mean,
that Intercourse and Communication which every reasonable
Creature ought to maintain with the great Author of his Being.
The Man who lives under an habitual Sense of the Divine
Presence keeps up a perpetual Cheerfulness of Temper, and
enjoys every Moment the Satisfaction of thinking himself in
Company with his dearest and best of Friends. The Time
never lies heavy upon him: It is impossible for him to be alone.
His Thoughts and Passions are the most busied at such Hours
when those of other Men are the most unactive. He no sooner
steps out of the World but his Heart burns with Devotion,
swells with Hope, and triumphs in the Consciousness of that
Presence which every where surrounds him; or, on the contrary,
pours out its Fears, its Sorrows, its Apprehensions, to the great
Supporter of its Existence.

I have here only considered the Necessity of a Man's being
Virtuous, that he may have something to do; but if we consider further that the Exercise of Virtue is not only an Amusement for the time it lasts, but that its Influence extends to
those Parts of our Existence which lie beyond the Grave, and
that our whole Eternity is to take its Colour from those Hours
which we here employ in Virtue or in Vice, the Argument
redoubles upon us for putting in Practice this Method of
passing away our Time.

When a Man has but a little Stock to improve, and has
Opportunities of turning it all to good Account, what shall we
think of him if he suffers nineteen Parts of it to lie dead, and
perhaps employs even the twentieth to his Ruin or Disadvantage? But because the Mind cannot be always in its Fervours,
nor strained up to a pitch of Virtue, it is necessary to find out
proper Employments for it in its Relaxations.

The next Method therefore that I would propose to fill up
our Time, should be useful and innocent Diversions. I must
confess I think it is below reasonable Creatures to be altogether
conversant in such Diversions as are meerly innocent, and have
nothing else to recommend them, but that there is no hurt in
them. Whether any kind of Gaming has even thus much to

say for it self, I shall not determine; but I think it is very wonderful to see Persons of the best Sense passing away a dozen Hours together in shuffling and dividing a Pack of Cards, with no other Conversation but what is made up of a few Game Phrases, and no other Ideas but those of black or red Spots ranged together in different Figures. Would not a Man laugh to hear any one of this Species complaining that Life is short?

The *Stage* might be made a perpetual Source of the most noble and useful Entertainments, were it under proper Regulations.

But the Mind never unbends it self so agreeably as in the Conversation of a well-chosen Friend. There is indeed no Blessing of Life that is any way comparable to the Enjoyment of a discreet and virtuous Friend. It eases and unloads the Mind, clears and improves the Understanding, engenders Thoughts and Knowledge, animates Virtue and good Resolutions, sooths and allays the Passions, and finds Employment for most of the vacant Hours of Life.

Next to such an Intimacy with a particular Person, one would endeavour after a more general Conversation with such as are able to entertain and improve those with whom they converse, which are Qualifications that seldom go asunder.

There are many other useful Amusements of Life, which one would endeavour to multiply, that one might on all Occasions have Recourse to something, rather than suffer the Mind to lie idle, or run adrift with any Passion that chances to rise in it.

A Man that has a Taste of Musick, Painting, or Architecture, is like one that has another Sense, when compared with such as have no Relish of those Arts. The Florist, the Planter, the Gardiner, the Husbandman, when they are only as Accomplishments to the Man of Fortune, are great Reliefs to a Country Life, and many ways useful to those who are possessed of them.

But of all the Diversions of Life, there is none so proper to fill up its empty Spaces as the reading of useful and entertaining Authors. But this I shall only touch upon, because it in some measure interferes with the third Method, which I shall propose in another Paper, for the Employment of our dead unactive Hours, and which I shall only mention in general to be the Pursuit of Knowledge. **L**

No. 94.
[ADDISON.]   Monday, June 18.

> . . . *Hoc est*
> *Vivere bis, vita posse priore frui.*—Mart.

THE last Method which I proposed in my *Saturday*'s Paper, for
filling up those empty Spaces of Life which are so tedious and
burthensome to idle People, is the employing our selves in the
Pursuit of Knowledge. I remember Mr. *Boyle*, speaking of a
certain Mineral, tells us, That a Man may consume his whole
Life in the Study of it, without arriving at the Knowledge of all
its Qualities. The Truth of it is, there is not a single Science,
or any Branch of it, that might not furnish a Man with Business
for Life, though it were much longer than it is.

I shall not here engage on those beaten Subjects of the Usefulness of Knowledge, nor of the Pleasure and Perfection it gives
the Mind, nor on the Methods of attaining it, nor recommend
any particular Branch of it, all which have been the Topicks
of many other Writers; but shall indulge my self in a Speculation that is more uncommon, and may therefore perhaps be
more entertaining.

I have before shewn how the unemployed Parts of Life
appear long and tedious, and shall here endeavour to shew
how those Parts of Life which are exercised in Study, Reading,
and the Pursuits of Knowledge, are long but not tedious, and
by that Means discover a Method of lengthening our Lives, and
at the same Time of turning all the Parts of them to our
Advantage.

Mr. *Lock* observes, 'That we get the Idea of Time, or Duration, by reflecting on that Train of Ideas which succeed one
another in our Minds: That for this Reason, when we sleep
soundly without dreaming, we have no Perception of Time, or
the Length of it, whilst we sleep; and that the Moment wherein
we leave off to think, till the Moment we begin to think again,
seem to have no Distance.' To which the Author adds; 'And
so, I doubt not, but it would be to a waking Man, if it were
possible for him to keep only one *Idea* on his Mind, without
Variation, and the Succession of others: And we see, that one
who fixes his Thoughts very intently on one thing, so as to
take but little Notice of the Succession of *Ideas* that pass in his
Mind whilst he is taken up with that earnest Contemplation,
lets slip out of his Account a good Part of that Duration, and
thinks that Time shorter than it is.'

We might carry this Thought further, and consider a Man
as, on one Side, shortening his Time by thinking on nothing, or

but a few things; so, on the other, as lengthening it, by employing his Thoughts on many Subjects, or by entertaining a quick and constant Succession of Ideas. Accordingly Monsieur *Mallebranche* in his *Enquiry after Truth*, (which was published several Years before Mr. *Lock*'s *Essay on Humane Understanding*) tells us, That it is possible some Creatures may think Half an Hour as long as we do a thousand Years; or look upon that Space of Duration which we call a Minute, as an Hour, a Week, a Month, or an whole Age.

This Notion of Monsieur *Mallebranche* is capable of some little Explanation from what I have quoted out of Mr. *Lock*; for if our Notion of Time is produced by our reflecting on the Succession of Ideas in our Mind, and this Succession may be infinitely accelerated or retarded, it will follow, that different Beings may have different Notions of the same Parts of Duration, according as their Ideas, which we suppose are equally distinct in each of them, follow one another in a greater or less Degree of Rapidity.

There is a famous Passage in the *Alcoran*, which looks as if *Mahomet* had been possessed of the Notion we are now speaking of. It is there said, That the Angel *Gabriel* took *Mahomet* out of his Bed one Morning to give him a Sight of all things in the seven Heavens, in Paradise, and in Hell, which the Prophet took a distinct View of; and after having held ninety thousand Conferences with God, was brought back again to his Bed. All this, says the *Alcoran*, was transacted in so small a Space of Time, that *Mahomet*, at his Return, found his Bed still warm, and took up an Earthen Pitcher (which was thrown down at the very Instant that the Angel *Gabriel* carried him away) before the Water was all spilt.

There is a very pretty Story in the *Turkish* Tales which relates to this Passage of that famous Impostor, and bears some Affinity to the Subject we are now upon. A Sultan of *Aegypt*, who was an Infidel, used to laugh at this Circumstance in *Mahomet*'s Life, as what was altogether impossible and absurd; But conversing one Day with a great Doctor in the Law, who had the Gift of working Miracles, the Doctor told him, he would quickly convince him of the Truth of this Passage in the History of *Mahomet*, if he would consent to do what he should desire of him. Upon this the Sultan was directed to place himself by an huge Tub of Water, which he did accordingly; and as he stood by the Tub, amidst a Circle of his great Men, the holy Man bid him plunge his Head into the Water, and draw it up again: The King accordingly thrust his Head into the Water, and at the same time found himself at the Foot of a Mountain on a Sea-shore. The King immediately began to rage against

his Doctor for this Piece of Treachery and Witchcraft; but at
length, knowing it was in vain to be angry, he set himself to
think on proper Methods for getting a Livelihood in this strange
Country: Accordingly he applied himself to some People whom
he saw at work in a neighbouring Wood; these People conducted him to a Town that stood at a little Distance from
the Wood, where after some Adventures he married a Woman
of great Beauty and Fortune. He lived with this Woman so
long till he had by her seven Sons and seven Daughters: He
was afterwards reduced to great Want, and forced to think of
plying in the Streets as a Porter for his Livelyhood. One
Day as he was walking alone by the Sea-Side, being seized with
many melancholy Reflections upon his former and his present
State of Life, which had raised a Fit of Devotion in him, he
threw off his Cloaths with a Design to wash himself, according to the Custom of the *Mahometans*, before he said his
Prayers.

After his first Plunge into the Sea, he no sooner raised his
Head above the Water, but he found himself standing by the
Side of the Tub, with the great Men of his Court about him,
and the holy Man at his Side: He immediately upbraided his
Teacher for having sent him on such a Course of Adventures,
and betray'd him into so long a State of Misery and Servitude;
but was wonderfully surprized when he heard that the State
he talked of was only a Dream and Delusion; that he had not
stirred from the Place where he then stood; and that he had
only dipped his Head into the Water, and immediately taken it
out again.

The *Mahometan* Doctor took this Occasion of instructing
the Sultan, that nothing was impossible with God; and that
He, with whom a Thousand Years are but as one Day, can if he
pleases make a single Day, nay a single Moment, appear to any
of his Creatures as a thousand Years.

I shall leave my Reader to compare these Eastern Fables
with the Notions of those two great Philosophers whom I have
quoted in this Paper; and shall only, by way of Application,
desire him to consider how we may extend Life beyond its
natural Dimensions, by applying ourselves diligently to the
Pursuits of Knowledge.

The Hours of a wise Man are lengthened by his Ideas, as
those of a Fool are by his Passions: The Time of the one
is long, because he does not know what to do with it; so
is that of the other, because he distinguishes every Moment
of it with useful or amusing Thought; or in other Words,
because the one is always wishing it away, and the other
always enjoying it.

How different is the View of past Life, in the Man who is
grown old in Knowledge and Wisdom, from that of him who
is grown old in Ignorance and Folly? The latter is like the
Owner of a barren Country, that fills his Eye with the Prospect
of naked Hills and Plains which produce nothing either profit-
able or ornamental; the other beholds a beautiful and spacious
Landskip, divided into delightful Gardens, green Meadows,
fruitful Fields, and can scarce cast his Eye on a single Spot of
his Possessions, that is not covered with some Beautiful Plant
or Flower.   L

No. 95.
[STEELE.]   Tuesday, June 19

Curae leves loquuntur, ingentes stupent.

HAVING read the two following Letters with much Pleasure,
I cannot but think the good Sense of them will be as agreeable
to the Town as any thing I could say either on the Topicks
they treat of, or any other. They both allude to former
Papers of mine, and I do not question but the first, which is
upon inward Mourning, will be thought the Production of a
Man who is well acquainted with the generous Earnings of
Distress in a Manly Temper, which is above the Relief of
Tears. A Speculation of my own on that Subject I shall defer
'till another Occasion.

The second Letter is from a Lady of a Mind as great as her
Understanding. There is, perhaps, something in the beginning
of it which I ought in Modesty to conceal; but I have so much
Esteem for this Correspondent, that I will not alter a Tittle of
what she writes, tho' I am thus Scrupulous at the Price of
being Ridiculous.

'*Mr.* SPECTATOR,

I was very well pleased with your Discourse upon General
Mourning; and should be obliged to you, if you would enter
into the Matter more deeply, and give us your Thoughts upon
the common Sense the ordinary People have of the Demonstra-
tions of Grief, who prescribe Rules and Fashions to the most
solemn Affliction; such as the Loss of the nearest Relations
and dearest Friends. You cannot go to visit a sick Friend,
but some impertinent Waiter about him observes the Muscles
of your Face, as strictly as if they were Prognosticks of his
Death or Recovery. If he happens to be taken from you, you

are immediately surrounded with Numbers of these Spectators, who expect a Melancholy Shrug of your Shoulders, a Pathetical Shake of your Head, and an Expressive Distortion of your Face, to measure your Affection and Value for the Deceased: But there is nothing, on these Occasions, so much in their Favour as immoderate Weeping. As all their Passions are superficial, they imagine the Seat of Love and Friendship to be placed visibly in the Eyes: They judge what Stock of Kindness you had for the Living, by the quantity of Tears you pour out for the Dead; so that if one Body wants that Quantity of Salt-water another abounds with, he is in great Danger of being thought insensible or ill-natured: They are Strangers to Friendship, whose Grief happens not to be moist enough to wet such a Parcel of Handkerchiefs. But Experience has told us nothing is so fallacious as this outward Sign of Sorrow; and the natural History of our Bodies will teach us, that this Flux of the eyes, this Faculty of weeping, is peculiar only to some Constitutions. We observe in the tender Bodies of Children, when crossed in their little Wills and Expectations, how dissolvable they are into Tears; If this were what Grief is in Men, Nature would not be able to support them in the Excess of it for one Moment. Add to this Observation, how quick is their Transition from this Passion to that of their Joy. I won't say we see often, in the next tender things to Children, Tears shed without much grieving. Thus it is common to shed Tears without much Sorrow, and as common to suffer much Sorrow without shedding Tears. Grief and Weeping are indeed frequent Companions, but, I believe, never in their highest Excesses. As Laughter does not proceed from profound Joy, so neither does Weeping from profound Sorrow. The Sorrow which appears so easily at the Eyes, cannot have pierced deeply into the Heart. The Heart, distended with Grief, stops all the Passages for Tears or Lamentations.

Now, Sir, what I would incline you to in all this, is, that you would inform the shallow Criticks and Observers upon Sorrow, that true Affliction labours to be invisible, that it is a Stranger to Ceremony, and that it bears in its own Nature a Dignity much above the little Circumstances which are affected under the Notion of Decency. You must know, Sir, I have lately lost a dear Friend, for whom I have not yet shed a Tear, and for that Reason your Animadversions on that Subject would be the more acceptable to,

> *Sir,*
>
> *Your most Humble Servant,*
>
> B. D.'

'Mr. Spectator,   *June the* 15*th.*

As I hope there are but few that have so little Gratitude as
not to acknowledge the Usefulness of your Pen, and to esteem
it a Publick Benefit; so I am sensible, be that as it will, you must
nevertheless find the Secret and Incomparable Pleasure of
doing Good, and be a great Sharer in the Entertainment you
give. I acknowledge our Sex to be much obliged, and I hope
improved by your Labours, and even your Intentions more
particularly for our Service. If it be true, as 'tis sometimes
said, that our Sex have an Influence on the other, your Paper
may be a yet more general Good. Your directing us to Reading is certainly the best Means to our Instruction; but I think,
with you, Caution in that Particular very useful, since the
Improvement of our Understandings may, or may not, be of
Service to us, according as it is managed. It has been thought
we are not generally so Ignorant as Ill-taught, or that our Sex
does so often want Wit, Judgment, or Knowledge, as the right
Application of them: You are so well-bred, as to say your fair
Readers are already deeper Scholars than the Beaus, and that
you could name some of them that talk much better than
several Gentlemen that made a Figure at *Will's*: This may
possibly be, and no great Compliment, in my Opinion, even
supposing your Comparison to reach *Tom's* and the *Grecian:*
Sure you are too wise to think That a Real Commendation of a
Woman. Were it not rather to be wished we improved in our
own Sphere, and approved our selves better Daughters, Wives,
Mothers, and Friends?

I can't but agree with the Judicious Trader in *Cheapside*
(though I am not at all prejudiced in his Favour) in recommending the Study of Arithmetick; and must dissent even
from the Authority which you mention, when it advises the
making our Sex Scholars. Indeed a little more Philosophy, in
order to the Subduing our Passions to our Reason, might be
sometimes serviceable, and a Treatise of that Nature I should
approve of, even in Exchange for *Theodosius, or the Force of
Love;* but as I well know you want not Hints, I will proceed no
further than to recommend the Bishop of *Cambray's* Education of a Daughter, as 'tis Translated into the only Language I
have any Knowledge of, tho' perhaps very much to its Disadvantage. I have heard it objected against that Piece, that
its Instructions are not of General Use, but only fitted for a
great Lady; but I confess I am not of that Opinion; for I don't
remember that there are any Rules laid down for the Expences
of a Woman, in which Particular only I think a Gentlewoman
ought to differ from a Lady of the best Fortune, or Highest
Quality, and nct in their Principles of Justice, Gratitude,

Sincerity, Prudence, or Modesty. I ought perhaps to make an
Apology for this long Epistle, but as I rather believe you a
Friend to Sincerity, than Ceremony, shall only assure you I am,

> *Sir,*
>
> *Your Most Humble Servant,*

T   Anabella.'

No. 96.

[STEELE.]   Wednesday, June 20.

> . . . *Amicum*
> *Mancipium domino & frugi . . .*—Hor.

'*Mr.* SPECTATOR,

I HAVE frequently read your Discourse upon Servants, and, as
I am one my self, have been much offended, that in that Variety
of Forms wherein you considered the Bad, you found no Place
to mention the Good. There is however one Observation of
yours I approve, which is, That there are Men of Wit and good
Sense among all Orders of Men: and that Servants report most
of the Good or Ill which is spoken of their Masters. That
there are Men of Sense who live in Servitude, I have the Vanity
to say I have felt to my woful Experience. You attribute very
justly the Source of our general Iniquity to Board-Wages, and
the Manner of living out of a domestick Way: But I cannot give
you my Thoughts on this Subject any Way so well, as by a
short Account of my own Life to this the Forty fifth Year of
my Age; that is to say, from my being first a Foot-boy at
Fourteen, to my present Station of a Nobleman's Porter in the
Year of my Age above-mentioned.

Know then, that my Father was a poor Tenant to the
Family of Sir *Stephen Rackrent*: Sir *Stephen* put me to School,
or rather made me follow his Son *Harry* to School, from my
Ninth Year; and there, though Sir *Stephen* paid something for
my Learning, I was used like a Servant, and was forc'd to get
what Scraps of Learning I could by my own Industry, for the
Schoolmaster took very little Notice of me. My young Master
was a Lad of very sprightly Parts; and my being constantly
about him and loving him, was no small Advantage to me. My
Master loved me extremely, and has often been whipped for
not keeping me at a Distance. He used always to say, That
when he came to his Estate I should have a Lease of my
Father's Tenement for nothing. I came up to Town with him
to *Westminster* School; at which Time he taught me, at Night,
all he learnt, and put me to find out Words in the Dictionary

when he was about his Exercise. It was the Will of Providence that Master *Harry* was taken very ill of a Fever, of which he died within ten Days after his first falling sick. Here was the first Sorrow I ever knew: and I assure you, Mr. SPECTATOR, I remember the beautiful Action of the sweet Youth in his Fever, as fresh as if it were Yesterday. If he wanted any thing, it must be given him by *Tom:* When I let any thing fall through the Grief I was under, he would cry, "Do not beat the poor Boy: Give him some more Julep for me, no Body else shall give it me." He would strive to hide his being so bad, when he saw I could not bear his being in so much Danger, and comforted me, saying, "*Tom, Tom,* have a good Heart." When I was holding a Cup at his Mouth he fell into Convulsions; and at this very Time I hear my dear Master's last Groan. I was quickly turned out of the Room, and left to sob and beat my Head against the Wall at my Leisure. The Grief I was in was inexpressible; and every Body thought it would have cost me my Life. In a few Days my old Lady, who was one of the Housewives of the World, thought of turning me out of Doors, because I put her in Mind of her Son. Sir *Stephen* proposed putting me to Prentice, but my Lady being an excellent Manager, would not let her Husband throw away his Money in Acts of Charity. I had Sense enough to be under the utmost Indignation, to see her discard with so little Concern one her Son had loved so much; and went out of the House to ramble wherever my Feet would carry me.

The third Day after I left Sir *Stephen*'s Family, I was strolling up and down the Walks in the *Temple*. A young Gentleman of the House, who (as I heard him say afterwards) seeing me half starved and well dressed, thought me an Equipage ready to his Hand, after very little Enquiry more than *did I want a Master?* bid me follow him: I did so, and in a very little while thought my self the happiest Creature in this World. My Time was taken up in carrying Letters to Wenches, or Messages to young Ladies of my Master's Acquaintance. We rambled from Tavern to Tavern, to the Play-house, the Mulberry-garden, and all Places of Resort; where my Master engaged every Night in some new Amour, in which and drinking he spent all his Time when he had Money. During these Extravagancies I had the Pleasure of lying on the Stairs of a Tavern half a Night, playing at Dice with other Servants, and the like Idlenesses. When my Master was moneyless, I was generally employed in transcribing amorous Pieces of Poetry, old Songs, and new Lampoons. This Life held till my Master married, and he had then the Prudence to turn me off because I was in the Secret of his Intreagues.

I was utterly at a Loss what Course to take next; when at last I applied my self to a Fellow-sufferer, one of his Mistresses, a Woman of the Town. She happening at that Time to be pretty full of Money, cloathed me from Head to Foot; and knowing me to be a sharp Fellow, employed me accordingly. Sometimes I was to go abroad with her, and when she had pitched upon a young Fellow she thought for her Turn, I was to be dropped as one she could not trust. She would often cheapen Goods at the *New Exchange*; and when she had a Mind to be attacked, she would send me away on an Errand. When an humble Servant and she were beginning a Parley, I came immediately, and told her Sir *John* was coming home; then she would order another Coach to prevent being dogged. The Lover makes Signs to me as I get behind the Coach, I shake my Head it was impossible: I leave my Lady at the next Turning, and follow the Cully to know how to fall in his way on another Occasion. Besides good Offices of this Nature, I writ all my Mistress's Love-Letters; some from a Lady that saw such a Gentleman at such a Place in such a coloured Coat, some shewing the Terrour she was in of a jealous old Husband, others explaining that the Severity of her Parents was such (tho' her Fortune was settled) that she was willing to run away with such a one tho' she knew he was but a younger Brother. In a Word, my Half-Education and Love of idle Books, made me outwrite all that made Love to her by way of Epistle; and as she was extreamly cunning, she did well enough in Company by a skilful Affectation of the greatest Modesty. In the Midst of all this, I was surprized with a Letter from her and a Ten Pound Note.

"*Honest* Tom,

You will never see me more. I am married to a very cunning Country-Gentleman, who might possibly guess something if I kept you still: therefore farewell."

When this Place was lost also in Marriage, I was resolved to go among quite another People for the Future; and got in Butler to one of those Families where there is a Coach kept, three or four Servants, a clean House, and a good general Outside upon a small Estate. Here I lived very comfortably for some Time, till I unfortunately found my Master, the very gravest Man alive, in the Garret with the Chambermaid. I knew the World too well to think of staying there; and the next Day pretended to have received a Letter out of the Country that my Father was dying, and got my Discharge with a Bounty for my Discretion.

The next I lived with was a peevish single Man, whom I

stay'd with for a Year and a Half. Most Part of the Time I passed very easily; for when I began to know him, I minded no more than he meant what he said: so that one Day in good Humour he said, *I was the best Man he ever had, by my want of Respect to him.*

These, Sir, are the chief Occurrences of my Life; and I will not dwell upon very many other Places I have been in, where I have been the strangest Fellow in the World, where no Body in the World had such Servants as they, where sure they were the unluckiest People in the World in Servants, and so forth. All I mean by this Representation, is, To shew you that we poor Servants are not (what you called us too generally) all Rogues; but that we are what we are, according to the Example of our Superiors. In the Family I am now in, I am guilty of no one Sin but Lying; which I do with a grave Face in my Gown and Staff every Day I live, and almost all Day long, in denying my Lord to impertinent Suitors, and my Lady to unwelcome Visitants. But, Sir, I am to let you know, that I am, when I can get abroad, a Leader of the Servants: I am he that keep Time with beating my Cudgel against the Boards in the Gallery at an Opera: I am he that am touched so properly at a Tragedy, when the People of Quality are staring at one another during the most important Incidents: When you hear in a Crowd a Cry in the right Place, an Humm where the Point is touched in a Speech, or an Hussa set up where it is the Voice of the People; you may conclude it is begun, or joined by,

Sir,

Your more than humble Servant,

T Thomas Trusty.'

No. 97.

[STEELE.] Thursday, June 21.

Projecere animas . . .—Virg.

AMONG the loose Papers which I have frequently spoken of heretofore, I find a Conversation between *Pharamond* and *Eucrate* upon the Subject of Duels, and the Copy of an Edict issued in Consequence of that Discourse.

Eucrate argued, That nothing but the most severe and vindictive Punishments, such as placing the Bodies of the Offenders in Chains, and putting them to Death by the most exquisite Torments, would be sufficient to extirpate a Crime which had so long prevailed and was so firmly fixed in the Opinion of the World as great and laudable; but the King answered, That indeed Instances of Ignominy were necessary in the Cure of

this Evil; but considering that it prevailed only among such
as had a Nicety in their Sense of Honour, and that it often
happened that a Duel was fought to save Appearances to the
World, when both Parties were in their Hearts in Amity and
Reconciliation to each other; it was evident, that Turning the
Mode another way would effectually put a Stop to what had
Being only as a Mode.   That to such Persons, Poverty and
Shame were Torments sufficient; That he would not go further
in punishing in others Crimes which he was satisfied he himself
was most guilty of, in that he might have prevented them
by speaking his Displeasure sooner.   Besides which the King
said, he was in general averse to Tortures, which was putting
Human Nature it self, rather than the Criminal, to Disgrace;
and that he would be sure not to use this Means where the
Crime was but an ill Effect arising from a laudable Cause, the
Fear of Shame.   The King, at the same time, spoke with much
Grace upon the Subject of Mercy; and repented of many Acts
of that kind which had a magnificent Aspect in the doing, but
dreadful Consequences in the Example.   Mercy to Particulars,
he observed, was Cruelty in the General: That tho' a Prince
could not revive a Dead Man by taking the Life of him who
killed him, neither could he make Reparation to the next
that should dye by the evil Example; or answer to himself
for the Partiality, in not pardoning the next as well as the
former Offender. 'As for me,' says *Pharamond*, 'I have
conquer'd *France*, and yet have given Laws to my People:
the Laws are my Methods of Life, they are not a Diminution but
a Direction to my Power.   I am still absolute to distinguish
the Innocent and the Virtuous, to give Honours to the Brave
and Generous; I am absolute in my Good-will, none can oppose
my Bounty, or prescribe Rules for my Favour.   While I can,
as I please, reward the Good, I am under no Pain that I cannot
pardon the Wicked: For which Reason,' continued *Pharamond*,
'I will effectually put a stop to this Evil, by exposing no more
the Tenderness of my Nature to the Importunity of having
the same Respect to those who are miserable by their Fault,
and those who are so by their Misfortune.   Flatterers (concluded the King smiling) repeat to us Princes, that we are
Heaven's Vicegerents: Let us be so, and let the only thing
out of our Power be *to do Ill.*'

Soon after the Evening, wherein *Pharamond* and *Eucrate*
had this Conversation, the following Edict was Publish'd.

Pharamond's Edict against Duels.

Pharamond, *King of the* Gauls, *to all his Loving Subjects
sendeth Greeting.*

Whereas it has come to our Royal Notice and Observation, that in Contempt of all Laws, Divine and Human, it is of late become a Custom among the Nobility and Gentry of this our Kingdom, upon slight and trivial, as well as great and urgent Provocations, to invite each other into the Field, there by their own Hands, and of their own Authority, to decide their Controversies by Combat; We have thought fit to take the said Custom into our Royal Consideration, and find, upon Enquiry into the usual Causes whereon such fatal Decisions have arisen, that by this wicked Custom, maugre all the Precepts of our Holy Religion, and the Rules of right Reason, the greatest Act of the Human Mind, *Forgiveness of Injuries*, is become vile and shameful; that the Rules of Good Society and Virtuous Conversation are hereby inverted; that the Loose, the Vain, and the Impudent, insult the Careful, the Discreet, and the Modest; that all Virtue is suppressed, and all Vice supported, in the one Act of being capable to dare to the Death. We have also further, with great Sorrow of Mind, observed that this Dreadful Action, by long Impunity, (our Royal Attention being employed upon Matters of more general Concern) is become Honourable, and the Refusal to engage in it Ignominious. In these our Royal Cares and Enquiries we are yet farther made to understand, that the Persons of most Eminent Worth, and most Hopeful Abilities, accompanied with the strongest Passion for true Glory, are such as are most liable to be involved in the Dangers arising from this Licence. Now taking the said Premises into our serious Consideration, and well weighing that all such Emergencies (wherein the Mind is incapable of commanding it self, and where the Injury is too sudden or too exquisite to be born) are particularly provided for by Laws heretofore enacted: and that the Qualities of less Injuries, like those of Ingratitude, are too nice and delicate to come under General Rules; We do resolve to Blot this Fashion, or Wantonness of Anger, out of the Minds of our Subjects, by our Royal Resolutions declared in this Edict as follow.

No Person who either sends or accepts a Challenge, or the Posterity of either, tho' no Death ensues thereupon, shall be, after the Publication of this our Edict, capable of bearing Office in these our Dominions.

The Person who shall prove the sending or receiving a Challenge, shall receive, to his own use and Property, the whole Personal Estate of both Parties; and their Real Estate shall be immediately vested in the next Heir of the Offenders, in as ample manner as if the said Offenders were actually Deceased.

In Cases where the Laws (which we have already granted to our Subjects) admit of an Appeal for Blood; when the Crimina is condemned by the said Appeal, he shall not only suffer Death, but his whole Estate, Real, Mixed and Personal, shall from the hour of his Death be vested in the next Heir of the Person whose Blood he spilt.

That it shall not hereafter be in our Royal Power, or that of our Successors, to pardon the said Offences, or restore the Offenders in their Estates, Honour, or Blood for ever.

Given at our Court at Blois *the* 8*th of* February 420. *In the Second Year of our Reign.*' T

No. 98.

[ADDISON.]   Friday, June 22.

. . . *Tanta est quaerendi cura decoris.*—Juv.

THERE is not so variable a thing in Nature as a Lady's Head-dress: Within my own Memory I have known it rise and fall above thirty Degrees. About ten Years ago it shot up to a very great Height, insomuch that the Female Part of our Species were much taller than the Men. The Women were of such an enormous Stature, that *we appeared as Grass-hoppers before them*: At present the whole Sex is in a Manner dwarfed and shrunk into a Race of Beauties that seems almost another Species. I remember several Ladies, who were once very near seven Foot high, that at present want some Inches of five: How they came to be thus curtailed I cannot learn: whether the whole Sex be at present under any Penance which we know nothing of, or whether they have cast their Head-dresses in order to surprize us with something in that Kind which shall be entirely new: or whether some of the tallest of the Sex, being too cunning for the rest, have contrived this Method to make themselves appear sizeable, is still a Secret; tho' I find most are of Opinion, they are at present like Trees new lopped and pruned, that will certainly sprout up and flourish with greater Heads than before. For my own Part, as I do not love to be insulted by Women who are taller than my self, I admire the Sex much more in their present Humilia-tion, which has reduced them to their natural Dimensions, than when they had extended their Persons, and lengthened them-selves out into formidable and gigantick Figures. I am not for adding to the beautiful Edifices of Nature, nor for raising any whimsical Superstructure upon her Plans: I must therefore repeat it, that I am highly pleased with the Coiffure now in Fashion; and think it shews the good Sense which at present very much reigns among the valuable Part of the Sex. One may observe, that Women in all Ages have taken more Pains than Men to adorn the Outside of their Heads; and indeed I very much admire, that those Female Architects who raise such wonderful Structures out of Ribbands, Lace and Wire, have not been recorded for their respective Inventions. It is certain there has been as many Orders in these Kinds of Building, as in those which have been made of Marble: Sometimes they rise in the Shape of a Pyramid, sometimes like a Tower, and sometimes like a Steeple. In *Juvenal's* Time the Building grew by several Orders and Stories, as he has very humorously described it.

> *Tot premit ordinibus, tot adhuc compagibus altum*
> *Aedificat caput: Andromachen a fronte videbis;*
> *Post minor est: credas aliam.*—Juv.

But I do not remember, in any Part of my Reading, that the Head-dress aspired to so great an Extravagance as in the fourteenth Century; when it was built up in a Couple of Cones or Spires, which stood so excessively high on each Side of the Head, that a Woman who was but a *Pygmy* without her Head-dress, appeared like a *Colossus* upon putting it on. Monsieur *Paradin* says, 'That these old fashioned Fontanges rose an Ell above the Head; that they were pointed like Steeples, and had long loose Pieces of Crape fastened to the Tops of them, which were curiously fringed and hung down their Backs like Streamers.'

The Women might possibly have carried this Gothick Building much higher, had not a famous Monk, *Thomas Conecte* by Name, attacked it with great Zeal and Resolution. This holy Man travelled from Place to Place to preach down this monstrous Commode; and succeeded so well in it, that as the Magicians sacrificed their Books to the Flames upon the Preaching of an Apostle, many of the Women threw down their Head-dresses in the Middle of his Sermon, and made a Bonfire of them within Sight of the Pulpit. He was so renowned, as well for the Sanctity of his Life as his Manner of Preaching, that he had often a Congregation of Twenty thousand People; the Men placing themselves on the one Side of his Pulpit, and the Women on the other that appeared (to use the Similitude of an ingenious Writer) like a Forrest of Cedars with their Heads reaching to the Clouds. He so warmed and animated the People against this monstrous Ornament, that it lay under a kind of Persecution; and whenever it appeared in publick was pelted down by the Rabble, who flung Stones at the Person that wore it. But notwithstanding this Prodigy vanished while the Preacher was among them, it began to appear again some Months after his Departure, or, to tell it in Monsieur *Paradin's* own Words, 'The Women that, like Snails in a Fright, had drawn in their Horns, shot them out again as soon as the Danger was over.' This Extravagance of the Women's Head-dresses in that Age is taken notice of by Monsieur *d'Argentre* in the History of *Bretagne*, and by other Historians as well as the Person I have here quoted.

It is usually observed, That a good Reign is the only proper Time for the making of Laws against the Exorbitance of Power; in the same Manner an excessive Head-dress may be attacked the most effectually when the Fashion is against it. I do therefore recommend this Paper to my female Readers by way of Prevention.

I would desire the fair Sex to consider, how impossible it is for them to add any thing that can be ornamental to what is already the Master-piece of Nature. The Head has the most beautiful Appearance, as well as the highest Station, in a humane Figure. Nature has laid out all her Art in beautifying the Face: She has touched it with Vermillion, planted in it a double Row of Ivory, made it the Seat of Smiles and Blushes, lighted it up and enlivened it with the Brightness of the Eyes, hung it on each Side with curious Organs of Sense, given it Aires and Graces that cannot be described, and surrounded it with such a flowing Shade of Hair as sets all its Beauties in the most agreeable Light: In short, she seems to have designed the Head as the Cupola to the most glorious of her Works; and when we load it with such a Pile of supernumerary Ornaments, we destroy the Symmetry of the humane Figure, and foolishly contrive to call off the Eye from great and real Beauties, to childish Gew-gaws, Ribbands, and Bone-lace.   L

No. 99.

[ADDISON.]
                                              Saturday, June 23.

> . . . *Turpi secernis honestum.*—Hor.

THE Club, of which I have often declar'd my self a Member, were last Night engaged in a Discourse upon that which passes for the chief Point of Honour among Men and Women; and started a great many Hints upon the Subject which I thought were entirely new. I shall therefore methodize the several Reflections that arose upon this Occasion, and present my Reader with them for the Speculation of this Day; after having promised, that if there is any thing in this Paper which seems to differ with any Passage of last *Thursday*'s, the Reader will consider this as the Sentiments of the Club, and the other as my own private Thoughts, or rather those of *Pharamond*.

The great Point of Honour in Men is Courage, and in Women Chastity. If a Man loses his Honour in one Rencounter, it is not impossible for him to regain it in another; a Slip in a Woman's Honour is irrecoverable. I can give no Reason for fixing the Point of Honour to these two Qualities; unless it be that each Sex sets the greatest Value on the Qualification which renders them the most amiable in the Eyes of the contrary Sex. Had Men chosen for themselves, without Regard to the Opinions of the Fair Sex, I should believe the Choice would have fallen on Wisdom or Virtue; or had Women determined their own Point of Honour, it is probable that Wit or Good-Nature would have carried it against Chastity.

Nothing recommends a Man more to the female Sex than Courage; whether it be that they are pleased to see one who is a Terror to others fall like a Slave at their Feet, or that this Quality supplies their own principal Defect, in guarding them from Insults and avenging their Quarrels, or that Courage is a natural Indication of a strong and sprightly Constitution. On the other Side, nothing makes a Woman more esteemed by the opposite Sex than Chastity; whether it be that we always prize those most who are hardest to come at, or that nothing besides Chastity, with its collateral Attendants, Truth, Fidelity, and Constancy, gives the Man a Property in the Person he loves, and consequently endears her to him above all things.

I am very much pleased with a Passage in the Inscription on a Monument erected in *Westminster Abby* to the late Duke and Dutchess of *Newcastle*, 'Her Name was *Margaret Lucas*, youngest Sister of the Lord *Lucas* of *Colchester; a noble Family, for all the Brothers were valiant, and all the Sisters virtuous.*'

In Books of Chivalry, where the Point of Honour is strained to Madness, the whole Story runs on Chastity and Courage. The Damsel is mounted on a white Palfrey, as an Emblem of her Innocence; and, to avoid Scandal, must have a Dwarf for her Page. She is not to think of a Man, till some Misfortune has brought a Knight-Errant to her Relief. The Knight falls in Love, and did not Gratitude restrain her from murdering her Deliverer, would die at her Feet by her Disdain. However, he must waste many Years in the Desart, before her Virgin Heart can think of a Surrender. The Knight goes off, attacks every thing he meets that is bigger and stronger than himself, seeks all Opportunities of being knock'd on the Head; and after seven Years Rambling returns to his Mistress, whose Chastity has been attacked in the mean Time by Giants and Tyrants, and undergone as many Trials as her Lover's Valour.

In *Spain*, where there are still great Remains of this romantick Humour, it is a transporting Favour for a Lady to cast an accidental Glance on her Lover from a Window, tho' it be two or three Stories high; as it is usual for the Lover to assert his Passion for his Mistress, in single Combat with a mad Bull.

The great Violation of the Point of Honour from Man to Man, is giving the Lie. One may tell another he whores, drinks, blasphemes, and it may pass unresented; but to say he lies, tho' but in jest, is an Affront that nothing but Blood can expiate. The Reason perhaps may be, because no other Vice implies a Want of Courage so much as the making of a Lie; and therefore telling a Man he lies, is touching him in the most sensible Part of Honour, and indirectly calling him a Coward. I cannot omit under this Head what *Herodotus* tells us of the ancient *Persians,* That from the Age of five Years to twenty they instruct their Sons only in three things, to manage the Horse, to make use of the Bow, and to speak Truth.

The placing the Point of Honour in this false kind of Courage, has given Occasion to the very Refuse of Mankind, who have neither Virtue nor common Sense, to set up for Men of Honour. An *English* Peer, who has not been long dead, used to tell a pleasant Story of a *French* Gentleman that visited him early one Morning at *Paris,* and after great Professions of Respect, let him know that he had it in his Power to oblige him; which, in short, amounted to this, that he believed he could tell his Lordship the Person's Name who justled him as he came out from the Opera; but before he would proceed, he begged his Lordship that he would not deny him the Honour of making him his Second. The *English* Lord, to avoid being drawn into a very foolish Affair, told him that he was under Engagements for his two next Duels to a Couple of particular Friends. Upon which the Gentleman immediately withdrew; hoping his Lordship would not take it ill, if he meddled no farther in an Affair from whence he himself was to receive no Advantage.

The beating down this false Notion of Honour, in so vain and lively a People as those of *France,* is deservedly looked upon as one of the most glorious Parts of their present King's Reign. It is Pity but the Punishment of these mischievous Notions should have in it some particular Circumstances of Shame and Infamy; that those who are Slaves to them may see, that instead of advancing their Reputations they lead them to Ignominy and Dishonour.

Death is not sufficient to deter Men, who make it their Glory to despise it; but if every one that fought a Duel were to stand in the Pillory, it would quickly lessen the Number of these imaginary Men of Honour, and put an End to so absurd a Practice.

When Honour is a Support to virtuous Principles, and runs parallel with the Laws of God and our Country, it cannot be too much cherished and encouraged: But when the Dictates of Honour are contrary to those of Religion and Equity, they are the greatest Depravations of human Nature, by giving wrong Ambitions and false Ideas of what is good and laudable; and should therefore be exploded by all Governments, and driven out as the Bane and Plague of human Society.   L

No. 100.
[STEELE.]   Monday, June 25.
Nil ego contulerim jucundo sanus amico.—Hor.

A MAN advanced in Years that thinks fit to look back upon his former Life, and calls that only Life which was passed with Satisfaction and Enjoyment, excluding all Parts which were not pleasant to him, will find himself very young, if not in his Infancy. Sickness, Ill Humour, and Idleness, will have robbed him of a great Share of that Space we ordinarily call our Life. It is therefore the Duty of every Man that would be true to himself, to obtain, if possible, a Disposition to be pleased, and place himself in a constant Aptitude for the Satisfactions of his Being. Instead of this, you hardly see a Man who is not uneasy in proportion to his Advancement in the Arts of Life. An affected Delicacy is the common Improvement we meet with in those who pretend to be refined above others: They do not aim at true Pleasures themselves, but turn their Thoughts upon observing the false Pleasures of other Men. Such People are Valetudinarians in Society, and they should no more come into Company than a sick Man should come into the Air: If a Man is too weak to bear what is a Refreshment to Men in Health, he must still keep his Chamber. When any one in Sir ROGER's Company complains he is out of Order, he immediately calls for some Posset-drink for him, for which Reason that Sort of People who are for ever bewailing their Constitution in other Places, are the Chearfullest imaginable when he is present.

It is a wonderful thing, that so many, and they not reckoned absurd, shall entertain those with whom they converse by giving them the History of their Pains and Aches; and imagine such Narrations their Quota of the Conversation. This is of all other the meanest Help to Discourse; and a Man must no think at all or think himself very insignificant, when he finds an Account of his Head-ach answered by another's asking what News in the last Mail? Mutual good Humour is a Dress we ought to appear in wherever we meet, and we should make no Mention of what concerns our selves, without it be of Matters wherein our Friends ought to rejoyce: But indeed there are Crowds of People who put themselves in no Method of pleasing themselves or others: such are those whom we usually call indolent Persons. Indolence is, methinks, an intermediate Stage between Pleasure and Pain, and very much unbecoming any Part of our Life after we are out of the Nurse's Arms. Such an Aversion to Labour creates a constant Weariness, and, one would think, should make Existence it self a Burthen. The indolent Man descends from the Dignity of his Nature, and makes that Being which was Rational meerly Vegetative: His Life consists only in the meer Encrease and Decay of a Body, which, with Relation to the rest of the World, might as well have been uninformed, as the Habitation of a reasonable Mind.

Of this Kind is the Life of that extraordinary Couple *Harry Tersett* and his Lady. *Harry* was in the Days of his Celibacy one of those pert Creatures who have much Vivacity and little Understanding; Mrs. *Rebecca Quickly*, whom he married, had all that the Fire of Youth and a lively Manner could do towards making an agreeable Woman. These two People of seeming Merit fell into each other's Arms; and Passion being sated, and no Reason or good Sense in either to succeed it, their Life is now at a Stand; their Meals are insipid, and their Time tedious; their Fortune has placed them above Care, and their Loss of Taste reduced them below Diversion. When we talk of these as Instances of Inexistence, we do not mean, that in order to live it is necessary we should always be in jovial Crews, or crowned with Chaplets of Roses, as the merry Fellows among the Antients are described; but it is intended by considering these Contraries to Pleasure, Indolence and too much Delicacy, to shew that it is Prudence to preserve a Disposition in our selves to receive a certain Delight in all we hear and see.

This portable Quality of good Humour seasons all the Parts and Occurrences we meet with, in such a Manner, that there are no Moments lost; but they all pass with so much Satisfaction, that the heaviest of Loads (when it is a Load) that of Time, is never felt by us. *Varilas* has this Quality to the highest Perfection, and communicates it wherever he appears: The Sad, the Merry, the Severe, the Melancholy, shew a new Chearfulness when he comes amongst them. At the same time no one can repeat any thing that *Varilas* has ever said, that deserves Repetition; but the Man has that innate Goodness of Temper, that he is welcome to every Body, because every Man thinks he is so to him. He does not seem to contribute any thing to the Mirth of the Company; and yet upon Reflection you find it all happened by his being there. I thought it was whimsically said of a Gentleman, That if *Varilas* had wit, it would be the best Wit in the World. It is certain, when a well corrected lively Imagination and good Breeding are added to a sweet Disposition, they qualify it to be one of the greatest Blessings, as well as Pleasures of Life.

Men would come into Company with ten Times the Pleasure they do, if they were sure of hearing nothing which should shock them, as well as expected what would please them. When we know every Person that is spoken of, is represented by one who has no ill Will, and every thing that is mentioned described by one that is apt to set it in the best Light, the Entertainment must be delicate; because the Cook has nothing brought to his Hand but what is the most excellent in its Kind. Beautiful Pictures are the Entertainments of pure Minds, and Deformities of the corrupted. It is a Degree towards the Life of Angels, when we enjoy Conversation wherein there is nothing presented but in its Excellence; and a Degree towards that of Daemons, wherein nothing is shewn but in its Degeneracy. T

No. 101.

[ADDISON.]　　　　　　　　　　　　　　　Tuesday, June 26.

> *Romulus & Liber pater & cum Castore Pollux,*
> *Post ingentia facta deorum in templa recepti,*
> *Dum terras hominumque colunt genus, aspera bella*
> *Componunt, agros assignant, oppida condunt;*
> *Ploravere suis non respondere favorem*
> *Speratum meritis. . . .*—Hor.

Censure, says a late ingenious Author, *is the Tax a Man pays to the Publick for being Eminent.* It is a Folly for an eminent Man to think of escaping it, and a Weakness to be affected with it. All the illustrious Persons of Antiquity, and indeed of every Age in the World, have passed through this fiery Persecution. There is no Defence against Reproach, but Obscurity; it is a kind of Concomitant to Greatness, as Satyrs and Invectives were an essential Part of a *Roman* Triumph.

If Men of Eminence are exposed to Censure on one hand, they are as much liable to Flattery on the other. If they receive Reproaches which are not due to them, they likewise receive Praises which they do not deserve. In a word, the Man in a high Post is never regarded with an indifferent Eye, but always considered as a Friend or an Enemy. For this Reason Persons in great Stations have seldom their true Characters drawn, till several Years after their Deaths. Their personal Friendships and Enmities must cease, and the Parties they were engaged in be at an end, before their Faults or their Virtues can have Justice done them. When Writers have the least Opportunity of knowing the Truth, they are in the best Disposition to tell it.

It is therefore the Privilege of Posterity to adjust the Characters of Illustrious Persons, and to set matters right between those Antagonists who by their Rivalry for Greatness divided a whole Age into Factions. We can now allow *Caesar* to be a great Man, without derogating from *Pompey;* and celebrate the Virtues of *Cato*, without detracting from those of *Caesar*. Every one that has been long dead has a due Proportion of Praise allotted him, in which whilst he lived his Friends were too profuse and his Enemies too sparing.

According to Sir *Isaac Newton*'s Calculations, the last Comet that made its Appearance in 1680, imbibed so much Heat by its Approaches to the Sun, that it would have been two thousand times hotter than red hot Iron, had it been a Globe of that Metal; and that supposing it as big as the Earth, and at the same Distance from the Sun, it would be fifty thousand Years in cooling, before it recover'd its natural Temper. In the like manner, if an *English* Man considers the great Ferment into which our Political World is thrown at present, and how intensely it is heated in all its Parts, he cannot suppose that it will cool again in less than three hundred Years. In such a Tract of Time it is possible that the Heats of the present Age may be extinguished, and our several Classes of great Men represented under their proper Characters. Some eminent Historian may then probably arise that will not write *recentibus odiis,* (as *Tacitus* expresses it,) with the Passions and Prejudices of a Contemporary Author, but make an impartial Distribution of Fame among the Great Men of the present Age.

I cannot forbear entertaining my self very often with the idea of such an imaginary Historian describing the Reign of *ANNE* the First, and introducing it with a Preface to his Reader, that he is now entring upon the most shining Part of the *English* Story. The great Rivals in Fame will be then distinguished according to their respective Merits, and shine in their proper Points of Light. Such an one (says the Historian) though variously represented by the Writers of his own Age, appears to have been a Man of more than ordinary Abilities, great Application, and uncommon Integrity: Nor was such an one (tho' of an opposite Party and Interest) inferior to him in any of these Respects. The several Antagonists who now endeavour to depreciate one another, and are celebrated or traduced by different Parties, will then have the same Body of Admirers, and appear Illustrious in the Opinion of the whole *British* Nation. The Deserving Man, who can now recommend himself to the Esteem of but half his Countrymen, will then receive the Approbations and Applauses of a whole Age.

Among the several Persons that flourish in this Glorious Reign, there is no Question but such a future Historian as the Person of whom I am speaking, will make mention of the Men of Genius and Learning, who have now any Figure in the *British* Nation. For my own part, I often flatter myself with the honourable Mention which will then be made of me; and have drawn up a Paragraph in my own Imagination, that I fancy will not be altogether unlike what will be found in some Page or other of this Imaginary Historian.

It was under this Reign, says he, that the SPECTATOR Published those little Diurnal Essays which are still extant. We know very little of the Name or Person of this Author, except only that he was a Man of a very short Face, extreamly addicted to Silence, and so great a Lover of Knowledge that he made a Voyage to *Grand Cairo* for no other Reason but to take the Measure of a Pyramid. His chief Friend was one Sir ROGER DE COVERLY, a whimsical Country Knight, and a *Templar* whose Name he has not transmitted to us. He lived as a Lodger at the House of a Widow-Woman, and was a great Humourist in all parts of his Life. This is all we can affirm with any Certainty of his Person and Character. As for his Speculations, notwithstanding the several obsolete Words and obscure Phrases of the Age in which he liv'd, we still understand enough of them to see the Diversions and Characters of the *English* Nation in his time: Not but that we are to make Allowance for the Mirth and Humour of the Author, who has doubtless strained many Representations of things beyond the Truth. For if we interpret his Words in their litteral Meaning, we must suppose that Women of the First Quality used to pass away whole Mornings at a Puppet-Show: That they attested their Principles by their *Patches*: That an Audience would sit out an Evening to hear a Dramatick Performance written in a Language which they did not understand: That Chairs and Flower-Pots were introduced as Actors upon the *British* Stage: That a Promiscuous Assembly of Men and Women were allowed to meet at Midnight in Masques within the Verge of the Court; with many Improbabilities of the like Nature. We must therefore, in these and the like Cases, suppose that these remote Hints and Allusions aimed at some certain Follies which were then in Vogue, and which at present we have not any Notion of. We may guess by several Passages in the *Speculations*, that there were Writers who endeavoured to detract from the Works of this Author; but as nothing of this nature is come down to us, we cannot guess at any Objections that could be made to his Paper. If we consider his Style with that Indulgence which we must shew to old *English* Writers, or if we look into the Variety of his Subjects, with those several Critical Dissertations, Moral Reflections,   *   *   *   *   *   *   *   *

*   *   *   *   *   *   *   *

*   *   *   *   *   *   *   *

*   *   *   *   *   *   *   *

*   *   *   *   *   *   *   *

The following Part of the Paragraph is so much to my Advantage, and beyond any thing I can pretend to, that I hope my Reader will excuse me for not inserting it.   L

No. 102.

[ADDISON.]

Wednesday, June 27.

> . . . *Lusus animo debent aliquando dari,*
> *Ad cogitandum melior ut redeat sibi.*—Phaed.

I DO not know whether to call the following Letter a Satyr upon Coquets, or a Representation of their several fantastical Accomplishments, or what other Title to give it; but as it is I shall communicate it to the Publick. It will sufficiently explain its own Intention, so that I shall give it my Reader at length, without either Preface or Postscript.

'*Mr.* SPECTATOR,

Women are armed with Fans as Men with Swords, and sometimes do more Execution with them: To the End therefore that Ladies may be entire Mistresses of the Weapon which they bear, I have erected an Academy for the training up of young Women in the *Exercise of the Fan*, according to the most fashionable Airs and Motions that are now practised at Court. The Ladies who *carry* Fans under me are drawn up twice a Day in my great Hall, where they are instructed in the Use of their Arms, and *exercised* by the following Words of Command,

> *Handle your Fans,*
> *Unfurl your Fans,*
> *Discharge your Fans,*
> *Ground your Fans,*
> *Recover your Fans,*
> *Flutter your Fans.*

By the right Observation of these few plain Words of Command, a Woman of a tolerable Genius who will apply her self diligently to her Exercise for the Space of but one half Year, shall be able to give her Fan all the Graces that can possibly enter into that little modish Machine.

But to the End that my Readers may form to themselves a right Notion of this *Exercise*, I beg Leave to explain it to them in all its Parts. When my female Regiment is drawn up in Array, with every one her Weapon in her Hand, upon my giving the Word to *handle their Fans*, each of them shakes her Fan at me with a Smile, then gives her Right-hand Woman a Tap upon the Shoulder, then presses her Lips with the Extremity of her Fan, then lets her Arms fall in an easy Motion, and stands in a Readiness to receive the next Word of Command. All this is done with a close Fan, and is generally learned in the first Week.

The next Motion is that of *unfurling the Fan*, in which are comprehended several little Flirts and Vibrations, as also gradual and deliberate Openings, with many voluntary Fallings asunder in the Fan it self, that are seldom learned under a Month's Practice. This Part of the *Exercise* pleases the Spectators more than any other, as it discovers on a Sudden an infinite Number of Cupids, Garlands, Altars, Birds, Beasts, Rainbows, and the like agreeable Figures, that display themselves to View, whilst every one in the Regiment holds a Picture in her Hand.

Upon my giving the Word to *discharge their Fans*, they give one general Crack that may be heard at a considerable Distance when the Wind sits fair. This is one of the most difficult Parts of the *Exercise*; but I have several Ladies with me, who at their first Entrance could not give a Pop loud enough to be heard at the further End of a Room, who can now *discharge a Fan* in such a Manner, that it shall make a Report like a Pocket-Pistol. I have likewise taken Care (in order to hinder young Women from letting off their Fans in wrong Places or unsuitable Occasions) to shew upon what Subject the Crack of a Fan may come in properly: I have likewise invented a Fan, with which a Girl of Sixteen, by the Help of a little Wind which is enclosed about one of the larges

Sticks, can make as loud a Crack as a Woman of Fifty with an ordinary Fan.

When the Fans are thus *discharged*, the Word of Command in Course is to *ground their Fans*. This teaches a Lady to quit her Fan gracefully when she throws it aside in order to take up a Pack of Cards, adjust a Curl of Hair, replace a falling Pin, or apply herself to any other Matter of Importance. This part of the *Exercise*, as it only consists in tossing a Fan with an Air upon a long Table (which stands by for that Purpose), may be learned in two Days Time as well as in a Twelve-month.

When my Female Regiment is thus disarmed, I generally let them walk about the Room for some Time; when on a sudden (like Ladies that look upon their Watches after a long Visit) they all of them hasten to their Arms, catch them up in a Hurry, and place themselves in their proper Stations upon my calling out *recover your Fans*. This Part of the *Exercise* is not difficult, provided a Woman applies her Thoughts to it.

The *Fluttering of the Fan* is the last, and indeed the Master-piece of the whole *Exercise*; but if a Lady does not mispend her Time, she may make herself Mistress of it in three Months. I generally lay aside the Dog-days and the hot Time of the Summer for the teaching this Part of the *Exercise*; for as soon as ever I pronounce *Flutter your Fans*, the place is filled with so many Zephyrs and gentle Breezes as are very refreshing in that Season of the Year, though they might be dangerous to Ladies of a tender Constitution in any other.

There is an infinite Variety of Motions to be made use of in the *Flutter of a Fan*: There is the angry Flutter, the modest Flutter, the timorous Flutter, the confused Flutter, the merry Flutter, and the amorous Flutter. Not to be tedious, there is scarce any Emotion in the Mind which does not produce a suitable Agitation in the Fan; insomuch, that if I only see the Fan of a disciplin'd Lady, I know very well whether she laughs, frowns, or blushes. I have seen a Fan so very angry, that it would have been dangerous for the absent Lover who provoked it to have come within the Wind of it; and at other Times so very languishing, that I have been glad for the Lady's Sake the Lover was at a sufficient Distance from it. I need not add, that a Fan is either a Prude or Coquet, according to the Nature of the Person who bears it. To conclude my Letter, I must acquaint you that I have from my own Observations compiled a little Treatise for the Use of my Scholars, entituled the *Passions of the Fan*; which I will communicate to you, if you think it may be of Use to the Publick. I shall have a general

Review on *Thursday* next; to which you shall be very welcome
if you will honour it with your Presence.

I am, &c.

P.S. I teach young Gentlemen the whole Art of Gallanting
a Fan.

N. B. I have several little plain Fans made for this Use, to
avoid Expence.'   L

No. 103.

[STEELE.]   Thursday, June 28.

. . . *Sibi quivis*
Speret idem, sudet multum frustraque laboret
Ausus idem . . .—Hor.

My Friend the Divine having been used with Words of Complaisance (which he thinks could be properly applied to no one
living, and I think could be only spoken of him, and that in his
Absence) was so extreamly offended with the excessive way of
speaking Civilities among us, that he made a Discourse against
it at the Club; which he concluded with this Remark, that he
had not heard one Compliment made in our Society since its
Commencement. Every one was pleased with his Conclusion;
and as each knew his good Will to the rest, he was convinced
that the many Professions of Kindness and Service, which we
ordinarily meet with, are not natural where the Heart is well
inclined; but are a Prostitution of Speech, seldom intended to
mean Any Part of what they express, never to mean All they
express. Our Reverend Friend, upon this Topick, pointed
to us two or three Paragraphs on this Subject in the first
Sermon of the first Volume of the late Arch-Bishop's Post-
humous Works. I do not know that I ever read any thing
that pleased me more; and as it is the Praise of *Longinus*, that
he speaks of the Sublime in a Stile suitable to it, so one may say
of this Author upon Sincerity, that he abhors any Pomp of
Rhetorick on this Occasion, and treats it with a more than
ordinary Simplicity, at once to be a Preacher and an Example.
With what Command of himself does he lay before us, in the
Language and Temper of his Profession, a Fault, which by the
least Liberty and Warmth of Expression would be the most
lively Wit and Satyr? But his Heart was better disposed,
and the good Man chastised the great Wit in such a manner,
that he was able to speak as follows.

'. . . Amongst too many other Instances of the great

Corruption and Degeneracy of the Age wherein we live, the great and general want of Sincerity in Conversation is none of the least. The World is grown so full of Dissimulation and Compliment, that Men's Words are hardly any Signification of their Thoughts; and if any Man measure his Words by his Heart, and speak as he thinks, and do not express more Kindness to every Man, than Men usually have for any Man, he can hardly escape the Censure of want of Breeding. The old *English* Plainness and Sincerity, that generous Integrity of Nature, and Honesty of Disposition, which always argues true Greatness of Mind, and is usually accompany'd with undaunted Courage and Resolution, is in a great measure lost amongst us: There hath been a long Endeavour to transform us into Foreign Manners and Fashions, and to bring us to a servile Imitation of none of the best of our Neighbours, in some of the worst of their Qualities. The Dialect of Conversation is now-a-days so swell'd with Vanity and Compliment, and so surfeited (as I may say) of Expressions of Kindness and Respect, that if a Man that lived an Age or two ago should return into the World again, he would really want a Dictionary to help him to understand his own Language, and to know the true intrinsick Value of the Phrase in Fashion, and wou'd hardly at first believe at what a low Rate the highest Strains and Expressions of Kindness imaginable do commonly pass in current Payment; and when he shou'd come to understand it, he wou'd be a great while before he could bring himself with a good Countenance and a good Conscience to converse with Men upon equal Terms, and in their own way.

And in truth it is hard to say, whether it should more provoke our Contempt or our Pity, to hear what solemn Expressions of Respect and Kindness will pass between Men, almost upon no Occasion; how great Honour and Esteem they will declare for one whom perhaps they never saw before, and how entirely they are all on the sudden devoted to his Service and Interest, for no Reason; how infinitely and eternally oblig'd to him, for no Benefit; and how extreamly they will be concern'd for him, yea and afflicted too, for no Cause. I know it is said, in Justification of this hollow kind of Conversation, that there is no Harm, no real Deceit in Compliment, but the matter is well enough, so long as we understand one another: *& Verba valent ut Nummi, Words are like Money*; and when the current Value of them is generally understood, no Man is cheated by them. This is something, if such Words were any thing; but being brought into the Accompt, they are meer Cyphers. However it is still a just Matter of Complaint, that Sincerity and Plainness are out of Fashion, and that our Language is running into a Lie; that Men have almost quite perverted the use of Speech, and made Words to signify nothing; that the greatest part of the Conversation of Mankind, is little else but driving a Trade of Dissimulation; insomuch that it would make a Man heartily sick and weary of the World, to see the little Sincerity that is in Use and Practice among Men.'

When the Vice is placed in this contemptible Light, he argues unanswerably against it, in Words and Thoughts so natural, that any Man who reads them would imagine he himself could have been the Author of them.

'If the Show of any thing be good for any thing, I am sure Sincerity is better; for why does any Man dissemble, or seem to be that which he is not, but because he thinks it good to have such a Quality as he pretends to? For to counterfeit and dissemble, is to put on the Appearance of some real Excellency. Now the best Way in the World to seem to be any thing, is really to be what he would seem to be. Besides, that it is many times as troublesome to make good the Pretence of a good Quality, as to have it; and if a Man have it not, it is ten to one but he is discovered to want it; and then all his Pains and Labour to seem to have it, is lost.'

In another Part of the same Discourse he goes on to shew, that all Artifice must naturally tend to the Disappointment of him that practises it.

'Whatsoever Convenience may be thought to be in Falshood and Dissimulation, it is soon over; but the Inconvenience of it is perpetual, because it brings a Man under an everlasting Jealousie and Suspicion, so that he is not believ'd when he speaks Truth, nor trusted when perhaps he means honestly: When a Man hath once forfeited the Reputation of his Integrity, he is set fast, and nothing will then serve his turn, neither Truth nor Falshood.' R

No. 104.
[STEELE.] Friday, June 29.

> . . . *Qualis equos Threissa fatigat*
> *Harpalyce* . . .—Virg.

IT would be a noble Improvement, or rather a Recovery of what we call good Breeding, if nothing were to pass amongst us for agreeable which was the least Transgression against that Rule of Life called Decorum, or a Regard to Decency. This would command the Respect of Mankind, because it carries in it Deference to their good Opinion; as Humility lodged in a worthy Mind, is always attended with a certain Homage which no haughty Soul, with all the Arts imaginable, will ever be able to purchase. *Tully* says, Virtue and Decency are so nearly related, that it is difficult to separate them from each other but in our Imagination. As the Beauty of the Body always accompanies the Health of it, so certainly is Decency concomitant to Virtue: As Beauty of Body, with an agreeable Carriage, pleases the Eye, and that Pleasure consists in that we observe all the Parts with a certain Elegance are proportioned to each other; so does Decency of Behaviour which appears in our Lives, obtain the Approbation of all with whom we converse, from the Order, Constancy, and Moderation of our Words and Actions. This flows from the Reverence we bear towards every good Man, and to the World in general; for to be negligent of what any one thinks of you, does not only shew you arrogant but abandoned. In all these Considerations we are to distinguish how one Virtue differs from another: As it is the Part of Justice never to do Violence, it is of Modesty never to commit Offence. In this last Particular lies the whole Force of what is called Decency; to this Purpose that excellent Moralist abovementioned talks of Decency; but this Quality is more easily comprehended by an ordinary Capacity, than expressed with all his Eloquence. This Decency of Behaviour is generally transgressed among all Orders of Men; nay, the very Women, tho' themselves created as it were for Ornament, are often very much mistaken in this ornamental Part of Life. It would methinks be a short Rule for Behaviour, if every young Lady in her Dress, Words, and Actions were only to recommend her self as a Sister, Daughter, or Wife, and make her self the more esteemed in one of those Characters. The Care of themselves, with regard to the Families in which Women are born, is the best Motive for their being courted to come into the Alliance of other Houses. Nothing can promote this End more than a strict Preservation of Decency. I should be glad if a certain Equestrian Order of Ladies, some of whom one meets in an Evening at every Outlet of the Town, would take this Subject into their serious Consideration: In Order thereunto the following Letter may not be wholly unworthy their Perusal.

'*Mr.* SPECTATOR,

Going lately to take the Air in one of the most beautiful Evenings this Season has produced; as I was admiring the Serenity of the Sky, the lively Colours of the Fields, and the Variety of the Landskip every Way around me, my Eyes were suddenly call'd off from these inanimate Objects by a little Party of Horsemen I saw passing the Road. The greater

Part of them escap'd my particular Observation, by reason that my whole Attention was fix'd on a very fair Youth who rode in the Midst of them, and seemed to have been dress'd by some Description in a Romance. His Features, Complexion, and Habit had a remarkable Effeminacy, and a certain languishing Vanity appear'd in his Air: His Hair, well curl'd and powder'd, hung to a considerable Length on his Shoulders, and was wantonly ty'd, as if by the Hands of his Mistress, in a Scarlet Ribbon, which play'd like a Streamer behind him: He had a Coat and Wastcoat of blue Camlet trimm'd and embroider'd with Silver: a Cravat of the finest Lace; and wore, in a smart Cock, a little Beaver Hat edg'd with Silver, and made more sprightly by a Feather. His Horse too, which was a Pacer, was adorn'd after the same airy Manner, and seem'd to share in the Vanity of the Rider. As I was pitying the Luxury of this young Person, who appear'd to me to have been educated only as an Object of Sight, I perceiv'd on my nearer Approach, and as I turn'd my Eyes downward, a Part of the Equipage I had not observ'd before, which was a Petticoat of the same with the Coat and Wastcoat. After this Discovery, I look'd again on the Face of the fair *Amazon* who had thus deceiv'd me, and thought those Features which had before offended me by their Softness, were now strengthen'd into as improper a Boldness; and tho' her Eyes, Nose, and Mouth seem'd to be formed with perfect Symmetry, I am not certain whether she, who in Appearance was a very handsome Youth, may not be in Reality a very indifferent Woman.

There is an Objection which naturally presents it self against these occasional Perplexities and Mixtures of Dress, which is, that they seem to break in upon that Propriety and Distinction of Appearance in which the Beauty of different Characters is preserv'd; and if they shou'd be more frequent than they are at present, wou'd look like turning our publick Assemblies into a general Masquerade. The Model of this *Amazonian* Hunting-habit for Ladies, was, as I take it, first imported from *France*, and well enough expresses the Gayety of a People who are taught to do any thing so it be with an Assurance; but I cannot help thinking it fits awkardly yet on our *English* Modesty. The Petticoat is a kind of Incumberance upon it; and if the *Amazons* should think fit to go on in this Plunder of our Sex's Ornaments, they ought to add to their Spoils, and complete their Triumph over us, by wearing the Breeches.

If it be natural to contract insensibly the Manners of those we imitate, the Ladies who are pleas'd with assuming our Dresses will do us more Honour than we deserve, but they will do it at their own Expence. Why should the lovely *Camilla*

deceive us in more Shapes than her own, and affect to be
represented in her Picture with a Gun and a Spaniel; while her
elder Brother, the Heir of a worthy Family, is drawn in Silks
like his Sister? The Dress and Air of a Man are not well to
be divided; and those who would not be content with the Latter
ought never to think of assuming the Former. There is so
large a Portion of natural Agreeableness among the fair Sex
of our Island, that they seem betray'd into these romantick
Habits without having the same Occasion for them with their
Inventors: All that needs to be desir'd of them is, that they
wou'd *be themselves*, that is, what Nature designed them: and to
see their Mistake when they depart from this, let them look
upon a Man who affects the Softness and Effeminacy of a
Woman, to learn how their Sex must appear to us when
approaching to the Resemblance of a Man.

<blockquote>
I am,
  Sir,
</blockquote>

T   *Your Most Humble Servant.'*

No. 105.
[ADDISON.]   Saturday, June 30.

<blockquote>
. . . *Id arbitror*
A dprime in vita esse utile, ut nequid nimis.—Ter. *Andr.*
</blockquote>

MY Friend WILL. HONEYCOMB values himself very much upon
what he calls the Knowledge of Mankind, which has cost him
many Disasters in his Youth; for WILL. reckons every Misfortune that he has met with among the Women, and every
Rencounter among the Men, as Parts of his Education, and
fancies he should never have been the Man he is, had not he
broke Windows, knocked down Constables, disturbed honest
People with his Midnight Serenades, and beat up a lewd
Woman's Quarters, when he was a young Fellow. The engaging in Adventures of this nature, WILL. calls the studying
of Mankind; and terms this Knowledge of the Town, the
Knowledge of the World. WILL. ingenuously confesses, that
for half his Life his Head ached every Morning with reading of
Men over-night; and at present comforts himself under certain
Pains which he endures from time to time, that without them
he could not have been acquainted with the Gallantries of the
Age. This WILL. looks upon as the Learning of a Gentleman,
and regards all other kinds of Science as the Accomplishments
of one whom he calls a Scholar, a Bookish Man, or a Philosopher.

For these Reasons WILL. shines in mixed Company, where he
has the Discretion not to go out of his Depth, and has often a

certain way of making his real Ignorance appear a seeming one. Our Club however has frequently caught him tripping, at which times they never spare him. For as WILL. often insults us with the Knowledge of the Town, we sometimes take our revenge upon him by our Knowledge of Books.

He was last Week producing two or three Letters which he writ in his Youth to a Coquet Lady. The Raillery of them was natural, and well enough for a meer Man of the Town; but, very unluckily, several of the Words were wrong spelt. WILL. laught this off at first as well as he could, but finding himself pushed on all sides, and especially by the *Templer*, he told us, with a little Passion, that he never liked Pedantry in Spelling, and that he spelt like a Gentleman, and not like a Scholar: Upon this WILL. had Recourse to his old Topick of shewing the narrow Spiritedness, the Pride, and Ignorance of Pedants; which he carried so far, that upon my retiring to my Lodgings, I could not forbear throwing together such Reflections as occurred to me upon that Subject.

A Man who has been brought up among Books, and is able to talk of nothing else, is a very indifferent Companion, and what we call a Pedant. But, methinks, we should enlarge the Title, and give it every one that does not know how to think out of his Profession, and particular way of Life.

What is a greater Pedant than a meer Man of the Town? Barr him the Play-houses, a Catalogue of the reigning Beauties, and an Account of a few fashionable Distempers that have befallen him, and you strike him Dumb. How many a pretty Gentleman's Knowledge lies all within the Verge of the Court? He will tell you the Names of the Principal Favourites, repeat the shrewd Sayings of a Man of Quality, whisper an Intreague that is not yet blown upon by common Fame; or, if the Sphere of his Observations is a little larger than ordinary, will perhaps enter into all the Incidents, Turns, and Revolutions in a Game of Ombre. When he has gone thus far he has shown you the whole Circle of his Accomplishments, his Parts are drained and he is disabled from any farther Conversation. What are these but rank Pedants? and yet these are the Men who value themselves most on their Exemption from the Pedantry of Colleges.

I might here mention the Military Pedant, who always talks in a Camp, and is storming Towns, making Lodgments, and fighting Battels from one end of the Year to the other. Every thing he speaks smells of Gunpowder; if you take away his Artillery from him, he has not a Word to say for himself. I might likewise mention the Law Pedant, that is perpetually putting Cases, repeating the Transactions of *Westminster-Hall*, wrangling with you upon the most indifferent Circumstances of Life, and not to be convinced of the Distance of a Place, or of the most trivial Point in Conversation, but by dint of Argument. The State-Pedant is wrapt up in News, and lost in Politicks. If you mention either of the Kings of *Spain* or *Poland*, he talks very notably; but if you go out of the *Gazette*, you drop him. In short, a meer Courtier, a meer Soldier, a meer Scholar, a meer any thing, is an insipid Pedantick Character, and equally ridiculous.

Of all the Species of Pedants, which I have mentioned, the Book-Pedant is much the most supportable; he has at least an exercised Understanding, and a Head which is full though confused, so that a Man who converses with him may often receive from him hints of things that are worth knowing, and what he may possibly turn to his own Advantage, tho' they are of little use to the Owner. The worst kind of Pedants among Learned Men, are such as are naturally endued with a very small Share of common Sense, and have read a great number of Books without Taste or Distinction.

The Truth of it is, Learning, like Travelling, and all other Methods of Improvement, as it finishes good Sense, so it makes a silly Man ten thousand times more insufferable, by supplying variety of Matter to his Impertinence, and giving him an Opportunity of abounding in Absurdities.

Shallow Pedants cry up one another much more than Men of solid and useful Learning. To read the Titles they give an Editor, or Collator of a Manuscript, you would take him for the Glory of the Common-Wealth of Letters, and the Wonder of his Age; when perhaps upon Examination you find that he has only Rectify'd a *Greek* Particle, or laid out a whole Sentence in proper Commas.

They are obliged indeed to be thus lavish of their Praises, that they may keep one another in Countenance; and it is no wonder if a great deal of Knowledge, which is not capable of making a Man Wise, has a natural Tendency to make him Vain and Arrogant. L

No. 106.

[ADDISON.]   Monday, July 2.

> . . . *Hinc tibi copia*
> *Manabit ad plenum benigno*
> *Ruris honorum opulenta cornu.*—Hor.

HAVING often received an Invitation from my Friend Sir ROGER DE COVERLY to pass away a Month with him in the

Country, I last Week accompanied him thither, and am settled with him for some Time at his Country-house, where I intend to form several of my ensuing Speculations. Sir ROGER, who is very well acquainted with my Humour, lets me rise and go to Bed when I please, dine at his own Table or in my Chamber as I think fit, sit still and say nothing without bidding me be merry. When the Gentlemen of the Country come to see him, he only shews me at a Distance: As I have been walking in his Fields I have observed them stealing a Sight of me over an Hedge, and have heard the Knight desiring them not to let me see them, for that I hated to be stared at.

I am the more at Ease in Sir ROGER's Family, because it consists of sober and staid Persons; for as the Knight is the best Master in the World, he seldom changes his Servants; and as he is beloved by all about him, his Servants never care for leaving him: By this Means his Domesticks are all in Years, and grown old with their Master. You would take his Valet de Chambre for his Brother, his Butler is gray-headed, his Groom is one of the gravest Men that I have ever seen, and his Coachman has the Looks of a Privy-Counsellor. You see the Goodness of the Master even in the old House-dog, and in a gray Pad that is kept in the Stable with great Care and Tenderness out of Regard to his past Services, tho' he has been useless for several Years.

I could not but observe with a great deal of Pleasure the Joy that appeared in the Countenances of these ancient Domesticks upon my Friend's Arrival at his Country-Seat. Some of them could not refrain from Tears at the Sight of their old Master; every one of them press'd forward to do something for him, and seemed discouraged if they were not employed. At the same Time the good old Knight, with a Mixture of the Father and the Master of the Family, tempered the Enquiries after his own Affairs with several kind Questions relating to themselves. This Humanity and Good-nature engages every Body to him, so that when he is pleasant upon any of them, all his Family are in good Humour, and none so much as the Person whom he diverts himself with: On the Contrary, if he coughs, or betrays any Infirmity of old Age, it is easy for a Stander-by to observe a secret Concern in the Looks of all his Servants.

My worthy Friend has put me under the particular Care of his Butler, who is a very prudent Man, and, as well as the rest of his Fellow-Servants, wonderfully desirous of pleasing me, because they have often heard their Master talk of me as of his particular Friend.

My chief Companion, when Sir ROGER is diverting himself in

the Woods or the Fields, is a very venerable Man who is ever with Sir ROGER, and has lived at his House in the Nature of a Chaplain above thirty Years. This Gentleman is a Person of good Sense and some Learning, of a very regular Life and obliging Conversation: He heartily loves Sir ROGER, and knows that he is very much in the old Knight's Esteem; so that he lives in the Family rather as a Relation than a Dependant.

I have observed in several of my Papers, that my Friend Sir ROGER, amidst all his good Qualities, is something of an Humourist; and that his Virtues, as well as Imperfections, are as it were tinged by a certain Extravagance, which makes them particularly *his*, and distinguishes them from those of other Men. This Cast of Mind, as it is generally very innocent in it self, so it renders his Conversation highly agreeable, and more delightful than the same Degree of Sense and Virtue would appear in their common and ordinary Colours. As I was walking with him last Night, he ask'd me how I liked the good Man whom I have just now mentioned? and without staying for my Answer, told me, That he was afraid of being insulted with Latin and Greek at his own Table; for which Reason, he desired a particular Friend of his at the University to find him out a Clergyman rather of plain Sense than much Learning, of a good Aspect, a clear Voice, a sociable Temper, and, if possible, a Man that understood a little of Back-Gammon. 'My Friend,' says Sir ROGER, 'found me out this Gentleman, who, besides the Endowments required of him, is, they tell me, a good Scholar though he does not shew it. I have given him the Parsonage of the Parish; and because I know his Value, have settled upon him a good Annuity for Life. If he outlives me, he shall find that he was higher in my Esteem than perhaps he thinks he is. He has now been with me thirty Years; and though he does not know I have taken Notice of it, has never in all that Time asked any thing of me for himself, tho' he is every Day solliciting me for something in Behalf of one or other of my Tenants his Parishioners. There has not been a Law-Suit in the Parish since he has lived among them: If any Dispute arises, they apply themselves to him for the Decision; if they do not acquiesce in his Judgment, which I think never happened above once, or twice at most, they appeal to me. At his first settling with me, I made him a Present of all the good Sermons which have been printed in *English*, and only begged of him that every *Sunday* he would pronounce one of them in the Pulpit. Accordingly, he has digested them into such a Series, that they follow one another naturally, and make a continued System of practical Divinity.'

As Sir ROGER was going on in his Story, the Gentleman we

were talking of came up to us; and upon the Knight's asking him who preached to Morrow (for it was *Saturday* Night) told us, the Bishop of St. *Asaph* in the Morning, and Doctor *South* in the Afternoon. He then shewed us his List of Preachers for the whole Year, where I saw with a great deal of Pleasure Archbishop *Tillotson*, Bishop *Saunderson*, Doctor *Barrow*, Doctor *Calamy*, with several living Authors who have published Discourses of Practical Divinity. I no sooner saw this venerable Man in the Pulpit, but I very much approved of my Friend's insisting upon the Qualifications of a good Aspect and a clear Voice; for I was so charmed with the Gracefulness of his Figure and Delivery, as well as with the Discourses he pronounced, that I think I never passed any Time more to my Satisfaction. A Sermon repeated after this Manner, is like the Composition of a Poet in the Mouth of a graceful Actor.

I could heartily wish that more of our Country-Clergy would follow this Example; and instead of wasting their Spirits in laborious Compositions of their own, would endeavour after a handsome Elocution, and all those other Talents that are proper to enforce what has been penned by greater Masters. This would not only be more easy to themselves, but more edifying to the People. L

No. 107.

[STEELE.]   Tuesday, July 3.

> *Aesopo ingentem statuam posuere Attici,*
> *Servumque collocarunt aeterna in basi,*
> *Patere honoris scirent ut cuncti viam.*—Phaed.

THE Reception, manner of Attendance, undisturb'd Freedom and Quiet, which I meet with here in the Country, has confirmed me in the Opinion I always had, that the general Corruption of Manners in Servants is owing to the Conduct of Masters. The Aspect of every one in the Family carries so much Satisfaction, that it appears he knows the happy Lot which has befallen him in being a Member of it. There is one Particular which I have seldom seen but at Sir ROGER's; it is usual in all other Places, that Servants fly from the parts of the House through which their Master is passing; on the contrary, here they industriously place themselves in his way; and it is on both sides, as it were, understood as a Visit when the Servants appear without calling. This proceeds from the Humane and equal Temper of the Man of the House, who also perfectly well knows how to enjoy a great Estate, with such Oeconomy as ever to be much before Hand. This makes his own Mind untroubled, and consequently unapt to vent peevish Expressions, or give passionate or inconsistent Orders to those about him. Thus Respect and Love go together; and a certain Chearfulness in Performance of their Duty, is the particular Distinction of the lower part of this Family. When a Servant is called before his Master, he does not come with an Expectation to hear himself rated for some trivial Fault, threatend to be stripp'd, or used with any other unbecoming Language, which mean Masters often give to worthy Servants; but it is often to know, what Road he took that he came so readily back according to Order: whether he passed by such a Ground; if the old Man who rents it is in good Health; or whether he gave Sir ROGER's Love to him, or the like.

A Man who preserves a Respect, founded on his Benevolence to his Dependants, lives rather like a Prince than a Master in his Family; his Orders are received as Favours, rather than Duties; and the Distinction of approaching him, is part of the Reward for executing what is commanded by him.

There is another Circumstance in which my Friend excells in his Management, which is the manner of rewarding his Servants: He has ever been of Opinion, that giving his cast Cloaths to be worn by Valets has a very ill Effect upon little Minds, and creates a silly Sense of Equality between the Parties, in Persons affected only with outward things. I have heard him often pleasant on this Occasion, and describe a young Gentleman abusing his Man in that Coat, which a Month or two before was the most pleasing Distinction he was conscious of in himself. He would turn his Discourse still more pleasantly upon the Ladies' Bounties of this kind; and I have heard him say he knew a fine Woman, who distributed Rewards and Punishments in giving becoming or unbecoming Dresses to her Maids.

But my good Friend is above these little Instances of Goodwill, in bestowing only Trifles on his Servants; a good Servant to him is sure of having it in his Choice very soon of being no Servant at all. As I before observed, he is so good an Husband, and knows so thoroughly that the Skill of the Purse is the Cardinal Virtue of this Life; I say, he knows so well that Frugality is the Support of Generosity, that he can often spare a large Fine when a Tenement falls, and give that Settlement to a good Servant who has a mind to go into the World, or make a Stranger pay the Fine to that Servant, for his more comfortable Maintenance, if he stays in his Service.

A Man of Honour and Generosity considers, it would be miserable to himself to have no Will but that of another, tho' it were of the best Person breathing, and for that Reason goes on as fast as he is able to put his Servants into independent Livelihoods. The greatest part of Sir ROGER's Estate is tenanted by Persons who have served himself or his Ancestors. It was to me extreamly pleasant to observe the Visitants from several parts to welcome his Arrival into the Country: and all the Difference that I could take notice of, between the late Servants who came to see him, and those who staid in the Family, was, that these latter were looked upon as finer Gentlemen and better Courtiers.

This Manumission and placing them in a way of Livelihood, I look upon as only what is due to a good Servant, which Encouragement will make his Successor be as diligent, as humble, and as ready as he was. There is something wonderful in the narrowness of those Minds, which can be pleased, and be barren of Bounty to those who please them.

One might, on this occasion, recount the Sense that Great Persons in all Ages have had of the Merit of their Dependants, and the Heroick Services which Men have done their Masters in the Extremity of their Fortunes; and shewn, to their un-done Patrons, that Fortune was all the Difference between them; but as I design this my Speculation only as a gentle Admonition to thankless Masters, I shall not go out of the Occurrences of common Life, but assert it as a general Observation, that I never saw, but in Sir ROGER's Family, and one or two more, good Servants treated as they ought to be. Sir ROGER's Kindness extends to their Children's Children, and this very Morning he sent his Coachman's Grandson to Pren-tice. I shall conclude this Paper with an Account of a Picture in his Gallery, where there are many which will deserve my future Observation.

At the very upper End of this handsome Structure I saw the Portraiture of two Young Men standing in a River, the one naked the other in a Livery. The Person supported seemed half Dead, but still so much alive as to shew in his Face exquisite Joy and Love towards the other. I thought the fainting Figure resembled my Friend Sir ROGER; and look-ing at the Butler, who stood by me, for an Account of it, he informed me that the Person in the Livery was a Servant of Sir ROGER's, who stood on the Shore while his Master was Swimming, and observing him taken with some sudden Illness, and sink under Water, jumped in and saved him. He told me Sir ROGER took off the Dress he was in as soon as he came home, and by a Great Bounty at that time, follow'd by his Favour ever since, had made him Master of that pretty Seat which we saw at a distance as we came to this House. I remember'd indeed Sir ROGER said there lived a very worthy Gentleman, to whom he was highly obliged, without mentioning any thing further. Upon my looking a little dissatisfyed at some part of the Picture, my Attendant informed me, that it was against Sir ROGER's Will, and at the earnest Request of the Gentleman himself, that he was Drawn in the Habit in which he had saved his Master.   R

No. 108.
[ADDISON.]   Wednesday, July 4.

Gratis anhelans, multa agendo nihil agens.—Phaed.

As I was Yesterday Morning walking with Sir ROGER before his House, a Country-Fellow brought him a huge Fish, which, he told him, Mr. *William Wimble* had caught that very Morning; and that he presented it, with his Service, to him, and intended to come and dine with him.   At the same Time he delivered a Letter, which my Friend read to me as soon as the Messenger left him.

'*Sir* ROGER,

I Desire you to accept of a Jack, which is the best I have caught this Season.   I intend to come and stay with you a Week, and see how the Perch bite in the *Black River.*   I observed, with some Concern, the last Time I saw you upon the Bowling-Green, that your Whip wanted a Lash to it: I will bring half a Dozen with me that I twisted last Week, which I hope will serve you all the Time you are in the Country.   I have not been out of the Saddle for six Days last past, having been at *Eaton* with Sir *John*'s eldest Son.   He takes to his Learning hugely.

           I am,
                       Sir,
                               Your humble Servant,
                                               Will Wimble.'

This extraordinary Letter, and Message that accompanied it, made me very curious to know the Character and Quality of the Gentleman who sent them; which I found to be as follows: *Will. Wimble* is younger Brother to a Baronet, and descended of the ancient Family of the *Wimbles.*   He is now between Forty and Fifty; but being bred to no Business and born to no Estate, he generally lives with his elder Brother as Superintendant of his Game.   He hunts a Pack of Dogs better than any Man in the Country, and is very famous for finding out a Hare.   He is extremely well versed in all the little

Handicrafts of an idle Man: He makes a *May*-fly to a Miracle; and furnishes the whole Country with Angle-Rods. As he is a good-natur'd officious Fellow, and very much esteemed upon Account of his Family, he is a welcome Guest at every House, and keeps up a good Correspondence among all the Gentlemen about him. He carries a Tulip-Root in his Pocket from one to another, or exchanges a Puppy between a couple of Friends that live perhaps in the opposite Sides of the County. *Will.* is a particular Favourite of all the young Heirs, whom he frequently obliges with a Net that he has weaved, or a Setting-dog that he has *made* himself: He now and then presents a Pair of Garters of his own knitting to their Mothers or Sisters; and raises a great deal of Mirth among them, by enquiring as often as he meets them *how they wear?* These Gentleman-like Manufactures and obliging little Humours, make *Will.* the Darling of the Country.

Sir ROGER was proceeding in the Character of him, when we saw him make up to us, with two or three Hazle-twigs in his Hand that he had cut in Sir ROGER's Woods, as he came through them, in his Way to the House. I was very much pleased to observe on one Side the hearty and sincere Welcome with which Sir ROGER received him, and on the other the secret Joy which his Guest discovered at Sight of the good old Knight. After the first Salutes were over, *Will.* desired Sir ROGER to lend him one of his Servants to carry a Set of Shuttlecocks he had with him in a little Box to a Lady that liv'd about a Mile off, to whom it seems he had promised such a Present for above this half Year. Sir ROGER's Back was no sooner turn'd, but honest *Will.* began to tell me of a large Cock-Pheasant that he had sprung in one of the neighbouring Woods, with two or three other Adventures of the same Nature. Odd and uncommon Characters are the Game that I look for, and most delight in; for which Reason I was as much pleased with the Novelty of the Person that talked to me, as he could be for his Life with the springing of a Pheasant, and therefore listned to him with more than ordinary Attention.

In the Midst of his Discourse the Bell rung to Dinner, where the Gentleman I have been speaking of had the Pleasure of seeing the huge Jack, he had caught, served up for the first Dish in a most sumptuous Manner. Upon our sitting down to it he gave us a long Account how he had hooked it, played with it, foiled it, and at length drew it out upon the Bank, with several other Particulars that lasted all the first Course. A Dish of Wild-fowl that came afterwards furnished Conversation for the rest of the Dinner, which concluded with a late Invention of *Will*'s for improving the Quail Pipe.

Upon withdrawing into my Room after Dinner, I was secretly touched with Compassion towards the honest Gentleman that had dined with us; and could not but consider with a great deal of Concern, how so good an Heart and such busy Hands were wholly employed in Trifles; that so much Humanity should be so little beneficial to others, and so much Industry so little advantageous to himself. The same Temper of Mind and Application to Affairs might have recommended him to the publick Esteem, and have raised his Fortune in another Station of Life. What Good to his Country or himself might not a Trader or Merchant have done with such useful tho' ordinary Qualifications?

Will. Wimble's is the Case of many a younger Brother of a great Family, who had rather see their Children starve like Gentlemen, than thrive in a Trade or Profession that is beneath their Quality. This Humour fills several Parts of *Europe* with Pride and Beggary. It is the Happiness of a trading Nation, like ours, that the younger Sons, tho' uncapable of any liberal Art or Profession, may be placed in such a Way of Life, as may perhaps enable them to vie with the best of their Family: Accordingly we find several Citizens that were launched into the World with narrow Fortunes, rising by an honest Industry to greater Estates than those of their elder Brothers. It is not improbable but *Will.* was formerly tried at Divinity, Law, or Physick; and that finding his Genius did not lie that Way, his Parents gave him up at length to his own Inventions: But certainly, however improper he might have been for Studies of a higher Nature, he was perfectly well turned for the Occupations of Trade and Commerce. As I think this is a Point which cannot be too much inculcated, I shall desire my Reader to compare what I have here written with what I have said in my Twenty first Speculation.   L

No. 109.
[STEELE.]   Thursday, July 5.

         . . . *Abnormis sapiens* . . .—Hor.

I was this Morning walking in the Gallery, when Sir ROGER enter'd at the end opposite to me, and advancing towards me, said, he was glad to meet me among his Relations the DE COVERLEYS, and hoped I liked the Conversation of so much good Company, who were as silent as my self. I knew he alluded to the Pictures, and as he is a Gentleman who does not a little value himself upon his ancient Descent, I expected he would give me some Account of them. We were now arrived at the upper End of the Gallery, when the Knight faced towards one of the Pictures, and as we stood before it, he entered into the Matter, after his blunt way of saying things, as they occur to his Imagination, without regular Introduction, or Care to preserve the Appearance of Chain of Thought.

'It is,' said he, 'worth while to consider the Force of Dress; and how the Persons of one Age differ from those of another, merely by that only. One may observe also that the General Fashion of one Age has been follow'd by one particular Set of People in another, and by them preserved from one Generation to another. Thus the vast Jetting Coat and small Bonnet, which was the Habit in *Harry* the Seventh's time, is kept on in the Yeomen of the Guard; not without a good and Politick View, because they look a Foot taller, and a Foot and an half broader; Besides, that the Cap leaves the Face expanded, and consequently more Terrible, and fitter to stand at the Entrance of Palaces.

This Predecessor of ours, you see, is dressed after this Manner, and his Cheeks would be no larger than mine were he in a Hat as I am. He was the last Man that won a Prize in the Tilt-Yard (which is now a Common Street before *Whitehall*). You see the broken Lance that lyes there by his right Foot: he shivered that Lance of his Adversary all to pieces: and bearing himself, look you Sir, in this manner, at the same time he came within the Target of the Gentleman who rode again him, and taking him with incredible Force before him on the Pummel of his Saddle, he in that manner rid the Turnament over, with an Air that shewed he did it rather to perform the Rule of the Lists, than Expose his Enemy; however, it appeared he knew how to make use of a Victory, and with a gentle Trot he marched up to a Gallery where their Mistress sat (for they were Rivals) and let him down with laudable Courtesy and pardonable Insolence. I don't know but it might be exactly where the Coffee-house is now.

You are to know this my Ancestor was not only of a military Genius but fit also for the Arts of Peace, for he play'd on the Base-viol as well as any Gentleman at Court; you see where his Viol hangs by his Basket-hilt Sword. The Action at the Tilt-yard you may be sure won the Fair Lady, who was a Maid of Honour, and the greatest Beauty of her time; here she stands the next Picture. You see, Sir, my Great Great Great Grand Mother has on the new-fashioned Petticoat, except that the Modern is gathered at the Waste; my Grandmother appear as if she stood in a large Drum, whereas the Ladies now wall as if they were in a Go-Cart. For all this Lady was bred a

Court, she became an Excellent Country-Wife, she brought ten
Children, and when I shew you the Library, you shall see in her
own hand (allowing for the Difference of the Language) the
best Receipt now in *England* both for an Hasty-Pudding and
a Whitepot.

If you please to fall back a little, because it is necessary to
look at the three next Pictures at one View; these are three
Sisters. She on the right Hand, who is so very beautiful,
dyed a Maid; the next to her, still handsomer, had the same
Fate, against her Will; this homely thing in the middle had both
their Portions added to her own, and was Stolen by a neighbouring Gentleman, a Man of Stratagem and Resolution, for
he poisoned three Mastiffs to come at her, and knocked down
two Dear-stealers in carrying her off. Misfortunes happen in
all Families: The Theft of this Romp and so much Money, was
no great matter to our Estate. But the next Heir that possessed it was this soft Gentleman, whom you see there: Observe
the small Buttons, the little Boots, the Laces, the Slashes about
his Cloaths, and above all the Posture he is drawn in, (which
to be sure was his own chusing); you see he sits with one Hand
on a Desk writing, and looking as it were another way, like an
easie Writer, or a Sonneteer: He was one of those that had too
much Wit to know how to live in the World; he was a Man of
no Justice, but great good Manners; he ruined every body
that had any thing to do with him, but never said a rude thing
in his Life; the most indolent Person in the World, he would
sign a Deed that passed away half his Estate with his Gloves
on, but would not put on his Hat before a Lady if it were to
save his Country. He is said to be the first that made Love
by squeezing the Hand. He left the Estate with ten thousand
Pounds Debt upon it, but however by all Hands I have been
informed that he was every way the finest Gentleman in the
World. That Debt lay heavy on our House for one Generation,
but it was retrieved by a Gift from that Honest Man you see
there, a Citizen of our Name, but nothing at all a-kin to us.
I know Sir ANDREW FREEPORT has said behind my Back,
that this Man was descended from one of the ten Children of
the Maid of Honour I shewed you above. But it was never
made out; we winked at the thing indeed, because Mony was
wanting at that time.'

Here I saw my Friend a little embarrassed, and turned my
Face to the next Portraiture.

Sir ROGER went on with his Account of the Gallery in the
following manner. 'This Man' (pointing to him I look'd at)
'I take to be the Honour of our House. Sir HUMPHREY DE
COVERLEY; he was in his Dealings as punctual as a Tradesman,

and as generous as a Gentleman. He would have thought himself as much undone by breaking his Word, as if it were to be followed by Bankruptcy. He served his Country as Knight of this Shire to his dying Day; He found it no easie matter to maintain an Integrity in his Words and Actions, even in things that regarded the Offices which were incumbent upon him, in the care of his own Affairs and Relations of Life, and therefore dreaded (tho' he had great Talents) to go into Employments of State, where he must be exposed to the Snares of Ambition. Innocence of Life and great Ability were the distinguishing Parts of his Character; the latter, he had often observed, had led to the Destruction of the former, and used frequently to lament that Great and Good had not the same Signification. He was an Excellent Husbandman, but had resolved not to exceed such a degree of Wealth; all above it he bestowed in secret Bounties many Years after the Sum he aimed at for his own use was attained. Yet he did not slacken his Industry, but to a decent old Age spent the Life and Fortune which was superfluous to himself, in the Service of his Friends and Neighbours.'

Here we were called to Dinner, and Sir ROGER ended the Discourse of this Gentleman, by telling me, as we followed the Servant, that this his Ancestor was a Brave Man, and narrowly escaped being killed in the Civil Wars; 'for,' said he, 'he was sent out of the Field upon a private Message the Day before the Battle of *Worcester.*' The Whim of narrowly escaping, by having been within a Day of Danger; with other Matters above-mentioned, mixed with good Sense, left me at a Loss whether I was more delighted with my Friend's Wisdom or Simplicity.   R

No. 110.

[ADDISON.]   Friday, July 6.

Horror ubique animos, simul ipsa silentia terrent.—Virg.

AT a little Distance from Sir ROGER's House, among the Ruins of an old Abby, there is a long Walk of aged Elms; which are shot up so very high, that when one passes under them, the Rooks and Crows that rest upon the Tops of them seem to be Cawing in another Region. I am very much delighted with this Sort of Noise, which I consider as a kind of natural Prayer to that Being who supplies the Wants of his whole Creation, and who, in the beautiful Language of the *Psalms*, feedeth the young Ravens that call upon him. I like this Retirement the better, because of an ill Report it lies under of being *haunted*; for which Reason (as I have been told in the Family) no living Creature ever walks in it besides the Chaplain. My good Friend the Butler desired me with a very grave Face not to venture myself in it after Sun-set, for that one of the Footmen had been almost frighted out of his Wits by a Spirit that appeared to him in the Shape of a black Horse without an Head: to which he added, that about a Month ago one of the Maids coming home late that Way with a Pail of Milk upon her Head, heard such a Rustling among the Bushes that she let it fall.

I was taking a Walk in this Place last Night between the Hours of Nine and Ten, and could not but fancy it one of the most proper Scenes in the World for a Ghost to appear in. The Ruins of the Abby are scattered up and down on every Side, and half covered with Ivy and Elder-Bushes, the Harbours of several solitary Birds which seldom make their Appearance till the Dusk of the Evening. The Place was formerly a Church-yard, and has still several Marks in it of Graves and Burying-Places. There is such an Eccho among the old Ruins and Vaults, that if you stamp but a little louder than ordinary you hear the Sound repeated. At the same Time the Walk of Elms, with the Croaking of the Ravens which from time to time are heard from the Tops of them, looks exceeding solemn and venerable. These Objects naturally raise Seriousness and Attention; and when Night heightens the Awfulness of the Place, and pours out her supernumerary Horrours upon every-thing in it, I do not at all wonder that weak Minds fill it with Spectres and Apparitions.

Mr. *Locke,* in his Chapter of the Association of Ideas, has very curious Remarks to shew how by the Prejudice of Educa-tion one Idea often introduces into the Mind a whole Set that bear no Resemblance to one another in the Nature of things. Among several Examples of this Kind, he produces the follow-ing Instance. *The Ideas of Goblins and Sprights have really no more to do with Darkness than Light: Yet let but a foolish Maid inculcate these often on the Mind of a Child, and raise them there together, possibly he shall never be able to separate them again so long as he lives; but Darkness shall ever afterwards bring with it those frightful Ideas, and they shall be so joyned, that he can no more bear the one than the other.*

As I was walking in this Solitude, where the Dusk of the Evening conspired with so many other Occasions of Terrour, I observed a Cow grazing not far from me, which an Imagina-tion that was apt to *startle* might easily have construed into a black Horse without an Head: and I dare say the poor Foot-man lost his Wits upon some such trivial Occasion.

My Friend Sir ROGER has often told me with a good deal of Mirth, that at his first coming to his Estate he found three Parts of his House altogether useless; that the best Room in it had the Reputation of being haunted, and by that Means was locked up; that Noises had been heard in his long Gallery, so that he could not get a Servant to enter it after eight a Clock at Night; that the Door of one of his Chambers was nailed up, because there went a Story in the Family that a Butler had formerly hanged himself in it; and that his Mother, who lived to a great Age, had shut up half the Rooms in the House, in which either her Husband, a Son, or Daughter had died. The Knight, seeing his Habitation reduced to so small a Compass, and himself in a Manner shut out of his own House, upon the Death of his Mother ordered all the Apartments to be flung open, and *exorcised* by his Chaplain, who lay in every Room one after another, and by that Means dissipated the Fears which had so long reigned in the Family.

I should not have been thus particular upon these ridiculous Horrours, did I not find them so very much prevail in all Parts of the Country. At the same Time I think a Person who is thus terrify'd with the Imagination of Ghosts and Spectres much more reasonable, than one who contrary to the Reports of all Historians sacred and prophane, ancient and modern, and to the Traditions of all Nations, thinks the Appearance of Spirits fabulous and groundless: Could not I give my self up to this general Testimony of Mankind, I should to the Relations of particular Persons who are now living, and whom I cannot distrust in other Matters of Fact. I might here add, that not only the Historians, to whom we may joyn the Poets, but likewise the Philosophers of Antiquity have favoured this Opinion. *Lucretius* himself, though by the Course of his Philosophy he was obliged to maintain that the Soul did not exist separate from the Body, makes no Doubt of the Reality of Apparitions, and that Men have often appeared after their Death. This I think very remarkable; he was so pressed with the Matter of Fact which he could not have the Confidence to deny, that he was forced to account for it by one of the most absurd un-philosophical Notions that was ever started. He tells us, That the Surfaces of all Bodies are perpetually flying off from their respective Bodies, one after another; and that these Surfaces or thin Cases that included each other while they were joined in the Body like the Coats of an Onion, are sometimes seen entire when they are separated from it; by which Means we often behold the Shapes and Shadows of Persons who are either dead or absent.

I shall dismiss this Paper with a Story out of *Josephus*, not

so much for the Sake of the Story it self as for the moral
Reflections with which the Author concludes it, and which I
shall here set down in his own Words. '*Glaphyra* the Daughter
of King *Archilaus*, after the Death of her two first Husbands
(being married to a third, who was Brother to her first Husband,
and so passionately in Love with her that he turn'd off his
former Wife to make Room for this Marriage) had a very odd
kind of Dream. She fancied that she saw her first Husband
coming towards her, and that she embraced him with great
Tenderness; when in the Midst of the Pleasure which she
expressed at the Sight of him, he reproached her after the
following Manner: *Glaphyra*, says he, thou has made good the
old Saying, That Women are not to be trusted. Was not I
the Husband of thy Virginity? Have I not Children by thee?
How couldst thou forget our Loves so far as to enter into a
second Marriage, and after that into a third, nay to take for
thy Husband a Man who has so shamelessly crept into the Bed
of his Brother? However, for the Sake of our passed Loves,
I shall free thee from thy present Reproach, and make thee
mine for ever. *Glaphyra* told this Dream to several Women of
her Acquaintance, and died soon after. I thought this Story
might not be impertinent in this Place, wherein I speak of those
Kings: Besides that, the Example deserves to be taken Notice
of, as it contains a most certain Proof of the Immortality of the
Soul, and of Divine Providence. If any Man thinks these Facts
incredible, let him enjoy his own Opinion to himself: but let
him not endeavour to disturb the Belief of others, who by
Instances of this Nature are excited to the Study of Virtue.' L

No. 111.
[ADDISON.] Saturday, July 7.

> . . . *Inter silvas Academi quaerere verum.*—Hor.

THE Course of my last Speculation led me insensibly into a
Subject upon which I always meditate with great Delight, I
mean the Immortality of the Soul. I was Yesterday walking
alone in one of my Friend's Woods, and lost my self in it very
agreeably, as I was running over in my Mind the several
Arguments that establish this great Point, which is the Basis
of Morality, and the Source of all the pleasing Hopes and secret
Joys that can arise in the Heart of a reasonable Creature. I
considered those several Proofs drawn,

First, From the Nature of the Soul it self, and particularly
its Immateriality; which, tho' not absolutely necessary to the

Eternity of its Duration, has, I think, been evinced to almost a Demonstration.

Secondly, From its Passions and Sentiments, as particularly from its Love of Existence, its Horrour of Annihilation, and its Hopes of Immortality, with that secret Satisfaction which it finds in the Practice of Virtue, and that Uneasiness which follows in it upon the Commission of Vice.

Thirdly, From the Nature of the Supreme Being, whose Justice, Goodness, Wisdom and Veracity are all concerned in this great Point.

But among these and other excellent Arguments for the Immortality of the Soul, there is one drawn from the perpetual Progress of the Soul to its Perfection, without a Possibility of ever arriving at it; which is a Hint that I do not remember to have seen opened and improved by others who have written on this Subject, tho' it seems to me to carry a great Weight with it. How can it enter into the Thoughts of Man, that the Soul, which is capable of such immense Perfections, and of receiving new Improvements to all Eternity, shall fall away into nothing almost as soon as it is created? Are such Abilities made for no Purpose? A Brute arrives at a Point of Perfection that he can never pass: In a few Years he has all the Endowments he is capable of; and were he to live ten thousand more, would be the same thing he is at present. Were a human Soul thus at a stand in her Accomplishments, were her Faculties to be full blown, and incapable of farther Enlargements, I could imagine it might fall away insensibly, and drop at once into a State of Annihilation. But can we believe a thinking Being, that is in perpetual Progress of Improvements, and travelling on from Perfection to Perfection, after having just looked abroad into the Works of its Creator, and made a few Discoveries of his infinite Goodness, Wisdom and Power, must perish at her first setting out, and in the very beginning of her Enquiries?

A Man, considered in his present State, seems only sent into the World to propagate his Kind. He provides himself with a Successor, and immediately quits his Post to make room for him.

> . . . *haeres*
> *Haeredem alterius, velut unda supervenit undam.*

He does not seem born to enjoy Life, but to deliver it down to others. This is not surprizing to consider in Animals, which are formed for our use, and can finish their Business in a short Life. The Silk-worm after having spun her Task, lays her Eggs and dies. But a Man can never have taken in his full measure of Knowledge, has not time to subdue his Passions, establish his Soul in Virtue, and come up to the Perfection of his Nature, before he is hurried off the Stage. Would an infinitely wise Being make such glorious Creatures for so mean a Purpose? Can he delight in the Production of such abortive Intelligences, such short-lived reasonable Beings? Would he give us Talents that are not to be exerted? Capacities that are never to be gratified? How can we find that Wisdom, which shines through all his Works, in the Formation of Man, without looking on this World, as only a Nursery for the next, and believing that the several Generations of rational Creatures, which rise up and disappear in such quick Successions, are only to receive their first Rudiments of Existence here, and afterwards to be transplanted into a more friendly Climate, where they may spread and flourish to all Eternity?

There is not, in my Opinion, a more pleasing and triumphant Consideration in Religion than this of the perpetual Progress which the Soul makes towards the Perfection of its Nature, without ever arriving at a Period in it. To look upon the Soul as going on from Strength to Strength, to consider that she is to shine for ever with new Accessions of Glory, and brighten to all Eternity; that she will be still adding Virtue to Virtue, and Knowledge to Knowledge; carries in it something wonderfully agreeable to that Ambition which is natural to the Mind of Man. Nay, it must be a Prospect pleasing to God himself, to see his Creation for ever beautifying in his Eyes, and drawing nearer to him, by greater degrees of Resemblance.

Methinks this single Consideration, of the Progress of a finite Spirit to Perfection, will be sufficient to extinguish all Envy in inferior Natures, and all Contempt in superior. That Cherubim, which now appears as a God to a human Soul, knows very well that the Period will come about in Eternity, when the Human Soul shall be as perfect as he himself now is: Nay when she shall look down upon that degree of Perfection, as much as she now falls short of it. It is true, the higher Nature still advances, and by that means preserves his Distance and Superiority in the Scale of Being; but he knows how high soever the Station is of which he stands possess'd at present, the inferior Nature will at length mount up to it, and shine forth in the same Degree of Glory.

With what Astonishment and Veneration may we look into our own Souls, where there are such hidden Stores of Virtue and Knowledge, such inexhausted Sources of Perfection? We know not yet what we shall be, nor will it ever enter into the Heart of Man to conceive the Glory that will be always in Reserve for him. The Soul considered with its Creator, is like

one of those Mathematical Lines that may draw nearer to
another for all Eternity, without a Possibility of touching it:
And can there be a Thought so transporting, as to consider
our selves in these perpetual Approaches to him, who is not
only the Standard of Perfection but of Happiness!   L

No. 112.

[ADDISON.]   Monday, July 9.

> 'Αθανάτους μὲν πρῶτα θεοὺς, νόμῳ ὡς διάκειται,
> Τίμα. . . .—Pyth.

I am always very well pleased with a Country *Sunday*; and
think, if keeping holy the Seventh Day were only a human
Institution, it would be the best Method that could have been
thought of for the polishing and civilizing of Mankind.   It is
certain the Country-People would soon degenerate into a kind
of Savages and Barbarians, were there not such frequent
Returns of a stated Time, in which the whole Village meet
together with their best Faces, and in their cleanliest Habits,
to converse with one another upon indifferent Subjects, hear
their Duties explained to them, and join together in Adoration
of the supreme Being.   *Sunday* clears away the Rust of the
whole Week, not only as it refreshes in their Minds the Notions
of Religion, but as it puts both the Sexes upon appearing in
their most agreeable Forms, and exerting all such Qualities as
are apt to give them a Figure in the Eye of the Village.   A
Country-Fellow distinguishes himself as much in the *Church-
yard*, as a Citizen does upon the *Change*; the whole Parish-
Politicks being generally discuss'd in that Place either after
Sermon or before the Bell rings.

My Friend Sir Roger being a good Church-man, has
beautified the Inside of his Church with several Texts of his
own chusing: He has likewise given a handsome Pulpit-Cloth,
and railed in the Communion-Table at his own Expence.   He
has often told me, that at his coming to his Estate he found his
Parishioners very irregular; and that in order to make them
kneel and join in the Responses, he gave every one of them a
Hassock and a Common-prayer Book: and at the same Time
employed an itinerant Singing-Master, who goes about the
Country for that Purpose, to instruct them rightly in the Tunes
of the Psalms; upon which they now very much value themselves, and indeed out-do most of the Country Churches that
I have ever heard.

As Sir Roger is Landlord to the whole Congregation, he keeps them in very good Order, and will suffer no Body to sleep in it besides himself; for if by Chance he has been surprized into a short Nap at Sermon, upon recovering out of it he stands up and looks about him, and if he sees any Body else nodding, either wakes them himself, or sends his Servants to them. Several other of the old Knight's Particularities break out upon these Occasions: Sometimes he will be lengthening out a Verse in the Singing-Psalms, half a Minute after the rest of the Congregation have done with it; sometimes, when he is pleased with the Matter of his Devotion, he pronounces *Amen* three or four times to the same Prayer; and sometimes stands up when every Body else is upon their Knees, to count the Congregation, or see if any of his Tenants are missing.

I was Yesterday very much surprized to hear my old Friend, in the Midst of the Service, calling out to one *John Matthews* to mind what he was about, and not disturb the Congregation. This *John Matthews* it seems is remarkable for being an idle Fellow, and at that Time was kicking his Heels for his Diversion. This Authority of the Knight, though exerted in that odd Manner which accompanies him in all Circumstances of Life, has a very good Effect upon the Parish, who are not polite enough to see any thing ridiculous in his Behaviour; besides that, the general good Sense and Worthiness of his Character, make his Friends observe these little Singularities as Foils that rather set off than blemish his good Qualities.

As soon as the Sermon is finished, no Body presumes to stir till Sir Roger is gone out of the Church. The Knight walks down from his Seat in the Chancel between a double Row of his Tenants, that stand bowing to him on each Side; and every now and then enquires how such an one's Wife, or Mother, or Son, or Father do whom he does not see at Church; which is understood as a secret Reprimand to the Person that is absent.

The Chaplain has often told me, that upon a Catechizing-day, when Sir Roger has been pleased with a Boy that answers well, he has ordered a Bible to be given him next Day for his Encouragement; and sometimes accompanies it with a Flitch of Bacon to his Mother. Sir Roger has likewise added five Pounds a Year to the Clerk's Place; and that he may encourage the young Fellows to make themselves perfect in the Church-Service, has promised upon the Death of the present Incumbent, who is very old, to bestow it according to Merit.

The fair Understanding between Sir Roger and his Chaplain, and their mutual Concurrence in doing Good, is the more remarkable, because the very next Village is famous for the Differences and Contentions that rise between the Parson and the 'Squire, who live in a perpetual State of War. The Parson is always preaching at the 'Squire, and the 'Squire to be revenged on the Parson never comes to Church. The 'Squire has made all his Tenants Atheists and Tithe-Stealers; while the Parson instructs them every *Sunday* in the Dignity of his Order, and insinuates to them in almost every Sermon, that he is a better Man than his Patron. In short, Matters are come to such an Extremity, that the 'Squire has not said his Prayers either in publick or private this half Year; and that the Parson threatens him, if he does not mend his Manners, to pray for him in the Face of the whole Congregation.

Feuds of this Nature, though too frequent in the Country, are very fatal to the ordinary People; who are so used to be dazled with Riches, that they pay as much Deference to the Understanding of a Man of an Estate, as of a Man of Learning; and are very hardly brought to regard any Truth, how important soever it may be, that is preached to them, when they know there are several Men of five hundred a Year who do not believe it.   L

No. 113.
[STEELE.]   Tuesday, July 10.
        . . . *Haerent infixi pectore vultus.*—Virg.

IN my first Description of the Company in which I pass most of my Time, it may be remembered that I mentioned a great Affliction which my Friend Sir ROGER had met with in his Youth, which was no less than a Disappointment in Love. It happened this Evening, that we fell into a very pleasing Walk at a Distance from his House: As soon as we came into it, 'It is,' quoth the good old Man, looking round him with a Smile, 'very hard, that any Part of my Land should be settled upon one who has used me so ill as the perverse Widow did; and yet I am sure I could not see a Sprig of any Bough of this whole Walk of Trees, but I should reflect upon her and her Severity. She has certainly the finest Hand of any Woman in the World. You are to know this was the Place wherein I used to muse upon her; and by that Custom I can never come into it, but the same tender Sentiments revive in my Mind, as if I had actually walked with that beautiful Creature under these Shades. I have been Fool enough to carve her Name on the Bark of several of these Trees; so unhappy is the Condition of Men in Love, to attempt the removing of their Passion by the Methods which serve only to imprint it deeper. She has certainly the finest Hand of any Woman in the World.'

Here followed a profound Silence; and I was not displeased to observe my Friend falling so naturally into a Discourse, which I had ever before taken Notice he industriously avoided. After a very long Pause, he entered upon an Account of this great Circumstance in his Life, with an Air which I thought raised my *Idea* of him above what I had ever had before; and gave me the Picture of that chearful Mind of his, before it received that Stroke which has ever since affected his Words and Actions. But he went on as follows.

'I came to my Estate in my Twenty second Year, and resolved to follow the Steps of the most worthy of my Ancestors, who have inhabited this spot of Earth before me, in all the Methods of Hospitality and good Neighbourhood, for the Sake of my Fame; and in Country Sports and Recreations, for the Sake of my Health. In my Twenty third Year I was obliged to serve as Sheriff of the County; and in my Servants, Officers, and whole Equipage, indulged the Pleasure of a young Man (who did not think ill of his own Person) in taking that publick Occasion of shewing my Figure and Behaviour to Advantage. You may easily imagine to your self what Appearance I made, who am pretty tall, rid well, and was very well dressed, at the Head of a whole County, with Musick before me, a Feather in my Hat, and my Horse well bitted. I can assure you I was not a little pleased with the kind Looks and Glances I had from all the Balconies and Windows, as I rode to the Hall where the Assizes were held. But when I came there, a beautiful Creature in a Widow's Habit sat in Court, to hear the Event of a Cause concerning her Dower. This commanding Creature (who was born for Destruction of all who behold her) put on such a Resignation in her Countenance, and bore the Whispers of all around the Court with such a pretty Uneasiness, I warrant you, and then recovered her self from one Eye to another, till she was perfectly confused by meeting something so wistful in all she encountered, that at last, with a Murrain to her, she cast her bewitching Eye upon me. I no sooner met it, but I bowed like a great surprized Booby; and knowing her Cause to be the first which came on, I cried, like a captivated Calf as I was, Make Way for the Defendant's Witnesses. This sudden Partiality made all the County immediately see the Sheriff also was become a Slave to the fine Widow. During the Time her Cause was upon Trial, she behaved her self, I warrant you, with such a deep Attention to her Business, took Opportunities to have little Billets handed to her Counsel, then would be in such a pretty Confusion, occasioned, you must know, by acting before so much Company, that not only I but the whole Court was prejudiced in her Favour; and all that the next Heir to her

Husband had to urge, was thought so groundless and frivolous, that when it came to her Counsel to reply, there was not half so much said as every one besides in the Court thought he could have urged to her Advantage. You must understand, Sir, this perverse Woman is one of those unaccountable Creatures that secretly rejoyce in the Admiration of Men, but indulge themselves in no further Consequences. Hence it is that she has ever had a Train of Admirers, and she removes from her Slaves in Town to those in the Country, according to the Seasons of the Year. She is a reading Lady, and far gone in the Pleasures of Friendship: She is always accompanied by a Confident, who is Witness to her daily Protestations against our Sex, and consequently a Bar to her first Steps towards Love, upon the Strength of her own Maxims and Declarations.

However, I must needs say this accomplished Mistress of mine has distinguished me above the rest, and has been known to declare Sir Roger de Coverley was the tamest and most human of all the Brutes in the Country. I was told she said so by one who thought he rallied me: but upon the Strength of this slender Encouragement of being thought least detestable, I made new Liveries, new paired my Coach-Horses, sent them all to Town to be bitted, and taught to throw their Legs well, and move altogether, before I pretended to cross the Country and wait upon her. As soon as I thought my Retinue suitable to the Character of my Fortune and Youth, I set out from hence to make my Addresses. The particular Skill of this Lady has ever been to inflame your Wishes, and yet command Respect. To make her Mistress of this Art, she has a greater Share of Knowledge, Wit, and good Sense, than is usual even among Men of Merit. Then she is beautiful beyond the Race of Women. If you won't let her go on with a certain Artifice with her Eyes, and the Skill of Beauty, she will arm her self with her real Charms, and strike you with Admiration instead of Desire. It is certain that if you were to behold the whole Woman, there is that Dignity in her Aspect, that Composure in her Motion, that Complacency in her Manner, that if her Form makes you hope, her Merit makes you fear. But then again, she is such a desperate Scholar, that no Country-Gentleman can approach her without being a Jest. As I was going to tell you, when I came to her House I was admitted to her Presence with great Civility; at the same Time she placed her self to be first seen by me in such an Attitude, as I think you call the Posture of a Picture that she discovered new Charms, and I at last came towards her with such an Awe as made me speechless. This she no sooner observed but she made her Advantage of it, and began

Discourse to me concerning Love and Honour, as they both
are followed by Pretenders, and the real Votaries to them.
When she discussed these Points in a Discourse, which I verily
believe was as learned as the best Philosopher in *Europe* could
possibly make, she asked me whether she was so happy as to
fall in with my Sentiments on these important Particulars.
Her Confident sat by her, and upon my being in the last Confusion and Silence, this malicious Aide of hers turning to her
says, I am very glad to observe Sir ROGER pauses upon this
Subject, and seems resolved to deliver all his Sentiments upon
the Matter when he pleases to speak. They both kept their
Countenances, and after I had sat half an Hour meditating
how to behave before such profound Casuists, I rose up and took
my Leave. Chance has since that Time thrown me very often
in her Way, and she as often has directed a Discourse to me
which I do not understand. This Barbarity has kept me ever
at a Distance from the most beautiful Object my Eyes ever
beheld. It is thus also she deals with all Mankind, and you
must make Love to her, as you would conquer the Sphinx, by
posing her. But were she like other Women, and that there
were any talking to her, how constant must the Pleasure of
that Man be, who could converse with a Creature—— But,
after all, you may be sure her Heart is fixed on some one or
other; and yet I have been credibly informed; but who can
believe half that is said! After she had done speaking to me,
she put her Hand to her Bosom and adjusted her Tucker.
Then she cast her Eyes a little down, upon my beholding her
too earnestly. They say she sings excellently: Her Voice in
her ordinary Speech has something in it inexpressibly sweet.
You must know I dined with her at a publick Table the Day
after I first saw her, and she helped me to some Tansy in the
Eye of all the Gentlemen in the Country: She has certainly the
finest Hand of any Woman in the World. I can assure you,
Sir, were you to behold her, you would be in the same Condition;
for as her Speech is Musick, her Form is Angelick. But I find
I grow irregular while I am talking of her; but indeed it would
be Stupidity to be unconcerned at such Perfection. Oh the
excellent Creature, she is as inimitable to all Women, as she is
inaccessible to all Men!'

I found my Friend begin to rave, and insensibly led him
towards the House, that we might be joined by some other
Company; and am convinced that the Widow is the secret
Cause of all that Inconsistency which appears in some Parts
of my Friend's Discourse; tho' he has so much Command of
himself as not directly to mention her, yet according to that of
Martial, which one knows not how to render into *English*,

Dum tacet hanc loquitur. I shall end this Paper with that whole Epigram, which represents with much Humour my honest Friend's Condition.

> *Quicquid agit Rufus, nihil est nisi Naevia Rufo:*
> *Si gaudet, si flet, si tacet, hanc loquitur;*
> *Caenat, propinat, poscit, negat, annuit, una est*
> *Naevia; si non sit Naevia, mutus erit.*
> *Scriberet hesterna patri cum luce salutem,*
> *Naevia lux, inquit, Naevia numen, ave.*

> *Let* Rufus *weep, rejoice, stand, sit, or walk,*
> *Still he can nothing but of* Naevia *talk;*
> *Let him eat, drink, ask Questions, or dispute,*
> *Still he must speak of* Naevia, *or be mute.*
> *He writ to his Father, ending with this Line,*
> *I am, my Lovely* Naevia, *ever thine.*

R

No. 114.
[STEELE.]   Wednesday, July 11.

>   . . . *Paupertatis pudor & fuga* . . .—Hor.

OECONOMY in our Affairs, has the same Effect upon our Fortunes which good Breeding has upon our Conversations. There is a pretending Behaviour in both Cases, which instead of making Men esteemed, renders them both miserable and contemptible. We had Yesterday at Sir ROGER's a Set of Country Gentlemen who dined with him: and after Dinner the Glass was taken, by those who pleased, pretty plentifully. Among others I observed a Person of a tolerable good Aspect, who seemed to be more greedy of Liquor than any of the Company, and yet, methought, he did not taste it with Delight. As he grew warm, he was suspicious of every thing that was said; and as he advanced towards being fudled, his Humour grew worse. At the same Time his Bitterness seemed to be rather inward Dissatisfaction in his own Mind, than any Dislike he had taken to the Company. Upon hearing his Name, I knew him to be a Gentleman of a considerable Fortune in this County, but greatly in Debt. What gives the unhappy Man this Peevishness of Spirit, is, that his Estate is dipp'd, and is eating out with Usury; and yet he has not the heart to sell any Part of it. His proud Stomach, at the Cost of restless Nights, constant inquietudes, Danger of Affronts, and a thousand nameless Inconveniences, preserves this Canker in his Fortune, rather than it shall be said he is a Man of fewer Hundreds a Year than he has been commonly reputed. Thus he endures the Torment of Poverty, to avoid the Name of being less rich. If you go to his House you see great Plenty; but served in a Manner that shows it is all unnatural, and that the Master's Mind is not at home. There is a certain Waste and Carelessness in the Air of every thing, and the whole appears but a covered Indigence, a magnificent Poverty. That Neatness and Chearfulness, which attends the Table of him who lives within Compass, is wanting, and exchanged for a libertine Way of Service in all about him.

This Gentleman's Conduct, tho' a very common way of Management, is as ridiculous as that Officer's would be, who had but few Men under his Command, and should take the Charge of an Extent of Country rather than of a small Pass. To pay for, personate, and keep in a Man's Hands, a greater Estate than he really has, is of all others the most unpardonable Vanity, and must in the End reduce the Man who is guilty of it to Dishonour. Yet if we look round us in any County of *Great-Britain*, we shall see many in this fatal Errour; if that may be call'd by so soft a Name, which proceeds from a false Shame of appearing what they really are, when the contrary Behaviour would in a short Time advance them to the Condition which they pretend to.

Laertes has fifteen hundred Pounds a Year; which is mortgaged for six thousand Pounds; but it is impossible to convince him, that if he sold as much as would pay off that Debt, he would save four Shillings in the Pound, which he gives for the Vanity of being the reputed Master of it. Yet if *Laertes* did this, he would, perhaps, be easier in his own Fortune; but then *Irus*, a Fellow of Yesterday, who has but twelve hundred a Year, would be his Equal. Rather than this shall be, *Laertes* goes on to bring well-born Beggars into the World, and every Twelve-month charges his Estate with at least one Year's Rent more by the Birth of a Child.

Laertes and *Irus* are Neighbours, whose Way of living are an Abomination to each other. *Irus* is moved by the Fear of Poverty, and *Laertes* by the Shame of it. Though the Motive of Action is of so near Affinity in both, and may be resolved into this, 'That to each of them Poverty is the greatest of all Evils,' yet are their Manners very widely different. Shame of Poverty makes *Laertes* launch into unnecessary Equipage, vain Expence, and lavish Entertainments; Fear of Poverty makes *Irus* allow himself only plain Necessaries, appear without a Servant, sell his own Corn, attend his Labourers, and be himself a Labourer. Shame of Poverty makes *Laertes* go every Day a Step nearer to it: and Fear of Poverty stirs up *Irus* to make every Day some further Progress from it.

These different Motives produce the Excesses which Men are guilty of in the Negligence of and Provision for themselves. Usury, Stock-Jobbing, Extortion and Oppression, have their Seed in the Dread of Want; and Vanity, Riot and Prodigality, from the Shame of it: But both these Excesses are infinitely below the Pursuit of a reasonable Creature. After we have taken Care to command so much as is necessary for maintaining our selves in the Order of Men suitable to our Character, the Care of Superfluities is a Vice no less extravagant, than the Neglect of Necessaries would have been before.

Certain it is that they are both out of Nature, when she is followed with Reason and good Sense. It is from this Reflexion that I always read Mr. *Cowley* with the greatest Pleasure: His Magnanimity is as much above that of other considerable Men, as his Understanding; and it is a true distinguishing Spirit in the elegant Author who published his Works, to dwell so much upon the Temper of his Mind and the Moderation of his Desires: By this Means he has rendered his Friend as amiable as famous. That State of Life which bears the Face of Poverty with Mr. *Cowley's great Vulgar*, is admirably described; and it is no small Satisfaction to those of the same Turn of Desire, that he produces the Authority of the wisest Men of the best Age of the World, to strengthen his Opinion of the ordinary Pursuits of Mankind.

It would methinks be no ill Maxim of Life, if, according to that Ancestor of Sir ROGER, whom I lately mentioned, every Man would point to himself what Sum he would resolve not to exceed. He might by this Means cheat himself into a Tranquility on this Side of that Expectation, or convert what he should get above it to nobler Uses than his own Pleasures or Necessities. This Temper of Mind would exempt a Man from an ignorant Envy of restless Men above him, and a more inexcusable Contempt of happy Men below him. This would be sailing by some Compass, living with some Design; but to be eternally bewildered in Prospects of future Gain, and putting on unnecessary Armour against improbable Blows of Fortune, is a Mechanick Being which has not good Sense for its Direction, but is carried on by a Sort of acquired Instinct towards things below our Consideration and unworthy our Esteem. It is possible that the Tranquility I now enjoy at Sir ROGER's may have created in me this Way of Thinking, which is so abstracted from the common Relish of the World: But as I am now in a pleasing Arbour surrounded with a beautiful Landskip, I find no Inclination so strong as to continue in these Mansions, so remote from the ostentatious Scenes o

Life; and am at this present Writing Philosopher enough to conclude with Mr. *Cowley*;

> *If e'er Ambition did my Fancy cheat,*
> *With any Wish so mean as to be Great;*
> *Continue, Heav'n, still from me to remove*
> *The humble Blessings of that Life I love.*

T

No. 115.

[ADDISON.] Thursday, July 12.

. . . *Ut sit mens sana in corpore sano.*—Juv.

BODILY Labour is of two kinds, either that which a Man submits to for his Livelihood, or that which he undergoes for his Pleasure. The latter of them generally changes the Name of Labour for that of Exercise, but differs only from ordinary Labour as it rises from another Motive.

A Country Life abounds in both these kinds of Labour, and for that Reason gives a Man a greater Stock of Health, and consequently a more perfect Enjoyment of himself, than any other way of Life. I consider the Body as a System of Tubes and Glands, or to use a more Rustick Phrase, a Bundle of Pipes and Strainers, fitted to one another after so wonderful a manner as to make a proper Engine for the Soul to work with. This Description does not only comprehend the Bowels, Bones, Tendons, Veins, Nerves, and Arteries, but every Muscle and every Ligature, which is a Composition of Fibres, that are so many imperceptible Tubes or Pipes interwoven on all sides with invisible Glands or Strainers.

This general Idea of a Human Body, without considering it in its Niceties of Anatomy, lets us see how absolutely necessary Labour is for the right Preservation of it. There must be frequent Motions and Agitations, to mix, digest, and separate the Juices contained in it, as well as to clear and cleanse that Infinitude of Pipes and Strainers of which it is composed, and to give their solid Parts a more firm and lasting Tone. Labour or Exercise ferments the Humours, casts them into their proper Channels, throws off Redundancies, and helps Nature in those secret Distributions, without which the Body cannot subsist in its Vigour, nor the Soul act with Chearfulness.

I might here mention the Effects which this has upon all the Faculties of the Mind, by keeping the Understanding clear, the Imagination untroubled, and refining those Spirits that are necessary for the proper Exertion of our intellectual Faculties, during the present Laws of Union between Soul and Body. It is to a Neglect in this Particular that we must ascribe the Spleen, which is so frequent in Men of studious and sedentary Tempers, as well as the Vapours to which those of the other Sex are so often subject.

Had not Exercise been absolutely necessary for our Well-being, Nature would not have made the Body so proper for it, by giving such an Activity to the Limbs, and such a Pliancy to every Part as necessarily produce those Compressions, Exten-tions, Contortions, Dilatations, and all other kinds of Motions that are necessary for the Preservation of such a System of Tubes and Glands as has been before mentioned. And that we might not want Inducements to engage us in such an Exercise of the Body as is proper for its Welfare, it is so ordered that nothing valuable can be procured without it. Not to mention Riches and Honour, even Food and Raiment are not to be come at without the Toil of the Hands and Sweat of the Brows. Providence furnishes Materials, but expects that we should work them up our selves. The Earth must be laboured before it gives its Encrease, and when it is forced into its several Products, how many Hands must they pass through before they are fit for Use? Manufactures, Trade, and Agri-culture, naturally employ more than nineteen Parts of the Species in twenty; and as for those who are not obliged to Labour, by the Condition in which they are born, they are more miserable than the rest of Mankind, unless they indulge themselves in that voluntary Labour which goes by the Name of Exercise.

My Friend Sir ROGER has been an indefatigable Man in Business of this kind, and has hung several Parts of his House with the Trophies of his former Labours. The Walls of his great Hall are covered with the Horns of several kinds of Deer that he has killed in the Chace, which he thinks the most valuable Furniture of his House, as they afford him frequent Topicks of Discourse, and shew that he has not been Idle. At the lower end of the Hall, is a large Otter's Skin stuffed with Hay, which his Mother ordered to be hung up in that manner, and the Knight looks upon with great Satisfaction, because it seems he was but nine Years old when his Dog killed him. A little Room adjoining to the Hall is a kind of Arsenal filled with Guns of several Sizes and Inventions, with which the Knight has made great Havock in the Woods, and destroyed many thousands of Pheasants, Partridges and Wood-Cocks. His Stable Doors are patched with Noses that belonged to Foxes of the Knight's own hunting down. Sir ROGER shewed me one of them that for Distinction sake has a Brass Nail struck through it, which cost him about fifteen Hours riding, carried him through half a dozen Counties, killed him a brace of Geldings, and lost above half his Dogs. This the Knight looks upon as one of the greatest Exploits of his Life. The perverse Widow, whom I have given some account of, was the Death of several Foxes; for Sir ROGER has told me that in the Course of his Amours he patched the Western Door of his Stable. Whenever the Widow was cruel, the Foxes were sure to pay for it. In proportion as his Passion for the Widow abated, and old Age came on, he left off Fox-hunting; but a Hare is not yet safe that sits within ten Miles of his House.

There is no kind of Exercise which I would so recommend to my Readers of both Sexes as this of Riding, as there is none which so much conduces to Health, and is every way accommodated to the Body, according to the *Idea* which I have given of it. Doctor *Sydenham* is very lavish in its Praises; and if the *English* Reader would see the Mechanical Effects of it described at length, he may find them in a Book published not many Years since, under the Title of *Medicina Gymnastica*. For my own part, when I am in Town, for want of these Opportunities, I exercise my self an Hour every Morning upon a dumb Bell that is placed in a Corner of my Room, and pleases me the more because it does every thing I require of it in the most profound Silence. My Landlady and her Daughters are so well acquainted with my Hours of Exercise, that they never come into my Room to disturb me whilst I am ringing.

When I was some Years younger than I am at present, I used to employ my self in a more laborious Diversion, which I learned from a *Latin* Treatise of Exercises that is written with great Erudition: It is there called the σκιομαχία, or the Fighting with a Man's own Shadow; and consists in the brandishing of two short Sticks grasped in each Hand, and Loaden with Plugs of Lead at either end. This opens the Chest, exercises the Limbs, and gives a Man all the Pleasure of Boxing, without the Blows. I could wish that several Learned Men would lay out that Time which they employ in Controversies and Disputes about nothing, in *this method* of fighting with their own Shadows. It might conduce very much to evaporate the Spleen, which makes them uneasy to the Publick as well as to themselves.

To conclude, As I am a Compound of Soul and Body, I consider my self as obliged to a double Scheme of Duties; and think I have not fulfilled the Business of the Day, when I do not thus employ the one in Labour and Exercise, as well as the other in Study and Contemplation. L

No. 116.
[BUDGELL.]   Friday, July 13.

> . . . *Vocat ingenti clamore Cithaeron,*
> *Taygetique canes* . . .—Virg.

THOSE who have searched into human Nature observe, that nothing so much shews the Nobleness of the Soul, as that its Felicity consists in Action. Every Man has such an active Principle in him, that he will find out something to employ himself upon in whatever Place or State of Life he is posted. I have heard of a Gentleman who was under close Confinement in the *Bastile* seven Years; during which Time he amused himself in scattering a few small Pins about his Chamber, gathering them up again, and placing them in different Figures on the Arm of a great Chair. He often told his Friends afterwards, that unless he had found out this Piece of Exercise, he verily believed he should have lost his Senses.

After what has been said, I need not inform my Readers, that Sir ROGER, with whose Character I hope they are at present pretty well acquainted, has in his Youth gone through the whole Course of those rural Diversions which the Country abounds in; and which seem to be extremely well suited to that laborious Industry a Man may observe here in a far greater Degree than in Towns and Cities. I have before hinted at some of my Friend's Exploits: He has in his youthful Days taken forty Coveys of Partridges in a Season; and tired many a Salmon with a Line consisting but of a single Hair. The constant Thanks and good Wishes of the Neighbourhood always attended him, on Account of his remarkable Enmity towards Foxes; having destroyed more of those Vermin in one Year, than it was thought the whole Country could have produced. Indeed the Knight does not scruple to own among his most intimate Friends, that in order to establish his Reputation this Way, he has secretly sent for great Numbers of them out of other Counties, which he used to turn loose about the Country by Night, that he might the better signalize himself in their Destruction the next Day. His Hunting-Horses were the finest and best managed in all these Parts: His Tenents are still full of the Praises of a grey Stone-horse that unhappily staked himself several Years since, and was buried with great Solemnity in the Orchard.

Sir ROGER, being at present too old for Fox-hunting; to keep himself in Action, has disposed of his Beagles and got a Pack of *Stop-Hounds*. What these want in Speed, he endeavours to make Amends for by the Deepness of their Mouths and the

Variety of their Notes, which are suited in such Manner to each other, that the whole Cry makes up a compleat Consort. He is so nice in this Particular, that a Gentleman having made him a Present of a very fine Hound the other Day, the Knight return'd it by the Servant with a great many Expressions of Civility; but desired him to tell his Master, that the Dog he had sent was indeed a most excellent *Base*, but that at present he only wanted a *Counter-Tenor*. Could I believe my Friend had ever read *Shakespear*, I should certainly conclude he had taken the Hint from *Theseus* in *the Midsummer-Night's Dream*.

> *My Hounds are bred out of the* Spartan *Kind,*
> *So flu'd, so sanded; and their Heads are hung*
> *With Ears that sweep away the Morning Dew.*
> *Crook-Knee'd and dew-lap'd like* Thessalian *Bulls;*
> *Slow in Pursuit, but match'd in Mouths like Bells,*
> *Each under each: A Cry more tuneable*
> *Was never hallow'd to, nor chear'd with Horn.*

Sir ROGER is so keen at this Sport, that he has been out almost every Day since I came down; and upon the Chaplain's offering to lend me his easy Pad, I was prevail'd on Yesterday Morning to make one of the Company. I was extremely pleas'd, as we rid along, to observe the general Benevolence of all the Neighbourhood towards my Friend. The Farmers' Sons thought themselves happy if they could open a Gate for the good old Knight as he passed by; which he generally requited with a Nod or a Smile, and a kind Inquiry after their Fathers and Uncles.

After we had rid about a Mile from home, we came upon a large Heath, and the Sports-men began to beat. They had done so for some time, when, as I was at a little Distance from the rest of the Company, I saw a Hare pop out from a small Furze-brake almost under my Horse's Feet. I marked the Way she took, which I endeavoured to make the Company sensible of by extending my Arm; but to no purpose, till Sir ROGER, who knows that none of my extraordinary Motions are insignificant, rode up to me, and asked me *if Puss was gone that Way?* Upon my answering *Yes* he immediately call'd in the Dogs, and put them upon the Scent. As they were going off, I heard one of the Country-Fellows muttering to his Companion, *That 'twas a Wonder they had not lost all their Sport, for want of the silent Gentleman's crying STOLE AWAY.*

This, with my Aversion to leaping Hedges, made me withdraw to a rising Ground, from whence I could have the Pleasure of the whole Chase, without the Fatigue of keeping in with the Hounds. The Hare immediately threw them above a

Mile behind her; but I was pleased to find, that instead of running straight forwards, or, in Hunter's Language, *Flying the Country*, as I was afraid she might have done, she wheeled about, and described a sort of Circle round the Hill where I had taken my Station, in such Manner as gave me a very distinct View of the Sport. I could see her first pass by, and the Dogs some Time afterwards unravelling the whole Track she had made, and following her thro' all her Doubles. I was at the same Time delighted in observing that Deference which the rest of the Pack paid to each particular Hound, according to the Character he had acquired amongst them: If they were at a Fault, and an old Hound of Reputation opened but once, he was immediately follow'd by the whole Cry; while a raw Dog, or one who was a noted *Liar*, might have yelped his Heart out, without being taken Notice of.

The Hare now, after having squatted two or three Times, and been put up again as often, came still nearer to the Place where she was at first started. The Dogs pursued her, and these were followed by the jolly Knight, who rode upon a white Gelding, encompassed by his Tenants and Servants, and chearing his Hounds with all the Gaiety of Five and Twenty. One of the Sports-men rode up to me, and told me that he was sure the Chase was almost at an End, because the old Dogs, which had hitherto lain behind, now headed the Pack. The Fellow was in the Right. Our Hare took a large Field just under us, follow'd by the full Cry *in View*. I must confess the Brightness of the Weather, the Chearfulness of every thing around me, the *Chiding* of the Hounds, which was returned upon us in a double Eccho from two neighbouring Hills, with the Hollowing of the Sports-men, and the Sounding of the Horn, lifted my Spirits into a most lively Pleasure, which I freely indulged because I was sure it was *innocent*. If I was under any Concern, it was on the Account of the poor Hare, that was now quite spent, and almost within the Reach of her Enemies; when the Hunts-man getting forward, threw down his Pole before the Dogs. They were now within eight Yards of that Game which they had been pursuing for almost as many Hours; yet on the Signal before-mentioned they all made a sudden Stand, and tho' they continued opening as much as before, durst not once attempt to pass beyond the Pole. At the same Time Sir Roger rode forward, and alighting, took up the Hare in his Arms; which he soon after delivered to one of his Servants, with an Order, if she could be kept alive, to let her go in his great Orchard, where, it seems, he has several of these Prisoners of War, who live together in a very comfortable Captivity. I was highly pleased to see the Discipline of the

Pack, and the Good-nature of the Knight, who could not find in his Heart to murder a Creature that had given him so much Diversion.

As we were returning home, I remembered that Monsieur *Paschal* in his most excellent Discourse on *the Misery of Man*, tells us, That *all our Endeavours after Greatness, proceed from nothing but a Desire of being surrounded by a Multitude of Persons and Affairs, that may hinder us from looking into our selves, which is a View we cannot bear.* He afterwards goes on to shew that our Love of Sports comes from the same Reason, and is particularly severe upon HUNTING. *What*, says he, *unless it be to drown Thought, can make Men throw away so much Time and Pains upon a silly Animal, which they might buy cheaper in the Market?* The foregoing Reflection is certainly just, when a Man suffers his whole Mind to be drawn into his Sports, and altogether loses himself in the Woods; but does not affect those who propose a far more laudable End from this Exercise, I mean, *The Preservation of Health, and keeping all the Organs of the Soul in a Condition to execute her Orders.* Had that incomparable Person whom I last quoted been a little more indulgent to himself in this Point, the World might probably have enjoyed him much longer; whereas thro' too great an Application to his Studies in his Youth, he contracted that ill Habit of Body, which, after a tedious Sickness, carried him off in the fortieth Year of his Age; and the whole History we have of his Life till that Time, is but one continued Account of the Behaviour of a noble Soul struggling under innumerable Pains and Distempers.

For my own Part, I intend to hunt twice a Week during my Stay with Sir ROGER; and shall prescribe the moderate use of this Exercise to all my Country Friends, as the best Kind of Physick for mending a bad Constitution, and preserving a good one.

I cannot do this better, than in the following Lines out of Mr. *Dryden.*

> *The first Physicians by Debauch were made,*
> *Excess began, and Sloth sustains the Trade.*
> *By Chace our long-liv'd Fathers earn'd their Food,*
> *Toil strung the Nerves, and purify'd the Blood:*
> *But we their Sons, a pamper'd Race of Men,*
> *Are dwindled down to threescore Years and ten.*
> *Better to hunt in Fields for Health unbought,*
> *Than fee the Doctor for a nauseous Draught.*
> *The Wise for Cure on Exercise depend,*
> *God never made his Work for Man to mend.*

No. 117.
[ADDISON.]   Saturday, July 14.

> . . . *Ipsi sibi somnia fingunt.*—Virg.

THERE are some Opinions in which a Man should stand Neuter, without engaging his Assent to one side or the other. Such a hovering Faith as this, which refuses to settle upon any Determination, is absolutely necessary in a Mind that is careful to avoid Errors and Prepossessions. When the Arguments press equally on both sides in Matters that are indifferent to us, the safest Method is to give up our selves to neither.

It is with this Temper of Mind that I consider the Subject of Witchcraft. When I hear the Relations that are made from all Parts of the World, not only from *Norway* and *Lapland*, from the *East* and *West Indies*, but from every particular Nation in *Europe*, I cannot forbear thinking that there is such an Intercourse and Commerce with Evil Spirits, as that which we express by the Name of Witchcraft. But when I consider that the ignorant and credulous Parts of the World abound most in these Relations, and that the Persons among us who are supposed to engage in such an Infernal Commerce are People of a weak Understanding and crazed Imagination, and at the same time reflect upon the many Impostures and Delusions of this Nature that have been detected in all Ages, I endeavour to suspend my Belief till I hear more certain Accounts than any which have yet come to my Knowledge. In short, when I consider the Question, Whether there are such Persons in the World as those we call Witches? my Mind is divided between the two opposite Opinions; or rather (to speak my Thoughts freely) I believe in general that there is, and has been such a thing as Witchcraft; but at the same time can give no Credit to any Particular Instance of it.

I am engaged in this Speculation, by some Occurrences that I met with Yesterday, which I shall give my Reader an Account of at large. As I was walking with my Friend Sir ROGER by the side of one of his Woods, an old Woman applied her self to me for my Charity. Her Dress and Figure put me in mind of the following Description in *Otway*.

> *In a close Lane as I pursu'd my Journey,*
> *I spy'd a wrinkled Hag, with Age grown double,*
> *Picking dry Sticks, and mumbling to her self.*
> *Her Eyes with scalding Rheum were gall'd and red;*
> *Cold Palsy shook her Head; her Hands seem'd wither'd;*
> *And on her Crooked Shoulders had she wrapp'd*
> *The tatter'd Remnants of an old striped Hanging,*
> *Which serv'd to keep her Carcass from the Cold:*

> *So there was nothing of a-piece about her.*
> *Her lower Weeds were all o'er coarsely patch'd*
> *With diff'rent-colour'd Rags, black, red, white, yellow,*
> *And seem'd to speak Variety of Wretchedness.*

As I was musing on this Description, and comparing it with the object before me, the Knight told me, that this very old Woman had the Reputation of a Witch all over the Country, that her Lips were observed to be always in Motion, and that there was not a Switch about her House which her Neighbours did not believe had carried her several hundreds of Miles. If she chanced to stumble, they always found Sticks or Straws that lay in the Figure of a Cross before her. If she made any Mistake at Church, and cryed *Amen* in a wrong Place, they never failed to conclude that she was saying her Prayers backwards. There was not a Maid in the Parish that would take a Pin of her, though she should offer a Bag of Money with it. She goes by the Name of *Moll White*, and has made the Country ring with several imaginary Exploits which are palmed upon her. If the Dairy Maid does not make her Butter come so soon as she would have it, *Moll White* is at the bottom of the Churn. If a Horse sweats in the Stable, *Moll White* has been upon his Back. If a Hare makes an unexpected Escape from the Hounds, the Huntsman curses *Moll White*. Nay, (says Sir ROGER) I have known the Master of the Pack, upon such an Occasion, send one of his Servants to see if *Moll White* had been out that Morning.

This Account raised my Curiosity so far, that I begged my Friend Sir ROGER to go with me into her Hovel, which stood in a solitary Corner under the side of the Wood. Upon our first entring Sir ROGER winked to me, and pointed at something that stood behind the Door, which upon looking that way I found to be an old Broomstaff. At the same time he whispered me in the Ear to take notice of a Tabby Cat that sat in the Chimney-Corner, which, as the old Knight told me, lay under as bad a Report as *Moll White* her self; for besides that *Moll* is said often to accompany her in the same Shape, the Cat is reported to have spoken twice or thrice in her Life, and to have played several Pranks above the Capacity of an ordinary Cat.

I was secretly concerned to see Human Nature in so much Wretchedness and Disgrace, but at the same time could not forbear smiling to hear Sir ROGER, who is a little puzzled about the old Woman, advising her as a Justice of Peace to avoid all Communication with the Devil, and never to hurt any of her Neighbours' Cattle. We concluded our Visit with a Bounty, which was very acceptable.

In our Return home Sir ROGER told me, that old *Moll* had

been often brought before him for making Children spit Pins, and giving Maids the Night-Mare; and that the Country People would be tossing her into a Pond and trying Experiments with her every Day, if it was not for him and his Chaplain.

I have since found, upon Enquiry, that Sir ROGER was several times staggered with the Reports that had been brought him concerning this old Woman, and would frequently have bound her over to the County Sessions, had not his Chaplain with much ado perswaded him to the contrary.

I have been the more particular in this Account, because I hear there is scarce a Village in *England* that has not a *Moll White* in it. When an old Woman begins to doat, and grow chargeable to a Parish, she is generally turned into a Witch, and fills the whole Country with extravagant Fancies, imaginary Distempers, and terrifying Dreams. In the mean time, the poor Wretch that is the innocent Occasion of so many Evils begins to be frighted at her self, and sometimes confesses secret Commerce and Familiarities that her Imagination forms in a delirious old Age. This frequently cuts off Charity from the greatest Objects of Compassion, and inspires People with a Malevolence towards those poor decrepid Parts of our Species, in whom Human Nature is defaced by Infirmity and Dotage. L

No. 118.
[STEELE.]   Monday, July 16.

. . . *Haeret lateri lethalis arundo.*—Virg.

THIS agreeable Seat is surrounded with so many pleasing Walks, which are struck out of a Wood, in the Midst of which the House stands, that one can hardly ever be weary of rambling from one Labyrinth of Delight to another. To one used to live in a City the Charms of the Country are so exquisite, that the Mind is lost in a certain Transport which raises us above ordinary Life, and yet is not strong enough to be inconsistent with Tranquility. This State of Mind was I in, ravished with the Murmur of Waters, the Whisper of Breezes, the Singing of Birds; and whether I looked up to the Heavens, down on the Earth, or turned on the Prospects around me, still struck with new Sense of Pleasure; when I found by the Voice of my Friend who walked by me, that we had insensibly strolled into the Grove sacred to the Widow. 'This Woman,' says he, 'is of all others the most unintelligible; she either designs to marry, or she does not. What is the most perplexing of all, is, that she does not either say to her Lovers she has any Resolution against that Condition of Life in general, or that she banishes them; but conscious of her own Merit, she permits their Addresses without Fear of any ill Consequence, or want of Respect, from their Rage or Despair. She has that in her Aspect, against which it is impossible to offend. A Man whose Thoughts are constantly bent upon so agreeable an Object, must be excused if the ordinary Occurrences in Conversation are below his Attention. I call her indeed perverse; but, alas! why do I call her so? because her superior Merit is such, that I cannot approach her without Awe, that my Heart is checked by too much Esteem: I am angry that her Charms are not more accessible, that I am more inclined to worship than salute her: How often have I wished her unhappy, that I might have an Opportunity of serving her? and how often troubled in that very imagination, at giving her the Pain of being obliged? Well, I have led a miserable Life in secret upon her Account: but fancy she would have condescended to have some Regard for me, if it had not been for that watchful Animal her Confident.

Of all Persons under the Sun (continued he, calling me by my Name) be sure to set a Mark upon Confidents: they are of all People the most impertinent. What is most pleasant to observe in them, is, that they assume to themselves the Merit of the Persons whom they have in their Custody. *Orestilla* is a great Fortune, and in wonderful Danger of Surprizes, therefore full of Suspicions of the least indifferent thing, particularly careful of new Acquaintance, and of growing too familiar with the old. *Themista*, her Favourite-Woman, is every whit as careful of whom she speaks to, and what she says. Let the Ward be a Beauty, her Confident shall treat you with an Air of Distance; let her be a Fortune, and she assumes the suspicious Behaviour of her Friend and Patroness. Thus it is that very many of our unmarried Women of Distinction, are to all Intents and Purposes married, except the Consideration of different sexes. They are directly under the Conduct of their Whisperer; and think they are in a State of Freedom, while they can prate with one of these Attendants of all Men in general, and still avoid the Man they most like. You do not see one Heiress in a hundred whose Fate does not turn upon this Circumstance of chusing a Confident. Thus it is that the Lady is addressed to, presented, and flattered, only by Proxy, in her Woman. In my Case, how is it possible that——' Sir ROGER was proceeding in his Harangue, when we heard the Voice of one speaking very importunately, and repeating these Words, 'What, not one

Smile?' We followed the Sound till we came to a close
Thicket, on the other Side of which we saw a young Woman
sitting as it were in a personated Sullenness just over a trans-
parent Fountain. Opposite to her Stood Mr. *William*, Sir
ROGER's Master of the Game. The Knight whispered me,
'Hist, these are Lovers.' The Huntsman looked earnestly at
the Shadow of the young Maiden in the Stream, 'Oh thou dear
Picture, if thou could'st remain there in the Absence of that
fair Creature whom you represent in the Water, how willingly
could I stand here satisfied for ever, without troubling my
dear *Betty* herself with any Mention of her unfortunate *William*,
whom she is angry with: But alas! when she pleases to be gone,
thou wilt also vanish. . . . Yet let me talk to thee while
thou dost stay. Tell my dearest *Betty*, thou dost not more
depend upon her, than does her *William*: Her Absence will
make away with me, as well as thee. If she offers to remove
thee, I'll jump into these Waves to lay hold on thee; her herself,
her own dear Person, I must never embrace again—Still
do you hear me without one Smile?—It is too much to
bear.—' He had no sooner spoke these Words, but he made
an Offer of throwing himself into the Water: At which his
Mistress started up, and at the next Instant he jumped across
the Fountain and met her in an Embrace. She half recovering from her Fright, said, in the most charming Voice imaginable, and with a Tone of Complaint, 'I thought how well you
would drown your self. No, no, you won't drown your self till
you have taken your leave of *Susan Holliday*.' The Hunts-
man, with a Tenderness that spoke the most passionate Love,
and with his Cheek close to hers, whispered the softest Vows
of Fidelity in her Ear; and cryed, 'Don't, my Dear, believe a
Word *Kate Willow* says; she is spiteful and makes Stories,
because she loves to hear me talk to herself for your sake.'
'Look you there,' quoth Sir ROGER, 'do you see there, all
Mischief comes from Confidents! But let us not interrupt
them; the Maid is honest, and the Man dare not be otherwise,
for he knows I loved her Father: I will interpose in this Matter,
and hasten the Wedding. *Kate Willow* is a witty mischievous
Wench in the Neighbourhood, who was a Beauty; and makes
me hope I shall see the perverse Widow in her Condition.
She was so flippant with her Answers to all the honest Fellows
that came near her, and so very vain of her Beauty, that she
has valued herself upon her Charms till they are ceased. She
therefore now makes it her Business to prevent other young
Women from being more Discreet than she was herself: However, the saucy Thing said the other Day well enough,"Sir
ROGER and I must make a Match, for we are both despised by

those we loved"; The Hussy has a great Deal of Power wherever she comes, and has her Share of Cunning.

'However, when I reflect upon this Woman, I do not know whether in the Main I am the worse for having loved her: Whenever she is recalled to my Imagination my Youth returns, and I feel a forgotten Warmth in my Veins. This Affliction in my Life has streaked all my Conduct with a Softness, of which I should otherwise have been incapable. It is. perhaps, to this dear Image in my Heart owing, that I am apt to relent, that I easily forgive, and that many desirable things are grown into my Temper, which I should not have arrived at by better Motives than the Thought of being one Day hers. I am pretty well satisfied such a Passion as I have had is never well cured; and between you and me, I am often apt to imagine it has had some whimsical Effect upon my Brain: For I frequently find, that in my most serious Discourse I let fall some comical Familiarity of Speech or odd Phrase that makes the Company laugh; However I cannot but allow she is a most excellent Woman. When she is in the Country I warrant she does not run into Dairies, but reads upon the Nature of Plants: She has a Glass Hive, and comes into the Garden out of Books to see them work, and observe the Policies of their Commonwealth. She understands every thing. I 'd give ten Pounds to hear her argue with my Friend Sir ANDREW FREEPORT about Trade. No, no, for all she looks so innocent as it were, take my Word for it she is no Fool.' T

No. 119.
[ADDISON.]   Tuesday, July 17.

> *Urbem quam dicunt Romam, Meliboee, putavi*
> *Stultus ego huic nostrae similem . . .*—Virg.

THE first and most obvious Reflections which arise in a Man who changes the City for the Country, are upon the different Manners of the People whom he meets with in those two different Scenes of Life. By Manners I do not mean Morals, but Behaviour and Good Breeding, as they shew themselves in the Town and in the Country.

And here, in the first place, I must observe a very great Revolution that has happened in this Article of Good Breeding. Several obliging Deferencies, Condescensions and Submissions, with many outward Forms and Ceremonies that accompany them, were first of all brought up among the politer Part of Mankind who lived in Courts and Cities, and distinguished themselves from the Rustick part of the Species (who on all Occasions acted bluntly and naturally) by such a mutual Complaisance and Intercourse of Civilities. These Forms of Conversation by degrees multiplied and grew troublesome; the Modish World found too great a Constraint in them, and have therefore thrown most of them aside. Conversation, like the *Romish* Religion, was so encumbered with Show and Ceremony, that it stood in need of a Reformation to retrench its Superfluities, and restore it to its natural good Sense and Beauty. At present therefore an unconstrained Carriage, and a certain Openness of Behaviour, are the height of Good Breeding. The Fashionable World is grown free and easie; our Manners sit more loose upon us: Nothing is so modish as an agreeable Negligence. In a word, Good Breeding shows it self most, where to an ordinary Eye it appears the least.

If after this we look on the People of Mode in the Country, we find in them the Manners of the last Age. They have no sooner fetched themselves up to the Fashion of the Polite World, but the Town has dropped them, and are nearer to the first State of Nature than to those Refinements which formerly reigned in the Court, and still prevail in the Country. One may now know a Man that never conversed in the World by his Excess of Good Breeding. A Polite Country Squire shall make you as many Bows in half an hour, as would serve a Courtier for a Week. There is infinitely more to do about Place and Precedency in a Meeting of Justices' Wives, than in an Assembly of Dutchesses.

This Rural Politeness is very troublesome to a Man of my Temper, who generally take the Chair that is next me, and walk first or last, in the Front or in the Rear, as Chance directs. I have known my Friend Sir ROGER's Dinner almost cold before the Company could adjust the Ceremonial, and be prevailed upon to sit down; and have heartily pitied my old Friend, when I have seen him forced to pick and cull his Guests, as they sat at the several Parts of his Table, that he might drink their Healths according to their respective Ranks and Qualities. Honest *Will. Wimble*, who I should have thought had been altogether uninfected with Ceremony, gives me abundance of Trouble in this Particular. Though he has been fishing all the Morning, he will not help himself at Dinner 'till I am served. When we are going out of the Hall, he runs behind me; and last Night, as we were walking in the Fields, stopped short at a Stile till I came up to it, and upon my making Signs to him to get over, told me, with a serious Smile, that sure I believed they had no Manners in the Country.

There has happened another Revolution in the Point of

Good Breeding, which relates to the Conversation among Men of Mode, and which I cannot but look upon as very extraordinary. It was certainly one of the first Distinctions of a well-bred Man, to express every thing that had the most remote Appearance of being obscene, in modest Terms and distant Phrases; whilst the Clown, who had no such Delicacy of Conception and Expression, clothed his *Ideas* in those plain homely Terms that are the most obvious and natural. This kind of Good Manners was perhaps carried to an Excess, so as to make Conversation too stiff, formal and precise; for which Reason (as Hypocrisy in one Age is generally succeeded by Atheism in another) Conversation is in a great measure relapsed into the first Extream; So that at present several of our Men of the Town, and particularly those who have been polished in *France*, make use of the most coarse uncivilized Words in our Language, and utter themselves often in such a manner as a Clown would blush to hear.

This infamous Piece of Good Breeding, which reigns among the Coxcombs of the Town, has not yet made its way into the Country; and as it is impossible for such an irrational way of Conversation to last long among a People that make any Profession of Religion, or Show of Modesty, if the Country Gentlemen get into it they will certainly be left in the Lurch. Their Good Breeding will come too late to them, and they will be thought a parcel of lewd Clowns, while they fancy themselves talking together like Men of Wit and Pleasure.

As the two Points of Good Breeding, which I have hitherto insisted upon, regard Behaviour and Conversation, there is a third which turns upon Dress. In this too the Country are very much behind hand. The Rural Beaus are not yet got out of the Fashion that took place at the time of the Revolution, but ride about the Country in red Coats and laced Hats, while the Women in many Parts are still trying to outvie one another in the Height of their Head Dresses.

But a Friend of mine who is now upon the Western Circuit, having promised to give me an Account of the several Modes and Fashions that prevail in the different Parts of the Nation through which he passes, I shall defer the enlarging upon this last Topick till I have received a Letter from him, which I expect every Post. **L**

No. 120.

[ADDISON.]   Wednesday, July 18.

> . . *Equidem credo, quia sit divinitus illis*
> *Ingenium* . . .—Virg.

My Friend Sir ROGER is very often merry with me, upon my passing so much of my Time among his Poultry: He has caught me twice or thrice looking after a Bird's Nest, and several times sitting an Hour or two together near an Hen and Chickens. He tells me he believes I am personally acquainted with every Fowl about his House; calls such a particular Cock my Favourite; and frequently complains that his Ducks and Geese have more of my Company than himself.

I must confess I am infinitely delighted with those Speculations of Nature which are to be made in a Country-Life; and as my Reading has very much lain among Books of natural History, I cannot forbear recollecting upon this Occasion the several Remarks which I have met with in Authors, and comparing them with what falls under my own Observation: The Arguments for Providence drawn from the natural History of Animals, being in my Opinion demonstrative.

The Make of every Kind of Animal is different from that of every other Kind; and yet there is not the least Turn in the Muscles or Twist in the Fibres of any one, which does not render them more proper for that particular Animal's Way of Life than any other Cast or Texture of them would have been.

The most violent Appetites in all Creatures are *Lust* and *Hunger*: The first, is a perpetual Call upon them to propagate their Kind; the latter, to preserve themselves.

It is astonishing to consider the different Degrees of Care that descend from the Parent to the Young, so far as is absolutely necessary for the leaving a Posterity. Some Creatures cast their Eggs as Chance directs them, and think of them no farther, as Insects and several Kinds of Fish: Others of a nicer Frame, find out proper Beds to deposite them in, and there leave them; as the Serpent, the Crocodile, and Ostrich: Others hatch their Eggs and tend the Birth, till it is able to shift for it self.

What can we call the Principle which directs every different Kind of Bird to observe a particular Plan in the Structure of its Nest, and directs all of the same Species to work after the same Model? It cannot be *Imitation*; for though you hatch a Crow under a Hen, and never let it see any of the Works of its own Kind, the Nest it makes shall be the same, to the laying of a Stick, with all the other Nests of the same Species. It cannot be *Reason*; for were Animals indued with it to as great a Degree as Man, their Buildings would be as different as ours, according to the different Conveniencies that they would propose to themselves.

Is it not remarkable, that the same Temper of Weather which raises this genial Warmth in Animals, should cover the Trees with Leaves and the Fields with Grass for their Security and Concealment, and produce such infinite Swarms of Insects for the Support and Sustenance of their respective Broods?

Is it not wonderful, that the Love of the Parent should be so violent while it lasts; and that it should last no longer than is necessary for the Preservation of the Young?

The Violence of this natural Love is exemplified by a very barbarous Experiment; which I shall quote at Length as I find it in an excellent Author, and hope my Readers will pardon the mentioning such an Instance of Cruelty, because there is nothing can so effectually shew the strength of that Principle in Animals of which I am here speaking. 'A Person who was well skilled in Dissections opened a Bitch, and as she lay in the most exquisite Tortures offered her one of her young Puppies, which she immediately fell a licking; and for the Time seemed insensible of her own Pain: On the Removal, she kept her Eye fixt on it, and began a wailing sort of Cry, which seemed rather to proceed from the Loss of her young one, than the Sense of her own Torments.'

But notwithstanding this natural Love in Brutes is much more violent and intense than in rational Creatures, Providence has taken Care that it should be no longer troublesome to the Parent than it is useful to the Young; for so soon as the Wants of the latter cease, the Mother withdraws her Fondness and leaves them to provide for themselves: And what is a very remarkable Circumstance in this Part of Instinct, we find that the Love of the Parent may be lengthened out beyond its usual Time if the Preservation of the Species requires it; as we may see in Birds that drive away their Young as soon as they are able to get their Livelihood, but continue to feed them if they are tied to the Nest or confined within a Cage, or by any other Means appear to be out of a Condition of supplying their own Necessities.

This natural Love is not observed in Animals to ascend from the Young to the Parent, which is not at all necessary for the Continuance of the Species: Nor indeed in reasonable Creatures does it rise in any Proportion, as it spreads it self downwards; for in all Family-Affection, we find Protection granted and Favours bestowed, are greater Motives to Love and Tenderness, than Safety, Benefits, or Life received.

One would wonder to hear Sceptical Men disputing for the

Reason of Animals, and telling us it is only our Pride and Prejudices that will not allow them the Use of that Faculty.

Reason shews it self in all Occurrences of Life; whereas the Brute makes no Discovery of such a Talent, but in what immediately regards his own Preservation, or the Continuance of his Species. Animals in their Generation are wiser than the Sons of Men; but their Wisdom is confined to a few Particulars, and lies in a very narrow Compass. Take a Brute out of his Instinct, and you find him wholly deprived of Understanding. To use an Instance that comes often under Observation.

With what Caution does the Hen provide her self a Nest in Places unfrequented, and free from Noise and Disturbance? When she has laid her Eggs in such a Manner that she can cover them, what Care does she take in turning them frequently, that all Parts may partake of the vital Warmth? When she leaves them to provide for her necessary Sustenance, how punctually does she return before they have Time to cool, and become incapable of producing an Animal? In the Summer you see her giving her self greater Freedoms, and quitting her Care for above two Hours together; but in Winter, when the Rigour of the Season would chill the Principles of Life, and destroy the young one, she grows more assiduous in her Attendance, and stays away but half the Time. When the Birth approaches, with how much Nicety and Attention does she help the Chick to break its Prison? Not to take Notice of her covering it from the Injuries of the Weather, providing it proper Nourishment, and teaching it to help it self; nor to mention her forsaking the Nest, if after the usual Time of reckoning the young one does not make its Appearance. A Chymical Operation could not be followed with greater Art or Diligence, than is seen in the hatching of a Chick; tho' there are many other Birds that shew an infinitely greater Sagacity in all the forementioned Particulars.

But at the same Time the Hen, that has all this seeming Ingenuity, (which is indeed absolutely necessary for the Propagation of the Species) considered in other Respects, is without the least Glimmerings of Thought or Common Sense. She mistakes a Piece of Chalk for an Egg, and sits upon it in the same Manner: She is insensible of any Increase or Diminution in the Number of those she lays: She does not distinguish between her own and those of another Species; and when the Birth appears of never so different a Bird, will cherish it for her own. In all these Circumstances, which do not carry an immediate Regard to the Subsistance of her self or her Species, she is a very Ideot.

There is not in my Opinion any thing more mysterious in Nature than this Instinct in Animals, which thus rises above Reason, and falls infinitely short of it. It cannot be accounted for by any Properties in Matter, and at the same Time works after so odd a Manner, that one cannot think it the Faculty of an intellectual Being. For my own Part, I look upon it as upon the Principle of Gravitation in Bodies, which is not to be explained by any known Qualities inherent in the Bodies themselves, nor from any Laws of Mechanism, but, according to the best Notions of the greatest Philosophers, is an immediate Impression from the first Mover, and the Divine Energy acting in the Creatures.

No. 121.
[ADDISON.]   Thursday, July 19.

. . . *Jovis omnia plena.*—Virg.

As I was walking this Morning in the great Yard that belongs to my Friend's Country House, I was wonderfully pleased to see the different Workings of Instinct in a Hen followed by a Brood of Ducks. The Young, upon the sight of a Pond, immediately ran into it; while the Step-mother, with all imaginable Anxiety, hovered about the Borders of it, to call them out of an Element that appeared to her so dangerous and destructive. As the different Principle which acted in these different Animals cannot be termed Reason, so when we call it *Instinct* we mean something we have no Knowledge of. To me, as I hinted in my last Paper, it seems the immediate Direction of Providence, and such an Operation of the Supreme Being as that which determines all the Portions of Matter to their proper Centres. A modern Philosopher, quoted by Monsieur *Bayle* in his Learned Dissertation on the Souls of Brutes, delivers the same Opinion, tho' in a bolder form of Words, where he says, *Deus est Anima Brutorum*, God himself is the Soul of Brutes. Who can tell what to call that seeming Sagacity in Animals, which directs them to such Food as is proper for them, and makes them naturally avoid whatever is noxious or unwholesome? *Tully* has observed that a Lamb no sooner falls from its Mother, but immediately and of his own accord applies it self to the Teat. *Dampier*, in his Travels, tells us, that when Seamen are thrown upon any of the unknown Coasts of *America*, they never venture upon the Fruit of any Tree, how tempting soever it may appear, unless they observe that it is marked with the Pecking of Birds; but fall on without any Fear or Apprehension where the Birds have been before them.

But notwithstanding Animals have nothing like the use of Reason, we find in them all the lower Parts of our Nature, the Passions and Senses in their greatest Strength and Perfection. And here it is worth our Observation, that all Beasts and Birds of Prey are wonderfully subject to Anger, Malice, Revenge, and all the other violent Passions that may animate them in search of their proper Food; as those that are incapable of defending themselves, or annoying others, or whose Safety lies chiefly in their Flight, are suspicious, fearful and apprehensive of every thing they see or hear; whilst others that are of Assistance and Use to Man, have their Natures softned with something mild and tractable, and by that means are qualified for a Domestick Life. In this case the Passions generally correspond with the Make of the Body. We do not find the Fury of a Lion in so weak and defenceless an Animal as a Lamb, nor the Meekness of a Lamb in a Creature so armed for Battle and Assault as the Lion. In the same manner, we find that particular Animals have a more or less exquisite Sharpness and Sagacity in those particular Senses which most turn to their Advantage, and in which their Safety and Welfare is the most concerned.

Nor must we here omit that great Variety of Arms with which Nature has differently fortifyed the Bodies of several kind of Animals, such as Claws, Hoofs and Horns, Teeth and Tusks, a Tail, a Sting, a Trunk, or a *Proboscis*. It is likewise observed by Naturalists, that it must be some hidden Principle distinct from what we call Reason, which instructs Animals in the Use of these their Arms, and teaches them to manage 'em to the best Advantage; because they naturally defend themselves with that part in which their Strength lies, before the Weapon be formed in it; as is remarkable in Lambs, which tho' they are bred within Doors, and never saw the Actions of their own Species, push at those who approach them with their Foreheads, before the first budding of a Horn appears.

I shall add to these general Observations an Instance which Mr. *Locke* has given us of Providence, even in the Imperfections of a Creature which seems the meanest and most despicable in the whole animal World. *We may*, says he, *from the Make of an Oyster, or Cockle, conclude, that it has not so many nor so quick Senses as a Man, or several other Animals: Nor, if it had, would it, in that State and Incapacity of transferring it self from one Place to another, be bettered by them. What good would Sight and Hearing do to a Creature, that cannot move it self to or from the Object, wherein at a distance it perceives Good or Evil? And would not Quickness of Sensation be an Inconvenience to an*

Animal, that still must be where Chance has once placed it; and there receive the Afflux of colder or warmer, clean or foul Water, as it happens to come to it?

I shall add to this Instance out of Mr. *Locke,* another out of the learned Dr. *Moor,* who cites it from *Cardan,* in relation to another Animal which Providence has left Defective, but at the same time has shewn its Wisdom in the Formation of that Organ in which it seems chiefly to have failed. *What is more obvious and ordinary than a Mole? and yet what more palpable Argument of Providence than she? The Members of her Body are so exactly fitted to her Nature and Manner of Life: For her Dwelling being under Ground, where nothing is to be seen, Nature has so obscurely fitted her with Eyes, that Naturalists can scarce agree whether she have any Sight at all or no. But for amends, what she is capable of for her Defence and Warning of Danger, she has very eminently conferred upon her; for she is exceeding quick of Hearing. And then her short Tail and short Legs, but broad Fore-feet armed with sharp Claws, we see by the Event to what purpose they are, she so swiftly working her self under Ground, and making her way so fast in the Earth, as they that behold it cannot but admire. Her Legs therefore are short, that she need dig no more than will serve the meer Thickness of her Body; and her Fore-Feet are broad that she may scoup away much Earth at a time; and little or no Tail she has, because she courses it not on the Ground, like the Rat or Mouse, of whose Kindred she is, but lives under the Earth, and is fain to dig her self a Dwelling there. And she making her way through so thick an Element, which will not yield easily, as the Air or the Water, it had been dangerous to have drawn so long a Train behind her; for her Enemy might fall upon her Rear, and fetch her out before she had compleated or got full Possession of her Works.*

I cannot forbear mentioning Mr. *Boyle*'s Remark upon this last Creature, who, I remember, somewhere in his Works observes, that though the Mole be not totally blind (as it is commonly thought,) she has not Sight enough to distinguish particular Objects. Her Eye is said to have but one Humour in it, which is supposed to give her the Idea of Light, but of nothing else, and is so formed that this Idea is probably painful to the Animal. Whenever she comes up into broad Day she might be in Danger of being taken, unless she were thus affected by a Light striking upon her Eye and immediately warning her to bury her self in her proper Element. More Sight would be useless to her, as none at all might be fatal.

I have only instanced such Animals as seem the most imperfect Works of Nature; and if Providence shews it self even in the Blemishes of these Creatures, how much more does it discover it self in the several Endowments which it has variously bestowed upon such Creatures as are more or less finished and compleated in their several Faculties, according to the Condition of Life in which they are posted?

I could wish our Royal Society would compile a body of Natural History, the best that could be gathered together from Books and Observations. If the several Writers among them took each his particular Species, and gave us a distinct Account of its Original Birth and Education; its Policies, Hostilities and Alliances, with the Frame and Texture of its inward and outward Parts, and particularly those that distinguish it from all other Animals, with their peculiar Aptitudes for the State of Being in which Providence has placed them, it would be one of the best Services their Studies could do Mankind, and not a little redound to the Glory of the All-wise Contriver.

It is true, such a Natural History, after all the Disquisitions of the Learned, would be infinitely short and Defective. Seas and Desarts hide Millions of Animals from our Observation. Innumerable Artifices and Stratagems are acted in the *Howling Wilderness* and in the *Great Deep*, that can never come to our Knowledge. Besides that there are infinitely more Species of Creatures which are not to be seen without, nor indeed with the help of the finest Glasses, than of such as are bulky enough for the naked Eye to take hold of. However, from the Consideration of such Animals as lie within the Compass of our Knowledge, we might easily form a Conclusion of the rest, that the same Variety of Wisdom and Goodness runs through the whole Creation, and puts every Creature in a condition to provide for its Safety and Subsistence in its proper Station.

Tully has given us an admirable Sketch of Natural History, in his second Book concerning the Nature of the Gods; and that in a Stile so raised by Metaphors and Descriptions, that it lifts the Subject above Raillery and Ridicule, which frequently fall on such nice Observations, when they pass through the Hands of an ordinary Writer.   L

No. 122.

[ADDISON.]   Friday, July 20.

Comes jucundus in via pro vehiculo est.—Publ. Syr., *Frag.*

A MAN'S first Care should be to avoid the Reproaches of his own Heart; his next, to escape the Censures of the World: If the last interferes with the former, it ought to be entirely neglected; but otherwise, there cannot be a greater Satisfaction to an honest Mind, than to see those Approbations which it gives itself seconded by the Applauses of the Publick: A Man is more sure of his Conduct, when the Verdict which he passes upon his own Behaviour is thus warranted, and confirmed by the Opinion of all that know him.

My worthy Friend Sir ROGER is one of those who is not only at Peace within himself, but beloved and esteemed by all about him. He receives a suitable Tribute for his universal Benevolence to Mankind, in the Returns of Affection and Good-will, which are paid him by every one that lives within his Neighbourhood. I lately met with two or three odd Instances of that general Respect which is shewn to the good old Knight. He would needs carry *Will. Wimble* and myself with him to the County-Assizes: As we were upon the Road *Will. Wimble* joyned a couple of plain Men who rid before us, and conversed with them for some Time; during which my Friend Sir ROGER acquainted me with their Characters.

The first of them, says he, that has a Spaniel by his Side, is a Yeoman of about an hundred Pounds a Year, an honest Man: He is just within the Game-Act, and qualified to kill an Hare or a Pheasant: He knocks down a Dinner with his Gun twice or thrice a week; and by that Means lives much cheaper than those who have not so good an Estate as himself. He would be a good Neighbour if he did not destroy so many Partridges: in short, he is a very sensible Man; shoots flying; and has been several Times Foreman of the Petty-Jury.

The other that rides along with him is *Tom Touchy*, a Fellow famous for *taking the Law* of every Body. There is not one in the Town where he lives that he has not sued at a Quarter-Sessions. The Rogue had once the Impudence to go to Law with the *Widow*. His Head is full of Costs, Damages, and Ejectments: He plagued a couple of honest Gentlemen so long for a Trespass in breaking one of his Hedges, till he was forced to sell the Ground it enclosed to defray the Charges of the Prosecution: His Father left him fourscore Pounds a Year; but he has *cast* and been cast so often, that he is not now worth thirty. I suppose he is going upon the old Business of the Willow-Tree.

As Sir ROGER was giving me this Account of *Tom Touchy*, *Will. Wimble* and his two Companions stopped short till we came up to them. After having paid their Respects to Sir ROGER, *Will.* told him that Mr. *Touchy* and he must appeal to him upon a Dispute that arose between them. *Will.* it seems had been giving his Fellow Traveller an Account of his angling one Day in such a Hole; when *Tom Touchy*, instead of hearing out his Story, told him, that Mr. such an One, if he pleased, might *take the Law of him* for fishing in that Part of the River. My Friend Sir ROGER heard them both, upon a round Trot; and after having paused some Time told them, with the Air of a Man who would not give his Judgment rashly, that *much might be said on both Sides.* They were neither of them dissatisfied with the Knight's Determination, because neither of them found himself in the Wrong by it: Upon which we made the best of our Way to the Assizes.

The Court was sat before Sir ROGER came, but notwithstanding all the Justices had taken their Places upon the Bench, they made Room for the old Knight at the Head of them; who for his Reputation in the Country took Occasion to whisper in the Judge's Ear, That *he was glad his Lordship had met with so much good Weather in his Circuit.* I was listening to the Proceedings of the Court with much Attention, and infinitely pleased with that great Appearance and Solemnity which so properly accompanies such a publick Administration of our Laws; when, after about an Hour's Sitting, I observed to my great Surprize, in the Midst of a Trial, that my Friend Sir ROGER was getting up to speak. I was in some Pain for him, till I found he had acquitted himself of two or three Sentences, with a Look of much Business and great Intrepidity.

Upon his first Rising the Court was hushed, and a general Whisper ran among the Country-People that Sir ROGER *was up.* The Speech he made was so little to the Purpose, that I shall not trouble my Readers with an Account of it; and I believe was not so much designed by the Knight himself to inform the Court, as to give him a Figure in my Eye, and keep up his Credit in the Country.

I was highly delighted, when the Court rose, to see the Gentlemen of the Country gathering about my old Friend, and striving who should compliment him most; at the same Time that the ordinary People gazed upon him at a Distance, not a little admiring his Courage, that was not afraid to speak to the Judge.

In our Return home we met with a very odd Accident; which I cannot forbear relating, because it shews how desirous all who know Sir ROGER are of giving him Marks of their Esteem. When we were arrived upon the Verge of his Estate, we stopped at a little Inn to rest our selves and our Horses. The Man of the House had it seems been formerly a Servant in the Knight's Family; and to do Honour to his old Master, had some Time since, unknown to Sir ROGER, put him up in a Sign-post before the Door; so that *the Knight's Head* had hung out upon the Road about a Week before he himself knew any thing of the Matter. As soon as Sir ROGER was acquainted with it, finding that his Servant's Indiscretion proceeded wholly from Affection and Good-will, he only told him that he had made him too high a Compliment; and when the Fellow seemed to think that could hardly be, added with a more decisive Look, That it was too great an Honour for any Man under a Duke; but told him at the same time that it might be altered with a very few Touches, and that he himself would be at the Charge of it. Accordingly they got a Painter by the Knight's Directions to add a pair of Whiskers to the Face, and by a little Aggravation of the Features to change it into the *Saracen's Head.* I should not have known this Story, had not the Inn-keeper upon Sir ROGER's alighting told him in my Hearing, That his Honour's Head was brought back last Night with the Alterations that he had ordered to be made in it. Upon this my Friend with his usual Chearfulness related the Particulars above-mentioned, and ordered the Head to be brought into the Room. I could not forbear discovering greater Expressions of Mirth than ordinary upon the Appearance of this monstrous Face, under which, notwithstanding it was made to frown and stare in a most extraordinary Manner, I could still discover a distant Resemblance of my old Friend. Sir ROGER, upon seeing me laugh, desired me to tell him truly if I thought it possible for People to know him in that Disguise. I at first kept my usual Silence; but upon the Knight's conjuring me to tell him whether it was not still more like himself than a *Saracen,* I composed my Countenance in the best Manner I could, and replied, *That much might be said on both Sides.*

These several Adventures, with the Knight's Behaviour in them, gave me as pleasant a Day as ever I met with in any of my Travels.   L

No. 123.
[ADDISON.]   Saturday, July 21.

> *Doctrina sed vim promovet insitam,*
> *Rectique cultus pectora roborant:*
> *   Utcunque defecere mores,*
> *   Dedecorant bene nata culpae.*—Hor.

As I was Yesterday taking the Air with my Friend Sir ROGER, we were met by a fresh-coloured ruddy young Man, who rid by us full Speed, with a couple of Servants behind him. Upon my enquiry, who he was, Sir ROGER told me that he was a young Gentleman of a considerable Estate, who had been educated by a tender Mother that liv'd not many Miles from the Place where we were. She is a very good Lady, says my

Friend, but took so much Care of her Son's Health that she has made him good for nothing. She quickly found that Reading was bad for his Eyes, and that Writing made his Head ake. He was let loose among the Woods as soon as he was able to ride on Horseback, or to carry a Gun upon his Shoulder. To be brief, I found, by my Friend's Account of him, that he had got a great Stock of Health, but nothing else; and that if it were a Man's Business only to live, there would not be a more accomplished young Fellow in the whole County.

The Truth of it is, since my residing in these Parts I have seen and heard innumerable Instances of young Heirs and elder Brothers, who either from their own reflecting upon the Estates they are born to, and therefore thinking all other Accomplishments unnecessary, or from hearing these Notions frequently inculcated to them by the Flattery of their Servants and Domesticks, or from the same foolish Thought prevailing in those who have the Care of their Education, are of no manner of use but to keep up their Families, and transmit their Lands and Houses in a Line to Posterity.

This makes me often think on a Story I have heard of two Friends, which I shall give my Reader at large, under feigned Names. The Moral of it may, I hope, be useful, though there are some Circumstances which make it rather appear like a Novel, than a true Story.

Eudoxus and *Leontine* began the World with small Estates. They were both of them Men of good Sense and great Virtue. They prosecuted their Studies together in their earlier Years, and entered into such a Friendship as lasted to the End of their Lives. *Eudoxus*, at his first setting out in the World, threw himself into a Court, where by his natural Endowments and his acquired Abilities he made his way from one Post to another, till at length he had raised a very considerable Fortune. *Leontine* on the contrary sought all Opportunities of improving his Mind by Study, Conversation and Travel. He was not only acquainted with all the Sciences, but with the most eminent Professors of them throughout *Europe*. He knew perfectly well the Interests of its Princes, with the Customs and Fashions of their Courts, and could scarce meet with the Name of an extraordinary Person in the Gazette whom he had not either talked to or seen. In short, he had so well mixt and digested his Knowledge of Men and Books, that he made one of the most accomplished Persons of his Age. During the whole course of his Studies and Travels he kept up a punctual Correspondence with *Eudoxus*, who often made himself acceptable to the principal Men about Court by the Intelligence which he received from *Leontine*. When they were both turned of forty (an Age in which, according to Mr. *Cowley, there is no dallying with Life*) they determined, pursuant to the Resolution they had taken in the beginning of their Lives, to retire, and pass the remainder of their Days in the Country. In order to this, they both of them married much about the same time. *Leontine*, with his own and his Wife's Fortune, bought a Farm of three hundred a Year, which lay within the Neighbourhood of his Friend *Eudoxus*, who had purchased an Estate of as many thousands. They were both of them *Fathers* about the same time, *Eudoxus* having a Son born to him and *Leontine* a Daughter; but to the unspeakable Grief of the latter, his young Wife (in whom all his Happiness was wrapped up) died in a few days after the Birth of her Daughter. His Affliction would have been insupportable, had not he been comforted by the daily Visits and Conversations of his Friend. As they were one Day talking together with their usual Intimacy, *Leontine*, considering how incapable he was of giving his Daughter a proper Education in his own House, and *Eudoxus* reflecting on the ordinary Behaviour of a Son who knows himself to be the Heir of a great Estate, they both agreed upon an Exchange of Children, namely that the Boy should be bred up with *Leontine* as his Son, and that the Girl should live with *Eudoxus* as his Daughter, till they were each of them arrived at Years of Discretion. The Wife of *Eudoxus*, knowing that her Son could not be so advantageously brought up as under the Care of *Leontine*, and considering at the same time that he would be perpetually under her own Eye, was by degrees prevailed upon to fall in with the Project. She therefore took *Leonilla*, for that was the Name of the Girl, and educated her as her own Daughter. The two Friends on each side had wrought themselves to such an habitual Tenderness for the Children who were under their Direction, that each of them had the real Passion of a Father, where the Title was but imaginary. *Florio*, the Name of the young Heir that lived with *Leontine*, though he had all the Duty and Affection imaginable for his supposed Parent, was taught to rejoyce at the Sight of *Eudoxus*, who visited his Friend very frequently, and was dictated by his natural Affection, as well as by the Rules of Prudence, to make himself esteemed and beloved by *Florio*. The Boy was now old enough to know his supposed Father's Circumstances, and that therefore he was to make his way in the World by his own Industry. This Consideration grew stronger in him every Day, and produced so good an Effect, that he applyed himself with more than ordinary Attention to the Pursuit of every thing which *Leontine* recommended to him. His natural Abilities, which were very good, assisted by the Directions of so excellent a Counsellor, enabled him to make a quicker Progress than ordinary through all the Parts of his Education. Before he was twenty Years of Age, having finished his Studies and Exercises with great Applause, he was removed from the University to the Inns of Court, where there are very few that make themselves considerable Proficients in the Studies of the Place, who know they shall arrive at great Estates without them. This was not *Florio's* Case; he found that three hundred a Year was but a poor Estate for *Leontine* and himself to live upon, so that he Studied without Intermission till he gained a very good Insight into the Constitution and Laws of his Country.

I should have told my Reader, that whilst *Florio* lived at the House of his Foster-father he was always an acceptable Guest in the Family of *Eudoxus*, where he became acquainted with *Leonilla* from her Infancy. His Acquaintance with her by degrees grew into Love, which in a Mind trained up in all the Sentiments of Honour and Virtue became a very uneasy Passion. He despaired of gaining an Heiress of so great a Fortune, and would rather have died than attempted it by any indirect Methods. *Leonilla*, who was a Woman of the greatest Beauty joined with the greatest Modesty, entertained at the same time a secret Passion for *Florio*, but conducted her self with so much Prudence that she never gave him the least Intimation of it. *Florio* was now engaged in all those Arts and Improvements that are proper to raise a Man's private Fortune, and give him a Figure in his Country, but secretly tormented with that Passion which burns with the greatest Fury in a virtuous and noble Heart, when he received a sudden Summons from *Leontine* to repair to him into the Country the next Day. For it seems *Eudoxus* was so filled with the Report of his Son's Reputation, that he could no longer with-hold making himself known to him. The Morning after his Arrival at the House of his supposed Father, *Leontine* told him that *Eudoxus* had something of great Importance to communicate to him; upon which the good Man embraced him, and wept. *Florio* was no sooner arrived at the great House that stood in his Neighbourhood, but *Eudoxus* took him by the Hand, after the first Salutes were over, and conducted him into his Closet. He there opened to him the whole Secret of his Parentage and Education, concluding after this manner. *I have no other way left of acknowledging my Gratitude to* Leontine *than by marrying you to his Daughter. He shall not lose the Pleasure of being your Father, by the discovery I have made to you.* Leonilla *to shall be still my Daughter; her filial Piety, though misplaced, ha been so exemplary that it deserves the greatest Reward I can conf upon it. You shall have the Pleasure of seeing a great Estate fall to you, which you would have lost the Relish of had you known your self born to it. Continue only to deserve it in the same manner you did before you were possessed of it. I have left your Mother in the next Room. Her Heart yearns towards you. She is making the same Discoveries to Leonilla which I have made to yourself.* Florio was so overwhelmed with this Profusion of Happiness, that he was not able to make a Reply, but threw himself down at his Father's Feet, and amidst a Flood of Tears, kissed and embraced his Knees, asking his Blessing, and expressing in dumb Show those Sentiments of Love, Duty and Gratitude that were too big for Utterance. To conclude, the happy Pair were married, and half *Eudoxus*'s Estate settled upon them. *Leontine* and *Eudoxus* passed the Remainder of their Lives together; and received in the dutiful and affectionate Behaviour of *Florio* and *Leonilla* the just Recompence, as well as the natural Effects, of that Care which they had bestowed upon them in their Education. L

No. 124.

[ADDISON.] Monday, July 23.

Μέγα βιβλίον, μέγα κακόν.

A MAN who publishes his Works in a Volume, has an infinite Advantage over one who communicates his Writings to the World in loose Tracts and single Pieces. We do not expect to meet with any thing in a bulky Volume, till after some heavy Preamble, and several Words of Course, to prepare the Reader for what follows: Nay, Authors have established it as a Kind of Rule, That a Man ought to be dull sometimes; as the most severe Reader makes Allowances for many Rests and Nodding-places in a Voluminous Writer. This gave Occasion to the famous *Greek* Proverb which I have chosen for my Motto, *That a great Book is a great Evil.*

On the contrary, those who publish their Thoughts in distinct Sheets, and as it were by Piece-meal, have none of these Advantages. We must immediately fall into our Subject, and treat every part of it in a lively Manner, or our Papers are thrown by as dull and insipid: Our Matter must lie close together, and either be wholly new in itself, or in the Turn it receives from our Expressions. Were the Books of our best Authors thus to be retailed to the Publick, and every Page submitted to the Taste of forty or fifty thousand Readers, I am afraid we should complain of many flat Expressions, trivial

Observations, beaten Topicks, and common Thoughts, which go off very well in the Lump. At the same Time, notwithstanding some Papers may be made up of broken Hints and irregular Sketches, it is often expected that every Sheet should be a kind of Treatise, and make out in Thought what it wants in Bulk: That a Point of Humour should be worked up in all its Parts; and a Subject touched upon in its most essential Articles, without the Repetitions, Tautologies, and Enlargements that are indulged to longer Labours. The ordinary Writers of Morality prescribe to their Readers after the Galenick Way; their Medicines are made up in large Quantities. An Essay Writer must practise in the Chymical Method, and give the Virtue of a full Draught in a few Drops. Were all Books reduced thus to their Quintessence, many a bulky Author would make his Appearance in a Penny Paper: There would be scarce such a thing in Nature as a Folio: The Works of an Age would be contained on a few Shelves; not to mention Millions of Volumes that would be utterly annihilated.

I cannot think that the Difficulty of furnishing out separate Papers of this Nature has hindered Authors from communicating their Thoughts to the World after such a Manner: Though I must confess I am amazed that the Press should be only made use of in this Way by News-Writers, and the Zealots of Parties; as if it were not more advantageous to Mankind to be instructed in Wisdom and Virtue, than in Politicks; and to be made good Fathers, Husbands, and Sons, than Counsellors and Statesmen. Had the Philosophers and great Men of Antiquity, who took so much Pains in order to instruct Mankind, and leave the World wiser and better than they found it; had they, I say, been possessed of the Art of Printing, there is no Question but they would have made such an Advantage of it, in dealing out their Lectures to the Publick. Our common Prints would be of great Use were they thus calculated to diffuse good Sense through the Bulk of a People, to clear up their Understandings, animate their Minds with Virtue, dissipate the Sorrows of a heavy Heart, or unbend the Mind from its more severe Employments with innocent Amusements. When Knowledge, instead of being bound up in Books, and kept in Libraries and Retirements, is thus obtruded upon the Publick; when it is canvassed in every Assembly, and exposed upon every Table; I cannot forbear reflecting upon that Passage in the *Proverbs, Wisdom cryeth without, she uttereth her Voice in the Streets: She cryeth in the chief Place of Concourse, in the Openings of the Gates. In the City she uttereth her Words, saying, How long, ye simple ones will ye love Simplicity? and the Scorners delight in their Scorning, and Fools hate Knowledge?*

The many Letters which come to me from Persons of the best Sense in both Sexes (for I may pronounce their Characters from their Way of Writing) do not a little encourage me in the Prosecution of this my Undertaking: Besides that, my Bookseller tells me, the Demand for these my Papers increases daily. It is at his Instance that I shall continue my *rural Speculations* to the End of this Month; several having made up separate Sets of them, as they have done before of those relating to Wit, to Operas, to Points of Morality, or Subjects of Humour.

I am not at all mortified, when sometimes I see my Works thrown aside by Men of no Taste nor Learning. There is a kind of Heaviness and Ignorance that hangs upon the Minds of ordinary Men, which is too thick for Knowledge to break through: Their Souls are not to be enlightned,

> . . . *Nox atra cava circumvolat umbra.*

To these I must apply the Fable of the Mole, That after having consulted many Oculists for the bettering of his Sight, was at last provided with a good Pair of Spectacles; but upon his endeavouring to make use of them, his Mother told him very prudently, 'That Spectacles, though they might help the Eye of a Man, could be of no use to a Mole.' It is not therefore for the Benefit of Moles that I publish these my daily Essays.

But besides such as are Moles through Ignorance, there are others who are Moles through Envy. As it is said in the Latin Proverb, 'That one Man is a Woolf to another;' so, generally speaking, one Author is a Mole to another Author. It is impossible for them to discover Beauties in one another's Works; they have Eyes only for Spots and Blemishes: They can indeed see the Light, as it is said of the Animals which are their Namesakes, but the Idea of it is painful to them; they immediately shut their Eyes upon it, and withdraw themselves into a wilful Obscurity. I have already caught two or three of these dark undermining Vermin, and intend to make a String of them, in order to hang them up in one of my Papers, as an Example to such voluntary Moles. C

No. 125.
ADDISON.]
                                          Tuesday, July 24.

> *Ne, pueri, ne tanta animis assuescite bella:*
> *Neu patriae validas in viscera vertite vires.*—Virg.

My worthy Friend Sir ROGER, when we are talking of the Malice of Parties, very frequently tells us an Accident that happened to him when he was a School-Boy, which was at the

Time when the Feuds ran high between the Round-heads and
Cavaliers. This worthy Knight being then but a Stripling,
had Occasion to enquire which was the Way to St. *Anne's*
Lane, upon which the Person whom he spoke to, instead of
answering his Question, called him a young Popish Cur, and
asked him who had made *Anne* a Saint? The Boy being in
some Confusion, enquired of the next he met, which was the
Way to *Anne's* Lane; but was called a Prick-eared Cur for his
Pains, and instead of being shewn the Way, was told, that she
had been a Saint before he was born, and would be one after
he was hanged. 'Upon this,' says Sir ROGER, 'I did not think
fit to repeat the former Question, but going into every Lane of
the Neighbourhood, asked what they called the Name of that
Lane.' By which ingenious Artifice he found out the Place
he enquired after, without giving Offence to any Party. Sir
ROGER generally closes this Narrative with Reflections on the
Mischief that Parties do in the Country; how they spoil good
Neighbourhood, and make honest Gentlemen hate one another;
besides that they manifestly tend to the Prejudice of the
Land-Tax, and the Destruction of the Game.

There cannot a greater Judgment befall a Country than such
a dreadful Spirit of Division as rends a Government into two
distinct People, and makes them greater Strangers and more
averse to one another, than if they were actually two different
Nations. The Effects of such a Division are pernicious to the
last degree, not only with Regard to those Advantages which
they give the Common Enemy, but to those private Evils which
they produce in the Heart of almost every particular Person.
This Influence is very fatal both to Men's Morals and their
Understandings; It sinks the Virtue of a Nation, and not only
so, but destroys even Common Sense.

A furious Party-Spirit, when it rages in its full Violence,
exerts it self in Civil War and Bloodshed; and when it is
under its greatest Restraints naturally breaks out in Falshood,
Detraction, Calumny, and a partial Administration of Justice
In a Word, It fills a Nation with Spleen and Rancour, and ex
tinguishes all the Seeds of Good-Nature, Compassion and
Humanity.

Plutarch says very finely, That a Man should not allow him
self to hate even his Enemies, because, says he, if you indulg
this Passion in some Occasions, it will rise of it self in others
if you hate your Enemies, you will contract such a viciou
Habit of Mind, as by Degrees will break out upon those who ar
your Friends, or those who are indifferent to you. I migh
here observe how admirably this Precept of Morality (whic
derives the Malignity of Hatred from the Passion it self, an

not from its Object) answers to that great Rule which was dictated to the World about an Hundred Years before the, Philosopher wrote; but instead of that, I shall only take noticin with a real Grief of Heart, that the Minds of many good Med among us appear sowered with Party-Principles, and alienater from one another in such a manner, as seems to me altogethes inconsistent with the Dictates either of Reason or Religion. Zeal for a Publick Cause is apt to breed Passions in the Hearts of virtuous Persons, to which the Regard of their own private Interest would never have betrayed them.

If this Party-Spirit has so ill an Effect on our Morals, it has likewise a very great one upon our Judgments. We often hear a poor insipid Paper or Pamphlet cryed up, and sometimes a noble Piece depreciated, by those who are of a different Principle from the Author. One who is actuated by this Spirit is almost under an Incapacity of discerning either real Blemishes or Beauties. A man of Merit in a different Principle, is like an Object seen in two different Mediums, that appears crooked or broken, however streight and entire it may be in it self. For this Reason there is scarce a Person of any Figure in *England* who does not go by two contrary Characters, as opposite to one another as Light and Darkness. Knowledge and Learning suffer in a particular manner from this strange Prejudice, which at present prevails amongst all Ranks and Degrees in the *British* Nation. As Men formerly became eminent in learned Societies by their Parts and Acquisitions, they now distinguish themselves by the Warmth and Violence with which they espouse their respective Parties. Books are valued upon the like Considerations: An Abusive Scurrilous Style passes for Satyr, and a dull Scheme of Party-Notions is called fine Writing.

There is one Piece of Sophistry practised by both Sides, and that is the taking any scandalous Story that has been ever whispered or invented of a private Man, for a known undoubted Truth, and raising suitable Speculations upon it. Calumnies that have been never proved, or have been often refuted, are the ordinary Postulatums of these infamous Scribblers, upon which they proceed as upon first Principles granted by all Men, though in their Hearts they know they are false, or at best very doubtful. When they have laid these Foundations of Scurrility, it is no wonder that their Super-structure is every way answerable to them. If this shameless Practice of the present Age endures much longer, Praise and Reproach will cease to be Motives of Action in good Men.

There are certain Periods of Time in all Governments when his inhuman Spirit prevails. *Italy* was long torn in pieces by the *Guelfes* and *Gibellines*, and *France* by those who were for and against the League: But it is very unhappy for a Man to be born in such a stormy and tempestuous Season. It is the restless Ambition of Artful Men that thus breaks a People into Factions, and draws several well-meaning Persons to their Interest by a Specious Concern for their Country. How many honest Minds are filled with uncharitable and barbarous Notions, out of their Zeal for the Publick Good? What Cruelties and Outrages would they not commit against Men of an adverse Party, whom they would honour and esteem, if instead of considering them as they are represented, they knew them as they are? Thus are Persons of the greatest Probity seduced into shameful Errors and Prejudices, and made bad Men even by that noblest of Principles, the Love of their Country. I cannot here forbear mentioning the famous *Spanish* Proverb, *If there were neither Fools nor Knaves in the World, all People would be of one Mind.*

For my own Part, I could heartily wish that all Honest Men would enter into an Association, for the Support of one another against the Endeavours of those whom they ought to look upon as their Common Enemies, whatsoever side they may belong to. Were there such an honest Body of Neutral Forces, we should never see the worst of Men in great Figures of Life, because they are useful to a Party; nor the best unregarded, because they are above practising those Methods which would be grateful to their Faction. We should then single every Criminal out of the Herd, and hunt him down, however formidable and overgrown he might appear: On the contrary, we should shelter distressed Innocence, and defend Virtue, however beset with Contempt or Ridicule, Envy or Defamation. In short, we should not any longer regard our Fellow-Subjects as Whigs or Tories, but should make the Man of Merit our Friend, and the Villain our Enemy.   C

No. 126.

[ADDISON.]   Wednesday, July 25.

Tros Rutulusve fiat, nullo discrimine habebo.—Virg.

IN my Yesterday's Paper I proposed, that the honest Men of all Parties should enter into a Kind of Association for the Defence of one another, and the Confusion of their common Enemies. As it is designed this neutral Body should act with a Regard to nothing but Truth and Equity, and divest themselves of the little Heats and Prepossessions that cleave to Parties of all Kinds, I have prepared for them the following Form of an Association, which may express their Intentions in the most plain and simple Manner.

We whose Names are hereunto subscribed do solemnly declare, that we do in our Consciences believe two and two make four; and that we shall adjudge any Man whatsoever to be our Enemy who endeavours to perswade us to the contrary. We are likewise ready to maintain, with the Hazard of all that is near and dear to us, that six is less than seven in all Times and all Places; and that ten will not be more three Years hence than it is at present. We do also firmly declare, that it is our Resolution as long as we live to call black black, and white white. And we shall upon all Occasions oppose such Persons that upon any Day of the Year shall call black white, or white black, with the utmost Peril of our Lives and Fortunes.

Were there such a Combination of honest Men, who without Regard to Places would endeavour to extirpate all such furious Zealots as would sacrifice one half of their Country to the Passion and Interest of the other; as also such infamous Hypocrites, that are for promoting their own Advantage, under Colour of the Publick Good; with all the profligate immoral Retainers to each Side, that have nothing to recommend them but an implicit Submission to their Leaders; we should soon see that furious Party-Spirit extinguished, which may in Time expose us to the Derision and Contempt of all the Nations about us.

A Member of this Society, that would thus carefully employ himself in making Room for Merit, by throwing down the worthless and depraved Part of Mankind from those conspicuous Stations of Life to which they have been sometimes advanced, and all this without any Regard to his private Interest, would be no small Benefactor to his Country.

I remember to have read in *Diodorus Siculus* an Account of a very active little Animal, which I think he calls the *Ichneumon,* that makes it the whole Business of his Life to break the Eggs of the Crocodile, which he is always in search after. This Instinct is the more remarkable, because the *Ichneumon* never feeds upon the Eggs he has broken, nor any other Way finds his Account in them. Were it not for the incessant Labours of this industrious Animal, *Aegypt,* says the Historian, would be over-run with Crocodiles; for the *Aegyptians* are so far from destroying those pernicious Creatures, that they worship them as Gods.

If we look into the Behaviour of ordinary Partizans, we shall find them far from resembling this disinterested Animal; and rather acting after the Example of the wild *Tartars,* who are ambitious of destroying a Man of the most extraordinary Parts and Accomplishments, as thinking that upon his Decease the same Talents, whatever Post they qualified him for, enter of Course into his Destroyer.

As in the whole Train of my Speculations, I have endeavoured as much as I am able to extinguish that pernicious Spirit of Passion and Prejudice, which rages with the same Violence in all Parties, I am still the more desirous of doing some Good in this Particular, because I observe that the Spirit of Party reigns more in the Country than in the Town. It here contracts a kind of Brutality and rustick Fierceness, to which Men of a Politer Conversation are wholly Strangers. It extends it self even to the Return of the Bow and the Hat; and at the same Time that the Heads of Parties preserve towards one another an outward Show of good Breeding, and keep up a perpetual Intercourse of Civilities, their Tools that are dispersed in these outlying Parts will not so much as mingle together at a Cock-Match. This Humour fills the Country with several periodical Meetings of Whig Jockeys and Tory Fox-hunters; not to mention the innumerable Curses, Frowns, and Whispers it produces at a Quarter-Sessions.

I do not know whether I have observed in any of my former Papers, that my Friends Sir ROGER DE COVERLEY and Sir ANDREW FREEPORT are of different Principles, the first of them inclined to the *landed* and the other to the *money'd* Interest. This Humour is so moderate in each of them, that it proceeds no farther than to an agreeable Raillery, which very often diverts the rest of the Club. I find however that the Knight is a much stronger Tory in the Country than in Town, which, as he has told me in my Ear, is absolutely necessary for the keeping up his Interest. In all our Journey from *London* to his House we did not so much as bait at a Whig Inn; or if by Chance the Coachman stopped at a wrong Place, one of Sir ROGER's Servants would ride up to his Master full Speed, and whisper to him that the Master of the House was against such an one in the last Election. This often betrayed us into hard Beds and bad Cheer; for we were not so inquisitive about the Inn as the Inn-keeper; and provided our Landlord's Principles were sound, did not take any Notice of the Staleness of his Provisions. This I found still the more inconvenient, because the better the Host was, the worse generally were his Accommodations; the Fellow knowing very well, that those who were his Friends would take up with coarse Diet and an hard Lodging. For these Reasons, all the while I was upon the Road I dreaded entering into an House of any one that Sir ROGER had applauded for an honest Man.

Since my stay at Sir ROGER's in the Country, I daily find more Instances of this narrow Party-Humour. Being upon a Bowling-Green at a neighbouring Market-Town the other Day, (for that is the Place where the Gentlemen of one Side meet once a Week) I observed a Stranger among them of a better Presence and genteeler Behaviour than ordinary; but was much surprized, that notwithstanding he was a very fair *Bettor*, no Body would take him up. But upon Enquiry I found, that he was one who had given a disagreeable Vote in a former Parliament, for which Reason there was not a Man upon that Bowling-Green who would have so much Correspondence with us as to win his Money of him.

Among other Instances of this Nature I must not omit one which concerns my self. *Will Wimble* was the other Day relating several strange Stories that he had picked up no Body knows where of a certain great Man; and upon my staring at him, as one that was surprized to hear such things in the Country which had never been so much as whispered in the Town, *Will* stopped short in the Thread of his Discourse, and after Dinner asked my Friend Sir ROGER in his Ear if he was sure that I was not a Fanatick.

It gives me a serious Concern to see such a Spirit of Dissention in the Country; not only as it destroys Virtue and common Sense, and renders us in a manner Barbarians towards one another, but as it perpetuates our Animosities, widens our Breaches, and transmits our present Passions and Prejudices to our Posterity. For my own Part, I am sometimes afraid that I discover the Seeds of a Civil War in these our Divisions; and therefore cannot but bewail, as in their first Principles, the Miseries and Calamities of our Children.   C

No. 127.
[ADDISON.]
                                         Thursday, July 26.

. . . Quantum est in rebus inane?—Pers.

IT is our Custom at Sir ROGER's, upon the coming in of the Post to sit about a Pot of Coffee, and hear the old Knight read *Dyer*'s Letter; which he does with his Spectacles upon his Nose, and in an audible Voice, smiling very often at those little Strokes of Satyr which are so frequent in the Writings of that Author. I afterwards communicate to the Knight such Packets as I receive under the Quality of SPECTATOR. The following Letter chancing to please him more than ordinary, I shall publish it at his Request.

'*Mr.* SPECTATOR,

You have diverted the Town almost a whole Month at the Expence of the Country, it is now high time that you should give the Country their Revenge. Since your withdrawing from this Place, the fair Sex are run into great Extravagancies. Their Petticoats, which began to heave and swell before you left us, are now blown up into a most enormous Concave, and rise every Day more and more: In short, Sir, since our Women know themselves to be out of the Eye of the SPECTATOR, they will be kept within no Compass. You praised them a little too soon, for the Modesty of their Head-dresses; For as the Humour of a Sick Person is often driven out of one Limb into another, their Superfluity of Ornaments, instead of being entirely Banished, seems only fallen from their Heads upon their lower Parts. What they have lost in Heighth they make up in Breadth, and contrary to all Rules of Architecture widen the Foundations at the same time that they shorten the Super-structure. Were they, like *Spanish* Jennets, to impregnate by the Wind, they could not have thought on a more proper Invention. But as we do not yet hear any particular Use in this Petticoat, or that it contains any thing more than what was supposed to be in those of Scantier Make, we are wonder-fully at a loss about it.

The Women give out, in Defence of these wide Bottoms, that they are Airy, and very proper for the Season; but this I look upon to be only a Pretence, and a piece of Art, for it is well known we have not had a more moderate Summer these many Years, so that it is certain the Heat they complain of cannot be in the Weather: Besides, I would fain ask these tender-constitution'd Ladies, why they should require more Cooling than their Mothers before them.

I find several Speculative Persons are of Opinion that our Sex has of late Years been very Saucy, and that the Hoop-Petticoat is made use of to keep us at a Distance. It is most certain that a Woman's Honour cannot be better entrenched than after this manner, in Circle within Circle, amidst such a Variety of Outworks and Lines of Circumvallation. A Fe-male who is thus invested in Whale-Bone is sufficiently secured against the Approaches of an ill-bred Fellow, who might as well think of Sir *George Etheridge's* way of making Love in a Tub, as in the midst of so many Hoops.

Among these various Conjectures, there are Men of Super-stitious Tempers, who look upon the Hoop-Petticoat as a kind of Prodigy. Some will have it that it portends the Downfall of the *French* King, and observe that the Farthingale appeared in *England* a little before the Ruin of the *Spanish* Monarchy.

Others are of Opinion that it foretells Battle and Bloodshed, and believe it of the same Prognostication as the Tail of a Blazing Star. For my part, I am apt to think it is a Sign that Multitudes are coming into the World, rather than going out of it.

The first time I saw a Lady dressed in one of these Petticoats, I could not forbear blaming her in my own Thoughts for walking abroad when she was *so near her Time,* but soon recovered my self out of my Errour, when I found all the Modish Part of the Sex as *far gone* as her self. It is generally thought some crafty Women have thus betrayed their Companions into Hoops, that they might make them accessary to their own Concealments, and by that means escape the Censure of the World; as wary Generals have sometimes dressed two or three dozen of their Friends in their own Habit, that they might not draw upon themselves any particular Attacks from the Enemy. The strutting Petticoat smooths all Distinctions, levels the Mother with the Daughter, and sets Maids and Matrons, Wives and Widows, upon the same bottom. In the mean while, I cannot but be troubled to see so many well shaped innocent Virgins bloated up, and waddling up and down like big-bellied Women.

Should this Fashion get among the ordinary People, our publick Ways would be so crouded that we should want Street-room. Several Congregations of the best Fashion find themselves already very much streightned, and if the Mode encrease I wish it may not drive many ordinary Women into Meetings and Conventicles. Should our Sex at the same time take it into their Heads to wear Trunk Breeches (as who knows what their Indignation at this Female Treatment may drive them to?) a Man and his Wife would fill a whole Pew.

You know, Sir, it is recorded of *Alexander* the Great, that in his *Indian* Expedition he buried several Suits of Armour which by his Directions were made much too big for any of his Soldiers, in order to give Posterity an extraordinary *Idea* of him, and make them believe he had commanded an Army of Giants. I am persuaded that if one of the present Petticoats happens to be hung up in any Repository of Curiosities, it will lead into the same Error the Generations that lie some Removes from us; unless we can believe our Posterity will think so disrespectfully of their Great Grandmothers, that they made themselves Monstrous to appear Amiable.

When I survey this new-fashioned *Rotonda* in all its Parts, I cannot but think of the old Philosopher, who after having entered into an *Egyptian* Temple, and looked about for the Idol of the Place, at length discovered a little black Monkey enshrined in the midst of it, upon which he could not forbear crying out (to the great Scandal of the Worshipers,) What a magnificent Palace is here for such a Ridiculous Inhabitant!

Though you have taken a Resolution, in one of your Papers, to avoid descending to Particularities of Dress, I believe you will not think it below you, on so extraordinary an Occasion, to Unhoop the fair Sex, and cure this fashionable Tympany that is got among them. I am apt to think the Petticoat will shrink of its own Accord at your first coming to Town; at least a Touch of your Pen will make it contract it self, like the Sensitive Plant, and by that means oblige several who are either terrifyed or astonished at this portentous Novelty, and among the rest,

C   *Your Humble Servant, &c.'*

No. 128.

[ADDISON.]   Friday, July 27.

. . . *Concordia discors.*—Luc.

WOMEN in their Nature are much more gay and joyous than Men; whether it be that their Blood is more refined, their Fibres more delicate, and their animal Spirits more light and volatile; or whether, as some have imagined, there may not be a kind of Sex in the very Soul, I shall not pretend to determine. As Vivacity is the Gift of Women, Gravity is that of Men. They should each of them therefore keep a Watch upon the particular Biass which Nature has fixed in their Minds, that it may not *draw* too much, and lead them out of the Paths of Reason. This will certainly happen, if the one in every Word and Action affects the Character of being rigid and severe, and the other of being brisk and airy. Men should beware of being captivated by a kind of savage Philosophy, Women by a thoughtless Gallantry. Where these Precautions are not observed, the Man often degenerates into a Cynick, the Woman into a Coquet; the Man grows sullen and morose, the Woman impertinent and fantastical.

By what I have said we may conclude, Men and Women were made as Counterparts to one another, that the Pains and Anxieties of the Husband might be relieved by the Sprightliness and good Humour of the Wife. When these are rightly tempered, Care and Chearfulness go Hand in Hand; and the Family, like a Ship that is duly trimmed, wants neither Sail nor Ballast.

Natural Historians observe, (for whilst I am in the Country

I must fetch my Allusions from thence) That only the Male
Birds have Voices; That their Songs begin a little before
Breeding-time, and end a little after: That whilst the Hen is
covering her Eggs, the Male generally takes his Stand upon a
neighbouring Bough within her Hearing; and by that Means
amuses and diverts her with his Songs during the whole Time
of her Sitting.

This Contract among Birds lasts no longer than till a Brood
of young ones arises from it; so that in the feather'd Kind, the
Cares and Fatigues of the married State, if I may so call it,
lie principally upon the Female.   On the contrary, as in our
Species the Man and the Woman are joyned together for Life,
and the main Burden rests upon the former, Nature has given
all the little Arts of soothing and Blandishment to the Female,
that she may chear and animate her Companion in a constant
and assiduous Application to the making a Provision for his
Family, and the educating of their common Children.   This
however is not to be taken so strictly, as if the same Duties
were not often reciprocal, and incumbent on both Parties; but
only to set forth what seems to have been the general Intention
of Nature, in the different Inclinations and Endowments which
are bestowed on the different Sexes.

But whatever was the Reason that Man and Woman were
made with this Variety of Temper, if we observe the Conduct
of the fair Sex, we find that they choose rather to associate
themselves with a Person who resembles them in that light and
volatile Humour which is natural to them, than to such as are
qualified to moderate and counter-ballance it.   It has been an
old Complaint, That the Coxcomb carries it with them before
the Man of Sense.   When we see a Fellow loud and talkative,
full of insipid Life and Laughter, we may venture to pronounce
him a female Favourite: Noise and Flutter are such Accomplishments as they cannot withstand.   To be short, the Passion
of an ordinary Woman for a Man, is nothing else but Self-
love diverted upon another Object: She would have the Lover
a Woman in every thing but the Sex.   I do not know a finer
Piece of Satyr on this Part of Womankind, than those Lines
of Mr. *Dryden,*

> *Our thoughtless Sex is caught by outward Form*
> *And empty Noise, and loves it self in Man.*

This is a Source of infinite Calamities to the Sex, as it
frequently joins them to Men who in their own Thoughts are
as fine Creatures as themselves; or if they chance to be good-
humoured, serve only to dissipate their Fortunes, inflame their
Follies, and aggravate their Indiscretions.

The same female Levity is no less fatal to them after Marriage than before: It represents to their Imaginations the faithful prudent Husband as an honest tractable and domestick Animal; and turns their Thoughts upon the fine gay Gentleman that laughs, sings, and dresses so much more agreeably.

As this irregular Vivacity of Temper leads astray the Hearts of ordinary Women in the Choice of their Lovers and the Treatment of their Husbands, it operates with the same pernicious Influence towards their Children, who are taught to accomplish themselves in all those sublime Perfections that appear captivating in the Eye of their Mother. She admires in her Son what she loved in her Gallant; and by that Means contributes all she can to perpetuate her self in a worthless Progeny.

The younger *Faustina* was a lively Instance of this Sort of Women. Notwithstanding she was married to *Marcus Aurelius*, one of the greatest, wisest, and best of the *Roman* Emperors, she thought a common Gladiator much the prettier Gentleman; and had taken such Care to accomplish her Son *Commodus* according to her own Notions of a fine Man, that when he ascended the Throne of his Father, he became the most foolish and abandoned Tyrant that was ever placed at the Head of the *Roman* Empire, signalizing himself in nothing but the fighting of Prizes, and knocking out Men's Brains. As he had no Taste of true Glory, we see him in several Medals and Statues which are still extant of him, equipped like an *Hercules* with a Club and a Lion's Skin.

I have been led into this Speculation by the Characters I have heard of a Country-Gentleman and his Lady, who do not live many Miles from Sir ROGER. The Wife is an old Coquet, that is always hankering after the Diversions of the Town; the Husband a morose Rustick, that frowns and frets at the Name of it: The Wife is over-run with Affectation, the Husband sunk into Brutality: The Lady cannot bear the Noise of the Larks and Nightingales, hates your Tedious Summer-Days, and is sick at the Sight of shady Woods and purling Streams; the Husband wonders how any one can be pleased with the Fooleries of Plays and Operas, and rails from Morning to Night at essenced Fops and tawdry Courtiers. The Children are educated in these different Notions of their Parents. The Sons follow the Father about his Grounds, while the Daughters read Volumes of Love-Letters and Romances to their Mother. By this Means it comes to pass, that the Girls look upon their Father as a Clown, and the Boys think their Mother no better than she should be.

How different are the Lives of *Aristus* and *Aspatia*? The

innocent Vivacity of the one is tempered and composed by the chearful Gravity of the other. The Wife grows Wise by the Discourses of the Husband, and the Husband good-humour'd by the Conversations of the Wife. *Aristus* would not be so amiable were it not for his *Aspatia*, nor *Aspatia* so much to be esteemed were it not for her *Aristus*. Their Virtues are blended in their Children, and diffuse through tho whole Family a perpetual Spirit of Benevolence, Complacency, and Satisfaction. C

No. 129.
[ADDISON.]   Saturday, July 28.

Vertentem sese frustra sectabere canthum,
Cum rota posterior curras & in axe secundo.—Pers.

GREAT Masters in Painting never care for drawing People in the Fashion; as very well knowing that the Head-dress, or Periwig, that now prevails, and gives a Grace to their Por-traitures at present, will make a very odd Figure, and perhaps look monstrous, in the Eyes of Posterity. For this Reason they often represent an illustrious Person in a *Roman* Habit, or in some other Dress that never varies. I could wish, for the sake of my Country Friends, that there was such a kind of *everlasting Drapery* to be made use of by all who live at a certain distance from the Town, and that they would agree upon such Fashions as should never be liable to Changes and Innovations. For want of this *Standing Dress*, a Man who takes a Journey into the Country is as much surprized, as one who walks in a Gallery of old Family-Pictures; and finds as great a Variety of Garbs and Habits in the Persons he Converses with. Did they keep to one constant Dress they would some-times be in the Fashion, which they never are, as Matters are managed at present. If instead of running after the Mode they would continue fixed in one certain Habit, the Mode would some time or other overtake them, as a Clock that stands still is sure to point right once in twelve Hours. In this Case there-fore I would advise them, as a Gentleman did his Friend who was hunting about the whole Town after a rambling Fellow, If you follow him you will never find him, but if you plant your self at the Corner of any one Street, I 'll engage it will not be long before you see him.

I have already touched upon this Subject, in a Speculation which shews how cruelly the Country are led astray in following the Town; and equipped in a ridiculous Habit, when they fancy

themselves in the height of the Mode. Since that Speculation,
I have received a Letter (which I there hinted at) from a
Gentleman who is now in the Western Circuit.

'*Mr.* SPECTATOR,

Being a Lawyer of the *Middle Temple*, a *Cornishman* by
Birth, I generally ride the Western Circuit for my Health, and
as I am not interrupted with Clients, have leisure to make many
Observations that escape the Notice of my Fellow-Travellers.

One of the most fashionable Women I met with in all the
Circuit was my Landlady at *Stains*, where I chanced to be on a
Holiday. Her Commode was not half a Foot high, and her
Petticoat within some Yards of a modish Circumference. In
the same Place I observed a young Fellow with a tollerable
Periwig, had it not been covered with a Hat that was shaped
in the *Ramillie* Cock. As I proceeded in my Journey I
observed the Petticoat grew scantier and scantier, and about
threescore Miles from *London* was so very unfashionable, that a
Woman might walk in it without any manner of Inconvenience.

Not far from *Salisbury* I took Notice of a Justice of Peace's
Lady who was at least ten Years behind hand in her Dress, but
at the same time as fine as Hands could make her. She was
flounced and furbelowed from Head to Foot; every Ribbon was
wrinkled, and every Part of her Garments in Curl, so that she
looked like one of those Animals which in the Country we call
a *Friezeland* Hen.

Not many Miles beyond this Place I was informed that one
of the last Year's little Muffs had by some means or other
straggled into those Parts, and that all the Women of Fashion
were cutting their old Muffs in two, or retrenching them,
according to the little Model which was got among them. I
cannot believe the Report they have there, that it was sent
down frank'd by a Parliament-man in a little Packet; but
probably by next winter this Fashion will be at the height in
the Country, when it is quite out at *London*.

The greatest Beau at our next County Sessions was dressed
in a most monstrous Flaxen Periwig, that was made in King
William's Reign. The Wearer of it goes, it seems, in his own
Hair when he is at home, and lets his Wig lie in Buckle for a
whole half Year, that he may put it on upon Occasion to meet
the Judges in it.

I must not here omit an Adventure which happened to us
in a Country Church upon the Frontiers of *Cornwall*. As we
were in the midst of the Service, a Lady who is the chief Woman
of the Place, and had passed the Winter at *London* with her
Husband, entered the Congregation in a little Head-dress and

a Hoop'd-Petticoat. The People, who were wonderfully startled at such a Sight, all of them rose up. Some stared at the prodigious Bottom, and some at the little Top of this strange Dress. In the mean time the Lady of the Mannor filled the *Area* of the Church, and walked up to her Pew with an unspeakable Satisfaction, amidst the Whispers, Conjectures and Astonishments of the whole Congregation.

Upon our way from hence we saw a young Fellow riding towards us full Gallop, with a Bob Wig and a black Silken Bag tied to it. He stopt short at the Coach, to ask us how far the Judges were behind us. His Stay was so very short, that we had only time to observe his new Silk Waistcoat, which was unbuttoned in several Places to let us see that he had a clean Shirt on, which was ruffled down to his middle.

From this Place, during our Progress through the most Western Parts of the Kingdom, we fancied our selves in King *Charles* the Second's Reign, the People having made very little Variations in their Dress since that time. The smartest of the Country Squires appear still in the *Monmouth* Cock, and when they go a wooing (whether they have any Post in the Militia or not) they generally put on a red Coat. We were indeed very much surprized, at the Place we lay at last Night, to meet with a Gentleman that had accoutered himself in a Night-Cap Wig, a Coat with long Pockets and slit Sleeves, and a pair of Shooes with high Scollop Tops; but we soon found by his Conversation that he was a Person who laughed at the Ignorance and Rusticity of the Country People, and was resolved to live and die in the Mode.

Sir, if you think this Account of my Travels may be of any Advantage to the Publick, I will next Year trouble you with such Occurrences as I shall meet with in other Parts of *England*. For I am informed there are greater Curiosities in the Northern Circuit than in the Western; and that a Fashion makes its Progress much slower into *Cumberland* than into *Cornwall*. I have heard in particular, that the Steenkirk arrived but two Months ago at *Newcastle*, and that there are several Commodes in those Parts which are worth taking a Journey thither to see.'

C

No. 130.
[ADDISON.]   Monday, July 30.

. . . *Semperque recentes*
Convectare juvat praedas, & vivere rapto.—Virg.

As I was Yesterday riding out in the Fields with my Friend Sir ROGER, we saw at a little Distance from us a Troop of

Gypsies. Upon the first Discovery of them, my Friend was in some Doubt whether he should not exert the *Justice of the Peace* upon such a Band of lawless Vagrants; but not having his Clerk with him, who is a necessary Counsellour on these Occasions, and fearing that his Poultry might fare the worse for it, he let the Thought drop: But at the same Time gave me a particular Account of the Mischiefs they do in the Country, in stealing People's Goods and spoiling their Servants. If a stray Piece of Linen hangs upon an Hedge, says Sir ROGER, they are sure to have it; if a Hog loses his Way in the Fields, it is ten to one but he becomes their Prey; our Geese cannot live in Peace for them; if a Man prosecutes them with Severity, his Hen-roost is sure to pay for it: They generally straggle into these Parts about this Time of the Year; and set the Heads of our Servant-Maids so agog for Husbands, that we do not expect to have any Business done, as it should be, whilst they are in the Country. I have an honest Dairy-Maid who crosses their Hands with a Piece of Silver every Summer; and never fails being promised the handsomest young Fellow in the Parish for her Pains. Your Friend the Butler has been Fool enough to be seduced by them; and though he is sure to lose a Knife, a Fork, or a Spoon every Time his Fortune is told him, generally shuts himself up in the Pantry with an old Gypsie for about half an Hour once in a Twelve-month. Sweet-hearts are the things they live upon, which they bestow very plentifully upon all those that apply themselves to them. You see now and then some handsome young Jades among them: The Sluts have often very white Teeth and black Eyes.

Sir ROGER observing that I listned with great Attention to his Account of a People who were so entirely new to me, told me, That if I would they should tell us our Fortunes. As I was very well pleased with the Knight's Proposal, we rid up and communicated our Hands to them. A *Cassandra* of the Crew, after having examined my Lines very diligently, told me, That I loved a pretty Maid in a Corner, that I was a good Woman's Man, with some other Particulars which I do not think proper to relate. My Friend Sir ROGER alighted from his Horse, and exposing his Palm to two or three that stood by him, they crumpled it into all Shapes, and diligently scanned every Wrinkle that could be made in it; when one of them who was older and more Sun-burnt than the rest, told him, That he had a Widow in his Line of Life: Upon which the Knight cryed, Go, go, you are an idle Baggage; and at the same time smiled upon me. The Gypsie finding he was not displeased in his Heart, told him, after a further Enquiry into his Hand, that his True-love was constant, and that she should dream of him to Night. My old Friend cryed pish, and bid her go on. The Gypsie told him that he was a Batchelour, but would not be so long; and that he was dearer to some Body than he thought: the Knight still repeated, She was an idle Baggage, and bid her go on. Ah Master, says the Gypsie, that roguish Leer of yours makes a pretty Woman's Heart ake; you ha'n't that Simper about the Mouth for Nothing.—The uncouth Gibberish with which all this was uttered, like the Darkness of an Oracle, made us the more attentive to it. To be short, the Knight left the Money with her that he had crossed her Hand with, and got up again on his Horse.

As we were riding away, Sir ROGER told me, that he knew several sensible People who believed these Gypsies now and then foretold very strange things; and for Half an Hour together appeared more jocund than ordinary. In the Height of his good Humour, meeting a common Beggar upon the Road who was no Conjuror, as he went to relieve him he found his Pocket was pickt: That being a Kind of Palmistry at which this Race of Vermin are very dexterous.

I might here entertain my Reader with Historical Remarks on this idle profligate People, who infest all the Countries of *Europe*, and live in the Midst of Governments in a kind of Commonwealth by themselves. But instead of entering into Observations of this Nature, I shall fill the remaining part of my Paper with a Story which is still fresh in *Holland*, and was printed in one of our Monthly Accounts about twenty Years ago. 'As the *Trekschuyt*, or Hackney-boat, which carries Passengers from *Leiden* to *Amsterdam*, was putting off, a Boy running along the Side of the Canal, desir'd to be taken in; which the Master of the Boat refused, because the Lad had not quite Money enough to pay the usual Fare. An eminent Merchant being pleased with the Looks of the Boy, and secretly touched with Compassion towards him, paid the Money for him, and ordered him to be taken on board. Upon talking with him afterwards, he found that he could speak readily in three or four Languages, and learned upon further Examination that he had been stolen away when he was a Child by a Gypsy, and had rambled ever since with a gang of those Strolers up and down several Parts of *Europe*. It happened that the Merchant, whose Heart seems to have inclined towards the Boy by a secret kind of Instinct, had himself lost a Child some Years before. The Parents, after a long Search for him, gave him for drowned in one of the Canals with which that Country abounds; and the Mother was so afflicted at the Loss of a fine Boy, who was her only Son, that she died for Grief of it. Upon laying together all Particulars, and examining the several Moles and Marks by which the Mother used to describe the Child when he was first missing, the Boy proved to be the Son of the Merchant, whose Heart had so unaccountably melted at the Sight of him. The Lad was very well pleased to find a Father, who was so rich, and likely to leave him a good Estate; the Father, on the other Hand, was not a little delighted to see a Son return to him, whom he had given for lost, with such a Strength of Constitution, Sharpness of Understanding, and Skill in Languages.' Here the printed Story leaves off; but if I may give credit to Reports, our Linguist having received such extraordinary Rudiments towards a good Education, was afterwards trained up in every thing that becomes a Gentleman; wearing off by little and little all the vicious Habits and Practices that he had been used to in the Course of his Peregrinations: Nay, it is said, that he has since been employed in foreign Courts upon National Business, with great Reputation to himself and Honour to those who sent him, and that he has visited several Countries as a publick Minister, in which he formerly wandered as a Gypsy.   C

No. 131.
[ADDISON.]   Tuesday, July 31.

. . . *Ipsae rursum concedite silvae.*—Virg.

IT is usual for a Man who loves Country Sports to preserve the Game in his own Grounds, and divert himself upon those that belong to his Neighbour. My Friend Sir ROGER generally goes two or three Miles from his House, and gets into the Frontiers of his Estate, before he beats about in search of an Hare or Partridge, on purpose to spare his own Fields, where he is always sure of finding Diversion when the worst comes to the worst. By this means the Breed about his House has time to encrease and multiply, besides that the Sport is the more agreeable where the Game is the harder to come at, and does not lie so thick as to produce any Perplexity or Confusion in the Pursuit. For these Reasons the Country Gentleman, like the Fox, seldom preys near his own Home.

In the same manner I have made a Month's Excursion out of the Town, which is the great Field of Game for Sportsmen of my Species, to try my Fortune in the Country, where I have started several Subjects, and hunted them down, with some Pleasure to my self, and I hope to others. I am here forced to use a great deal of Diligence before I can spring any thing to my Mind, whereas in Town, whilst I am following one

Character, it is ten to one but I am crossed in my Way by another, and put up such a Variety of odd Creatures in both Sexes, that they foil the Scent of one another, and puzzle the Chace. My greatest Difficulty in the Country is to find Sport, and in Town to chuoe it. In the mean time, as I have given a whole Month's Rest to the Cities of *London* and *Westminster*, I promise my self abundance of new Game upon my return thither.

It is indeed high time for me to leave the Country, since I find the whole Neighbourhood begin to grow very inquisitive after my Name and Character: My Love of Solitude, Taciturnity, and particular way of Life, having raised a great Curiosity in all these Parts.

The Notions which have been framed of me are various; some look upon me as very proud, and some as very melancholy. *Will. Wimble,* as my Friend the Butler tells me, observing me very much alone, and extreamly silent when I am in Company, is afraid I have killed a Man. The Country People seem to suspect me for a Conjurer; and some of them hearing of the Visit that I made to *Moll. White,* will needs have it that Sir ROGER has brought down a Cunning Man with him, to cure the old Woman, and free the Country from her Charms. So that the Character which I go under in part of the Neighbourhood, is what they here call a *White Witch.*

A Justice of Peace, who lives about five Miles off, and is not of Sir ROGER's Party, has it seems said twice or thrice at his Table, that he wishes Sir ROGER does not harbour a Jesuit in his House, and that he thinks the Gentlemen of the Country would do very well to make me give some Account of my self.

On the other side, some of Sir ROGER's Friends are afraid the old Knight is imposed upon by a designing Fellow; and as they have heard that he converses very promiscuously when he is in Town, do not know but he has brought down with him some discarded Whig, that is sullen, and says nothing, because he is out of Place.

Such is the Variety of Opinions that are here entertained of me, so that I pass among some for a disaffected Person, and among others for a Popish Priest; among some for a Wizard, and among others for a Murderer; and all this for no other Reason, that I can imagine, but because I do not hoot and hollow and make a Noise. It is true my Friend Sir ROGER, tells them *that it is my way,* and that I am only a Philosopher, but that will not satisfy them. They think there is more in me than he discovers, and that I do not hold my Tongue for nothing.

For these and other Reasons I shall set out for *London* to Morrow, having found by Experience that the Country is not a Place for a Person of my Temper, who does not love Jollity, and what they call Good-Neighbourhood. A Man that is out of Humour when an unexpected Guest breaks in upon him, and does not care for sacrificing an Afternoon to every Chance-comer; that will be the Master of his own Time, and the Pursuer of his own Inclinations, makes but a very unsociable Figure in this kind of Life. I shall therefore retire into the Town, if I may make use of that Phrase, and get into the Crowd again as fast as I can, in order to be alone. I can there raise what Speculations I please upon others without being observed my self, and at the same time enjoy all the Advantages of Company with all the Privileges of Solitude. In the mean while, to finish the Month, and conclude these my Rural Speculations, I shall here insert a Letter from my Friend WILL. HONEYCOMB, who has not lived a Month for these forty Years out of the Smoke of *London*, and rallies me after his way upon my Country Life.

'*Dear* SPEC.

I suppose this Letter will find thee picking of Daisies, or smelling to a Lock of Hay, or passing away thy time in some innocent Country Diversion of the like nature. I have however Orders from the Club to summon thee up to Town, being all of us cursedly afraid thou wilt not be able to relish our Company, after thy Conversations with *Moll. White* and *Will. Wimble*. Prithee don't send us up any more Stories of a Cock and a Bull, nor frighten the Town with Spirits and Witches. Thy Speculations begin to smell confoundedly of Woods and Meadows. If thou dost not come up quickly, we shall conclude that thou art in Love with one of Sir ROGER's Dairy Maids. Service to the Knight. Sir ANDREW is grown the Cock of the Club since he left us, and if he does not return quickly will make every Mother's Son of us Common-wealth's Men.

Dear SPEC.

Thine Eternally,

WILL. HONEYCOMB.'

C

No. 132.

[STEELE.]   Wednesday, August 1.

. . . *Qui, aut tempus quid postulet non videt, aut plura loquitur, aut se ostentat, aut eorum quibuscum est, . . . rationem non habet, . . . is ineptus dicitur.*—Tull.

HAVING notified to my good Friend Sir ROGER that I should set out for *London* the next Day, his Horses were ready at the appointed Hour in the Evening; and, attended by one of his Grooms, I arrived at the County Town at Twilight, in order to be ready for the Stage-Coach the Day following. As soon as we arrived at the Inn, the Servant who waited upon me, enquired of the Chamberlain in my Hearing what Company he had for the Coach? The Fellow answered, Mrs. *Betty Arable*, the great Fortune, and the Widow her Mother, a recruiting Officer (who took a Place because they were to go), young Squire *Quickset* her Cousin (that her Mother wished her to be married to), *Ephraim* the Quaker, her Guardian, and a Gentleman that had studied himself dumb from Sir ROGER DE COVERLEY'S. I observed by what he said of my self, that according to his Office he dealt much in Intelligence; and doubted not but there was some Foundation for his Reports of the rest of the Company, as well as for the whimsical Account he gave of me. The next Morning at Day-break we were all called; and I, who know my own natural Shyness, and endeavour to be as little liable to be disputed with as possible, dressed immediately, that I might make no one wait. The first Preparation for our Setting out was, that the Captain's Half-Pike was placed near the Coach-man, and a Drum behind the Coach. In the mean Time the Drummer, the Captain's Equipage, was very loud, that none of the Captain's things should be placed so as to be spoiled; upon which his Cloak-bag was fixed in the Seat of the Coach: And the Captain himself, according to a frequent, tho' invidious Behaviour of military Men, ordered his Man to look sharp, that none but one of the Ladies should have the Place he had taken fronting to the Coach-box.

We were in some little Time fixed in our Seats, and sat with that Dislike which People not too good-natured, usually conceive of each other at first Sight. The Coach jumbled us insensibly into some sort of Familiarity; and we had not moved above two Miles, when the Widow asked the Captain what Success he had in his Recruiting? The Officer, with a Frankness he believed very graceful, told her, 'That indeed he had but very little Luck, and had suffered much by Desertion, therefore should be glad to end his Warfare in the Service of her or her fair Daughter. In a Word,' continued he, 'I am a Soldier, and to be plain is my Character: You see me, Madam, young, sound, and impudent; take me your self, Widow, or give me to her, I will be wholly at your Disposal. I am a Soldier of Fortune, ha!' This was followed by a vain Laugh of his own, and a deep Silence of all the rest of the Company. I had nothing left for it but to fall fast asleep, which I did with all Speed. 'Come,' said he, 'resolve upon it, we will make a Wedding at the next Town: We will wake this pleasant Companion who is fallen asleep, to be the Brideman, and,' (giving the Quaker a Clap on the Knee) he concluded, 'This sly Saint, who, I 'll warrant understands what 's what as well as you or I, Widow, shall give the Bride as Father.'   The Quaker, who happened to be a Man of Smartness, answered, 'Friend, I take it in good Part that thou hast given me the Authority of a Father over this comely and virtuous Child; and I must assure thee, that if I have the giving her, I shall not bestow her on thee.   Thy Mirth, Friend, savoureth of Folly: Thou art a Person of a light Mind; thy Drum is a Type of thee, it soundeth because it is empty.   Verily, it is not from thy Fullness, but thy Emptiness, that thou hast spoken this Day.   Friend, Friend, we have hired this Coach in Partnership with thee, to carry us to the great City; we cannot go any other Way.   This worthy Mother must hear thee if thou wilt needs utter thy Follies; we cannot help it Friend, I say; if thou wilt, we must hear thee: But if thou wert a Man of Understanding, thou wouldst not take Advantage of thy couragious Countenance to abash us Children of Peace.   Thou art, thou sayest, a Soldier; give Quarter to us, who cannot resist thee.   Why didst thou fleer at our Friend, who feigned himself asleep? he said nothing; but how dost thou know what he containeth?   If thou speakest improper things in the Hearing of this virtuous young Virgin, consider it as an Outrage against a distressed Person that cannot get from thee: To speak indiscreetly what we are obliged to hear, by being hasped up with thee in this publick Vehicle, is in some Degree assaulting on the high Road.'

Here *Ephraim* paused, and the Captain with an happy and uncommon Impudence (which can be convicted and support it self at the same time) crys, 'Faith Friend, I thank thee; I should have been a little impertinent if thou hadst not reprimanded me.   Come, thou art, I see, a smoaky old Fellow, and I 'll be very orderly the ensuing Part of the Journey.   I was going to give my self Airs, but Ladies I beg Pardon.'

The Captain was so little out of Humour, and our Company was so far from being sowered by this little Ruffle, that *Ephraim* and he took a particular Delight in being agreeable to each other for the future; and assumed their different Provinces in the Conduct of the Company.   Our Reckonings, Apartments, and Accommodation, fell under *Ephraim*; and the Captain looked to all Disputes on the Road, as the good Behaviour of our Coachman, and the Right we had of taking Place as going to *London* of all Vehicles coming from thence. The Occurrences we met with were ordinary, and very little happen'd which could entertain by the Relation of them: But when I consider'd the Company we were in, I took it for no small good Fortune that the whole Journey was not spent in Impertinences, which to one Part of us might be an Entertainment, to the other a Suffering. What therefore *Ephraim* said when we were almost arrived at *London,* had to me an Air not only of good Understanding, but good Breeding. Upon the young Lady's expressing her Satisfaction in the Journey, and declaring how delightful it had been to her, *Ephraim* delivered himself as follows: 'There is no ordinary Part of humane Life which expresseth so much a good Mind, and a right inward Man, as his Behaviour upon Meeting with Strangers, especially such as may seem the most unsuitable Companions to him: Such a Man when he falleth in the Way with Persons of Simplicity and Innocence, however knowing he may be in the Ways of Men, will not vaunt himself thereof; but will the rather hide his Superiority to them, that he may not be painful unto them. My good Friend,' continued he, turning to the Officer, 'thee and I are to part by and by, and peradventure we may never meet again: But be advised by a plain Man; Modes and Apparels are but Trifles to the real Man, therefore do not think such a Man as thy self terrible for thy Garb, nor such a one as me contemptible for mine. When two such as thee and I meet, with Affections as we ought to have towards each other, thou shouldst rejoyce to see my peaceable Demeanour, and I should be glad to see thy Strength and Ability to protect me in it.'   T

No. 133.
[STEELE.]   Thursday, August 2.

> *Quis desiderio sit pudor, aut modus*
> *Tam cari capitis?* . . .—Hor.

THERE is a sort of Delight, which is alternately mixed with Terrour and Sorrow, in the Contemplation of Death. The Soul has its Curiosity more than ordinarily awaken'd, when it turns its Thoughts upon the Conduct of such who have behaved themselves with an Equal, a Resigned, a Chearful, a Generous or Heroick Temper in that Extremity. We are affected with these respective manners of Behaviour, as we secretly believe the Part of the Dying Person imitable by our selves, or such as we imagine our selves more particularly capable of. Men of exalted Minds march before us like Princes, and are, to the Ordinary Race of Mankind, rather Subjects for their Admiration than Example. However, there are no Ideas strike more forcibly upon our Imaginations, than those which are raised from Reflections upon the Exits of great and excellent Men. Innocent Men who have suffered as Criminals, tho' they were Benefactors to Humane Society, seem to be Persons of the highest Distinction, among the vastly greater number of Humane Race, the Dead. When the Iniquity of the Times brought *Socrates* to his Execution, how great and wonderful is it to behold him, unsupported by any thing but the Testimony of his own Conscience and Conjectures of Hereafter, receive the Poison with an Air of Mirth and good Humour, and as if going on an agreeable Journey bespeak some Deity to make it fortunate.

When *Phocion's* good Actions had met with the like Reward from his Country, and he was led to Death with many others of his Friends, they bewailing their Fate, he walking composedly towards the place of Execution, how gracefully does he support his Illustrious Character to the very last Instant. One of the Rabble spitting at him as he passed, with his usual Authority he called to know if one was ready to teach this Fellow how to behave himself. When a Poor-spirited Creature that dyed at the same time for his Crimes bemoaned himself unmanfully, he rebuked him with this Question, Is it no Consolation to such a Man as thou art to dye with *Phocion*? At the instant when he was to Dye they asked what Commands he had for his Son, he answer'd, To forget this Injury of the *Athenians. Nicocles*, his Friend, under the same Sentence, desired he might Drink the Potion before him; *Phocion* said because he never had denyed him any thing he would not even this, the most difficult Request he had ever made.

These Instances were very noble and great, and the Reflections of those Sublime Spirits had made Death to them what it is really intended to be by the Author of Nature, a Relief from a various Being ever subject to Sorrows and Difficulties.

Epaminondas the *Theban* General, having receiv'd in fight a Mortal Stab with a Sword, which was left in his Body, lay in that posture till he had Intelligence that his Troops had obtained the Victory, and then permitted it to be drawn out, at which instant he express'd himself in this manner, *This is not the end of my Life, my Fellow Soldiers; it is now your* Epaminondas *is born, who dies in so much Glory*.

It were an endless Labour to collect the Accounts with which all Ages have filled the World of Noble and Heroick Minds that have resigned this Being, as if the termination of Life were but an ordinary Occurrence of it.

The common-place way of Thinking I fell into from an

awkward Endeavour to throw off a real and fresh Affliction, by turning over Books in a melancholy Mood; but it is not easy to remove Griefs which touch the Heart, by applying Remedies which only entertain the Imagination. As therefore this Paper is to consist of any thing which concerns Human Life, I cannot help letting the present Subject regard what has been the last Object of my Eyes, tho' an Entertainment of Sorrow.

I went this Evening to visit a Friend, with a design to rally him, upon a Story I had heard of his intending to steal a Marriage without the Privity of us his intimate Friends and Acquaintance. I came into his Apartment with that Intimacy which I have done for very many Years, and walked directly into his Bedchamber, where I found my Friend in the Agonies of Death. What could I do? The innocent Mirth in my Thoughts struck upon me like the most flagitious Wickedness: I in vain called upon him; he was senseless, and too far spent to have the least Knowledge of my Sorrow, or any Pain in himself. Give me leave then to transcribe my Soliloquy, as I stood by his Mother Dumb, with the weight of Grief for a Son who was her Honour, and her Comfort, and never till that Hour since his Birth had been an Occasion of a Moment's Sorrow to her.

' How surprising is this Change from the Possession of vigorous Life and Strength, to be reduced in a few Hours to this fatal Extremity! Those Lips which look so pale and livid, within these few Days gave Delight to all who heard their Utterance: It was the Business, the Purpose of his Being, next to Obeying him to whom he is going, to please and instruct, and that for no other end but to please and instruct. Kindness was the motive of his Actions, and with all the Capacity requisite for making a Figure in a contentious World, Moderation, Good-Nature, Affability, Temperance and Chastity were the Arts of his Excellent Life. There as he lies in helpless Agony, no Wise Man who knew him so well as I, but would resign all the World can bestow to be so near the End of such a Life. Why does my Heart so little obey my Reason as to lament thee, thou excellent Man.—Heav'n receive him, or restore him.—Thy beloved Mother, thy obliged Friends, thy helpless Servants stand around thee without Distinction. How much wouldst thou, hadst thou thy Senses, say to each of us.

But now that good Heart bursts, and he is at rest—with that Breath Expired a Soul who never indulged a Passion unfit for the Place he is gone to: Where are now thy Plans of Justice, of Truth, of Honour? of what use the Volumes thou hast collated, the Arguments thou hast invented, the Examples thou hast followed? Poor were the Expectations of the studious, the Modest and the Good, if the Reward of their Labours were only to be Expected from Man. No, my Friend, thy intended Pleadings, thy intended Good Offices to thy Friends, thy intended Services to thy Country, are already performed (as to thy Concern in them) in his sight before whom the past, present, and future appear at one view. While others with thy Talents were tormented with Ambition, with vain Glory, with Envy, with Emulation, how well didst thou turn thy Mind to its own Improvement in things out of the Power of Fortune; in Probity, in Integrity, in the Practice and Study of Justice; how silent thy Passage, how private thy Journey, how Glorious thy End! *Many have I known more Famous, some more knowing, not one so Innocent.*' R

No. 134.
[STEELE.]   Friday, August 3.

. . . *Opiferque per orbem*
Dicor . . .—Ovid.

DURING my Absence in the Country several Packets have been left for me, which were not forwarded to me, because I was expected every Day in Town. The Author of the following Letter dated from *Tower-hill*, having some times been entertain'd with some Learned Gentlemen in Plush Doublets, who have Vended their Wares from a Stage in that Place, has pleasantly enough addressed to Me, as no less a Sage in Morality, than those are in Physick. To comply with his kind Inclination to make my Cures famous, I shall give you his Testimonial of my great Abilities at large in his own Words.

'*Sir*,

Your saying t'other Day there is something wonderful in the Narrowness of those Minds, which can be pleas'd, and be barren of Bounty to those who please them, makes me in pain that I am not a Man of Power: If I were, you should soon see how much I approve your Speculations. In the mean time I beg leave to supply that Inability with the empty Tribute of an honest Mind, by telling you plainly I love and thank you for your daily Refreshments. I constantly peruse your Paper as I smoke my Morning's Pipe (tho' I can't forbear reading the Motto before I fill and light), and really it gives a grateful Relish to every Whif; each Paragraph is freight either with useful or delightful Notions, and I never fail of being highly diverted or improv'd. The Variety of your Subjects surprizes me as much as a Box of Pictures did formerly, in which there was only one Face, that by pulling some Pieces of Isinglass over it, was chang'd into a grave Senator or a *Merry Andrew*, a Patch'd Lady or a Nun, a Beau or a Black-a-moor, a Prude or a Coquet, a Country 'Squire or a Conjurer, with many other different Representations very entertaining (as you are) tho' still the same at the Bottom. This was a childish Amusement when I was carried away with outward Appearance, but you make a deeper Impression, and affect the secret Springs of the Mind; you charm the Fancy, sooth the Passions, and insensibly lead the Reader to that Sweetness of Temper that you so well describe; you rouse Generosity with that Spirit, and inculcate Humanity with that Ease, that he must be miserably Stupid that is not affected by you. I can't say indeed that you have put Impertinence to Silence, or Vanity out of Countenance; but methinks you have bid as fair for it, as any Man that ever appear'd upon a Publick Stage; and offer an infallible Cure of Vice and Folly, for the Price of one Penny. And since it is usual for those who receive Benefit by such famous Operators, to publish an Advertisement, that others may reap the same Advantage, I think my self obliged to declare to all the World, that having for a long time been splenatick, ill-natur'd, froward, suspicious and unsociable, by the Application of your Medicines, taken only with half an Ounce of right *Virginia* Tobacco for six successive Mornings, I am become open, obliging, officious, frank and hospitable.

I am,

Tower-hill,   *Your humble Servant,*
July 5, 1711.   *and great Admirer,*

George Trusty.'

The careful Father and humble Petitioner hereafter mentioned, who are under Difficulties about the just Management of Fans, will soon receive proper Advertisements relating to the Professors in that behalf, with their Places of Abode and Methods of Teaching.

'*Sir,*   *July the 5th,* 1711.

In your Spectator of *June* the 7th you Transcribe a Letter sent to you from a new sort of Muster-master, who teaches Ladies the whole Exercise of the Fan; I have a Daughter just come to Town, who tho' she has always held a Fan in her Hand at proper times, yet she knows no more how to use it according to true Discipline, than an awkward School-boy does to make use of his new Sword: I have sent for her on purpose to learn the Exercise, she being already very well accomplished in all other Arts which are necessary for a young Lady to understand; my Request is, that you will speak to your Correspondent on my behalf; and in your next Paper let me know what he expects, either by the Month, or the Quarter, for teaching; and where he keeps his place of Rendezvous. I have a Son too, whom I wou'd fain have taught to gallant Fans, and should be glad to know what the Gentleman will have for teaching them both, I finding Fans for Practice at my own Expence. This Information will in the highest manner oblige,

Sir,

Your Most Humble Servant,

William Wiseacre.

As soon as my Son is perfect in this Art (which I hope will be in a Year's time, for the Boy is pretty apt), I design he shall learn to ride the great Horse, (altho' he is not yet above twenty Years old) if his Mother, whose Darling he is, will venture him.'

'*To the* SPECTATOR.

The Humble Petition of Benjamin Easie, *Gent.*

Sheweth,

That it was your Petitioner's Misfortune to walk to *Hackney* Church last *Sunday*, where to his great Amazement he met with a Soldier of your own training; she furls a Fan, recovers a Fan, and goes through the whole Exercise of it to Admiration. This well-managed Officer of yours has, to my Knowledge, been the Ruin of above five young Gentlemen besides my self, and still goes on laying waste wheresoever she comes, whereby the whole Village is in great danger. Our humble Request is therefore that this bold Amazon be ordered immediately to lay down her Arms, or that you would issue forth an Order that we who have been thus Injured may meet at the Place of General Rendezvous, and there be taught to manage our Snuff-Boxes in such manner as we may be an equal Match for her:

And your Petitioner shall ever Pray, &c.'

R

No. 135.

[ADDISON.]   Saturday, August 4.

Est brevitate opus, ut currat sententia . . .—Hor.

I HAVE somewhere read of an eminent Person, who used in his
private Offices of Devotion to give Thanks to Heaven that he
was Born a *Frenchman*: For my own part I look upon it as a
peculiar Blessing that I was born an *Englishman*. Among
many other Reasons, I think my self very happy in my Country,
as the *Language* of it is wonderfully adapted to a Man who is
sparing of his Words, and an Enemy to Loquacity.

As I have frequently reflected on my good Fortune in this
Particular, I shall communicate to the Publick my Speculations upon the *English* Tongue, not doubting but they will
be acceptable to all my curious Readers.

The *English* delight in Silence more than any other *European*
Nation, if the Remarks which are made on us by Foreigners
are true. Our Discourse is not kept up in Conversation, but
falls into more Pauses and Intervals than in our Neighbouring
Countries; as it is observed, that the matter of our Writings is
thrown much closer together, and lies in a narrower Compass
than is usual in the Works of Foreign Authors: For, to favour
our Natural Taciturnity, when we are obliged to utter our
Thoughts, we do it in the shortest way we are able, and give as
quick a Birth to our Conceptions as possible.

This Humour shews it self in several Remarks that we may
make upon the *English* Language. At first of all by its
abounding in Monosyllables, which gives us an Opportunity of
delivering our Thoughts in few Sounds. This indeed takes off
from the Elegance of our Tongue, but at the same time expresses
our Ideas in the readiest manner, and consequently answers
the first Design of Speech better than the Multitude of Syllables,
which make the Words of other Languages more Tunable and
Sonorous. The Sounds of our *English* Words are commonly
like those of String Musick, short and transient, which rise and
perish upon a single Touch; those of other Languages are like
the Notes of Wind Instruments, sweet and swelling, and
lengthen'd out into variety of Modulation.

In the next place we may observe, that where the Words are
not Monosyllables, we often make them so, as much as lies
in our Power, by our Rapidity of Pronunciation; as it generally
happens in most of our long Words which are derived from the
Latin, where we contract the length of the Syllables that gives
them a grave and solemn Air, in their own Language, to make
them more proper for Dispatch, and more conformable to the

Genius of our Tongue. This we may find in a Multitude of Words, as *Liberty, Conspiracy, Theatre, Orator,* &c.

The same natural Aversion to Loquacity has of late Years made a very considerable Alteration in our Language, by closing in one Syllable the Termination of our Praeterperfect Tense, as in these Words, *drown'd, walk'd, arriv'd,* for *drowned, walked, arrived,* which has very much disfigured the Tongue, and turned a tenth part of our smoothest Words into so many Clusters of Consonants. This is the more remarkable, because the want of Vowels in our Language has been the general Complaint of our politest Authors, who nevertheless are the Men that have made these Retrenchments, and consequently very much increased our former Scarcity.

This Reflection on the Words that end in *ed,* I have heard in Conversation from one of the greatest Genius's this Age has produced. I think we may add to the foregoing Observation, the Change which has happened in our Language, by the Abbreviation of several words that are terminated in *eth,* by substituting an *s* in the room of the last Syllable, as in *drowns, walks, arrives,* and innumerable other Words, which, in the Pronunciation of our Fore-fathers were *drowneth, walketh, arriveth.* This has wonderfully multiplied a Letter which was before too frequent in the *English* Tongue, and added to that *hissing* in our Language, which is taken so much notice of by Foreigners; but at the same time humours our Taciturnity, and eases us of many superfluous Syllables.

I might here observe, that the same single Letter on many occasions does the Office of a whole Word, and represents the *His* and *Her* of our Forefathers. There is no doubt but the Ear of a Foreigner, which is the best Judge in this Case, would very much disapprove of such Innovations, which indeed we do our selves in some measure, by retaining the old Termination in Writing, and in all the Solemn Offices of our Religion.

As in the Instances I have given we have epitomized many of our particular Words to the Detriment of our Tongue, so on other Occasions we have drawn two Words into one, which has likewise very much untuned our Language, and clogged it with Consonants, as *mayn't, can't, sha'n't, wo'n't,* and the like, for *may not, can not, shall not, will not,* &c.

It is perhaps this Humour of speaking no more than we needs must, which has so miserably curtailed some of our Words, that in familiar Writings and Conversations, they often lose all but their first Syllables, as in *mob. rep. pos. incog.* and the like; and as all ridiculous Words make their first Entry into a Language by familiar Phrases, I dare not answer for these that they will not in time be looked upon as a part of our Tongue.

We see some of our Poets have been so indiscreet as to imitate *Hudibras*'s Doggrel Expressions in their serious Compositions, by throwing out the Signs of our Substantives, which are essential to the *English* Language. Nay, this Humour of shortning our Language had once run so far, that some of our celebrated Authors, among whom we may reckon Sir *Roger L' Estrange* in particular, began to prune their Words of all superfluous Letters, as they termed them, in order to adjust the Spelling to the Pronunciation; which would have confounded all our Etymologies, and have quite destroyed our Tongue.

We may here likewise observe, that our Proper Names, when familiarized in *English*, generally dwindle to Monosyllables, whereas in other Modern Languages they receive a softer Turn on this occasion, by the Addition of a new Syllable. *Nick* in *Italian* is *Nicolini, Jack* in *French Janot;* and so of the rest.

There is another Particular in our Language which is a great Instance of our Frugality of Words, and that is the suppressing of several Particles, which must be produced in other Tongues to make a Sentence intelligible: This often perplexes the best Writers, when they find the Relatives *whom, which,* or *they,* at their Mercy whether they may have Admission or not; and will never be decided till we have something like an Academy, that by the best Authorities and Rules drawn from the Analogy of Languages shall settle all Controversies between Grammar and Idiom.

I have only considered our Language as it shews the Genius and natural Temper of the *English,* which is modest, thoughtful and sincere, and which perhaps may recommend the People, though it has spoiled the Tongue. We might perhaps carry the same Thought into other Languages, and deduce a great part of what is peculiar to them from the Genius of the People who speak them. It is certain the light talkative Humour of the *French* has not a little infected their Tongue, which might be shewn by many Instances; as the Genius of the *Italians,* which is so much addicted to Musick and Ceremony, has moulded all their Words and Phrases to those particular Uses. The Stateliness and Gravity of the *Spaniards* shews itself to Perfection in the Solemnity of their Language; and the blunt honest Humour of the *Germans* sounds better in the Roughness of the *High Dutch,* than it would in a politer Tongue. C

No. 136.

[STEELE.]   Monday, August 6.

> . . . *Parthis mendacior* . . .—Hor.

ACCORDING to the Request of this strange Fellow, I shall print the following Letter.

'*Mr.* SPECTATOR,

I shall without any manner of Preface or Apology acquaint you, that I am, and ever have been from my Youth upward, one of the greatest Liars this Island has produced. I have read all the Moralists upon the Subject, but could never find any effect their Discourses had upon me, but to add to my Misfortune by new Thoughts and Ideas, and making me more ready in my Language, and capable of sometimes mixing seeming Truths with my Improbabilities. With this strong Passion towards Falshood in this kind, there does not live an honester man or a sincerer Friend; but my Imagination runs away with me, and whatever is started I have such a Scene of Adventures appears in an instant before me, that I cannot help uttering them, tho' to my immediate Confusion I cannot but know I am liable to be detected by the first Man I meet.

Upon occasion of the mention of the Battle of *Pultowa*, I could not forbear giving an Account of a Kinsman of mine, a young Merchant who was bred at *Mosco*, that had too much Metal to attend Books of Entries and Accounts, when there was so active a Scene in the Country where he resided, and followed the Czar as a Volunteer: This warm Youth, born at the Instant the thing was spoke of, was the Man who unhorsed the *Swedish* General, he was the Occasion that the *Moscovites* kept their Fire in so Soldier-like a manner, and brought up those Troops which were cover'd from the Enemy at the beginning of the Day; besides this, he had at last the good Fortune to be the Man who took Count *Piper*. With all this Fire I knew my Cousin to be the Civilest Creature in the World. He never made any impertinent Show of his Valour, and then he had an excellent Genius for the World in every other kind. I had Letters from him (here I felt in my Pockets) that exactly spoke the Czar's Character, which I knew perfectly well; and I could not forbear concluding, that I lay with his Imperial Majesty twice or thrice a Week all the while he lodged at *Deptford*. What is worse than all this, it is impossible to speak to me, but you give me some occasion of coming out with one Lie or other, that has neither Wit, Humour, prospect of Interest, or any other Motive that I can think of in Nature.

The other Day, when one was commending an Eminent and
Learned Divine, what occasion in the World had I to say, Methinks he would look more Venerable if he were not so fair a
Man? I remember the Company smiled. I have seen the
Gentleman since, and he is Cole Black. I have Intimations
every Day in my Life that no Body believes me, yet I am
never the better. I was saying something the other Day to an
old Friend at *Will's* Coffee-house, and he made me no manner
of Answer; but told me, that an Acquaintance of *Tully* the
Orator having two or three times together said to him, without
receiving any Answer, That upon his Honour he was but that
very Month forty years of Age; *Tully* answer'd, Surely you
think me the most incredulous Man in the World, if I don't
believe what you have told me every Day this ten Years. The
Mischief of it is, I find my self wonderfully inclin'd to have been
present at every Occurrence that is spoken of before me; this
has led me into many Inconveniencies, but indeed they have
been the fewer, because I am no ill-natur'd Man, and never
speak things to any Man's Disadvantage. I never directly
defame, but I do what is as bad in the Consequence, for I have
often made a Man say such and such a lively Expression, who
was born a mere Elder Brother. When one has said in my
hearing, Such a one is no wiser than he should be, I immediately have reply'd, Now 'faith I can't see that, he said a very
good thing to my Lord such a one upon such an occasion, and
the like. Such an honest Dolt as this has been watch'd in
every Expression he utter'd, upon my Recommendation of
him, and consequently been subject to the more Ridicule.
I once endeavour'd to Cure my self of this impertinent Quality,
and resolv'd to hold my Tongue for seven Days together; I
did so, but then I had so many Winks and unnecessary Distortions of my Face upon what any body else said, that I
found I only forebore the Expression, and that I still lied in
my Heart to every Man I met with. You are to know one
thing (which I believe you 'll say is a Pity considering the use
I should have made of it) I never Travell'd in my Life; but I
do not know whether I could have spoken of any Foreign
Country with more familiarity than I do at present, in Company
who are Strangers to me. I have cursed the Inns in *Germany*;
commended the Brothels at *Venice*; the Freedom of Conversation in *France*; and tho' I never was out of this dear Town, and
fifty Miles about it, have been three Nights together dogged by
Bravoes for an Intreague with a Cardinal's Mistress at *Rome*.

It were endless to give you Particulars of this kind, but I
can assure you, Mr. SPECTATOR, there are about Twenty or
Thirty of us in this Town, I mean by this Town the cities of

London and *Westminster*; I say there are in Town a sufficient Number of us to make a Society among our selves; and since we cannot be believed any longer, I beg of you to print this my Letter, that we may meet together, and be under such Regulation as there may be no Occasion for Belief or Confidence among us. If you think fit, we might be called *The Historians*, for *Liar* is become a very harsh Word. And that a Member of the Society may not hereafter be ill received by the rest of the World, I desire you would explain a little this sort of Men, and let not us *Historians* be ranked, as we are in the Imaginations of ordinary People, among common Liars, Make-bates, Impostors, and Incendiaries. For your Instruction herein, you are to know that an *Historian*, in Conversation, is only a Person of so pregnant a Fancy that he cannot be contented with ordinary Occurrences. I know a Man of Quality of our Order, who is of the wrong side of Forty three, and has been of that Age, according to *Tully*'s Jest, for some Years since, whose Vein is upon the Romantick. Give him the least Occasion, and he will tell you something so very particular that happened in such a Year and in such Company, where by the by was present such a one, who was afterwards made such a thing. Out of all these Circumstances, in the best Language in the World, he will join together with such probable Incidents an Account that shews a Person of the deepest Penetration, the honestest Mind, and withal something so Humble when he speaks of himself, that you would Admire. Dear Sir, why should this be Lying? There is nothing so instructive. He has withal the gravest Aspect; something so very venerable and great! Another of these Historians is a young Man whom we would take in, tho' he extreamly wants Parts; as People send Children (before they can learn any thing) to School, to keep them out of Harm's way. He tells things which have nothing at all in them, and can neither please nor displease, but merely take up your Time to no manner of Purpose, no manner of Delight; but he is Good-natured, and does it because he loves to be saying something to you, and entertain you.

I could name you a Soldier that hath done very great things without Slaughter; he is prodigiously dull and slow of Head, but what he can say is for ever false, so that we must have him.

Give me leave to tell you of one more who is a Lover; he is the most afflicted Creature in the World lest what happened between him and a Great Beauty should ever be known. Yet again, he comforts himself. *Hang the Jade her Woman. If Mony can keep Slut trusty I will do it, tho' I mortgage every Acre;* Anthony *and* Cleopatra *for that: All for Love, and the World well lost.* . . .

Then, Sir, there is my little Merchant, honest *Indigo* of the *Change*, there 's my Man for Loss and Gain, there 's Tare and Tret, there 's lying all round the Globe; he has such a prodigious Intelligence he knows all the *French* are doing, and what we intend or ought to intend, and has it from such hands. But alas whither am I running! While I complain, while I remonstrate to you, even all this is a Lie, and there is not one such Person of Quality, Lover, Soldier, or Merchant, as I have now described in the whole World that I know of. But I will catch my self once in my Life, and in spite of Nature speak one Truth, to wit that I am

Your Humble Servant, &c.'

T

No. 137.
[STEELE.]   Tuesday, August 7.

At haec etiam servis semper libera fuerunt, timerent, gauderent, dolerent, suo potius quam alterius arbitrio.—Tull. *Epist.*

It is no small Concern to me, that I find so many Complaints from that Part of Mankind whose Portion it is to live in Servitude, that those whom they depend upon will not allow them to be even as happy as their Condition will admit of. There are, as these unhappy Correspondents inform me, Masters who are offended at a chearful Countenance, and think a Servant is broke loose from them, if he does not preserve the utmost Awe in their Presence. There is one who says, if he looks satisfied, his Master asks him what makes him so pert this Morning; if a little sower, Hark ye, Sirrah, are not you paid your Wages? The poor Creatures live in the most extreme Misery together: The Master knows not how to preserve Respect, nor the Servant how to give it. It seems this Person is of so sullen a Nature, that he knows but little Satisfaction in the Midst of a plentiful Fortune, and secretly frets to see any Appearance of Content in one that lives upon the hundredth Part of his Income, who is unhappy in the Possession of the Whole. Uneasy Persons, who cannot possess their own Minds, vent their Spleen upon all who depend upon them; which, I think, is expressed in a lively manner in the following Letters.

'*Sir*,   *August 2, 1711.*

I have read your *Spectator* of the 3d of the last Month, and wish I had the Happiness of being preferred to serve so good a Master as Sir ROGER. The Character of my Master is the very

Reverse of that good and gentle Knight's. All his Directions
are given, and his Mind revealed by way of Contraries: As when
any thing is to be remembered, with a peculiar Cast of Face he
cries, *Be sure to forget now.* If I am to make Haste back,
*Don't come these two Hours; be sure to call by the Way upon some
of your Companions.* Then another excellent Way of his is,
if he sets me any thing to do, which he knows must necessarily
take up Half a Day, he calls ten times in a Quarter of an Hour
to know whether I have done yet. This is his Manner, and the
same Perverseness runs through all his Actions, according as the
Circumstances vary. Besides all this, he is so suspicious, that
he submits himself to the Drudgery of a Spy. He is as unhappy himself as he makes his Servants: He is constantly
watching us, and we differ no more in Pleasure and Liberty
than as a Gaoler and a Prisoner. He lays Traps for Faults, and
no sooner makes a Discovery, but falls into such Language, as
I am more ashamed of for coming from him, than for being
directed to me. This, Sir, is a short Sketch of a Master I have
served upwards of nine Years; and tho' I have never wronged
him, I confess my Despair of pleasing him has very much
abated my Endeavour to do it. If you will give me Leave
to steal a Sentence out of my Master's *Clarendon,* I shall
tell you my Case in a Word, *Being used worse than I deserved,
I cared less to deserve well than I had done.*

I am,

Sir,

Your humble Servant,

RALPH VALET.'

'*Dear Mr.* SPECTER,

I am the next Thing to a Lady's Woman, and am under both
my Lady and her Woman. I am so used by them both, that
I should be very glad to see them in the SPECTER. My Lady
her self is of no Mind in the World, and for that Reason her
Woman is of twenty Minds in a Moment. My Lady is one that
never knows what to do with her self; she pulls on and puts
off every thing she wears twenty times before she resolves
upon it for that Day. I stand at one End of the Room, and
reach things to her Woman. When my Lady asks for a thing,
I hear and have half brought it, when the Woman meets me
in the Middle of the Room to receive it, and at that Instant she
says No she will not have it. Then I go back, and her Woman
comes up to her, and by this Time she will have that, and two
or three things more in an Instant: The Woman and I run to
each other; I am loaded and delivering the things to her when
my Lady says she wants none of all these things, and we are

the dullest Creatures in the World, and she the unhappiest Woman living, for she shan't be dress'd in any time.   Thus we stand not knowing what to do, when our good Lady with all the Patience in the World tells us as plain as she can speak, that she will have Temper because we have no manner of Understanding, and begins again to dress, and see if we can find out of our selves what we are to do.   When she is Dressed she goes to Dinner, and after she has disliked every thing there, she calls for the Coach, then commands it in again, and then she will not go out at all, and then will go too, and orders the Chariot. Now good Mr. SPECTER, I desire you would, in the Behalf of all who serve froward Ladies, give out in your Paper, that nothing can be done without allowing Time for it, and that one cannot be back again with what one was sent for if one is called back before one can go a Step for that they want.   And if you please let them know that all Mistresses are as like as all Servants.

I am

Your loving Friend,

PATIENCE GIDDY.'

These are great Calamities; but I met the other Day in the five Fields towards *Chelsea*, a pleasanter Tyrant than either of the above represented.   A fat Fellow was puffing on in his open Wastcoat; a Boy of fourteen in a Livery carrying after him his Cloak, upper Coat, Hat, Wig, and Sword.   The poor Lad was ready to sink with the Weight, and could not keep up with his Master, who turned back every half Furlong, and wondered what made the lazy young Dog lag behind.

There is something very unaccountable, that People cannot put themselves in the Condition of the Persons below them when they consider the Commands they give.   But there is nothing more common, than to see a Fellow (who, if he were reduced to it, would not be hired by any Man living) lament that he is troubled with the most worthless Dogs in Nature.

It would, perhaps, be running too far out of common Life to urge, that he who is not Master of himself and his own Passions, cannot be a proper Master of another.   Aequanimity in a Man's own Words and Actions, will easily diffuse it self through his whole Family.   *Pamphilio* has the happiest Household of any Man I know, and that proceeds from the human Regard he has to them in their private Persons, as well as in respect that they are his Servants.   If there be any Occasion, wherein they may in themselves be supposed to be unfit to attend their Master's Concerns, by reason of any Attention to their own, he is so good as to place himself in their Condition. thought it very becoming in him, when at Dinner the other

Day he made an Apology for want of more Attendants. He said, *One of my Footmen is gone to the Wedding of his Sister, and the other I don't expect to Wait, because his Father died but two Days ago.* T

No. 138.

[STEELE.] Wednesday, August 8.

Utitur in re non dubia testibus non necessariis.—Tull.

ONE meets now and then with Persons who are extreamly learned and knotty in Expounding clear Cases. *Tully* tells us of an Author that spent some Pages to prove that Generals could not perform the Great Enterprizes which have made them so Illustrious, if they had not had Men. He asserted also, it seems, that a Minister at home, no more than a Commander abroad, could do any thing without other Men were his Instruments and Assistants. On this Occasion he produces the Example of *Themistocles, Pericles, Cyrus,* and *Alexander* himself, whom he denies to have been capable of effecting what they did, except they had been followed by others. It is pleasant enough to see such Persons contend without Opponents, and triumph without Victory.

The Author above-mention'd by the Orator, is placed for ever in a very ridiculous Light, and we meet every Day in Conversation such as deserve the same kind of Renown for troubling those with whom they Converse with the like Certainties. The Persons that I have always thought to deserve the highest Admiration in this kind are your ordinary Story-tellers, who are most religiously careful of keeping to the Truth in every particular Circumstance of a Narration, whether it concern the main end, or not. A Gentleman whom I had the Honour to be in Company with the other Day, upon some Occasion that he was pleas'd to take, said, He remember'd a very pretty Repartee made by a very Witty Man in King *Charles*'s time upon the like Occasion. I remember (said he, upon entring into the Tale) much about the time of *Oates*'s Plot, that a Cousin-German of mine and I were at the *Bear* in *Holborn*: No, I am out, it was at the *Cross Keys*; but *Jack Thomson* was there, for he was very great with the Gentleman who made the Answer. But I am sure it was spoken somewhere thereabouts, for we drank a Bottle in that Neighbourhood every Evening. But no matter for all that, the thing is the same; but——

He was going on to settle the Geography of the Jest when I left the Room, wondering at this odd turn of Head which can play away its Words, with uttering nothing to the purpose, still observing its own Impertinences, and yet proceeding in them. I do not question but he inform'd the rest of his Audience, who had more Patience than I, of the Birth and Parentage, as well as the Collateral Alliances of his Family, who made the Repartee, and of him who provoked him to it.

It is no small Misfortune to any who have a just value for their Time, when this Quality of being so very Circumstantial, and careful to be exact, happens to shew it self in a Man whose Quality obliges them to attend his Proofs, that it is now Day, and the like. But this is augmented when the same Genius gets into Authority, as it often does. Nay, I have known it more than once ascend the very Pulpit. One of this sort taking it in his Head to be a great Admirer of Dr. *Tillotson* and Dr. *Beveridge*, never fail'd of proving out of these great Authors things which no Men living would have denied him upon his own single Authority. One Day resolving to come to the Point in hand, he said, According to that excellent Divine, I will enter upon the Matter, or in his Words in his fifteenth Sermon of the Folio Edition, Page 160,

I shall briefly explain the Words, and then consider the Matter contained in them.

This honest Gentleman needed not, one would think, strain his Modesty so far as to alter his design of *Entring upon the Matter*, to that of *Briefly explaining*. But so it was, that he would not even be contented with that Authority, but added also the other Divine to strengthen his Method, and told us, With the Pious and Learned Dr. *Beveridge*, Page 4th of his 9th Volume, *I shall endeavour to make it as plain as I can from the Words which I have now read, wherein for that Purpose we shall consider——* This Wiseacre was reckoned by the Parish, who did not understand him, a most Excellent Preacher, but that he read too much, and was so Humble that he did not trust enough to his own Parts.

Next to these ingenious Gentlemen, who argue for what no body can deny them, are to be ranked a sort of People who do not indeed attempt to prove insignificant things, but are ever labouring to raise Arguments with you about Matters you will give up to them without the least Controversy. One of these People told a Gentleman who said he saw Mr. such a one go his Morning at nine a Clock towards the *Gravel-Pits*, Sir, I must beg your Pardon for that, for tho' I am very loath to have any Dispute with you, yet I must take the Liberty to tell you it was nine when I saw him at St. *James's*. When Men of this Genius are pretty far gone in Learning they will put you to prove that Snow is White, and when you are upon that Topick can say that there is really no such thing as Colour in Nature; in a Word, they can turn what little Knowledge they have, into a ready Capacity of raising Doubts; into a Capacity of being always frivolous and always unanswerable. It was of two Disputants of this impertinent and laborious kind that the Cynick said, *One of these Fellows is Milking a Ram, and the other holds the Pail.*

ADVERTISEMENT.

The Exercise of the Snuff-Box, according to the most fashionable Airs and Motions, in opposition to the Exercise of the Fan, will be Taught with the best plain or perfum'd Snuff, at Charles Lillie's, *Perfumer, at the Corner of* Bauford-Buildings *in the* Strand, *and Attendance given for the benefit of the young Merchants about the Exchange for two Hours every Day at Noon, except* Saturdays, *at a Toy-Shop near* Garraway's *Coffee-house. There will be likewise Taught* The Ceremony of the Snuff-box, *or Rules for offering Snuff to a Stranger, a Friend, or a Mistress, according to the Degrees of Familiarity or Distance; with an Explanation of the Careless, the Scornful, the Politick, and the Surly Pinch, and the Gestures proper to each of them.*

N. B. The Undertaker does not question but in a short time to have form'd a Body of Regular Snuff-Boxes ready to meet and make Head against all the Regiment of Fans which have been lately Disciplin'd, and are now in Motion. T

No. 139.

[STEELE.] Thursday, August 9.

Vera gloria radices agit, atque etiam propagatur. Ficta omnia celeriter, tanquam flosculi, decidunt, nec simulatum potest quid quam esse diuturnum.—Tull.

OF all the Affections which attend Human Life, the Love o Glory is the most Ardent. According as this is Cultivated in Princes, it produces the greatest Good or the greatest Evi Where Sovereigns have it by Impressions received from Educa tion only, it creates an Ambitious rather than a Noble Mind where it is the natural Bent of the Prince's Inclination, i prompts him to the Pursuit of Things truly Glorious. The tw greatest Men now in *Europe* (according to the common accepta tion of the Word *Great*) are *Lewis* King of *France,* and *Peter* Emperor of *Russia.* As it is certain that all Fame does not arise from the Practice of Virtue, it is, methinks, no unpleasing Amusement to examine the Glory of these Potentates, and distinguish that which is empty, perishing and frivolous, from what is solid, lasting and important. *Lewis* of *France* had his Infancy attended by Crafty and Worldly Men, who made Extent of Territory the most glorious Instances of Power, and mistook the spreading of Fame for the Acquisition of Honour. The young Monarch's Heart was by such Conversation easily deluded into a fondness for Vain glory, and upon these unjust Principles to form or fall in with suitable Projects of Invasion, Rapine, Murder, and all the Guilts that attend War when it is unjust. At the same time this Tyranny was laid, Sciences and Arts were encouraged in the most generous Manner, as if Men of higher Faculties were to be bribed to permit the Massacre of the rest of the World. Every Superstructure which the Court of *France* built upon their first Designs, which were in themselves Vicious, was suitable to its false Foundation. The Ostentation of Riches, the Vanity of Equipage, Shame of Poverty, and Ignorance of Modesty, were the common Arts of Life. The Generous Love of one Woman was changed into Gallantry for all the Sex, and Friendships among Men turned into Commerces of Interest, or mere Professions. *While these were the Rules of Life, Perjuries in the Prince, and a general Corruption of Manners in the Subject, were the Snares in which* France *has Entangled all her Neighbours.* With such false Colours have the Eyes of *Lewis* been Enchanted from the Debauchery of his early Youth, to the Superstition of his present old Age. Hence it is, that he has the Patience to have Statues erected to his Prowess, his Valour, his Fortitude; and in the Softnesses and Luxury of a Court, to be applauded for Magnanimity and Enterprize in Military Atchievements.

Peter Alexovitz of *Russia,* when he came to Years of Manhood, though he found himself Emperor of a vast and numerous People, Master of an endless Territory, absolute Commander of the Lives and Fortunes of his Subjects, in the midst of this unbounded Power and Greatness turned his Thoughts on Himself and People with Sorrow. Sordid Ignorance and a Brute Manner of Life this Generous Prince beheld, and Condemned from the Light of his own *Genius.* His Judgment suggested this to him, and his Courage prompted him to amend it. In order to this he did not send to the Nation from whence the rest of the World has borrowed its Politeness, but himself left his Diadem to learn the true Way to Glory and Honour, and Application to useful Arts, wherein to employ the Laborious, the Simple, the Honest part of his People. Mechanick Employments and Operations were very justly the first Objects of his Favour and Observation. With this glorious Intention he travelled into Foreign Nations in an obscure Manner, above receiving little Honours where he sojourned, but prying into what was of more Consequence, their Arts of Peace and of War. By this means has this great Prince laid the Foundation of a great and lasting Fame, by personal Labour, personal Knowledge, personal Valour. It would be Injury to any of Antiquity to Name them with him. Who, but himself, ever left a Throne to learn to sit in it with more Grace? Who ever thought himself mean in Absolute Power, 'till he had learned to use it?

If we consider this wonderful Person, it is Perplexity to know where to begin his Encomium. Others may in a Metaphorical or Philosophick Sense be said to command themselves, but this Emperor is also literally under his own Command. How Generous and how Good was his entring his own Name as a Private Man in the Army he raised, that none in it might expect to out-run the Steps with which he himself advanced? By such Measures this god-like Prince learned to Conquer, learned to use his Conquests. How Terrible has he appeared in Battle, how gentle in Victory? Shall then the base Arts of the *Frenchman* be held Polite, and the honest Labours of the *Russian,* Barbarous? No: Barbarity is the Ignorance of true Honour, or placing any thing instead of it. The unjust Prince is Ignoble and Barbarous, the Good Prince only Renowned and Glorious.

Tho' men may impose upon themselves what they please by their corrupt Imaginations, Truth will ever keep its Station: and as Glory is nothing else but the Shadow of Virtue, it will certainly disappear at the Departure of Virtue. But how carefully ought the true Notions of it to be preserved, and how industrious should we be to encourage any Impulses towards it? The *Westminster* School-boy that said the other Day he could not sleep or play for the Colours in the Hall, ought to be free from receiving a Blow for ever.

But let us consider what is truly Glorious, according to the Author I have to Day quoted in the Front of my Paper.

The Perfection of Glory, says *Tully,* consists in these three Particulars: *That the People love us; that they have Confidence in us; that being affected with a certain Admiration towards us, they think we deserve Honour.* This was spoken of Greatness in a Commonwealth: But if one were to form a Notion of Consummate Glory under our Constitution, one must add to the above-mentioned Felicities a certain necessary Inexistence, and

Disrelish of all the rest, without the Prince's Favour. He should, methinks, have Riches, Power, Honour, Command, Glory; but Riches, Power, Honour, Command and Glory should have no Charms, but as accompanied with the Affection of his Prince. He should, methinks, be Popular because a Favourite, and a Favourite because Popular. Were it not to make the Character too imaginary, I would give him Sovereignty over some Foreign Territory, and make him esteem that an empty Addition without the kind Regards of his own Prince. One may merely have an *Idea* of a Man thus composed and circumstantiated, and if he were so made for Power without an Incapacity of giving Jealousy, he would be also Glorious without Possibility of receiving Disgrace. This Humility and this Importance must make his Glory immortal.

These Thoughts are apt to draw me beyond the usual Length of this Paper, but if I could suppose such Rhapsodies could out-live the common Fate of ordinary things, I would say these Sketches and faint Images of Glory were drawn in *August* 1711, when *John* Duke of *Marlborough* made that memorable March wherein he took the *French* Lines without Blood-shed. T

No. 140.

[STEELE.] Friday, August 10.

. . Animum nunc huc celerem nunc dividit illuc.—Virg.

WHEN I acquaint my Reader that I have many other Letters not yet acknowledged, I believe he will own, what I have a mind he should believe, that I have no small Charge upon me, but am a Person of some Consequence in this World. I shall therefore employ the present Hour only in reading Petitions, in the Order as follows.

'*Mr.* SPECTATOR,

I have lost so much Time already, that I desire, upon the Receipt hereof, you would sit down immediately and give me your Answer. I would know of you whether a Pretender of mine really loves me. As well as I can I will describe his Manners. When he sees me he is always talking of Constancy, but vouchsafes to visit me but once a Fortnight, and then is always in haste to be gone. When I am sick, I hear, he says he is mightily concerned, but neither comes nor sends, because, as he tells his Acquaintance with a Sigh, he does not care to let me know all the Power I have over him, and how impossible it is for him to live without me. When he leaves the Town he writes once in six Weeks, desires to hear from me, complains of the Torment of Absence, speaks of Flames, Tortures, Languishings and Extasies. He has the Cant of an impatient Lover, but keeps the Pace of a Lukewarm one. You know I must not go faster than he does, and to move at this rate is as tedious as counting a great Clock. But you are to know he is rich, and my Mother says, As he is slow he is sure; He will love me long, if he love me little: But I appeal to you whether he loves at all

Your Neglected

Humble Servant,

Lydia Novell.

All these Fellows who have Mony are extreamly sawcy and cold; Pray Sir, tell them of it.'

'*Mr.* SPECTATOR,

I have been delighted with nothing more through the whole Course of your Writings than the substantial Account you lately gave of Wit, and I could wish you would take some other Opportunity to express further the Corrupt Taste the Age is run into; which I am chiefly apt to attribute to the Prevalency of a few popular Authors, whose Merit in some respects has given a Sanction to their Faults in others. Thus the Imitators of *Milton* seem to place all the Excellency of that sort of Writing either in the uncouth or antique Words, or something else which was highly vicious, tho' pardonable, in that Great Man. The Admirers of what we call Point, or Turn, look upon it as the peculiar Happiness to which *Cowley, Ovid* and others owe their Reputation, and therefore endeavour to imitate them only in such Instances; what is Just, Proper and Natural does not seem to be the Question with them, but by what Means a quaint Antithesis may be brought about, how one Word may be made to look two ways, and what will be the Consequence of a forced Allusion. Now tho' such Authors appear to me to resemble those who make them selves fine, instead of being well dressed or graceful; yet the Mischief is that these Beauties in them, which I call Blemishes, are thought to proceed from Luxuriance of Fancy, and overflowing of good Sense: In one Word, they have the Character of being too Witty; but if you would acquaint the World they are not Witty at all, you would among many others, oblige,

Sir,

Your Most Benevolent Reader,

R. D.'

'*Sir,*

I am a young Woman, and reckoned Pretty, therefore you 'll
pardon me that I trouble you to decide a Wager between me
and a Cousin of mine, who is always contradicting one because
he understands *Latin*   Pray, Sir, is Dimple spelt with a single
or a double P?

I am, Sir,

Your very Humble Servant,

Betty Saunter.

Pray Sir *direct thus,* To the kind Querist, *and leave it at Mr.*
Lillie*'s, for I don't care to be known in the thing at all.*

I am, Sir, again Your Humble Servant.'

'*Mr.* SPECTATOR,

I must needs tell you there are several of your Papers I do
not much like. You are often so Nice there is no enduring
you, and so Learned there is no understanding you. What
have you to do with our Petticoats?

Your Humble Servant,

Parthenope.'

'*Mr.* SPECTATOR,

Last Night as I was walking in the Park I met a Couple of
Friends: Prithee *Jack,* says one of them, let us go drink a
Glass of Wine, for I am fit for nothing else. This put me upon
reflecting on the many Miscarriages which happen in Con-
versations over Wine, when Men go to the Bottle to remove
such Humours as it only stirs up and awakens. This I could
not attribute more to any thing than to the Humour of putting
Company upon others which Men do not like themselves.
Pray, Sir, declare in your Papers, that he who is a troublesome
Companion to himself, will not be an agreeable one to others.
Let People reason themselves into good Humour, before they
impose themselves upon their Friends. Pray, Sir, be as
Eloquent as you can upon this Subject, and do Humane Life
so much good, as to argue powerfully, that it is not every one
that can swallow who is fit to drink a Glass of Wine.

Your most humble Servant.'

'*Sir,*

I this Morning cast my Eye upon your Paper concerning the
Expence of Time. You are very obliging to the Women,
especially those who are not Young and past Gallantry, by
touching so gently upon Gaming: Therefore I hope you do not
think it wrong to employ a little leisure time in that Diversion:

but I should be glad to hear you say something upon the Behaviour of some of the Female Gamesters.

I have observed Ladies who in all other respects are gentle, Good-humoured, and the very Pinks of good Breeding; who as soon as the Ombre Table is called for, and set down to their Business, are immediately Transmigrated into the veriest Wasps in Nature.

You must know I keep my Temper and win their Money; but am out of Countenance to take it, it makes them so very uneasie. Be pleased, dear Sir, to instruct them to lose with a better Grace and you will oblige

Yours,

Rachel Basto.'

'*Mr.* Spectator,

Your Kindness to *Eleonora,* in one of your Papers, has given me Encouragement to do my self the Honour of Writing to you. The great Regard you have so often expressed for the Instruction and Improvement of our Sex, will, I hope, in your own Opinion sufficiently excuse me from making any Apology for the Impertinence of this Letter. The great desire I have to Embellish my Mind with some of those Graces which you say are so becoming, and which you assert Reading helps us to, has made me uneasie 'till I am put in a Capacity of attaining them: This, Sir, I shall never think my self in, 'till you shall be pleased to recommend some Author or Authors to my Perusal.

I thought indeed, when I first cast my Eye on *Eleonora's* Letter, that I should have had no occasion for requesting it of you; but, to my very great Concern, I found, on the Perusal of that *Spectator,* I was entirely disappointed, and am as much at a loss how to make use of my Time for that end as ever. Pray, Sir, oblige me at least with one Scene, as you were pleased to entertain *Eleonora* with your Prologue. I write to you not only my own Sentiments, but also those of several others of my Acquaintance, who are as little pleased with the ordinary manner of spending one's Time as my self: And if a fervent Desire after Knowledge, and a great Sense of our present Ignorance, may be thought a good presage and earnest of Improvement, you may look upon your Time you shall bestow in answering this Request not thrown away to no purpose. And I can't but add, that unless you have a particular and more than ordinary Regard for *Eleonora,* I have a better Title to your Favour than she; since I do not content my self with Tea-Table Reading of your Papers, but it is my Entertainment very often when alone in my Closet. To shew you I am capable of Improvement and hate Flattery, I acknowledge I do not like some of your Papers; but even there I am readier

to call in question my own shallow Understanding, than Mr.
Spectator's profound Judgment.

> *I am, Sir, your already (and in hopes*
> *of being more your) obliged Servant,*

> PARTHENIA.'

This last Letter is written with so urgent and serious an Air,
that I cannot but think it incumbent upon me to comply with
her Commands, which I shall do very suddenly.   T

No. 141.

[STEELE.]   Saturday, August 11.

> . . . *Migravit ab aure voluptas*
> *Omnis* . . .—Hor.

In the present Emptiness of the Town, I have several Applications from the lower Parts of the Players, to admit Suffering to
pass for Acting. They in very obliging Terms desire me to let
a Fall on the Ground, a Stumble, or a good Slap on the Back,
be reckoned a Jest. These Gambols I shall tolerate for a
Season, because I hope the Evil cannot continue longer than
till the People of Condition and Taste return to Town. The
Method, some time ago, was to entertain that Part of the
Audience who have no Faculty above Eyesight, with Rope-
Dancers and Tumblers; which was a way discreet enough, because it prevented Confusion, and distinguished such as could
show all the Postures which the Body is capable of, from those
who were to represent all the Passions to which the Mind is
subject. But tho' this was prudently settled, Corporeal and
Intellectual Actors ought to be kept at a still wider Distance
than to appear on the same Stage at all: For which Reason I
must propose some Methods for the Improvement of the Bear-
Garden, by dismissing all Bodily Actors to that Quarter.

In Cases of greater Moment, where Men appear in Publick,
the Consequence and Importance of the thing can bear them
out. And tho' a Pleader or Preacher is Hoarse or Awkward,
the weight of their Matter commands Respect and Attention;
but in Theatrical Speaking, if the Performer is not exactly
proper and graceful, he is utterly ridiculous. In Cases where
there is little else expected, but the Pleasure of the Ears and
Eyes, the least Diminution of that Pleasure is the highest
Offence. In Acting, barely to perform the Part is not commendable, but to be the least out is contemptible. To avoid
these Difficulties and Delicacies, I am informed, that while I
was out of Town the Actors have flown in the Air, and play'd

such Pranks, and run such Hazards, that none but the Servants of the Fire-Office, Tilers and Masons, could have been able to perform the like. The Author of the following Letter, it seems, has been of the Audience at one of these Entertainments, and has accordingly complained to me upon it; but I think he has been to the utmost degree Severe against what is exceptionable in the Play he mentions, without dwelling so much as he might have done on the Author's most excellent Talent of Humour. The pleasant Pictures he has drawn of Life, should have been more kindly mentioned, at the same time that he banishes his Witches, who are too dull Devils to be attacked with so much Warmth.

'Mr. SPECTATOR,

Upon a Report that *Moll White* had follow'd you to Town, and was to act a Part in the *Lancashire Witches*, I went last Week to see that Play. It was my Fortune to sit next to a Country Justice of the Peace, a Neighbour (as he said) of Sir ROGER'S, who pretended to shew her to us in one of the Dances. There was Witchcraft enough in the Entertainment almost to incline me to believe him; *Ben. Johnson* was almost lamed; young *Bullock* narrowly saved his Neck; the Audience was astonish'd, and an old Acquaintance of mine, a Person of Worth, whom I wou'd have bow'd to in the Pit, at two Yards distance did not know me.

If you were what the Country People reported you, a white Witch, I cou'd have wish'd you had been there to have exorcis'd that Rabble of Broomsticks, with which we were haunted for above three Hours. I cou'd have allow'd them to set *Clod* in the Tree, to have scared the Sportsmen, plagu'd the Justice, and employ'd honest *Teague* with his Holy Water. This was the proper Use of them in Comedy, if the Author had stopp'd here; but I cannot conceive what Relation the Sacrifice of the Black Lamb, and the Ceremonies of their Worship to the Devil, have to the Business of Mirth and Humour.

The Gentleman who writ this Play, and has drawn some Characters in it very justly, appears to have been mis-led in his Witchcraft by an unwary following the inimitable *Shakespear*. The Incantations in *Mackbeth* have a Solemnity admirably adapted to the Occasion of that Tragedy, and fill the Mind with a suitable Horror; besides, that the Witches are a part of the Story itself, as we find it very particularly related in *Hector Boetius*, from whom he seems to have taken it. This therefore is a proper Machine where the Business is dark, horrid and bloody; but is extreamly foreign from the Affair of Comedy. Subjects of this kind, which are in themselves disagreeable, can at no time become entertaining, but by passing thro' an Imagination like *Shakespear*'s to form them; for which Reason Mr. *Dryden* wou'd not allow even *Beaumont* and *Fletcher* capable of imitating him.

> *But* Shakespear's *Magick cou'd not copy'd be,*
> *Within that Circle none durst Walk but He.*

I should not however have troubled you with these Remarks, if there were not something else in this Comedy, which wants to be exorcis'd more than the Witches. I mean the Freedom of some Passages, which I should have overlook'd, if I had not observed that those Jests can raise the loudest Mirth, tho' they are painful to right Sense, and an Outrage upon Modesty.

We must attribute such Liberties to the Taste of that Age, but indeed by such Representations a Poet sacrifices the best Part of his Audience to the worst; and, as one wou'd think, neglects the Boxes, to write to the Orange Wenches.

I must not conclude till I have taken notice of the Moral with which this Comedy ends. The two young Ladies having given a notable Example of outwitting those who had a Right in the Disposal of them, and marrying without Consent of Parents, one of the injur'd Parties, who is easily reconcil'd, winds up all with this Remark,

> *. . . Design whate'er we will,*
> *There is a Fate which over-rules us still.*

We are to suppose that the Gallants are Men of Merit, but if they had been Rakes the Excuse might have serv'd as well. *Hans Carvel*'s Wife was of the same Principle, but has express'd it with a Delicacy which shews she is not serious in her Excuse, but in a sort of Humorous Philosophy turns off the Thought of her Guilt, and says

> *That if weak Women go astray*
> *Their Stars are more in fault than they.*

This no doubt is a full Reparation, and dismisses the Audience with very edifying Impressions.

These things fall under a Province you have partly pursu'd already, and therefore demand your Animadversion, for the regulating so Noble an Entertainment as that of the Stage. It were to be wished that all who write for it hereafter wou'd raise their Genius, by the Ambition of pleasing People of the best Understanding; and leave others who shew nothing of the Human Species but Risibility, to seek their Diversion at the Bear-Garden, or some other Privileg'd Place, where Reason and good Manners have no Right to disturb them.

August 8, 1711.   *I am,* &c.'

T

No. 142.

[STEELE.] Monday, August 13.

. . . Irrupta tenet copula . . .—Hor.

THE following Letters being Genuine, and the Images of a Worthy Passion, I am willing to give the old Lady's Admonition to my self, and the Representation of her own Happiness, a Place in my Writings.

'*Mr.* SPECTATOR, *August* 9, 1711.

I am now in the Sixty seventh Year of my Age, and read you with Approbation; but methinks you do not strike at the Root of the greatest Evil in Life, which is the false Notion of Gallantry in Love. It is, and has long been, upon a very ill foot; but I who have been a Wife Forty Years, and was bred in a way that has made me ever since very happy, see through the Folly of it. In a Word, Sir, When I was a young Woman, all who avoided the Vices of the Age were very carefully educated, and all Phantastical Objects were turned out of our Sight. The Tapistry Hangings, with the great and venerable Simplicity of the Scripture Stories, had better Effects than now the Loves of *Venus* and *Adonis*, or *Bacchus* and *Ariadne* in your fine present Prints. The Gentleman I am Married to made Love to me in Rapture, but it was the Rapture of a Christian and a Man of Honour, not a Romantick Hero, or a Whining Coxcomb: This put our Life upon a right Basis. To give you an Idea of our Regard one to another, I enclose to you several of his Letters writ Forty Years ago, when my Lover; and one writ t'other Day, after so many Years Cohabitation.

Your Servant,

Andromache.'

"*Madam,* *August* 7, 1671.

If my Vigilance and ten thousand Wishes for your Welfare and Repose could have any force, you last Night slept in Security, and had every good Angel in your Attendance. To have my Thoughts ever fix'd on you, to live in constant Fear of every Accident to which Human Life is liable, and to send up my hourly Prayers to avert 'em from you; I say, Madam, thus to think and thus to suffer, is what I do for Her who is in Pain at my Approach, and calls all my tender Sorrow Impertinence. You are now before my Eyes, my Eyes that are ready to flow with Tenderness, but cannot give Relief to my gushing Heart, that dictates what I am now saying, and yearns to tell you all its Achings. How art thou, oh my Soul, stoln from thy self! How is all thy Attention broken! My Books are blank Paper, and my Friends Intruders. I have no hope of Quiet but from your Pity. To grant it would make more for your Triumph. To give Pain is the Tyranny, to make Happy the true Empire of Beauty. If you would consider aright, you'd find an agreeable Change in dismissing the Attendance of a Slave, to receive the Complaisance of a Companion. I bear the former in hopes of the latter Condition: As I live in Chains without murmuring at the Power which inflicts 'em, so I could enjoy Freedom without forgetting the Mercy that gave it.

> *Madam,*
>
> *I am,*
>
> *your most Devoted,*
>
> *most obedient Servant."*

Tho' I made him no Declarations in his Favour, you see he had hopes of Me when he writ this in the Month following.

"*Madam,*   *September* 3, 1671.

Before the Light this Morning dawned upon the Earth I awak'd, and lay in expectation of its return, not that it cou'd give any new Sense of Joy to me, but as I hop'd it would bless you with its chearful Face, after a Quiet which I wish'd you last Night. If my Prayers are heard, the Day appear'd with all the Influence of a Merciful Creator upon your Person and Actions. Let others, my lovely Charmer, talk of a Blind Being that disposes their Hearts, I contemn their low Images of Love. I have not a Thought which relates to you, that I cannot with Confidence beseech the All-seeing Power to bless Me in. May he direct you in all your Steps, and reward your Innocence, your Sanctity of Manners, your prudent Youth, and becoming Piety, with the Continuance of his Grace and Protection. This is an unusual Language to Ladies; but you have a Mind elevated above the giddy Notions of a Sex insnared by Flattery, and mis-led by a false and short Adoration into a solid and long Contempt. Beauty, my fairest Creature, palls in the Possession, but I love also your Mind; your Soul is as dear to me as my own; and if the Advantages of a liberal Education, some Knowledge, and as much Contempt of the World, join'd with the Endeavours towards a Life of strict Virtue and Religion, can qualify me to raise new Ideas in a Breast so well dispos'd as yours is, our Days will pass away with Joy; and old Age instead of introducing melancholy Prospects of Decay, give us hope of Eternal Youth in a better Life. I have but few Minutes from the Duty of my Employment to write in, and without time to read over what I have writ, therefore beseech you to pardon the first Hints of my Mind, which I have express'd in so little Order.

I am,

Dearest Creature,

your most Obedient,

most Devoted Servant."

The two next were Written after the Day for our Marriage was fix'd.

 "*Madam,*   *September 25, 1671.*

It is the hardest thing in the World to be in Love, and yet attend Business. As for me, all that speak to me find me out, and I must lock my self up, or other People will do it for me. A Gentleman ask'd me this Morning what News from *Holland,* and I answer'd She 's exquisitely handsome. Another desir'd to know when I had been last at *Windsor,* I reply'd She designs to go with me. Prethee allow me at least to kiss your Hand before the appointed Day, that my Mind may be in some Composure. Methinks I could write a Volume to you, but all the Language on Earth would fail in saying how much, and with what dis-interested Passion,

I am ever Yours."

September 30, 1671.

Seven in the Morning.

 "*Dear Creature,*

Next to the Influence of Heav'n, I am to thank you that I see the returning Day with Pleasure. To pass my Evenings in so sweet a Conversation, and have the Esteem of a Woman of your Merit, has in it a Particularity of Happiness no more to be express'd than return'd. But I am, my Lovely Creature, contented to be on the oblig'd Side, and to employ all my Days in new Endeavours to convince you and all the World of the Sense I have of your Condescension in Chusing,

Madam,

Your most Faithful,

Most Obedient Humble Servant."

He was, when he writ the following Letter, as agreeable and pleasant a Man as any in England.

 "*Madam,*   *October 20, 1671.*

I beg Pardon that my Paper is not Finer, but I am forc'd to write from a Coffee-house where I am attending about Business. There is a dirty Croud of Busie Faces all around me talking of Mony, while all my Ambition, all my Wealth is Love: Love, which animates my Heart, sweetens my Humour, enlarges my Soul, and affects every Action of my Life. 'Tis to my Lovely Charmer I owe that many noble Ideas are continually affix'd to my Words and Actions: 'Tis the natural Effect of that Generous Passion to create in the Admirers some Similitude of the Object admired; thus, my Dear, am I every Day to improve from so sweet a Companion. Look up, my Fair One, to that Heaven which made thee such, and join with me to implore its Influence on our tender innocent Hours, and beseech the Author of Love to bless the Rights he has ordain'd, and mingle with our Happiness a just Sense of our Transient Condition, and a Resignation to his Will, which only can regulate our Minds to a steady Endeavour to please him and each other.

I am, for Ever,

Your faithful Servant."

I will not trouble you with more Letters at this time, but if you saw the poor withered Hand which sends you these Minutes, I am sure you would smile to think that there is one who is so gallant as to speak of it still as so welcome a Present, after forty Years Possession of the Woman whom he writes to.

   "Madam,   *June 23, 1711.*

I heartily beg your Pardon for my Omission to write Yesterday. It was no Failure of my tender Regard for you; but having been very much perplexed in my Thoughts on the Subject of my last, made me determine to suspend speaking of it till I came my self. But, my lovely Creature, know it is not in the Power of Age, or Misfortune, or any other Accident which hangs over human Life, to take from me the pleasing Esteem I have for you, or the Memory of the bright Figure you appeared in when you gave your Hand and Heart to,

Madam,

Your most grateful Husband,

and obedient Servant."'

T

No. 143.

[STEELE.]

Tuesday, August 14.

Non est vivere sed valere vita.—Mart.

It is an unreasonable thing some Men expect of their Acquaintance. They are ever complaining that they are out of Order, or displeas'd, or they know not how; and are so far from letting that be a Reason for retiring to their own Homes, that they make it their Argument for coming into Company. What has any Body to do with Accounts of a Man's being indispos'd but his Physician? If a Man laments in Company, where the rest are in Humour enough to enjoy themselves, he should not take it ill if a Servant is order'd to present him with a Porringer of Cawdle or Posset-Drink, by way of Admonition that he go home to Bed. That Part of Life which we ordinarily understand by the Word Conversation, is an Indulgence to the sociable Part of our Make; and should incline us to bring our Proportion of good Will or good Humour among the Friends we meet with, and not to trouble them with Relations which must of Necessity oblige them to a real or feign'd Affliction. Cares, Distresses, Diseases, Uneasinesses, and Dislikes of our own, are by no Means to be obtruded upon our Friends. If we would consider how little of this Vicissitude of Motion and Rest, which we call Life, is spent with Satisfaction; we should be more tender of our Friends, than to bring them little Sorrows which do not belong to them. There is no real Life, but chearful Life; therefore Valetudinarians should be sworn, before they enter into Company, not to say a Word of themselves till the Meeting breaks up. It is not here pretended, that we should be always sitting with Chaplets of Flowers round our Heads, or be crowned with Roses, in order to make our Entertainments agreeable to us; but if (as it is usually observed) they who resolve to be merry, seldom are so; it will be much more unlikely for us to be well pleased, if they are admitted who are always complaining they are sad. Whatever we do we should keep up the Chearfulness of our Spirits, and never let them sink below an Inclination at least to be well pleased: The Way to this, is to keep our Bodies in Exercise, our Minds at Ease. That insipid State wherein neither are in Vigour, is not to be accounted any Part of our Portion of Being. When we are in the Satisfaction of some innocent Pleasure, or Pursuit of some laudable Design, we are in the Possession of Life, of human Life. Fortune will give us Disappointments enough, and Nature is attended with Infirmities enough, without our adding to the unhappy Side of our Account by our Spleen or ill Humour. Poor *Cottilus*, among so many real Evils, a chronical Distemper and a narrow Fortune, is never heard to complain: That equal Spirit of his, which any Man may have that, like him, will conquer Pride, Vanity, and Affectation, and follow Nature, is not to be broken, because it has no Points to contend for. To be anxious for nothing but what Nature demands as necessary, if it is not the way to an Estate, is the way to what Men aim at by getting an Estate. This Temper will preserve Health in the Body, as well as Tranquility in the Mind. *Cottilus* sees the World in an Hurry, with the same Scorn that a sober Person sees a Man drunk. Had he been contented with what he ought to have been, how could, says he, such a one have met with such a Disappointment? If another had valued his Mistress for what he ought to have loved her, he had not been in her Power: If her Virtue had had a Part of his Passion, her Levity had been his Cure; she could not then have been false and amiable at the same Time.

Since we cannot promise our selves constant Health, let us endeavour at such a Temper as may be our best Support in the Decay of it. *Uranius* has arrived at that Composure of Soul, and wrought himself up to such a Neglect of every thing with which the Generality of Mankind is enchanted, that nothing but acute Pains can give him Disturbance, and against those too he will tell his intimate Friends he has a Secret which gives him present Ease. *Uranius* is so thoroughly perswaded of another Life, and endeavours so sincerely to secure an Interest in it, that he looks upon Pain but as a quickening of his Pace to an Home, where he shall be better provided for than in his present Apartment. Instead of the melancholy Views which others are apt to give themselves, he will tell you that he has forgot he is mortal, nor will he think of himself as such. He thinks at the Time of his Birth he entered into an eternal Being; and the short Article of Death he will not allow an Interruption of Life, since that Moment is not of half the Duration as is his ordinary Sleep. Thus is his Being one uniform and consistent Series of chearful Diversions and moderate Cares, without Fear or Hope of Futurity. Health to him is more than Pleasure to another Man, and Sickness less affecting to him than Indisposition is to others.

I must confess, if one does not regard Life after this Manner, none but Ideots can pass it away with any tolerable Patience. Take a fine Lady who is of a delicate Frame, and you may observe from the Hour she rises a certain Weariness of all that passes about her. I know more than one who is much too nice to be quite alive. They are sick of such strange frightful People that they meet; one is so awkward and another so disagreeable, that it looks like a Penance to breathe the same Air with them. You see this is so very true, that a great Part of Ceremony and Good-breeding among the Ladies turns upon their Uneasiness; and I 'll undertake, if the How-d'ye Servants of our Women were to make a weekly Bill of Sickness, as the Parish Clerks do of Mortality, you would not find in an Account of seven Days, one in thirty that was not downright Sick or indisposed, or but a very little better than she was, and so forth.

It is certain, that to enjoy Life and Health as a constant Feast, we should not think Pleasure necessary; but, if possible, to arrive at an Equality of Mind. It is as mean to be over-joy'd upon Occasions of good Fortune, as to be dejected in Circumstances of Distress. Laughter in one Condition, is as unmanly as Weeping in the other. We should not form our Minds to expect Transport on every Occasion, but know how to make Enjoyment to be out of Pain. Ambition, Envy, vagrant Desire, or impertinent Mirth will take up our Minds, without we can possess our selves in that Sobriety of Heart which is above all Pleasures, and can be felt much better than described: But the ready Way, I believe, to the right Enjoyment of Life, is by a Prospect towards another to have but a very mean Opinion of it. A great Author of our Time has set this in an excellent Light, when with a philosophick Pity of human Life he spoke of it in his Theory of the Earth in the following Manner.

For what is this Life but a Circulation of little mean Actions? We lie down and rise again, dress and undress, feed and wax hungry, work or play, and are weary, and then we lie down again, and the Circle returns. We spend the Day in Trifles, and when the Night comes we throw our selves into the Bed of Folly, amongst Dreams and broken Thoughts and wild Imaginations. Our Reason lies asleep by us, and we are for the Time as arrant Brutes as those that sleep in the Stalls or in the Field. Are not the Capacities of Man higher than these? and ought not his Am-bition and Expectations to be greater? Let us be Adventurers for another World: 'Tis at least a fair and noble Chance; and there is nothing in this worth our Thoughts or our Passions. If we should be disappointed, we are still no worse than the rest of our Fellow-Mortals; and if we succeed in our Expectations, we are eternally happy. T

No. 144.

[STEELE.]   Wednesday, August 15.

. . . Noris quam elegans formarum spectator siem.—Ter.

BEAUTY has been the Delight and Torment of the World ever since it began. The Philosophers have felt its Influence so sensibly, that almost every one of them has left us some Say-ing or other, which intimated that he too well knew the Power of it. One has told us, that a graceful Person is a more powerful Recommendation, than the best Letter that can be writ in your Favour. Another desires the Possessor of it to consider it is a meer Gift of Nature, and not any Perfection of his own. A Third calls it a short liv'd Tyranny; a Fourth, a silent Fraud, because it imposes upon us without the help of Language; but, I think, *Carneades* spoke as much like a Philosopher as any of them, tho' more like a Lover, when he call'd it Royalty without Force. It is not indeed to be denied, that there is something irresistible in a Beauteous Form; the most Severe will not pretend, that they do not feel an immediate Praepossession in Favour of the Handsome. No one denies them the Privilege of being first heard, and being regarded before others in Matters of ordinary Consideration. At the same time the Handsome should consider that it is a Possession, as it were, foreign to them. No one can give it himself, or preserve it when they have it. Yet so it is, that People can bear any Quality in the World than Beauty. It is the Consolation of all who are naturally too much affected with the Force of it, that a little Attention, if a Man can attend with Judgment, will cure them. Handsom People usually are so Phantastically pleas'd with themselves, that if they do not kill at first Sight, as the Phrase is, a second Interview disarms them of all their Power. But I shall make this Paper rather a Warning-piece to give Notice where the Danger is, than to propose Instructions how to avoid it when you have fallen in the way of it. Handsome Men shall be the Subjects of another Chapter, the Women shall take up the present Discourse.

Amaryllis, who has been in Town but one Winter, is extreamly improved with the Arts of Good-Breeding, without leaving Nature. She has not lost the Native Simplicity of her Aspect, to substitute that Patience of being stared at, which is the usual Triumph and Distinction of a Town Lady. In Publick Assemblies you meet her careless Eye diverting it self with the Objects around her, insensible that she her self is one of the brightest in the Place.

Dulcissa is quite of another Make, she is almost a Beauty by Nature, but more than one by Art. If it were possible for her to let her Fan or any Limb about her rest, she would do some part of the Execution she meditates; but tho' she designs her self a Prey, she will not stay to be taken. No Painter can give you Words for the different Aspects of *Dulcissa* in half a Moment, wherever she appears: So little does she accomplish what she takes so much Pains for, to be gay and careless.

Merab is attended with all the Charms of Woman and Accomplishments of Man. It is not to be doubted but she has a great deal of Wit, if she were not such a Beauty; and she would have more Beauty had she not so much Wit. Affectation prevents her Excellencies from walking together. If she has a mind to speak such a Thing, it must be done with such an Air of her Body; and if she has an Inclination to look very careless, there is such a smart Thing to be said at the same time, that the design of being admired destroys it self. Thus the Unhappy *Merab*, tho' a Wit and Beauty, is allowed to be neither, because she will always be both.

Albacinda has the Skill as well as Power of pleasing. Her Form is majestick, but her Aspect humble. All good Men should beware of the Destroyer. She will speak to you like your Sister, till she has you sure; but is the most vexatious of Tyrants when you are so. Her Familiarity of Behaviour, her indifferent Questions, and general Conversation, make the silly part of her Votaries full of hopes, while the wise fly from her Power. She well knows she is too Beautiful and too Witty to be indifferent to any who converse with her, and therefore knows she does not lessen her self by Familiarity, but gains occasions of Admiration, by seeming Ignorance of her Perfections.

Eudosia adds to the height of her Stature a Nobility of Spirit which still distinguishes her above the rest of her Sex. Beauty in others is lovely, in others agreeable, in others attractive; but in *Eudosia* it is commanding: Love towards *Eudosia* is a Sentiment like the Love of Glory. The Lovers of other Women are soften'd into Fondness, the Admirers of *Eudosia* exalted into Ambition.

Eucratia presents her self to the Imagination with a more kindly Pleasure, and as she is Woman, her Praise is wholly Feminine. If we were to form an Image of Dignity in a Man, we should give him Wisdom and Valour, as being essential to the Character of Manhood. In like manner if you describe a right Woman in a laudable Sense, she should have gentle Softness, tender Fear, and all those parts of Life, which distinguish her from the other Sex; with some Subordination to it, but such an Inferiority that makes her still more lovely. *Eucratia* is that Creature, she is all over Woman, Kindness is all her Art, and Beauty all her Arms. Her Look, her Voice, her Gesture, and whole Behaviour is truly Feminine. A Goodness mixed with Fear, gives a Tincture to all her Behaviour. It would be Savage to offend her, and Cruelty to use Art to gain her. Others are Beautiful, but *Eucratia* thou art Beauty!

Omnamante is made for Deceit, she has an Aspect as Innocent as the famed *Lucrece*, but a Mind as Wild as the more famed *Cleopatra*. Her face speaks a Vestal, but her Heart a *Messalina*. Who that beheld *Omnamante's* negligent unobserving Air, would believe that she hid under that regardless Manner the witty Prostitute, the rapacious Wench, the prodiga

Curtizan? She can, when she pleases, adorn those Eyes with Tears like an Infant that is chid: She can cast down that pretty Face in Confusion, while you rage with Jealousie, and storm at her Perfidiousness; she can wipe her Eyes, tremble and look frighted, till you think your self a Brute for your Rage, own your self an Offender, beg Pardon, and make her new Presents.

But I go too far in reporting only the Dangers in beholding the Beauteous, which I design for the Instruction of the Fair as well as their Beholders; and shall end this Rhapsody with mentioning what I thought was well enough said of an Antient Sage to a Beautiful Youth, whom he saw admiring his own Figure in Brass. What, said the Philosopher, could that Image of yours say for it self if it could speak? It might say, (answer'd the Youth) *That it is very Beautiful. And are not you asham'd*, replyed the Cynick, *to value your self upon that only of which a Piece of Brass is capable?*

T

No. 145.

[STEELE.]

Thursday, August 16.

Stultitiam patiuntur opes . . . Hor.

IF the following Enormities are not amended upon the first Mention, I desire farther Notice from my Correspondents.

'Mr. SPECTATOR,

I am obliged to you for your Discourse the other Day upon frivolous Disputants, who with great Warmth, and Enumeration of many Circumstances and Authorities, undertake to prove Matters which no Body living denies. You cannot employ your self more usefully than in adjusting the Laws of Disputation in Coffee-houses and accidental Companies, as well as in more formal Debates. Among many other things which your own Experience must suggest to you, it will be very obliging if you please to take Notice of Wagerers. I will not here repeat what *Hudibras* says of such Disputants, which is so true, that it is almost Proverbial; but shall only acquaint you with a Set of young Fellows of the Inns of Court, whose Fathers have provided for them so plentifully, that they need not be very anxious to get Law into their Heads for the Service of their Country at the Bar; but are of those who are sent (as the Phrase of Parents is) to the *Temple* to know how to keep their own. One of these Gentlemen is very loud and captious at a Coffee-ouse which I frequent, and being in his Nature troubled with a Humour of Contradiction, though withal excessive Ignorant, he has found a way to indulge this Temper, go on in Idleness and Ignorance, and yet still give himself the Air of a very learned and knowing Man by the Strength of his Pocket. The Misfortune of the thing is, I have, as it happens sometimes, a greater Stock of Learning than of Money. The Gentleman I am speaking of, takes Advantage of the Narrowness of my Circumstances in such a manner, that he has read all that I can pretend to, and runs me down with such a positive Air, and with such powerful Arguments, that from a very Learned Person I am thought a mere Pretender. Not long ago I was relating that I had read such a Passage in *Tacitus*, up starts my young Gentleman in a full Company, and pulling out his Purse offered to lay me ten Guineas, to be staked immediately in that Gentleman's Hands, (pointing to one smoking at another Table) that I was utterly mistaken. I was Dumb for want of ten Guineas; he went on unmercifully to triumph over my Ignorance how to take him up, and told the whole Room he had read *Tacitus* twenty times over, and such a remarkable Incident as that could not escape him. He has at this time three considerable Wagers depending between him and some of his Companions, who are rich enough to hold an Argument with him. He has five Guineas upon Questions in Geography, two that the *Isle of Wight* is a Peninsula, and three Guineas to one that the World is round. We have a Gentleman comes to our Coffee-house who deals mightily in Antique Scandal; my Disputant has laid him twenty Pieces upon a Point of History, to wit, that *Caesar* never lay with *Cato*'s Sister, as is scandalously reported by some People.

There are several of this sort of Fellows in Town, who Wager themselves into Statesmen, Historians, Geographers, Mathematicians, and every other Art, when the Persons with whom they talk have not Wealth equal to their Learning. I beg of you to prevent, in these Youngsters, this Compendious Way to Wisdom, which costs other People so much Time and Pains, and you will oblige

Your Humble Servant.'

Coffee-House near the
Temple, Aug. 12, 1711.

'*Mr.* SPECTATOR,

Here 's a Young Gentleman that sings Opera-Tunes, or Whistles in a full House. Pray let him know that he has no Right to act here as if he were in an empty Room. Be pleased to divide the Spaces of a Publick Room, and certifie Whistlers, Singers and Common Orators, that are heard further than their Portion of the Room comes to, that the Law is open, and that there is an Equity which will relieve us from such as interrupt

us in our Lawful Discourse, as much as against such as stop us
on the Road. I take these Persons, Mr. SPECTATOR, to be such
Trespassers as the Officer in your Stage Coach, and am of the
same Sentiment with Councellor *Ephraim*. It is true the
Young Man is rich, and, as the Vulgar say, needs not care for
any Body; but sure that is no Authority for him to go whistle
where he pleases.

I am, Sir,

Your Most Humble Servant.

P.S. I have Chambers in the *Temple*, and here are Students
that learn upon the Hautboy; pray desire the Benchers, that
all Lawyers who are Proficients in Wind-Musick may lodge to
the *Thames.*'

'*Mr.* SPECTATOR,

We are a Company of Young Women who pass our Time very
much together, and obliged by the Mercenary Humour of the
Men to be as Mercenarily inclined as they are. There visits
among us an old Batchelor whom each of us had a Mind to.
The Fellow is rich, and knows he may have any of us, therefore
is particular to none, but excessively ill-bred. His Pleasantry
consists in Romping, he snatches Kisses by surprise, put his
Hand in our Necks, tears our Fans, robs us of Ribbons, forces
Letters out of our Hands, looks into any of our Papers, and a
thousand other Rudenesses. Now what I'll desire of you is
to acquaint him, by Printing this, that if he does not marry one
of us very suddenly, we have all agreed, the next time he
pretends to be merry, to affront him, and use him like a Clown
as he is. In the Name of the Sisterhood I take my leave of
you, and am, as they all are,

Your Constant Reader,

and Well-wisher.'

'*Mr.* SPECTATOR,

I and several others of your Female Readers, have con-
formed our selves to your Rules, even to our very Dress.
There is not one of us but has reduced our outward Petticoat
to its ancient Sizable Circumference, tho' indeed we retain
still a Quilted one underneath, which makes us not altogether
unconformable to the Fashion; but 'tis on Condition Mr.
SPECTATOR extends not his Censure so far. But we find you
Men secretly approve our Practice, by imitating our Pira-
midical Form. The Skirt of your fashionable Coats forms as
large a Circumference as our Petticoats; as these are set out
with Whalebone, so are those with Wire, to encrease and sustain the Bunch of Fold that hangs down on each side; and the

Hat, I perceive, is decreased in just Proportion to our Head-dresses. We make a regular Figure, but I defy your Mathematicks to give Name to the Form you appear in. Your Architecture is mere *Gothick*, and betrays a worse Genius than ours; therefore if you are partial to your own Sex, I shall be less than I am now

T   *Your Humble Servant.'*

No. 146.

[STEELE.]   Friday, August 17.

Nemo vir magnus sine aliquo afflatu divino unquam fuit.—Tull.

WE know the highest Pleasure our Minds are capable of enjoying with Composure, when we read sublime Thoughts communicated to us by Men of great Genius and Eloquence. Such is the Entertainment we meet with in the philosophick Parts of *Cicero*'s Writings. Truth and good Sense have there so charming a Dress, that they could hardly be more agreeably represented with the Addition of poetical Fiction and the Power of Numbers. This ancient Author, and a modern one, have fallen into my Hands within these few Days; and the Impressions they have left upon me, have at the present quite spoiled me for a merry Fellow. The Modern is that admirable Writer, the Author of the Theory of the Earth. The Subjects with which I have lately been entertained in them both bear a near Affinity; they are upon Enquiries into Hereafter, and the Thoughts of the latter seem to me to be raised above those of the former in proportion to his Advantages of Scripture and Revelation. If I had a Mind to it, I could not at present talk of any thing else; therefore I shall translate a Passage in the one, and transcribe a Paragraph out of the other, for the Speculation of this Day. *Cicero* tells us, that *Plato* reports *Socrates*, upon receiving his Sentence, to have spoken to his Judges in the following Manner.

'I have great Hopes, oh my Judges, that it is infinitely to my Advantage that I am sent to Death: For it must of Necessity be, that one of these two things must be the Consequence. Death must take away all these Senses, or convey me to another Life. If all Sense is to be taken away, and Death is no more than that profound Sleep without Dreams, in which we are sometimes buried, oh Heavens! how desirable is it to die? how many Days do we know in Life preferable to such a State? But if it be true that Death is but a Passage to Places which they who lived before us do now inhabit, how much still happier is it to go from those who call themselves Judges, to appear before those that really are such; before *Minos, Rhadamanthus, Aeacus* and *Triptolemus,* and to meet Men who have lived with Justice and Truth? Is this, do you think, no happy Journey? Do you think it nothing to speak with *Orpheus, Musaeus, Homer* and *Hesiod?* I would, indeed, suffer many Deaths to enjoy these Things. With what particular Delight should I talk to *Palamedes, Ajax,* and others, who like me have suffered by the Iniquity of their Judges. I should examine the Wisdom of that great Prince, who carried such mighty Forces against *Troy;* and argue with *Ulysses* and *Sisyphus,* upon difficult Points, as I have in Conversation here, without being in Danger of being condemned. But let not those among you who have pronounced me an innocent Man be afraid of Death. No Harm can arrive at a good Man whether dead or living: his Affairs are always under the Direction of the Gods; nor will I believe the Fate which is allotted to me my self this Day to have arrived by Chance; nor have I ought to say either against my Judges or Accusers, but that they thought they did me an Injury.—But I detain you too long, it is Time that I retire to Death, and you to your Affairs of Life; which of us has the Better is known to the Gods, but to no mortal Man.'

The divine *Socrates* is here represented in a Figure worthy his great Wisdom and Philosophy, worthy the greatest mere Man that ever breath'd. But the modern Discourse is written upon a Subject no less than the Dissolution of Nature it self. Oh how glorious is the old Age of that great Man, who has spent his Time in such Contemplations as has made this Being, what only it should be, an Education for Heaven! He has, according to the Lights of Reason and Revelation, which seem'd to him clearest, traced the Steps of Omnipotence: He has, with a Celestial Ambition, as far as it is consistent with Humility and Devotion, examined the Ways of Providence, from the Creation to the Dissolution of the visible World. How pleasing must have been the Speculation, to observe Nature and Providence move together, the physical and moral World march the same Pace: To observe Paradice and eternal Spring the Seat of Innocence, troubled Seasons and angry Skies the Portion of Wickedness and Vice. When this admirable Author has reviewed all that has passed, or is to come, which relates to the habitable World, and run through the whole Fate of it, how could a Guardian Angel, that had attended it through all its Courses or Changes, speak more emphatically at the End of his Charge than does our Author, when he makes, as it were, a

Funeral Oration over this Globe, looking to the Point where it once stood?

'Let us only, if you please, to take Leave of this Subject, reflect upon this Occasion on the Vanity and transient Glory of this habitable World. How by the Force of one Element breaking loose upon the rest, all the Vanities of Nature, all the Works of Art, all the Labours of Men, are reduced to Nothing. All that we admired and adored before as great and magnificent, is obliterated or vanished; and another Form and Face of things, plain, simple, and every where the same, overspreads the whole Earth. Where are now the great Empires of the World, and their great imperial Cities? Their Pillars, Trophies, and Monuments of Glory? Shew me where they stood, read the Inscription, tell me the Victor's Name. What Remains, what Impressions, what Difference, or Distinction, do you see in this Mass of Fire? *Rome* it self, eternal *Rome*, the great City, the Empress of the World, whose Domination and Superstition ancient and modern, make a great Part of the History of this Earth; what is become of her now? She laid her Foundations deep, and her Palaces were strong and sumptuous; *She glorified her self, and lived deliciously, and said in her Heart I sit a Queen, and shall see no Sorrow:* But her Hour is come, she is wiped away from the Face of the Earth, and buried in everlasting Oblivion. But it is not Cities only, and Works of Men's Hands, but the everlasting Hills, the Mountains and Rocks of the Earth are melted as Wax before the Sun, and *their Place is no where found.* Here stood the *Alpes*, the Load of the Earth, that covered many Countries, and reached their Arms from the Ocean to the Black Sea; this huge Mass of Stone is softned and dissolved as a tender Cloud into Rain. Here stood the *African* Mountains, and *Atlas* with his Top above the Clouds; there was frozen *Caucasus*, and *Taurus*, and *Imaus*, and the Mountains of *Asia*; and yonder towards the North stood the *Riphaean* Hills, cloath'd in Ice and Snow. All these are vanished, dropt away as the Snow upon their Heads. *Great and marvellous are thy Works, just and true are thy Ways, thou King of Saints! Hallelujah.'* **T**

No. 147.
[STEELE.]   Saturday, August 18.

Pronuntiatio est vocis & vultus & gestus moderatio cum venustate.—Tull.

'Mr. SPECTATOR,

THE well Reading of the Common Prayer is of so great Importance, and so much neglected, that I take the Liberty to offer to your Consideration some Particulars on that Subject; And what more worthy your Observation than this? A thing so Publick, and of so high Consequence. It is indeed wonderful, that the frequent Exercise of it should not make the Performers of that Duty more expert in it. This Inability, as I conceive, proceeds from the little Care that is taken of their Reading, while Boys and at School, where when they are got into *Latin*, they are look'd upon as above *English*, the Reading of which is wholly neglected, or at least read to very little purpose, without any due Observations made to them of the proper Accent and manner of Reading; by this means they have acquir'd such ill Habits as won't easily be remov'd. The only way that I know of to remedy this, is to propose some Person of great Ability that way as a Pattern for them; Example being most effectual to convince the Learned, as well as instruct the Ignorant.

You must know, Sir, I've been a constant Frequenter of the Service of the Church of *England* for above these four Years last past, and 'till *Sunday* was sevennight never discover'd, to so great a Degree, the Excellency of the Common Prayer. When being at St. *James*'s *Garlick-hill* Church, I heard the Service read so distinctly, so emphatically, and so fervently, that it was next to an Impossibility to be unattentive. My Eyes and my Thoughts could not wander as usual, but were confin'd to my Prayers: I then consider'd I address'd my self to the Almighty, and not to a beautiful Face. And when I reflected on my former Performances of that Duty, I found I had run it over as a matter of Form, in comparison to the Manner in which I then discharged it. My Mind was really affected, and fervent Wishes accompanied my Words. The Confession was read with such a resign'd Humility, the Absolution with such a comfortable Authority, the Thanksgivings with such a Religious Joy, as made me feel those Affections of the Mind in a manner I never did before. To remedy therefore the Grievance above complain'd of, I humbly propose, that this excellent Reader, upon the next and every Annual Assembly of the Clergy of *Sion College*, and all other Conventions, should read Prayers before them. For then those, that are afraid of stretching their Mouths, and spoiling their soft Voice, will learn to Read with Clearness, Loudness, and Strength. Others that affect a rakish negligent Air by folding their Arms, and lolling on their Book, will be taught a decent Behaviour, and comely Erection of Body. Those that Read so fast as if impatient of their Work, may learn to speak Deliberately. There is another sort of Persons whom I call Pindarick Readers, as being confin'd to no set measure; these Pronounce five or six Words with great Deliberation, and the five or six Subsequent ones with as great Celerity: The first part of a Sentence with a very exalted Voice, and the latter part with a Submissive one: Sometime again with one sort of a Tone, and immediately after with a very different one. These Gentlemen will learn of my admired Reader an Evenness of Voice and Delivery. And all who are Innocent of these Affectations, but Read with such an Indifference as if they did not understand the Language, may then be inform'd of the Art of Reading movingly and fervently, how to place the Emphasis, and give the proper Accent to each Word, and how to vary the Voice according to the Nature of the Sentence. There is certainly a very great Difference between the Reading a Prayer and a Gazette, which I beg of you to inform a Sett of Readers, who affect, forsooth, a certain Gentleman-like Familiarity of Tone, and mend the Language as they go on, crying instead of Pardoneth and Absolveth, Pardons and Absolves. These are often pretty Classical Scholars, and would think it an unpardonable Sin to read *Virgil* or *Martial* with so little Taste as they do Divine Service.

This Indifference seems to me to arise from the Endeavour of avoiding the Imputation of Cant, and the false Notion of it. It will be proper therefore to trace the Original and Signification of this Word. Cant, is by some People, derived from one *Andrew Cant* who, they say, was a Presbyterian Minister in some illiterate part of *Scotland*, who by Exercise and Use had obtained the Faculty, *alias* Gift, of Talking in the Pulpit in such a Dialect, that it 's said he was understood by none but his own Congregation, and by not all of them. Since *Mas. Cant*'s time, it has been understood in a larger Sense, and signifies all sudden Exclamations, Whinings, unusual Tones, and in fine all Praying and Preaching like the unlearned of the Presbyterians. But I hope a proper Elevation of Voice, a due Emphasis and Accent, are not to come within this description: So that our Readers may still be as unlike the Presbyterians as they please. The Dissenters (I mean such as I have heard) do indeed elevate their Voices, but it is with sudden Jumps from the lower to the higher part of them; and that with so little Sense or Skill, that their Elevation and Cadence is Bawling and Muttering. They make use of an Emphasis, but so improperly, that it is often placed on some very insignificant Particle, as upon *if*, or *and*. Now if these Improprieties have so great an Effect on the People, as we see they have, how great an Influence would the Service of our Church, containing the best Prayers that ever were Compos'd, and that in Terms most affecting, most humble, and most expressive of our Wants and Dependance on the Object of our Worship, dispos'd in most proper Order, and void of all Confusion; what Influence, I say, would these Prayers have, were they delivered with a due Emphasis, an apposite Rising and Variation of Voice, the Sentence concluded with a gentle Cadence, and, in a Word, with such an Accent and turn of Speech as is peculiar to Prayer?

As the matter of Worship is now managed in Dissenting Congregations, you find insignificant Words and Phrases raised by a lively Vehemence; in our own Churches, the most exalted Sense depreciated, by a dispassionate Indolence. I remember to have heard Dr. *S——e* say in his Pulpit, of the Common Prayer, that, at least, it was as perfect as any thing of Human Institution: If the Gentlemen who err in this kind would please to recollect the many Pleasantries they have read upon those who recite good Things with an ill Grace, they would go on to think that what in that case is only Ridiculous, in themselves is Impious. But leaving this to their own Reflections, I shall conclude this Trouble with what *Caesar* said upon the Irregularity of Tone in one who read before him, *Do you read or sing? If you sing, you sing very ill.*

T   *Your Most Humble Servant.'*

No. 148.

[STEELE.]   Monday, August 20.

. . . *Exempta juvat spinis de pluribus una.*—Hor.

MY Correspondents assure me, that the Enormities which they lately complained of, and I published an Account of, are so far from being amended, that new Evils arise every Day to interrupt their Conversation, in Contempt of my Reproofs. My Friend who writes from the Coffee-house near the *Temple*, informs me, that the Gentleman who constantly sings a Voluntary in spite of the whole Company, was more musical than ordinary after reading my Paper; and has not been contented with that, but has danced up to the Glass in the Middle of the Room, and practised Minuet-steps to his own Humming. The incorrigible Creature has gone still further, and in the open Coffee-house, with one Hand extended as leading a Lady in it, he has danced both *French* and Country-Dances, and admonished his supposed Partner by Smiles and Nods to hold up her Head and fall back, according to the respective Facings and Evolutions of the Dance. Before this Gentleman began this his Exercise, he was pleased to clear his Throat by coughing and spitting a full half Hour; and as soon as he struck up, he appealed to an Attorney's Clerk in the Room, whether he hit as he ought *Since you from Death have saved me?* and then ask'd the young Fellow, pointing to a Chancery-Bill under his Arm, whether that was an Opera-Score he carried or not? Without staying for an Answer he fell into the Exercise abovementioned, and practised his Airs to the full House who were turned upon him, without the least Shame or Repentance for his former Transgressions.

I am to the last Degree at a Loss what to do with this young Fellow, except I declare him an Outlaw, and pronounce it penal for any one to speak to him in the said House which he frequents, and direct that he be obliged to drink his Tea and Coffee without Sugar, and not receive from any Person whatsoever any thing above mere Necessaries.

As we in *England* are a sober People, and generally inclined rather to a certain Bashfulness of Behaviour in Publick, it is amazing whence some Fellows come whom one meets with in this Town; They do not all seem to be the Growth of our Island; the pert, the talkative, all such as have no Sense of the Observation of others, are certainly of foreign Extraction. As for my Part, I am as much surpriz'd when I see a talkative *Englishman,* as I should be to see the *Indian* Pine growing on one of our quick-set Hedges: where these Creatures get Sun enough, to make them such lively Animals and dull Men, is above my Philosophy.

There are another Kind of Impertinents which a Man is perplexed with in mixed Company, and those are your loud Speakers: These treat Mankind as if we were all deaf; they do not express but declare themselves. Many of these are guilty of this Outrage out of Vanity, because they think all they say is well; or that they have their own Persons in such Veneration, that they believe nothing which concerns them can be insignificant to any Body else. For these People's Sake, I have often lamented that we cannot close our Ears with as much Ease as we can our Eyes: It is very uneasy that we must necessarily be under Persecution. Next to these Bawlers, is a troublesome Creature who comes with the Air of your Friend and your

Intimate, and that is your Whisperer. There is one of them at a Coffee-house which I my self frequent, who observing me to be a Man pretty well made for Secrets, gets by me, and with a Whisper tells me things which all the Town knows. It is no very hard Matter to guess at the Source of this Impertinence, which is nothing else but a Method or Mechanick Art of being wise. You never see any frequent in it, whom you can suppose to have any thing in the World to do. These Persons are worse than Bawlers, as much as a secret Enemy is more dangerous than a declared one. I wish this my Coffee-house Friend would take this for an Intimation, that I have not heard one Word he has told me for these several Years; whereas he now thinks me the most trusty Repository of his Secrets. The Whisperers have a pleasant Way of ending the close Conversation, with saying aloud, *Do not you think so?* Then whisper again, and then aloud, *but you know that Person*; then whisper again. The thing would be well enough, if they whispered to keep the Folly of what they say among Friends, but alas they do it to preserve the Importance of their Thoughts. I am sure I could name you more than one Person whom no Man living ever heard talk upon any Subject in Nature, or ever saw in his whole Life with a Book in his Hand, that I know not how can whisper something like Knowledge of what has and does pass in the World; which you would think he learned from some familiar Spirit that did not think him worthy to receive the whole Story. But in Truth Whisperers deal only in half Accounts of what they entertain you with. A great Help to their Discourse is, 'That the Town says, and People begin to talk very freely, and they had it from Persons too considerable to be named, what they will tell you when things are riper.' My Friend has winked upon me any Day since I came to Town last, and has communicated to me as a Secret, that he designed in a very short Time to tell me a Secret; but I shall know what he means, he now assures me, in less than a Fortnight's Time.

But I must not omit the dearer Part of Mankind, I mean the Ladies, to take up a whole Paper upon Grievances which concern the Men only; but shall humbly propose, that we change Fools for an Experiment only. A certain Set of Ladies complain they are frequently perplexed with a Visitant who affects to be wiser than they are; which Character he hopes to preserve by an obstinate Gravity, and great Guard against discovering his Opinion upon any Occasion whatsoever. A painful Silence has hitherto gained him no further Advantage, than that as he might, if he had behaved himself with Freedom, been excepted against, but as to this and that Particular, he now offends in the whole. To relieve these Ladies, my good Friends and Correspondents, I shall exchange my dancing Outlaw for their dumb Visitant, and assign the silent Gentleman all the Haunts of the Dancer: In order to which I have sent them by the Penny-Post the following Letters for their Conduct in their new Conversations.

'*Sir,*

I have, you may be sure, heard of your Irregularities without regard to my Observations upon you; but shall not treat you with so much Rigour as you deserve. If you will give your self the Trouble to repair to the Place mentioned in the Postscript to this Letter at Seven this Evening, you will be conducted into a spacious Room well lighted, where there are Ladies and Musick. You will see a young Lady laughing next the Window to the Street; you may take her out, for she loves you as well as she does any Man, tho' she never saw you before. She never thought in her Life any more than your self. She will not be surprized when you accost her, nor concerned when you leave her. Hasten from a Place where you are laughed at, to one where you will be admired. You are of no Consequence, therefore go where you will be welcome for being so.

Your most Humble Servant.'

'*Sir,*

The Ladies whom you visit, think a wise Man the most impertinent Creature living, therefore you cannot be offended that they are displeased with you. Why will you take Pains to appear wise, where you would not be the more esteemed for being really so? Come to us; forget the Gigglers; and let your Inclination go along with you whether you speak or are silent; and let all such Women as are in a Clan or Sisterhood, go their own way; there is no Room for you in that Company who are of the common Taste of the Sex.

> *For Women born to be controll'd*
> *Stoop to the forward and the bold;*
> *Affect the haughty and the proud,*
> *The gay, the frolick, and the loud.*

T

No. 149.

[STEELE.]   Tuesday, August 21.

> *Cui in manu sit, quem esse dementem velit,*
> *Quem supere, quem sanari, quem in morbum injici,*
> *Quem contra amari, quem accersiri, quem expeli.*
>
> —Caecil. apud Tull.

THE following Letter and my Answer shall take up the present Speculation.

'*Mr.* SPECTATOR,

I am the young Widow of a Country Gentleman, who has left me entire Mistress of a large Fortune, which he agreed to as an Equivalent for the Difference in our Years. In these Circumstances it is not extraordinary to have a Crowd of Admirers; which I have abridg'd in my own Thoughts, and reduc'd to a Couple of Candidates only, both young and neither of 'em disagreeable in their Persons; according to the common Way of computing, in one the Estate more than deserves my Fortune, in the other my Fortune more than deserves the Estate. When I consider the first, I own I am so far a Woman I cannot avoid being delighted with the Thoughts of living great; but then he seems to receive such a Degree of Courage from the Knowledge of what he has, he looks as if he was going to confer an Obligation on me; and the Readiness he accosts me with, makes me jealous I am only hearing a Repetition of the same things he has said to a hundred Women before. When I consider the other, I see my self approach'd with so much Modesty and Respect, and such a Doubt of himself, as betrays methinks an Affection within, and a Belief at the same Time that he himself would be the only Gainer by my Consent. What an unexceptionable Husband could I make out of both! But since that 's impossible, I beg to be concluded by your Opinion; it is absolutely in your Power to dispose of

Your most obedient Servant,

Sylvia.'

Madam,

You do me great Honour in your Application to me on this important Occasion; I shall therefore talk to you with the Tenderness of a Father, in Gratitude for your giving me the Authority of one. You do not seem to make any great Distinction between these Gentlemen as to their Persons; the whole Question lies upon their Circumstances and Behaviour: If the one is less respectful because he is rich, and the other more obsequious because he is not so, they are in that Point moved by the same Principle, the Consideration of Fortune, and you must place them in each other's Circumstances before you can judge of their Inclination. To avoid Confusion in discussing this Point, I will call the richer Man *Strephon* and the other *Florio*. If you believe *Florio* with *Strephon's* Estate would behave himself as he does now, *Florio* is certainly your Man; but if you think *Strephon*, were he in *Florio's* Condition, would be as obsequious as *Florio* is now, you ought for your own sake to choose *Strephon*; for where the Men are equal, there is no Doubt Riches ought to be a Reason for Preference. After this Manner, my dear Child, I would have you abstract them from their Circumstances; for you are to take it for granted, that he who is very humble only because he is poor, is the very same Man in Nature with him who is haughty because he is rich.

When you have gone thus far, as to consider the Figure they make towards you; you will please, my Dear, next to consider the Appearance you make towards them. If they are Men of Discerning, they can observe the Motives of your Heart; and *Florio* can see when he is disregarded only upon Account of Fortune, which makes you to him a mercenary Creature; and you are still the same thing to *Strephon*, in taking him for his Wealth only: You are therefore to consider whether you had rather oblige, than receive an Obligation.

The Marriage-Life is always an insipid, a vexatious, or an happy Condition. The first is, when two People of no Genius or Taste for themselves meet together, upon such a Settlement as has been thought reasonable by Parents and Conveyancers from an exact Valuation of the Land and Cash of both Parties: In this Case the young Lady's Person is no more regarded, than the House and Improvements in Purchase of an Estate; but she goes with her Fortune, rather than her Fortune with her. These make up the Crowd or Vulgar of the rich, and fill up the Lumber of humane Race, without Beneficence towards those below them, or Respect towards those above them; and lead a despicable, independent and useless Life, without Sense of the Laws of Kindness, Good-nature, mutual Offices, and the elegant Satisfactions which flow from Reason and Virtue.

The vexatious Life arises from a Conjunction of two People of quick Taste and Resentment, put together for Reasons well known to their Friends, in which especial Care is taken to avoid (what they think the chief of Evils) Poverty, and ensure to them Riches, with every Evil besides. These good People live in a constant Constraint before Company, and too great Familiarity alone; when they are within Observation they fret at each others Carriage and Behaviour, when alone they revile each others Person and Conduct; In Company they are in a Purgatory, when only together in an Hell.

The happy Marriage is, where two Persons meet and voluntarily make Choice of each other, without principally regarding or neglecting the Circumstance of Fortune or Beauty. These may still love in spite of Adversity or Sickness: The former we may in some Measure defend our selves from, the other is the Portion of our very Make. When you have a true Notion of this sort of Passion, your humour of living great will vanish out of your Imagination, and you will find Love has nothing to do with State. Solitude, with the Person beloved, has a Pleasure, even in a Woman's Mind, beyond Show or Pomp. You are therefore to consider which of your Lovers will like you best undress'd, which will bear with you most when out of Humour; and your Way to this is to ask of your self, which of them you value most for his own Sake? and by that judge which gives the greater Instances of his valuing you for your self only.

After you have expressed some Sense of the humble Approach of *Florio*, and a little Disdain at *Strephon's* Assurance in his Address, you cry out, *What an unexceptionable Husband could I make out of both!* It would therefore methinks be a good Way to determine your self: Take him in whom what you like is not transferable to another; for if you chuse otherwise, there is no Hopes your Husband will ever have what you liked in his Rival; but intrinsick Qualities in one Man may very probably purchase every thing that is adventitious in another. In plainer Terms: he whom you take for his personal Perfections will sooner arrive at the Gifts of Fortune, than he whom you take for the Sake of his Fortune attain to personal Perfections. If *Strephon* is not as accomplish'd and agreeable as *Florio*, Marriage to you will never make him so; but Marriage to you may make *Florio* as rich as *Strephon*: Therefore to make a sure Purchase, employ Fortune upon Certainties, but do not sacrifice Certainties to Fortune.

> *I am,*
>
> *You most obedient*
> *Humble Servant.*

T

No 150.
[BUDGELL.] Wednesday, August 22.

> *Nil habet infelix paupertas durius in se,*
> *Quam quod ridiculos homines facit* . . .—Juv.

As I was walking in my Chamber the Morning before I went last into the Country, I heard the Hawkers with great Vehemence crying about a Paper, entit'led *The ninety nine Plagues of an empty Purse.* I had indeed some Time before observed, that the Orators of *Grub-street* had dealt very much in *Plagues*: They have already published in the same Month *The Plagues of Matrimony, The Plagues of a single Life, The nineteen Plagues of a Chambermaid, The Plagues of a Coachman, The Plagues of a Footman,* and *The Plague of Plagues.* The Success these several *Plagues* met with, probably gave Occasion to the abovementioned Poem on an *empty Purse.* However that be, the same Noise so frequently repeated under my Window, drew me insensibly to think on some of those Inconveniences and Mortifications which usually attend on Poverty, and in short gave Birth to the present Speculation; for after my Fancy had run over the most obvious and common Calamities which Men of mean Fortunes are liable to, it descended to those little Insults and Contempts, which, tho' they may seem to dwindle into nothing when a Man offers to describe them, are perhaps in themselves more cutting and insupportable than the former. *Juvenal* with a great deal of Humour and Reason tells us, that nothing bore harder upon a poor Man in his Time, than the continual Ridicule which his Habit and Dress afforded to the Beaus of *Rome.*

> *Quid, quod materiam praebet causasque jocorum*
> *Omnibus hic idem, si foeda & scissa lacerna,*
> *Si toga sordidula est, & rupta calceus alter*
> *Pelle patet, vel si consuto vulnere crassum*
> *Atque recens linum ostendit non una cicatrix*—Juv. *Sat.* 3.

> *Add, that the Rich have still a Gibe in Store,*
> *And will be monstrous witty on the Poor;*
> *For the torn Surtout and the tatter'd Vest,*
> *The Wretch and all his Wardrobe are a Jest;*
> *The greasy Gown sully'd with often turning,*
> *Gives a good Hint to say the Man's in Mourning;*
> *Or if the Shoe be ript, or patch is put,*
> *He's wounded! see the Plaister on his Foot.*—Dryd.

'Tis on this Occasion that he afterwards adds the Reflection which I have chosen for my Motto.

> *Want is the Scorn of ev'ry wealthy Fool,*
> *And Wit in Rags is turn'd to Ridicule.*—Dryd.

It must be confess'd, that few things make a Man appear more despicable, or more prejudice his Hearers against what he is going to offer, than an awkward or pitiful Dress; insomuch that I fancy, had *Tully* himself pronounced one of his Orations with a Blanket about his Shoulders, more People would have laughed at his Dress than have admired his Eloquence. This last Reflection made me wonder at a Set of Men, who, without being subjected to it by the Unkindness of their Fortunes, are contented to draw upon themselves the Ridicule of the World in this Particular; I mean such as take it into their Heads, that the first regular Step to be a Wit is to commence a Sloven. It is certain nothing has so much debased that, which must have been otherwise so great a Character; and I know not how to account for it, unless it may possibly be in Complaisance to those narrow Minds who can have no Notion of the same Person's possessing different Accomplishments; or that it is a sort of Sacrifice which some Men are contented to make to Calumny, by allowing it to fasten on one Part of their Character, while they are endeavouring to establish another. Yet however unaccountable this foolish Custom is, I am afraid it could plead a long Prescription; and probably gave too much Occasion for the vulgar Definition still remaining among us of an *Heathen Philosopher*.

I have seen the Speech of a *Terrae-filius*, spoken in King *Charles* II's Reign; in which he describes two very eminent Men, who were perhaps the greatest Scholars of their Age; and after having mentioned the intire Friendship between them, concludes, That *they had but one Mind, one Purse, one Chamber, and one Hat*. The Men of Business were also infected with a sort of Singularity little better than this. I have heard my Father say, that a broad-brimm'd Hat, short Hair, and an unfolded Handkerchief, were in his Time absolutely necessary to denote a *notable Man*; and that he had known two or three who aspired to the Characters of *very notable*, wear Shooe-strings with great Success.

To the Honour of our present Age it must be allowed, that some of our greatest Genius's for *Wit* and *Business* have almost intirely broke the Neck of these Absurdities.

Victor, after having dispatched the most important Affairs of the Commonwealth, has appear'd at an Assembly, where all the Ladies have declared him the genteelest Man in the Company; and in *Atticus*, tho' every way one of the greatest Genius's the Age has produc'd, one sees nothing particular in his Dress or Carriage to denote his Pretensions to Wit and Learning: So that at present a Man may venture to cock up his Hat, and wear a fashionable Wig, without being taken for a Rake or a Fool.

The Medium between a Fop and a Sloven is what a Man of Sense would endeavour to keep; yet I remember Mr. *Osbourn* advises his Son to appear in his Habit rather above than below his Fortune; and tells him, that he will find an handsome Suit of Cloaths always procures some additional Respect. I have indeed my self observed, that my Banker ever bows lowest to me when I wear my full-bottom'd Wig; and writes me *Mr.* or *Esq.* accordingly as he sees me dress'd.

I shall conclude this Paper with an Adventure which I was my self an Eye-witness of very lately.

I happened the other Day to call in at a celebrated Coffee-house near the *Temple*. I had not been there long when there came in an elderly Man very meanly dress'd, and sat down by me; he had a thread-bare loose Coat on, which it was plain he wore to keep himself warm, and not to favour his under Suit, which seemed to have been at least its Contemporary: His short Wig and Hat were both answerable to the rest of his Apparel. He was no sooner seated than he called for a Dish of Tea; but as several Gentlemen in the Room wanted other things, the Boys of the House did not think themselves at Leisure to mind him. I could observe the old Fellow was very uneasy at the Affront, and at his being obliged to repeat his Commands several Times to no Purpose; till at last one of the Lads presented him with some stale Tea in a broken Dish, accompanied with a Plate of brown Sugar; which so raised his Indignation, that after several obliging Appellations of Dog and Rascal, he asked him aloud before the whole Company, *Why he must be used with less Respect than that Fop there?* pointing to a well-dress'd young Gentleman who was drinking Tea at the opposite Table. The Boy of the House reply'd with a good deal of Pertness, That his Master had two sorts of Customers, and that the Gentleman at the other Table had given him many a Six Pence for wiping his Shooes. By this time the young *Templar* who found his Honour concerned in the Dispute, and that the Eyes of the whole Coffee-house were upon him, had thrown aside a Paper he had in his Hand and was coming towards us, while we at the Table made what Haste we could to get away from the impending Quarrel, but were all of us surprized to see him as he approached nearer put on an Air of Deference and Respect. To whom the old Man said, *Hark you, Sirrah, I'll pay off your extravagant Bills once more; but will take effectual Care for the future, that your Prodigality shall not spirit up a Parcel of Rascals to insult your Father.*

Tho' I by no Means approve either the Impudence of the Servants or the Extravagance of the Son, I cannot but think the old Gentleman was in some Measure justly served for walking in Masquerade, I mean appearing in a Dress so much beneath his Quality and Estate.　　　　　　　　　　**X**

No. 151.

[STEELE.]　　　　　　　　　　　　　　Thursday, August 23.

> *Maximas virtutes jacere omnes necesse est voluptate*
> *dominante.*—Tull. *De Fin.*

I KNOW no one Character that gives Reason a greater Shock, at the same Time that it presents a good ridiculous Image to the Imagination, than that of a Man of Wit and Pleasure about the Town. This Description of a Man of Fashion, spoken by some with a Mixture of Scorn and Ridicule, by others with great Gravity as a laudable Distinction, is in every Body's Mouth that spends any Time in Conversation. My Friend WILL. HONEYCOMB has this Expression very frequently; and I never could understand by the Story which follows, upon his Mention of such a one, but that his Man of Wit and Pleasure was either a Drunkard too old for Wenching, or a young lewd Fellow with some Liveliness, who would converse with you, receive kind Offices of you, and at the same time debauch your Sister or lye with your Wife. According to his Description, a Man of Wit when he could have Wenches for Crowns a Piece which he liked quite as well, would be so extravagant as to bribe Servants, make false Friendships, fight Relations; I say according to him plain and simple Vice was too little for a Man of Wit and Pleasure; but he would leave an easy and accessible Wickedness, to come at the same thing with only the Addition of certain Falshood, and possible Murder. WILL. thinks the Town grown very dull, in that we do not hear so much as we used to do of these Coxcombs, whom (without observing it) he describes as the most infamous Rogues in Nature, with Relation to Friendship, Love, or Conversation.

When Pleasure is made the chief Pursuit of Life, it will necessarily follow that such Monsters as these will arise from a constant Application to such Blandishments as naturally root out the Force of Reason and Reflexion, and substitute in their Place a general Impatience of Thought, and a constant Pruriency of inordinate Desire.

Pleasure, when it is a Man's chief Purpose, disappoints it self; and the constant Application to it palls the Faculty of enjoying it, tho' it leaves the Sense of our Inability for that we wish, with a Disrelish of every thing else. Thus the intermediate Seasons of the Man of Pleasure, are more heavy than one would impose upon the vilest Criminal. Take him when he is awaked too soon after a Debauch, or disappointed in following a worthless Woman without Truth, and there is no Man living whose Being is such a Weight or Vexation as his is. He is an utter Stranger to the pleasing Reflexions in the Evening of a well-spent Day, or the Gladness of Heart or Quickness of Spirit in the Morning after profound Sleep or indolent Slumbers. He is not to be at Ease any longer than he can keep Reason and good Sense without his Curtains; otherwise he will be haunted with the Reflection, that he could not believe such a one the Woman that upon Tryal he found her. What has he got by his Conquest, but to think meanly of her for whom a Day or two before he had the highest Honour? and of himself for, perhaps, wronging the Man whom of all Men living he himself would least willingly have injured?

Pleasure seizes the whole Man who addicts himself to it, and will not give him Leisure for any good Office in Life which contradicts the Gayety of the present Hour. You may indeed observe in People of Pleasure a certain Complacency and Absence of all Severity, which the Habit of a loose unconcerned Life gives them; but tell the Man of Pleasure your secret Wants, Cares, or Sorrows, and you will find he has given up the Delicacy of his Passions to the Cravings of his Appetites. He little knows the perfect Joy he loses, for the disappointing Gratifications which he pursues. He looks at Pleasure as she approaches, and comes to you with the Recommendation of warm Wishes, gay Looks, and graceful Motion; but he does not observe how she leaves his Presence with Disorder, Impotence, downcast Shame, and conscious Imperfection. She makes our Youth inglorious, our Age shameful.

WILL. HONEYCOMB gives us twenty Intimations in an Evening of several Hags whose Bloom was given up to his Arms; and would raise a Value to himself for having had, as the Phrase is, very good Women. WILL's good Women are the Comfort of his Heart, and support him, I warrant, by the Memory of past Interviews with Persons of their Condition. No, there is not in the World an Occasion wherein Vice makes so phantastical a Figure, as at the Meeting of two old People who have been Partners in unwarrantable Pleasure. To tell a toothless old Lady that she once had a good Set, or a defunct Wencher that he once was the admired Thing of the Town, are Satyrs instead of Applauses; but on the other Side, consider the old Age of those who have passed their Days in Labour, Industry, and Virtue, their Decays make them but appear the more venerable, and the Imperfections of their Bodies are beheld as a Misfortune to humane Society that their Make is so little durable.

But to return more directly to my Man of Wit and Pleasure. In all Orders of Men where-ever this is the chief Character, the Person who wears it is a negligent Friend, Father, and Husband, and intails Poverty on his unhappy Descendants. Mortgages, Diseases, and Settlements are the Legacies a Man of Wit and Pleasure leaves to his Family. All the poor Rogues that make such lamentable Speeches after every Sessions at *Tyburn*, were, in their Way, Men of Wit and Pleasure before they fell into the Adventures which brought them thither.

Irresolution and Procrastination in all a Man's Affairs, are the natural Effects of being addicted to Pleasure: Dishonour to the Gentleman and Bankrupcy to the Trader, are the Portion of either whose chief Purpose of Life is Delight. The chief Cause that this Pursuit has been in all Ages received with so much Quarter from the soberer Part of Mankind, has been that some Men of great Talents have sacrificed themselves to it: The shining Qualities of such People have given a Beauty to whatever they were engaged in, and a Mixture of Wit has recommended Madness. For let any Man who knows what it's to have passed much Time in a Series of Jollity, Mirth, Wit, or humourous Entertainments, look back at what he was all that while a doing, and he will find that he has been at one Instant sharp to some Man he is sorry to have offended, impertinent to some one it was Cruelty to treat with such Freedom, ungracefully noisie at such a Time, unskilfully open at such a Time, unmercifully calumnious at such a Time; and from the whole Course of his applauded Satisfactions, unable in the End to recollect any Circumstance which can add to the Enjoyment of his own Mind alone, or which he would put his Character upon with other Men. Thus it is with those who are best made for becoming Pleasures; but how monstrous is it in the Generality of Mankind who pretend this Way, without Genius or Inclination towards it? The Scene then is wild to an Extravagance; this is as if Fools should mimick Madmen. Pleasure of this Kind is the intemperate Meals and loud Jollities of the common Rate of Country Gentlemen, whose Practice and Way of Enjoyment is to put an End as fast as they can to that little Particle of Reason they have when they are sober: These Men of Wit and Pleasure dispatch their Senses as fast as possible, by drinking till they cannot taste, smoaking till they cannot see, and roaring till they cannot hear.   T

No. 152.

[STEELE.]   Friday, August 24.

Οΐη περ φύλλων γενεή τοΐη δὲ καὶ ἀνδρῶν.—Hom.

THERE is no sort of People whose Conversation is so pleasant as that of military Men, who derive their Courage and Magnanimity from Thought and Reflection. The many Adventures which attend their Way of Life makes their Conversation so full of Incidents, and gives them so frank an Air in speaking of what they have been Witnesses of, that no Company can be more amiable than that of Men of Sense who are Soldiers. There is a certain irregular Way in their Narrations or Discourse, which has something more warm and pleasing than we meet with among Men who are used to adjust and methodize their Thoughts.

I was this Evening walking in the Fields with my Friend Captain SENTREY, and I could not, from the many Relations which I drew him into of what passed when he was in the Service, forbear expressing my Wonder, that the Fear of Death, which we, the rest of Mankind, arm our selves against with so much Contemplation, Reason and Philosophy, should appear so little in Camps, that common Men march into open Breaches, meet opposite Battallions, not only without Reluctance but with Alacrity. My Friend answered what I said in the following manner: 'What you wonder at may very naturally be the Subject of Admiration to all who are not conversant in Camps; but when a Man has spent some Time in that Way of Life, he observes a certain Mechanick Courage which the ordinary Race of Men become Masters of from acting always in a Crowd: They see indeed many drop, but then they see many more alive; they observe themselves escape very narrowly, and they do not know why they should not again. Besides which general way of loose thinking, they usually spend the other Part of their Time in Pleasures, upon which their Minds are so entirely bent, that short Labours or Dangers are but a cheap Purchase of Jollity, Triumph, Victory, fresh Quarters, new Scenes, and uncommon Adventures. Such are the Thoughts of the Executive Part of an Army, and indeed of the Gross of Mankind in general; but none of these Men of Mechanical Courage have ever made any great Figure in the Profession of Arms. Those who are formed for Command, are such as have reasoned themselves, out of a Consideration of greater Good than Length of Days, into such a Negligence of their Being, as to make it their first Position. That it is one Day to be resigned; and since it is, in the Prosecution of worthy Actions and Service of Mankind they can put it to habitual Hazard. The Event of our Designs, say they, as it relates to others, is uncertain; but as it relates to our selves it must be prosperous, while we are in the Pursuit of our Duty, and within the Terms upon which Providence has ensured our Happiness, whether we die or live. All that Nature has prescribed must be good; and as Death is natural to us, it is Absurdity to fear it. Fear loses its Purpose when we are sure it cannot preserve us, and we should draw Resolution to meet it from the Impossibility to escape it. Without a Resignation to the Necessity of dying, there can be no Capacity in Man to attempt any thing that is glorious; but when they have once attained to that Perfection, the Pleasures of a Life spent in Martial Adventures are as great as any of which the human Mind is capable. The Force of Reason gives a certain Beauty, mixed with the Conscience of Well-doing and Thirst of Glory, to all which before was terrible and ghastly to the Imagination. Add to this, that the Fellowship of Danger, the common Good of Mankind, the general Cause, and the manifest Virtue you may observe in so many Men, who made no Figure till that Day, are so many Incentives to destroy the little Consideration of their own Persons. Such are the Heroick Part of Soldiers who are qualified for Leaders: As to the rest whom I before spoke of, I know not how it is, but they arrive at a certain Habit of being void of Thought, insomuch that on Occasion of the most imminent Danger they are still in the same Indifference: Nay I remember an Instance of a gay *Frenchman* who was led on in Battle by a superior Officer (whose Conduct it was his Custom to speak of always with Contempt and Raillery), and in the Beginning of the Action received a Wound he was sensible was mortal; his Reflection on this Occasion was, *I wish I could live another Hour, to see how this blundering Coxcomb will get clear of this Business.*

I remember two young Fellows who rid in the same Squadron of a Troop of Horse, who were ever together; they eat, they drank, they intreagued; in a Word, all their Passions and Affections seem'd to tend the same Way, and they appear'd serviceable to each other in them. We were in the Dusk of the Evening to march over a River, and the Troop these Gentlemen belonged to were to be transported in a Ferry-boat as fast as they could. One of the Friends was now in the Boat, while the other was drawn up with others by the Water-side waiting the Return of the Boat. A Disorder happened in the Passage by an unruly Horse: and a Gentleman who had the Rein of his Horse negligently under his Arm, was forced into the Water by his Horse's jumping over. The Friend on the Shore cry'd out, who 's that is drowned trow? He was immediately answered, your Friend, *Harry Thompson*. He very gravely replyed, *Ay, he had a mad Horse*. This short Epitaph from such a Familiar without more Words, gave me, at that Time under Twenty, a very moderate Opinion of the Friendship of Companions. Thus is Affection and every other Motive of Life in the Generality, rooted out by the present busy Scene about them: They lament no Man whose Capacity can be supplied by another; and where Men converse without Delicacy, the next Man you meet will serve as well as he whom you have lived with half your Life. To such the Devastation of Countries, the Misery of Inhabitants, the Cries of the Pillaged, and the silent Sorrow of the great Unfortunate, are ordinary Objects; their Minds are bent upon the little Gratifications of their own Senses and Appetites, forgetful of Compassion, insensible of Glory, avoiding only Shame; their whole Hearts taken up with the trivial Hope of meeting and being merry. These are the People who make up the Gross of the Soldiery: But the fine Gentleman in that Band of Men, is such a one as I have now in my Eye, who is foremost in all Danger to which he is ordered. His Officers are his Friends and Companions, as they are Men of Honour and Gentlemen; the private Men his Brethren, as they are of his Species. He is beloved of all that behold him: They wish him in Danger as he views their Ranks, that they may have Occasions to save him at their own Hazard. Mutual Love is the Order of the Files where he commands; every Man afraid for himself and his Neighbour, not lest their Commander should punish them, but lest he should be offended. Such is his Regiment who knows Mankind, and feels their Distresses so far as to prevent them. Just in distributing what is their Due, he would think himself below their Taylor to wear a Snip of their Cloaths in Lace upon his own; and below the most rapacious Agent, should he enjoy a Farthing above his own Pay. Go on, brave Man, immortal Glory is thy Fortune, and immortal Happiness thy Reward.' T

No. 153.

[STEELE.] Saturday, August 25.

Habet natura ut aliarum omnium rerum sic vivendi modum; senectus autem peractio aetatis est tanquam fabulae. Cujus defatigationem fugere debemus, praesertim adjuncta satietate.—Tull. *De Senect.*

OF all the impertinent Wishes which we hear expressed in Conversation, there is not one more unworthy a Gentleman or a Man of liberal Education, than that of wishing one's self younger. I have observed this Wish is usually made upon Sight of some Object which gives the Idea of a past Action, that it is no Dishonour to us that we cannot now repeat; or else on what was in it self shameful when we performed it. It is a certain Sign of a foolish or a dissolute Mind, if we want our Youth again only for the Strength of Bones and Sinews which we once were Masters of. It is (as my Author has it) as absurd in an old Man to wish for the Strength of a Youth, as it would be in a young Man to wish for the Strength of a Bull or a Horse. These Wishes are both equally out of Nature, which should direct in all things that are not contradictory to Justice, Law and Reason. But tho' every old Man has been Young, and every young one hopes to be old, there seems to be a most unnatural Misunderstanding between those two Stages of Life. This unhappy Want of Commerce arises from the insolent Arrogance or Exultation in Youth, and the irrational Despondence or self-pity in Age. A young Man whose Passion and Ambition is to be good and wise, and an old one who has no Inclination to be lewd or debauched, are quite unconcerned in this Speculation; but the Cocking young Fellow who treads upon the Toes of his Elders, and the old Fool who envyes the sawcy Pride he sees him in, are the Objects of our present Contempt and Derision. Contempt and Derision are harsh Words; but in what manner can one give advice to a Youth in the pursuit and Possession of sensual Pleasures, or afford Pity to an old Man in the impotence and desire of Enjoying them? When young Men in publick Places betray in their Deportment an abandoned Resignation to their Appetites, they give to sober Minds a Prospect of a despicable Age, which, if not interrupted by Death in the midst of their Follies, must certainly come. When an old Man bewails the Loss of such Gratifications which are passed, he discovers a monstrous Inclination to that which it is not in the Course of Providence to recall. The State of an old Man, who is dissatisfi'd merely for his being such, is the most out of all Measures of Reason and good Sense of any Being we have any Account of from the highest Angel to the lowest Worm. How miserable is the Contemplation to consider a libidinous old Man (while all Created things, beside himself and Devils, are following the order of Providence) fretting at the Course of things, and being almost the sole Malecontent in the Creation. But let us a little reflect upon what he has lost by the number of Years: The Passions which he had in Youth are not to be obeyed as they were then, but Reason is more powerful now without the Disturbance of them. An old Gentleman t'other day in Discourse with a Friend of his, (reflecting upon some

Adventures they had in Youth together) cry'd out, *Oh Jack those were happy Days! That is true*, replyed his Friend, *but methinks we go about our Business more quietly than we did then.* One would think it should be no small Satisfaction to have gone so far in our Journey that the Heat of the Day is over with us. When Life it self is a Feaver, as it is in licentious Youth, the Pleasures of it are no other than the Dreams of a Man in that Distemper; and it is as absurd to wish the Return of that Season of Life, as for a Man in Health to be sorry for the Loss of gilded Palaces, fairy Walks, and flowery Pastures, with which he remembers he was entertained in the troubled Slumbers of a Fit of Sickness.

As to all the rational and worthy Pleasures of our Being, the Conscience of a good Fame, the Contemplation of another Life, the Respect and Commerce of honest Men, our Capacities for such Enjoyments are enlarged by Years. While Health endures, the latter Part of Life, in the Eye of Reason, is certainly the more eligible. The Memory of a well-spent Youth gives a peaceable, unmixed, and elegant Pleasure to the Mind; and to such who are so unfortunate as not to be able to look back on Youth with Satisfaction, they may give themselves no little Consolation that they are under no Temptation to repeat their Follies, and that they at present despise them. It was prettily said, 'He that would be long an old Man, must begin early to be one': It is too late to resign a thing after a Man is robbed of it: therefore it is necessary that before the Arrival of Age we bid adieu to the Pursuits of Youth, otherwise sensual Habits will live in our Imaginations when our Limbs cannot be subservient to them. The poor Fellow who lost his Arm last Siege will tell you, he feels the Fingers that are buried in *Flanders* ake every cold Morning at *Chelsea*.

The fond Humour of appearing in the gay and fashionable World, and being applauded for trivial Excellencies, is what makes Youth have Age in Contempt, and makes Age resign with so ill a Grace the Qualifications of Youth: But this in both Sexes is inverting all things, and turning the natural Course of our Minds, which should build their Approbations and Dislikes upon what Nature and Reason dictate, into Chimera and Confusion.

Age in a virtuous Person, of either Sex, carries in it an Authority which makes it preferable to all the Pleasures of Youth. If to be saluted, attended, and consulted with Deference, are Instances of Pleasure, they are such as never fail a virtuous old Age. In the Enumeration of the Imperfections and Advantages of the younger and later Years of Man they are so near in their Condition that, methinks, it should be incredible we see so little Commerce of Kindness between them. If we consider Youth and Age with *Tully,* regarding the Affinity to Death, Youth has many more Chances to be near it than Age; what Youth can say more than an old Man, He shall live till Night? Youth catches Distempers more easily, its Sickness is more violent, and its Recovery more doubtful. The Youth indeed hopes for many more Days, so cannot the old Man: The Youth's Hopes are ill grounded; for what is more foolish than to place any Confidence upon an Uncertainty? But the old Man has not Room so much as for Hope; he is still happier than the Youth, he has already enjoyed what the other does but hope for; One wishes to live long, the other has lived long. But alas, is there any thing in humane Life, the Duration of which can be called long? There is nothing which must end to be valued for its Continuance. If Hours, Days, Months, and Years pass away, it is no Matter what Hour, what Day, what Month, or what Year we dye. The Applause of a good Actor is due to him at whatever Scene of the Play he makes his Exit. It is thus in the Life of a Man of Sense, a short Life is sufficient to manifest himself a Man of Honour and Virtue: when he ceases to be such he has lived too long; and while he is such, it is of no Consequence to him how long he shall be so, provided he is so to his Life's End. T

No. 154.
[STEELE.]   Monday, August 27.

Nemo repente fuit turpissimus . . .—Juv.

'*Mr.* SPECTATOR,

YOU are frequent in the Mention of Matters which concern the feminine World, and take upon you to be very severe against Men upon all those Occasions: But all this while I am afraid you have been very little conversant with Women, or you would know the Generality of them are not so angry as you imagine at the general Vices amongst us. I am apt to believe (begging your Pardon) that you are still what I my self was once, a queer modest Fellow; and therefore, for your Information, shall give you a short Account of my self, and the Reasons why I was forced to wench, drink, play, and do every thing which are necessary to the Character of a Man of Wit and Pleasure, to be well with the Ladies.

You are to know then that I was bred a Gentleman, and had the finishing Part of my Education under a Man of great Probity, Wit, and Learning in one of our Universities. I will not deny but this made my Behaviour and Mein bear in it a Figure of Thought rather than Action; and a Man of quite contrary Character, who never thought in his Life, rallied me one Day upon it, and said He believ'd I was still a Virgin. There was a young Lady of Virtue present, and I was not displeased to favour the Insinuation: But it had a quite contrary Effect from what I expected; I was ever after treated with great Coldness both by that Lady and all the rest of my Acquaintance. In a very little Time I never came into a Room but I could hear a Whisper, Here comes the Maid: A Girl of Humour would on some Occasion say, Why how do you know more than any of us? An Expression of that kind was generally followed by a loud Laugh: In a Word, for no other Fault in the World than that they really thought me as innocent as themselves, I became of no Consequence among them, and was receiv'd always upon the Foot of a Jest. This made so strong an Impression upon me, that I resolv'd to be as agreeable as the best of the Men who laugh'd at me; but I observed it was Nonsense for me to be impudent at first among those who knew me; My Character for Modesty was so notorious wherever I had hitherto appeared, that I resolved to shew my new Face in new Quarters of the World. My first Step I chose with Judgment, for I went to *Astrop*; and came down among a Crowd of Academicks, at one Dash, the impudentest Fellow they had ever seen in their Lives. Flushed with this Success, I made Love and was happy. Upon this Conquest I thought it would be unlike a Gentleman to stay long with my Mistress, and crossed the Country to *Bury*: I could give you a very good Account of my self at that Place also. At these two ended my first Summer of Gallantry. The Winter following, you would wonder at it, but I relapsed into Modesty upon coming among People of Figure in *London*, yet not so much but that the Ladies who had formerly laughed at me said, Bless us! how wonderfully that Gentleman is improved? Some Familiarities about the Play-houses towards the End of the ensuing Winter, made me conceive new Hopes of Adventures; and instead of returning the next Summer to *Astrop* or *Bury*, I thought my self qualified to go to *Epsom*; and followed a young Woman, whose Relations were jealous of my Place in her Favour, to *Scarborough*. I carried my Point, and in my third Year aspired to go to *Tunbridge*, and in the Autumn of the same Year made my Appearance at *Bath*. I was now got into the Way of Talk proper for Ladies, and was run into a vast Acquaintance among them, which I always improved to the *best Advantage*. In all this Course of Time, and some Years following, I found a sober modest Man was always looked upon by both Sexes as a precise unfashioned Fellow of no Life or Spirit. It was ordinary for a Man who had been drunk in good Company, or passed a Night with a Wench, to speak of it next Day before Women for whom he had the greatest Respect. He was reproved, perhaps, with a Blow of the Fan or an oh Fie, but the angry Lady still preserved an apparent Approbation in her Countenance: He was called a strange wicked Fellow, a sad Wretch; he shrugs his Shoulders, swears, receives another Blow, swears again he did not know he swore, and all was well. You might often see Men game in the presence of Women, and throw at once for more than they were worth, to recommend themselves as Men of Spirit. I found by long Experience, that the loosest Principles and most abandoned Behaviour, carried all before them in Pretentions to Women of Fortune. The Encouragement given to People of this Stamp, made me soon throw off the remaining Impressions of a sober Education. In the above-mentioned Places, as well as in Town, I always kept Company with those who lived most at large; and in due Process of Time I was a very pretty Rake among the Men, and a very pretty Fellow among the Women. I must confess I had some melancholy Hours upon the Account of the Narrowness of my Fortune, but my Conscience at the same Time gave me the Comfort that I had qualified my self for marrying a Fortune.

When I had lived in this Manner for some Time, and became thus accomplished, I was now in the Twenty seventh Year of my Age, and about the Forty seventh of my Constitution, my Health and Estate wasting very fast; when I happened to fall into the Company of a very pretty young Lady in her own Disposal. I entertained the Company, as we Men of Gallantry generally do, with the many Haps and Disasters, Watchings under Windows, Escapes from jealous Husbands, and several other Perils. The young thing was wonderfully charmed with one that knew the World so well and talked so fine; with *Desdemona,* all her Lover said affected her; *it was strange, 'twas wond'rous strange.* In a Word, I saw the Impression I had made upon her, and with a very little Application the pretty thing has married me. There is so much charm in her Innocence and Beauty, that I do now as much detest the Course I have been in for many Years, as ever I did before I entred into it.

What I intend, Mr. SPECTATOR, by writing all this to you, is, that you would, before you go any further with your Panegyricks on the fair Sex, give them some Lectures upon their silly Approbations. It is that I am weary of Vice, and that it was not in my natural Way, that I am now so far recovered as not to bring this believing dear Creature to Contempt and Poverty for her Generosity to me. At the same Time tell the Youth of good Education of our Sex, that they take too little Care of improving themselves in little things: A good Air at entring into a Room, a proper Audacity in expressing himself with Gayety and Gracefulness, would make a young Gentleman of Virtue and Sense capable of discountenancing the shallow impudent Rogues that shine among the Women.

Mr. SPECTATOR, I don't doubt but you are a very sagacious Person, but you are so great with *Tully* of late, that I fear you will contemn these things as Matters of no Consequence: But believe me, Sir, they are of the highest Importance to humane Life; and if you can do any thing towards opening fair Eyes, you will lay an Obligation upon all your Contemporaries who are Fathers, Husbands, or Brothers to Females.

Your most affectionate humble Servant,
Simon Honeycomb.'

T

No. 155.
[STEELE.] Tuesday, August 28.

. . . *Hae nugae seria ducent*
In mala . . .—Hor.

I HAVE more than once taken Notice of an indecent License taken in Discourse, wherein the Conversation on one Part is involuntary, and the Effect of some necessary Circumstance. This happens in travelling together in the same hired Coach, sitting near each other in any publick Assembly, or the like. I have upon making Observations of this sort received innumerable Messages, from that Part of the fair Sex whose Lot in Life is to be of any Trade or publick Way of Life. They are all to a Woman urgent with me to lay before the World the unhappy Circumstances they are under, from the unreasonable Liberty which is taken in their Presence, to talk on what Subject it is thought fit by every Coxcomb who wants Understanding or Breeding. One or two of these Complaints I shall set down.

'Mr. SPECTATOR,

I keep a Coffee-house, and am one of those whom you have thought fit to mention as an Idol some Time ago. I suffered a good deal of Raillery upon that Occasion; but shall heartily forgive you, who were the Cause of it, if you will do me Justice in another Point. What I ask of you, is, to acquaint my Customers (who are otherwise very good ones) that I am unavoidably hasped in my Bar, and cannot help hearing the improper Discourses they are pleased to entertain me with. They strive who shall say the most immodest things in my Hearing: At the same Time half a Dozen of them loll at the Bar staring just in my Face, ready to interpret my Looks and Gestures according to their own Imaginations. In this passive Condition I know not where to cast my Eyes, place my Hands, or what to employ my self in: But this Confusion is to be a Jest, and I hear them say in the End, with an insipid Air of Mirth and Subtlety, Let her alone, she knows as well as we for all she looks so. Good Mr. SPECTATOR, perswade Gentlemen that it is out of all Decency: Say it is possible a Woman may be modest, and yet keep a publick House. Be pleas'd to argue, that in Truth the Affront is the more unpardonable because I am obliged to suffer it, and cannot fly from it. I do assure you, Sir, the Chearfulness of Life which would arise from the honest Gain I have, is utterly lost to me from the endless, flat, impertinent Pleasantries which I hear from Morning to Night. In a Word, it is too much for me to bear; and I desire you to acquaint them, that I will keep Pen and Ink at the Bar, and write down all they say to me, and send it to you for the Press. It is possible when they see how empty what they speak, without the Advantage of an impudent Countenance and Gesture, will appear, they may come to some Sense of themselves, and the Insults they are guilty of towards me. I am,

Sir,

Your most humble Servant,

The Idol.'

This Representation is so just, that it is hard to speak of it without an Indignation which perhaps would appear too elevated to such as can be guilty of this inhuman Treatment, where they see they affront a modest, plain, and ingenuous Behaviour. This Correspondent is not the only Sufferer in this Kind, for I have long Letters both from the *Royal* and *New Exchange* on the same Subject. They tell me that a young Fop cannot buy a Pair of Gloves, but he is at the same Time straining for some ingenious Ribaldry to say to the young Woman who helps them on. It is no small Addition to the Calamity, that the Rogues buy as hard as the plainest and modestest Customers they have; besides which they loll upon their Counters half an Hour longer than they need, to drive away other Customers, who are to share their Impertinencies with the Milliner, or go to another Shop. Letters from *'Change-Alley* are full of the same Evil, and the Girls tell me except I can chace some eminent Merchants from their Shops they shall in a short Time fail. It is very unaccountable, that Men can have so little Deference to all Mankind who pass by them, as to bear being seen toying by twos and threes at a Time, with no other Purpose but to appear gay enough to keep up a light Conversation of common-place Jests, to the Injury of her whose Credit is certainly hurt by it, tho' their own may be strong enough to bear it. When we come to have exact Accounts of these Conversations, it is not to be doubted but that their Discourses will raise the usual Stile of buying and selling: Instead of the plain down-right lying, and asking and bidding so unequally to what they will really give and take, we may hope to have from these fine Folks an Exchange of Complements. There must certainly be a great deal of pleasant Difference between the Commerce of Lovers, and that of all other Dealers, who are, in a Kind, Adversaries. A sealed Bond or a Bank Note, would be a pretty Gallantry to convey unseen into the Hands of one whom a Director is charmed with; otherwise the City Loiterers are still more unreasonable than those at the other End of the Town: At the *New Exchange* they are eloquent for want of Cash, but in the City they ought with Cash to supply their want of Eloquence.

If one might be serious on this prevailing Folly, one might observe, that it is a melancholy thing, when the World is mercenary even to the buying and selling our very Persons, that young Women, tho' they have never so great Attractions from Nature, are never the nearer being happily disposed of in Marriage; I say, it is very hard under this Necessity, it shall not be possible for them to go into a Way of Trade for their Maintenance, but their very Excellencies and personal Perfections shall be a Disadvantage to them, and subject them to be treated as if they stood there to sell their Persons to Prostitution. There cannot be a more melancholy Circumstance to one who has made any Observation in the World, than one of these erring Creatures exposed to Bankruptcy. When that happens, none of these toying Fools will do any more than any other Man they meet to preserve her from Infamy, Insult, and Distemper. A Woman is naturally more helpless than the other Sex; and a Man of Honour and Sense should have this in his View in all Manner of Commerce with her. Were this well weighed, Inconsideration, Ribaldry, and Nonsense would not be more natural to entertain Women with than Men; and it would be as much Impertinence to go into a Shop of one of these young Women without buying, as into that of any other Trader. I shall end this Speculation with a Letter I have received from a pretty Milliner in the City.

'Mr. SPECTATOR,

I have read your Account of Beauties, and was not a little surprized to find no Character of my self in it. I do assure you I have little else to do but to give Audience as I am such. Here are Merchants of no small Consideration, who call in as certainly as they go to 'Change to say something of my roguish Eye: And here is one who makes me once or twice a Week tumble over all my Goods, and then owns it was only a Gallantry to see me act with these pretty Hands; then lays out three Pence in a little Ribbon for his Wrist-bands, and thinks he is a Man of great Vivacity. There is an ugly thing not far off me, whose Shop is frequented only by People of Business, that is all Day long as busy as possible. Must I that am a Beauty be treated with for nothing but my Beauty? Be pleased to assign Rates to my kind Glances, or make all pay who come to see me, or I shall be undone by my Admirers for want of Customers. *Albacinda*, *Eudosia*, and all the rest would be used just as we are, if they were in our Condition; therefore pray consider the Distress of us the lower Order of Beauties, and I shall be

T   *Your oblig'd humble Servant.'*

No. 156.

[STEELE.]   Wednesday, August 29.

> *. . . Sed tu simul obligasti*
> *Perfidum votis caput, enitescis*
> *Pulchrior multo . . .*—Hor.

I DO not think any thing could make a pleasanter Entertainment, than the History of the reigning Favourites among the Women from Time to Time about this Town. In such an Account we ought to have a faithful Confession of each Lady for what she liked such and such a Man, and he ought to tell us by what particular Action or Dress he believed he should be most successful. As for my Part, I have always made as easy a Judgment when a Man dresses for the Ladies, as when he is equipped for Hunting or Coursing. The Woman's Man is a Person in his Air and Behaviour quite different from the rest of our Species; His Garb is more loose and negligent, his Manner more soft and indolent; that is to say, in both these Cases there is an apparent Endeavour to appear unconcerned and careless. In catching Birds the Fowlers have a Method of imitating their Voices to bring them to the Snare; and your Women's Men have always a Similitude of the Creature they hope to betray, in their own Conversation. A Woman's Man is very knowing in all that passes from one Family to another, has little pretty Officiousnesses, is not at a Loss what is good for a Cold, and it is not amiss if he has a Bottle of Spirits in his Pocket in case of any sudden Indisposition.

Curiosity having been my prevailing Passion, and indeed the sole Entertainment of my Life, I have sometimes made it my Business to Examine the Course of Intreagues, as well as the Manners and Accomplishments of such as have been most successful that Way. In all my Observation, I never knew a Man of good Understanding a general Favourite; some Singularity in his Behaviour, some Whim in his Way of Life, and what would have made him ridiculous among the Men, has recommended him to the other Sex. I should be very sorry to offend a People so fortunate as these of whom I am speaking; but let any one look over the old Beaux, and he will find the Man of Success was remarkable for quarrelling impertinently for their Sakes, for dressing unlike the rest of the World, or passing his Days in an insipid Assiduity about the fair Sex, to gain the Figure he made amongst them. Add to this that he must have the Reputation of being well with other Women, to please any one Woman of Gallantry; for you are to know, that there is a mighty Ambition among the light Part of the Sex to gain Slaves from the Dominion of others. My Friend WILL. HONEYCOMB says it was a common Bite with him, to lay Suspicions that he was favoured by a Lady's Enemy, that is some rival Beauty, to be well with her herself. A little Spite is natural to a great Beauty; and it is ordinary to snap up a disagreeable Fellow lest another should have him. That impudent Toad *Bareface* fares well among all the Ladies he converses with, for no other Reason in the World but that he has the Skill to keep them from Explanation with one another. Did they know there is not one who likes him in her Heart, each would declare her Scorn of him the next Moment; but he is well received by them because it is the Fashion, and Opposition to each other brings them insensibly into an Imitation of each other. What adds to him the greatest Grace is, that the pleasant Thief, as they call him, is the most inconstant Creature living, has a wonderful deal of Wit and Humour, and never wants something to say; besides all which, he has a most spiteful dangerous Tongue if you should provoke him.

To make a Woman's Man, he must not be a Man of Sense or a Fool; the Business is to entertain, and it is much better to have a Faculty of arguing than a Capacity of judging right. But the pleasantest of all the Women's Equipage are your regular Visitants; these are Volunteers in their Service withou

Hopes of Pay or Preferment: It is enough that they can lead out from a publick Place, that they are admitted on a publick Day, and can be allowed to pass away part of that heavy Load, their Time, in the Company of the Fair. But commend me above all others to those who are known for your Ruiners of Ladies; these are the choicest Spirits which our Age produces. We have several of these irresistible Gentlemen among us when the Company is in Town. These Fellows are accomplished with the Knowledge of the ordinary Occurrences about Court and Town, have that sort of good Breeding which is exclusive of all Morality, and consists only in being publickly decent, privately dissolute.

It is wonderful how far a fond Opinion of herself can carry a Woman to make her have the least Regard to a professed known Woman's Man: But as scarce one of all the Women who are in the Tour of Gallantries ever hears any thing of what is the common Sense of sober Minds, but are entertained with a continual Round of Flatteries, they cannot be Mistresses of themselves enough to make Arguments for their own Conduct from the Behaviour of these Men to others. It is so far otherwise, that a general Fame for Falshood in this kind, is a Recommendation; and the Coxcomb, loaded with the Favours of many others, is received like a Victor that disdains his Trophies, to be a Victim to the present Charmer.

If you see a Man more full of Gesture than ordinary in a publick Assembly, if loud upon no Occasion, if negligent of the Company round him, and yet laying wait for destroying by that Negligence, you may take it for granted that he has ruined many a fair One. The Woman's Man expresses himself wholly in that Motion which we call Strutting: An elevated Chest, a pinched Hat, a measurable Step, and a sly surveying Eye, are the Marks of him. Now and then you see a Gentleman with all these Accomplishments; but alas any one of them is enough to undo thousands: When a Gentleman with such Perfections adds to it suitable Learning, there should be publick Warning of his Residence in Town, that we may remove our Wives and Daughters. It happens sometimes that such a fine Man has read all the Miscellany Poems, a few of our Comedies, and has the Translation of *Ovid*'s Epistles by Heart. Oh if it were possible that such a one could be as true as he is charming! but that is too much, the Women will share such a dear false Man: 'A little Gallantry to hear him Talk one would indulge one's self in, let him reckon the Sticks of one's Fan, say something of the Cupids in it, and then call one so many soft Names which a Man of his Learning has at his Fingers-Ends. There sure is some Excuse for Frailty, when attack'd by such Force

against a weak Woman.' Such is the Soliloquy of many a
Lady one might name, at the Sight of one of these who makes
it no Iniquity to go on from Day to Day in the Sin of Woman-
slaughter.

It is certain that People are got into a way of Affection, with
a manner of overlooking the most solid Virtues, and admiring
the most trivial Excellencies. The Woman is so far from expecting to be contemned for being a very injudicious silly
Animal, that while she can preserve her Features and her
Mein, she knows she is still the Object of Desire; and there is a
sort of secret Ambition, from reading frivolous Books, and
keeping as frivolous Company, each side to be amiable in
Imperfection, and arrive at the Characters of the dear Deceiver
and the perjured Fair.

T

No. 157.
[STEELE.]   Thursday, August 30.

> . . . *Genius, natale comes qui temperat astrum,*
> *Naturae deus humanae, mortalis in unum*
> *Quodque caput* . . .—Hor.

I am very much at a Loss to express by any Word that occurs
to me in our Language that which is understood by *Indoles* in
Latin. The natural Disposition to any particular Art, Science,
Profession, or Trade, is very much to be consulted in the Care
of Youth, and studied by Men for their own Conduct when
they form to themselves any Scheme of Life. It is wonderfully hard indeed for a Man to judge of his own Capacity impartially; that may look great to me which may appear little
to another, and I may be carried by Fondness towards my self
so far, as to attempt things too high for my Talents and
Accomplishments: But it is not methinks so very difficult a
Matter to make a Judgment of the Abilities of others, especially
of those who are in their Infancy. My common-place Book
directs me on this Occasion to mention the Dawning of Greatness in *Alexander*, who being asked in his Youth to contend for
a Prize in the Olympick Games, answered he would if he had
Kings to run against him. *Cassius*, who was one of the Con-
spirators against *Caesar*, gave as great a Proof of his Temper,
when in his Childhood he struck a Play-fellow, the Son of
Sylla, for saying his Father was Master of the *Roman* People.
Scipio is reported to have answered (when some Flatterers at
Supper were asking him what the *Romans* should do for a

General after his Death), Take *Marius*. *Marius* was then a very Boy, and had given no Instances of his Valour; but it was visible to *Scipio* from the Manners of the Youth, that he had a Soul formed for the Attempt and Execution of great Undertakings. I must confess I have very often with much Sorrow bewailed the Misfortune of the Children of *Great Britain*, when I consider the Ignorance and Undiscerning of the Generality of School-masters. The boasted Liberty we talk of is but a mean Reward for the long Servitude, the many Heart Aches and Terrours, to which our Childhood is exposed in going through a Grammar-School: Many of these stupid Tyrants exercise their Cruelty without any Manner of Distinction of the Capacities of Children, or the Intention of Parents in their Behalf. There are many excellent Tempers which are worthy to be nourished and cultivated with all possible Diligence and Care, that were never designed to be acquainted with *Aristotle, Tully,* or *Virgil*; and there are as many who have Capacities for understanding every Word those great Persons have writ, and yet were not born to have any Relish of their Writings. For want of this common and obvious discerning in those who have the Care of Youth, we have so many Hundred unaccountable Creatures every Age whipped up into great Scholars, that are for ever near a right Understanding, and will never arrive at it. These are the Scandal of Letters, and these are generally the Men who are to teach others. The Sense of Shame and Honour is enough to keep the World it self in Order without Corporal Punishment, much more to train the Minds of uncorrupted and innocent Children. It happens, I doubt not, more than once in a Year, that a Lad is chastised for a Blockhead, when it is good Apprehension that makes him incapable of knowing what his Teacher means: A brisk Imagination very often may suggest an Errour, which a Lad could not have fallen into if he had been as heavy in conjecturing as his Master in explaining: But there is no Mercy even towards a wrong Interpretation of his Meaning; the Sufferings of the Scholar's Body are to rectify the Mistakes of his Mind.

I am confident that no Boy who will not be allured to Letters without Blows, will ever be brought to any thing with them. A great or good Mind must necessarily be the worse for such Indignities: and it is a sad Change to lose of its Virtue for the Improvement of its Knowledge. No one who has gone through what they call a great School, but must remember to have seen Children of excellent and ingenuous Natures (as has afterwards appeared in their Manhood); I say no Man has passed through this Way of Education, but must have seen an ingenuous Creature expiring with Shame, with pale Looks, beseeching

Sorrow, and silent Tears, throw up its honest Eyes, and kneel on its tender Knees to an inexorable Blockhead, to be forgiven the false Quantity of a Word in making a Latin Verse: The Child is punished, and the next Day he commits a like Crime, and so a third with the same Consequence. I would fain ask any reasonable Man whether this Lad, in the Simplicity of his native Innocence, full of Shame, and capable of any Impression from that Grace of Soul, was not fitter for any Purpose in this Life, than after that Spark of Virtue is extinguished in him, tho' he is able to write twenty Verses in an Evening?

Seneca says, after his exalted Way of talking, *As the immortal Gods never learnt any Virtue, tho' they are endued with all that is good; so there are some Men who have so natural a Propensity to what they should follow, that they learn it almost as soon as they hear it.* Plants and Vegetables are cultivated into the Production of finer Fruit than they would yield without that Care; and yet we cannot entertain Hopes of producing a tender conscious Spirit into Acts of Virtue, without the same Methods as is used to cut Timber, or give new Shape to a Piece of Stone.

It is wholly to this dreadful Practice that we may attribute a certain Hardness and Ferocity which some Men, tho' liberally educated, carry about them in all their Behaviour. To be bred like a Gentleman, and punished like a Malefactor, must, as we see it does, produce that illiberal Sauciness which we see sometimes in Men of Letters.

The *Spartan* Boy who suffered the Fox (which he had stolen and hid under his Coat) to eat into his Bowels, I dare say had not half the Wit or Petulance which we learn at great Schools among us: But the glorious Sense of Honour, or rather Fear of Shame, which he demonstrated in that Action, was worth all the Learning in the World without it.

It is methinks a very melancholy Consideration, that a little Negligence can spoil us, but great Industry is necessary to improve us; the most excellent Natures are soon depreciated, but evil Tempers are long before they are exalted into good Habits. To help this by Punishments, is the same thing as killing a Man to cure him of a Distemper; when he comes to suffer Punishment in that one Circumstance, he is brought below the Existence of a rational Creature, and is in the State of a Brute that moves only by the Admonition of Stripes. But since this Custom of educating by the Lash is suffered by the Gentry of *Great Britain*, I would prevail only that honest heavy Lads may be dismissed from Slavery sooner than they are at present, and not whipped on to their fourteenth or fifteenth Year, whether they expect any Progress from them or not. Let the Child's Capacity be forthwith examined, and he sent to some Mechanick Way of Life, without Respect to his Birth, if Nature design'd him for nothing higher; let him go before he has innocently suffered, and is debased into a Dereliction of Mind for being what it is no Guilt to be, a plain Man. I would not here be supposed to have said, that our learned Men of either Robe who have been whipped at School, are not still Men of noble and liberal Minds; but I am sure they had been much more so than they are, had they never suffered that Infamy.

But tho' there is so little Care, as I have observed, taken, or Observation made of the natural Strain of Men, it is no small Comfort to me, as a SPECTATOR, that there is any right Value set upon the *bona Indoles* of other Animals; as appears by the following Advertisement handed about the County of *Lincoln*, and subscribed by *Enos Thomas*, a Person whom I have not the Honour to know, but suppose to be profoundly learned in Horse-Flesh.

A Chesnut Horse called Caesar, *bred by* James Darcey, *Esq; at* Sedbury *near* Richmond *in the County of* York; *his Grandam was his old royal Mare, and got by* Blunderbuss, *which was got by* Hemsly Turk, *and he got Mr.* Courant's Arabian, *which got Mr.* Minshul's Jewstrump. *Mr.* Caesar *sold him to a Nobleman (coming five Years old, when he had but one Sweat) for three hundred Guineas. A Guinea a Leap and Trial, and a Shilling the Man.*

T   Enos Thomas.

No. 158.
[STEELE.]   Friday, August 31

        . . . *Nos haec novimus esse nihil.*—Mart.

OUT of a firm Regard to Impartiality I print these Letters, let them make for me or not.

'Mr. SPECTATOR,

I have observed through the whole Course of your Rhapsodies, (as you once very well called them) you are very industrious to overthrow all that many your Superiours who have gone before you have made their Rule of writing. I am now between fifty and sixty, and had the Honour to be well with the first Men of Taste and Gallantry in the joyous Reign of *Charles* the Second: We then had, I humbly presume, as good Understandings among us as any now can pretend to. As for your self, Mr. SPECTATOR, you seem with the utmost Arrogance to undermine the very Fundamentals upon which we conducted our selves. It is monstrous to set up for a Man of Wit, and yet deny that Honour in a Woman is any thing else but Peevishness, that Inclination is the best Rule of Life, or Virtue and Vice any thing else but Health and Disease. We had no more to do but to put a Lady in good Humour, and all we could wish followed of Course. Then again, your *Tully*, and your Discourses of another Life, are the very Bane of Mirth and good Humour. Prithee don't value thy self on thy Reason at that exorbitant Rate, and the Dignity of humane Nature; take my Word for it, a Setting-dog has as good Reason as any Man in *England*. Had you (as by your Diurnals one would think you do) set up for being in vogue in Town, you should have fallen in with the Bent of Passion and Appetite; your Songs had then been in every pretty Mouth in *England*, and your little Distichs had been the Maxims of the Fair and the Witty to walk by: But alas, Sir, what can you hope for from entertaining People with what must needs make them like themselves worse than they did before they read you? Had you made it your Business to describe *Corinna* charming, though inconstant; to find something in humane Nature it self to make *Zoilus* excuse himself for being fond of her; and to make every Man in good Commerce with his own Reflections, you had done something worthy our Applause; but indeed, Sir, we shall not commend you for disapproving us. I have a great deal more to say to you, but I shall sum it up all in this one Remark, In short, Sir, you do not write like a Gentleman.

> I am,
>
> > Sir,
> >
> > > *Your most humble Servant.'*

'*Mr.* SPECTATOR,

The other Day we were several of us at a Tea-Table, and according to Custom and your own Advice had the *Spectator* read among us: It was that Paper wherein you are pleased to treat with great Freedom that Character which you call a Woman's Man. We gave up all the Kinds you have mentioned, except those who, you say, are our constant Visitants. I was upon the Occasion commissioned by the Company to write to you, and tell you, That we shall not part with the Men we have at present, till the Men of Sense think fit to relieve them, and give us their Company in their Stead. You cannot imagine but that we love to hear Reason and good Sense better than the Ribaldry we are at present entertained with; but we must have Company, and among us very inconsiderable is

better than none at all. We are made for the Cements of
Society, and came into the World to create Relations among
Mankind; and Solitude is an unnatural Being to us. If the
Men of good Understanding would forget a little of their
Severity, they would find their Account in it; and their Wisdom
would have a Pleasure in it, to which they are now Strangers.
It is natural among us, when Men have a true Relish of our
Company and our Value, to say every thing with a better
Grace; and there is without designing it something ornamental
in what Men utter before Women, which is lost or neglected
in Conversations of Men only. Give me Leave to tell you Sir,
it would do you no great Harm if you your self came a little
more into our Company; it would certainly cure you of a
certain positive and determining Manner in which you talk
sometimes. In hopes of your Amendment,

I am,

Sir,

Your gentle Reader.'

'*Mr.* Spectator,

Your professed Regard to the fair Sex, may perhaps make
them value your Admonitions when they will not those of other
Men. I desire you, Sir, to repeat some Lectures upon Subjects
which you have now and then in a cursory Manner only just
touched. I would have a *Spectator* wholly writ upon good
Breeding; and after you have asserted that Time and Place
are to be very much considered in all our Actions, it will be
proper to dwell upon Behaviour at Church. On *Sunday* last a
grave and reverend Man preached at our Church: There was
something particular in his Accent, but without any Manner
of Affectation. This Particularity a Set of Gigglers thought
the most necessary thing to be taken Notice of in his whole
Discourse, and made it an Occasion of Mirth during the whole
Time of Sermon: You should see one of them ready to burst
behind a Fan, another pointing to a Companion in another
Seat, and a fourth with an arch Composure, as if she would if
possible stifle her Laughter. There were many Gentlemen who
looked at them stedfastly, but this they took for ogling and
admiring them: There was one of the merry ones in particular,
that found out but just then that she had but five Fingers, for
she fell a reckoning the pretty Pieces of Ivory over and over
again, to find her self Employment and not laugh out. Would
it not be expedient, Mr. Spectator, that the Church-Warden
should hold up his Wand on these Occasions, and keep the
Decency of the Place as a Magistrate does the Peace in a
Tumult elsewhere?'

'*Mr.* SPECTATOR,

I am a Woman's Man, and read with a very fine Lady your Paper wherein you fall upon us whom you envy: What do you think I did? you must know she was dressing, I read the *Spectator* to her, and she laughed at the Places where she thought I was touched; I threw away your Moral, and taking up her Girdle cryed out,

> *Give me but what this Ribbon bound,*
> *Take all the rest the Sun goes round.*

She smiled, Sir, and said you were a Pedant; so say of me what you please, read *Seneca*, and quote him against me if you think fit.

I am,

Sir,

T   *Your humble Servant.*'

No. 159.

[ADDISON.]   Saturday, September 1.

> . . . *Omnem, quae nunc obducta tuenti*
> *Mortales hebetat visus tibi, & humida circum*
> *Caligat, nubem eripiam* . . .—Virg.

WHEN I was at *Grand Cairo* I picked up several Oriental Manuscripts, which I have still by me. Among others I met with one, entitled *The Visions of Mirzah*, which I have read over with great Pleasure. I intend to give it to the Publick when I have no other Entertainment for them; and shall begin with the first Vision, which I have translated Word for Word as follows.

'On the fifth Day of the Moon, which according to the Custom of my Forefathers I always keep holy, after having washed my self and offered up my Morning Devotions, I ascended the high Hills of *Bagdat*, in order to pass the rest of the Day in Meditation and Prayer. As I was here airing my self on the Tops of the Mountains, I fell into a profound Contemplation on the Vanity of humane Life; and passing from one Thought to another, Surely, said I, Man is but a Shadow and Life a Dream. Whilst I was thus musing, I cast my Eyes towards the Summit of a Rock that was not far from me, where I discovered one in the Habit of a Shepherd, with a little Musical Instrument in his Hand. As I looked upon him he applied it to his Lips, and began to play upon it. The Sound of it was exceeding sweet, and wrought into a Variety of Tunes that were inexpressibly melodious, and altogether different from any thing I had ever heard. They put me in mind of those heavenly Airs that are played to the departed Souls of good Men upon their first Arrival in Paradise, to wear out the Impressions of the last Agonies, and qualify them for the Pleasures of that happy Place. My Heart melted away in secret Raptures.

I had been often told that the Rock before me was the Haunt of a Genius; and that several had been entertained with Musick who had passed by it, but never heard that the Musician had before made himself visible. When he had raised my Thoughts, by those transporting Airs which he played, to taste the Pleasures of his Conversation, as I looked upon him like one astonished, he beckoned to me, and by the waving of his Hand directed me to approach the Place where he sat. I drew near with that Reverence which is due to a superior Nature; and as my Heart was entirely subdued by the captivating Strains I had heard, I fell down at his Feet and wept. The Genius smiled upon me with a Look of Compassion and Affability that familiarized him to my Imagination, and at once dispelled all the Fears and Apprehensions with which I approached him. He lifted me from the Ground, and taking me by the Hand, *Mirzah*, said he, I have heard thee in thy Soliloquies, follow me.

He then led me to the highest Pinnacle of the Rock, and placing me on the Top of it, Cast thy Eyes Eastward, said he, and tell me what thou seest. I see, said I, a huge Valley and a prodigious Tide of Water rolling through it. The Valley that thou seest, said he, is the Vale of Misery, and the Tide of Water that thou seest is Part of the great Tide of Eternity. What is the Reason, said I, that the Tide I see rises out of a thick Mist at one End, and again loses it self in a thick Mist at the other? What thou seest, said he, is that Portion of Eternity which is called Time, measured out by the Sun, and reaching from the Beginning of the World to its Consummation. Examine now, said he, this Sea that is bounded with Darkness at both Ends, and tell me what thou discoverest in it. I see a Bridge, said I, standing in the Midst of the Tide. The Bridge thou seest, said he, is humane Life; consider it attentively. Upon a more leisurely Survey of it, I found that it consisted of threescore and ten entire Arches, with several broken Arches, which added to those that were entire, made up the Number about an hundred. As I was counting the Arches, the Genius told me that this Bridge consisted at first of a thousand Arches; but that a great Flood swept away the rest, and left the Bridge in the ruinous Condition I now beheld it. But tell me further, said he, what thou discoverest on it. I see Multitudes of People passing over it, said I, and a black Cloud hanging on each End of it. As I looked more attentively, I saw several of the Passengers dropping thro' the Bridge, into the great Tide that flowed underneath it; and upon further Examination, perceived there were innumerable Trap-doors that lay concealed in the Bridge, which the Passengers no sooner trod upon, but they fell through them into the Tide and immediately disappeared. These hidden Pit-falls were set very thick at the Entrance of the Bridge, so that Throngs of People no sooner broke through the Cloud, but many of them fell into them. They grew thinner towards the Middle, but multiplied and lay closer together towards the End of the Arches that were entire.

There were indeed some Persons, but their Number was very small, that continued a kind of hobbling March on the broken Arches, but fell through one after another, being quite tired and spent with so long a Walk.

I passed some Time in the Contemplation of this wonderful Structure, and the great Variety of Objects which it presented. My Heart was filled with a deep Melancholy to see several dropping unexpectedly in the Midst of Mirth and Jollity, and catching at every thing that stood by them to save themselves. Some were looking up towards the Heavens in a thoughtful Posture, and in the Midst of a Speculation stumbled and fell out of Sight. Multitudes were very busy in the Pursuit of Bubbles that glittered in their Eyes and danced before them, but often when they thought themselves within the Reach of them their Footing failed and down they sunk. In this Confusion of Objects, I observed some with Scymetars in their Hands, and others with Urinals, who ran to and fro upon the Bridge, thrusting several Persons on Trap-doors which did not seem to lie in their Way, and which they might have escaped had they not been thus forced upon them.

The Genius seeing me indulge my self in this melancholy Prospect, told me I had dwelt long enough upon it: Take thine Eyes off the Bridge, said he, and tell me if thou yet seest any thing thou dost not comprehend. Upon looking up, What mean, said I, those great Flights of Birds that are perpetually hovering about the Bridge, and settling upon it from Time to Time? I see Vultures, Harpyes, Ravens, Cormorants; and among many other feathered Creatures several little winged Boys, that perch in great Numbers upon the middle Arches. These said the Genius, are Envy, Avarice, Superstition, Despair, Love, with the like Cares and Passions that infest humane Life.

I here fetched a deep Sigh. Alas, said I, Man was made in vain! How is he given away to Misery and Mortality! tortured in Life, and swallowed up in Death! The Genius being moved with Compassion towards me, bid me quit so uncomfortable a Prospect: Look no more, said he, on Man in the first Stage of his Existence, in his setting out for Eternity; but cast thine Eye on that thick Mist into which the Tide bears the several Generations of Mortals that fall into it. I directed my Sight as I was ordered, and (whether or no the good Genius strengthened it with any supernatural Force, or dissipated Part of the Mist that was before too thick for the Eye to penetrate) I saw the Valley opening at the further End, and spreading forth into an immense Ocean, that had a huge Rock of Adamant running through the Midst of it, and dividing it into two equal Parts. The Clouds still rested on one Half of it, insomuch that I could discover nothing in it; but the other appeared to me a vast Ocean planted with innumerable Islands, that were covered with Fruits and Flowers, and interwoven with a thousand little shining Seas that ran among them. I could see Persons dressed in glorious Habits, with Garlands upon their Heads, passing among the Trees, lying down by the Sides of Fountains, or resting on Beds of Flowers; and could hear a confused Harmony of singing Birds, falling Waters, humane Voices, and musical Instruments. Gladness grew in me upon the Discovery of so delightful a Scene. I wished for the Wings of an Eagle, that I might fly away to those happy Seats; but the Genius told me there was no Passage to them, except through the Gates of Death that I saw opening every Moment upon the Bridge. The Islands, said he, that lie so fresh and green before thee, and with which the whole Face of the Ocean appears spotted as far as thou canst see, are more in Number than the Sands on the Sea-shore; there are Myriads of Islands behind those which thou here discoverest, reaching further than thine Eye or even thine Imagination can extend it self. These are the Mansions of good Men after Death, who according to the Degree and Kinds of Virtue in which they excelled, are distributed among these several Islands, which abound with Pleasures of different Kinds and Degrees, suitable to the Relishes and Perfections of those who are settled in them; every Island is a Paradise accommodated to its respective Inhabitants. Are not these, O *Mirzah*, Habitations worth contending for? Does Life appear miserable, that gives thee Opportunities of earning such a Reward? Is Death to be feared, that will convey thee to so happy an Existence? Think not Man was made in vain, who has such an Eternity reserved for him. I gazed with inexpressible Pleasure on these happy

Islands. At length, said I, shew me now, I beseech thee, the
Secrets that lie hid under those dark Clouds which cover the
Ocean on the other Side of the Rock of Adamant. The Genius
making me no Answer, I turned about to address my self to
him a second time, but I found that he had left me; I then
turned again to the Vision which I had been so long contemplating, but instead of the rolling Tide, the arched Bridge, and
the happy Islands, I saw nothing but the long hollow Valley
of *Bagdat*, with Oxen, Sheep, and Camels grazing upon the
Sides of it.

The End of the first Vision of Mirzah. C

No. 160.

[ADDISON.] Monday, September 3.

. . . *Cui mens divinior, atque os*
Magna sonaturum, des nominis hujus honorem.—Hor.

THERE is no Character more frequently given to a Writer, than
that of being a Genius. I have heard many a little Sonneteer
called a *fine Genius*. There is not an Heroick Scribler in the
Nation, that has not his Admirers who think him a *great
Genius*; and as for your Smatterers in Tragedy, there is scarce
a Man among them who is not cried up by one or other for a
prodigious Genius.

My Design in this Paper is to consider what is properly a
great Genius, and to throw some Thoughts together on so
uncommon a Subject.

Among great Genius's, those few draw the Admiration of all
the World upon them, and stand up as the Prodigies of Mankind, who by the mere Strength of natural Parts, and without
any Assistance of Art or Learning, have produced Works that
were the Delight of their own Times and the Wonder of Posterity. There appears something nobly wild and extravagant
in these great natural Genius's, that is infinitely more beautiful
than all the Turn and Polishing of what the *French* call a *Bel
Esprit*, by which they would express a Genius refined by
Conversation, Reflection, and the Reading of the most polite
Authors. The greatest Genius which runs through the Arts
and Sciences, takes a kind of Tincture from them, and falls
unavoidably into Imitation.

Many of these great natural Genius's that were never dis-
ciplined and broken by Rules of Art, are to be found among the

Ancients, and in particular among those of the more Eastern Parts of the World. *Homer* has innumerable Flights that *Virgil* was not able to reach, and in the Old Testament we find several Passages more elevated and sublime than any in *Homer*. At the same Time that we allow a greater and more daring Genius to the Ancients, we must own that the greatest of them very much failed in, or, if you will, that they were much above the Nicety and Correctness of the Moderns. In their Similitudes and Allusions, provided there was a Likeness, they did not much trouble themselves about the Decency of the Comparison: Thus *Solomon* resembles the Nose of his Beloved to the Tower of *Libanon* which looketh toward *Damascus*; as the Coming of a Thief in the Night, is a Similitude of the same Kind in the New Testament. It would be endless to make Collections of this Nature: *Homer* illustrates one of his Heroes encompassed with the Enemy, by an Ass in a Field of Corn that has his Sides belaboured by all the Boys of the Village without stirring a Foot for it; and another of them tossing to and fro in his Bed and burning with Resentment, to a Piece of Flesh broiled on the Coals. This particular Failure in the Ancients, opens a large Field of Raillerie to the little Wits, who can laugh at an Indecency but not relish the Sublime in these Sorts of Writings. The present Emperor of *Persia*, conformable to this Eastern way of Thinking, amidst a great many pompous Titles, denominates himself the Sun of Glory, and the *Nutmeg of Delight*. In short, to cut off all Cavelling against the Ancients, and particularly those of the warmer Climates, who had most Heat and Life in their Imaginations, we are to consider that the Rule of observing what the *French* call the *Bienseance* in an Allusion, has been found out of latter Years and in the colder Regions of the World; where we would make some Amends for our want of Force and Spirit, by a scrupulous Nicety and Exactness in our Compositions. Our Countryman *Shakespear* was a remarkable Instance of this first kind of great Genius's.

I cannot quit this Head without observing that *Pindar* was a great Genius of the first Class, who was hurried on by a Natural Fire and Impetuosity to vast Conceptions of things, and noble Sallies of Imagination. At the same time, can any thing be more ridiculous than for Men of a sober and moderate Fancy to imitate this Poet's Way of Writing in those monstrous Compositions which go among us under the Name of Pindaricks? When I see People copying Works, which, as *Horace* has represented them, are singular in their Kind and inimitable; when I see Men following Irregularities by Rule, and by the little Tricks of Art straining after the most unbounded Flights of Nature, I cannot but apply to them that Passage in *Terence*.

> . . . *incerta haec si tu postules*
> *Ratione certa facere, nihilo plus agas.*
> *Quam si des operam, ut cum ratione insanias.*

In short a modern Pindarick Writer compared with *Pindar*, is like a Sister among the *Camisars* compared with *Virgil's* Sybil: There is the Distortion, Grimace, and outward Figure, but nothing of that divine Impulse which raises the Mind above it self, and makes the Sounds more than humane.

There is another kind of Great Genius's which I shall place in a second Class, not as I think them inferior to the first, but only for distinction's sake as they are of a different kind. This second Class of great Genius's are those that have formed themselves by Rules, and submitted the Greatness of their natural Talents to the Corrections and Restraints of Art. Such among the *Greeks* were *Plato* and *Aristotle*, among the *Romans Virgil* and *Tully*, among the *English Milton* and Sir *Francis Bacon*.

The Genius in both these Classes of Authors may be equally great, but shews it self after a different Manner. In the first it is like a rich Soil in a happy Climate, that produces a whole Wilderness of noble Plants rising in a thousand beautiful Landskips without any certain Order or Regularity. In the other it is the same rich Soil under the same happy Climate, that has been laid out in Walks and Parterres, and cut into Shape and Beauty by the Skill of the Gardener.

The great Danger in these latter kind of Genius's, is, least they cramp their own Abilities too much by Imitation, and form themselves altogether upon Models, without giving the full Play to their own natural Parts. An Imitation of the best Authors is not to compare with a good Original; and I believe we may observe that very few Writers make an extraordinary Figure in the World, who have not something in their Way of thinking or expressing themselves that is peculiar to them and entirely their own.

It is odd to consider what great Genius's are sometimes thrown away upon Trifles.

I once saw a Shepherd, says a famous *Italian* Author, who used to divert himself in his Solitudes with tossing up Eggs and catching them again without breaking them: In which he had arrived to so great a Degree of Perfection, that he would keep up four at a Time for several Minutes together playing in the Air, and falling into his Hand by Turns. I think, says the Author, I never saw a greater Severity than in this Man's Face;

for by his wonderful Perseverance and Application, he had
contracted the Seriousness and Gravity of a Privy-Councellour;
and I could not but reflect with my self, that the same Assiduity
and Attention, had they been rightly applied, might have made
him a greater Mathematician than *Archimedes.*

C

No. 161.

[BUDGELL.]   Tuesday, September 4.

> *Ipse dies agitat festos; fususque per herbam,*
> *Ignis ubi in medio & socii cratera coronant,*
> *Te libans, Lenaee, vocat; pecorisque magistris*
> *Velocis jaculi certamina ponit in ulmo:*
> *Corporaque agresti nudat praedura palaestra,*
> *Hanc olim veteres vitam coluere Sabini,*
> *Hanc Remus & frater: sic fortis Etruria crevit,*
> *Scilicet & rerum facta est pulcherrima Roma.*—Virg. *G.* 2.

I AM glad that my late going into the Country has encreased
the Number of my Correspondents, one of whom sends me the
following Letter.

'Sir,

Though you are pleased to retire from us so soon into the
City, I hope you will not think the Affairs of the Country altogether unworthy of your Inspection for the Future.   I had the
Honour of seeing your short Face at Sir ROGER DE COVERLEY'S,
and have ever since thought your Person and Writings both
extraordinary.   Had you stayed there a few Days longer you
would have seen a Country *Wake,* which you know in most
Parts of *England* is the *Eve-Feast of the Dedication of our
Churches.*   I was last Week at one of these Assemblies, which
was held in a neighbouring Parish, where I found their *Green*
covered with a promiscuous Multitude of all Ages and both
Sexes, who esteem one another more or less the following Part
of the Year according as they distinguish themselves at this
Time.   The whole Company were in their Holy-day Cloaths,
and divided into several Parties, all of them endeavouring to
shew themselves in those Exercises wherein they excelled, and
to gain the Approbation of the Lookers on.

I found a Ring of Cudgel-Players, who were breaking one
another's Heads in order to make some impression on their
Mistresses' Hearts.   I observed a lusty young Fellow who had
the Misfortune of a broken Pate; but what considerably added
to the Anguish of the Wound, was his over-hearing an old Man,

who shook his Head and said, *That he questioned now if black* Kate *would marry him these three Years.* I was diverted from a further Observation of these Combatants, by a Foot ball Match which was on the other side of the *Green*; where *Tom Short* behaved himself so well, that most People seemed to agree *it was impossible that he should remain a Batchelour till the next Wake.* Having played many a Match my self, I could have looked longer on this Sport, had I not observed a Country Girl who was posted on an Eminence at some Distance from me, and was making so many odd Grimaces, and writhing and distorting her whole Body in so strange a Manner, as made me very desirous to know the Meaning of it. Upon my coming up to her, I found that she was over-looking a Ring of Wrestlers, and that her Sweet-heart, a Person of small Stature, was contending with an huge brawny Fellow, who twirled him about, and shook the little Man so violently, that by a secret Sympathy of Hearts it produced all those Agitations in the Person of his Mistress, who I dare say, like *Caelia* in *Shakespear* on the same Occasion, could have *wished herself invisible to catch the strong Fellow by the Leg.* The Squire of the Parish treats the whole Company every Year with a Hogshead of Ale; and proposes a *Beaver Hat* as a Recompence to him who gives most *Falls.* This has raised such a Spirit of Emulation in the Youth of the Place, that some of them have rendered themselves very expert at this Exercise; and I was often surprized to see a Fellow's Heels fly up, by a Trip which was given him so smartly that I could scarce discern it. I found that the old Wrestlers seldom enter'd the Ring, till some one was grown formidable by having thrown two or three of his Opponents; but kept themselves as it were in a reserved Body to defend the *Hat*, which is always hung up by the Person who gets it in one of the most conspicuous Parts of the House, and looked upon by the whole Family as something redounding much more to their Honour than a Coat of Arms. There was a Fellow who was so busy in regulating all the Ceremonies, and seemed to carry such an Air of Importance in his Looks, that I could not help inquiring who he was; and was immediately answer'd, *That he did not value himself upon nothing, for that he and his Ancestors had won so many Hats, that his Parlour looked like a Haberdasher's Shop:* However this Thirst of Glory in them all, was the Reason that no one Man stood *Lord of the Ring* for above three *Falls* while I was amongst them.

The young Maids, who were not Lookers on at these Exercises, were themselves engaged in some Diversion; and upon my asking a Farmer's Son of my own Parish what he was gazing at with so much Attention, he told me, *That he was seeing* Betty Welch, whom I knew to be his Sweet-heart, *pitch a Bar.*

In short, I found the Men endeavour'd to shew the Women they were no Cowards, and that the whole Company strived to recommend themselves to each other, by making it appear that they were all in a perfect State of Health, and fit to undergo any Fatigues of bodily Labour.

Your Judgment upon this Method of *Love* and *Gallantry*, as it is at present practised amongst us in the Country, will very much oblige,

Sir,

Yours, &c.'

If I would here put on the Scholar and Politician, I might inform my Readers how these bodily Exercises or Games were formerly encouraged in all the Commonwealths of Greece; from whence the *Romans* afterwards borrow'd their *Pentathlum*, which was compos'd of *Running, Wrestling, Leaping, Throwing,* and *Boxing,* tho' the Prizes were generally nothing but a Crown of Cypress or Parsley, Hats not being in fashion in those Days; That there is an old Statute, which obliges every Man in *England,* having such an Estate, to keep and exercise the long Bow; by which Means our Ancestors excelled all other Nations in the Use of that Weapon, and we had all the real Advantages, without the Inconvenience of a standing Army: And that I once met with a Book of Projects, in which the Author considering to what noble Ends that Spirit of Emulation, which so remarkably shews it self among our common People in these Wakes, might be directed, proposes that for the Improvement of all our handicraft Trades there should be annual Prizes set up for such Persons as were most excellent in their several Arts. But laying aside all these political Considerations, which might tempt me to pass the Limits of my Paper, I confess the greatest Benefit and Convenience that I can observe in these Country Festivals, is the bringing young People together, and giving them an Opportunity of shewing themselves in the most advantageous Light. A Country Fellow that throws his Rival upon his Back, has generally as good Success with their common Mistress; as nothing is more usual than for a nimble-footed Wench to get a Husband at the same Time she wins a Smock. Love and Marriages are the natural Effects of these anniversary Assemblies. I must therefore very much approve the Method by which my Correspondent tells me each Sex endeavours to recommend it self to the other, since nothing seems more likely to promise a healthy Offspring or a happy Cohabitation.

And I believe I may assure my Country Friend, that there has been many a Court Lady who would be contented to exchange her crazy young Husband for *Tom Short*, and several Men of Quality who would have parted with a tender Yoke-fellow for *Black Kate*.

I am the more pleased with having *Love* made the principal End and Design of these Meetings, as it seems to be most agreeable to the Intent for which they were at first instituted, as we are informed by the learned Dr. *Kennet*, with whose Words I shall conclude my present Paper.

These Wakes, says he, *were in Imitation of the ancient* ἀγάπαι, *or Love-feasts; and were first established in* England *by Pope Gregory the Great, who in an Epistle to* Melitus *the Abbot, gave Order that they should be kept in Sheds or Arbories made up with Branches and Boughs of Trees round the Church.*

He adds, *That this laudable Custom of Wakes prevailed for many Ages, till the nice Puritans began to exclaim against it as a Remnant of Popery; and by Degrees the precise Humour grew so popular, that at an* Exeter *Assizes the Lord Chief Baron* Walter *made an Order for the Suppression of all Wakes; but on Bishop* Laud's *complaining of this innovating Humour, the King commanded the Order to be reversed.* X

No. 162.
[ADDISON.] Wednesday, September 5.

. . . *Servetur ad imum,*
Qualis ab incepto processerit, & sibi constet.—Hor.

NOTHING that is not a real Crime makes a Man appear so contemptible and little in the Eyes of the World as Inconstancy, especially when it regards Religion or Party. In either of these Cases, tho' a Man perhaps does but his Duty in changing his Side, he not only makes himself hated by those he left, but is seldom heartily esteemed by those he comes over to.

In these great Articles of Life therefore a Man's Conviction ought to be very strong, and if possible so well timed that worldly Advantages may seem to have no Share in it, or Mankind will be ill-natured enough to think he does not change Sides out of Principle, but either out of Levity of Temper or Prospects of Interest. Converts and Renegadoes of all kinds should take particular care to let the World see they act upon honourable Motives; or whatever Approbations they may receive from themselves, and Applauses from those they converse with, they may be very well assured that they are the Scorn of all good Men, and the publick Marks of Infamy and Derision.

Irresolution on the Schemes of Life which offer themselves to our Choice, and Inconstancy in pursuing them, are the greatest and most universal Causes of all our Disquiet and Unhappiness. When Ambition pulls one Way, Interest another, Inclination a third, and perhaps Reason contrary to all, a Man is likely to pass his Time but ill who has so many different Parties to please When the Mind hovers among such a Variety of Allurements, one had better settle on a Way of Life that is not the very best we might have chosen, than grow old without determining our Choice, and go out of the World as the greatest Part of Mankind do, before we have resolved how to live in it. There is but one Method of setting our selves at Rest in this Particular, and that is by adhering stedfastly to one great End as the chief and ultimate Aim of all our Pursuits. If we are firmly resolved to live up to the Dictates of Reason, without any Regard to Wealth, Reputation, or the like Considerations, any more than as they fall in with our principal Design, we may go through Life with Steddiness and Pleasure; but if we act by several broken Views, and will not only be virtuous, but wealthy, popular, and every thing that has a Value set upon it by the World, we shall live and die in Misery and Repentance.

One would take more than ordinary Care to guard one's self against this particular Imperfection, because it is that which our Nature very strongly inclines us to; for if we examine our selves throughly, we shall find that we are the most changeable Beings in the Universe. In Respect of our Understanding, we often embrace and reject the very same Opinions; whereas Beings above and beneath us have probably no Opinions at all, or at least no Wavering and Uncertainties in those they have. Our Superiours are guided by Intuition, and our Inferiours by Instinct. In Respect of our Wills, we fall into Crimes and recover out of them, are amiable or odious in the Eyes of our great Judge, and pass our whole Life in offending and asking Pardon. On the contrary, the Beings underneath us are not capable of sinning, nor those above us of repenting. The one is out of the Possibilities of Duty, and the other fixed in an eternal Course of Sin, or an eternal Course of Virtue.

There is scarce a State of Life, or Stage in it, which does not produce Changes and Revolutions in the Mind of Man. Our Schemes of Thought in Infancy are lost in those of Youth; these two take a different Turn in Manhood, till old Age often leads us back into our former Infancy. A new Title or an unexpected Success throws us out of ourselves, and in a Manner destroys our Identity. A cloudy Day or a little Sun-shine have as great an Influence on many Constitutions, as the most real Blessings or Misfortunes. A Dream varies our Being, and changes our Condition while it lasts; and every Passion, not to mention Health and Sickness, and the greater Alterations in Body and Mind, makes us appear almost different Creatures. If a Man is so distinguished among other Beings by this Infirmity, what can we think of such as make themselves remarkable for it even among their own Species? It is a very trifling Character to be one of the most variable Beings of the most variable Kind, especially if we consider that he who is the great Standard of Perfection has in him no Shadow of Change, but is the same Yesterday, to Day, and for ever.

As this Mutability of Temper and Inconsistency with our selves is the greatest Weakness of humane Nature, so it makes the Person who is remarkable for it in a very particular Manner more ridiculous than any other Infirmity whatsoever, as it sets him in a greater Variety of foolish Lights, and distinguishes him from himself by an Opposition of party-coloured Characters. The most humourous Character in *Horace* is founded upon this Unevenness of Temper and Irregularity of Conduct.

> . . . *Sardus habebat*
> *Ille Tigellius hoc. Caesar qui cogere posset*
> *Si peteret per amicitiam patris atque suam, non*
> *Quidquam proficeret; Si collibuisset, ab ovo*
> *Usque ad mala citaret Io Bacche, modo summa*
> *Voce, modo hac, resonat quae chordis quatuor ima.*
> *Nil aequale homini fuit illi: Saepe velut qui*
> *Currebat fugiens hostem; persaepe velut qui*
> *Junonis sacra ferret. Habebat saepe ducentos,*
> *Saepe decem servos. Modo reges atque tetrarchas,*
> *Omnia magna loquens. Modo, sit mihi mensa tripes, &*
> *Concha salis puri, & toga, quae defendere frigus,*
> *Quamvis crassa, queat. Decies centena dedisses*
> *Huic parco paucis contento, quinque diebus*
> *Nil erat in loculis. Noctes vigilabat ad ipsum*
> *Mane: diem totam stertebat. Nil fuit unquam*
> *Sic impar sibi . . .*—Hor. *Sat.* 3, Lib. 1.

Instead of translating this Passage in *Horace,* I shall entertain my *English Reader* with the Description of a Parallel Character, that is wonderfully well finished by Mr. *Dryden,* and raised upon the same Foundation.

> *In the first Rank of these did* Zimri *stand:*
> *A Man so various, that he seem'd to be*
> *Not one, but all Mankind's Epitome.*

> *Stiff in Opinions, always in the wrong;*
> *Was every thing by Starts, and Nothing long*
> *But, in the Course of one revolving Moon,*
> *Was Chymist, Fidler, Statesman, and Buffoon:*
> *Then all for Women, Painting, Rhiming, Drinking;*
> *Besides ten thousand Freaks that dy'd in thinking.*
> *Blest Madman, who cou'd every Hour employ,*
> *With something New to wish, or to enjoy!*

C

No. 163.

[ADDISON.]   Thursday, September 6.

> . . . *Si quid ego adjuero, curamve levasso,*
> *Quae nunc te coquit, & versat in pectore fixa,*
> *Ecquid erit pretii?*—Enn. ap. Tullium.

ENQUIRIES after Happiness, and Rules for attaining it, are not so necessary and useful to Mankind as the Arts of Consolation, and supporting one's self under Affliction. The utmost we can hope for in this World is Contentment; if we aim at any thing higher, we shall meet with nothing but Grief and Disappointments. A man should direct all his Studies and Endeavours at making himself easie now, and happy hereafter.

The Truth of it is, if all the Happiness that is dispersed through the whole Race of Mankind in this World were drawn together, and put into the Possession of any single Man, it would not make a very happy Being. Though, on the contrary, if the Miseries of the whole Species were fixed in a single Person, they would make a very miserable one.

I am engaged in this Subject by the following Letter, which, though Subscribed by a fictitious Name, I have reason to believe is not Imaginary.

'*Mr.* SPECTATOR,

I am one of your Disciples, and endeavour to live up to your Rules, which I hope will encline you to pity my Condition: I shall open it to you in a very few Words. About three Years since a Gentleman, whom, I am sure, you your self would have approved, made his Addresses to me. He had every thing to recommend him but an Estate, so that my Friends, who all of them applauded his Person, would not for the sake of both of us favour his Passion. For my own part I resigned my self up entirely to the Direction of those who knew the World much better than my self, but still lived in hopes that some Juncture or other would make me happy in the Man whom, in my Heart, I preferred to all the World; being determined

if I could not have him to have no Body else. About three
Months ago I received a Letter from him, acquainting me,
that by the death of an Unkle he had a considerable Estate
left him, which he said was welcome to him upon no other
Account but as he hoped it would remove all Difficulties that
lay in the Way to our mutual Happiness. You may well
suppose, Sir, with how much Joy I received this Letter, which
was followed by several others filled with those Expressions
of Love and Joy, which I verily believe no Body felt more
sincerely, nor knew better how to describe, than the Gentleman I am speaking of. But, Sir, how shall I be able to tell it
you! by the last Week's Post I received a Letter from an
intimate Friend of this unhappy Gentleman, acquainting me,
that as he had just settled his Affairs, and was preparing for
his Journey, he fell sick of a Fever and died. It is impossible
to express to you the Distress I am in upon this Occasion. I
can only have Recourse to my Devotions, and to the reading
of good Books for my Consolation; and as I always take a
particular Delight in those frequent Advices and Admonitions
which you give the Publick, it would be a very great piece of
Charity in you to lend me your Assistance in this Conjuncture.
If after the reading of this Letter you find your self in a
Humour rather to Rally and Ridicule, than to Comfort me, I
desire you would throw it into the Fire, and think no more of
it; but if you are touched with my Misfortune, which is greater
than I know how to bear, your Counsels may very much
Support, and will infinitely Oblige the afflicted

                                        LEONORA.'

A Disappointment in Love is more hard to get over than any
other; the Passion it self so softens and subdues the Heart,
that it disables it from struggling or bearing up against the
Woes and Distresses which befal it. The Mind meets with
other Misfortunes in her whole Strength; she stands collected
within her self, and sustains the Shock with all the force which
is natural to her; but a Heart in Love has its Foundations
sapped, and immediately sinks under the Weight of Accidents
that are disagreeable to its Favourite Passion.

In Afflictions Men generally draw their Consolations out of
Books of Morality, which indeed are of great use to fortifie
and strengthen the Mind against the Impressions of Sorrow.
Monsieur St. *Evremont,* who does not approve of this Method,
recommends Authors who are apt to stir up Mirth in the Mind
of the Readers, and fancies Don *Quixote* can give more Relief
to an heavy Heart than *Plutarch* or *Seneca,* as it is much easier
to divert Grief than to conquer it. This doubtless may have

its Effects on some Tempers. I should rather have recourse to Authors of a quite contrary kind, that give us Instances of Calamities and Misfortunes, and shew Human Nature in its greatest Distresses.

If the Affliction we groan under be very heavy, we shall find some Consolation in the Society of as great Sufferers as our selves, especially when we find our Companions Men of Virtue and Merit. If our Afflictions are light, we shall be comforted by the Comparison we make between our selves and our Fellow-Sufferers. A Loss at Sea, a Fit of Sickness, or the Death of a Friend, are such Trifles when we consider whole Kingdoms laid in Ashes, Families put to the Sword, Wretches shut up in Dungeons, and the like Calamities of Mankind, that we are out of Countenance for our own Weakness, if we sink under such little Strokes of Fortune.

Let the Disconsolate *Leonora* consider, that at the very time in which she languishes for the Loss of her Deceas'd Lover, there are Persons in several parts of the World just perishing in a Shipwreck; others crying out for Mercy in the Terrors of a Death-bed Repentance; others lying under the Tortures of an Infamous Execution, or the like dreadful Calamities; and she will find her Sorrows vanish at the appearance of those which are so much greater and more astonishing.

I would further propose to the Consideration of my afflicted Disciple, that possibly what she now looks upon as the greatest Misfortune, is not really such in it self. For my own part, I question not but our Souls in a separate State will look back on their Lives in quite another View, than what they had of them in the Body; and that what they now consider as Misfortunes and Disappointments, will very often appear to have been Escapes and Blessings.

The Mind that hath any Cast towards Devotion, naturally flies to it in its Afflictions.

When I was in *France* I heard a very remarkable Story of two Lovers, which I shall relate at length in my to Morrow's Paper, not only because the Circumstances of it are extra-ordinary, but because it may serve as an Illustration to all that can be said on this last Head, and shew the Power of Religion in abating that particular Anguish which seems to lie so heavy on *Leonora*. The Story was told me by a Priest, as I travelled with him in a Stage-Coach. I shall give it my Reader, as well as I can remember, in his own Words, after having premised, that if Consolations may be drawn from a wrong Religion and a misguided Devotion, they cannot but flow much more naturally from those which are founded upon Reason, and established in good Sense.

No. 164.

[ADDISON.]   Friday, September 7.

> *Illa, Quis & me, inquit, miseram, & te perdidit, Orpheu?*
> *Jamque vale: feror ingenti circumdata nocte,*
> *Invalidasque tibi tendens, heu! non tua, palmas.*—Virg.

CONSTANTIA was a Woman of extraordinary Wit and Beauty, but very unhappy in a Father, who having arrived at great Riches by his own Industry, took Delight in nothing but his Money. *Theodosius* was the younger Son of a decayed Family, of great Parts and Learning, improved by a genteel and virtuous Education. When he was in the twentieth Year of his Age he became acquainted with *Constantia*, who had not then passed her fifteenth. As he lived but a few Miles Distance from her Father's House, he had frequent Opportunities of seeing her; and by the Advantages of a good Person and a pleasing Conversation, made such an Impression in her Heart as it was impossible for Time to efface: He was himself no less smitten with *Constantia*. A long Acquaintance made them still discover new Beauties in each other, and by Degrees raised in them that mutual Passion which had an Influence on their following Lives. It unfortunately happened, that in the Midst of this Intercourse of Love and Friendship between *Theodosius* and *Constantia*, there broke out an irreparable Quarrel between their Parents, the one valuing himself too much upon his Birth, and the other upon his Possessions. The Father of *Constantia* was so incensed at the Father of *Theodosius*, that he contracted an unreasonable Aversion towards his Son, insomuch that he forbad him his House, and charged his Daughter upon her Duty never to see him more. In the mean Time, to break off all Communication between the two Lovers, who he knew entertained secret Hopes of some favourable Opportunity that should bring them together, he found out a young Gentleman of a good Fortune and an agreeable Person, whom he pitched upon as a Husband for his Daughter. He soon concerted this Affair so well, that he told *Constantia* it was his Design to marry her to such a Gentleman, and that her Wedding should be celebrated on such a Day. *Constantia*, who was over-awed with the Authority of her Father, and unable to object any thing against so advantageous a Match, receiv'd the Proposal with a profound Silence; which her Father commended in her, as the most decent Manner of a Virgin's giving her Consent to an Overture of that Kind. The Noise of this intended Marriage soon reached *Theodosius*, who after a long Tumult of Passions, which naturally rise in a

Lover's Heart on such an Occasion, writ the following Letter
to *Constantia.*

'The Thought of my *Constantia,* which for some Years has
been my only Happiness, is now become a greater Torment to
me than I am able to bear. Must I then live to see you
another's? The Streams, the Fields, and Meadows, where
we have so often talked together, grow painful to me; Life
it self is become a Burden. May you long be happy in the
World, but forget that there was ever such a Man in it as

THEODOSIUS.'

This Letter was conveyed to *Constantia* that very Evening,
who fainted at the reading of it; and the next Morning she was
much more alarmed by two or three Messengers, that came to
her Father's House one after another to enquire if they had
heard any thing of *Theodosius,* who it seems had left his
Chamber about Midnight, and could no where be found. The
deep Melancholy which had hung upon his Mind some Time
before, made them apprehend the worst that could befall him.
Constantia, who knew that nothing but the Report of her
Marriage could have driven him to such Extremities, was not
to be comforted: She now accused herself for having so tamely
given an Ear to the Proposal of a Husband, and looked upon
the new Lover as the Murderer of *Theodosius:* In short, she
resolved to suffer the utmost Effects of her Father's Displeasure, rather than comply with a Marriage which appeared
to her so full of Guilt and Horrour. The Father seeing himself
entirely rid of *Theodosius,* and likely to keep a considerable
Portion in his Family, was not very much concerned at the
obstinate Refusal of his Daughter; and did not find it very
difficult to excuse himself upon that Account to his intended
Son-in-Law, who had all along regarded this Alliance rather
as a Marriage of Convenience than of Love. *Constantia* had
now no Relief but in her Devotions and Exercises of Religion,
to which her Afflictions had so entirely subjected her Mind,
that after some Years had abated the Violence of her Sorrows,
and settled her Thoughts in a kind of Tranquility, she resolved
to pass the Remainder of her Days in a Convent. Her Father
was not displeased with a Resolution, which would save Money
in his Family, and readily complied with his Daughter's Intentions. Accordingly in the Twenty-fifth Year of her Age,
while her Beauty was yet in all its Height and Bloom, he
carried her to a neighbouring City, in order to look out a Sisterhood of Nuns among whom to place his Daughter. There
was in this Place a Father of a Convent who was very much
renowned for his Piety and exemplary Life; and as it is usual

in the *Romish* Church for those who are under any great Affliction or Trouble of Mind to apply themselves to the most eminent Confessors for Pardon and Consolation, our beautiful Votary took the Opportunity of confessing herself to this celebrated Father.

We must now return to *Theodosius*, who the very Morning that the above-mentioned Enquiries had been made after him, arrived at a religious House in the City where now *Constantia* resided; and desiring that Secrecy and Concealment of the Fathers of the Convent which is very usual upon any extraordinary Occasion, he made himself one of the Order, with a private Vow never to enquire after *Constantia*, whom he looked upon as given away to his Rival upon the Day on which, according to common Fame, their Marriage was to have been solemnized. Having in his Youth made a good Progress in Learning, that he might dedicate himself more entirely to Religion he entered into holy Orders, and in a few Years became renowned for his Sanctity of Life, and those pious Sentiments which he inspired into all who conversed with him. It was this holy Man to whom *Constantia* had determined to apply herself in Confession, tho' neither she nor any other besides the Prior of the Convent knew any thing of his Name or Family. The gay, the amiable *Theodosius* had now taken upon him the Name of Father *Francis*; and was so far concealed in a long Beard, a shaven Head, and a religious Habit, that it was impossible to discover the Man of the World in the venerable Conventual.

As he was one Morning shut up in his Confessional, *Constantia* kneeling by him, opened the State of her Soul to him; and after having given him the History of a Life full of Innocence, she burst out in Tears, and entered upon that Part of her Story in which he himself had so great a Share. My Behaviour, says she, has I fear been the Death of a Man who had no other Fault but that of loving me too much. Heaven only knows how dear he was to me whilst he lived, and how bitter the Remembrance of him has been to me since his Death. She here paused, and lifted up her Eyes that streamed with Tears towards the Father; who was so moved with the Sense of her Sorrows, that he could only command his Voice, which was broke with Sighs and Sobbings, so far as to bid her proceed. She followed his Directions, and in a Flood of Tears poured out her Heart before him. The Father could not forbear weeping aloud, insomuch that in the Agonies of his Grief the Seat shook under him. *Constantia*, who thought the good Man was thus moved by his Compassion towards her, and by the Horrour of her Guilt, proceeded with the utmost

Contrition to acquaint him with that Vow of Virginity in which she was going to engage herself, as the proper Atonement for her Sins, and the only Sacrifice she could make to the Memory of *Theodosius*.   The Father, who by this time had pretty well composed himself, burst out again in Tears upon hearing that Name to which he had been so long disused, and upon receiving this Instance of an unparallel'd Fidelity from one who he thought had several Years since given herself up to the Possession of another.   Amidst the Interruptions of his Sorrow, seeing his Penitent overwhelmed with Grief, he was only able to bid her from time to time be comforted— To tell her that her Sins were forgiven her—That her Guilt was not so great as she apprehended—That she should not suffer herself to be afflicted above Measure.   After which he recovered himself enough to give her the Absolution in Form; directing her at the same time to repair to him again the next Day, that he might encourage her in the pious Resolutions she had taken, and give her suitable Exhortations for her Behaviour in it.   *Constantia* retired, and the next Morning renewed her Applications.   *Theodosius* having mann'd his Soul with proper Thoughts and Reflections, exerted himself on this Occasion in the best Manner he could, to animate his Penitent in the Course of Life she was entering upon, and wear out of her Mind those groundless Fears and Apprehensions which had taken Possession of it; concluding, with a Promise to her, that he would from time to time continue his Admonitions when she should have taken upon her the holy Veil.   The Rules of our respective Orders, says he, will not permit that I should see you, but you may assure your self not only of having a Place in my Prayers, but of receiving such frequent Instructions as I can convey to you by Letters. Go on chearfully in the glorious Course you have undertaken, and you will quickly find such a Peace and Satisfaction in your Mind which it is not in the Power of the World to give.

Constantia's Heart was so elevated with the Discourse of Father *Francis*, that the very next Day she entered upon her Vow.   As soon as the Solemnities of her Reception were over, she retired, as it is usual, with the Abbess into her own Apartment.

The Abbess had been informed the Night before of all that had passed between her Novitiate and Father *Francis*: From whom she now delivered to her the following Letter.

'As the First Fruits of those Joys and Consolations which you may expect from the Life you are now engaged in, I must acquaint you that *Theodosius*, whose Death sits so heavy upon your Thoughts, is still alive; and that the Father to whom you have confessed yourself, was once that *Theodosius*, whom you so much lament. The Love which we have had for one another will make us more happy in its Disappointment, than it could have done in its Success. Providence has disposed of us for our Advantage, tho' not according to our Wishes. Consider your *Theodosius* still as dead, but assure your self of one who will not cease to pray for you in Father

FRANCIS.'

Constantia saw that the Hand-writing agreed with the Contents of the Letter; and upon reflecting on the Voice of the Person, the Behaviour, and above all the extreme Sorrow of the Father during her Confession, she discovered *Theodosius* in every Particular. After having wept with Tears of Joy, It is enough, says she, *Theodosius* is still in Being: I shall live with Comfort and die in Peace.

The Letters which the Father sent her afterwards are yet extant in the Nunnery where she resided; and are often read to the young Religious, in order to inspire them with good Resolutions and Sentiments of Virtue. It so happened, that after *Constantia* had lived about ten Years in the Cloyster, a violent Fever broke out in the Place, which swept away great Multitudes, and among others *Theodosius*. Upon his Death-bed he sent his Benediction in a very moving Manner to *Constantia*; who at that time was her self so far gone in the same fatal Distemper, that she lay delirious. Upon the Interval which generally precedes Death in Sicknesses of this Nature, the Abbess finding that the Physicians had given her over, told her that *Theodosius* was just gone before her, and that he had sent her his Benediction in his last Moments. *Constantia* receiv'd it with Pleasure: And now, says she, If I do not ask any thing improper, let me be buried by *Theodosius*. My Vow reaches no farther than the Grave. What I ask is, I hope, no Violation of it.—She died soon after, and was interred according to her Request.

Their Tombs are still to be seen, with a short Latin Inscription over them to the following Purpose.

Here lie the Bodies of Father *Francis* and Sister *Constance*. *They were lovely in their Lives, and in their Death they were not divided.*

C

No. 165.

[ADDISON.] Saturday, September 8.

> . . . *Si forte necesse est* .*.*
> *Fingere cinctutis non exaudita Cethegis*
> *Continget: dabiturque licentia sumpta pudenter.* —Hor.

I HAVE often wished, that as in our Constitution there are several Persons whose Business it is to watch over our Laws, our Liberties and Commerce, certain Men might be set apart, as Super-intendants of our Language, to hinder any Words of a Foreign Coin from passing among us; and in particular to prohibit any *French* Phrases from becoming Current in this Kingdom, when those of our own stamp are altogether as valuable. The present War has so adulterated our Tongue with strange Words, that it would be impossible for one of our Great Grandfathers to know what his Posterity have been doing, were he to read their Exploits in a Modern News-Paper. Our Warriors are very Industrious in Propagating the *French* Language, at the same time that they are so gloriously success-ful in beating down their Power. Our Soldiers are Men of strong Heads for Action, and perform such Feats as they are not able to express. They want Words in their own Tongue to tell us what it is they Atchieve, and therefore send us over Accounts of their Performances in a Jargon of Phrases, which they learn among their Conquered Enemies. They ought however to be provided with Secretaries, and assisted by our Foreign Ministers, to tell their Story for them in plain *English*, and to let us know in our Mother-Tongue what it is our brave Countrymen are about. The *French* would indeed be in the right to publish the News of the present War in *English* Phrases, and make their Campaigns unintelligible. Their People might flatter themselves that things are not so bad as they really are, were they thus palliated with Foreign Terms, and thrown into Shades and Obscurity. But the *English* cannot be too clear in their Narrative of those Actions, which have raised their Country to a higher Pitch of Glory than it ever yet arrived at, and which will be still the more admired the better they are explained.

For my part, by that Time a Siege is carried on two or three Days, I am altogether lost and bewildered in it, and meet with so many inexplicable Difficulties, that I scarce know which Side has the better of it, till I am informed by the Tower Guns that the Place is surrendred. I do indeed make some Allowances for this Part of the War, Fortifications having been Foreign Inventions, and upon that Account abounding in Foreign Terms. But when we have won Battels which may be described in our own Language, why are our Papers filled with so many unintelligible Exploits, and the *French* obliged to lend us a part of their Tongue before we can know how they are Conquered? They must be made accessary to their own Disgrace, as the *Britains* were formerly so artificially wrought in the Curtain of the *Roman* Theatre, that they seemed to draw it up, in order to give the Spectators an Opportunity of seeing their own Defeat celebrated upon the Stage: For so Mr. *Dryden* has translated that Verse in *Virgil*.

> *Purpurea intexti tollant aulaea Britanni.*
>
> *Which interwoven* Britains *seem to raise,*
> *And show the Triumph that their Shame displays.*

The Histories of all our former Wars are transmitted to us in our Vernacular Idiom, to use the Phrase of a great Modern Critick. I do not find in any of our Chronicles, that *Edward* the Third ever reconnoitred the Enemy, tho' he often discover'd the Posture of the *French*, and as often vanquish'd them in Battel. The *Black Prince* passed many a River without the help of Pontoons, and filled a Ditch with Faggots as successfully as the Generals of our Times do it with Fascines. Our Commanders lose half their Praise, and our People half their Joy, by means of those hard Words and dark Expressions in which our News-Papers do so much abound. I have seen many a prudent Citizen, after having read every Article, enquire of his next Neighbour what News the Mail had brought.

I remember in that remarkable Year when our Country was delivered from the greatest Fears and Apprehensions, and raised to the greatest height of Gladness it had ever felt since it was a Nation, I mean the Year of *Blenheim*, I had the Copy of a Letter sent me out of the Country, which was written from a young Gentleman in the Army to his Father, a Man of a good Estate and plain Sense: As the Letter was very modishly checquered with this Modern Military Eloquence, I shall present my Reader with a Copy of it.

'*Sir*,

Upon the Junction of the *French* and *Bavarian* Armies they took Post behind a great Morass which they thought impracticable. Our General the next Day sent a Party of Horse to reconnoitre them from a little Hauteur, at about a quarter of an Hour's distance from the Army, who return'd again to the Camp unobserved through several Defiles, in one of which they met with a Party of *French* that had been Marauding, and made them all Prisoners at Discretion.   The Day after a drum arrived at our Camp, with a Message which he would communicate to none but the General; he was followed by a Trumpet, who they say behaved himself very saucily, with a Message from the Duke of *Bavaria*.   The next Morning our Army being divided into two Corps, made a Movement towards the Enemy: You will hear in the publick Prints how we treated them, with the other Circumstances of that glorious Day.   I had the good Fortune to be in the Regiment that pushed the *Gens d' Arms*.   Several *French* Battalions, who some say were a Corps de Reserve, made a Show of Resistance; but it only proved a Gasconade, for upon our preparing to fill up a little Fosse, in order to attack them, they beat the Chamade, and sent us *Charte Blanche*.   Their Commandant, with a great many other General Officers, and Troops without number, are made Prisoners of War, and will I believe give you a Visit in *England*, the Cartel not being yet settled.   Not questioning but these Particulars will be very welcome to you, I congratulate you upon them, and am your most dutiful Son,' &c.

The Father of the young Gentleman upon the Perusal of the Letter found it contained great News, but could not guess what it was.   He immediately communicated it to the Curate of the Parish, who upon the reading of it, being vexed to see any thing he could not understand, fell into a kind of a Passion, and told him, that his Son has sent him a Letter that was neither Fish, Flesh, nor good Red Herring.   I wish, says he, the Captain may be *Compos Mentis*, he talks of a saucy Trumpet, and a Drum that carries Messages: Then who is this *Charte Blanche*: He must either banter us, or he is out of his Senses.   The Father, who always look'd upon the Curate as a learned Man, began to fret inwardly at his Son's Usage, and producing a Letter which he had written to him about three Posts afore, You see here, says he, when he writes for Mony he knows how to speak intelligibly enough; there is no Man in *England* can express himself clearer, when he wants a new Furniture for his Horse.   In short, the old Man was so puzzled upon the Point, that it might have fared ill with his Son, had he not seen all the Prints about three Days after filled with the same Terms of Art, and that *Charles* only writ like other Men.   L

No. 166.

[ADDISON.]   Monday, September 10.

> . . . Quod nec Jovis ira, nec ignis,
>   Nec poterit ferrum, nec edax abolere vetustas.—Ovid.

ARISTOTLE tells us, that the World is a Copy or Transcript of
those Ideas which are in the Mind of the first Being; and that
those Ideas which are in the Mind of Man, are a Transcript of
the World: To this we may add, that Words are the Transcript
of those Ideas which are in the Mind of Man, and that Writing
or Printing are the Transcript of Words.

As the supreme Being has expressed, and as it were printed
his Ideas in the Creation, Men express their Ideas in Books,
which by this great Invention of these latter Ages may last as
long as the Sun and Moon, and perish only in the general
Wreck of Nature. Thus *Cowley* in his Poem on the Resur-
rection, mentioning the Destruction of the Universe, has those
admirable Lines.

> Now all the wide-extended Sky,
>   And all th' harmonious Worlds on high,
>   And Virgil's sacred Work shall die.

There is no other Method of fixing those Thoughts which
arise and disappear in the Mind of Man, and transmitting them
to the last Periods of Time; no other Method of giving a Per-
manency to our Ideas, and preserving the Knowledge of any
particular Person, when his Body is mixed with the common
Mass of Matter, and his Soul retired into the World of Spirits.
Books are the Legacies that a great Genius leaves to Mankind,
which are delivered down from Generation to Generation, as
Presents to the Posterity of those who are yet unborn.

All other Arts of perpetuating our Ideas continue but a short
Time: Statues can last but a few Thousands of Years, Edifices
fewer, and Colours still fewer than Edifices. *Michael Angelo*,
Fontana, and *Raphael*, will hereafter be what *Phidias*, *Vitruvius*, and *Apelles* are at present; the Names of great Statuaries,
Architects, and Painters, whose Works are lost. The several
Arts are expressed in mouldring Materials; Nature sinks under
them, and is not able to support the Ideas which are imprest
upon it.

The Circumstance which gives Authors an Advantage above
all these great Masters, is this, that they can multiply their
Originals; or rather can make Copies of their Works, to what
Number they please, which shall be as valuable as the Originals
themselves. This gives a great Author something like a
Prospect of Eternity, but at the same Time deprives him of

those other Advantages which Artists meet with. The Artist finds greater Returns in Profit, as the Author in Fame. What an inestimable Price would a *Virgil* or a *Homer*, a *Cicero* or an *Aristotle* bear, were their Works like a Statue, a Building, or a Picture, or to be confined only in one Place, and made the Property of a single Person?

If Writings are thus durable, and may pass from Age to Age throughout the whole Course of Time, how careful should an Author be of committing any thing to Print that may corrupt Posterity, and poyson the Minds of Men with Vice and Errour? Writers of great Talents, who employ their Parts in propagating Immorality, and seasoning vicious Sentiments with Wit and Humour, are to be looked upon as the Pests of Society and the Enemies of Mankind: They leave Books behind them (as it is said of those who die in Distempers which breed an ill Will towards their own Species) to scatter Infection and destroy their Posterity. They act the Counterparts of a *Confucius* or a *Socrates*; and seem to have been sent into the World to deprave humane Nature, and sink it into the Condition of Brutality.

I have seen some Roman-Catholick Authors, who tell us that vicious Writers continue in Purgatory so long as the Influence of their Writings continues upon Posterity: For Purgatory, say they, is nothing else but a cleansing us of our Sins, which cannot be said to be done away, so long as they continue to operate and corrupt Mankind. The vicious Author, say they, sins after Death, and so long as he continues to sin, so long must he expect to be punished. Though the Roman-Catholick Notion of Purgatory be indeed very ridiculous, one cannot but think that if the Soul after Death has any Knowledge of what passes in this World, that of an immoral Writer would receive much more Regret from the Sense of corrupting, than Satisfaction from the Thought of pleasing his surviving Admirers.

To take off from the Severity of this Speculation, I shall conclude this Paper with a Story of an Atheistical Author, who at a time when he lay dangerously sick and had desired the Assistance of a neighbouring Curate, confessed to him with great Contrition, that nothing sat more heavy at his Heart than the Sense of his having seduced the Age by his Writings, and that their evil Influence was likely to continue even after his Death. The Curate upon further Examination finding the Penitent in the utmost Agonies of Despair, and being himself a Man of Learning, told him, that he hoped his Case was not so desperate as he apprehended, since he found that he was so very sensible of his Fault, and so sincerely repented of it.

The Penitent still urged the evil Tendency of his Books to subvert all Religion, and the little Ground of Hope there could be for one whose Writings would continue to do Mischief when his Body was laid in Ashes. The Curate finding no other Way to comfort him, told him, that he did well in being afflicted for the evil Design with which he published his Book; but that he ought to be very thankful that there was no Danger of its doing any Hurt. That his Cause was so very bad and his Arguments so weak, that he did not apprehend any ill Effects of it. In short, that he might rest satisfied his Book could do no more Mischief after his Death, than it had done whilst he was living. To which he added, for his further Satisfaction, that he did not believe any besides his particular Friends and Acquaintance had ever been at the Pains of reading it, or that any Body after his Death would ever enquire after it. The dying Man had still so much the Fraility of an Author in him, as to be cut to the Heart with these Consolations; and without answering the good Man, asked his Friends about him (with a Peevishness that is natural to a sick Person) where they had picked up such a Block-head? And whether they thought him a proper Person to attend one in his Condition? The Curate finding that the Author did not expect to be dealt with as a real and sincere Penitent, but as a Penitent of Importance, after a short Admonition withdrew; not questioning but he should be again sent for if the Sickness grew desperate. The Author however recovered, and has since written two or three other Tracts with the same Spirit, and very luckily for his poor Soul, with the same Success. C

No. 167.
[STEELE.]   Tuesday, September 11.

> . . . *Fuit haud ignobilis Argis,*
> *Qui se credebat miros audire tragoedos,*
> *In vacuo laetus sessor plausorque theatro;*
> *Caetera qui vitae servaret munia recto*
> *More; bonus sane vicinus, amabilis hospes,*
> *Comis in uxorem, posset qui ignoscere servis,*
> *Et signo laeso non insanire lagenae;*
> *Posset qui rupem & puteum vitare patentem.*
> *Hic ubi cognatorum opibus curisque refectus*
> *Expulit elleboro morbum bilemque meraco,*
> *Et redit ad sese: Pol me occidistis, amici,*
> *Non servastis, ait, cui sic extorta voluptas,*
> *Et demptus per vim mentis gratissimus error.*—Hor.

THE unhappy Force of an Imagination unguided by the Check of Reason and Judgment, was the Subject of a former Specu-

lation. My Reader may remember that he has seen in one of
my Papers a Complaint of an unfortunate Gentleman, who
was unable to contain himself, (when any ordinary Matter
was laid before him) from adding a few Circumstances to
enliven plain Narrative. That Correspondent was a Person
of too warm a Complexion to be satisfied with things merely
as they stood in Nature, and therefore formed Incidents which
should have happened to have pleased him in the Story. The
same ungoverned Fancy which pushed that Correspondent on,
in Spite of himself, to relate publick and notorious Falshoods,
makes the Author of the following Letter do the same in
Private; one is a prating the other a silent Liar.

There is little pursued in the Errors of either of these Worthies
but mere present Amusement: But the Folly of him who lets
his Fancy place him in distant Scenes untroubled and unin-
terrupted, is very much preferable to that of him who is ever
forcing a Belief, and defending his Untruths with new Inventions. But I shall hasten to let this Liar in Soliloquy,
who calls himself a CASTLE-BUILDER, describe himself with the
same Unreservedness as formerly appeared in my Correspondent above-mention'd. If a Man were to be serious on this
Subject, he might give very grave Admonitions to those who
are following any thing in this Life, on which they think
to place their Hearts, and tell them that they are really
CASTLE-BUILDERS. Fame, Glory, Wealth, Honour, have in
the Prospect pleasing Illusions; but they who come to possess
any of them will find they are Ingredients towards Happiness,
to be regarded only in the second Place, and that when they
are valued in the first Degree, they are as disappointing as
any of the Phantoms in the following Letter.

'*Mr.* SPECTATOR,   *Sept.* 6, 1711.

I am a Fellow of a very odd Frame of Mind, as you will find
by the Sequel; and think my self Fool enough to deserve a
Place in your Paper. I am unhappily far gone in Building,
and am one of that Species of Men who are properly denomi-
nated Castle-Builders, who scorn to be beholden to the Earth
for a Foundation, or dig in the Bowels of it for Materials; but
rest their Structures in the most unstable of Elements, the
Air; Fancy alone laying the Line, marking the Extent, and
shaping the Model. It would be difficult to enumerate what
august Palaces and stately Porticoes have grown under my
forming Imagination, or what verdant Meadows and shady
Groves have started into Being by the powerful Feat of a
warm Fancy. A Castle-Builder is even just what he pleases,
and as such I have grasped imaginary Scepters, and delivered

uncontroulable Edicts, from a Throne to which conquer'd Nations yielded Obeisance. I have made I know not how many Inroads into *France*, and ravaged the very Heart of that Kingdom; I have dined in the *Louvre*, and drank Champaign at *Versailles*; and I would have you take Notice, I am not only able to vanquish a People already cowed and accustomed to Flight, but I could, *Almanzor* like, drive the *British* General from the Field, were I less a Protestant, or had ever been affronted by the Confederates. There is no Art or Profession, whose most celebrated Masters I have not eclipsed. Wherever I have afforded my salutary Presence, Fevers have ceased to burn, and Agues to shake the human Fabrick. When an eloquent Fit has been upon me, an apt Gesture and proper Cadence has animated each Sentence, and gazing Crowds have found their Passions worked up into Rage, or soothed into a Calm. I am short, and not very well made; yet upon Sight of a fine Woman, I have stretch'd into proper Stature, and killed with a good Air and Mein. These are the gay Phantoms that dance before my waking Eyes, and compose my Day-Dreams. I should be the most contented happy Man alive, were the chimerical Happiness which springs from the Paintings of Fancy less fleeting and transitory. But alas! it is with Grief of Mind I tell you, the least Breath of Wind has often demolished my magnificent Edifices, swept away my Groves, and left no more Trace of them than if they had never been. My Exchequer has sunk and vanished by a Rap on my Door, the Salutation of a Friend has cost me a whole Continent, and in the same Moment I have been pulled by the Sleeve, my Crown has fallen from my Head. The ill Consequence of these Reveries is inconceivably great, seeing the Loss of imaginary Possessions makes Impressions of real Woe. Besides, bad Oeconomy is visible and apparent in Builders of invisible Mansions. My Tenant's Advertisements of Ruins and Dilapidations often cast a Damp on my Spirits, even in the Instant when the Sun, in all his Splendor, gilds my Eastern Palaces. Add to this the pensive Drudgery in Building, and constant grasping Aerial Trowels, distracts and shatters the Mind, and the fond Builder of *Babells* is often cursed with an incoherent Diversity and Confusion of Thoughts. I do not know to whom I can more properly apply my self for relief from this Fantastical Evil, than to your self; whom I earnestly implore to accommodate me with a Method how to settle my Head and cool my Brain-pan. A Dissertation on Castle-Building may not only be serviceable to my self, but all Architects, who display their Skill in the thin Element. Such a Favour would oblige me to make my next Soliloquy not contain the Praises of my dear self but of the Spectator, who shall, by complying with this, make me

His Obliged, Humble Servant,

T   Vitruvius.'

No. 168.

[STEELE.]   Wednesday, September 12.

> . . . *Pectus praeceptis format amicis.*—Hor.

IT would be Arrogance to neglect the Application of my Correspondents, so far as not sometimes to insert their Animadversions upon my Paper; that of this Day shall be therefore wholly composed of the Hints which they have sent me.

'Mr. SPECTATOR,

I send you this to congratulate your late Choice of a Subject, for treating on which you deserve publick Thanks; I mean that on those licensed Tyrants the School-masters. If you can disarm them of their Rods, you will certainly have your old Age reverenced by all the young Gentlemen of *Great Britain* who are now between seven and seventeen years. You may boast that the incomparably wise *Quintilian* and you are of one Mind in this Particular. *Si cui est* (says he) *mens tam illiberalis ut objurgatione non corrigatur, is etiam ad plagas, ut pessima quaeque mancipia, durabitur,*—If any Child be of so disingenuous a Nature, as not to stand corrected by Reproof, he, like the very worst of Slaves, will be hardened even against Blows themselves; and afterwards, *Pudet dicere in quae probra nefandi homines isto caedendi jure abutantur,* i.e. *I blush to say how shamefully those wicked Men abuse the Power of Correction.*

I was bred my self, Sir, in a very great School, of which the Master was a *Welchman,* but certainly descended from a *Spanish* Family, as plainly appear'd from his Temper as well as his Name. I leave you to judge what a sort of a Schoolmaster a *Welchman* ingrafted on a *Spaniard* would make. So very dreadful had he made himself to me, that altho' it is above twenty Years since I felt his heavy Hand, yet still once a Month at least I dream of him, so strong an Impression did he make on my Mind. 'Tis a Sign he has fully terrified me waking, who still continues to haunt me sleeping.

And yet I may say, without Vanity, that the Business of the School was what I did without great Difficulty; and I was not remarkably unlucky; and yet such was the Master's Severity, that once a Month, or oftner, I suffered as much as would have satisfied the Law of the Land for a *Petty-Larceny*.

Many a white and tender Hand, which the fond Mother had passionately kiss'd a thousand and a thousand Times, have I seen whipped till it was covered with Blood: perhaps for smiling, or for going a Yard and half out of a Gate, or for writing an O for an A, or an A for an O: These were our great Faults! Many a brave and noble Spirit has been there broken; others have run from thence and were never heard of afterwards. It is a worthy Attempt to undertake the Cause of distrest Youth; and it is a noble Piece of *Knight-Errantry* to enter the Lists against so many armed Paedagogues. 'Tis pity but we had a Set of Men, polite in their Behaviour and Method of teaching, who should be put into a Condition of being above flattering or fearing the Parents of those they instruct. We might then possibly see Learning become a Pleasure, and Children delighting themselves in that, which now they abhor for coming upon such hard Terms to them: What would be still a greater Happiness arising from the Care of such Instructors, would be, that we should have no more Pedants, nor any bred to Learning who had not Genius for it. I am, with the utmost Sincerity,

Sir,

Your most affectionate
humble Servant.'

'Mr. SPECTATOR, *Richmond, Sept.* 5th, 1711.

I am a Boy of fourteen Years of Age, and have for this last Year been under the Tuition of a Doctor of Divinity, who has taken the School of this Place under his Care. From the Gentleman's great Tenderness to me and Friendship to my Father, I am very happy in learning my Book with Pleasure. We never leave off our Diversions any further than to salute him at Hours of Play when he pleases to look on. It is impossible for any of us to love our own Parents better than we do him. He never gives any of us an harsh Word, and we think it the greatest Punishment in the World when he will not speak to any of us. My Brother and I are both together inditing this Letter: He is a Year older than I am, but is now ready to break his Heart that the Doctor has not taken any Notice of him these three Days. If you please to print this he will see it, and, we hope, taking it for my Brother's earnest Desire to be restored to his Favour, he will again smile upon him.

Your most obedient Servant,

T. S.

'Mr. SPECTATOR,

You have represented several sorts of *Impertinents* singly, I wish you would now proceed, and describe some of them in Sets. It often happens in publick Assemblies, that a Party who came thither together, or whose Impertinencies are of an equal Pitch, act in Concert, and are so full of themselves as to give Disturbance to all that are about them. Sometimes you have a Set of Whisperers who lay their Heads together in order to sacrifice every Body within their Observation; sometimes a Set of Laughers, that keep up an insipid Mirth in their own Corner, and by their Noise and Gestures shew they have no Respect for the rest of the Company. You frequently meet with these Sets at the Opera, the Play, the Water-works, and other publick Meetings, where their whole Business is to draw off the Attention of the Spectators from the Entertainment, and to fix it upon themselves; and it is to be observ'd that the Impertinence is ever loudest, when the Set happens to be made up of three or four Females who have got what you call a Woman's Man among them.

I am at a Loss to know from whom People of Fortune should learn this Behaviour, unless it be from the Footmen who keep their Places at a new Play, and are often seen passing away their Time in Sets at *All-fours* in the Face of a full House, and with a perfect Disregard to the People of Quality sitting on each side of them.

For preserving therefore the Decency of publick Assemblies, methinks it would be but reasonable that those who disturb others should pay at least a double Price for their Places; or rather Women of Birth and Distinction should be inform'd, that Levity of Behaviour in the Eyes of People of Understanding degrades them below their meanest Attendants; and Gentlemen should know that a fine Coat is a Livery, when the Person who wears it discovers no higher Sense than that of a Footman. I am,

Sir,

Your most humble Servant.'

'Mr. SPECTATOR,   *Bedfordshire, Sept.* 1st, 1711.

I am one of those whom every Body calls a Pocher, and sometimes go out to course with a Brace of Greyhounds, a Mastiff, and a Spaniel or two; and when I am weary with Coursing, and have killed Hares enough, go to an Ale-house to refresh myself. I beg the Favour of you (as you set up for a Reformer) to send us Word how many Dogs you will allow us to go with, how many Full-Pots of Ale to drink, and how

many Hares to kill in a Day, and you will do a great Piece of
Service to all the Sports-men: Be quick then, for the Time of
Coursing is come on.

Yours in Haste,

T   Isaac Hedgeditch.'

No. 169.

[ADDISON.]   **Thursday, September 13.**

> *Sic vita erat; facile omnes perferre ac pati:*
> *Cum quibus erat cunque una, his sese dedere,*
> *Eorum obsequi studiis: advorsus nemini;*
> *Nunquam praeponens se aliis: Ita facillime*
> *Sine invidia invenias laudem.*—Ter. *Andr.*

MAN is subject to innumerable Pains and Sorrows by the very
Condition of Humanity, and yet, as if Nature had not sown
evils enough in Life, we are continually adding Grief to Grief,
and aggravating the common Calamity by our cruel Treatment of one another. Every Man's natural Weight of Affliction is still made more heavy by the Envy, Malice, Treachery,
or Injustice of his Neighbour. At the same time that the
Storm beats upon the whole Species, we are falling foul upon
one another.

Half the Misery of Human Life might be extinguished,
would Men alleviate the general Curse they lie under, by
mutual Offices of Compassion, Benevolence and Humanity.
There is nothing therefore which we ought more to encourage
in our selves and others, than that Disposition of Mind which
in our Language goes under the Title of Good-nature, and
which I shall chuse for the Subject of this Day's Speculation.

Good-nature is more agreeable in Conversation than Wit,
and gives a certain Air to the Countenance which is more
amiable than Beauty. It shows Virtue in the fairest Light,
takes off in some measure from the Deformity of Vice, and
makes even Folly and Impertinence supportable.

There is no Society or Conversation to be kept up in the
World without Good-nature, or something which must bear
its Appearance, and supply its Place. For this Reason Mankind have been forced to invent a kind of Artificial Humanity,
which is what we express by the Word *Good-Breeding.* For
if we examine thoroughly the Idea of what we call so, we shall
find it to be nothing else but an Imitation and Mimickry of
Good-nature, or in other Terms, Affability, Complaisance and
Easiness of Temper reduced into an Art.

These exterior Shows and Appearances of Humanity render a Man wonderfully popular and beloved, when they are founded upon a real Good-nature; but without it are like Hypocrisy in Religion, or a bare Form of Holiness, which, when it is discovered, makes a Man more detestable than professed Impiety.

Good-nature is generally born with us: Health, Prosperity and kind Treatment from the World are great Cherishers of it where they find it, but nothing is capable of forcing it up, where it does not grow of it self. It is one of the Blessings of a happy Constitution, which Education may improve but not produce.

Xenophon in the Life of his Imaginary Prince, whom he describes as a Pattern for Real ones, is always celebrating the *Philanthropy* or Good-nature of his Hero, which he tells us he brought into the World with him, and gives many remarkable Instances of it in his Childhood, as well as in all the several Parts of his Life. Nay, on his Death-bed, he describes him as being pleased, that while his Soul returned to him who made it, his Body should incorporate with the great Mother of all things, and by that means become beneficial to Mankind. For which reason, he gives his Sons a positive Order not to enshrine it in Gold or Silver, but to lay it in the Earth as soon as the Life was gone out of it.

An Instance of such an Overflowing of Humanity, such an exuberant Love to Mankind, could not have entered into the Imagination of a Writer, who had not a Soul filled with great Ideas, and a general Benevolence to Mankind.

In that celebrated Passage of *Salust*, where *Caesar* and *Cato* are placed in such beautiful, but opposite Lights; *Caesar's* Character is chiefly made up of Good-nature, as it show'd it self in all its Forms towards his Friends or his Enemies, his Servants or Dependants, the Guilty or the Distressed. As for *Cato's* Character, it is rather awful than amiable. Justice seems most agreeable to the Nature of God, and Mercy to that of Man. A Being who has nothing to Pardon in himself, may reward every Man according to his Works; but he whose very best Actions must be seen with Grains of Allowance, cannot be too mild, moderate, and forgiving. For this reason, among all the monstrous Characters in Human Nature, there is none so odious, nor indeed so exquisitely Ridiculous, as that of a rigid severe Temper in a Worthless Man.

This Part of Good-nature, however, which consists in the pardoning and over-looking of Faults, is to be exercised only in doing our selves Justice, and that too in the ordinary Commerce and Occurrences of Life; for in the Publick

Administrations of Justice, Mercy to one may be Cruelty to others.

It is grown almost into a Maxim, that Good-natured Men are not always Men of the most Wit. This Observation, in my Opinion, has no Foundation in Nature. The greatest Wits I have conversed with, are Men eminent for their Humanity. I take therefore this Remark to have been occasioned by two Reasons. First, Because Ill-nature among ordinary Observers passes for Wit. A spightful Saying gratifies so many little Passions in those who hear it, that it generally meets with a good Reception. The Laugh rises upon it, and the Man who utters it is look'd upon as a shrewd Satyrist. This may be one Reason why a great many pleasant Companions appear so surprizingly dull, when they have endeavoured to be Merry in Print; the Publick being more just than Private Clubs or Assemblies, in distinguishing between what is Wit and what is Ill-nature.

Another Reason why the Good-natured Man may sometimes bring his Wit in Question, is, perhaps, because he is apt to be moved with Compassion for those Misfortunes or Infirmities, which another would turn into Ridicule, and by that Means gain the Reputation of a Wit. The Ill-natured Man, though but of equal Parts, gives himself a larger Field to expatiate in, he exposes those Failings in Human Nature which the other would cast a Veil over, laughs at Vices which the other either excuses or conceals, gives Utterance to Reflections which the other stifles, falls indifferently upon Friends or Enemies, exposes the Person who has obliged him, and in short sticks at nothing that may establish his Character of a Wit. It is no wonder therefore he succeeds in it better than the Man of Humanity, as a Person who makes use of indirect Methods is more likely to grow rich than the fair Trader.   L

The End of the Second Volume.

NOTES

A = Original Daily Issue.

B. I. = Biographical Index.

Dedication. PAGE 1. Addison dedicated his *Poem to His Majesty* (1695) and his *Remarks on Several Parts of Italy* (1705) to Lord Somers. He wrote a fuller appreciation in No. 39 of the *Free-holder*, published on the day of Somers's funeral. Steele, in No. 438 of the *Spectator*, speaks of him as 'one of the greatest Souls now in the World.' Cf. Swift's 'Bookseller's Dedication' prefixed to the *Tale of a Tub*, and Pope's panegyrical footnote to line 77 of the *Epilogue to the Satires*.

I. PAGE 3. *Motto.* Horace, *Ars Poetica*, 143.

Below the motto of No. 1 of the original issue is printed: 'To be Continued every Day.'

PAGE 4. The 'taciturnity' of Mr. Spectator, which would appear to be a good-natured transcript of Addison's personal manner, is humorously sustained throughout the subsequent papers. The 'dumb man' is the counterpart of the 'old astrologer' of the *Tatler*. 'She gave out, with good Success, that I was an Old Astrologer; after that a Dumb Man; and last of all she made me pass for a Lion.' (*Guardian*, No. 141.)

Addison alludes, in the second paragraph, to the oriental savant, John Greaves (1602–52), Professor of Geometry at Gresham College, London, and afterwards Savilian Professor of Astronomy at Oxford, who published *Pyramidographia or A Discourse of the Pyramids of Egypt* (1646) and several other works, chiefly on weights and measures (collected and edited by Birch, 1737). His argument, an anticipation of that of Piazzi Smyth, is explained in the title of a pamphlet printed in 1706: *The Origine and Antiquity of our English Weights & Measures discovered by their near agreement with such Standards that are now found in one of the Egyptian Pyramids.* Addison returns, in Nos. 8, 17, 69, 101, 159, etc., to his joke about the voyage to Grand Cairo.

With the third paragraph cf. the announcement in No. 1 of the *Tatler*: 'All accounts of Gallantry, Pleasure, and Entertainment shall be under the article of White's Chocolate-house; Poetry, under that of Will's Coffee-house; Learning, under the title of Grecian; Foreign and Domestic News you will have from Saint James's Coffee - house.' Will's Coffee - house, in Russell Street, Covent Garden, had been the chief rendezvous of the wits since Dryden's association with it, but by 1711 its literary reputation was on the decline. Swift, in his rhapsody *On Poetry*, pictures its 'tribe of circling Wits,' and, in the *Tale of a Tub*, refers satirically to the low tone of conversation at this house at this time. So, too, in Pope's correspondence of this period there are several references to the house and to its ruling spirit Tidcombe, whose 'beastly laughable life' was 'at once nasty and diverting' (Elwin and Courthope, vi. 84). Addison, who had been a *habitué*, withdrew in 1712 to Button's, a new house on the other side of the street. Child's, in St. Paul's Churchyard, had, from its proximity to Doctors' Commons, the Royal Society (then at Gresham College), and the College of Physicians, a large clientele among the clergy and professional classes, mostly of the Tory party (cf. Nos. 556 and 609). St. James's was a fashionable Whig house at the south-west corner of St. James's Street; and the Cocoa-Tree, in the same street, attracted the Tories. The Grecian, in Devereux Street in the Strand (originally carried on by a Greek who had come to England with an English merchant in 1652), was chiefly a lawyers' resort, but was frequented by the learned for the discussion of questions of philosophy and scholarship (cf. Nos. 49 and 403). Pope addresses his paper 'To the learned Inquisitor Martinus Scriblerus: the Society of Free Thinkers Greeting' from the Grecian, and satirizes the pedantic symposia of the college sophs and 'pert' Templars in the second book of *The Dunciad* (lines 379 et sqq.). There is a companion sketch in the humorous advertisement in the 78th *Tatler*, which describes the 'seat of learning' in the Smyrna Coffee-house in Pall Mall. Jonathan's, in Change Alley, was the favourite coffee-house of the merchant and stock-jobbing class ('that General Mart of Stock-jobbers,' *Tatler*, No. 38), just as Garraway's, in the same street, well known for its wine sales, was the recognized rendezvous of their more fashionable customers.

The *Post-Man* newspaper—which, according to the 'Upholsterer,' wrote 'like an angel' (*Tatler*, No. 232), and was 'the best for everything,' according to John Dunton (*Life and Errors,* 1705)—was carried on by a M. Fonvive, described in the *General Postscript* (1709, No. 12), as 'M. Hugonotius, Politicus Gallo-Anglus, a spiteful Commentator.' It had some reputation for its foreign news and correspondence (cf. *Tatler*, No. 178). Steele imputed the loss of the 'Upholsterer's' intellect to its 'Way of going on in the Words, and making no Progress in the Sense' (*Tatler*, No. 178); and Defoe criticized it in his *Review of the Affairs of France*. See Swift's *Journal to Stella*, 26th October 1710: also Nichols's *Literary Anecdotes*, iv. 61 et sqq., 84.

PAGE 6. The letters of correspondents became a feature of the *Spectator*. Addison states his editorial position in Nos. 16, 46, 428, and 442 (with 450); in No. 271 he pleasantly refers to the critical readers who, like Nick Doubt of the *Tatler* (No. 91), suspected the genuineness of these contributions. Steele was, as Johnson tells us, much beholden to outside 'copy' (*Lives*, 1790 edition, ii. 343, 365). Two volumes of *Original and Genuine Letters sent to the Tatler and Spectator* were published in 1725 by Lillie, the perfumer, with Steele's name on the title-page.

2   *Motto.* Juvenal, *Satires*, vii. 167.

Johnson's statement (based on a paragraph by Budgell, which Addison is said to have revised) that the personages of

the *Spectator* were not 'merely ideal,' but 'known and conspicuous in various stations' (*Lives*, ii. 348), is probably re-
sponsible for the almost morbid ingenuity of later editors in
identifying the characters of these papers. Sir Roger's original
appears to have been Sir John Pakington, a Tory squire of
Worcestershire (1671–1727). Captain Sentry and Will Honeycomb are said to be portraits of Colonels Kempenfelt and
Cleland. Will Wimble, like Tom Folio of the *Tatler*, has been
traced (No. 108, note), and even the 'perverse beautiful widow'
has been discovered (No. 113, note). 'Theophrastus,' says
Budgell, 'was the *Spectator* of the age he lived in. He drew
the pictures of particular men; and while he was describing,
for example, a miser, having some remarkable offender of this
kind in his eye, he threw in a circumstance or two, which, tho'
they might not possibly be proper examples of Avarice, served
to make the Picture of the man Compleat' (Preface to *The
Moral Characters of Theophrastus*, 1714). The popular interpretation of this passage would appear to be somewhat forced;
and the difficulty of finding biographical analogies, especially
in the case of Sir John Pakington (see *Dictionary of National
Biography*), is a very serious argument against its justness.
Steele anticipated this antiquarian ingenuity, and endeavoured
to thwart it (see No. 262), just as Fielding later declared against
the 'malicious applications' to his characters in *Joseph Andrews*
(III. i). The characters are general, as Addison hints in No. 34,
and their literary kinship with Sir Jeoffrey Notch and the company of the *Tatler* is obvious. And if we consider that in the
Spectator these personal types take the place of the interests
associated in the *Tatler* with each coffee-house—that the gossip
of the Grecian is in the *Spectator* the wisdom of the Templar,
and that of White's the opinions of Will Honeycomb—we are
still further at issue with the antiquaries. The literary intention of the *Spectator* is so manifest, that there is as little to
be gained by speculating on the models as by individualizing
the earlier 'humours' of Jonson and Etherege, or the characters
of the later novel.

PAGE 6. In a tract of 1648 against a knight, Sir Hugh *Caulverley*,
there is reference to a tune called *Roger of Caulverley* (Ashton's
Social Life in the Reign of Queen Anne, ii. 268–9). It appears as
Roger of Coverly in the *Second Part of the Dancing Master* (1696),
and is referred to as a popular air in *The History of Robert
Powel, the Puppet-Showman* (see note on page 524). It is
called *Roger de Caubly* in the 34th *Tatler*. The tune was later
associated with the country dance, known since the days of the
Spectator by that name. Country dances became fashionable
in France during the Regency (1715–23), under the name *contre-
danse*, which has been erroneously supposed to be the original
form of the word. See Budgell's references in No. 67; also
No. 148.

Soho Square, originally King Square, built in 1681, was still
a fashionable quarter for 'Lady Dainty' and her set (*Tatler*,
No. 37). See Shadwell's plays, *passim*.

PAGE 6. *My Lord Rochester.* John Wilmot, Earl of Rochester (1648-80). His verses on *Nothing* are referred to in No. 305, and his *Imitation of Horace* is quoted in No. 91. See the advertisement in No. 87, *A*.

Sir George Etherege (1635-91), author of *The Comical Revenge or Love in a Tub* (see Nos. 44 and 127), *She Would if she Could* (No. 51), and *The Man of Mode or Sir Fopling Flutter* (No. 65).

A Duel. See page 521.

Bully Dawson is, on the authority of Oldys (received at second hand) the model of Captain Hackum, a 'Block-headed Bully,' in Shadwell's *Squire of Alsatia* (1688).

PAGE 7. The *Treatise on the Sublime* had been edited by Langbaine (1636), and Hudson (1710), and translated by Hall (1662), by Pulteney (1680), and anonymously (1690); but it was chiefly through the French editions and translations, too numerous to mention, and notably the translation and commentary of Boileau (Englished in 1711), that the *Treatise* of Longinus affected critical theory and literary practice in England. At the time of this paper, Edmund Smith's translation, which Johnson has praised highly (*Lives*, ii. 242), was in MS., and Welsted was preparing his version for the press (1712). Cf. Swift's lines on the cult of Longinus in his rhapsody *On Poetry*.

The Templar treats his father's wishes after the manner of Young Maggot in Shadwell's *True Widow* (I. ii).

PAGE 8. *The Rose Tavern* (cf. No. 36) was an actors' house in Brydges Street, close to Drury Lane Theatre. It is referred to by Swift in his *Verses on the Death of Dr. Swift*, line 299, and frequently in Shadwell's plays (especially in *The Scowrers*), for its rowdy scenes; and it is probably depicted in the third plate of Hogarth's *Rake's Progress*.

Captain Sentry is said to be, as hinted above, a sketch of Colonel Kempenfelt, the father of the hero of the *Royal George* (see Steele's reference to Colonel Camperfelt in No. 544).

PAGE 9. *Will. Honeycomb* has been explained to be a Colonel Cleland, who seems to have had the amorous bent of his more notorious namesake, the 'biographer' of Fanny Hill. See the *Dictionary of National Biography*, Pope's works (*passim*), and Steele's *Correspondence*, edited by Nichols, page 358. The last volume of the *Spectator* is dedicated to Will. Honeycomb.

3. PAGE 10. *Motto.* Lucretius, iv. 962.

PAGE 11. Addison's allegory alludes to the financial crisis following the Revolution. The Whigs, supported by 'Sir Andrew Freeport' and his friends, represented the moneyed interests; the Tories, with 'Sir Roger,' upheld the landed interests (cf. No. 174). It was the obvious policy of the former to maintain that *Public Credit* (as expressed by the Bank of England and the National Debt) would be imperilled if the Stuarts gained the ascendant. The 'young man of about twenty-two years of age' menacing the Act of Settlement, is James, son of James II, whose probable policy of repudiation is signified by the 'spunge.' The third person, whom the dreamer 'had never seen,' is the

Elector of Hanover, who came to the throne in 1714. With him is associated the Whig 'Toleration' ('Moderation leading in Religion') which Locke had enunciated in 1689. Cf. the reference to the 'Figure of Moderation' in the 257th *Tatler*. The happy change from 'Heaps of Paper' to 'Pyramids of Guineas' finds its historical original in Montagu's scheme for the restoration of the currency. One of the characters in Steele's allegory in the 48th *Tatler* is 'Umbra, the Daemon or Genius of Credit.' The Tory hatred of 'commodious gold' and 'blest paper credit' has its full expression later in Pope's third epistle of the *Moral Essays*. See also Pope's *Imitations of Horace* (*Epistles*, I. i. 65–133), his versified *Satires of Donne*, and Swift's letter to Pope, 10th January 1721.

PAGE 12. *Rehearsal*. The reference is to the scene in the last act, where an eclipse, Luna, Orbis, and Sol are introduced.

Et neque, etc. Ovid, *Metamorphoses*, iii. 491–3.

Last line. Homer, *Odyssey*, x. 19.

4. PAGE 13. *Motto*. Horace, *Satires*, II. vi. 58.

PAGE 14. *Jesuit*. See page 240.

'Nunquam se minus otiosum esse, quam cum otiosus, nec minus solum, quam cum solus esset.'—Cicero, *De Officiis*, III. i (cf. Rogers's *Human Life* (Aldine edition, page 130), and Byron's *Childe Harold's Pilgrimage*, III. xc). A fair proportion of the many allusions to Cicero (which so embarrassed Simon Honeycomb) refers to the *De Officiis*. Cockman's *Tully's Offices in English*, published by Buckley, reached a third edition in 1714.

PAGE 15. *Young thing*. 'Blooming Beauty' in *A*.

PAGE 16. The *Tatler* in its opening number had likewise announced its interest in feminine affairs. The *Spectator's* polite attention to the ladies prompted Swift to say, 'I will not meddle with the *Spectator*. Let him fair sex it to the world's end' (*Journal to Stella*, 8th February 1711–12). Compare Addison's further plea in No. 10, and Belvidera's letter in No. 205. Addison's delicate pleasantries on feminine foibles, in the *Tatler* and *Spectator*, so took the public fancy that they became the prevailing topics of the humorous and light literature of his time. Much of *The Rape of the Lock*, for example, is distinctly inspired by these witty sketches (see note to page 213). The 'Tea-Table' represented the domestic and feminine interests in contrast to those associated with the 'Coffee-house.' References to this antithesis are numerous in the *Spectator* and contemporary literature ('Here no *Chit-Chat*, here no *Tea-Tables* are.'—Shadwell's *Squire of Alsatia*, Epilogue). Steele wrote a short-lived paper called the *Tea-Table* (founded on 17th December 1715), and another called *Chit-Chat* (6th March 1716); and Allan Ramsay, in 1724, published his *Tea-Table Miscellany*. The *Tea-Table* (36 numbers) appeared in London in 1724.

5. PAGE 17. *Motto*. Horace, *Ars Poetica*, 5.

Addison's papers on the opera and dramatic *mise en scène* generally emphasize the sentiments of the *Tatler* and anticipate the criticism of Pope (*Dunciad*, book iii, and *Epistle to*

Augustus). They may have a personal interest in connection with the disaster to Addison's opera of *Rosamond* in April 1706. See also No. 18. The raillery of the *Spectator* recalls the gibes in Saint-Evremond's *Les Opéras*.

PAGE 17. *Nicolini.* See Grimaldi, Nicolino, in *B. I.*

Addison illustrates his criticism of histrionic absurdities from the opera of *Rinaldo* (see below), in which we have fire-spitting dragons (I. v, vii), a boat in an open sea (II. iii), a 'real' waterfall (III. i), and thunder and lightning (III. ii). In his satire on the introduction of living birds, he is referring to the stage direction in I. vi, where 'birds are heard to sing, and seen flying up and down among the trees,' during the flute symphony to *Augelletti che cantate*. See also No. 14, and the advertisement to No. 36.

Sir Martin Mar-all or The Feigned Innocence, a popular comedy (first acted on 16th August 1776), adapted by Dryden from the Duke of Newcastle's translation of Molière's *L'Étourdi*, and from Quinault's *L'Amant indiscret*. The reference is to the first scene of the fifth act, where Sir Martin, after the conclusion of the serenade to Mrs. Millisent, sung and played by his man Warner in the next room, 'continues fumbling and gazing on his mistress.' Whereupon she says: 'A pretty humoured song. But stay, methinks he plays and sings still, and yet we cannot hear him. Play louder, Sir Martin, that we may have the fruits on 't.'

PAGE 18. The opera of *Rinaldo*, Handel's first venture on the English stage, was produced at the Haymarket on 24th February 1711, and ran for fifteen nights. The libretto, which is founded on a well-known episode in Tasso's *Gerusalemme liberata*, was by Giacomo Rossi, and was translated by Aaron Hill: hence 'the two Poets of different Nations.' See No. 14. Addison refers to, and quotes from, the English and Italian edition of the libretto published in 1711 by Thomas Howlatt.

Hendel or Händel, the composer, known as *Handel* to later generations in England. Aaron Hill writes *Hendel* in his preface to *Rinaldo*. In the original issue Addison had given Handel the *Italian* title of *Seignior*, which he corrected in an erratum in the following number.

PAGE 19. *Monsieur Boileau. Satires*, ix:

> Tous les jours à la cour un sot de qualité
> Peut juger de travers avec impunité;
> A Malherbe, à Racan, préférer Théophile,
> *Et le clinquant du Tasse à tout l'or de Virgile.*

See also *L'Art poétique*, iii. 205 et sqq.; *Réflexions sur Longin*, ii. Addison makes a like comparison in Nos. 279 and 369.

Whittington and his Cat. Cf. No. 14, which informs us that Powell, the showman, had (probably on this hint from Addison) set up *Whittington* against *Rinaldo and Armida*; also *Tatler*, No. 78.

Christopher Rich, manager of Drury Lane, the 'Kitt Crotchet' of No. 258, and the 'Divito' of the *Tatler* (Nos. 12, 42, and 99).

He was the father of 'Harlequin' Rich, the 'immortal Rich' of *The Dunciad* (iii. 261). See *B. I.*

PAGE 19. *London and Wise*, a famous firm of gardeners, referred to at greater length in No. 477, and eulogized by Evelyn in the Advertisement to his translation of Quintinye's *Compleat Gard'ner* (1693). Their nursery at Brompton Park, near Kensington, so impressed the author of *Sylva Sylvarum*, that he wrote: 'I cannot therefore forbear to publish . . . what we can and are able to perform in this part of *Agriculture*; and have some Amoenities and advantages peculiar to our own, which neither France, nor any other *Country* can attain to; and is much due to the industry of Mr. London and Mr. Wise, and to such as shall imitate their Laudable Undertakings.' London and Wise expounded their views in *The Retir'd Gard'ner* (a translation of Sieur Louis Liger's book) in 1711, and gave a minute description of Count Tallard's formal garden at Nottingham. See the description of Leonora's garden in No. 37. They made fashionable the formal Dutch style, which in its later years of excess was satirized by Pope in his fourth *Moral Essay* (lines 113–26). Pope, too, 'twisted and twirled' (to borrow Horace Walpole's phrase) his Twickenham garden in direct protest to the formal ideas of the earlier decades. This later and contrary style, practised by the gardeners Bridgeman and Kent, and applauded by Walpole, gave to the Continent, through the Duke of Nivernois's translation of Walpole's *Essay on Modern Gardening*, the *jardin à l'anglaise*. For information on orange groves and orange-trees, so frequently named in these papers, the reader is referred to Evelyn's supplementary *Treatise of Orange-trees*, which deals with this 'Master-Piece of Gard'ning.' An interesting copperplate of a formal garden introduces the essay. Cf. also Sir W. Temple's description of the garden of Moor Park (*Miscellanea*); *The Dutch Gardener or The Compleat Florist*, from the Dutch of Henry Van Oosten, 'the Leiden Gardener,' advertised in No. 32 (*A*); and Kip's plates in Atkyns's *Gloucestershire* (folio, 1712).

6. PAGE 20. *Motto.* Juvenal, *Satires*, xiii. 54.

PAGE 21. The words in italics are not, as Henry Morley has stated, a résumé of Blackmore's forthcoming poem on the *Creation*, but a quotation from three sentences of the Preface to his *Prince Arthur* (third edition, 'corrected,' 1696). Steele's approving reference supplements the Tatler's quizzical apology for the ridicule of the *Advice to the Poets* (Nos. 3, 14), and may be considered as a puff preliminary to Sir Richard's 'philosophical poem,' which Addison, prompted by stronger religious sympathies, praises in No. 339 of the *Spectator*. This approval and that shown by Dennis, and later by Johnson (*Lives*, iii. 74), stand in marked contrast to the contempt entertained for 'Quack Maurus' by Dryden, Swift, Pope, and Grub Street generally—a contempt which may not be entirely explained by Blackmore's attack on the coterie at Will's in his *Satyr against Wit* (1700). Addison, if we believe Swift, heartily despised the *man* (Scott's *Swift*, xii. 140).

PAGE 21. Budgell apologizes for the coarseness of the character of the sloven from Theophrastus—a coarseness 'which the *Politeness of the present age* would never have endured' (*Characters of Theophrastus*, Preface).

7. PAGE 22. *Motto.* Horace, *Epistles*, II. ii. 207.

PAGE 23. *Childermas* or Innocents' Day (28th December) was, like Friday, a 'cross day,' on which 'it was impossible to have good luck,' especially if work was attempted (cf. Swift, *Directions to Servants*: 'The Cook'). If the 'little boy' had comported himself according to Strype (1720), he would have gone to 'Paul's Church' on that day. Mr. Spectator's reflection on the losing of a day 'in every week' is not clear. J. Rayner, the well-known writing-master at Paul's School, published at this time, from his house at the sign of the Hand and Pen, 'The Paul's Scholars Copy-Book, containing the Round and Round-Text hands, with Alphabets at large of the Greek and Hebrew, and *Joyning pieces of each.* . . .'

Lord Galway was defeated at Almanza on 25th (14th, O.S.) April 1707.

Line 35. *Quitting.* 'Cleaning' in *A*.

8. PAGE 25. *Motto.* Virgil, *Aeneid*, i. 411.

The Society for the Reformation of Manners (founded in 1690) was, in the words of antiquary Strype, 'designed to controul Looseness' and to punish those 'distempering themselves by excess of drink and breaking the Sabbath.' It boasted, in the report for 1708, of having prosecuted no fewer than 3,299 persons. This number fell in 1714 to 2,571, and in 1716 to 1,820: which decline is accepted as a proof that 'a visible reformation hath ensued,' despite the opposition of the 'advocates for Debauchery.' (See Strype's edition of Stowe's *Survey*, 1720, II. v. 30.) Steele, in No. 3 of the *Tatler*, confesses his sympathy with the society.

PAGE 26. The masquerades, referred to again in Nos. 14, 22 (advertisement), and 158, had become a cause of scandal under the management of the notorious Swiss Count Heidegger (see *B. I.*). Hogarth satirizes these entertainments in his engravings, 'Masquerades and Operas,' on the 'Taste of the Town' (1724) and the 'Large Masquerade Ticket' (1727); and Fielding attacks them in his *Masquerade* (1728). Pope alludes in *The Dunciad* to the 'strange bird from Switzerland' (i. 290). An advertisement in No. 53 announces that a masquerade will be held 'at the request of several foreigners' on 1st May at Old Spring Garden.

The *Counter* was a prison attached to a city court.

PAGE 27. *Waller. To Vandyck*, lines 5–8.

PAGE 28. *Grand Cairo.* See page 513.

Mr. Spectator's humorous decision to visit the masquerade is in exact parallel with Mr. Bickerstaff's reply to the petition of the linendrapers against low dresses (*Tatler*, No. 215).

9. *Motto.* Juvenal, *Satires*, xv. 163.

Addison's description of the eccentric clubs (perhaps in part mythical) will readily be compared with Goldsmith's humorous sketches in his *Essays* (especially i) and in his *Citizen of the World* (29, 30). The more fantastic of these clubs call to mind others in the Edinburgh of that day—the Easy, the Pious (for pies, not piety), the Dirty, the Black-Wig, the Hell-Fire, the Industrious, and many others.

PAGE 29. *Hum-Drum Club.* Goldsmith refers to a club of this name in his *Essays*, i. 'If he be phlegmatic, he may sit in silence at the Humdrum Club in Ivy Lane.'

The Club of Duellists. The subject of the duello is discussed in Nos. 84, 91, 97, 99, and more fully in the *Tatler*, Nos. 25, 26, 28, 29, 31, 38, 39, and in the Preface to the fourth volume of the collected *Tatlers*. Steele returns to his criticism of it in the *Guardian*, and in *The Lying Lover* (v. i).

PAGE 30. The *Kit-Cat Club*, founded in 1700, was composed of a number of Whig peers and men of letters, who met weekly at the house of one Christopher Kat, a pastry-cook in Shire Lane. Christopher was an artist in mutton pies, and so tempted the public palate that, says the Prologue to *The Reformed Wife* (1700):

> though the town all delicates afford,
> A Kit-Kat is a supper for a lord.

Jacob Tonson *primus*, 'obstetrix Musarum,' acted as secretary, and about 1703 transferred the club to his villa at Barn Elms in Surrey. In this house were hung the famous set of portraits of the members by Kneller, which had been presented to Tonson by the sitters. The membership of forty included the Whig leaders Halifax and Somers, and Dryden, Vanbrugh, Congreve, Addison, Garth, Steele, and Walsh. Pope and Gay sometimes visited the club, and on one occasion drank the health of Swift, who had set up the Tory Society of Brothers as an antidote to the political influence of the Kit-Cat. The verses written to be engraved on the 'toasting-glasses' are perhaps the only literary records of the club, but the literature of the time is strewed with witty references to its proceedings. See, in especial, Blackmore's verses on the Kit-Cat and the epigram (by Pope?) in the *Miscellanies* of 1727 (Elwin and Courthope, iv. 446). A handsome volume by Faber, entitled *The Kit-Cat Club, done from the original paintings of Sir Godfrey Kneller*, was published by Tonson in 1735. See Nichols, *Anecdotes*, i. 293, etc. The name is preserved in the familiar size of canvas (36 inches by 28 inches), which Tonson's space is said to have made Kneller's choice.

The *Beef-Steak Club*, the first of that name, met in a tavern in Old Jewry, and had Dick Estcourt, the actor, for its *provedore* (see No. 264, etc., and *B. I.*). Cf. Dr. King's *Art of Cookery*:

> He that of honour, wit, and mirth partakes,
> May be a fit companion o'er beef steaks.
> His name may be to future times enrolled
> In Estcourt's book, whose gridiron's made of gold.

Estcourt wore a small gold gridiron as his badge of office.

The *October Club*, the Tory rival of the Kit-Cat, met at the Bell Tavern in King Street, Westminster, and drank to the confusion of Whig politics in October ale. See Swift's *Advice to the Members of the October Club*. *The Secret History of the October Club*, by a member, was published in 1711 (advertisement in No. 45, *A*).

PAGES 30-1. Cf. Goldsmith's account of the club of Moral Philosophers (*Essays*, i). Ben Jonson's *Leges Convivales* were cut in gold letters over the chimney of the Apollo Club room in the old Devil Tavern at Temple Bar. The text is printed in Langbaine (1691), page 284, in Gifford's *Jonson*, ix, and in Cunningham's, iii. 364. See also No. 72, and *Tatler*, No. 79.

PAGE 31. *Justus Lipsius*, commentator and antiquary. His works were published in three thick volumes in 1675. His *De Ritu Conviviorum apud Romanos* will be found in volume iii, page 1476.

10. *Motto*. Virgil, *Georgics*, i. 201.

The circulation of the *Spectator* is said to have risen from 3,000 to 4,000, to 20,000, and even to 30,000 copies. 10,000 copies probably represented the average issue during the closing months of the daily issue. See the particulars in *Addisoniana* in Hurd's edition, vi. 688, and Drake's *Essays*, i. 82, iii. 326. To this must be added the sale in volume form, which up to the date of the cessation of the daily issue amounted to 9,000 copies. (Nos. 227 (advertisement), 283 (advertisement), 488, and 555.)

PAGE 32. For the phrase 'Tea Equipage' cf. *Tatler*, No. 86.

Bacon. Advancement of Learning, ii, Introduction, § 14. Pope uses the simile, but more correctly, in the *Essay on Man*, ii. 132.

Muscovy or Poland. This is a sly reference to the 'Upholsterer' of the *Tatler*, whose 'crack towards politics' made him 'much more inquisitive to know what passed in *Poland* than in his own family,' and caused him to be concerned 'by some news he had lately read from *Muscovy*' (Nos. 155, 160, and 178). 'Oh, I love Gazettes extreamly . . .,' says Clodpate, in Shadwell's *Epsom Wells*, 'they are such pretty penn'd Things; and I do love to hear of *Wisnowisky*, *Potosky*, General *Wrangle*, and Count *Tot*, and all those brave fellows' (I. i).

PAGE 33. *The Female World*. See No. 4 and note, and No. 205.

11. PAGE 34. *Motto*. Juvenal, *Satires*, ii. 63.

The story of the Ephesian matron is first told in the *Satyricon* of Petronius Arbiter (Paris edition, 1587, page 64). It reappears in the Middle Ages in the popular *Historia Septem Sapientum* (edited by G. Buchner, 1889, page 64). La Fontaine's *La Matrone d'Éphèse* was printed with the twelfth book of *Fables*, published by Barbin, Paris, 1694. See also Chapman's *Widow's Tears* and Otway's *Venice Preserved* (II. i).

PAGE 35. *The Fable of the Lion and the Man* is La Fontaine's *Le Lion abattu par l'Homme* (*Fables*, III. x).

A True and Exact History of the Island of Barbados. By Richard Ligon, Gent. was published in folio, in 1657, and in a second edition in 1673. Steele's reference applies to either edition. Poor Yarico, who 'for her love lost her liberty,' is thus described: 'An Indian woman, a slave in the house, who was of excellent shape and colour, for it was a pure bright bay; small breasts, with the niples of a porphyrie colour: this woman would not be woo'd by any means to wear Cloaths.' Inkle does not appear in Ligon's book, and may have been satirically invented, as Austin Dobson suggests (*Selections from Steele*, page 483), from the name of an inferior kind of tape. The word, here so suitably applied to such a haberdasher, will be found in its ordinary sense on page 143 (see note). Steele's interest in Barbados was more than literary, for he had inherited, in 1706, from his first wife, Mrs. Margaret Stretch, a plantation there, worth £850 per annum.

12. PAGE 37. *Motto*. Persius, *Satires* ii. 63.

The *Daily Courant*, printed by Samuel Buckley, 'the learned printer' of the *Gazette*, the *Monthly Register*, and the *Spectator*. Steele praises it in the 178th *Tatler*.

PAGE 40. This paper gives the first hint in the *Spectator* of Addison's interest in *Paradise Lost* (No. 262 onwards), of which he had already shown a youthful appreciation in the *Account of the Greatest English Poets* (1693). The quotation is from iv. 675–88, and the reference is to i. 252–3 of Hesiod's *Works and Days*:

τρὶς γὰρ μύριοί εἰσιν ἐπὶ χθονὶ πουλυβοτείρῃ
ἀθάνατοι Ζηνὸς φύλακες θνητῶν ἀνθρώπων.

Addison's admiration of *Paradise Lost* had been anticipated in the *Tatler* (*passim*, especially No. 237); and both authors may have known Patrick Hume's *Commentary*, London, 1695.

13. *Motto*. Martial, *Epigrams*, XII. xciii.

Hydaspes (*L'Idaspe fedele*), an opera in three acts, was first produced on 23rd May 1710. The addition of the Italian-English libretto (1712) contains a dedication by Nicolino Grimaldi (*ante*, page 17), who took the part of Hydaspes. He is thrown naked to a lion and, after expostulation in the minor key, overcomes the stage brute by the musical valour of the major. (See Sutherland Edwards, *History of the Opera*, i. 117.) Addison's 'exhortation' to English actors is on the lines of Steele's account of Grimaldi in the 115th *Tatler*: 'Our best Actors are somewhat at a loss to support themselves with proper Gesture, as they move from any considerable Distance to the Front of the Stage.'

Recitative. See page 87 and note. Cf. *Rehearsal*: 'I make 'em, sirs, play the battle *in recitativo*' (v. i).

PAGE 42. *The famous Equestrian Statue*. This is the earlier equestrian statue of Henry IV on the Pont Neuf. It was erected in 1635, and demolished and melted into cannon in 1792.

14. PAGE 43. *Motto*. Ovid, *Metamorphoses*, iv. 590.

Fable of the Lion, etc. See page 35.

PAGE 44. Addison in his college days had made merry in Latin hexameters on *Machinae Gesticulantes*, *anglice a Puppet-show* (Hurd, i. 249), and Fielding, eighteen years after the writing of this paper, complains: 'When the theatres are puppet-shows, and the comedians ballad-singers, when fools lead the town, would a man think to thrive by his wit?' (*The Author's Farce*).

These years were, in the words of Charles Magnin, the historian of marionettes, the golden age of puppets in England.

Martin Powell had already (1709) supplied the *Tatler* with a subject for satire (Nos. 44, 50, 77, and 115), and his continued success as the leading puppet-showman is further borne out by the satirical attentions of the *Spectator*. He was then exhibiting in the Little Piazza, on the east side of Covent Garden south of the present Russell Street, to the great hurt of the regular drama (cf. Hogarth's plate of a *Just View of the British Stage*, 1725). He wrote a number of plays for his puppets, and established the traditions of action of the modern 'Punch and Judy,' though his Punchinello retained many of the characteristics of its Italian ancestry. See the engraving in Burnet's *Second Tale of a Tub or The History of Robert Powel, the Puppet-Showman* (1715). He is called simply 'Powell' or 'Mr. Powell' in the *Tatler* and *Spectator*: the name 'Robert' appears in Burnet's pamphlet, which was a satire on *Robert* Harley, Earl of Oxford. He must not be confounded with his contemporary George Powell, the actor. (See *B. I.*)

The undertaker of the masquerade is referred to *ante*, page 520.

PAGE 45. *Arcadia*. See note, page 533.

Motion is the old word for either a puppet or a puppet-show. Cf. Shakespeare, *Winter's Tale*, IV. iii. 103, *Two Gentlemen of Verona*, II. i. 100, etc.; Ben Jonson, *Bartholomew Fair*, v. i and iii.

See the reference to the representation of *Rinaldo*, page 518. *Whittington and his Cat*, ib. Defoe in his *Groans of Great Britain*, 1713, gives Powell's advertisement of *Whittington* (H. Morley's *Spectator*, 52, note).

PAGE 46. *Pig*. Powell's repertoire included 'the pleasant and comical humours of Valentini, Nicolini, and the tuneful warbling *pig* of Italian race.' (Dedication to Burnet's pamphlet, mentioned above.)

Susanna was a favourite subject for puppet plays. Henry Morley quotes a copy of verses, dated 1665, describing these entertainments:

> Their Sights are so rich, is able to bewitch
> The heart of a very fine man-a;
> Here 's *Patient Grisel* here, and *Fair Rosamond* there,
> And the *History of Susanna*.

Punch soon set himself up as a *censor morum* and gained no little reputation as a political oracle. Perhaps his most successful blow was levelled against the French Prophets of Moorfields. Addison, in No. 34, threatens to reprimand the puppet-moralist if he grows too extravagant. The *Tatler* had complained of the attacks of the 'rake-hell' puppet.

The original issue contains the following advertisement: '*On the first of April will be performed at the Play-house in the* Haymarket, *an Opera call'd* The Cruelty *of* Atreus. N.B. *The Scene wherein* Thyestes *eats his own children, is to be performed by the famous Mr.* Psalmanazar, *lately arrived from* Formosa: *The whole Supper being set to Kettle-drums.*' This joke at the expense of the notorious George Psalmanazar, the 'Formosan convert' (1680–1763), was not reprinted till some time after Steele's death. Swift introduces him in his *Modest Proposal for Preventing the Children of Poor People in Ireland from being a Burden to their Parents or Country* (1729).

15. PAGE 47. *Motto.* Ovid, *Ars Amatoria*, i. 159.

This paper shows at many points a kinship with La Bruyère's 'Des Femmes' in the *Caractères* (iii). See especially No. 77. La Bruyère was a favourite also with the *Tatler*: cf. the transcription in No. 57.

PAGE 49. *Totumque*, etc. *Aeneid*, xi. 781–2.

16. *Motto.* Horace, *Epistles*, I. i. 11.

The *muff* was an ornament of the male fashionable. 'Cibber ingross'd the fops, the men of muffs, red heels and ribbons' (*Original Letters to the Tatler*, etc., 1725). It is named among the 'shabby superfluities' of the 'Upholsterer' (*Tatler*, No. 155).

PAGE 50. The *Rainbow* in Fleet Street, near the gate of the Inner Temple, was established in 1656 by a barber, James Farr, who carried on his double business for a time (H. Morley).

Fringed Gloves. See Nos. 30 and 311. *Red heels* and red stockings were fashionable. Cf. *Tatler*, No. 113. The 'rivers' in No. 29 appeared in red stockings.

PAGE 51. *Drawcansir*, the hero of *The Rehearsal*, whose bombast is intended as a parody of the extravagances of the character of Almanzor in Dryden's *Conquest of Granada*.

17. PAGE 52. *Motto.* Juvenal, x. 191.

Further disquisitions on 'Ugly Clubs' will be found in Nos. 32, 48, 52, 78, and 87.

PAGE 53. Paul Scarron (1610–60), author of the *Roman comique*, married in 1652 Mlle d'Aubigné, afterwards Madame de Maintenon. He was deformed by rheumatism from his twenty-seventh year. His pleasantries on himself are in the Preface to the Reader 'who has never seen me' (prefixed to the *Relation véritable*): 'Les autres [disent] que mon chapeau tient à une corde qui passe dans une poulie, et que je le hausse et baisse pour saluer ceux qui me visitent. Je pense être obligé en conscience de les empêcher de mentir plus longtemps, et c'est pour cela que j'ai fait faire la planche que tu vois au commencement de mon livre . . . Mes cuisses et mon corps en sont un autre, et ma tête se penchant sur mon estomac, je ne ressemble pas mal à un Z.'

The Prince and Falstaff in *2 Henry IV*, II. iii. 235–40.

For my own part. Steele is quizzing at his own expense. The portraits by Kneller and Thornhill show the 'shortness of his face' to which there is constant reference throughout these papers.

PAGE 54. *Grand Cairo.* See page 513.

Aesop's ugliness is described with realistic detail in his *Life* by Maximus Planudes, and is referred to in the life by La Fontaine, prefixed to the *Fables*. The ill-favoured Thersites appears in the second book of the *Iliad*. The deformities of Duns Scotus were probably the exaggeration of his opponents the

Thomists, and through them became a tradition. The personal appearance of Hudibras is drawn in I. i. 240 et sqq. 'The old Gentleman' is Loyola in Oldham's *Satyrs upon the Jesuits* (III).

PAGE 55. Mother Shipton's prophecies, first published in 1641, were a favourite chap-book subject. See Ashton's *Chap Books of the Eighteenth Century*, page 88.

18. *Motto.* Horace, *Epistles*, II. i. 187.

PAGE 56. The English opera of *Arsinoe, Queen of Cyprus*, partly a translation from the Italian and partly an adaptation of a piece by Peter Motteux, was produced at Drury Lane on 16th January 1705. The score was written by Thomas Clayton, whose musical incapacity, two years later, ruined Addison's *Rosamond*. The Spectator's italics, which may be compared with Cibber's statement in the note to page 121, recall the disaster. In concert advertisements in the *Spectator*, Clayton is described as 'the author of Arsinoe' (*A*).

Nothing is capable, etc. Cf. the later phrase from Beaumarchais: 'Aujourd'hui ce qui ne vaut pas la peine d'être dit on le chante' (*Le Mariage de Figaro*). Boileau, speaking of Quinault's verses, had said: 'C'était leur faiblesse même qui les rendait d'autant plus propres pour le musicien' (*Réflexions sur Longin*, iii).

Camilla was the second opera in the Italian manner sung in England. It was composed by Marcantonio Buononcini, and was produced at Drury Lane by subscription on 29th March 1706. It was sung half in English and half in Italian. Mrs. Tofts, who had taken the part in *Arsinoe*, played Camilla in English, while Valentini, as the hero, sang in Italian. (See Edwards, *History of the Opera*, i. 109.) The libretto, supposed to be by Owen MacSwiney, bears the imprint 'London 1706.'

PAGE 57. Addison's friend Edmund Smith (see page 516) produced *Phaedra and Hippolitus* in 1709—'a consummate tragedy' excelling the Greek and Latin *Phaedra* and 'the French one,' says Johnson (*Lives*, ii. 236). It ran only four nights, even with Betterton, Booth, Mrs. Barry, and Mrs. Oldfield in the cast. Addison wrote the Prologue, in which he joined issue with the lovers of Italian opera. See Genest, ii. 368–72.

PAGE 58. Plato, *Republic*, iii.

19. *Motto.* Horace, *Satires*, I. iv. 17.

Sir Francis Bacon. *Essays*, ix ('Of Envy'), § 1.

20. PAGE 60. *Motto.* Homer, *Iliad*, i. 225.

This is a companion paper to No. 145 of the *Tatler*, which discusses these 'professed Enemies to the Repose of the Fair Sex.' It may be compared with Nos. 22 and 262 of the *Tatler*, and Nos. 46, 53, and 250 of the *Spectator*.

21. PAGE 63. *Motto.* Horace, *Epistles*, I. v. 28.

PAGE 64. *Virgil's Army.* *Aeneid*, x. 432–3.

PAGE 65. *Northern Hive.* 'This part of Scythia, in its whole *northern* extent, I take to have been the vast hive out of which issued so mighty swarms of barbarous nations,' etc.—Temple's *Works* (1754 edition), ii. 273.

A more elaborate hit at the virtuosi had been made in the

Tatler (Nos. 210, 221), where Steele gave the will of Sir Nicholas Gimcrack, whom Shadwell had introduced to the public in his comedy *The Virtuoso.*

22. PAGE 66. *Motto.* Horace, *Ars Poetica,* 188.

The wild boar in *Camilla* (page 56) is slain by a dart thrown by the heroine, played by Mrs. Tofts. It is included in the humorous inventory of stage effects in No. 42 of the *Tatler.*

PAGE 67. *Lion in Hydaspes.* See page 523.

The Emperor of the Moon, a three-act farce, was an adaptation by Mrs. Aphra Behn of a French Harlequin play, entitled *Harlequin l'Empereur dans le Monde de la Lune.* It was produced in 1687, and was often revived. See below.

The Fortune Hunters or Two Fools Well Met, by James Carlile, was first played at Drury Lane in 1689. The reference is to the farcical situation in Act II, where the inebriated Mr. Spruce encounters his wife's gallant by the pump in the garden and mistakes an arm for a pump-handle. (See Genest, i. 473.) It was performed at the Haymarket on 10th June and 31st October 1707.

The last line of Ralph Simple's letter refers to Act II, sc. iii of *The Emperor of the Moon.* There Scaramouch places a company of masqueraders 'all in the Hanging, in which they make the Figures, where they stand without Motion in Postures.' Harlequin is 'placed on a Tree in the Hangings,' and the ambitious Simple hopes to pose by an orange-tree in this fantastic tapestry. See the account in Genest, i. 457–8.

PAGE 68. Fletcher's *Pilgrim,* III. v, 'the interior of a madhouse.' Mr. Spectator's correspondent played the part of the English madman, who calls from his cell: 'Give me some drink.' The first keeper interposes: 'Oh, there's the Englishman,' who thereupon exclaims: 'Fill me a thousand pots and froth 'em, froth 'em.' The piece had been recently played at the Haymarket, on 10th October 1710.

Line 22. *Ass.* 'Horse' in *A.*

King Latinus is a character in the opera of *Camilla* (page 56) who speaks a number of lines in recitative in II. x, including these given in the text. The unfortunate actor, who had been sent off to the French war, is not named in the book of the play (see No. 53). He is also the butt of the *Tatler* (see No. 145).

PAGE 69. The *Advertisement* satirizes the masquerade (page 26).

23. *Motto.* Virgil, *Aeneid,* ix. 420.

PAGE 70. *A Passage.* Plato, *Phaedo,* § 40; Aristophanes, *The Clouds. Catullus. Carmina,* xxxi.

Claude Quillet's (Calvidii Leti) *Callipaedia,* in Latin verse (Leyden, 1655), contained a scoffing reference to Cardinal Mazarin's Sicilian origin, iv, page 48 (10–13) and page 50 (21–2), the latter as follows:

Quid loquar ut blande Galla excipiatur in Aula
Advena, Trinacriis etiam devectus ab oris.

This was omitted in the second (1656) and later Paris editions. Quillet's recompense was, as Addison says, a 'good Abby' worth 400 pistoles. An English verse translation, conjoined with one of Sainte-Marthe's *Paedotrophia*, appeared on 5th May 1711 (see advertisement in *A*).

PAGE 70. The statue of Pasquin in the Piazza di Pasquino by the Braschi Palace in Rome, so called from its having been found below the stall of the satirical cobbler Pasquino, was a place dear to the Roman populace for the publication of lampoons ('pasquinades,' 'pasquils') on public men and events (cf. No. 427). Opposite this idle corner stood the statue of Marforio, which, according to the ready wit of the mob, conversed with its neighbour. In this lively play of question and answer on the pedestals of the statues the public preserved the tradition of the libellous gossip of the cobbler's booth. Pope Sixtus V had by his elevation brought fortune and state to his sister Camilla, who, like the later Madame Sans-Gêne, had been a laundress. Hence the joke about the 'dirty shirt.' For the historical evidences of this tale see Ranke's *History of the Popes*, III, § iv, and the notes in Thomas Arnold's *Addison* (Clarendon Press), pages 487–8. Steele introduces Pasquin in the *Tatler*, notably in Nos. 129, 140, and 187 (letters from Pasquin of Rome to Isaac Bickerstaff of Great Britain) and the Advertisement to No. 130: and Fielding entitled one of his minor pieces *Pasquin; a dramatick satire on the Times* (1736).

PAGE 71. *Aretine.* Pietro d'Arezzo (1492–1557), known as Aretino.

PAGE 72. *A Fable.* Sir Roger L'Estrange's *Fables of Aesop, etc.*, second edition, 1694, page 368.

Easter Day in 1711 fell on 1st April (O.S.) or 5th April (N.S.).

24. *Motto.* Horace, *Satires*, I. ix. 3.

Such Fellows. 'These People' in *A*.

PAGE 73. *Clinch of Barnet*, showman, referred to in No. 31.

PAGE 75. *The Day I keep.* References to this new fashion are plentiful in contemporary literature. Cf. 'Visiting Days' in the advertisement on page 109; also page 248. 'A well-bred Man would as soon call upon a Lady (who keeps a Day) at Midnight, as on any Day but that on which she professes being at home' (*Tatler*, No. 166). Cf. also *Tatler*, No. 109, and Shadwell's *True Widow*, III. i. *The Ladies Visiting Day*, attributed to Burnaby, from which Cibber took material for his *Double Gallant*, was played in 1701 (see Genest, ii. 241).

Kidney. The waiter at the St. James's Coffee-house (see *Tatler, passim*).

25. *Motto.* Virgil, *Aeneid*, xii. 46.

Mr. Spectator returns to his fun at the expense of the *Valetudinarians* in Nos. 143, 429, 440, and 573. See also No. 100; and *Tatler*, Nos. 16 and 77.

Thomas Sydenham, the physician, wrote a treatise on fevers which appeared in Latin (*Methodus Curandi Febres*) in 1666. A brief account of his life was written by Samuel Johnson (Boswell's *Johnson*, edited by Hill, i. 153).

PAGE 76. Santorio (Sanctorius Sanctorius) of Padua (died 1636) first demonstrated the bearing of perspiration in the 'animal economy' in his *De Medicina Statica Aphorismorum Sectiones vii*, octavo, Venice, 1614. A reprint, with a Latin commentary by M. Lister, was published in London in 1701, but it had been Englished by ' J. D.' as early as 1676. It was again translated into English, in 1712, by John Quincy. Cf. Shadwell's *True Widow*, in which young Maggot cures his fatness by 'the exercise of the mind,' and has 'an engine to weigh himself when he sits down to write or think.'

PAGE 77. *Stavo*, etc. Addison probably borrowed this from Dryden. It is given in the *Dedication of the Aeneis* (*Works*, edited by Scott and Saintsbury, xiv. 149). Henry Morley says: 'The old English reading is: "I was well; I would be better; and here I am."' Cf. Shakespeare's 'Striving to better, oft we mar what 's well' (*King Lear*, I. i. 347).

That Point of Felicity. Addison refers to a line in Martial's *Epigrams*, x. xlvii: 'Summum nec metuas diem nec optes,' a sentiment expressed by Milton in *Paradise Lost*, xi. 553.

26. PAGE 78. *Motto.* Horace, *Odes*, I. iv. 13.

PAGE 79. Γλαῦκον, etc. Homer, *Iliad*, xvii. 216. *Glaucumque*, etc. Virgil, *Aeneid*, vi. 483.

Sir Cloudesley Shovel's monument stands in the south aisle of the choir of St. Paul's.

PAGE 80. Austin Dobson has compared the concluding paragraph with the well-known apostrophe to Death by Raleigh, to show the difference in style between the eighteenth century and the seventeenth (*Eighteenth Century Essays*, page 260).

27. PAGE 81. *Motto.* Horace, *Epistles*, I. i. 20.

PAGE 82. The Clergyman is introduced in the second paper.

28. PAGE 83. *Motto.* Horace, *Odes*, II. x. 19.

PAGE 84. In *A* the sentence, lines 1–3, reads: 'It is as follows.'

Cf. with this paper No. 18 of the *Tatler*, where the supervision of street signs is humorously proposed. The prevalence of signboards in London is a familiar feature of Hogarth's street scenes. The numbering of the doors in the streets was almost unknown. Prescott Street, Goodman's Fields, is mentioned as being marked by numbers in 1708 (Halton's *New View*, quoted by Henry Morley), but the fashion did not set in till Parliament had, in 1762, condemned the swinging signboards as a public nuisance. In 1764 New Burlington Street was numbered in the modern way.

PAGE 85. The ingenious Mrs. Salmon's waxworks are referred to again in Nos. 31 and 609, and are advertised in the *Tatler* of 30th November 1710. She had just opened her new premises in Fleet Street at the sign of the Golden Salmon.

The rebus of Abel Drugger's sign will be found in Ben Jonson's *Alchemist*, II. i.

29. PAGE 86. *Motto.* Horace, *Satires*, I. x. 23.

PAGE 87. Addison justly marks the contrast between Henry Purcell's musical dramas and the Italian operas. It is nevertheless interesting to note that in Purcell's opera *Dido and Aeneas* all the dialogue is recitative, not spoken. Purcell died in November 1695, aged 36.

PAGE 88. *Dying Falls.* 'That strain again! it had a dying fall' (*Twelfth Night*, I. i. 4).

PAGE 88. Jean Baptiste Lully (1633–87), *surintendant de la musique* to Louis XIV, set himself, as Addison says, to add the grace and modulation of the Italian opera to the national music of his adopted country. He wrote twenty operas, one of which, *Proserpine*, in five acts (produced 19th November 1680), is referred to by Addison in the next paragraph. An account of Lully will be found in Grove's *Dictionary of Music*, third edition, iii. 245–8. Is the '*lulling* softness' (lines 5–6 above) a pun?

PAGE 89. First paragraph. Cf. page 46, third paragraph.

Red Stockings. See note on page 525.

An advertisement in the original issue informs readers that they can have 'Compleat setts' of the *Spectator* for March. Other monthly parts followed.

30. *Motto.* Horace, *Epistles*, I. vi. 65.

PAGE 90. For other references to the modish *Fringe-Glove* see note on page 525.

PAGE 91. *Duelling.* See page 521.

The line is from Martial, *Epigrams*, i. 71. 'Naevia' is generally read 'Laevia.'

31. PAGE 92. *Motto.* Virgil, *Aeneid*, vi. 266.

The dancing Monkies. See page 86. *The Lions.* See page 40.

The popular *Rival Queens or Alexander the Great*, by Nat Lee (see No. 92), had been burlesqued at the Haymarket (29th June 1710) by Colley Cibber, with Bullock as Roxana, and Bullock junior as Statira (Genest, ii. 455).

PAGE 93. *The dumb Conjurer.* Duncan Campbell, referred to in Nos. 323 and 474. See *B. I.*

Clench or Clinch of Barnet. See page 73.

Mrs. Salmon. See page 85 and note.

Quintus Curtius. IX. i. 31–3.

Hockley-in-the-Hole, now Ray Street (formerly Rag Street), near Clerkenwell Green, was in great repute with the mob for its bear-baiting and prize-fights. In No. 436 Steele refers to it as a 'Place of no small Renown for the Gallantry of the lower Order of Britons,' and describes an encounter there between 'two Masters of the Noble Science of Defence'; and the writer of No. 630 alludes to 'the Gladiators of Hockley in the Hole.' Cf. *Tatler*, No. 28: '. . . till oblig'd to leave the Bear-garden on the Right, to avoid being borne down by Fencers, Wild Bulls, and Monsters, too terrible for the Encounter of any Heroes, but such whose Lives are their Livelihood'; also *Dunciad*, i. 326, *The Beggar's Opera*, I. vi, and Johnson's *Letters*, ii. 30. Jonathan Wild was son-in-law of 'Scragg Hollow, of Hockley in the Hole, Esq.' (*Jonathan Wild*, I. ii).

William Pinkethman, comedian and showman, is referred to in Nos. 36, 370, 455, 502, 539 (see *B. I.*). In No. 44, and in subsequent sheets at intervals, appears the following advertisement: 'Mr. Penkethman's Wonderful Invention call'd the Pantheon: or, the Temple of the Heathen Gods. The work of several years, and great Expense, is now perfected; being a most surprising and magnificent Machine, consisting of 5 several curious Pictures, the Painting and contrivance whereof is beyond expression admirable. The Figures, which are above 100, and move their Heads, Legs, Arms, and Fingers, so exactly to what they perform, and setting one Foot before another, like living Creatures, that it justly deserves to be esteem'd the greatest Wonder of the Age. . . . In the Little Piazza, Covent Garden, in the same House where Punch's Opera is. . . .'

PAGE 93. Pope satirizes the popular liking for 'spectacle' in *Imitations of Horace, Epistles*, II. i, and there refers to the 'bear or elephant.'

Powell. George Powell, the actor. See *B. I.*

The German Artist. The *Tatler* gives an imaginary account of a waxwork of the religions of Great Britain, exhibited by a German artist (No. 257). Shadwell in *Bury Fair* makes fun of German jugglers.

PAGE 94. The satire is directed against Heidegger (see page 520).

32. PAGE 95. *Motto.* Horace, *Satires*, I. v. 64.

Ugly Club. See page 54.

PAGE 97. *Alexander the Great's* wry neck. Cf. *Tatler*, No. 77.

Eighty eight (1688). An allusion to William III, who had, in Burnet's words, 'a *Roman* Eagle Nose.'

The frontispiece of the third edition of Dryden's *Juvenal and Persius* (1702) represents Apollo giving the mask of Satire to Juvenal. The first edition, 1693, is without 'Sculptures.'

PAGE 98. *Larvati*, in the primary sense, 'bewitched.' *Larva*, a ghost; then a mask.

33. *Motto.* Horace, *Odes*, I. xxx. 5.

PAGE 99. Saint-Evremond's *Essays* were done into English in 1694 by Brown. The sentiment will be found in the section of vol. ii, 'Of the Pleasure that Women take in their Beauty.' *Saint-Evremoniana* was published in 1710.

PAGE 100. *Porcelain Clay:*

> Ay; these look like the workmanship of heaven;
> This is the porcelain clay of humankind,
> And therefore cast into these noble moulds.
>
> *Don Sebastian*, I. i.

PAGE 101. *Kneller's.* See the letter in No. 555.

Paradise Lost, viii. 488–9. More correctly: 'In every gesture.'

A short Epitaph. From Ben Jonson's *Epitaph on Elizabeth, L. H.* (*Epigrams*, cxxiv). Steele's memory is out; it runs:

> Underneath this stone doth lie
> As much *beauty* as could die:
> Which *in life* did *harbour* give
> To more *virtue than doth* live.

Chalmers suggests John Hughes (*B. I.*) as the author of the letter and of one in No. 53. May not this be the moral vein of Richard Blackmore?

34. *Motto.* Juvenal, *Satires*, xv. 159.

For the first and last paragraphs of this paper see note on pages 514–15.

PAGE 104. *The Roman Triumvirate.* Cf. Shakespeare, *Julius Caesar*, IV. i.

Punch. See notes on page 524.

35. PAGE 104. *Motto.* Catullus, *Carmina*, xxix. 16; erroneously ascribed to Martial in the original.

PAGE 105. 'Window-breaking' and 'scouring,' as the humour of the 'gay empty sparks,' are frequent topics in Shadwell's plays. See *The Woman-Captain*, *The Squire of Alsatia*, *The Scowrers*, *passim.* In the fiddler's song in his *Epsom Wells* Shadwell speaks of

> The cheats of the City,
> The rattling of coaches,
> And the Noise of the Men they call Witty!

The *Tatler* describes the breaking of windows with halfpence as 'a generous Piece of Wit' (No. 77).

Wit by Negatives. In Cowley's ode, *Of Wit* (Grosart's edition, i. 135–6), where these lines occur in the seventh stanza:

> What is it then, which like the Power Divine
> We only can by Negatives define?

Last line, 'are several imposters,' *A*.

PAGE 106. Line 3. *Cheats.* 'Counterfeits,' *A*.

PAGE 107. Last paragraph. See note to page 101.

36. *Motto.* Virgil, *Aeneid*, iii. 583.

April the 9th must be intended: the letter refers to No. 31 (page 92).

PAGE 108. *The Hangings*, page 67 and note; *The Rose Tavern*, page 8; *Make Love*, etc., cf. page 127; *King Porus*, page 93; *Mr. Pinkethman*, ib.; *Oracle of Delphos*, ib.; *Hercules*, etc., page 84.

'T. D.' may stand for Thomas Doggett (see *B. I.*).

The Rehearsal, I. i:

Enter Thunder and Lightning.

Thun. I am the bold Thunder.

Bayes. Mr. Cartwright, prithee speak that a little louder, and with a hoarse voice. I am the bold *Thunder*: pshaw! speak it me in a voice that thunders it out indeed: I am the bold Thunder.

Thun. I am the bold *Thunder*.

The Rehearsal was played at the Haymarket on 18th November 1709, with Johnson in the part of Thunder, and at Drury Lane on 29th January 1711, with Johnson in the same part and Miss Younger as Lightning.

PAGE 109. The *nom de guerre* 'Salmoneus' is happily chosen, for the son of Aeolus had imitated lightning, and had been hurled to the nether world by a thunderbolt from Jove. See Dryden's *Aeneis*, vi. 787.

Chr. Rich. See page 518.

For William Bullock see *B. I.* At Pinkethman's Summer Theatre at Greenwich, *The Rival Queens* had been played on 6th July 1710, with Powell as Alexander, and Bullock junior as Hephestion. On 7th April 1711, Bullock had appeared as Sir Bookish Outside, and Pinkethman as Tipple, a servant, in *Injured Love*, a new play by an anonymous author (see Genest, ii. 478).

Visiting Days. See page 528.

PAGE 110. *Enchanted Woods.* See Nos. 5 and 14.

PAGE 110. *Card-matches.* Matches made of card dipped in sulphur. The cry of the vendors is referred to in No. 251, and in the *Tatler*, No. 4.

37. *Motto.* Virgil, *Aeneid*, vii. 805.

PAGES 111–12. John Ogilby, who is satirized in *Mac Flecknoe* and *The Dunciad*, published two translations of Virgil, one in 1649, the other in 1654. The 1684 edition of the second had 'such excellent sculptures; and (what added great grace to his works) he printed them all on special good paper, and in a very good letter' (note to *Dunciad*, i. 141). Dryden's *Juvenal* (*ante*, page 97 and note) first appeared in 1693.

Cassandre, by La Calprenède (1642, 10 vols.), was translated by Charles Cotterell (folio, London, 1676), and 'By several Hands' (3 vols., 8vo, London, 1703); *Cléopâtre*, by the same (1647–63, 10 vols.), by Robert Loveday (vols. i–vi), John Coles (vii), James Webbe (viii), and J. Davies (ix–xii) from 1652 to 1665, and in a two-volume folio edition in 1674; *Astrée*, by Honoré d'Urfé (1616–20), by a 'Person of Quality,' with the Preface signed J. D. (3 vols., 1657); *Artamène ou Le Grand Cyrus*, by Mlle de Scudéry (1649–53, 10 vols.), by 'F. G.' in five folio volumes; and *Clélie*, by the same (1656–60, 10 vols.), in five parts by John Davies (i–iii), and by G. Havers (iv–v), 1656–61. These 'vast French romances,' for the most part in folio, enjoyed great popularity in England, especially among the women. In Steele's *Tender Husband* (I. i) Captain Clerimont says knowingly: '*Cassandra*, *Astraea*, and *Clelia* are my intimate acquaintance,' in reply to the warning that the young lady 'has spent all her solitude in reading romances' and has her head 'full of shepherds, knights, flowery meads, groves, and streams.' So, too, *Tatler*, Nos. 75 and 139. Many of the most popular English plays were derived from them (see the list in Ward's *English Dramatic Literature*, iii. 309). The thirteenth edition of Sidney's *Countess of Pembroke's Arcadia* (*ante*, page 45), appeared in 1674. This romance is studied by Lettice, 'by a small candle,' in Steele's *Lying Lover* (IV. ii): 'the faithful Argalus was renowned all over the plains of Arca—Arca—Arcadia—for his loyal and true affection to his charming paramour, Parthenia.'

Of the works of Newton, Locke, Temple, and Taylor, which find a place in this catalogue, nothing need be said. The *Dictionary* may refer to *Glossographia Anglicana Nova ; or a Dictionary interpreting such hard words of whatever language as are at present used in the English Tongue* (London, 1707). Sherlock's *Practical Discourses concerning Death*, which passed through many editions, is referred to in No. 289. *The Fifteen Comforts of Matrimony*, an English version (published anonymously in 1682) of the popular fifteenth-century *Quinze Joies de mariage*, was the first of a series of books of its kind. Its antidote, *The Fifteen Comforts of Real Matrimony*, appeared in 1683; and *The Fifteen Comforts of Rash and Inconsiderate Marriage*, fourth edition in 1694, and another in 1706, and *The Fifteen Comforts of Cuckoldom* in 1706. Malebranche's

Recherche de la Vérité was Englished by Thomas Taylor in 1694, and by R. Sault in the same year. (See No. 94.) There were many editions of *The Academy of Compliments*. Two appeared before 1713, viz. *The Academy of Compliments 'or A New Way of Wooing* . . . (London, 1685, 8vo), and *The Compleat Academy of Compliments, containing choice sentences* . . . (London, 1705, 12mo). Nicholas Culpeper's *Compleat Midwife's Practice* appeared in an 'enlarged edition' in 1663, and again in 1698, and his *Directory for Midwives* in 1651 and 1693. The *Ladies Calling, by the Author of the Whole Duty of Man*, was a popular octavo, of which the seventh edition was published at Oxford in 1700. Abigail, in Shadwell's *Scowrers*, praises it as one of 'these godly Books [which] quiet the Conscience mightily' (I. i). Thomas D'Urfey, 'that ancient Lyrick' of the *Tatler* (No. 214), published, among other pieces, *Tales Tragical and Comical*, in verse, in 1704. It may add point to the satire to quote Pope (*Letters*, 10th April 1710): 'Any man of any quality is heartily welcome to the best toping-table of our gentry who can roundly hum out some fragment or rhapsodies of his works.' Baker's *Chronicle of the Kings of England*, printed in 1643, and in a ninth edition in 1696, is mentioned in No. 269 as always to be found on Sir Roger's hall window (cf. also *Tatler*, No. 264). The *Advice to a Daughter*, by George Savile, Marquess of Halifax, will be found in his *Miscellanies* (1700 edition, pages 1–84). *Secret Memoirs and Manners of Several Persons of Quality of both Sexes from the New Atalantis* . . . appeared in 1709 from the pen of the notorious Mary Manley. A second edition, in two volumes, was published in 1709; and her *Court Intrigues* in 1711. The 'Key' may be supposed to be in MS. like the one, in the Rawlinson collection in the Bodleian Library, noted by Thomas Arnold (*Addison*, page 496). References will be found in the *Tatler*, No. 243, and Pope's *Rape of the Lock*, iii. 165. Steele's *Christian Hero* was published in 1701. *The Speech of Henry Sacheverell D.D. upon his Impeachment* . . . is a small folio of ten pages (London, 1710); see *infra*, page 175. Of the trial of Robert ('Handsome') Fielding for 'having two wives, three different short accounts appeared in 1706; but the reference is probably to *The Arraignment, Tryal, and Conviction*, published in 1708. *Seneca's Morals*, by Sir Roger L'Estrange, appeared in a seventh edition in 1699, and in a tenth in 1711. La Ferte's *Instructions* may not refer to a book, though there appeared in 1696 a *Second Part of the Dancing Master* [1652], *or Directions for Country Dances*. Mr. Ferte advertises his school in Compton Street, Soho, in No. 52 and later numbers of the *Spectator*.

PAGE 112. *Hungary Water* was a popular compound of spirits of wine, lavender, and rosemary, which was used as a cure-all and as a perfume. See ii. 484. It was applied for a squirrel bite (*Tatler*, 266); Swift rubbed his rheumatic shoulder with it (*Journal to Stella*, 29th March 1712); and Mr. Bickerstaff grouped it as a necessary with tea and snuff (*Tatler*, No. 125). Cf. *Tatler*, No. 245: 'A spunge dipped in *Hungary Water* left but the Night before by a young Lady going upon a Frolick *Incog.*'

PAGE 113. Addison makes good in No. 92 his promise to discuss the equipment of a lady's library. See also page 247. The *Tatler*, in No. 248, had introduced the subject of a 'Female Library.' In 1714 Steele published, or gave his name to, *The Ladies Library* (3 vols., 12mo), in the preface of which he wrote: 'The Reader is to understand that the Papers which compose the following volumes came into my hands upon the frequent mention in the *Spectator* of a *Ladies Library.*' The volumes do not deal with books but with topics, as Employment, Dress, Chastity, and Charity, 'supposed to be collected out of the several writings of our greatest Divines.'

38. *Motto.* Martial, *Epigrams*, VI. xxix. 8.

PAGE 114. Dr. Thomas Burnet's *Telluris Theoria Sacra* appeared in translation in 1690. Its thesis, that the primitive records may be interpreted allegorically, was opposed by Whiston in 1696 in his *New Theory of the Earth*, which maintained that they were 'perfectly agreeable to religion and philosophy.' See Leslie Stephen's *English Thought in the Eighteenth Century*, I. ii.

PAGE 115. Eighth line from foot. *A man.* Lord Cowper.

39. PAGE 116. *Motto.* Horace, *Epistles*, II. ii. 102.

Tragedy is the noblest, etc. Addison here follows Aristotle (*Poetics*, xxvi) in defiance of Dryden (*Dedication of the Aeneis*) and the French critics, notably Chapelain, Rapin, and Le Bossu.

Seneca. De Providentia, § 2.

PAGE 117. *Aristotle observes. Poetics*, iv (Vahlen, page 12), and *Rhetoric*, iii. 1. The question of iambic and blank verse had been already discussed by Dryden in his *Essay of Dramatic Poesy*, xv, pages 359, 364, and 369; that of plays in rhyme, ib., page 355 onwards; that of the hemistich, the pauses, and 'variety of cadences,' ib., pages 363, 371, and 372. Addison probably had in mind the closing speeches of the third act of Dryden's *Oedipus*, which illustrate all the points of his thesis. He quotes a portion in his next paper.

PAGE 118. *Plain English.* Cf. Boileau, *Réflexions sur Longin*, xi, § 1.

Aristotle's 'observation' is reproduced in Horace, *Ars Poetica*, lines 95–8.

PAGE 119. Nathaniel Lee (1650–90). His popular play of *The Rival Queens or The Death of Alexander the Great* (1677) has been referred to (page 530). He collaborated with Dryden in *Oedipus* (1679). Dryden's fifth *Epistle* is addressed to 'Mr. Lee, on his tragedy of the *Rival Queens.*'

Thomas Otway (1651–85). *Venice Preserved or A Plot Discovered*, was first acted at the Duke's Theatre in 1682.

Si pro patria, etc. Florus, IV. i. Cf. Ben Jonson's *Catiline*, v. vi.

40. PAGE 120. *Motto.* Horace, *Epistles*, II. i. 208.

Poetical Justice. This paper was, according to Pope, the occasion of John Dennis's 'deplorable frenzy' in Lintot's bookshop on 27th March 1712. 'Opening one of the volumes of the

Spectator, in large paper, [he] did suddenly, without the least provocation, tear out that of No. —, where the author treats of poetical justice, and cast it into the street' (Pope's *Works*, edited by Elwin and Courthope, x. 459). For Dennis's reply see his *Original Letters* (1721, page 407).

PAGE 120. *Aristotle*. *Poetics*, xiii.

PAGE 121. *The Orphan or The Unhappy Marriage*, by Otway (1680); *Venice Preserved*, ante, No. 39; *Alexander the Great*, ib.; *Theodosius or The Force of Love*, by Nat Lee, drawn from the romance of *Pharamond* (1680); *All for Love or The World Well Lost*, by Dryden (1678), a transcript of Shakespeare's *Antony and Cleopatra*; *Oroonoko*, by Thomas Southerne (1696), founded on Mrs. Aphra Behn's novel of that name.

King Lear, 'as Shakespeare wrote it,' had been acted at Lincoln's Inn Fields Theatre between 1662 and 1665. Since 1681 Nahum Tate's wretched adaptation had held the stage.

The Mourning Bride, Congreve's only tragedy (1697); *Tamerlane*, by Rowe (1702); *Ulysses*, by the same (1705); *Phaedra and Hippolitus* (ante, page 526).

Tragi-Comedy. Sidney, in his *Apologie for Poetrie*, denounces 'the mingling Kings and Clownes' in 'mungrell Tragy-comedie,' and adds: 'I knowe the Auncients have one or two examples of Tragy-comedies, as *Plautus* hath *Amphitrio*. But if we marke them well, we shall find that they never, or very daintily, match Horn-pypes and Funeralls' (*Elizabethan Critical Essays*, edited by Gregory Smith, i. 199). See the Introduction to the same, page xliv, and references (by Index). Dryden discusses the subject in his Dedications to *The Spanish Friar* (vi. 410), *Love Triumphant* (viii. 376), and *The Rival Ladies*, but especially in the *Essay of Dramatic Poesy*, which directly suggests the passage in the *Spectator*. 'There is no theatre in the world,' says Lisideius, 'has anything so absurd as the English tragi-comedy; 'tis a drama of our own invention, and the fashion of it is enough to proclaim it so' (xv. 317, 321). 'I cannot but conclude, to the honour of our nation,' replies Neander (i.e. Dryden) 'that we have invented, increased, and perfected a more pleasant way of writing for the stage, than was ever known to the ancients or moderns of any nation, which is tragi-comedy' (page 332).

For the *Double Plot* and *Under Plot* see the dialogue between Lisideius and Neander in Dryden's *Essay of Dramatic Poesy*; also the Preface to *Cleomenes* and to *Love Triumphant*.

Rants. Cf. Colley Cibber's remarks on *The Rival Queens* (*Apology*, page 89): 'When these flowing Numbers come from the Mouth of a Betterton, the Multitude no more desired Sense to them, than our musical *Connoisseurs* think it essential in the celebrated Airs of the Italian Opera.'

PAGE 122. *Powell*. George Powell, the actor. See *B. I.*

PAGES 122-3. In the first extract from *Oedipus* (III. i) Scott and Saintsbury's edition reads, 'If wandering in the maze of fate I run,' and '*the* paths'; in the second (iv. i), 'pond'rous *earth*.' The third act was written by Dryden; the fourth by Lee.

PAGE 123. Dryden's *Conquest of Mexico* (Powell's benefit piece) is advertised in the next number by its first and better known title, *The Indian Emperor*.

41. *Motto.* Ovid, *Metamorphoses*, i. 653. The usual reading is without 'es,' but the Codex Harl. and other MSS. preserve it (see Robinson Ellis, *Anecdota Oxoniensia*, Classical Series, i, part 5)

Ben Jonson's *Epicoene or The Silent Woman*, v. i.

> *Cut.* The first is *impedimentum erroris.*
> *Ott.* Of which there are several species.
> *Cut.* Ay, as *error personae.*
> *Ott.* If you contract yourself to one person, thinking her another.

PAGE 124. *Picts.* Cf. Dennis's *Essay upon Publick Spirit* (1711): 'Men, who like Women are come to use Red and White, and part of the Nation are turning Picts again' (page 15).

PAGE 125. Cowley's 'Wayting Maid,' in *The Mistress*, stanza iv. 'The exact manner of *Lindamira*.' *Tatler*, No. 9.

PAGE 126. Donne's *Anatomy of the World* (*The Second Anniversary*), lines 244–6: 'That one *might* almost say.'

42. *Motto.* Horace, *Epistles*, II. i. 202.

Aristotle. *Poetics*, xiv.

PAGE 127. Cf. Sidney's *Apologie for Poetrie*: 'Two Armies flye in, represented with foure swords and bucklers' (*Elizabethan Critical Essays, u.s.* i. 197); Shakespeare's *Henry V*: 'With four or five most vile and ragged foils,' etc. (Act IV, Prologue, 50 et sqq.); Ben Jonson's *Every Man in his Humour*: 'With three rusty swords,' etc. (Prologue, 9 et sqq.). See also *The Rehearsal*, v. i.

PAGE 128. *Non tamen*, etc. Horace, *Ars Poetica*, 182–4.

The additional notion of *Admiration* appears in Sidney's *Apologie*: 'Tragedy . . . that with sturring the affects of admiration and commiseration teacheth the uncertainety of this world.' See the note in *Elizabethan Critical Essays, u.s.* (1904), i. 392–3.

43. PAGE 129. *Motto.* Virgil, *Aeneid*, vi. 854.

PAGES 129–30. The formula, which granted unlimited authority to the consuls, included these words: 'Ne quid respublica detrimenti capiat.' Henry Morley is wrong in stating that Abraham Froth's Act 'for importing French Wines' is a muddle-headed reference to the Methuen Treaty of 1703, which favoured port at the expense of claret. An Act was passed in 1711 for the importation of French wine. See Burnet's reflections upon it (*History of his Own Time*, ii. 565–6). The 'Northern Prince' is Charles XII of Sweden, and the references are to the campaign with the Tsar Peter. *Palmquist* may be, as Henry Morley suggests, the 'Hebdomadal Meeting' variant for Count Poniatowski. The 'Neutrality Army' may refer to England, Germany, and Holland, which were signatories to a treaty of neutrality after Poltava.

PAGE 130. *Dyer's News-Letter* (cf. Nos. 127 and 457), published by John Dyer, was discontinued on his death in September 1713.

PAGE 131. *The British Princess: an Heroick Poem*, by Edward Howard, one of the butts of *The Rehearsal*, was ridiculed by Rochester and by Sprat. It was the latter who called it an 'incomparable, incomprehensible Poem.' Henry Morley quotes Howard's lines:

> A vest as admir'd Vortager had on
> Which from this Island's foes his Grandsire won.

Edward King took it upon him to defend the burlesque couplet as sober sense (*Munimenta Antiqua*, iii. 186).

44. PAGE 132. Motto. Horace, *Ars Poetica*, 153.

Sounding of the Clock. In the fifth act of Otway's *Venice Preserv'd* (1682), where, during the scene between Jaffier and Belvidera, the 'passing bell' tolls for Pierre.

Hamlet, I. iv. 38–54 (second, or later, folio).

PAGE 133. 'Les Anglois nos voisins aiment le sang, dans leurs jeux, par le qualité de leur tempérament: ce sont des insulaires, séparés du reste des hommes; nous sommes plus humains. . . . Les peuples, qui paroissent avoir plus de génie pour la Tragédie de tous nos voisins, sont les Anglois, par l'esprit de leur nation qui se plaist aux choses atroces, et par le caractère de leur langue qui est propre aux grandes expressions.'—René Rapin's *Réflexions sur la Poétique d'Aristote, etc.*, 1674, pages 183, 201. The same reference occurs in the 134th *Tatler*. Vavasseur controverts Rapin's statement about 'grandes expressions' in his *Remarques sur les nouvelles Réflexions* (Paris, 1675, page 117). See note to page 192.

PAGE 134. *The famous play.* Corneille's *Horace* (1640).

A Tragedy. Electra. See the Remarks in Roscommon, at the passage referred to below.

PAGE 135. Horace, *Ars Poetica*, 185. The second version of the Latin and English is as in Roscommon, but with the second line ('And spill,' etc.), given in the first quotation, omitted.

Bullock, Norris. See *B. I.*

PAGE 136. Etherege's *Comical Revenge or Love in a Tub* was played at Lincoln's Inn Fields in 1664.

45. Motto. Juvenal, *Satires*, iii. 100.

Shadwell, in *A True Widow* (I. i, *passim*), jests at 'French Fopperies.'

Visits in their Beds. The *ruelle du lit* is originally the narrow passage on either side of the bed, but under Louis XIV it came to signify the bedrooms or boudoirs of fashionable ladies, where morning conversation was held with their visitors. See also iv. 272. Cf. Molière, *Les Précieuses ridicules, L'École des femmes*; Boileau, *Satires*, xii; and the humorous anecdote in *Menagiana*, ii. 334. Hence the phrases, *courir les ruelles, homme de ruelle* (*Spectator*, No. 530). Cf. Dryden, *Dedication of the Aeneis*, page 139, and Pope, *Rape of the Lock*, iii. 166.

PAGE 137. Line 34. *Awaken'd.* French *éveillé*. Cf. Etherege's *Sir Fopling Flutter*, IV. i.

Macbeth (Davenant's version) was acted at the Haymarket on 27th December 1707. Betterton played Macbeth; and Norris, Bullock, and Bowen the Witches.

46. PAGE 139. *Motto.* Ovid, *Metamorphoses*, I. i. 9.

Edward Lloyd's Coffee-house, originally in Tower Street, from which it was removed in 1692 to Lombard Street, was a well-known house for wine sales (see advertisements, *A*) and ship-broking business. It attracted customers from John's in Birchin Lane, and even from Garraway's, and acquired a reputation with merchant shippers. See *Tatler*, No. 268.

Charles Lillie, perfumer, at the corner of Beaufort Buildings in the Strand, acted as agent for the sale of the *Spectator* (see advertisements in *A*, No. 16 onwards), as he had done for the *Tatler* (see Nos. 138 and 142). He issued two volumes of *Original and Genuine Letters sent to the Tatler and Spectator* (1725).

PAGE 141. *The Postman.* See page 514.

The Bishop of Salisbury. Gilbert Burnet, the historian, wrote a description, in the form of letters, of his continental travels in 1685-6.

The Art of Ogling. Cf. *ante*, No. 20.

The Ring. A fashionable resort in Hyde Park for promenaders and horsemen. Cf. Nos. 73, 88, 377.

47. PAGE 142. *Motto.* Martial, *Epigrams*, II. xli.

Hobbes's *Human Nature*, ix, § 13 (Molesworth, iv. 46).

PAGE 143. *A Satyr.* Boileau's fourth *Satire*. See Dennis, *Original Letters* (1721, page 417).

The sobriquet *Jack-Pudding*, for a merry andrew, which appears in Milton's *Defence of the People of England*, i, was much in vogue in the literature at the end of the seventeenth century. Cf. Shadwell's plays, *passim*; Jones's *Elymas* (1682). Addison has not added the German equivalent *Hans Wurst*.

Sleeveless Errand. Cf. *Troilus and Cressida*, v. iv. 9.

Inkle. See note to page 35. The burning of *blue Inkle* as a restorative is referred to in Shadwell's *Sullen Lovers*, II, and *The Amorous Bigot*, v. i.

PAGE 144. *The Biter* is discussed in No. 504. A *bite* (as in No. 156) is the eighteenth-century word for our 'sell'; a *biter*, one who *humbugs*. 'I'll teach you a way to outwit Mrs. Johnson,' writes Swift to Dr. Tisdall (16th December 1703): 'it is a new-fashioned way of being witty, and they call it a *bite*. You must ask a bantering question, or tell some damned lie in a serious manner, and then she will answer or speak as if you were in earnest; and then cry you, "Madam, there's a *bite*!"' See Swift's verses, *passim*. Rowe's comedy *The Biter* was produced on 4th December 1704, when the author, according to Dr. Johnson, 'sat in the house laughing with great vehemence, whenever he had in his own opinion produced a jest' (*Lives*, ii. 313).

PAGES 144-5. *2 Henry IV*, I. ii. 6.

48. PAGE 145. *Motto.* Ovid, *Metamorphoses*, xiv. 652.

PAGE 147. *The Unhappy Favourite or The Earl of Essex*, by Banks, was first produced at the Theatre Royal in 1682, and was played at Drury Lane on 25th December 1709. It was a popular piece, and supplied the basis for the later plays, *The Earl of Essex*, by Jones (1753) and Brooke (1761). See the Preface to Fielding's *Tom Thumb the Great* (1730). *Lord*

Foppington was Colley Cibber's part in his own play, *The Careless Husband*, acted on 7th December 1704. *Justice Clodpate*, 'an immoderate hater of London,' is a character in Shadwell's *Epsom Wells* (1672), revived at Drury Lane on 18th December 1798, with Powell, Johnson (as the Justice), Bullock, and Pinkethman in the cast. *Justice Overdo* is in Ben Jonson's *Bartholomew Fair* (1614), which was acted at the Haymarket on 12th August 1707.

49. PAGE 148. *Motto.* Martial, *Epigrams*, x. iv.

Beaver the Haberdasher is James Heywood, linen-draper, Fish Street Hill, the 'James Easy' of the letter in No. 268, and the author of a volume of *Letters and Poems*. (See Austin Dobson's *Steele*, pages 467, 473.)

PAGE 149. *The Grecian.* See page 514. *Squire's* was near Gray's Inn, and *Searle's* was at Lincoln's Inn. See Nos. 269 and 271.

PAGE 150. *Dinner-Time.* 'In my own Memory the Dinner has crept by Degrees from Twelve a Clock to Three, and where it will fix no Body knows' (*Tatler*, No. 263). Lady Dainty, conceiving 'it necessary for a Gentlewoman to be out of order,' dined in her closet at twelve (ib., No. 77). Cf. Swift's *Journal of a Modern Lady* (1728).

Tom the Tyrant was the head waiter at White's Coffee-house, of sufficient authority to be classed with Mr. Kidney of the St. James's. He is the 'Sir Thomas' of the *Tatler* (Nos. 16, 26, and 36).

50. *Motto.* Juvenal, *Satires*, xiv. 321.

On the morning after the appearance of this paper, Swift wrote in his *Journal to Stella*: 'The Spectator is written by Steele with Addison's help; 'tis often very pretty. Yesterday it was made of a noble hint I gave him long ago for his Tatlers, about an Indian supposed to write his travels into England. I repent he ever had it. I intended to have written a book on that subject. I believe he has spent it all in one paper, and all the under hints there are mine too; but I never see him or Addison.' Addison, who, it will be noted, is the author of the paper, cannot well have been indebted to Swift for the 'under hints.' The paper in the *Tatler* (No. 171, 12th May 1710) gives an account of the manner in which the Indian kings 'who were lately in Great Britain' did honour to their landlord, the upholsterer in King Street, Covent Garden. This man, whom they styled 'Cadaroque,' is the 'Upholsterer' of the present paper. The four Iroquois chiefs (including Tee Yee Neen Ho Ga Row, 'Emperor of the Mohocks') had come to England to hear

their doom

Secur'd against the threats of France and Rome.

See the Epilogue spoken 'before the four Indian Kings' at the Haymarket after the performance of *Macbeth* on 24th April 1710 (Genest, ii. 452). As to the distinction between the 'Upholsterer' and the 'Political Upholsterer,' and the identification of the former with one of the Arnes, see *Dictionary of National Biography*, article Thomas Arne.

This paper may have helped Goldsmith in his plan of *The Citizen of the World*; but Montesquieu's *Lettres persanes* (1721), named by Thomas Arnold as indebted to this happy 'hint,' more probably drew directly from du Fresny's *Amusements sérieux et comiques d'un Siamois* (1707) and Galland's translation of the *Thousand and One Nights* (1708).

PAGE 151. Line 29. *The Surface of a Pebble.* 'Polished Marble,' *A*.

PAGE 152. Fifth line from foot. *Persons*, etc. 'Men of the greatest Perfections in their Country,' *A*.

PAGE 153. For the 'black spots' or patches, see No. 81.

51. *Motto.* Horace, *Epistles*, II. i. 127.

Steele criticizes his own play by way of prelude to his strictures on several popular comedies. (See Nos. 65, 75.) The passage is from the first edition of *The Funeral* (published December 1701). The later text, Act II, sc. i, reads:

> *Campley.* O that Harriot! to embrace that beauteous——
> *Lord Hardy.* Ay Tom, etc.

PAGE 154. Line 20. *About him to delight.* 'Else to gratify,' *A*.

She Would if she Could, by Sir George Etherege, had been last acted on 5th December 1706, at the Haymarket.

PAGE 155. *Ibrahim, 13th Emperour of the Turks* (corrected in the Preface to '12th') was written by Mrs. Pix. It was produced at Drury Lane in 1696, and again on 20th October 1702 (see Genest, ii. 74). Settle had written a play entitled *Ibrahim* in 1676, founded on Scudéry's romance of that name.

The 'throwing of the handkerchief' supplied many a metaphor in the plays of the day. Cf. Shadwell's *Scowrers*, I. i. It is probable that not a little of the eastern 'colour' of contemporary literature was derived from a treatise on the seraglio written by John Greaves (*ante*, page 513).

The Rover or The Banished Cavaliers, by Mrs. Aphra Behn, of which the first part was licensed on 2nd July 1677, and the second acted in 1681. The first part was the better, and was more popular. The scene where Blunt falls 'into the common shore' is taken from Boccaccio, *Decameron*, II. v (Genest, ii. 210).

At Bartholomew Fair. This may refer to the popular acrobatic exhibitions at the fair, or, according to some editors, to the display of figure by 'Lady Mary,' a rope-dancer of the time.

52. PAGE 157. *Motto.* Virgil, *Aeneid*, i. 78.

Tacta places, etc. Martial, vii. 101; one of the three doubtful epigrams not printed in the later texts.

PAGE 158. *The Postman.* See page 514. The *Spectator* (*A*) frequently advertises 'rosy' cosmetics, especially 'the famous Bavarian Red Liquor.'

53. PAGE 159. *Motto.* Horace, *Ars Poetica*, 359.

PAGE 160. *Epictetus his Morals, with Simplicius his Comment*, was done into English, in 1694, by George Stanhope. A second edition was printed in 1700. The passage in italics is a resumé of c. 62. For Saint-Evremond see *ante*, page 531.

PAGE 160. *R. B.* Cf. note to letter in No. 33, where there is also a reference to Saint-Evremond.

PAGE 162. *King Latinus.* See page 527.

54. PAGE 163. *Motto.* Horace, *Epistles*, I. xi. 28.

PAGE 164. *That great Man.* See Plato's *Apology*, vi.

PAGE 165. *Hudibras*, III. ii. 175–6. '*Shin'd* upon.'

'This Letter [and that in No. 78] may be by Laurence Eusden.'—H. Morley.

PAGE 166. Any distinction between *Coffee-house* and *Chocolate-house*, in respect of their names, must be more or less doubtful. Pepys says: 'To a coffee-house to drink jocolatte' (*Diary*, 24th November 1664). At the coffee-houses, which became more numerous and more club-like, 'the guests were supplied with newspapers' (Johnson's *Dictionary*). White's and the Cocoa-Tree were chocolate-houses.

55. *Motto.* Persius, *Satires*, v. 129.

PAGES 166–7. The passage is lines 132–55 of the same satire. The quotation from Dryden's translation will be found in Scott and Saintsbury's edition, xiii. 258. Line 5: '*The tyrant Lucre* no denial takes'; lines 20–1:

> Nothing retards thy voyage now, *unless*
> The other lord forbids, *Voluptuousness.*

[*Brown George*=a brown loaf (Johnson); *Borachio*='a bottle commonly of a pigges skin, with the hair inward, dressed inwardly with rozen, to keep wine or liquor sweet' (Minsheu, cf. Jonson's *The Devil is an Ass*, II. i); *Jack*=the old English waxed leather bottle or cup.]

PAGE 168. *One who coveted*, etc. Sallust, *Bellum Catilinarium*, v: 'alieni appetens, sui profusus.'

56. PAGE 169. *Motto.* Lucan, *Pharsalia*, i. 454.

PAGE 170. The works of *Albertus Magnus* (1193–1280) were published in twenty-one volumes at Leyden in 1651.

A Friend of mine. See page 150.

PAGE 173. *That precious Metal.* Cf. the Christian 'thirst for gold' in the well-known passage on the 'poor Indian' in Pope's *Essay on Man*, i. 107–8.

57. *Motto.* Juvenal, *Satires*, vi. 252–3.

The Wife of Hector. Iliad, vi. 490.

The 'rural Andromache' recalls Mrs. Alse Copswood, 'the Yorkshire Huntress,' who is described in the 37th *Tatler* as 'come to town lately, and moves as if she were on her Nag, and going to take a Five-Bar Gate; and is as loud as if she were following her Dogs.'

PAGE 175. The Whig *Dr. Titus Oates* is a clever disguise for the Tory Dr. Henry Sacheverell. The enthusiasm of the Tory ladies for the doctor during his trial (27th February–23rd March 1710) is described in the *Tatler* (No. 142). 'In the mean Time it is not to be expressed, how many cold Chickens the Fair Ones have eaten since this day [6th March] seven-night for the Good of their Country.' Dr. Sacheverell's *Speech* had its place in Leonora's library, see page 534.

PAGE 175. *Snuff-box.* See note on page 547.

58. PAGE 176. *Motto.* Horace's words (*Ars Poetica*, 361) are 'Ut pictura poesis: erit,' but Addison is quoting the opening lines of du Fresnoy's *De Arte Graphica* (1658). See the editor's *Elizabethan Critical Essays* (1904), i. 386–7.

Longinus begins his *Treatise on the Sublime* with an adverse critique of the book on that subject by Caecilius, the Sicilian rhetorician and friend of Dionysius of Halicarnassus. He holds that it is written in a *humbler* style than the argument demands.

PAGES 177–8. The 'short poems printed among the minor Greek Poets' will be found on pages 314–99 of *Poetae Minores Graeci*, edited by Ralph Winterton, Cambridge, 1684. Addison must have had these pages before him when he wrote the paper, as the 'Figures' are given by him in the same order, and as all the details refer to the texts in that edition. A full account of these and other 'Figures' will be found in Puttenham's *Art of English Poesie*. (See *Elizabethan Critical Essays*, *u.s.*, ii. 95 et seq. and 416.)

PAGE 178. *Chuse*, etc. Dryden's *Mac Flecknoe*, lines 205–8.

Mr. Herbert's Poems. George Herbert's *Temple*: as in *The Altar* (No. 1) and *Easter Wings* (No. 11).

The Translation of Du Bartas. Joshua Sylvester's (Dedication).

PAGE 179. Cowley in his *Pindarique Odes* had set a fashion of *déshabillé* in English verse, to which the later Caroline poets, Dryden, and the contemporaries of Addison turned for relaxation from the rigorous heroic couplet. A more ample denunciation of 'Pindarick Writers' will be found in No. 160. Addison expresses too, in No. 147, his 'classical' hatred of those whom he calls 'Pindarick Readers.'

59. *Motto.* Seneca, *De Brevitate Vitae*, xiii.

The work of Tryphiodorus (*c.* A.D. 400), a grammarian and epic poet, is described by Hesychius of Miletus as follows: Νέστωρ ἐποποιός, ὁ ἐκ Λυκίας, ἔγραψεν, Ἰλιάδα λειπογράμματον. Ἔστι γὰρ ἐν τῷ α μὴ εὑρίσκεσθαι α, καὶ κατὰ ῥαψῳδίαν οὕτω τὸ ἐκάστης ἐκλιμπάνειν στοιχεῖον. Ἐποίησε δὲ καὶ Τρυφιόδωρος Ὀδύσσειαν ὁμοίως αυτῷ (*Fragmenta Historicorum Graecorum*, edited by Müller, iv. 171). His only extant work, on the *Fall of Troy*, was printed by H. Stephanus, in folio, in 1566.

PAGES 180–1. Addison has borrowed most of his details in illustration of the rebus from Camden's *Remains concerning Britain*, first published anonymously in 1605.

PAGE 181. *In Ovid. Metamorphoses*, 356–69.

Erasmus. Colloquia Familiaria, 'Echo.'

Hudibras, I. iii. 183–220. It is Orsin who bewails his loss. Butler, according to Warburton, refers in the lines about 'splay-foot rhymes,' to Sidney's *Arcadia*. He may have had in mind such poems as Herbert's *Heaven* (*The Temple*, No. 159).

60. PAGE 182. *Motto.* Persius, *Satires*, iii. 85.

PAGE 183. The making of anagrams (ἀναγραμματίζειν of the Greek grammarians) was older than monkish times, though the word 'anagram' (French, *anagramme*) came in in the sixteenth century. See Puttenham's *Art of English Poesie* ('of the Ana-grame or Poesie transposed') and Camden, both *ut supra*.

PAGE 183. *Anagram of a Man.* Cf.:

> Though all her parts be not in th' usual place,
> She hath yet an anagram of a good face.
>
> Donne, *Elegies*, ii. 15–16.

Cf. also *Hudibras*, III. i. 771–2.

Ibi omnis, etc. Virgil, *Georgics*, iv. 491–2.

PAGE 184. *Like a Seam.* E.g. No. 58 in Herbert's *Temple*.

The *Mercure galant*, by Visé, was established for the criticism of *belles-lettres* and those lighter matters which the *Journal des Sçavans* did not discuss.

PAGE 185. See *Menagiana*, i. 174–5 (third edition, 1713). An account of the 'learned' Gilles Ménage (died 1692) will be found in Bayle. He was probably Molière's model for Vadius in *Les Femmes savantes*.

Played booty. 'Played double' in *A*.

The works of Jean François Sarazin were printed by Ménage in 1656, after their author's death (*Menagiana*, i. 30, 447).

PAGE 186. *Hudibras*, I. i. 11–12; I. ii. 1–2. Cf. *Tatler*, No. 132.

61. *Motto.* Persius, *Satires*, v. 19.

One of the most deliberate and lengthy exercises in punning by the 'learned monarch' is his speech to the professors of the college of Edinburgh during his visit in 1617 (see *The Muses Welcome*, 1618).

PAGE 187. *Bishop Andrews.* Lancelot Andrewes (1555–1626).

Paronomasia, pun; *Ploce* (πλοκή), literally a twining, more familiarly the Aristotelian dramatic antithesis to λύσις; *Antanaclasis*, the repetition of the same word in a different, if not in a contrary sense.

PAGE 189. The saying of Aristaenetus, with the rendering by Mercerus, is taken by Addison from *Menagiana*, i. 321. Mercerus, or Mercier, was the father-in-law of Salmasius, or Saumaise, the opponent of Milton.

62. *Motto.* Horace, *Ars Poetica*, 309.

And hence, etc. Locke's *Essay concerning Human Understanding*, 1690, 'Of Discerning,' etc.

PAGE 190. Cf. Addison on Cowley, in *An Account of the Greatest English Poets*, Hurd, i. 22–7: 'He more had pleased us, had he pleased us less,' which is borrowed from Boileau (*Epistles*, ix).

PAGE 191. *Cowley. The Mistress, passim.*

PAGE 192. 'The definition of Wit . . . is only this: That it is a propriety of thoughts and words: or, in other terms, thoughts and words elegantly adapted to the subject.'—Dryden's *Apology for Heroic Poetry*, prefixed to *The State of Innocence*. Dryden, in the Preface to *Albion and Albanius*, states that this definition, if true, 'will extend to all sorts of poetry.' In the Preface to the second *Miscellany* he says that he drew his definition from the consideration of Virgil's art. 'This evening,' says the 62nd *Tatler*, 'was spent at our Table in Discourse of Propriety of Words and Thoughts, which is Mr. *Dryden's* Definition of Wit.'

The dialogues of Bouhours, entitled *La Manière de bien penser dans les ouvrages d'esprit,* wherein this sentiment occurs, appeared in 1687, and were translated into English in 1705 by a 'Person of Quality.' Bouhours quotes from the ninth *Epistle* of Boileau, 'Rien n'est beau que le vrai,' etc., an idea which is familiar enough in Boileau's *Art of Poetry.* The vogue of Bouhours and Rapin among the lesser wits is illustrated in the *Tatler,* No. 87. Rapin was translated by Rymer.

PAGE 193. *Dryden. Dedication of the Aeneis,* Scott and Saintsbury, xiv. 180. *Segrais* (1624–1701), the friend of Mme de la Fayette, translated the *Aeneid* and *Georgics* into French verse, to which he prefixed a dissertation. Dryden makes ample reference to this in his *Dedication of the Aeneis.*

63. PAGE 194. *Motto.* Horace, *Ars Poetica,* I.

Pulvillio (Italian *polviglio*: Latin *pulvillus*), a sachet of scented powder. 'All sorts of Essences, Perfumes, Pulvilios, Sweet-Bags, perfum'd Boxes for your Hoods and Gloves' (Shadwell's *Bury Fair,* II. ii).

PAGE 195. *Dullness,* the eighteenth-century antithesis to *Wit, Good Sense,* etc., which dwelt in 'Caves' and fantastic 'Temples.' See, especially, the passages in Pope's *Dunciad* and *Essay on Criticism.*

Tryphiodorus. See page 543.

64. PAGE 198. *Motto.* Juvenal, *Satires,* iii. 182–3.

This day Swift enters in his *Journal to Stella*: 'Dr. Freind was with me, and pulled out a twopenny pamphlet just published, called "The State of Wit," giving a character of all the papers that have come out of late. The author seems to be a Whig. . . . But above all things he praises the Tatlers and Spectators; and I believe Steele and Addison were privy to the printing of it. Thus is one treated by these impudent dogs.'

PAGE 199. Charles II of Spain had died in 1700; Peter II of Portugal in 1706; and the Emperor Joseph I on 17th April 1711, a few weeks before the publication of this paper.

65. PAGE 200. *Motto.* Horace, *Satires,* I. x. 90.

PAGE 201. Sir George Etherege's popular comedy, *The Man of Mode or Sir Fopling Flutter* (licensed 3rd June 1676), is referred to in Dryden's *Mac Flecknoe,* 151–4. See No. 75.

PAGE 203. In *A* is an advertisement, in large type, of Pope's *Essay on Criticism.* 'This day is publish'd. An Essay on Criticism. . . . Price 1s.'

66. *Motto.* Horace, *Odes,* III. vi. 21–4.

Belle Sauvage. See page 85.

'John Hughes is the author of these two letters, and, Chalmers thinks, also of the letters signed R. B. in Nos. 33 and 53' (H. Morley). See note to page 101.

67. PAGE 205. *Motto.* Sallust, *Bellum Catilinarium,* xxv.

Lucian's *Dialogue on Dancing* was translated, in the *Works,* by Ferrard Spence (1684), and again 'By several Eminent Hands' (1711).

PAGES 206–7. Budgell, in the name 'Monsieur Rigadoon,' hints, probably correctly, at the French origin of this lovely dance; and he appears to be right in stating that the country dance (called *contre-danse* on its introduction into France) is 'an invention of our own country.' The rigadoon was a dance for two. Cf. *Guardian*, No. 154. *Mol. Pately* was a popular English dance of the early sevententh century. The description of the French dancing may be compared with that in the *Tatler*, No. 88. See also note *ante*, page 534 (La Ferte).

PAGE 207. 'In foul weather, it would not be amiss for them to learn to dance, that is, to learn just so much (for all beyond is superfluous, if not worse) as may give them a graceful comportment of their bodies.'—Cowley's *Proposition for the Advancement of Experimental Philosophy* (§ 'The School').

PAGE 208. The sale of Italian paintings at the 'Three Chairs' is advertised in No. 64 and subsequent papers.

68. PAGE 209. *Motto.* Ovid, *Metamorphoses*, i. 355.

> *Tully.* De Amicitia, vi. 22.
> *Bacon.* Essays ('Of Friendship'), edited by Wright, page 107.

PAGE 210. See Ecclesiasticus, vi, ix, xxii, and xxvii.

PAGE 211. *Morum comitas.* Cicero, *passim*, especially *De Officiis*, ii. Cf. the motto of the 112th *Tatler*.

> *Difficilis*, etc. Martial, *Epigrams*, xii. 47.

69. PAGE 212. *Motto.* Virgil, *Georgics*, i. 54.

With this paper on the power of trade compare No. 174.

The old Philosopher. A reference to Diogenes the Cynic, who claimed to be of no country but κοσμοπολίτης (Diogenes Laertius, vi. 63). Goldsmith later adopted the phrase 'Citizen of the World' as a title to the papers which appeared in the *Public Ledger*.

PAGE 213. *Grand Cairo.* See page 513.

The description of the toilet, which may be compared with that in the 116th *Tatler*, may have suggested lines 129–36 of *The Rape of the Lock*, canto i. See note to page 16.

PAGE 214. *Pyramids of China.* Cf. No. 37, page 110.

70. PAGE 215. *Motto.* Horace, *Epistles*, II. i. 63.

Boileau gives this well-known anecdote of Molière in his *Réflexions sur Longin*, i.

Cf. Sidney's *Apology for Poetry* (*Elizabethan Critical Essays*, i. 178). 'Addison,' says Percy, in his *Reliques*, 'is mistaken with regard to the antiquity of the common-received copy; for this, if one may judge from the style, cannot be older than the time of Elizabeth, and was probably written after the eulogium of Sir Philip Sidney: perhaps in consequence of it' (i. 19). Percy gives the text of 'the genuine antique poem' (ib.); the errors in it are corrected in Skeat's *Specimens of English Literature*.

PAGE 216. *The greatest Modern Criticks* would seem to be a generality for Le Bossu, the author of the *Traité du Poëme épique* (1675). I am indebted to Mr. Nichol Smith for pointing out the following passages which Addison adopts: 'La première chose . . . est de choisir l'instruction et le point de Morale' (page 37); '. . . il emploie moins la force du raisonnement que l'insinuation et le plaisir, s'accommodant aux coûtumes et aux inclinations particulières de ses auditeurs' (page 44). Chapters viii and xi of Book I show that Homer and Virgil 'formed their plans in this view.' The allusion to the Greek States is also borrowed (page 66).

PAGE 218. *A Passage*. Virgil, *Aeneid*, xi. 820-6.

PAGE 219. *Vicisti*, etc., *Aeneid*, xii. 936-7; *At vero*, etc., *Aeneid*, x. 821-3.

Addison returns to this ballad in No. 74.

71. PAGE 220. *Motto*. Ovid, *Heroic Epistles*, iv. 10.

Dryden. *Works* (Scott and Saintsbury), xi, 488, lines 79-116. Steele omits line 81 (after the second in the quotation),

For Cymon shunned the Church, and used not much to pray,

and lines 102-3 (after the twenty-second in the same),

> Where two beginning paps were scarcely spied,
> For yet their places were but signified.

PAGE 221. The letter of the 'enamoured footman' is believed to be genuine. James Hirst, a servant of Steele's (and Addison's) friend the Hon. Edward Wortley, had by mistake enclosed a letter to his 'mistress' in a parcel which he delivered to his master. Mr. Wortley refused to return it, saying: 'No, James. You shall be a great man. This letter must appear in the *Spectator*' (Chalmers, i. 434).

72. PAGE 223. *Motto*. Virgil, *Georgics*, iv. 208-9.

Whet. Cf. advertisement in the *Tatler* (No. 138): 'Whereas Mr. Bickerstaff . . . has received Information, That there are in and about the Royal-Exchange a sort of Persons commonly known by the name of *Whetters*, who drink themselves into an intermediate State of being neither drunk or sober . . .' See also *Tatler*, No. 141.

PAGE 224. *Ben Johnson's Club*. See page 522. The twenty-fourth and last rule ran: 'Neminem reum pocula faciunto. Focus perennis esto.'

Kit-Cat and October. See page 521.

PAGE 225. *Whisk* or whist. It is so spelt in *The Country Gentleman's Vade-Mecum*, London, 1699, page 63 (Halliwell).

To moisten (or 'wet') *their Clay*, as a humorous synonym for 'to drink,' does not seem to be older than the first decade of the eighteenth century. (See the *Oxford English Dictionary*.)

73. *Motto*. Virgil, *Aeneid*, i. 328.

PAGE 226. *Cicero*. *Tusculan Disputations*, v. xxiv.

The Ring. See page 539.

PAGE 227. *Paradise Lost*, i. 376 et sqq.

In the Apocrypha. Bel and the Dragon, 3 et sqq.

A Tale of Chaucer. From the pesudo-Chaucerian poem, *The Remedie of Love* (c. 1530), printed in Chalmers's *Poets*, i. 539 stanzas 8 and 9).

Snuff-taking by ladies was quite *à la mode* in the days of the *Spectator*. See Nos. 57, 91, and especially 344. 'My sister . . . sits with her nose full of snuff . . . reading Plays and Romances' (*Tatler*, No. 75). 'After this, we turned our Discourse into a more gay style, and parted: But before we did so, I made her resign her Snuff-box for ever, and half drown her self with washing away the Stench of the Musty' (*Tatler*, No. 79).

See also Nos. 35 and 140; Swift's *Journal to Stella*, 3rd November 1711.

74. PAGE 228. *Motto.* Virgil, *Aeneid*, iv. 88.

The earlier paper will be found on pages 215-19. See notes thereon.

PAGE 229. *Audiet*, etc. Horace, *Odes*, I. ii. 23-4.

Vocat, etc. Virgil, *Georgics*, iii. 43-5.

PAGE 230. The lines *Adversi*, etc., are printed by Addison and his editors as one passage. Lines 1-2 are from *Aeneid*, xi. 605-6; 3-5, *Aeneid*, vii. 682-4; and 5-8, ib. 712-15.

Turnus, etc. *Aeneid*, ix. 47. *Vidisti*, etc. Ib. 269-70.

'A deep and *deeply* Blow,' a printer's error in the original edition.

PAGE 231. *Has inter*, etc. *Aeneid*, xii. 318-20.

Cadit, etc. *Aeneid*, ii. 426-8. The 1712 text prints *est* after *visum*.

PAGE 232. *Hudibras*, I. iii. 94-6.

> And, being down, still laid about:
> As Widdrington in doleful dumps
> Is said to fight upon his stumps.

Non pudet, etc. *Aeneid*, xii. 229-31.

75 PAGE 233. *Motto.* Horace, *Epistles*, I. xvii. 23.

This paper is supplementary to No. 65.

76 PAGE 236. *Motto.* Horace, *Epistles*, I. viii. 17.

La Calprenède's romance of *Pharamond* was published in Paris in 1661, and was translated into English in 1677 by John Phillips, Milton's nephew.

77 PAGE 238. *Motto.* Martial, *Epigrams*, I. lxxxvi. 8-10. In the 1712 text it is printed in two lines: 'Non convivere licet,' etc.

The sketch of Will Honeycomb as a *rêveur* or *distrait* is borrowed from La Bruyère: 'Il se promène sur l'eau, et il demande quelle heure il est: on lui présente une montre, à peine l'a-t-il reçue, que ne songeant plus ni à l'heure, ni à la montre, il la jette dans la rivière, comme une chose qui l'embarrasse' (*Caractères*, xi, 'De l'Homme'). Budgell gives this episode an English colour; the other freaks of Menalcas he acknowledges (page 240) as a direct transcript from his French original (ib.). De Brancas, brother of the Duc de Villars, is said to have been La Bruyère's model for Menalcas.

PAGE 239. *Great Wit.* *Absalom and Achitophel*, i. 163-4:

> *Great wits are sure to madness* near allied, etc.

'Nullum magnum ingenium sine mixtura dementiae.'— Seneca, *De Tranquillitate Animi*, xv.

Mathematicians. Perhaps an allusion to the familiar tales about Sir Isaac Newton.

PAGE 240. *Jesuit.* See page 14.

78. PAGE 242. *Motto.* See first paragraph.

Laurence Eusden has been named as Steele's Cambridge correspondent (H. Morley). See No. 54.

PAGE 244. *The Lowngers.* Cf. page 165.

You, your self. Steele doubtless revised the humorous

'petition' and 'remonstrance' (No. 80) with increased amusement, for the chief task of emendation which fell to him and his collaborators in the preparation of these volumes was the readjustment of the *Whos* and *Thats*. For example, in No. 72, of eight alterations seven are the substitution of 'who' and 'which' for 'that.'

79. PAGE 245. *Motto.* Horace, *Epistles*, I. xvi. 52.
   PAGE 246. *M. T.* Is this 'Mary Tuesday' of No. 24?
   PAGE 247. *Hecatissa.* See page 146.
      Female Library. See page 112.
      Together, etc. Dr. Johnson quotes the first line of this couplet, and adds '*Anon*.'
      Weekly Preparations. This is perhaps a reference to *A Week's Preparation*, etc. (London, 1679; forty-seventh edition, second part, 1736), a popular devotional work, one of several of its kind bearing similar titles.
   PAGE 248. *To say black is the eye*, to find fault with. 'I defy anybody to say black is my eye' (Fielding, *Tom Jones*, IX. iv).
80. *Motto.* Horace, *Epistles*, I. xi. 27.
      Babies, dolls. Cf. Nos. 478 and 500 ('little Girls tutoring their Babies'), and *Tatler*, No. 95.
      Visitings. See page 528.
   PAGE 250. Line 2. *Hands.* So the early texts. Several later editions read 'Bands.'
   PAGE 251. Line 4. So punctuated in the original texts. A better reading is obtained by placing the second comma after the second 'That.'
      The line, which Steele gives incorrectly, is not in *The Indian Emperor*, but in *Aureng-Zebe* (IV. i):

> You love the name
> So well, your every question ends in that;
> You force me still to answer you, Morat.

      '*Egad*,' '*I vow to gad*,' '*And all that*' are constantly on the lips of Failer, the 'hanger-on' of Sir Timorous in Dryden's *Wild Gallant*. These mannerisms are burlesqued in *The Rehearsal* in the speeches of Bayes.

Dedication. PAGE 252. Charles Montagu, first Earl of Halifax, had been praised by Addison in his *Account of the Greatest English Poets*, and by Tickell in the Dedication to his *Homer*. Steele dedicated the fourth volume of the *Tatler* to him (April 1711). Halifax succeeded Bubb Dodington as Pope's

> full-blown Bufo, puff'd by every quill;
> Fed with soft dedication all day long.
> *Epistle to Dr. Arbuthnot*, 232--3.

81 PAGE 253. *Motto.* Statius, *Thebaid*, ii. 128.
      It was the custom of the playhouse at this time for the wits and men about town to go to the side boxes, and for the ladies to sit in the front or middle boxes (cf. Nos. 88, 311, 377). Steele epitomizes an audience thus: 'Three of the fair sex for the front boxes, two gentlemen of wit and pleasure for the side-boxes, and

three substantial citizens for the pit' (*Theatre*, No. 3).   Cf. Congreve's *Double-Dealer*, II. ii; *Tatler*, Nos. 77 and 217; *Rape of the Lock*, v. 14; and Gay's *Toilette*, 27.   At the first performance of *Cato*, Addison entertained Bishop Berkeley and some friends in a side box with 'two or three flasks of burgundy and champagne.'   Dr. Johnson's definition of a side box as the 'seat for the ladies on the side of the theatre' shows that by his time that part of the house was no longer reserved for only the bolder or less reputable of their sex.   He and his party occupied the 'front row in a side-box' at Covent Garden on the first night of *She Stoops to Conquer* (Forster's *Goldsmith*, IV. xv, quoted by Austin Dobson).

PAGE 253. *Patches.* See page 153.   The 'setting' of the headdress was also symbolic of political leanings.   Cf. the *Freeholder*, No. 8: 'She has contrived to shew her principles by the setting of her commode.'

PAGE 254. Addison quotes from Cowley's *Davideis*, iii. 403–4, but changes the sex of the tiger for his present purpose.   He borrows the quotation from Statius from Cowley's notes.

PAGE 255. *Oration of Pericles.* Thucydides, II. xlv.

82. PAGE 256. *Motto.* Juvenal, *Satires*, iii. 33.
Ludgate was, till the order for its removal in July 1760, a prison for debtors who were freemen of the city, lawyers, or clergymen.

PAGE 257. *Where with like Haste*, etc. Denham's *Cooper's Hill*, lines 31–2. 'Tho' several ways.'

83. PAGE 259. *Motto.* Virgil, *Aeneid*, i. 464.

PAGE 261. *An old Man.* Hogarth has satirized this image in his 'Time smoking a Picture' (1761).   See also his *Analysis of Beauty* (1753 edition, page 118).

84. *Motto.* Virgil, *Aeneid*, ii. 6–8.
Duelling. See page 29 and note.
Pharamond. See page 236 and note.   The names *Eucrate* (ib.) and *Spinamont* are coined by Steele to give point to his modern application, the former signifying 'temperate' (εὔκρατος), the latter being a disguise for Mr. Richard Thornhill, who shot Sir Cholmondeley Dering in a duel in Tothill Fields on 9th May 1711.   This encounter, which according to Swift, 'made a noise' at the time, is referred to by him in his *Journal to Stella* under that date.   See *B. I.* (Thornhill, Richard).   Jeremy Collier had already anticipated some of Steele's arguments in his conference 'Of Duelling' between Philotimus and Philalethes (*Essays*, second edition, 1697, page 103).

PAGE 263. Line 11. '. . . which spoke *the utmost sense of his Majesty without ability to express it*,' *A*.

85. PAGE 264. *Motto.* Horace, *Ars Poetica*, 319–22.

PAGE 265. *Pye, piety*, a very ancient pun. Cf. page 521.
The evergreen 'History of the Two Children in the Wood' was printed with 'The old Song upon the Same' in chap-book form in 1700.   See Ashton's *Chapbooks of the Eighteenth Century*, page 369 et sqq., for an account of this rare pamphlet.   The earliest version of the ballad in the British Museum is dated 1640.

PAGE 265. Fourth line from foot. '. . . such as *Virgil himself would have touched upon had the like story been told by that Divine Poet.* For which . . .' *A.* With this allusion to Virgil in *A* cf. Nos. 70 and 74. Addison's emendations throughout this paper are for the most part a reduction of the emphasis of the first issue—e.g. 'wonderfully natural' becomes 'natural'—a peace-offering to the 'little conceited Wits' who had not relished his praise of the Ballads. In the concluding paragraph Addison may refer to an anonymous threepenny pamphlet, ascribed to Dr. William Wagstaffe, *A Comment upon the History of Tom Thumb*, which reached a second edition in 1711. 'It is a surprising thing,' writes the satirist, 'that in an Age so Polite as this, in which we have such a number of Poets, Criticks, and Commentators, some of the best things that are extant in our language should pass unobserv'd. . . . Indeed we had an *Enterprising Genius* of late, that has thought fit to disclose the Beauties of some Pieces to the World, that might have been otherwise indiscernable, and believ'd trifling and insipid, for no other Reason but their unpolish'd Homeliness of Dress. And if we were to apply our selves, instead of the *Classicks*, to the *Study of Ballads* . . . it is impossible to say what improvement might be made to Wit in general and the art of Poetry in particular.' The story of Tom Thumb will be found 'superior to either of those incomparable Poems of *Chevy Chase* or *The Children in the Wood*' (pages 1, 2). He commends 'the Beauty, Regularity, and Majestic Simplicity of the Relation' (page 18) and adds: 'tho' I am very well satisfied with this Performance, yet according to the usual modesty of Authors, I am oblig'd to tell the World *it will be a great Satisfaction to me, knowing my own insufficiency*, if I have given but some hints of the Beauties of this Poem' (page 21). And again: 'The most *refin'd Writers* of this Age have been delighted with the reading it. Mr. Tho. D'Urfey, I am told, is an Admirer, and Mr. John Dunton has been heard to say, more than once, "He had rather be the Author of it than all his Works"' (page 23).

PAGE 266. Line 9. ' . . . for a *goodnatured Reader* not,' *A.*

Horace. Odes, III. iv. 9–13.

The Late Lord Dorset. Charles Sackville, the 'Eugenius' of Dryden's *Essay of Dramatic Poesy.*

Greatest Candour. 'Greatest Humanity' in *A.*

Moliere's Thoughts. See *Le Misanthrope*, I. ii, where Alceste quotes an old song, and declares its superiority to a sonnet about Phillis, just recited. He adds:

> La rime n'est pas riche, et le style en est **vieux:**
> Mais ne voyez-vous pas que cela vaut bien mieux
> Que ces colifichets dont le bon sens murmure,
> Et que la passion parle-là toute pure?

See also the Prologue to Rowe's *Jane Shore* (1713) for the expression of the same notion.

86. PAGE 267. *Motto.* Ovid, *Metamorphoses*, ii. 447.

Speak that I may see thee. 'Ut te videam aliquid eloquere,' a saying ascribed to Socrates by Apuleius in his *Florida* (ii).

PAGE 268. Martial, *Epigrams*, XII. liv.

The *ingenious Author* is probably Baptista della Porta, whose *De Humana Physiognomia*, in four books, appeared in 1586.

Nahum Tate translated P. Coste's life of Condé in 1693, under the title *The Life of Louis of Bourbon, late Prince of Condé, digested into Annals. . . . Done out of French.*

PAGE 269. *Socrates was an extraordinary Instance.* The first half of the paragraph is a transcript from Cicero's *De Fato*, v, which recounts the diagnosis of Zopyrus the physiognomist; the second, concerning Socrates conquering his 'particular vices,' from the *Tusculan Disputations*, IV. xxxvii.

Silenus. Plato, *Symposium*, 215A.

Dr. Moore. Henry More, 'the Platonist,' author of the *Enchiridion Ethicum* (1669).

87. PAGE 270. *Motto.* Virgil, *Eclogues*, ii. 17.

Ugly Club. See page 52 and note. *Idols.* See page 226.

PAGE 271. *Hecatissa.* See page 146.

Sacrificed my Necklace, etc. See page 255.

PAGE 272. '*T. T.*' has been identified with Laurence Eusden.

This paper in *A* concludes with the following advertisement: '*This is to give Notice, That the three Criticks who last Sunday settled the Characters of my Lord Rochester and Boileau, in the Yard of a Coffee-house in Fuller's Rents, will meet this next Sunday at the same Time and Place, to finish the Merits of several Dramatick Writers: And will also make an End of the Nature of True Sublime.*'

88. *Motto.* Virgil, *Eclogues*, iii. 16.

This paper, which is a companion to Nos. 96, 107, and 137, may be compared in many of its details with Act I, sc. i of Steele's *Conscious Lovers*, and with his dramatic fragment, *The Gentleman.* Townley's *High Life below Stairs* (Drury Lane, October 1759) is said to have been founded on it.

PAGE 274. *Purle*, 'a kind of medicated malt liquor, in which wormwood and aromaticks are infused' (Johnson). Cf. also Purl-royal (Halliwell).

The Ring. See page 539.

White's. See pages 513, 542. It was situated at the lower end of St. James's Street, and was notorious as a resort of fashionable gamesters. It is the building in the background of the fourth plate of Hogarth's 'Rake's Progress' against which the artist has directed a streak of lightning.

Side-boxes. See page 253 and note.

89. PAGE 275. *Motto.* Persius, *Satires*, v. 64–71. Addison printed *juvenesque* for *puerique* in the first line.

PAGE 276. *Philander* and *Strephon* had been introduced by the *Tatler.* See especially Nos. 13 and 245.

PAGE 278. *Paradise Lost*, viii. 469–95, 500–11.

90. *Motto.* Virgil, *Georgics*, iii. 90–100.

Notions of Plato. Republic (towards the end), *Gorgias* (524), but especially *Phaedo* (81).

PAGE 279. *The Platonists.* So, too, Henry More, referred to on page 269.

PAGE 280. *Virgil. Aeneid*, vi. 604–7. Dryden's translation. vi. 818–23: 'By their *sides* is set.'

Monsieur Pontignan. Addison's learned author is Bayle, and 'the other occasion' is his article on the abbey of Fonte-vrault [Frontevaux]. Pontignan, the hero of the adventure, is introduced in a footnote (in the editions after that of 1697) thus: 'This brings to my mind an adventure I read in a little book which was printed at Paris and Holland anno 1682,' i.e. the *Académie galante.* The 'gay rambler,' runs the footnote, found 'these ladies, how immodest soever they may be repre-sented, were more prudent than the Devotees of Frontevaux.'

91. PAGE 282. *Motto.* Virgil, *Georgics*, iii. 244. This paper, accord-ing to Chalmers (ii. 10, iv. 128, notes), was written by Hughes.

Her Snuff-Box. See page 547.

PAGE 283. *Fine Gentleman.* See No. 75.

PAGE 284. *Sidley* (Sedley), etc. From Rochester's *Allusion to the Tenth Satire of the First Book of Horace*, lines 64–70. The original reads (2) 'resistless Power' and (5) '*Betwixt* declining Virtue.'

Celia the Fair. Dryden, *A New Song* (xi, page 176). Cor-rectly, '*Sylvia* the fair, in the bloom of fifteen.'

Barn Elms, a favourite duelling ground. The Kit-Cat club-house was there (see page 521).

PAGE 285. *Rival Mother.* There were *Rival Brothers, Rival Fools, Rival Kings, Rival Ladies, Rival Queens, Rival Sisters* familiar to playgoers of Steele's day. Perhaps this hit at the popular epithet would specially recall Dryden's *Rival Ladies*, in which there is a character named Honoria.

92. *Motto.* Horace, *Epistles*, II. ii. 61–3.

Tea-Equipage. See page 517.

Leonora (see page 110) has been identified as Mrs. Perry, sister of Miss Shepheard, the 'Parthenia' of No. 140 and 'Leonora' of No. 163. Both were kinswomen of Sir Fleetwood Shepheard.

Dalton's *Countrey Justice* first appeared in 1630, and ran through many editions before that of 1690, the last preceding the publication of this paper.—*The Compleat Jockey* may refer to *The Experienced Jockey, Compleat Horseman, or Gentleman's Delight*, a duodecimo of 1684.—The *Clavis Apocalyptica* (second edition, 1632) of the 'sublime genius' Joseph Mede was trans-lated by Richard More in 1643, and was the occasion of an extensive literature of 'observations' and 'analyses,' continuing even to the nineteenth century.

PAGE 286. The first volume of *The Secret Letters and Negociations of the Mareschal d'Estrades, Monsieur Colbert, and the Count d'Avaux* . . . had just been published (1710).—Bayle's *Dic-tionnaire historique et critique* (Rotterdam, 1697, second edition, 1702) appeared in an English translation 'with corrections by the Author' in 1710 (4 vols. fol.). Mr. Spectator and his con-temporaries were much beholden for their illustrations to Bayle, which, according to Dennis, was 'now spread throughout Europe' (*An Essay upon Public Spirit*, 1711).—William Wall's

History of Infant Baptism, in two parts, appeared in 1705, and in a second edition in 1707. One *Thomas* Wall wrote on the same subject a few years earlier (1691–2).—*The Finishing Stroke, Being a vindication of the Patriarchal Scheme of Government*, was written by Charles Leslie (London, 1711, 8vo). It deals with Hoadley's *Institution of Civil Government* (1710) and Higden's *Defence.*—The husbands' list of books of *Dissuasives*, etc., is, of course, mostly fictitious; but the subject of Susanna was a favourite of the cheap press (cf. page 524), and the *Pleasures of a Country Life* may be the sub-title of J. Pomfret's *Choice* (1709).—There was a *Government of the Tongue, by the Author of the Whole Duty of Man* (sixth edition, 1697).— Edmund Wingate's *Arithmetique made Easie* was a popular text-book which had reached an eleventh edition in 1704.— Elizabeth Grey, Countess of Kent, gave her name to a popular collection, entitled *A Choice Manuell or Rare and Select Secrets in Physick and Chyrurgery, etc.* The second part called *A True Gentlewoman's Delight* had reached a nineteenth edition in 1687. —*Pharamond* (page 548).—*Cassandra* (page 533).

PAGE 286. *Prudes.* See No. 217 and *Tatler*, Nos. 102 and 126.

All for Love or The World well Lost, a tragedy by Dryden (1678).—*Sophonisba or Hannibal's Overthrow*, a tragedy by Nat Lee (1676), which, according to Langbaine, 'always appeared on the stage with applause, especially from the fair sex'; its performance at Drury Lane is advertised in No. 119, A. *The Fatal Marriage or The Innocent Adultery*, by Southerne (1694), known later in the century under the name of *Isabella.*—*Mithridates, King of Pontus*, by Nat Lee (1678).—*The Rival Queens or The Death of Alexander the Great* (pages 535, 536).—*Aureng-Zebe*, a tragedy by Dryden (1676), referred to on page 549.— *Theodosius or The Force of Love*, by Nat Lee (page 536).

PAGE 287. *Will's.* See page 513.

93. *Motto.* Horace, *Odes*, I. xi. 6–8.

Seneca. Epistles, x, and *De Brevitate Vitae*, § 1. Cf. motto, No. 59 (page 179).

PAGE 290. Line 30. The sense is clear, though the syntax is incomplete.

94. PAGE 291. *Motto.* Martial, *Epigrams*, X. xxiii. 7–8.

Mr. Boyle. 'Basilius Valentinus . . . publisht long since an excellent Treatise of Antimony, inscribed *Currus Triumphalis Antimonii.* . . . He gives this account of his leaving many things unmentioned, that the Shortness of Life makes it impossible for one Man thoroughly to learn Antimony, in which every Day something of new is discovered' (*Some Considerations touching the Usefulness of Experimental Naturall Philosophy*, Oxford, 1664, pages 13, 14).

Locke's *Essay concerning Human Understanding*, II. xiv. 4.

PAGE 292. *Malebranche.* See pages 533–4.

Alcoran . . . Turkish Tales. The journey of Mahomet is referred to in the seventeenth sura of the *Koran*, but the details were derived by Addison from the *Turkish Tales*, published by Tonson in 1708.

95. PAGE 294. *Motto.* Seneca, *Hippolytus*, ii. 607.

 General Mourning. See No. 64.

 PAGE 296. *Deeper Scholars*, etc. See page 287.

  Tom's, a well-known coffee-house in Russell Street, Covent Garden, almost opposite Button's. There was a 'Tom's' in Cornhill, and another in the Strand. See Austin Dobson's *Eighteenth Century Vignettes*, iii. 340.

  Grecian. See page 514.

  Trader in Cheapside. See page 286.

  Theodosius. See page 286 and note.

  Bishop of Cambray. Fénelon.

 PAGE 297. *Anabella.* Cf. *ante*, page 161.

96. *Motto.* Horace, *Satires*, II. vii. 2–3.

 PAGE 298. *Mulberry Garden*, on the site of Buckingham Palace, succeeded Spring Garden as a fashionable resort. In Evelyn's time it was 'the only place of refreshment about the town for persons of the best quality to be exceeding cheated at' (*Diary*, 10th May 1654). See Pepys's *Diary, passim*. It gave the title to a comedy by Sir Charles Sedley (1668). See Shadwell's *Humourists* (1670), Act III.

 PAGE 299. The *New Exchange* was a fashionable fancy goods mart in the Strand, on the site of the stables of Durham House, over against the modern Bedford Street. It was much frequented by the men about town after the Restoration. Young Bookwit in Steele's *Lying Lover* calls it 'a seraglio, a living gallery of beauties staring from side to side' (II. ii). It is constantly alluded to in the Restoration drama. See No. 155.

97. PAGE 300. *Motto.* Virgil, *Aeneid*, vi. 436.

  Steele has already discussed the duello, *ante*, page 261. See note there.

98. PAGE 303. *Motto.* Juvenal, *Satires*, vi. 501.

  As Grass-hoppers, etc. Numbers, xiii. 33.

 PAGE 304. *Tot premit*, etc. Juvenal, *Satires*, vi. 502–4. Addison printed '*Aliam credas.*'

  Fontange, Commode. The commode was a tall head-dress fashionable with ladies in England during the closing decades of the seventeenth century. Mlle de Fontanges introduced the coiffure in France in 1679. It consisted of a wire framework decorated with lace or silk, to which lappets or streamers were sometimes affixed. See Nos. 263, 265, also note on page 550 of this volume.

  Addison's account of the head-dress and of Thomas Conecte, Carmelite monk (burned 1434), and his references to Guillaume Paradin's *Annales de Bourgoigne* (1566) and Bertrand d'Argentré's *Histoire de Bretagne* (1582) are taken from Bayle's *Dictionary* (article 'Conecte'), referred to *ante*, page 286.

99. PAGE 305. *Motto.* Horace, *Satires*, I. vi. 63.

 PAGE 307. Lines 16–19. *I cannot . . . Truth*, not in *A*. The reference is to Herodotus, I. cxxxvi.

  An English Peer. Bishop Percy was informed that Addison here alludes to William Cavendish, first Duke of Devonshire (1640–1707).

100. PAGE 308. *Motto.* Horace, *Satires*, I. v. 44.
    Valetudinarians. See page 528.
101. PAGE 310. *Motto.* Horace, *Epistles*, II. i. 5–10.
    Censure, etc., is one of Swift's *Thoughts on Various Subjects,
Moral and Diverting* (1706).
    PAGE 311. *Recentibus odiis.* Tacitus, *Annals*, I. i.
102. PAGE 313. *Motto.* Phaedrus, *Fables*, III. xiv. 12–13.
    This paper on the art of the fan is a sequel to Steele's account
of the 'Management of that Utensil' in the 52nd *Tatler*, and
recalls the verses on Flavia's 'instrument' quoted in the 239th
Tatler.
103. PAGE 316. *Motto.* Horace, *Ars Poetica*, 240–2.
    Late Archbishop's Posthumous Works. Tillotson's sermon
'On Sincerity.' See also page 326.
    PAGE 317. *Words are like Money.* Cf. the metaphor in Hobbes's
Leviathan, I. iv: 'Words are wise men's counters, they do but
reckon by them; but they are the money of fools.'
104. PAGE 318. *Motto.* Virgil, *Aeneid*, i. 316–17.
    PAGE 319. *Tully says.* *De Officiis*, I. xxvii.
    The *Spectator* returns to the subject of ladies' riding costumes
in Nos. 331, 435, and 485 (advertisement). A 'Compleat
Riding Suit for a Lady' is described in an advertisement to
No. 81, *A*.
    The letter has been ascribed to John Hughes.
105. PAGE 321. *Motto.* Terence, *Andria*, i. 60–1.
    Broke Windows. See page 532.
    PAGE 322. *Ombre.* See the description in *The Rape of the Lock*,
iii. 25 et sqq.; and Prior's *Upon Playing at Ombre with Two
Ladies*.
106. PAGE 323. *Motto.* Horace, *Odes*, I. xvii. 14–16.
    Roger de Coverley. See page 515.
    PAGE 324. *Press'd forward.* See page 326.
    PAGE 325. *A Clergyman . . . that understood a little of Back-
Gammon.* So, too, Swift in his correspondence with Gay: 'In
what esteem are you with the vicar of the parish? Can you
play with him at backgammon?' (4th May 1732). And again:
'I believe I formerly desired to know whether the vicar of
Amesbury can play at backgammon' (12th August 1732).
    PAGE 326. W. Fleetwood had been Bishop of St. Asaph since
1708; but there may be no point in the reference.
107. *Motto.* Phaedrus, *Fables*, II, Epilogue, 1–3.
    Place themselves in his way. Cf. page 324.
    In No. 124 (*A*) is advertised 'A Quarterly Contribution for
the Benefit of Faithful Servants.' See also page 562.
    PAGE 327. *An Husband.* By the will of the 'perverse widow,' only
in the old sense of a thrifty man or economist.
108. PAGE 329. *Motto.* Phaedrus, *Fables*, II. v. 3.
    Mr. William Wimble was identified, even as far back as 1741,
with Thomas Morecraft, described in an obituary notice in the
Gentleman's Magazine as 'a Baronet's younger Son, the Person
mentioned by the Spectator in the character of *Will*. Wimble'
(2nd July 1741). This is repeated in a note to the edition of

1766. We may dismiss this biographical guess, as we have others of its kind (see page 515). If there be any prototype, it must be found in the 'Honourable Mr. Thomas Gules, of Gule-Hall, in the County of Salop,' who is introduced in the *Tatler* (No. 256). He, too, 'had chosen to starve like a man of Honour,' as became a 'cadet of a very ancient family,' and was fond of 'twisting a whip,' and of making nut-crackers 'for his Diversion, in order to make a present now and then to his Friends.'

PAGE 330. *He carries a Tulip-Root.* The tulip mania was abating its seventeenth-century extravagance, but it was still a dangerous snare to enthusiasts. See the 218th *Tatler* (30th August 1710).

109. PAGE 331. *Motto.* Horace, *Satires*, II. ii. 3.

PAGE 332. The *Tilt-Yard* lay in front of the old Banqueting Hall, towards Charing Cross. It covered a portion of the present parade of St. James's. (See Fisher's *Ground Plan of Whitehall*, 1680; also Stow's *Survey*, edited by Strype.)

Jenny Mann's *Tilt-Yard Coffee-House*, a military rendezvous, stood on the site on which the office of the Paymaster-General was afterwards built. It was in high repute as late as Boswell's time (*Correspondence*, 16th February 1762).

My Grandmother appears. Planché discusses the description of the old costume in this essay in his *History of British Costume* (1874), page 351.

PAGE 333. *Whitepot.* 'A dish made of cream, sugar, rice, currants, cinnamon, etc. It was formerly much eaten in Devonshire' (Halliwell). Cf. *Hudibras*, I. i. 299; *Tatler*, No. 245; Gay's *Shepherd's Week* ('Monday').

110. PAGE 334. *Motto.* Virgil, *Aeneid*, ii. 755.
Feedeth the young Ravens. Psalm cxlvii. 9.

PAGE 335. Locke's *Essay concerning Human Understanding*, II. xxxiii. 10.

PAGE 336. *Lucretius.* De Rerum Natura, iv. 33 et sqq.
Josephus. Antiquities of the Jews, XVII. xiii. 4.

111. PAGE 337. *Motto.* Horace, *Epistles*, II. ii. 45.

PAGE 338. Line 36. '. . . propagate his Kind, and provide himself,' *A.*

Haeres, etc. Horace, *Epistles*, II. ii. 175–6.

112. PAGE 340. *Motto.* Pythagoras, *Carmina Aurea*, 1–2.

113. PAGE 342. *Motto.* Virgil, *Aeneid*, iv. 4.
The perverse Widow. Cf. *ante*, page 6. A persistent tradition identifies her with a widow, Mrs. Catherine Beevey, to whom Steele dedicated the second volume of *The Ladies Library* (*ante*, page 535). She was described by Mrs. Manley as 'one of those dark and lasting beauties that strike with reverence and yet delight.' The reader desirous to know the pros and cons may refer to Nichols's *Illustrations*, iv. 820; W. Henry Wills's *Sir Roger de Coverley* (1850), pages 196–99; and to an article in *Longman's Magazine*, April 1897. Some editors, with a like ingenuity, have fixed on Lady Warwick, whom Addison was to marry in 1716.

PAGE 345. *Tansy.* Old receipts for tansy cakes and tansy puddings will be found in Halliwell's *Dictionary.* Cf. Herrick's *Hesperides*, No. 691; Chambers's *Book of Days*, i. 425, 429.

PAGE 346. Martial, *Epigrams*, I. lxviii. 1–6.

114. *Motto.* Horace, *Epistles*, I. xviii. 24.

Dipp'd. Mortgaged.

PAGE 347. *Four Shillings in the Pound.* The land tax.

PAGE 348. The *elegant Author* is Thomas Sprat, who prefixed a Latin life to the edition of Cowley's Latin poems, afterwards enlarged and printed with Cowley's English works.

Great Vulgar. From Cowley's rendering of Horace's *Odi profanum vulgus et arceo*, 'not exactly copied, but rudely imitated' by him at the conclusion of his essay 'Of Greatness':

Hence ye profane; I hate ye all,
Both the great vulgar, and the small.

PAGE 349. *If e'er Ambition.* From a verse passage in Cowley's essay 'Of Greatness.' Line 4, '*Blessing.*'

115. *Motto.* Juvenal, *Satires*, x. 356.

PAGE 351. *Perverse Widow.* See No. 113.

Dr. Sydenham. See page 528.

Medicina Gymnastica or A Treatise concerning the power of Exercise, with respect to the Animal Economy, by Francis Fuller (1705).

Treatise of Exercises. Artis Gymnasticae apud Antiquos . . . Libri vi (Venice, 1569). By Hieronymus Mercurialis. See iv. 5, and vi. 2. This book passed through many editions and latterly included a description of the Palaestra by the Roman architect Vitruvius. Cf. pages 487 and 502 of this volume.

116. PAGE 352. *Motto.* Virgil, *Georgics*, iii. 43–4.

PAGE 353. *My hounds are bred*, etc. *Midsummer Night's Dream*, IV. i. 116–22. The later description of the 'chiding' of the hounds and of the 'double echo' show that Mr. Spectator himself was indebted to Shakespeare. Cf.:

And mark the musical confusion
Of hounds and echo in conjunction.
Ib., lines 109–10.

Never did I hear
Such gallant chiding.
Ib., lines 113–14.

Cf. Gervase Markham's *Countrey Contentments* (1615), page 6, as to the selection of the dogs' 'mouths' for 'sweetness of cry.' Also Somerville's *Chace*, i. 127. 'Mr. Budgell has shown himself to be no sportsman, by fixing the date of his hunting-party in the month of July, and by making Sir Roger hunt with stop-hounds, which are, I believe, peculiar to stag-hunting' (note in Chalmers's edition).

PAGE 355. Dryden's *Epistle to John Driden*, lines 73–4, 88–95.

117. PAGE 356. *Motto.* Virgil, *Eclogues*, viii. 108.

It is hardly necessary to believe that Addison was prompted to this paper on witchcraft by the misfortunes of some local 'Moll White,' such as the Jane Wenham of Henry Morley's note. The 'tabby cat,' the 'pins,' the 'saying of prayers backwards,' etc., were by tradition the necessary horrors of every successful prosecution.

PAGE 356. Line 37. '. . . in *Ottway*, which I could not forbear repeating on this occasion,' *A.* The quotation is from a speech of Chamont in *The Orphan*, Act II. Line 1 runs: '*Through* a close lane.'

118. PAGE 358. *Motto.* Virgil, *Aeneid*, iv. 73.

PAGE 360. *We followed the Sound*, etc. 'A little water-colour sketch by Mr. Thackeray of this scene was not long since in the market. It is now [1896] in the possession of Sir Henry Thompson' (Dobson's *Selections from Steele*, page 460).

119. PAGE 361. *Motto.* Virgil, *Eclogues*, i. 19–20.

120. PAGE 364. *Motto.* Virgil, *Georgics*, i. 415–16.

Line 34. *Deposite.* 'Depose' in *A.*

121. PAGE 367. *Motto.* Virgil, *Eclogues*, iii. 60.

Tully has observed. De Natura Deorum, ii. 51. See the concluding paragraph of this essay.

Dampier's *Voyages*, i. 39 (fourth edition, 1699).

PAGE 368. Locke's *Essay concerning Human Understanding*, II. ix. 13.

PAGE 369. Henry More's *Antidote against Atheisme* (1653), ii. 10, § 5.

Boyle's *Disquisition about the Final Causes of Natural Things*, section ii.

122. PAGE 370. *Motto.* Publilius Syrus, *Fragments.* Some texts read 'facundus.'

PAGE 371. *Game-Act.* See page 7.

PAGE 372. *The Knight's Head.* Portrait signs were not uncommon. Pontack, the famed purveyor, had a likeness of his father on his signboard. Cf. the sign of the Swiss Count, 'the features being strong, and fit for hanging high (*Tatler*, No. 18).

123. PAGE 373. *Motto.* Horace, *Odes*, IV. iv. 33–6.

PAGE 375. Cowley's words are: 'But there is no fooling with life, when it is once turn'd beyond forty' (*Essays*, 'The Danger of Procrastination').

Addison wrote to Mr. Wortley Montagu, on the day of the publication of this paper: 'Being very well pleased with this day's *Spectator*, I cannot forbear sending you one of them, and desiring your opinion of the story in it. When you have a son I shall be glad to be his Leontine, as my circumstances will probably be like his. . . .'

124. PAGE 377. The *Motto* is an adaptation of Callimachus, *Fragmenta*, ccclix, τὸ μέγα βιβλίον ἴσον τῷ μεγάλῳ κακῷ. Athenaeus quotes it (III. i) as a saying of Callimachus.

Forty or fifty thousand Readers. Has this any bearing on the circulation of the *Spectator*, which was increasing (page 379)? See page 522.

PAGE 378. *Wisdom*, etc. Proverbs, i. 20–2.

PAGE 379. *Nox atra*, etc. Virgil, *Aeneid*, ii. 360.

Latin Proverb. 'Lupus est homo homini,' Plautus, *Asinaria*, II. iv. 88.

125. *Motto.* Virgil, *Aeneid*, vi. 833–4.

PAGE 380. *Plutarch. De Inimicorum Utilitate, passim*; *Moralia*, ii. 91; *Life of Pericles* (towards the end).

PAGE 381. *That great Rule.* Luke, vi. 27.

126. PAGE 382. *Motto.* Virgil, *Aeneid*, x. 108.

PAGE 383. Diodorus Siculus, I. xxxv.

PAGE 384. *Landed and money'd* interests. See page 516.

127. PAGE 385. *Motto.* Persius, I. i.

Dyer's. See page 537.

PAGE 386. *Petticoats.* 'I was in Hopes that I had brought them [the ladies] to some Order, and was employing my Thoughts on the Reformation of their Petticoats' (*Tatler*, No. 115). Cf. *ante*, page 332. No. 118 (*A*) advertises, as just published, *The Farthingale reviv'd, or More Work for a Cooper : A Panegyrick on the late, but most admirable Invention of the Hoop-Petticoat. Written at the Bath.*

Etherege's *Love in a Tub.* Cf. pages 136 and 538.

PAGE 387. *Suits of Armour.* Plutarch's *Life of Alexander* (towards the end).

128. PAGE 388. *Motto.* Lucan, *Pharsalia*, i. 98.

PAGE 390. *Romances.* See page 533.

129. PAGE 391. *Motto.* Persius, v. 71–2.

PAGE 392. *Commode.* See note on page 555.

Petticoat. See No. 127 and note.

The Ramillie Cock was the mode in 1706.

PAGE 393. *Monmouth Cock*, fashionable from 1667. See Pepys's *Diary*, 3rd June 1667 (Globe edition, page 502, note).—The *Steenkirk* was properly a kerchief of silk or lace, fashionable in Paris in the winter of 1692–3 after the battle at Steinkirk, though the name was freely applied to the newest whims of the milliners.

130. *Motto.* Virgil, *Aeneid*, vii. 748–9.

131. PAGE 395. *Motto.* Virgil, *Eclogues*, x. 63.

PAGE 397. *A White Witch*, of a species which, in Dryden's words, was 'mischievously good.' See W. Henry Wills's *Sir Roger de Coverley*, page 207.

Jesuit. Cf. pages 14 and 240.

132. PAGE 398. *Motto.* Cicero, *De Oratore*, ii. iv. Steele printed the passage continuously without indicating the omissions, and added 'esse' after 'ineptus.'

PAGE 399. *Ephraim*, 'who cannot resist' (page 400); a reference to Psalm lxxviii. 9.

Captain's Equipage, satirically applied to a single orderly.

All the essays from No. 132 to No. 158 are, with two exceptions (No. 135 by Addison and No. 150 by Budgell), by Steele. Some light may be thrown on this by ' J. G.'s' remarks on the *Tatlers* in his *Present State of Wit*, written in May 1711: 'I am assur'd from good hands, That all the *Visions* and other Tracts in that way of writing, with a very great number of the most exquisite Pieces of Wit and Raillery throughout the Lucubrations, are intirely of this Gentleman's Composing; which may in some Measure account for that different Genius, which appears in the Winter Papers from those of the Summer; at which time, as the *Examiner* often hinted, this Friend of Mr. Steele's was in Ireland.' Was Addison on holiday, or indisposed, or was he in Ireland looking after his threatened interests?

PAGE 400. *The Right we had of taking Place*, etc., a contentious question which naturally arose from the bad condition of the highways. Cf. the pedestrian worry about 'taking the wall,' humorously introduced in the *Tatler* (No. 256).

133. PAGE 401. *Motto.* Horace, *Odes*, I. xxiv. 1-2.

PAGE 402. *These Instances.* Plutarch's *Life of Phocion.* The anecdote of *Nicocles* is near the end.

PAGE 403. *A Friend.* Stephen Clay of the Inner Temple, son of Edmund Clay, haberdasher. Steele refers to him frequently in his correspondence, chiefly in connection with his affairs in the West Indies. See Nichols's edition of the *Letters*, volume i, where at page 222 are printed two sets of verses by Clay, *The Maid's Complaint* and *A Song in Imitation of an Ode of Horace.*

134. PAGE 404. *Motto.* Ovid, *Metamorphoses*, i. 521-2.

PAGE 406. *Manage our Snuff-Boxes.* The sequel is in No. 138.

135. PAGE 407. *Motto.* Horace, *Satires*, I. x. 9.

PAGE 408. *One of the greatest Genius's.* This reference to Swift is an interesting clue to the origin of Addison's paper. Swift, in a letter in the *Tatler* (No. 230, 27th September 1710), exposes 'the corruption of our style,' and gives a sample letter showing the fashionable 'abbreviations and elisions.' He also discusses the 'refinement' of giving but the first syllable of a word, taking as examples from the said letter the words *mob, rep, pozz*, which with *incog.* (also in the letter) are specially noted by Addison. He returns to the subject in *A Proposal for Correcting, Improving, and Ascertaining the English Tongue*, in a letter addressed to Lord Oxford in February 1712 (published May 1712). It is a plea for the establishment of an academy 'to correct and fix the English language.' Towards the conclusion he says: 'I would willingly avoid repetition, having, about a year ago, communicated to the public much of what I had to offer upon this subject, by the hands of an ingenious gentleman, who for a long time did thrice a week divert or instruct the kingdom by his papers, and is supposed to pursue the same design at present, under the title of Spectator.' There are several references to the subject of this letter in the *Journal to Stella*, from 21st February to 17th July; and Voltaire discusses it in his twenty-fourth letter (*Lettres philosophiques*, 1734). It is hardly necessary to follow Thomas Arnold in showing how wrongly Addison, or Steele (No. 147), understood the mysteries of *es* and *eth* or *his* and *her*. It might be more to the point to speculate on the amusing inconsistency between the doctrine of the essay and the practice of the revisers.

136. PAGE 410. *Motto.* Horace, *Epistles*, II. i. 112.

My Imagination, etc. The sentences may be made clearer by the insertion of 'which' after 'adventures.'

Pultowa. 8th July 1709.

Count Piper was Prime Minister of Charles XII of Sweden.

Deptford. In the spring of 1698.

PAGE 412. 'A *make-bate*, a busie-bodie, a pick-thanke, a seeke-trouble' (Florio).

All for Love, etc., by Dryden. See page 286.

137. PAGE 413. *Motto.* Cicero?

The *Spectator* deals with the question of master and servant, *ante*, No. 107. The letters of Ralph Valet and Patience Giddy call to mind some of the points in Swift's *Directions to Servants*.

PAGE 415. *The five Fields towards Chelsea*, on the site of the modern Belgravia and Pimlico. This was a favourite country walk towards Chelsea, even though it was, as Mr. Bickerstaff tells us, a place 'where the Robbers lie in wait.' See *Tatler*, No. 34.

138. PAGE 416. *Motto.* Cicero, *De Officiis*, II. v.

Tully tells us. *De Inventione Rhetorica.*

PAGE 417. *Dr. Beveridge*, Bishop of St. Asaph (1637–1708).

PAGE 418. The *Advertisement* is the sequel to the petition on page 406.

Charles Lillie. See page 539.

Garraway's. See page 514. Also Nos. 403 and 457; *Tatler*, No. 147; Steele's *Tender Husband*, II. i.

139. *Motto.* Cicero, *De Officiis*, II. xii. 43.

PAGE 420. *Mechanick Employments.* See the reference to Deptford, *ante*, page 410.

The Colours in the Hall were those taken at Blenheim.

The Perfection of Glory, etc. Cicero, *Philippics*, i.

PAGE 421. *August* 1711, when Marlborough passed the French lines on his march on Bouchain.

140. *Motto.* Virgil, *Aeneid*, iv. 285. Steele prints it thus: *Animum curis nunc huc nunc dividit illuc.*

PAGE 422. *Account of Wit.* See pages 176 et sqq.

Imitators of Milton. E.g. John Philips in his *Cyder*.

PAGE 423. *Mr. Lillie's.* See page 418.

PAGE 424. *Ombre Table.* See page 322 and note.

PAGE 425. *Parthenia.* See note to page 285.

141. *Motto.* Horace, *Epistles*, II. i. 187–8.

PAGE 426. *Moll White.* See page 357.

Shadwell's comedy *The Lancashire Witches, and Tegue O'Divelly, the Irish Priest*, produced in 1681, had, according to Downes, 'several *Machines* of flyings for the Witches.' It was acted at the Haymarket (July 1707) 'with all the risings, sinkings, and flyings of the Witches.' Performances at Drury Lane are advertised in Nos. 132, 137, 144, etc. (*A*). Steele refers to episodes in Acts IV and V.

Ben Johnson and *Bullock*, actors. See *B. I.*

Bellenden's translation of Hector Boece's *Historia Scotorum* supplied many of the details of Holinshed's *Chronicle*, from which Shakespeare borrowed.

PAGE 427. *But Shakespeare's Magick.* Dryden and Davenant's *Tempest*, Prologue, 19–20.

Design whate'er. The concluding line of Act V of *The Lancashire Witches*.

Hans Carvel, by Prior. Steele quotes lines 11–12, but puts the verbs in the present tense.

PAGE 427. *I am*, etc. John Hughes is said to have written this letter.

142. PAGE 428. *Motto.* Horace, *Odes*, I. xiii. 18.

Steele's phrase 'being genuine' need not be interpreted by the note on page 514, for the originals have been preserved. They were addressed by Steele to his wife, 'Dear Prue,' four years previously, not forty. They are printed in Nichols's edition of the *Epistolary Correspondence*. The letter dated 'Aug. 7, 1671' reproduces the letter of 'Aug. 22, 1707' (Nichols, i. 105) verbatim, with the change of 'Madam' for 'Mrs. Scurlock' at the close. The letter of 'Sept. 3' is that of Aug. 16 (altered to Aug. 23), 1707 (Nichols, i. 97). The interpolation '*Though I made*,' etc., is added on the MS. The letter of 'Sept. 25' is that of Sept. 1, 1707 (Nichols, i. 109). The sentence '*The two next*,' etc., is added on the MS. In the original, '*Holland*' reads '*Lisbon*'; '*Windsor*,' '*Hampton-court*'; '*She designs to go with me*,' '*It will be on Tuesday come se'nnight*'; '*the appointed day*,' '*that day*.' After 'composure' the original reads: 'Oh Love!

> A thousand Torments dwell about thee,
> Yet who would Live, to Live without thee?'

The letter 'of Sept. 30' is that of Sept. 3, 1707 (Nichols, i. 111). The next letter, of 'Oct. 20,' is that of Aug. 30, 1707 (Nichols, i. 108), on the MS. of which is added, '*He was, when he writ*,' etc. The last letter, dated 'June 23,' had been written quite recently, on June 20 (Nichols, i. 218).

143. PAGE 431. *Motto.* Martial, *Epigrams*, VI. lxx. 15.

PAGE 432. *Valetudinarians.* See note, page 528.

Cottilus and *Uranius* have been unmasked by ingenious editors. The former is said to be Henry Martyn (of No. 555), who had a house at Blackheath 'perhaps called his Cot,' and the latter 'was probably Mr. John Hughes'! See No. 180.

PAGE 433. *How-d'ye Servants.* A *howd'ee* was the colloquial term for a servant whose duty it was to pass this phrase of formal civility to his master's friends. Cf. *Bridget Howd'ee*, the 'lively serving wench' of the *Tatler* (No. 245). 'I have been returning,' says Swift, in his *Journal to Stella*, 'the visits of those that sent howdees in my sickness' (10th May 1712). See also Swift's *Verses on his Own Death*, line 123.

PAGE 434. *A great Author*, etc. Burnet's *Theory of the Earth*. See *ante*, pages 114 and 440, and notes.

144. *Motto.* Terence, *Eunuchus*, III. v. 18.

PAGE 437. Steele's *Antient Sage* is Antisthenes, described in Diogenes Laertius, VI. i, from whom he borrows his preceding learned allusions to Aristotle, Plato, Socrates, Theophrastus, and Carneades.

145. *Motto.* Horace, *Epistles*, I. xviii. 29.

Hudibras, II. i. 297–8.

> Quoth she, I've heard old cunning stagers
> Say, Fools for arguments use wagers.

PAGE 439. *Your Stage Coach.* See page 399.

Sizable Circumference. Cf. No. 127.

146. PAGE 440. *Motto.* Cicero, *De Natura Deorum*, II. lxvi. 166.
    Such is the Entertainment. Cf. pages 517 and 565.
    The Theory of the Earth. Cf. page 563. The quotation to-wards the close is from III. xi. 110–11, edition of 1684.
    Cicero tells us. Tusculan Disputations, i.

147. PAGE 443. *Motto.* From the pseudo-Ciceronian treatise *Rhetorica ad C. Herennium*, I. ii.
    St. James's Garlick-hill (Garlickhithe), rebuilt in 1676–82, was near Thames Street in Vintry Ward. The reader referred to is the Rev. Philip Stubbs, afterwards Archdeacon of St. Albans.
    Sion College, London Wall.
    PAGE 444. *Pindarick Readers.* Cf. page 483 and note, page 543.
    Cant. Steele is out in his etymology. See the *Oxford English Dictionary.*
    PAGE 445. *Dr. S——e.* Probably Dr. George Smalridge, after-wards Bishop of Bristol, the 'Favonius' of the 114th *Tatler.* See Austin Dobson's *Selections from Steele*, page 456.
    Do you read, etc. *Si cantas, male cantas; si legis, cantas*, a saying of Caesar's, quoted by Quintilian, *De Institutione Oratoria*, I. viii.

148. *Motto.* Horace, *Epistles*, II. ii. 212.
    PAGE 446. *French and Country Dances.* See pages 545–6.
    PAGE 448. *For Women*, etc. Waller, *Of Love*, lines 13–16.

149. PAGE 449. *Motto.* Cicero, *Tusculan Disputations*, IV. xxxii. 68.

150. PAGE 452. *Motto.* Juvenal, *Satires*, iii. 152–3.
    Plagues. Budgell probably refers to some pamphlets, now difficult to trace. The British Museum Catalogue describes an 1800 edition of the *Fifteen Plagues of a Footman, Coachman, &c.*, and also the *Pleasures of a Single Life* (1701). Cf. *The Fifteen Comforts*, etc., in note, page 533.
    Juvenal, *Satires*, iii. 147–51. Dryden's translation, lines 248–55. Scott and Saintsbury's edition reads '*patches*' for '*patch is.*'
    Want is the Scorn, etc., ib. 256–7.
    PAGE 453. *Sloven.* Budgell, the writer of this paper, included a translation of *The Sloven* in his Theophrastus. See page 520.
    Atticus. Did this suggest to Pope his sobriquet for Addison?
    PAGE 454. *Mr. Osbourn. Advice to a Son*, I. xxiii.

151. PAGE 455. *Motto.* Cicero, *De Finibus*, II. xxxv. 117.

152. PAGE 458. *Motto.* Homer, *Iliad*, vi. 146.
    PAGE 459. *A gay Frenchman*, etc. The anecdote is of the Chevalier de Flourilles, killed at Sénef in 1674. It is told in the *Memoirs of Condé* (referred to *ante*, page 268 and note).

153. PAGE 460. *Motto.* Cicero, *De Senectute*, xxiii.
    PAGE 461. *My author.* Cicero.
    Line 13. So *A*, but the 1712 text reads 'a Young.'

154. PAGE 463. *Motto.* Juvenal, *Satires*, ii. 83.
    PAGE 464. Simon Honeycomb's visits to the watering-places are in an ascending scale of modishness from Astrop Wells near Oxford to Tunbridge and Bath. St. Edmundsbury is the scene of Shadwell's *Bury Fair*; and Epsom Wells gives the title to another comedy by the same hand.

PAGE 466. *Great with Tully of late.* Cf. note, page 517; also page 476.

155. In *A* this paper is numbered '156,' and subsequent papers are incorrectly numbered. The error is rectified from '166' onwards. *Motto.* Horace, *Ars Poetica*, 451.

> *Idol.* Cf. page 271.

PAGE 467. *New Exchange.* See page 299 and note.

PAGE 469. *Your Account of Beauties.* See pages 434 et sqq.

156. *Motto.* Horace, *Odes*, II. viii. 5–7.

PAGE 470. *A common Bite.* See page 539.

PAGE 472. *Affection.* Either in the obsolete sense of *affectation*, as used by Maria in *The School for Scandal* (I. i), or a misprint for that word, which is given in its usual form on page 22.

157. *Motto.* Horace, *Epistles*, II. ii. 187–9.

PAGE 474. *Seneca says. Epistles*, xcv (about the middle).

PAGE 475. *That Infamy.* Steele is at issue with public opinion, which found its most straightforward expression in the later utterances of Dr. Johnson (see Birkbeck Hill's edition of Boswell's *Johnson*, i. 46, ii. 407, v. 99). Steele returns to the 'licensed Tyrants, the Schoolmasters' in No. 168.

158. *Motto.* Martial, *Epigrams*, XIII. ii. 8.

> *The Present State of Wit* (1711) points out that Steele, instead of falling in with the customs of the day, like the other papers of the time, took the new course of attacking them.

PAGE 476. *Is the best Rule.* 'Is not the best Rule,' *A.*

> *Your Tully.* Cf. page 466 and note.

PAGE 478. *Give me but what*, etc. Waller, *On a Girdle*, lines 11–12.

159. *Motto.* Virgil, *Aeneid*, ii. 604–6.

> *Grand Cairo.* See note, page 513.

> *The Visions of Mirzah.* Cf. Steele's *Conscious Lovers*, I. ii. 1: 'These Moral Writers practise Virtue after Death: This charming Vision of *Mirza!* Such an Author consulted in a Morning sets the Spirit for the Vicissitudes of the Day, better than the Glass does a Man's Person.'

160. PAGE 482. *Motto.* Horace, *Satires*, I. iv. 43–4.

PAGE 483. *Bienséance.* Cf. Boileau, *L'Art poétique*, iii. 122–3.

> *Pindaricks.* See note to page 444.

PAGE 484. Terence, *Eunuchus*, I. i. 16–18.

> *Camisars.* The name given to the Calvinists of the Cévennes during the religious troubles following the revocation of the Edict of Nantes. They are represented in the waxwork of English religions in the 257th *Tatler*. They were known as the French Prophets (page 524). See also *Tatler*, No. 11.

161. *Motto.* Virgil, *Georgics*, ii. 527–34.

PAGE 486. *Like Caelia. As You Like It*, I. ii. 190.

PAGE 488. *Dr. Kennet. Parochial Antiquities* (1695), pages 610 et sqq.

162. *Motto.* Horace, *Ars Poetica*, 126–7.

PAGE 490. *Character in Horace. Satires*, I. iii. 3–19.

> *Character . . . by Mr. Dryden.* The well-known description of George, Duke of Buckingham, in *Absalom and Achitophel* (i 544–54).

163. PAGE 491. *Motto.* Cicero, *De Senectute*, i.
     PAGE 492. *Leonora.* See note to page 285.
        Monsieur St. Evremont. See page 531.
164. PAGE 494. *Motto.* Virgil, *Georgics*, iv. 494, 497–8.
     PAGE 498. *They were lovely*, etc. 2 Samuel, i. 23.
        Langhorne has a short poem entitled *Theodosius to Constantia* (1760), and two volumes of the *Correspondence of Theodosius and Constantia* (1764–5), which were suggested by this paper.
165. PAGE 499. *Motto.* Horace, *Ars Poetica*, 48, 50–1. The motto in *A* was *Semivirumque bovem, semibovemque virum* (misquoted from Ovid, *Ars Amatoria*, ii. 24).
        Cf. the attack on French fopperies, pages 136 et sqq.; also Dennis's *Essay upon Public Spirit* (1711), page 13. This paper occasioned a pamphlet, *The Spectator Inspected or A Letter to the Spectator from an Officer in Flanders*.
     PAGE 500. Virgil, *Georgics*, iii. 25. Addison printed '*Atque intertexti tollant*,' etc. Dryden's translation, lines 39–40.
        Great Modern Critick. Bentley. See Jebb's *Bentley*, page 174.
166. PAGE 502. *Motto.* Ovid, *Metamorphoses*, xv. 871–2.
     PAGE 503. This anecdote of the Freethinker is cousin german to that of 'the Atheist' in the *Tatler*, No. 111. Steele's further attacks on the 'Minute Philosophers' in the *Tatler*, and in No. 234 of the *Spectator*, have been supposed to be directed against John ('Janus Junius') Toland (1669–1722), author of the *Pantheisticon* (1705), whom Pope satirized in *The Dunciad* (ii. 399, iii. 212).
167. PAGE 504. *Motto.* Horace, *Epistles*, ii. ii. 128–40.
     PAGE 505. *Unable to contain himself.* See No. 136.
     PAGE 506. *Almanzor like.* As that character in Dryden's *Almanzor and Almahide or The Conquest of Granada.* See *Drawcansir*, *ante*, page 51, and note.
     PAGE 507. *Vitruvius.* The original of this *nom de guerre* is referred to on pages 502 and 558.
168. *Motto.* Horace, *Epistles*, ii. i. 128.
        Licensed Tyrants the Schoolmasters. See No. 157.
        Quintilian. De Institutione Oratoria, i. iii.
        The *very great School* is Eton. The master was Dr. Charles Roderick, afterwards Provost of King's College, Cambridge.
     PAGE 508. The school at Richmond was under the charge of Dr. Nicholas Brady, who, with Tate, versified the Psalms.
     PAGE 509. *The Water-works.* This is 'the famous Water Theatre of the ingenious Mr. Winstanly,' which is frequently advertised by his widow in the original issue. It stood at the lower end of Piccadilly, and was known 'by the Wind-mill on the Top of it.'
169. PAGE 510. *Motto.* Terence, *Andria*, i. i. 35–9.
     PAGE 511. *Xenophon. Cyropaedia*, viii. vii. 25.
        Salust. Sallust, *Bellum Catilinarium*, lvii.